Library Catalogue of the American Numismatic Association

Library Catalogue of the American Numismatic Association

second edition

GENEVA KARLSON, *librarian*

International Standard Book Number: 0-89637-000-3
Library of Congress Catalog Card Number: 77-93078
American Numismatic Association
818 N. Cascade Ave., Colorado Springs, Colorado 80903
©1977 by American Numismatic Association. All rights reserved.
Printed in United States of America

Aaron R. Feldman

BUY THE BOOK BEFORE THE COIN

Friends or relatives of a deceased person often want to show appreciation for the departed by setting up some form of memorial. In most cases such an act is commendable, especially when the remembrance has a practical value to survivors with common or related interests.

Aaron R. Feldman, ANA 14033, passed away on March 16, 1976, and left behind many friends and an untold number of collectors who had been influenced by his slogan, "Buy the book before the coin." One of these many friends expressed a desire to fund a suitable memorial to this student of numismatics who had been so unselfishly helpful to others.

Fate seemed to show the way to an auspicious solution: the anonymous friend contributed generously to the cost of producing this new library catalogue. A man of modest means himself, Aaron Feldman waived his profit on many a book to encourage the collector to further study. Now his special friend has come forth with a contribution that will continue the influence Aaron so conscientiously fostered.

Aaron R. Feldman was a native and lifelong resident of the New York City area who signed his application for ANA membership as a "retail merchant" and "general" collector, and who had only three mailing addresses in 29 years of ANA membership. He spent many years in the millinery business before opening "the world's smallest coin shop" in the New York City Jewelry Exchange in the 1950's. As a dealer, he spent more time imparting information than selling coins and counted many highly regarded numismatists among his personal friends. He gave up his beloved hobby only after Parkinson's disease incapacitated him. To this modest man, the American Numismatic Association dedicates this catalogue of the world's largest circulating numismatic library.

CONTENTS

ACKNOWLEDGMENTS

      This catalogue has been produced in part through an
anonymous gift in memory of Aaron Feldman. Kaman Sciences
Corporation produced the computer listing from which this
reference has been printed. Western Interstate Commission
for Higher Education generously furnished a grant allowing
us to use the services of graduate student Steve Milligan
for several months to update our periodical records. Special
thanks go to Edward C. Rochette, Executive Vice-President of
the ANA, for his inspiration and guidance in the production
of both the 1972 and 1978 editions and to Glenn B. Smedley,
ANA Board member, for giving so freely of his time and talents.
Several ANA staff members have been instrumental in making
this edition possible; N. Neil Harris for supervising the
printing; Ruthann Brettell for engineering the computer phases;
John Watson for graphics; and library staffers Catherine Mundy
and Nancy Stith, catalogers; Kathy Tatchio and Debbie Brooks,
library assistants; for their endless hours of cataloging
and proofing.

LIBRARIANS OF THE ANA

S. H. Chapman	1891
William C. Stone	1892
Fred B. Stebbens	1899
S. C. Stevens	1901
Ben Green	1904
J. L. Zerbe	1908
Ludger Gravel	1909
Harry H. Yawger	1912
E. D. Putnam	1921
Paul M. Lange	1924
Charles W. Foster	1931
William S. Dewey	1937
T. R. Hammer	1940
D. Dee DeNise	1951
John J. Gabarron	1956
Geneva Karlson	1967

LIBRARY SERVICES AND HOW TO USE THEM

One of the first resolutions of the founders of the ANA in 1891 was to provide for a library so that its members could be well informed in the field of their chosen hobby. From its small beginnings of copies of <u>Plain Talk</u> and <u>The Numismatist</u>, it has grown into the world's largest circulating library on numismatics. Individual members and member clubs may use its research facilities through our "borrow by mail" service.

Borrowing Regulations

Please request all books by number, author and title when ever possible in the following manner:

Dear Librarian:

> *I wish to borrow the following books:*
> *BC30   Sear - Roman Coins and Their Values.*
> *S41*
>
> *GB30   Sheldon - Penny Whimsy.*
> *S5p*
> *My ANA number is 19811.*
>
> *Sincerely,*
>
> *Mike Smith*
> *403 So. Main St.*
> *Detroit, MI   48234*

Book requests from member clubs must come from an official whose name is furnished for our records as having this authority.

Members pay postage and insurance both ways. Insurance rates are based on the value of the books and may vary from 40¢ to $1.20. Please use the same rate of insurance that was necessary to mail the books from the library to you. This amount will be noted on the envelope included with your shipment as will the postal charge. This envelope containing the total amount of money due the library should be enclosed with your return shipment. Each book should be individually wrapped for added protection.

If you do not have a library catalogue showing the call number, author and title, you may request books by subject. Be specific as to your research requirements.

The continuation of this service depends on you, its user. Books must be returned promptly, carefully wrapped, properly insured, with fees included. It is important that all "receipts for insured mail" are retained for at least three months after mailing books to us. The borrower must pay replacement costs of uninsured books lost in the mails or books lost while in the possession of the borrower.

Books are checked out for a period of six weeks and they may be renewed upon request unless on reserve for another member. An overdue notice will be mailed for material not returned within two weeks of the date due. If no response is received within another two week time lapse, records will be forwarded to the proper office for executive action.

Copying Services

Copying services are available for material when this is more feasible than mailing a large volume, or when desired material does not circulate as is the case with Rare Books and Reference Copies. Copyright regulations will be observed. Copying charges are as follows:

        10¢ per page for members
        15¢ per page for non-members

Numismatic Research Inquires

We welcome numismatic research inquires, however, the librarian cannot undertake detailed research requiring an extensive amount of time. Please enclose a self addressed stamped envelope for a reply. Address all correspondence to: Librarian, American Numismatic Association, P.O. Box 2366, Colorado Springs, CO 80901.

Reprints, Books and Magazines For Sale

The ANA has approximately 90 titles of reprints, books, and back issues of <u>The Numismatist</u>, <u>The Numismatic Scrapbook Magazine</u> and <u>World Coins</u> for sale. The reprints are of articles previously published in <u>The Numismatist</u> and are priced from 25¢ to $7.50 each.

A list of publications available for purchase may be obtained by writing to: Librarian, American Numismatic Association, P.O. Box 2366, Colorado Springs, CO 80901.

CLASSIFICATION SYSTEM

NUMISMATICS AND COINS

General Coins

AA 10 Societies
   20 Collections, museums
   30 Catalogues
   40 General works - historical, etc.
   45 General (Foreign Language)
   50 Dictionaries, encyclopedias, bibliographies, manuals,
      directories
   55 Numismatics - Education and teaching
   58 Numismatists, A-Z
   60 Coin collecting
   70 Special aspects - counterfeiting, etc.
   72 Numismatics - displays and exhibits
   73 Coin clubs
   75 Dealers and dealerships; mail-order coin business, etc.
   78 Investment
   80 Iconography, heraldry, inscriptions, art in numismatics
   90 Technical aspects - weights and measures
   95 Coin preservation; cleaning
   96 Grading
   97 Coin photography
   99 Philately and numismatics

Metals, Mines and Mining

AB 10 Societies
   15 Bibliographies, directories, dictionaries, etc.
   20 General
   25 Technical
   26 By country, A-Z
   28 United States
   29 United States, by state, A-Z
   30 Gold - General
   32 Gold - Technical
   36 Gold - United States
   39 Gold - United States, by state, A-Z
   40 Silver - same as for Gold
   50 Nickel - same as for Gold
   60 Copper - same as for Gold
   70 Iron and Steel, Alloys - same as for Gold

Ancient Coins

BA 10
   20 Collections
   30 Catalogues
   40 General
   45 Dictionaries, etc.
   50 Collecting
   60 Technical - includes cleaning and preservation
   65 Special aspects - Coins of the Bible, etc.
   70 Iconography
   80 Finds, by place, A-Z
   90

Ancient Greek Coins

BB 10
   20 Collections
   30 Catalogues
   40 General
   45 Bibliographies, etc.
   50 Collecting
   55 Special, technical
   56 Gold
   57 Silver
   58 Bronze, etc.
   60 Iconography
   70 Finds
   80 By period
   90 By region - Greece
   94 By country - Europe
   97 By country - Asia, Africa

Ancient Roman Coins

BC   10
     20   Collections
     30   Catalogues
     40   General
     45   Bibliographies, etc.
     50   Collecting
     60   Technical
     63   Gold
     65   Silver
     67   Bronze, copper
     70   Iconography
     75   Finds
     80   By period - Republican 449BC-31BC
     85   By period - Imperial 27BC-476AD
     90   By region - Italy
     93   By country - Africa
     95   By country - Asia
     97   By country - Europe

Ancient Asian and African Coins (except China, see KC50)

BD   10   India - collections
     15   India - general
     20   Ceylon
     30   Parthia
     32   Persia (Sassanian)
     34   Seleucid empire
     36   Syria
     38   Other cities or regions A-Z
     40   Israel - General
     45   Israel - Collections
     50   Israel - Special; by period
     60   Israel, Regional, A-Z
     70   Africa - General and special
     80   Carthage
     83   Egypt
     85   Mauretania
     87   Other, A-Z
     90

Byzantine Coins

BE   10
     20   Collections
     30   Catalogues
     40   General
     50   Dictionaries
     60   Special; iconography
     70   Technical
     80   By period
     90   By place

World Coins - Medieval and Modern

Coins of North and South America

Mexico

Central America

          30 Special
          40 Technical
          43 Gold
          45 Silver
          47 Copper
          50 Costa Rica
          55 Guatemala
          60 Honduras
          65 Panama
          70 British Honduras
          75 El Salvador
          80 Nicaragua

West Indies

    FD 20 Catalogues
        30 General
        35 Special
        40 Bermuda
        45 Cuba
        50 Dominican Republic
        53 Haiti
        55 Jamaica
        60 Puerto Rico
        65 Virgin Islands
        70 Other, A-Z

South America

    FE 10
        20 General, catalogues
        30 Argentina
        35 Bolivia
        40 Brazil
        50 Chile
        55 Columbia
        60 Ecuador
        65 Guiana
        70 Paraguay
        75 Peru
        80 Uruguay
        85 Venezuela

United States

    GA 10 Societies
        20 Collections - Public
        25 Collections - Private
        30 Catalogues
        40 General
        50 Guides for collecting
        55 Investment

XVII

       60
       70   Special - includes counterfeiting
       80   Technical, minting
       85   Government Reports
       90   Patterns, oddities, mint errors, etc.

GB   10   Gold
       15   Private gold
       20   Silver
       30   Copper
       35   Nickel
       40   Iconography (commemoratives), heraldry
       50   Colonial
       60   Post Colonial to 1860
       70   1860 to present
       80   Local, A-Z

Canada

HA   10   Societies
       20
       30   Catalogues, bibliographies, directories
       35   Collecting
       40   General
       50   Special, technical
       53   Gold
       55   Silver
       57   Copper
       60   Iconography
       70   History
       80   New Brunswick
       85   Nova Scotia
       90   Other, A-Z

Europe

JA   10   Societies
       20   Collections
       30   Catalogues
       40   General
       50   Special
       55   Hoards
       60   Technical
       63   Gold
       65   Silver
       67   Copper, etc.
       70   Iconography, inscriptions, commemoratives
       79   By period - Ancient
       80   By period - Medieval
       83   Early modern
       85   18th century
       87   19th and 20th centuries

        90 Regional, A-Z
        95 Colonies

Great Britain, Ireland, Scotland

JB same as JA except for:

        40 General works written before 1910
        45 Since 1910
        80 Ancient, Anglo-Saxon
        83 Medieval, Anglo-Gallic (1066-1485)
        85 Early modern to 1800
        87 19th, 20th centuries
        90 Ireland
        93 Scotland
        94 Isle of Man, Lundy
        95 Channel Islands
        96 Commonwealth
        97 Other, A-Z

Scandinavia

JC 10 General (more than one country)
    20 Denmark - General
    30 Special, technical
    40 Iceland, Greenland
    50 Norway - General, historical
    60 Special, technical
    70 Sweden - General
    75 Sweden - catalogues
    80 Special - historical, technical
    85 Swedish possessions
    90 Finland

Spain, Portugal, Andorra

JD 10 Spain - Collections, catalogues
    15 Societies
    20 Spain - General
    30 Special, technical
    33 Gold
    35 Silver
    37 Copper
    40 Ancient
    43 Medieval
    44 Post Medieval through 18th Century
    45 Modern - 19th century on
    50 Local, A-Z
    60 Portugal - Collections, catalogues
    70 General
    80 Special, technical
    83 Gold

XIX

    85 Silver
    87 Copper
    90 Prior to 1640
    93 1640-1900
    95 Since 1900
    97 Andorra

France

JE same as JA except for:
    80 Gaul (ancient)
    82 Medieval
    83 Early modern up to time of Napoleon
    85 Napoleonic era
    87 To present
    95 Colonies
    97 Monaco

Netherlands, Belgium, Luxembourg, Liechtenstein

JF same as JA

Germany

JG Same as JA except for:
    67 Procelain as well as copper
    90 Bavaria
    92 Brandenburg-Prussia
    94 Saxony
    96 Wurtemburg
    98 Other provinces and towns, A-Z

Switzerland

JH same as JA

Italy

JI same as JA except for:
    93 Papal coins
    97 Regional, A-Z

Poland, Czechoslovakia, Hungary, Rumania, Yugoslavia

JJ 10
    20 Poland - General
    30 Special
    40 Yugoslavia
    50 Czechoslovakia - General

```
60  Special
70  Hungary - General
80  Special
85  Rumania
90
```

Austria

```
JK  Same as for JA
```

Greece and Balkan States

```
JL  10  General
    20  Balkans - Catalogues, etc.
    30  General
    40  Special
    50
    60  Greece - Catalogues, etc.
    70  General
    80  Special
    90  Cyprus - General
    92  Cyprus - Societies
```

Soviet Union, Latvia, Lithuania, Estonia

```
JM  Same as for JA except for:
    90  Russia, provinces A-Z
    91  Uzbek SSR
    92  Ukranian SSR
    93  Latvia
    95  Lithuania
    97  Other
```

Malta - use if majority of book covers since independence,
    1964; if former, use JB96

```
JN  Same as for JA
```

Coins - Modern Asia, Near and Middle East

```
KA  10  General
    20  Regional, A-Z (Afghanistan, Armenia, Arabia, Khokand,
        Turkey) (Turkey includes Ottoman Empire, etc.)
    30  Iran, medieval Persia (Saffarids)
    40  Israel, Modern
    45  Lebanon
    50  Mohammedan Empire, modern and medieval
    55  Mohammedan Empire - regional, A-Z
    60  India and Ceylon - Collections
    70  India and Ceylon - General
```

75 India and Ceylon - Special, technical
80 India and Ceylon - Medieval
83 India and Ceylon - Early modern
85 India and Ceylon - Modern
90 India and Ceylon - Regional, A-Z (Ceylon KA 90.C4)

Coins - Far East

KB 10 Far East - General
    20 Indonesia, Malaysia - General
        (Dutch East Indies)
    25 Indonesia - Regional
    30 Philippines - General
    40 Philippines - Special
    50 Philippines - Historical
    60 Philippines - Local
    70 Indochina, A-Z (includes Annam, Hong Kong,
        Nepal, Thailand, Tibet, Vietnam, etc.)

China

KC 10 Societies, bibliographies, directories, etc.
    20 General
    30 Special
    40 Technical
    43 Gold
    45 Silver
    47 Copper
    50 Ancient
    55 Early modern
    60 Modern
    70 Regional, A-Z

Japan and Korea

KD 10 Japan - Catalogues, collections
    20   General
    30   Special
    40   Technical
    43   Gold
    45   Silver
    47   Copper
    50   Historical
    60   Regional, A-Z
    70 Korea - General
    80   Special

Modern Africa

LA 10 General
    20 British possessions, former and current (Zanzibar,
        Nigeria)
    30 South Africa (Griqualand)
    40 Portuguese possessions, former and current (An-
        gola, Mozambique, Sao Tome)
    50 Ethiopia
    60 Egypt
    70 French possessions, former and current
    80 Italian possessions, former and current
    90 Belgian possessions, former and current
    95 German possessions, former and current

Australia, New Zealand, Pacific Islands

MA 20 Australia and New Zealand - General
    30 Special
    40 Australia - General
    50 Special
    60 Early history
    70 New Zealand - General
    80 Special
    90 Pacific Islands, New Guinea, Fiji

EXONUMIA: TOKENS, POLITICANA, PRIMITIVE MONEY, SEALS & SCARABS

General Tokens

NA 10 Periodicals, societies, collections
    20 General
    30 Special
    40 Ancient
    50 Medieval
    60 16th - 18th Centuries
    70 19th - 20th Centuries

Tokens - Special Uses

NB 20 Commercial
    40 Religious
    60 Jetons, counters
    80 Other uses

United States - Tokens

PA 10 Collections
    20 Catalogues
    30 General works
    40 Special uses or forms
    50 Colonial
    60 Early national (18th Century)
    70 19th - 20th Centuries
    73 Hard times tokens
    75 Civil War
    80 Local, A-Z

Canada - Tokens

PB 10 Collections
    20 Catalogues
    30 General works
    40 Special aspects
    50 Medieval
    60 16th - 18th Centuries
    70 19th - 20th Centuries
    80 Local, A-Z
    90 Cities and towns, A-Z

Western Hemisphere - Tokens

PC 20 Mexico
    35 Panama and Canal Zone
    37 Guatemala
    80 South America, by country A-Z

Europe - Tokens

PD 10 Collections
    20 Catalogues
    30 General

Great Britain - Tokens

PE 10 Collections
    20 Catalogues
    30 General works
    40 Special aspects
    50 Medieval
    55 17th Century
    60 18th Century
    70 19th - 20th Centuries
    80 London
    85 Ireland
    90 Scotland
    95 Local, A-Z

France - Tokens

PF 10 Collections
    20 Catalogues
    30 General works
    40 Special aspects
    50 Medieval
    60 16th-18th Centuries
    70 19th-20th Centuries
    80 Local, A-Z
    90 Cities, towns, and provinces, A-Z

Germany - Tokens

PG 10 Collections
    20 Catalogues
    30 General works
    40 Special aspects
    50 Medieval
    60 16th-18th Centuries
    70 19th-20th Centuries, includes notgeld
    80 Local, A-Z
    90 Cities and towns, A-Z

Netherlands - Tokens

PH 10 Collections
    20 Catalogues
    30 General works
    40 Special aspects

       50   Medieval
       60   16th-18th Centuries
       70   19th-20th Centuries
       80   Local, A-Z
       90   Cities and towns, A-Z

Western Europe - Tokens

PI   30   Iberia
     50   Italy
     60   Scandinavia
     62   Sweden
     64   Norway
     66   Denmark

Eastern Europe - Tokens

PJ   10   Collections
     20   Catalogues
     30   General works
     40   Special aspects
     50   Medieval
     60   16th - 18th Centuries
     70   19th - 20th Centuries
     80   Local, A-Z
     90   Cities and towns, A-Z

Asia - Tokens

PL   20   China
     30   Dutch East Indies
     40   India & Ceylon
     50   Korea
     60   Thailand
     70   Philippines

Africa - Tokens

PM   10   Collections
     20   Catalogues
     30   General works
     40   Special aspects
     50   Medieval
     60   16th - 18th Centuries
     70   19th - 20th Centuries
     80   Local, A-Z
     90   Cities and towns, A-Z

Australia, New Zealand - Tokens

PN 10   General
    20   Australia
    40   New Zealand

U.S. Politicana (Tokens, Medals, Buttons)

QA 20   General works
    40   18th - 19th Centuries
    60   20th Century

Primitive Money

QB 20   Collections
    30   General works
    40   Economic, anthropological treatment
    50   Africa
    60   Asia and Pacific
    70   Americas

Seals and Scarabs

QC 20   Ancient Asia
    30   Ancient Egypt
    40   Europe
    50   Great Britain
    60   United States

MEDALS

Modern World - Medals (Also Europe Alone)

RA 10   Collections
    20   Catalogues
    30   General works
    40   Special aspects
    50   Artists, A-Z
    60   Iconography: Persons, families, A-Z
    70   Iconography: Events, A-Z
    80   Iconography: Subjects, A-Z

Ancient - Medals

RB 10   Collections
    20   General works
    30   Special aspects
    40   Greek
    50   Roman (collections, general)
    60   Roman, by place or period
    70   Iconography
    80
    90   Other countries, A-Z

RC (for future expansion)

Western Europe - Medals

RD 10
    20   Netherlands
    30   Belgium
    40   Scandinavia
    45   Denmark
    50   Sweden
    60   Switzerland

Great Britain - Medals

RE 10   Collections
    15   Catalogues
    20   General works
    30   Special aspects
    35   Individual artists, A-Z
    40   Medieval
    50   Renaissance
    60   18th Century
    70   19th-20th Centuries
    80   Persons, Families, A-Z

85   Events, subjects, A-Z
90   Local, A-Z

France - Medals

RF 10   Collections
    15   Catalogues
    20   General works
    30   Special aspects
    35   Individual artists, A-Z
    40   Medieval
    50   Renaissance
    60   18th Century
    70   19th - 20th Centuries
    80   Persons, Families A-Z
    85   Events, subjects, A-Z
    90   Local, A-Z

Germany - Medals

RG 10   Collections
    15   Catalogues
    20   General works
    30   Special aspects
    35   Individual artists, A-Z
    40   Medieval
    50   Renaissance
    60   18th Century
    70   19th-20th Centuries
    80   Persons, families A-Z
    85   Events, subjects, A-Z
    90   Local, A-Z

Spain, Portugal, Andorra

RH 10   Societies; collections
    15   Catalogues
    20   General works
    30   Special aspects
    35   Individual artists A-Z
    40   Medieval
    50   Renaissance
    60   18th Century
    65   Early modern 16th-18th Centuries
    70   19th-20th Centuries
    80   Persons, families, A-Z
    85   Events, subjects, A-Z
    90   Local, A-Z

Italy - Medals

```
RI   10   Collections
     15   Catalogues
     20   General works
     30   Special aspects
     35   Individual artists, A-Z
     40   Medieval
     50   Renaissance
     60   18th  Century
     70   19th-20th Centuries
     80   Persons, families, A-Z
     85   Events, subjects, A-Z
     90   Local, A-Z
```

Russia, USSR, Ukranian SSR, Latvia, etc. (those
    communist states in the USSR)

```
RJ   same as RH except for:

     88   Russia, local, A-Z
     90   USSR countries, by country, A-Z
```

Eastern Europe - Medals

```
RK   10
     20   Austria
     30
     40   Czechoslovakia
     50
     60   Hungary
     70   Rumania
     80
```

RL   (for future expansion)

United States - Medals

```
RM   10   Collections
     15   Catalogues
     20   General works
     30   Special aspects
     35   Individual artists, A-Z
     40   Medieval
     50   Colonial
     60   Early national
     70   19th-20th Centuries
     80   Persons, families, A-Z
     85   Events, subjects, A-Z (includes Indian medals)
     90   Local, A-Z
```

xxx

Latin America - Medals

RN 10   General
    20   Mexico
    30   Central America, A-Z
    40   West Indies, A-Z
    50   South America, A-Z
    60   Brazil
    70   Chile

Canada - Medals

RO 10   Collections
    15   Catalogues
    20   General works
    30   Special aspects
    35   Individual artists, A-Z
    40   Medieval
    50   Renaissance
    60   18th Century
    70   19th - 20th Centuries
    80   Persons, families, A-Z
    85   Events, subjects, A-Z
    90   Local, A-Z

Asia - Medals

RP 20   Philippines
    50   China

Africa - Medals

RQ 10   Collections
    15   Catalogues
    20   General works
    30   Special aspects
    35   Individual artists, A-Z
    40   Medieval
    50   Renaissance
    60   18th Century
    70   19th-20th Centuries
    80   Persons, families, A-Z
    85   Events, subjects, A-Z
    90   Local, A-Z

Australia, New Zealand - Medals

RR 10   Collections
    15   Catalogues
    20   General works
    30   Special aspects

35   Individual artists, A-Z
40   Medieval
50   Renaissance
60   18th Century
70   19th-20th Centuries
80   Persons, families, A-Z
85   Events, subjects, A-Z
90   Local, A-Z

ORDERS AND DECORATIONS

World - Orders and Decorations

SA 20 Catalogues
    30 General works
    40 Specific orders, groups, etc.
    50 18th-19th Centuries
    60 20th Century
    70 Local, A-Z

Europe - Orders and Decorations

SB 20 Western A-Z
    60 Eastern A-Z

France - Orders & Decorations

SC 20 Catalogues
    30 General works
    40 Specific orders, groups, etc.
    50 18th-19th Centuries
    60 20th Century
    70 Colonies

Germany - Orders & Decorations

SD 20 Catalogues
    30 General works
    40 Specific orders, groups, etc.
    50 18th - 19th Centuries
    60 20th Century
    70 Local, A-Z

Great Britain - Orders & Decorations

SE 20 Catalogues
    30 General works
    40 Specific orders, groups, etc.
    50 18th - 19th Centuries
    60 20th Century
    70 Local A-Z

Italy - Orders & Decorations

SF 20 Catalogues
    30 General works
    40 Specific orders, groups, etc.
    50 18th - 19th Centuries

          60 20th Century
          70 Local, A-Z

Russia - Orders & Decorations

SG   20 Catalogues
     30 General works
     40 Specific orders, groups, etc.
     50 18th - 19th Centuries
     60 20th Century
     70 Local, A-Z

United States - Orders & Decorations

SH   20 Catalogues
     30 General works
     40 Specific orders, groups, etc.
     50 18th - 19th Centuries
     60 20th Century
     70 Local, A-Z

Western Hemisphere except U.S. - Orders & Decorations

SI   20 Canada
     40 Mexico
     60 South America
     80 Other, A-Z

Asia - Orders & Decorations

SJ   20 China
     40 Japan
     60 Korea
     80 Other, Far East, A-Z
     85 Near East, A-Z

Africa - Orders & Decorations

SK   20 South Africa

PAPER MONEY

World - Paper Money

UA 20 Catalogues
    30 General works
    31 Before 1800
    32 19th Century
    33 20th Century
    40 Special aspects
    50 Collecting
    60 Military currency

Western Europe - Paper Money

UB 20 General works
    30 Great Britain
    40 France
    50 Italy
    53 Spain
    55 Portugal
    60 Scandinavia
    70 Netherlands, low countries

Germany - Paper Money

UC 20 General
    40 Notgeld
    55 18th-19th Centuries
    60 20th Century
    80 Colonies

Eastern Europe - Paper Money

UF 20 General works
    30 Soviet Union
    40 Baltic States
    50 Balkan States
    60 Hungary, Austria
    70 Poland, Czechoslovakia, Yugoslavia

North and South America

UH same as UA

Canada - Paper Money

UI 30 General works
    40 Special aspects

```
50   18-19th Centuries
60   20th Century
```

Mexico - Paper Money

```
UJ   30   General works
     40   Special aspects
     60   20th Century
```

Latin America - paper Money

```
UK   10   South America - A-Z, except below
     20   Central America
     30   West Indies
     40   Brazil
     50   paraguay, Uruguay
```

Asia - Paper Money

```
UM   20   Near East, A-Z
     30   Middle East, A-Z
     35   Far East:  India, Ceylon, A-Z
     40   Philippines
     45   Southeast Asia:  Cambodia, Laos, Thailand, Vietnam,
          etc., A-Z
```

China, Korea, Japan - Paper Money

```
UN   20   China, general
     30   Special, ancient
     40   20th Century
     50   Japan, general
     60   20th Century
     70   Korea
```

Africa (Modern)

```
UP   10   General
     20   British possessions, current and former
     30   South Africa
     40   Portuguese possessions, current and former
     50   Ethiopia
     60   Egypt
     70   French possessions, current and former
     80   Italian possessions, current and former
     90   Belgian possessions, current and former
     95   German possessions, current and former
```

Australia - Paper Money

UQ 10   Societies
    20
    30   General
    35   Special, technical
    37   By period
    38   By state, A-Z
    40   New Zealand, general
    45   Special, technical
    47   By period
    48   Geographical, A-Z (North Island, South Island,
         Chatham Island, Stewart Island)
    50   New Guinea, etc.

United States - Paper Money

US 10   Societies, reports of agencies, etc.
    15   Catalogues
    20   General works
    25   Engraving and printing
    30   Counterfeiting
    35   Scrip, emergency money
    40   Colonial, continental
    45   Colonial, by state, A-Z
    50   Fractional currency, encased postage stamps, postal
         notes
    60   Civil War, Confederacy
    70   National Bank notes, 1860's-1930's
    75   State bank notes, county scrip
    77   Subjects and events on notes, A-Z
    80   By state, A-Z
    85   persons on notes, A-Z
    90   20th Century (small size)

BANKS & BANKING

United States - Banks & Banking

VA 30 General
    35 Government reports, laws, etc.
    40 Specific banks and bankers
    45 Special aspects
    50 19th Century
    60 East, A-Z
    70 Midwest, A-Z
    80 West, A-Z
    90 South, A-Z

Western Hemisphere except U.S. - Banks & Banking

VB 30 Canada
    40 Mexico
    50 South America
    60 West Indies
    70 Central America

Europe - Banks & Banking

VC 30 Great Britain
    40 France
    50 Germany
    55 Netherlands, Belgium, Liechtenstein, Luxembourg
    60 Italy

World - Banks & Banking

VD 10 Societies, commissions, etc.
    30 General
    40

Asia

VE 10
    20
    30 China

CHECKS

STOCKS & BONDS

VR 10 General Works
    20
    30 United States - General
    40 United States by State A-Z
    50 Western Hemisphere except U.S. by Country A-Z
    60 Europe by Country A-Z
    70 Africa by Country A-Z
    80 Asia by Country A-Z
    90 Far East by Country A-Z

ECONOMICS

World Economics

WA 30 General works
    50 Ancient monetary systems

United States - Economics

WB 30 General
    40 Special
    50 Colonial
    60 19th Century
    70 20th Century
    80 Regional

Europe - Economics

WC 10 General
    30 Great Britain
    40 France
    50 Germany
    52 Switzerland
    60 Italy

Western Hemisphere - Economics

WD 30 Canada
    40 Mexico
    50 West Indies
    60 Central America
    70 South America

Asia - Economics

WE 30 India
    60 China
    70 Near East

ABBREVIATIONS

AJN - American Journal of Numismatics

ANA - American Numismatic Association,
Colorado Springs

ANS - American Numismatic Society,
New York

Bibl. - Bibliography

Col. - Colored

Comp. - Compiler

Ed. - Editor

Ill., Illus. - Illustrated

Inc. - Included

N.D. - No publication date

N.P. - No place of publication

N. Pub. - No publisher

P. - Pages

Pl. - Plates

V., Vol. - Volume

LEGEND

Rare Book. - is not loaned out

Reference - is not loaned out

PART I

Coins and Coin Collecting

<u>NUMISMATICS</u> (<u>GENERAL</u>)

SOCIETIES

AA10
A4
	American Numismatic Society.
	     The American Numismatic Society. New York, American Numismatic Society, n.d.
	     36p. illus. 16cm.

AA10
A44
	Alexander, David Thomason
	     From Dan to Eilat...deep roots of Israel. Originally published in Coin World, 1976. Reprinted-Sidney, Ohio, Amos Press; American Israel Numismatic Assn., 1976.
	     35p. photographs. 21cm.

AA10
C3
	Castellane, MM. le Compte de
	     Congres International de Numismatique, rouni a Paris en 1900. Proces-verbaux & memoires publies par MM. le Compte de Castellane et Adrien Blanchet. Paris, au Siege de la Societe Francaise de Numismatique, 1900.
	     449p. plates XXXIV. 25cm.

AA10
H6
Rare
Books
	Hooper, Joseph
	     Numismatic foundation stones by Joe. Hooper. Detroit, Mich., Geo. F. Heath, 1891. The Numismatist and Year Book for 1891. Vol. 3, #19 & 20. First paper.
	     19p. 20cm.

AA10
I5
	International Association of Professional numismatists.
	     List of members. London, The Assn., 1969.
	     32p. 14cm.

AA10
W4
	Weeks, William R.
	     The American Numismatic Society. New York, 1910.
	     20p. photograph. 24cm.

AA20
B5
      Bibliotheque Royale Albert, Brussels.
        Cinq annees d'acquisitions;
1969-1973; exposition organisee a
la Bibliotheque royale Albert I du
18 Janvier au 1 Mars 1975. Brussels,
1975.
      495p. illus. 26cm.

AA20
B7
      British museum. Dept. of coins and medals.
        A guide to the Department of coins and
medals in the British museum. 3d ed.,
London, The Trustees, 1922.
      94p. illus. 8pl. 21cm.

AA20
C5
      Clain-Stefanelli, Vladimir.
        Hall of monetary history and medallic
art, Smithsonian Institution, Washington
D.C.
In: Museum. Published by Unesco.
      v. xv, no. 3, 1962
      6p. (191-196), illus. 31cm.

AA20
F5
      Fiala, Eduard
        Beschreibung der Sammlung Bohmischer
munzen und medaillen des Max Donebauer;
anhang von Eduard Fiala. Austria,
Akademische Druck-u. Verlagsanstalt, 1970.
      2v. illus. 28cm.

AA20
J6
      [Johnston, Elizabeth Bryant], 1833-1907.
        A visit to the cabinet of the United
States Mint, at Philadelphia. [Philadelphia
Press of J. B. Lippincott & co., 1876.]
      92p. illus. 20cm.

AA20
N3
      National Bank of Detroit
        The money museum. Detroit,
the author, 1971.
      unpaged. illus. 23cm.

AA20
S6
      Smithsonian Institution-National
Museum of History and Technology.
        The history of money and medals.
Washington, 1972.
      20p. illus. 22cm.

AA20   U. S. Treasury Dept. Bureau of the Mint
U5   A description of ancient and modern
         coins, in the cabinet collection at the
         Mint of the United States. Prepared and
         arranged under the direction of James Ross
         Snowden ... Philadelphia, J.B. Lippincott,
         1860.
             xix, 412p. illus. xxvii pl. 23cm.

AA20   U. S. Treasury Dept. Bureau of the Mint.
U5g   Guide to the numismatic collection of
         the Mint of the United States at Philadel-
         phia, Pa. ... Washington, Govt. print.
         off., 1913.
             106p. front., illus., diagr. 20cm.

AA20   Yale College. New Haven, Conn.
Y3   Catalogue of the cabinet of coins
         belonging to Yale College. New Haven,
         Tuttle, Morehouse & Taylor, 1863.
             48p.   23cm

CATALOGUES

AA30   Chaffers, William, 1811-1892
C45   A catalogue of ancient and modern coins
         and medals, which may be obtained, at the
         prices attached to each, of ... to which
         is added a list of antiquities, etc. 4th
         ed. London, J. Davy & Sons, 1855.
             iv, 148p. ill. 22cm.

AA30   Coins of the world ancient and modern; the
C6   collection of John Story Jenks;
         catalogued by Henry Chapman.
         Philadelphia, Henry Chapman, 1921.
             653p. 32cm.

AA30   Dye, John S.
D8   Dye's gold and silver coin
         chart manual; embracing all that
         have been in use from the days of
         Julius Caesar to the present time.
         N.Y., John S. Dye, [1849?]
             52p. illus. 23cm.

AA30   Friedberg, Robert, 1912
F7   International coin catalogue and price
         list. New York, Coin and Currency Publishing
         Institute, 1949-1960.
             175p. ill. 23cm.

AA30   Mackay, James Alexander
M3   Value in coins and medals. 1st Amer. ed.
         New York, Transatlantic Arts [1969, c1968].
             224p. 12 plates. 23cm.

AA30   Scott, J. W.
S3c   Standard coin catalogue, no. 2. Copper.
         New York, 1878-1913.
             illus. 22cm.
             Library has 1878, 1880, 1882, 1884, 1907, 1913,
         and addenda.

AA30   Scott stamp and coin company
S3s   Standard coin catalogue, no. 1, silver
         and gold, New York, 1880-1916.
             illus. 22cm.
             Library has: 1880, 1882, 1883, 1890, 1893,
         1906, 1910, 1916.

GENERAL WORKS - HISTORICAL, ETC.

AA40   Akerman, John Yonge, 1806-1873.
A4   An introduction to the study of ancient
         and modern coins by John Yonge Akerman...
         London, J. R. Smith, 1848.
             vii, 22p. illus. 18cm.
             Bibliography: p. vi-vii

AA40   American Numismatic Association.
A54   Introduction to numismatics, a sympos-
         ium. [Edited by] Elston G. Bradfield and
         Glenn B. Smedley, [Phoenix, ANA, 1962].
             48p. illus. 23cm.
             "A reprint of articles that appeared in
         the May, June, July 1962 issues of the
         Numismatist.

AA40   American Numismatic Society.
A55   Centennial publication. Edited by Harald
         Ingholt. New York, 1958.
             xii, 712p. 50 plates. 29cm.

AA40   Angell, Norman, 1874-
A6   The story of money. Garden City, N.Y.,
            Garden City Publishing, [c1929].
                411p. plate. 21cm.
                Bibliography: p. 387-389

AA40   Angus, Ian.
A67   Fell's guide to coins and money tokens of
            the world. New York, F. Fell Publishers
            [1974, c1973].
                128p. illus. 27cm.
            Bibliography: p. 125

AA40   Becker, Thomas W.
B4   The heritage of coins. N.p., International
            Program Development Corporation, 1970.
                64p. illus. 18 slides 28cm. (Inter-
            national Numismatic Collector Society, Library
            1, Volume 1.)

AA40   Betton, James L.
B42   Money talks, a numismatic anthology
            selected from Calcoin NEWS. California
            State Numismatic Assoc., [1970].
                372p. illus. 22cm.

AA40   Brown, Laurence A.
B7   Coins through the ages. New York,
            Sterling Pub. Co. [1962, c1961].
                185p. 16 plates. 20cm. (Sterling
            collectors series).

AA40   Brown and Bigelow
B76   All about money. St. Paul, Minn.,
Vert.   Brown and Bigelow, 1960.
File   unpaged. illus. 23cm.

AA40   Burgess, Frederick William, 1855-
B8   Chats on old coins. London, T. F. Unwin,
            [1913], New York, Toronto.
                393p. illus. plates. 20cm.
                Bibliography: p. 385-386

AA40   Burks, Paul Dore.
B87   Fireside yarns; 1001 nights, reminis-
            cences of an old coin man. 1st ed. Los
            Angeles, priv. print, 1932.
                82p. illus. 22cm.

AA40   Carson, Robert Andrew Glindinning.
C3   Coins of the world. New York, Harper,
            [1962], and London, Hutchinson, 1962.
                xiii, 642p. 64 plates. 24cm.
                Bibliography: p. 571-586

AA40   Carlson, Carl
C37   Through history with coins.
Vert.   Taken from Johns Hopkins Magazine,
File   Baltimore, 1974.
                pp. 4-11. illus. 28cm.

AA40   Chase Manhattan Bank
C5   The story of money from barter to
            banking. New York, Chase Manhattan Bank,
            1966.
                16p. illus. 16cm.

AA40   Clain-Stefanelli, Elvira Eliza.
C5g   Numismatics: an ancient science, a survey
            of its history. [Washington, Govt. Print.
            Off., 1965]
                101p. illus. 28cm.
                Bibliography: p. 68-94

AA40   Clain-Stefanelli, Elvira Eliza.
C53   The beauty and lore of coins, currency
            and medals [by] Elvira and Vladimir Clain-
            Stefanelli. Photography by Lee Boltin.
            Croton-on-Hudson, N.Y., Riverwood Pub.,
            1974.
                256p. illus. part. col. 29cm..

AA40   Coin World, ed.
C6   A bicentennial numismatic quiz.
            Sidney, Ohio, Amos Press, 1975.
                36p. 22cm.

AA40   Dodson, Oscar H.
D6   Money tells the story. Racine, Wis.,
            Whitman Pub. Co. [1962].
                64p. illus. 20cm.

AA40   Elder, Thomas L., ed.
E3e   The Elder rare coin book. N.Y.
            Thom. L. Elder, 1913.
                166p. illus. 24cm.

AA40   Del Monte, Jacques, 1902-
F3   Fell's international coin book. New
            York, Fell, 1953, 1961, 1975.
                192p. illus. 20cm.

AA40   Fink, Clarence M.
F5m   Modern coin collectors' history
            of the world. Dallas, Royal Pub-
            lishing Co., n.d.
                unpaged. 21cm. (Coin
            Series, #1)

AA40   Fink, Clarence M.
F5p   Pieces of fate; (gem coin stories
            of information with illustrations for
            collectors and numismatists.) Dallas,
            Royal Publishing Co., 1959.
                146p. illus. 24cm.

AA40   Gelinas, Paul J.
G4   The how and why wonder book of coins and
            currency. New York, Wonder Books [1965].
                48p. illus. 28cm.

AA40   Graham, Frank D.
G7   Money; what it is and what it does by
            Frank D. Graham and Charles H. Seaver.
            New York, Newson & Co., 1936.
                158p. illus. 18cm.

AA40   Gross, Ruth Belov.
G73   Money, money, money. Illustrated
            by Leslie Jacobs. New York, Four Winds
            Press [1971]
                [37] p. illus. 24cm.

AA40   Grierson, Philip
G75   Numismatics. London, Oxford
            University Press, 1975.
                211p. illus. 21cm.

AA40   Groom, Arthur
G76   How money has developed.
            London, Routledge and Kegan Paul,
            1958.
                129p. illus. 19cm.

AA40   Hammer, Ted
H3   Romance of money. Releases; May 6,
Vert.   13, 20, 27. (one page each)
File   looseleaf. 28cm.

AA40   Haskin, Frederic J., 1872-
H38   Everybody's coin book, by Frederic J.
          Haskin. Origin and development of coins,
          famous collections, rare, curious and valu-
          able pieces, with suggestions for amateur
          collectors. [Washington, D. C., rev. ed.
          1939, c1935].
             32p. 23cm.

AA40   [Homans, Isaac Smith, Jr.].
H6   The coin book, comprising a history of
          coinage; a synopsis of the mint laws of the
          United States; statistics of the coinage from
          1792 to 1870; list of current gold and silver
          coins, and their custom house values; a
          dictionary of all coins known in ancient and
          modern times, with their values; the gold and
          silver product of each state to 1870; list of
          works on coinage; the daily price of gold
          from 1862 to 1871. Philadelphia, J. B.
          Lippincott & Co., 1872, 1874 [c1872].
             139p. xvi pl. 23cm.

AA40   Hobson, Burton.
H62   Hidden values in coins: what you should
          know about coins and coin collecting.
          London, Melbourne, Oak Tree P., 1966.
             124p. illus. 22cm.

AA40   Humphreys, Henry Noel, 1810-1879.
H8   The coin collector's manual; ...
          especially of Great Britain. London, H.
          G. Bohn, 1853, 1880, 1883.
             2v. illus. 11 pl. 19cm.

AA40   Hutchinson, William H.
H88   A child's book of coins and currency
          old and new. New York, Maxton, 1957.
             [28]p. illus. 26cm.

AA40   International Numismatic Commission.
I5   A survey of numismatic research, 1960-
          1965. Copenhagen, International Numisma-
          tic Commission, 1967.
             3v. 25cm.

AA40   International Numismatic Commission.
I5   A survey of numismatic research, 1966-
1973   1971. New York, International Numismatic
        Commission, 1973.
            3v. 25cm.

AA40   Keary, Charles Francis, 1848-1917.
K4   The morphology of coins. Chicago,
        Argonaut, 1970.
            89p. ill. pl. 24cm.
            Bibliography included.

AA40   Lane-Poole, Stanley, 1854-1931, ed.
L3   Coins and medals; their place in history
        and art. British Museum, 1892, 1894;
        Chicago, Argonaut, 1968.
            156p. illus. 25cm.

AA40   Leeming, Joseph.
L4   From barter to banking; the story
        of the world's coinage and money.
        N.Y., D. Appleton-Century Co., 1940.
            138p. illus. 20cm.

AA40   Lindheim, Leon.
L5   Facts & fictions about coins. New York,
        Funk & Wagnells, [1968, c1967].
            viii, 280p. illus. 18cm.
            Bibliography: p. 273-276.

AA40   Linecar, Howard W. A.
L55   Coins. London, E. Benn, 1955, 1962
            183p. illus. 22cm. (Practical hand-
        books for collectors).
            Bibliography: p. 184-185.

AA40   Macdonald, George.
M3   The evolution of coinage. Cambridge
        [Eng.], the University press; New York,
        Putnam's Sons, 1916.
            vi, 148p. illus. 7 pl. 16cm.

AA40   Masters, Robert V., 1914-
M34   Coinometry; an instructive historical
        introduction to coins and currency for the
        young collector. Illustrated by Howard
        Simon. New York, Sterling Pub. Co., 1952,
        Rev. ed., c 1958.
            93p. illus. 23 x 26cm.

AA40   Mathews, George D.
M35   The coinages of the world; ancient and
            modern. Illustrated with several hundred
            engravings of the principal coins. New York,
            Scott & Co., 1876.
                vi, 305p. illus. 22cm.

AA40   The money and stamp manual...
M65   N.Y., Money and Stamp Brokerage
                Co., Inc., [1909].
                123p. illus. 16cm.

AA40   New York. Federal Reserve Bank.
N4   A brief summary of coins and
Vert.   currency. N.Y., the author, n.d.
File   15p. illus. 10cm.

AA40   Perez, Gilbert S.
P4   The history of money. Manila,
            The Philippine Numismatic and Antiquarian
            Society, 1950.
                16p. 23cm. (Philippine Numismatic
            Monographs, #7).

AA40   Porteous, John.
P6c   Coins. London, Weidenfeld & Nicolson,
                [1964].
                128p. illus. (part col.), ports. 22cm.

AA40   Porteous, John.
P6h   Coins in history: a survey of coinage
            from the reform of Diocletian to the Latin
            Monetary Union. New York, Putnam, 1969.
                251p. illus. (some col.), facsims,
            maps, ports. 26cm.
                Bibliography: p. [250]-251.

AA40   Prime, William Cowper, 1825-1905.
P7   Coins, medals, and seals, ancient and
            modern, with a sketch of the history of
            coins and coinage, instructions for young
            collectors, tables of comparative rarity,
            price lists of English and American coins,
            medals and tokens... Ed. by W.C. Prime ...
            New York, Harper & brothers, 1861.
                292p. 23cm.

AA40   Quiggin, Alison Hingston.
Q8   The story of money, by A. H. Quiggin.
            London, Methuen & Co., Ltd., 1958.
                73p. illus. 22cm. (Methuen's
            Outlines).

AA40   Rawlings, Gertrude Burford.
R2   Coins and how to know them. London,
           Methuen, New York, Stokes, [1908], 1966.
               xix, 374p. 206 illus. on xxxv pl.
           19cm.
               1966 edition: Ancient, medieval, modern
           coins and how to know them.

AA40   Raymond, D.
R28   Coins and the story they tell.
           Sydney, [1948?].
               23p. 5 pl. 23cm.

AA40   Raymond, Wayte.
R3   The coin collector's series. [Twelve
           monographs bound together]. New York,
           1940-46.
               Contents: U.S. Commemorative coins;
           Coins of Mexico, Silver ecus of France,
           Early medals of Washington, Coins of Cen.
           America; Silver crowns of Gr. Brit & Ire-
           land; Standard ptolemaic silver; U.S.
           cents; Coins of S. Amer; Coins of W. Indies;
           Guide to Ancient coins; Coins of Canada.

AA40   Reinfeld, Fred, 1910-1964.
R4   Treasury of the world's coins. New
           York, Sterling Pub. Co. [c1953, rev. ed.
           c1955], 1967.
               221p. illus. 27cm.
               1967 edition revised by Burton Hobson.

AA40   Reinfeld, Fred.
R42   A catalogue of the world's most
           popular coins. Revised edition.
           New York, Sterling Pub. Co. [1960], 63, 65, 69, 76.
               265p. illus. 26cm.

AA40   The romance of money.
R64   N.Y., Natamsa Publishing Co.,
Vert.   1937.
File   unpaged. illus. 16cm.

AA40   Russell, Solveig Paulson.
R8   From barter to gold, the story of money.
           New York, Rand McNally [1961].
               64p. illus. 24cm.

AA40   Saeman, C. C.
S2   The evolution of money. N.p., N.pub., 1951.
               17p. 23cm.

AA40   Schwarz, Ted.
S3   Coins as living history. N.Y.,
          Arco Pub., 1976.
              224p. illus. 24cm.

AA40   Seidler, Ned.
S5   The story of money. New York, Odyssey,
          [1965].
              44p. illus. 11 x 17cm.

AA40   Smithsonian Institution.
S6   Contributions from the Museum of His-
          tory and Technology. Papers 31-33 on
          Numismatics. Washington, 1970.
              108, 102, 68p. illus. 28cm.

AA40   Stockvis, Albert.
S7   Standard coin and medal
V.3   catalogue of the world; from the
          earliest times (1000 BC) to the
          present day with illustrations
          of coins and coats of arms.
          Cleveland, the author, 1945.
              V.3 39p. illus. 23cm.

AA40   Stockvis, Albert.
S7   Catalogue of coins, medals and
V.4   tokens; from BC 2000 to the present
          day. With illustrations of coins
          and coat of arms. Cleveland,
          the author, 1945.
              V.4 66p. illus. 23cm.

AA40   The story of money.
S77   St. Paul, Louis F. Dow Co.,
Vert.   1953.
File   unpaged. illus. 23cm.

AA40   Thomas, Eleanor.
T5   The story of money. Columbus,
          Ohio, American Education Press,
          Inc., 1935.
              36p. illus. 23cm. (Weekly
          Reader unit study book, #606).

AA40   White, Benjamin.
W5   The romance of currency. Tunbridge,
          Wells, n.d.
              38p. pl. 18cm.

AA45
B8
Buchenau, Heinrich.
    Grundriss der Munzkunde.
II: Die Munze in ihrer geschichtlichen
entwicklung vom altertum bis zur
gegenwart. Leipzig, Teubner, 1920.
    128p. ill. 18cm.

AA45
C5
Chijs, Pieter Otto van der, 1802-1867.
    Beknopte verhandeling over het nut der
beoefening van de Algemeene, dat is: oude,
middeleeuwsche en hedendaagsche munt-en
penningkunde. Leiden, Cyfveer, 1829.
    84p. 22cm.
    Bibliography: p. 53-84.

AA45
D3
Dannenberg, Hermann.
    Grundzuge der munzkunde, von Hermann
Dannenberg. Zweite, Vermehrte und
Verbesserbe Auflage. Mit 11 tafeln
abbildungen. Leipzig, J. J. Weber, 1899
    ix, 307p. 11 pl. 17cm.

AA45
D6
Dozy, Charles M.
    Het verzamelen van munten en penningen.
Handboek tot het aanleggen van eene munt-en
penning-verzameling. Door Mr. Ch. M. Dozy.
Leiden, A. W. Sijthoff [1884].
    209p. 51 illus. 21cm.
    Bibliography: p. 194-198

AA45
D8
Dupriez, Charles.
    Monnaies et medailles, du. VII
siecle before J.C. jusqu'a a nos
jours [par] Ch. Dupriez. Bruzelles,
the author, 1928.
    32p. plates. 25cm.

AA45
F7
Friedensburg, Ferdinand.
    Die Munze in der kulturgeschichte,
von Ferdinand Friedensburg...Berlin, Weid-
mannsche buchhandlung, 1909.
    viii, 241p. illus. 21cm.

AA45
G6
Gomez, Don Jose Justo, Conde de la
Cortina.
    Nociones elementales de Numismatica
para el use de las aficionados a
esta ciencia [par] Don Jose Gomez
de la Cortina. Facsimile ed.
Mexico City, Academia Mexicana de
Estudios Numismatics, 1975. Originally
published in 1843.
    36p. scattered illus. 24cm.

AA45   Joachim, Johann Friedrich.
J6   Unterricht von dem munzweaen ...
        den Juden, Griechen und Romern ... Europ-
        aischen Landern. Halle, Renger, 1754.
            288p. 18cm.

AA45   Karys, Jonas.
K3   Numismatika, dictionary, studies.
        Putnam, Conn., Immaculata, 1970.
            340p. illus. 24cm.
            In Lithuanian.

AA45   Lenormant, Francois 1837-1883.
L4   Monnaies et medailles, par Fr. Lenormant
        ... Paris, A. Quantin, Nouvelle edition,
        [188-].
            328p. illus. 21cm. (Bibliotheque de
        l'enseignement des beaux-arts).

AA45   Loon, Gerard van, 1683-1758.
L6   Inleiding tot de Heedendaagsche penning-
Rare   kunde ofte verhandeling van den oorsprong
Books   van 't geld. Amsterdam, Pieter de Coup,
        1717.
            184p. 6 pl. 19cm.

AA45   Loehr, August O.
L63   Numismatik und geldgeschichte.
        Vienna, Rudolf M. Rohrer, 1944.
            47p. XVI plates. 22cm.

AA45   Prober, Kurt.
P7   Manual de numismatica. 1st ed & 2nd ed,
        revista e aumentada. [Rio de Janeiro,
        Leuzinger, 1944, 1945].
            189p. illus. 24cm. (Monografias
        Numismaticas)

AA45   Renauldin, Leop Jes.
R4   Etudes historiques et critiques sur
        les medecins numismatistes, contenant
        leur biographie et l'analyse de
        leurs ecrits. Paris, J. B. Bailliere,
        1851.
            576p. 23cm.

AA45   Scaligeri, Joseph.
S3   De re nummaria dissertatio,
Rare   liber posthumus: ex bibliotheca
Books   academia Lugd. Bat. N.P.,
        Raphelengis, 1616.
            72p. 17cm.

AA45   Sey, Katalin B.
S4   Munzen und medaillen [by] Katalin B.
          Sey [and] Istvan Gedai. Budapest, Magyer
          Helikon-Corvina, 1973.
              52p.; unpaged plates. Illus. 26cm.

AA45   Suhle, Arthur.
S9   Die munze, von den an fangen bis zur
          Europaischen neuzeit. [von] Arthur Suhle.
          Leipzig, Koehler & Amelang, n.d.
              227p. illus. 22cm.

AA45   Ting, Fu-Pao.
T5   Ku Chien Hsuch Kang Yao, by Ting
          Fu-Pao. Originally published in 1940.
          Reprinted: n.p., n. pub., 1975.
              198p. illus. 27cm.
              English title: An outline of
          Numismatology.

DICTIONARIES, BIBLIOGRAPHIES, ETC.

AA50   Akerman, John Yonge, 1806-1873.
A3   A numismatic manual. London, Taylor &
          Walton, 1840, 1890.
              xiv, 420p. illus. xvii pl. 22cm.

AA50   Alexander and Co's New hub coin book;
A4   an absolute and reliable and up-
              to-date handbook of American and
              foreign coins illustrated with
              reproductions of photographs of the
              actual coins. various ed.
              Baltimore, I. & M. Ottenheimer,
              n.d.
              119p. illus. 15cm.

AA50   American Numismatic Association.
A45   Dictionary of Numismatic terms.
          Colorado Springs, 1968, 1970.
              20p. 23cm.

AA50   Amoros, Jose.
A5   Enciclopedia Grafica-la moneda.
          Barcelona, 1931.
              64p. illus. 24cm.

AA50
A8

Attinelli, Emmanuel Joseph.
     A bibliography of American
numismatic auction catalogues, 1828-
1875; by Emmanuel Joseph Attinelli.
Reprint of the N.Y. 1876 edition titled
Numisgraphics. Lawrence, Mass.,
Quarterman Publications, 1976.
     149p. 24cm.

AA50
B5

Bowman, Fred.
     A bibliography of Canadian
numismatists. n.p., n. pub., n.d.
     34p., IVp. 29cm.

AA50
B7

Brunk, Gregory G.
     A bibliography of numismatic
literature on countermarked coins,
Waterloo, Iowa, the author, 1975.
     122p. 28cm.

AA50
C4

Chamberlain, Christopher Churchill.
     Coin dictionary and guide. New York,
Sterling, [1961, c1960].
     251p. illus. 19cm.

AA50
C4t
REF

Chamberlain, Christopher Churchill.
     The teach yourself guide to
numismatics; an A.B.C. of coins and
coin collecting, by C. C. Chamberlain.
London, The English Universities Press,
Ltd., 1960.
     180p. illus. 18cm. (Teach yourself
books)

AA50
C55

Clain-Stafanelli, Elvira Eliza.
     Select numismatic bibliography. New York
Stack [1965]
     406p. 26cm.

AA50
C6

Coin World, ed.
     Coin world almanac; a handbook
for coin collectors; compiled
and edited by the staff of Coin
World. Sidney, Ohio, Amos
Press, 1975.
     833p. charts. graphs. 22cm.

AA50
D8

Dye, John S.
     Dye's coin encyclopaedia: a complete
illustrated history of the coins of the world
...To which is added an appendix, by E. Mason
Jr. ...presenting an authenticated statement
of the coinage of the late Southern confederacy, at New Orleans, in 1861 ... Philadelphia, Bradley & company, 1883.
     1152p. illus. 22cm.

AA50   Frey, Albert Romer, 1858-
F7   Dictionary of numismatic names, with
        Glossary of numismatic terms in English,
        French, German, Italian, Swedish by Mark M.
        Salton. [New York] Barnes & Noble [1947], 1973
             ix, 311, 94p. 26cm.

AA50   Grierson, Philip.
G7   Coins and medals; a select bibliography.
        [London] Published for the Historical
        Association by G. Philip, 1954.
             88p. 19cm.

AA50   Grossman, Lee.
G76   Numismatic listing of modern &
        medi[e]val countries. San Antonio,
        Almanzar's Coins of the World [c1972]
             65, [1]p. illus. 22cm.
             bibliography: p. [66]

AA50   Gnecchi, Francesco ed E.
G8   Guida numismatica universale by
        F. ed., E. Gnecchi. Quarta edizione.
        Milano, Ulrico Hoepli, 1903.
             608p; 64p. 16cm.

AA50   Heyde, Gilbert Christoph.
H4   Coins; information for all interested in
        coins, from beginners to advanced collectors
        By ... [Sydney, E. Baxter] 1945.
             51p. 22cm.

AA50   Hobson, Burton.
H6   Illustrated encyclopedia of world
        coins by Burton Hobson and Robert Obojski.
        Garden City, New York, Doubleday, [1970].
             512p. illus. 24cm.

AA50   Johnson, D. Wayne.
J6   Anonymous Numismatic works; a list of
Ref.   141 books ... published anonymously but
        whose authorship is hereby revealed.
        University City, Mo., 1956.
             20p. 28cm.

AA50   Johnson, D. Wayne, comp.
J6n   Numismatic directory for 1957, compiled
1957   by ... and Walter H. Breen. St. Louis,
        Missouri, D. Wayne Johnson, 1957.
             101p. 22cm.

AA50   Krasnodebski, Jan J., ed.
K7   International numismatic directory.
Ref.   Foreward by C. H. V. Sutherland. London,
         1973.
             272p. 22cm.

AA50   Krause, Hermann.
K73   Numismatic dictionary; English-
Ref.   German; German-English. Munchen, Ernst
         Battenberg, 1971.
             87p. 21cm. (Kleine numismatische
         bibliothek, #8)

AA50   Leroux, Joseph.
L42   Vade mecum du collectionneur par Joseph
         Leroux, M.D. ... Montreal, Beauchemin &
         Valois, 1885.
             94p. 12 pl. 25cm.
         French and English

AA50   New York. Public library.
N4   ... List of works relating to numismatics
         New York, 1914.
             195p. 26cm.
         Reprinted from the Bulletin of the New
         York public library.

AA50   Nop, Vladimir.
N6   Soupis numismaticke literatury;
         V Kromerizske Zamecke Knihovne.
         Brne, Czechoslovakia, Moravske
         Museum, 1974.
             114p. 48 plates. 25cm.
         (Numismatica Noravica, #4)
             Written in Czech and German with one
         preface, index and various other
         sections in English.

AA50   Numismatic News Weekly.
N8   Coin club roster and information
         booklet. 1974 ed. Iola, Wisc,
         Krause Publications, 1974.
             79p. 28cm.

AA50   Probszt, Gunther.
P7   Numismatische literatur Osteuropas
         und des Balkans. Graz, Austria,
         Akademische Druck, 1960.
             87p. 27cm.

AA50   Rosichan, Richard H.
R6   Stamps and coins / Richard H. Rosichan.
        -Littleton, Colo. : Libraries Unlimited, 1974.
            404p. 24cm. (Spare time guides; no. 5)

AA50   Sigler, Phares O.
S5   Numismatic bibliography. Dearborn,
        Mich., Dearborn Press [1951]
            iv. 189p. 23cm.

AA50   Smith, Andrew Madsen, 1841-1915.
S6   Illustrated encyclopaedia of gold and
        silver coins of the world; illustrating the
        modern, ancient, current and curious,
        from A.D. 1885 back to B.C. 700 ...
        Philadelphia, A.M. Smith, 1886.
            511p. illus. 25cm.

AA50   Spink and Son Ltd., London.
S62   A selected list of books on coins and
        medals arranged in series ... together
        with a catalogue of works on numismatics.
        London, Spink, 1932.
            74p. 23cm.

AA50   The Star coin book; an encyclopedia
S7   of rare American and foreign coins
            giving the dates of all rare U.S.
            coins, paper money, etc.,
            showing prices paid for them and by
            whom bought. Various eds. Ft.
            Worth, Texas, Numismatic Co., of
            Texas, n.d.
            112p. illus. 18cm.

AA50   The star rare coin encyclopedia;
S7s   an elaborate encyclopedia of
            the coins of the world from 600
            BC down to the present time,
            giving the dates and amounts
            paid for rare United States and
            foreign coins. Various eds.,
            Ft. Worth, Texas, Numismatic
            Co., of Texas, B. Max Mehl,
            various dates, 1924-
            208p. illus. 19cm.

AA50   Sydney. Public library of New South Wales.
S9   ... Books and articles on coins, medals,
        and tokens in the General reference library
        and Mitchell library collections. Sydney,
        A. J. Kent, government printer, 1923.
            102p. 24cm.

AA50   Les monnaies d'or d'argent et de platine.
T3   internationales, 3-5th ed. documentation
            reunie par tardy. Paris [1963].
            2v. 32 pl. v.1: 16cm. x 12cm. v.2:
            16 x 26cm.

AA50   Von Bergen, William.
V6   The rare coin encyclopedia;
            [in three parts]. [Boston], W. Von
            Bergen, 1901.
                 116p. illus. 18cm.

NUMISMATICS - EDUCATION AND TEACHING

AA55   Whitting, Philip D.
W5   Coins in the classroom; an introduction
            to numismatics for teachers, by P. D.
            Whitting. London, Historical Association,
            1966.
                 46p. 4 pl. 22cm.
                 Bibliography: p. 44-46.

AA55   Wormser, Moritz.
W6   Numismatics, government support and
            university instruction, a plea for recog-
            nition; an address by Moritz Wormser, pres.
            American numismatic assoc. at its annual
            convention New York, August 1922. [New
            York, American numismatic association, 1922]
                 16p. 23cm.

NUMISMATISTS, A-Z

AA58   DeWitt, John Doyle, 1902-
R6D4   Alfred S. Robinson, Hartford numismatist.
            by J. Doyle DeWitt. #[Hartford] Conn. His-
            torical Society, 1968.
                 28p. illus. 20cm.
                 Bibliography: p. 28

AA60 Bolt, Conway A.
B5   Collector to numismatist. Address
Vert. given before the Cape Fear Coin Club,
File   Marshville, N.C., 1962.
      3p. photo. 22cm.

AA60 Botsford, Robert K.
B6   Coin collecting pleasures and profits.
Vert. Chicago, Hewitt Bros., n.d.
File   16p. illus. 16cm.

AA60 Boy Scouts of America.
B68   Coin collecting. New York, Boy Scouts of
    America, 1938, 1949, 1954, 1975.
      83p. ill. 21cm. (Merit Badge Series)

AA60 Bressett, Kenneth E.
B7   Let's collect coins; an introduction to
    a fascinating hobby, with price guide of
    valuable coins, by Ken Bressett. Racine,
    Wis., Whitman Pub. Co., 1966-1976.
      64p. illus. 19cm.

AA60 Brown, Laurence A.
B76   Coins and coin collecting made
    simple [by] Laurence A. Brown.
    Drawings by Ann Pemberton. Garden
    City, Doubleday, 1963.
      180p. illus. 26cm.

AA60 Chamberlain, Christopher Churchill.
C45   Collecting coins by C. C. Chamberlain...
    2nd enl. ed. London, Reven Books, 1956.
      90p. illus. 18cm.

AA60 Coffin, Joseph.
C7c   Coin collecting. New York, Coward-
    McCann, Inc., 1938.
      155p. illus. 19cm.

AA60 Coffin, Joseph, 1899-
C7c2   The complete book of coin collecting.
    New York, Coward McCann, 1959, 1967, 1973,
    1976.
      251p. ill. 21cm.

AA60 Del Monte, Jacques, 1902-
D4   Coins; a complete guide to collecting.
    [Los Angeles, Trend Books, 1959].
      128p. illus. 25cm. (Trend book, 180)

AA60   Elder Numismatic Press.
E3   Collecting and hobbies; with special
          reference to coin, medal and paper money
          collecting; being a series of addresses.
          N.Y., Elder Numismatic Press, 1917.
              63p. scattered illus. 24cm.

AA60   Evans, Eva Knox.
E8a   The adventure book of money. New York,
          Capital Publ. Co., 1956.
              93p. illus. 25cm.

AA60   Evans, Eva Knox.
E8q   Question and answer adventures-Coins.
          New York, Golden Press, 1965.
              96p. illus. 25cm. (1956 edition under
          title: Question and answer book of coins).

AA60   Felix, Ervin J.   1918-
F4   How to collect stamps, coins, and paper
          money. [Chicago] Windsor Press [1954].
              160p. illus. 24cm.

AA60   Forrer, Leonard Steyning.
F6   The art of collecting coins; a practical
          guide to numismatics. Foreword by C. H. V.
          Sutherland. London, Arco Publishers, 1955,
          and New York, Citadel Press.
              183p. 16 plates. 22cm.
              Bibliography: p. 157-183.

AA60   Gould, Maurice M.
G6   Gould's gold and silver guide to coins.
          New York, Fleet Press Corp. [1969], 1970.
              255p. illus. 21cm.

AA60   Hanson, T.
H25   Coin collecting. London, Glasgow,
          Collins, [1965].
              128p. illus., photog. 15cm. (Collins
          Nutshell Books)

AA60   Hazlitt, William Carew, 1834-1913.
H3   The coin collector. London, G. Redway,
          1896.
              304p. plates. 21cm. (The Collector
          series)
              Bibliography: p. [286]-294

AA60   Head, Don.
H35   So you want to be a coin collector.
          Seattle, Wash., The author, 1964.
              32p. illus. 19cm.

AA60   Herndon, James E.
H4   How to start collecting coins.
        Shreveport, La., The author, 1964.
            59p. illus. 21cm.

AA60   Hobson, Burton.
H6   Coin collecting as a hobby. New York,
        Sterling Pub. Co. [1967].
            128p. illus. 21cm.

AA60   Hobson, Burton.
H6c   Coins you can collect. New and rev. ed.
        New York, Hawthorn Books [1970]
            128p. illus. 24cm.

AA60   Hobson, Burton.
H6i   International guide to coin collecting.
        New York, New American Library [1966].
            142p. illus. 18cm.

AA60   Hobson, Burton.
H6w   What you should know about coins & coin
        collecting. Greenwich, Conn., Fawcett
        Publications [1965].
            192p. illus. 18cm. (Gold medal books,
        d1554)

AA60   Jacob, Kenneth A.
J3   Coin collecting for beginners. Cambridge
        [Eng.], Weatherheads, [1952]
            52p. illus. 22cm.

AA60   Joachim, E. E.
J6   Coins beautiful, containing photographs
        of over 200 of the world's most beautiful
        coins. Photography by Shirley Hecht.
        Atlanta, Capitol Press; distributed by
        International Import Co., Stone Mountain,
        Ga. [1968]
            100 l. illus. 22cm.
            Includes bibliographical references.

AA60   Mills, Brad.
M45   The official guide to coin collecting
        N. Y., House of Collectibles, 1974.
            192p. 19cm.

AA60   Milne, Joseph Grafton, 1867-
M5   Coin collecting, by J. G. Milne, G. H. V.
        Sutherland and J. D. A. Thompson. [London]
        Oxford University Press [1950]
            xii, 152p. 44 plates. 21cm.
            Bibliography: p. 133-134.

AA60
P8

Purvey, Frank.
    Collecting coins; illustrated with
photographs by the author. 1st edition.
London, W. & G. Foyle Ltd., 1963, 1971.
    96p. VIII plates. 18cm.
    Bibliography: pp. 92-96

AA60
R41

Reed, Fred Morton.
    Coins: an investor's & collector's
guide [by] Mort Reed. Chicago,
Regnery [1973]
    x, 403p. illus. 24cm.

AA60
R42h

Reinfeld, Fred, 1910-1964.
    How to build a coin collection. New
York, Sterling Pub. Co., 1958, 1959, 1965,
1973.
    159p. illus. 21cm.

AA60
S3

Schulman, Hans M. F., 1914-
    The coin collectors' almanac, by H.M.F.
Schulman and H. W. Holzer, with contributions by leading experts. New York,
1946.
    372p. illus. 25cm.

AA60
S34
Vert.
File

Schermerhorn, Charles W.
    A penny saved - a penny earned.
[history of "toy" banks] n.p., n.
pub., 1947.
    4p. 27cm.

AA60
S4

Sears, Deane.
    Coin collectors' guide, by Deane Sears
and Martin Rywell. Harriman, Tenn., Pioneer
Press, 1958, 1960.
    76p. ill. 22cm.

AA60
S5

Sherwood, Earle D.
    What shall I collect? Reprinted from
Numismatic Scrapbook Magazine, 1961.
    52p. illus. 19cm.

AA60
W3

Watson, James.
    Collecting coins and paper
money [by] James Watson. London,
Stanley Gibbons Publ., 1975.
    32p. illus. 20cm. (Stanley
Gibbons guides, #2.)

AA60   Wie ich zum sammeln kam; munz-
W53   sammler berichten. Munchen.
              Ernst Battenberg, 1972.
              159p. illus. 21cm.

AA60   Winskowsky, Horst.
W55   Wie sammelt man munzen? Munchen,
              Ernst Battenberg, 1974.
                  154p. illus. tables. 19cm.

AA60   Zimmerman, Walter J., 1910-
Z5   The coin collector's fact book, by
              Walter J. Zimmerman. New York, Arco
              [1974]
                  135p. illus. 25cm.
                  Bibliography: p. 9-11.

SPECIAL ASPECTS - COUNTERFEITING, ETC.

AA70   Hill, George Francis, 1867-
B4   Becker, the counterfeiter, by George
              F. Hill ... London, Spink and Son, ld.,
              1925, 1955.
                  27 pl. 24cm.

AA70   Brunetti, Lodovico.
B7   Opus monetale Cigoi, by Lodovico
              Brunetti. [Bologna, Editore Arnaldo
              Forni, 1966]
                  158p. illus. 14 pl. 32cm.
                  Bibliographical footnotes.

AA70   Low, Lyman Hayes.
L6   Observations on the practice of counter-
              feiting coins and medals. New York, 1895.
                  14p. 23cm.
                  Reprinted from the American Journal of
              Numismatics, July 1895.

AA70   Newman, Eric P.
N4   Lessons in modern day counter-
Vert.   feiting. From "Coin Forgery
File   approaches perfection": International
              Numismatic Congress, Copenhagen,
              1967. Xeroxed from The Numismatist,
              Nov., 1967.
                  pp. 1380-1388. illus. 24cm.

AA70   Svoronos, John N.
S9   Christodoulos the counterfeiter
            [by] J. Svoronos. Originally published
            Athens, 1922. Reprinted Chicago,
            Ares, 1974.
                36p. 16 plates. 28cm.

NUMISMATICS - DISPLAYS AND EXHIBITS

AA72   Heisterkamp, David P.
H4   The exhibition of numismatic
            materials. University of N. Iowa,
            the author, 1973.
                23p. photos. 29cm.

DEALERS AND DEALERSHIPS; MAIL-ORDER COIN BUSINESS, ETC.

AA75   Bowers, Q. David.
B6   How to be a successful coin dealer,
            by Q. David Bowers. [Sidney, Ohio, Coin
            World, 1973]
                47p. 22cm.

AA75   Heath, G. A.
H3   How to sell coins by mail. Toronto,
            Ontario, G.A. Heath, 1973, 1975.
                35p. 28cm.

AA75   Jensen, Chris.
J4   How to build your own mail order coin
Vert.   business. Yonkers, N.Y., the author, 1973.
File   7p. 22cm.

AA75   Reagan, Lewis Martin, 1904-
R4   Numismatics (coin collecting) Cambridge,
            Mass., Bellman Pub. Co. [c1955].
                16p. illus. 23cm. (Vocational and
            professional monographs, no. 86)

AA75   Saxton, Burton H.
S2   Effective advertising. N.P.,
            the American Numismatic Assn., 1953.
                15p. 23cm.

INVESTMENT

AA78   Bowers and Ruddy Galleries.
B6   Rare coins as an investment ... collection/
            investment program. [Los Angeles, Bowers and
            Ruddy Galleries, Inc., 1976.]
                24p. illus. 28cm.

AA78   Forman, Harry J.
F6   How you can make big profits investing in
            coins [by] Harry J. Forman. New York, Nummus
            Press [1972]
                160p. 24cm.

AA78   Romano, Don C. A.
R6   Decisions, a monograph, discourses on
            the economy in general and probable numis-
            matic investments. N.p., Don C.A. Romano,
            1976.
                89p. illus. 28cm.

AA80   Abbott, George Henry.
A2   The elephant on coins. By...president of
       the Australian numismatic society. (Read
       before the society at Sydney on 24th July
       and 28th August, 1919) [Sydney, Sydney and
       Melbourne publishing co., 1919].
           15p. illus. 24cm.

AA80   Allan, William.
A5   The Christian teaching of coin mottoes;
       with a supplementary chapter on the religious
       character of ancient coins by...Jeremiah
       Zimmerman. London, Society for Promoting
       Christian Knowledge, 1911.
           184p. illus. 19cm.

AA80   Broeker, Peter W.
B2   Olympic coins from antiquity to the
       present, by Peter W. Broeker. 1st ed.
       Pointe Claire, Quebec, Stebro, 1973.
           101p. illus. 21cm.

AA80   Babelon, Jean, 1889-
B3   Great coins and medals. Photos. by J.
       Roubier. [Translated from the French by
       Stuart Hood. London, Thames & Hudson,
       [1959]
           37p. 167 plates. 28cm.

AA80   Becker, Thomas William.
B4   Art in commemorative coins. Published by
       the author, 1962.
           53p. illus. 19cm.

AA80   Conservation coin collection. [London,
C6   Spink & Son, n.d.]
           2v. ill. 21cm.

AA80   Davis, Bruce.
D3   A currency zoo. Colorado Springs,
       Colorado, the author, 1974.
           12p. illus. 29cm.

AA80   Eads, Ora.
E2   Cats on coins. Series taken from
       Cattus, various issues, Nashville,
       Tennessee, 1974-75.
           variously paged. illus. 22cm.

AA80   Gentleman, David.
G4   Design in miniature. New York,
            Watson-Guptill [1972]
                 104p. illus. 22cm.

AA80   Hoober, Richard T.
H6   Ships on coins and medals. Reprinted
            from The Numismatist, vol. 61, Jan. 1948.
                 12p. illus. 23cm.

AA80   Hobson, Burton.
H62   Coin identifier. New York, Sterling
            Pub. Co. [1966].
                 88p. illus. 21cm.

AA80   Jacob, Kenneth A.
J3   Coins and Christianity. London, Seaby,
            1959.
                 40p. illus. 21cm.
                 Reprinted from Seaby's Coins and Medal
            Bulletin, 1957-1958.

AA80   McNaught, James B.
M3   Physicians on coins. Reprinted from the
            Stanford Medical Bulletin, May, 1944.
                 8p. illus. 24cm.

AA80   Medical coins and medals. [Articles in] Ciba.
M4   Symposia, vol. 9, no. 10, January-February
                 1948. Ciba Pharmaceutical Products.
                 30p. illus. 23cm.

AA80   Mosher, Stuart.
M6   Coin mottoes and their translations.
            Reprinted from The Numismatist, 1948.
                 38p. 23cm.

AA80   Murray, John.
M8   The truth of revelation demonstrated by an
            appeal to existing monuments, sculptures,
            gems, coins and medals. 2nd. ed. London,
            Wm. Smith, 1840.
                 380p. 3 pl. 22cm.

AA80   Rentzmann, Wilhelm.
R4   Numismatisches legenden-lexicon des mittel-
            alters und der neuzeit. Von Wilhelm
            Rentzmann ... Berlin, R. Wegener,
            1865-66. Reprint, Dusseldorf, Schenk,
            1965.
                 2v. 24cm. 2v. in 1

AA80   Rentzmann, Wilhelm.
R4w   Numismatisches wappen-lexicon des mittel-
          alters und der neuzeit, index. Reprint.
          Dusseldorf, Schenk, 1965.
             viii, 113p. pl. 24cm.

AA80   Schwarz-Winklhofer, I.
S3   Das buch der zeichen und symbole;
          herausgegeben von I. Schwarz-
          Winklhofer und H. Biedermann. Graz,
          Austria, Verlag fur Sammler, 1972.
             281p. illus. 19cm.

AA80   Sutherland, Carol Humphrey Vivian.
S8   Art in coinage; the aesthetics of money
          from Greece to the present day. London,
          B.T. Batsford [1955]; New York, Philos-
          ophical Library, 1956.
             223p. illus. 23cm.

AA80   Thurman, Harrison E.
T45   Heraldry and world coinage. The author,
          privately printed, 1964.
             74p. 201 illus. 21cm.

AA80   Wenzel, Alexander.
W4   Auflosungen Lateinischer legenden
          auf munzen und medaillen. Braunschweig,
          Klinkhardt & Biermann, 1974.
             327p. 27cm.
             -in German & English

AA80   Ziegesar, Anton Von.
Z5   Tiermotiv katalog. Munchen,
          Ernst Battenberg, 1970.
             153p. illus. 21cm. (Kleine
          Numismatische Bibliothek, #5)

TECHNICAL ASPECTS - WEIGHTS AND MEASURES

AA90   Becker, Thomas W.
B4   The coin makers [by] Thomas W. Becker.
          Garden City, N.Y., Doubleday [1969].
             178p. illus.(part col.) ports. 24cm.

AA90   Berriman, A. E.
B42   Historical metrology; a new analysis of
          the archaeological and the historical
          evidence relating to weights and measures.
          London, Dent, [1953].
             224p. illus. 19cm.
             Bibliography: p. 200-215

AA90   Bowring, Sir John.
B6   The decimal system in numbers, coins
        and accounts; especially with reference to
        the decimalisation of the currency and
        accountancy of the United Kingdom. London,
        Nathaniel Cook, 1854.
            245p. illus. 19cm.

AA90   British Museum. Dept. of Coins & Medals.
B7   Grains and grammes. A table of equiva-
        lents for the use of numismatists. Oxford,
        for the trustees, 1920.
            35p. tables. 20cm.

AA90   Caley, Earle Radcliffe.
C3   Metrological tables. New York, American
        Numismatic Society, 1965.
            119p. 2 pl. 22cm. (Numismatic Notes and
        monographs no. 154)

AA90   Egleston, Thomas, Comp.
E3   Tables of weights, measures, coins
        etc. of the U.S. and England with
        their equivalents in the metric
        system. Boston, American Metric
        Bureau, 1880.
            60p. 17cm.

AA90   Holt, Susan Fraker.
H5   The United States and the metric
        system. Minneapolis, Federal Reserve
        Bank of Minneapolis, 1973.
            32p. charts. 23cm.
            Bibliography.

AA90   Kelly, P.
K4   The universal cambist and commercial in-
        structor: being a full and accurate treatise
        on the exchanges, coins, weights, and meas-
        ures, of all trading nations and their colo-
        nies. Second edition. London, Longman,
        1835.
            2 v. in 1 (xl, 422, xxiv, 380p.) map 28cm.

AA90   Kisch, Bruno.
K5   Scales and weights; a historical outline.
        New Haven, Yale University, 1965.
            297p. illus. 26cm.
            Bibliography: p. 268-281

AA90
M3
Vert.
File
	Mandel, Bill.
	    Jimmy Chin's miraculous coins;...
	metal plating will never be the
	same. Taken from "Today" section,
	Philadelphia Inquirer, April 6,
	1975.
	    pp. 14, 18-21. illus. 32cm.

AA90 Mandel, Bill.
M3   Jimmy Chin's miraculous coins;...
Vert. metal plating will never be the
File   same. Taken from "Today" section,
       Philadelphia Inquirer, April 6,
       1975.
           pp. 14, 18-21. illus. 32cm.

AA90 Monnoyage (Minting).
M6   [Plates depicting early coin making
Vert. processes and equipment]
File   xix pl.

AA90 Ridgeway, William.
R5   The origin of metallic currency and
       weight standards. Detroit, Singing Tree,
       1970.
           417p. illus. 22cm.
           Reprint of 1892 ed.

AA90 Sheppard, Thomas.
S5   Money scales and weights; by
       T. Sheppard and J. F. Musham.
       Originally published in the Numismatic
       Circular 1920-1923. Reprinted-London,
       Spink & Son, Ltd., 1975.
           221p. illus. 25cm.

COIN PRESERVATION, CLEANING

AA95 Frank, Charles.
F7   Coin preservation handbook. 1st ed.
       [Brooklyn] Coingard Industries, 1964.
           xx, 135p. illus., maps. 21cm.
           Bibliography: p. 134-135.

AA95 Johnson, R. A.
J6   Security storage containers: design, con-
       struction, concealment. Dripping Springs,
       Texas, R.A. Johnson, 1976.
           28p. ill. 22cm.

AA95 Mervis, Clyde D.
M4   Cleaning coins. Reprinted from the
       Numismatic Scrapbook Magazine, 1962, 1963.
           22p. 19cm.

AA95   Molnar, Irme.
M6   The cleaning of silver coins. Reprinted
          from Numismatic Scrapbook, [1946].
               47p. 20cm.

AA95   Welter, Gerhard.
W4   Cleaning and preservation of coins and
          medals. With an Appendix, Grading coins.
          New York, H. Schulman, 1970.
               xi, 123p. 23cm.

AA95   Winskowsky, Horst.
W5   Munzen pflegen; sachgerechte
          reinigung konservierung und aufbewahrung.
          Munchen, Ernst Battenberg, 1974.
               133p. illus. 21cm. (Kleine
          Numismatische Bibliothek, #3)

GRADING

AA96   Hobson, Burton.
H6   Pictorial guide to coin conditions, by
          Burton Hobson and Fred Reinfeld. New York,
          Sterling Pub. Co.; distributed to the coin
          trade by President Coin Corp. [1962].
               128p. illus. 17cm.

AA96   Raisig, L. Miles.
R2   The weight grading of coins. From:
          Numismatic Scrapbook Magazine, v. 27, no.
          10; October 1961.
               p. 2561-2575. illus. 19cm.

PHILATELY AND NUMISMATICS

AA99   Vose, Donald R.
V6   A guidebook to first day $2.00
          cancellations and valuations; featuring
          Illinois certified notes. 1st ed. Freeport,
          Ill., the author, 1976.
               24p. illus. 22cm.

AA99   Walker, Doris.
W3   A guide book of philatelic
          numismatic covers. 1st ed. San Clemente,
          Calif., 99 Co., 1970.
               1 vol. (unpaged). illus. 20cm.

<u>METALS</u>, <u>MINES</u>, <u>MINING</u>

BIBLIOGRAPHIES, DIRECTORIES, ETC.

AB15   Merlub-Sobel, M.
M4   Metals and alloys dictionary.
Ref   Brooklyn, Chemical Publ. Co.,
        1944.
            238p. 22cm.

TECHNICAL ASPECTS

AB25   American Metal Market.
A5   Metal Statistics. 58th ed.-
        New York, the author, 1965-
            799p. 16cm.

AB25   Gray, Allen G., ed.
G7   Modern electroplating. Sponsored
        by the Electrochemical Society, Inc.,
        New York, John Wiley & Sons, Inc.,
        1953.
            563p. 24cm.

AB25   Hoyt, Samuel L.
H5   Metals and alloys data book.
        New York, Reinhold Publ. Corp., 1943.
            334p. charts. 26cm.

AB25   Hoke, C. M.
H6   Testing precious metals with
        the touchstone. N.Y., Jeweler's
        Technical Advice Co., n.d.
            24p. illus. 21cm.

AB25   Liddell, Donald M.
L5   Handbook of nonferrous metallurgy;
        recovery of the metals. 2d ed. N.Y.,
        McGraw Hill, 1945.
            721p. illus. 23cm.

AB25   Smith, Ernest A.
S6   The sampling and assay of the
        precious metals; comprising gold,
        silver, platinum...2d Rev. ed.
        London, Charles Griffin & Co., Ltd.
        1947.
            505p. scattered illus. 23cm.

UNITED STATES

AB28   Raymond, Rossiter W.
R3   Mineral resources of the states and
        territories west of the Rocky Mountains.
        Washington, Govt. Printing Office.,
        1869.
            256p. maps. 23cm.

AB28   U.S. Treasury Dept. Bureau of the Mint.
U5   Report of the director of the mint upon
        the statistics of the production of the
        precious metals in the United States.
        Washington, GPO, 1881, 1900.
            443p. 24cm.

GOLD - GENERAL WORKS

AB30   Allen, Gina.
A4   Gold! New York, Crowell, [1964].
            275p. illus. 22cm.
            Bibliography: p. 257-266.

AB30   Burkett, Russell.
B8   Everything you wanted to know about
        gold and other precious metals; a non-
        professional's guide to profit
        and protection. 2d ed. Glendora,
        Ca., Russell Burkett Investor
        Books, 1975.
            99p. illus. 28cm.
            -Bibliography

AB30   Flueler, Niklaus, ed.
F5   Das buch vom gold [von] Gunter
        Breitling et. al. [edited by]
        Niklaus Flueler und Sebastian
        Speich. Luzern, Switzerland,
        Verlag C. J. Bucher, 1975.
            287p. illus. part. col. 31cm.

AB30   Hammett, A. B. J.
H3   The history of gold. Kerrville, Tex.,
        Braswell, [1966].
            vi, 107p. illus. 24cm.

AB30   Hobbs, Franklyn.
H6   Gold; the real ruler of the world.
         Chicago, the Business Foundation Publishers,
         1943.
             271p.   23cm.

AB30   Los Angeles. County Museum.
L6   Gold before Columbus; a survey
         exhibition of 2300 years of the
         art of the goldsmith in ancient
         America. Presented by the Los
         Angeles County Museum. L.A., the
         Museum, 1964.
             79p.   illus.   25cm.

AB30   Sutherland, Carol Vivian Humphrey.
S9   Gold; its beauty, power and
         allure [by] C.H.V. Sutherland. N.Y.,
         McGraw Hill, 1960, c1959.
             195p.   illus., part. col.   24cm.

AB30   Vicker, Ray.
V5   The realms of gold [by] Ray Vicker.
         N.Y., Charles Scribner's Sons,
         1975.
             244p.   24cm.

AB30   White, Peter T.
W5   The eternal treasure, Gold.   Photographs
Vert.   by James L. Stanfield.
File   (In the National Geographic Magazine,
         Washington D.C., Jan., 1974. V. 145, No. 1)
         51p.   illus.   26cm.

GOLD - TECHNICAL ASPECTS

AB32   Dewey, Frederic P.
D4   The solubility of gold in
Vert.   nitric acid. Reprinted from the
File   Journal of the American Chemical
         Society. Vol. XXXI, #3, Mar., 1910.
             pp. 318-323.   24cm.

AB32   Horn, Howard.
H6   The goldhorn book for jewelers; a
         reference book of helpful information
         for jewelers...of special interest to
         those who buy old gold, platinum and
         silver [by] Howard Horn and Arie
         Goldstein. N.Y., Goldhorn Refiners,
         n.d.
             unpaged.   charts.   23cm.

AB32   Kaufman, Jerroll D.
K3   Panning gold. 1st printing.
            Colorado Springs, Colo., Springs
            Treasure Hunters League, 1975.
                24cm. illus. 22cm.

AB32   Rickard, T. A.
R5   The stamp milling of gold ores. 2nd ed.
            New York, London, Scientific Pub. Co., 1898.
                xi, 260p. illus. tables. 23cm.

GOLD - UNITED STATES, BY STATE, A-Z

AB39   Egenhoff, Elisabeth L.
C2E4   The elephant as they saw it, a collection
            of contemporary pictures and statements
            on gold mining in California, assembled by
            E. L. Egenhoff. California, Division of
            Mines, 1949.
                128p. illus. 23cm.

AB39   Missouri Numismatic Society.
C2M5   A romance of gold rush days and the
            forty-niners, as told at the coin festival
            of the ... . St. Louis, Missouri, Missouri
            Numismatic Society, 1969.
                27p. illus. 28cm.

AB39   Sunset Books, ed.
C2S9   Gold rush country; guide to
            California's mother lode and northern
            mines; by the editors of Sunset
            Books and Sunset Magazine. Menlo Park,
            Ca., Lane Books, 1968.
                96p. illus. 28cm.

AB39   [Cooper, Ben Green].
G4C6   Dahlonega gold. Atlanta, Roberts,
            1962.
                32p. illus. 18cm.

SILVER - GENERAL WORKS

AB40   Butts, Allison, ed.
B8   Silver-economics, metallurgy,
            and use; edited by Allison Butts with
            the collaboration of Charles D.
            Coxe, sponsored by Handy and Harmon.
            Princeton, N. J., D. Van Nostrant Co.,
            Inc., 1967.
                448p. graphs. 24cm.

AB40   Mendenhall, W. E.
M4   The vital need for free silver.
        n.p., the author, 1938.
            68p. 15cm.

SILVER - TECHNICAL ASPECTS

AB42   Dewey, Frederic P.
D4 .   The Gay-Lussac method of silver
        determination. Reprinted from the
        Journal of Industrial and Engineering
        Chemistry, Vol. 5, #3, Mar., 1913.
            15p. 24cm.

SILVER - UNITED STATES, BY STATE, A-Z

AB49   Smith, Grant H.
N3S6   The history of the Comstock Lode, 1850-
        1920. Reno, Nevada Bureau of Mines, 1943.
            297p. illus. 23cm. (University of
        Nevada Bulletin, v.37, no.3, July, 1943)

NICKEL - GENERAL WORKS

AB50   Howard-White, F. B.
H6   Nickel, an historical review.
        Princeton, N.J.; New York, Van Nostrand,
        [1963].
            xiii, 350p. fronts. illus. 22cm.
            Bibliography: p. 259-302.

AB50   International Nickel Company.
I5   This is International Nickel.
        [Toronto, n.d.].
            [32]p. col. illus. 28 x 28cm.

COPPER - TECHNICAL ASPECTS

AB62   Elwell, W. T.
E3   Analysis of copper and its
          alloys [by] W. T. Elwell and I. R.
          Scholes. 1st ed. Oxford,
          Pergamon Press, Ltd., 1967.
              183p. illus. charts. 23cm.

AB62   Finlay, Walter L.
F5   Silver-bearing copper; a
          compendium of the origin, character-
          istics, uses and future of copper
          containing 12-25 ounces per ton of
          silver. New York, Copper Range Co.-
          Corinthian Ed., 1968.
              356p. illus. 24cm.

COPPER - UNITED STATES

AB66   Ranie, Hans.
S9R3   The great copper mountain; Hans Ranie's
          Mine Map of 1683. [Sweden, Bengtsons
          Litografiska ab sthlm, 1961]
              unpaged. 21cm.

IRON AND STEEL, ALLOYS - GENERAL WORKS

AB70   Brick, R. M.
B7   Structure and properties of
          alloys,...by R. M. Brick and Arthur
          Phillips. 1st ed. N.Y., McGraw-
          Hill Book Co., 1942.
              227p. illus. 22cm. (Metallurgy
          and Metallurgical Engineering Series)

AB70   Harrington, Richard H.
H3   The modern metallurgy of alloys
          [by] R. H. Harrington. New York,
          John Wiley & Sons, inc., 1948.
              209p. charts. 22cm.

AB70   International Nickel Co., Inc.
I5   The platinum metals. Reprinted
          from Interscience Encyclopedia, Inc.,
          New York, n.d.
              pp. 819-860. 23cm.

AB70   Societa Italiana Acciai Speciali.
S6   L'acmonital e la monetazione
        in acciaio inossidabile. Milan,
        n.d.
            50p. illus. 30cm.

IRON AND STEEL, ALLOYS - TECHNICAL ASPECTS

AB72   Rice, L. P.
R5   A study of alloys suitable for use as
        United States coinage, by ..., M.E. Emerson,
        H.J. Wagner, R.W. Hale, and A.M. Hall. Co-
        lumbus, Ohio, Battelle Memorial Institute,
        1965.
            46p. charts 29cm.

<u>ANCIENT</u> <u>COINS</u>

COLLECTIONS

BA20   Oxford, England. Oxford University.
A8   Ashmolean Museum.
             Report of the visitors. Oxford,
          University Press, 1947, 1950.
             variously paged. illus. 22cm.

BA20   Baramki, Dimitri.
B3   The coins exhibited in the
          archaeological museum of the
          American University of Beirut.
          Beirut, American University of
          Beirut, 1968.
             186p. XI plates. 25cm.

BA20   Boston. Museum of Fine Arts.
B6   Guide to the Catherine Page Perkins
          collection of Greek and Roman coins.
          Boston, Houghton, Mifflin, 1902.
             111p. 5 pl. 19cm.

BA20   British Museum. Dept. of Coins and Medals.
B7   Guide to the principal gold and silver
          coins of the ancients, from circa B.C. 700
          to A.D. 1, by Barclay V. Head. London,
          The Trustees ... 1889 (3rd ed.), 1895
          (4th ed). Chicago, Argonaut, 1968.
             128p. 70 pl. 22cm.
             1968 ed. is reprint of 2nd ed. of 1881,
          with new preface & select bibliography.
             Bibliography: p. xv-xviii

BA20   British Museum. Dept. of Coins & Medals.
B7s   Synopsis of the contents of the British
          museum; Dept. of coins & medals. A guide
          to the select Greek & Roman coins exhibited
          in electrotype. New ed. by Barclay V. Head.
          London, the Trustees, 1880.
             128p. vii pl. 21cm.

BA20   Copenhagen. Nationalmuseets. (Mont. og
C5   medalle-Samlingen).
             Orientalske, graeske og romerske monter.
          2nd ed. Kobenhavn, 1952.
             108p. illus. 22cm.

BA20   Cox, Dorothy Hannah, 1893-
C6   A Tarsus coin collection in the Adana mus-
        eum, by D.H. Cox. New York, The American
        numismatic society, 1941.
            67p. plates. 17cm. (Numismatic notes
        and monographs, no. 92)

BA20   Freeman, Sarah Elizabeth.
F7   Coins: Treasure trove of history. In:
        The Johns Hopkins magazine, v. ix, no. 3,
        Dec. 1957, p. 14-18.
            5p. illus. 28cm.

BA20   Harvard University. Fogg Art Museum.
H3   Ancient coins. Cambridge, Mass., 1956.
            [40]p. illus. 19 x 13cm. (Fogg
        picture book no. 4)

BA20   Holloway, R. Ross.
H6   The ancient coins [in] the Frederick M.
        Watkins Collection, Fogg Art Museum, Harvard
        University. Reprint from the [collection],
        Boston, Harvard University, 1973.
            pp. 101-153. illus. 25cm.

BA20   Holzer, Hans.
H64   The Thomas Ollive Mabbott collection of
        coins of the Greek world and coins of the
        Roman world ... sold at auction at Hans M.F.
        Schulman Gallery, 1969. New York, Sanford
        J. Durst, 1976.
            148, 95p. pl. 27cm.
        Contains prices realized.

BA20   Iliescu, O.
I3   Cabinetul numismatic...Romine,
        Biblioteca Academici Republicii
        Populare Romine., [1957?]
            pp. 179-189. VIII plates. 26cm.

BA20   Manhattan college, New York.
M3   The Bishop Bonaventure F. Broderick
        collection of ancient coins, catalogued by
        Frederick S. Knobloch ... New York city,
        Manhattan college [pref. 1942].
            28p. 23cm.

BA20   Mosser, Sawyer McArthur, 1905-
M6   The Endicott gift of Greek & Roman coins,
        incl. the "Catacombs" hoard, by Sawyer McA.
        Mosser. New York, The American numismatic
        society, 1941.
            53p. plates. 17cm. (Numismatic notes
        and monographs. No. 97).

BA20   Oxford. University. Ashmolean Museum.
O8   Exhibition of antiquities and coins,
            purchased from the collection of the late
            Capt. E.G. Spencer-Churchill. (Published
            by the Museum), 1965.
                 24p. 20 plates. 24cm.

BA20   Raymond, Wayte, 1886-
R3   The J. Pierpont Morgan collection;
            catalogue of the Greek and Roman coins,
            Abukir medallions [and] Roman gold bar.
            With an introd. by Sydney P. Noe. New York,
            W. Raymond, Inc. [1953].
                 59p. illus. 23cm.

CATALOGUES

BA30   Raymond, Wayte, 1886-1956.
R3a   Ancient coins, Greek, Roman and Byzan-
            tine, guide and price list, with over 250
            illustrations, published by Wayte Raymond,
            Inc. New York [1936]
                 28p. illus. 23cm.

BA30   Raymond, Wayte, 1886-1956.
R3g   ... Guide to ancient coins ... with over
            250 illustrations. New York, Wayte Raymond,
            Inc., [1944].
                 28p. illus. 23cm. (The Coin collector
            series, no. 11).

GENERAL WORKS

BA40   Babelon, Jean.
B3   La numismatique antique. ("Que sais-
            je?"), Paris, Preases Universitaires de
            France, 1949.
                 127p. illus. 17cm.

BA40   Cardwell, Edward, 1787-1861.
C3   Lectures on the coinage of the Greeks
            and Romans, delivered in the Univ. of Ox-
            ford ... Oxford, S. Collingwood for J.
            Murray, London, 1832.
                 xvi, 238p. 22cm.
                 Bibliography: p. xi-xii

BA40   Cervin, David R.
C4   The first twenty-eight anno Domini
          dated European coins and their
          present existence worldwide. Privately
          reprinted from The Numismatist, July
          1973, Vol. 86, no. 7. Amarillo,
          Texas, the author, 1973.
               pp. 1141-1165. illus. 21cm.

BA40   Corolla numismatica, numismatic essays in
C6   honour of Barclay V. Head.
               London, New York, H. Frowde,
               1906.
               xvi, 386p. illus. 18 pl. 28cm.

BA40   Eckhel, Josepho, 1737-1798.
E25   Doctrina numorum veterum conscripta a
          Josepho Eckhel. Vindobonae (Leipzig)
          Sumptibus I. V. Degen, etc. 1792-1828.
               8v. 24cm.
               Contents: 1. Spain, Gaul, Britain, Germany,
          Italy. 2. Europe, Asia Minor. 3. Asia. 4. Egypt,
          Africa. 5. Roman, Consular & family coins
          6-8. Roman Empire.

BA40   Fritze, Hans von.
F7   Nomisma; Untersuchungen auf dem
          Gebiete der antiken Munzkunde; heraus-
          gegeben von Hans von Fritze und Hugo
          Gaebler. Berlin, Mayer & Muller, 1907.
               28p. pl. 31cm.

BA40   Grasse, Johann Georg Theodor, 1814-1885.
G7   Handbuch der alten numismatik von den
Rare   altesten zeiten bis auf Constantine. ...
Books   Leipzig, E. Schafer, 1854.
               vi, 241p. 72 pl. 23cm.

BA40   Humphreys, Henry Noel.
H8   Ancient coins and medals. London,
Rare   Grant and Griffith, 1850.
Books   208p. 10 pl. 23cm.

BA40   Laing, Lloyd Robert.
L3   Coins and archaeology [by] Lloyd R.
          Laing. New York, Schocken Books [1970,
          c1969]
               xvi, 336p. illus., maps. 23cm.
               Bibliography: p. [300]-326.

BA40   Lenormant, Francois.
L4   La monnaie dans l'antiquite. ...
          Bologna, Forni Editore, [1969].
              3v. 21cm.
              [Reprint of Paris ed., 1878-79].

BA40   Macdonald, George, 1862-1940.
M3   Coin types, their origin and development;
          being the Rhind lectures for 1904 ...
          Glasgow, J. Maclehose, 1905. Reprinted,
          1969, Argonaut.
              x, 275p. illus. 10 pl. 22cm.

BA40   Martin, Peter-Hugo.
M37   Die anonymen munzen des jahres
          68 nach Christus [von] Peter-Hugo
          Martin. Mainz, Philipp von Zabern,
          1974.
              95p. 12 plates. 30cm.

BA40   Miller, Max.
M45   Munzen des altertums von Max Miller.
1963   3d rev. ed, by Tyll Kroha. Braunschweig,
          Klinkhardt & Biermann [1963]
              198p. illus. 33 pl. 1 map. 25cm.
          (Bibliothek fur kunst- und antiquitaten
          freunde, band 43)
              Bibliography: pp. 193-195.

BA40   Milne, Joseph Grafton, 1867-1951.
M5   Greek and Roman coins and the study of
          history. London, Methuen & Co., [1939].
              128p. 16 pl. 19cm.

BA40   Newell, Edward Theodore, 1886-1941.
N4   Miscellanea numismatica: Cyrene to
          India. New York, American numismatic
          society, 1938.
              101p. pl. 17cm. (Numismatic notes
          and monographs, no. 82)

BA40   American Numismatic Association.
N8   Selections from the Numismatist, ancient
          and medieval coins. Racine, Wisc., Whitman,
          1960.
              318p. ill. 24cm. (The Numismatist reprint
          series)

BA40   Regling, Kurt Ludwig, 1876-1935.
R4   Ancient numismatics; the coinage of
          ancient Greece and Rome. Translation by
          Terry Merz. Chicago, Argonaut Inc., 1969.
              79p. 22cm. (The Argonaut library of
          antiquities)

BA40   Recuil de medailles de peuples et de villes;
R42   qui n'ont point encore ete publiees,
Rare   ou qui sont peu connues. Paris, H.L.
Books   Guerin & L.F. Delatour, 1763.
             5 vols. illus. 29cm.

BA40   Reinach, Theodore.
R45   L'histoire par les monnaies; essais de
         numismatique ancienne. Paris, E. Leroux,
         1902.
             iv, 269p. illus. 6 pl. 28cm.

BA40   Spanheim, Ezechiel.
S6   Dissertationes de praestantia et us u
Rare   numismatum antiquorum. London, Richard
Books   Smith, 1717.
             2v. ill. 37cm.

DICTIONARIES, BIBLIOGRAPHIES, ETC.

BA45   [Hill, George Francis].
H5   A tribute to Sir George Hill on his
         eightieth birthday, 1867-1947. Oxford
         Univ. Press, priv. print., 1948.
             43p. front. 23cm.

BA45   Vermeule, Cornelius Clarkson, 1925-
V4   A bibliography of applied numismatics in
         the fields of Greek and Roman archaeology
         and the fine arts. London, Spink, 1956.
             viii, 172p. 19cm.

COLLECTING

BA50   Head, Barclay Vincent, 1844-1914.
H4   Handbook of Greek and Roman coins.
         New York, Attic Books, 1969.
             32p. illus. 18cm.

BA50   Hill, Sir George Francis, 1867-1948.
H5   Ancient Greek and Roman coins; a hand-
         book, by G. F. Hill. New and enl. ed. [1st
         American ed.] Chicago, Argonaut, 1964,
         New York, Macmillan, 1899.
             xv. 302p. illus., 16 plates. 22cm.
             Bibliography: p. [297]-302.

BA50   Pennington, Paul.
P4   Ancient coins, an introduction to a
          fascinating hobby, by Paul Pennington.
          [Chicago, Hewitt bros., 1942].
              67p. illus. 20cm.
              Bibliography: p. 3-4.

BA50   Reinfeld, Fred, 1910-
R4   Picture book of ancient coins, by Fred
          Reinfeld and Burton Hobson. London, Oak
          Tree Press; New York, Sterling Pub. Co.
          [1963].
              64p. illus. 26cm. (Visual history
          series)

BA50   Sutherland, Carol Humphrey Vivian.
S8   Ancient numismatics: a brief introduction.
          New York, American Numismatic Society, 1958.
              29p. 23cm.

BA50   Wear, Ted Graham, 1902-
W4   Ancient coins; how to collect for fun
          and profit [by] Ted G. Wear. [1st ed.]
          Garden City, N.Y., Doubleday, 1965.
              viii, 152p. illus. 22cm.

TECHNICAL ASPECTS

BA60   Bloesch, H.
B5   Cleaning ancient coins. New York,
Vert.   n.p., 1963.
File   7p. chart. 27cm.

BA60   Campbell, William, 1876-
C3   Greek and Roman plated coins, by William
          Campbell. New York, The American numismatic
          society, 1933.
              174p. illus., plates, diagrs. 17cm.
          (Numismatic notes and monographs, [no. 57])

BA60   Hall, E. T., ed.
H3   Methods of chemical and metallurigical
          investigation of ancient coinage; a
          symposium held by the Royal Numismatic
          Society at ... London,...1970, edited
          by E. T. Hall and D. M. Metcalf.
          London, Royal Numismatic Society, 1972.
              448p. XX plates. 26cm. (Royal
          Numismatic Society Special Publication
          Number 8).

BA60   Hoskins, Charles R., comp.
H6   Notes from: The conservation of anti-
          quities and works of art, by H. J. Plender-
          leith. New York, Oxford Univ. Press, 1956.
              [23]p. 28cm.

BA60   Meyers, P.
M4   Non-destructive activation analysis of
Vert.   ancient coins using charged particles
File   and fast neutrons. From Archaeometry,
          Volume ii, 1969.
              [17]p. 25cm.

BA60   Nichols, Henry W.
N5   Restoration of ancient bronzes and cure
          of malignant patina. Chicago, Field
          Museum of National History, 1930.
              50p. 11 pl. 24cm. (Museum Technique
          Series, no. 3)

BA60   Vermeule, Cornelius C.
V4   Some notes on ancient dies and coining
          methods. London, Spink & Son, 1954.
              51p. illus. 19cm.
              Reprinted from The Numismatic Circular,
          1953-54.

SPECIAL ASPECTS

BA65   Akerman, John Yonge, 1803-1873.
A4   Numismatic illustrations of the narrat-
          ive portions of the New Testament. Chicago,
          Argonaut, 1966.
              vii, 62p. illus. 22cm.

BA65   Banks, Florence Aiken.
B3   Coins of Bible days. New York,
          Macmillan, 1955.
              178p. illus. 24cm.

BA65   Biblical Museums Bulletin.
B5   Eisenberg issue. Louisville, Ky,
          Southern Baptist Theological Seminary,
          Fall, 1962.
              29p. illus. 21cm.

BA65   Cahn, Herbert A., ed.
C3   Kleine schriften zur munzkunde
          und archaologie. Basel, Arch-
          aologischer, 1975.
              172p. illus. 26cm.

BA65   Halliday, G. R.
H3   Money talks about the Bible. Hollywood,
        CA., The author, 1948.
            28p. illus. 21cm.

BA65   Matsson, G. O.
M3   The gods, goddesses and heroes on the
        ancient coins of Bible lands. Stockholm,
        Numismatiska Bokforlaget, 1969.
            267p. illus. 24cm.

BA65   Tuckwood, Charles E.
T8   Ancient coins associated with Christian-
        ity. Philadelphia. The Philadelphia Trans-
        portation Co. [1946].
            13p. illus. 17cm.

BA65   Tuckwood, Charles E.
T82   Ancient coins associated with Chris-
Vert.   tianity. From the Numismatist, July
File   1947.
            [11]p. illus.

BA65   Walsh, Robert, 1772-1852.
W3   An essay on ancient coins, medals, and
        gems, as illus. the progress of Christianity
        in the early ages, by the Rev. R. Walsh ...
        Second ed. greatly enlarged. London, Howell
        and Stewart, 1828.
            viii, 140p. 38 pl. 18cm.

BA65   Wirgin, Wolf.
W5   The widow's mite story. Reprinted
Vert.   from the Numismatist, April, 1955.
File   8p. 2 pl. 23cm.

BA65   Yeoman, Richard S.
Y4   Moneys of the Bible; an illustrated
        digest of the coinage of Biblical times
        with scriptural references. Racine, Wis.,
        Whitman, 1961.
            61p. illus. 20cm.

ICONOGRAPHY

BA70   Akerman, John Yonge, 1806-1873.
A55   Ancient coins of cities and princes,
        geographically arranged and described. By
        John Yonge Akerman ... Hispania-Gallia-
        Britannia. London, J.R. Smith, 1846.
            iv, 203p. xxiv pl. 28cm.

BA70   Babelon, Jean, 1889-
B3   Le portrait dans l'antique d'apres les
         monnaies. ... Nouvelle ed. rev. & comp.
         Paris, Payot, 1950.
             202p. 32 pl. 23cm.

BA70   Bellinger, Alfred Raymond, 1893-
B4   Victory as a coin type, by Alfred
         Bellinger and Marjoeie Alkins Berlincourt.
         New York, American Numismatic Society, 1962.
             68, xiii p. illus. 23cm. (Numismatic
         notes and monographs, no. 149)

BA70   Bieber, Margarete.
B5a   Alexander the Great in Greek and Roman
         art. Chicago, Argonaut, 1964.
             98p. 63 plates. 22cm.

BA70   Bieber, Margarete.
B5p   The portraits of Alexander the Great.
         Reprinted from the Proceedings of the Ameri-
         can Philosophical Society, v.93, No. 5, 1949.
             p. 373-427. illus. 26cm.

BA70   Donaldson, Thomas Leverton, 1795-1885.
D6   Architectura numismatica or, architectu-
1859   ral medals of classic antiquity. ... London,
         Day and Son, 1859.
             xxxi, 349p. illus. 26cm.

BA70   Donaldson, Thomas Leverton, 1795-1885.
D6   Ancient architecture on Greek coins and
1966   medals; architectura numismatica. Chicago,
         Argonaut, 1966.
             A-M, xxi, 349p. pl. 24cm.

BA70   Magnaguti, Alexander.
M3   Hadrianus in nummis. Reprinted from
         the Numismatic Circular, 1934.
             136p. illus. 25cm.
             Bibliography

BA70   Regling, Kurt Ludwig.
R4   Die antike munze als kunstwerk. Berlin,
         Schoetz & Parrhysius, 1924.
             148p. 45 pl. 23cm.

BA70   Trell, Bluma L.
T7   "Architecture on ancient coins."
Vert.   Taken from Archaeology, V. 29, #1.
File   N.Y., 1976.
             pp. 7-13, illus. 27cm.

BA80   Cox, Dorothy Hannah, 1893-
C8C6   Coins from the excavations at Curium,
           1932-1953. New York, American Numismatic
           Society, 1959.
                xii, 125p. 10 pl. 23cm. (Numismatic
           notes and monographs, no. 145)

BA80   Weber, Shirley Howard, 1883-
E3W4   An Egyptian hoard of the second cen-
           tury, A.D., by Shirley H. Weber. New
           York, American numismatic society, 1932.
                41p. pl. 17cm. (Numismatic notes and
           monographs, no. 54)

BA80   Hrbas, Milos.
O5H7   Ancient coins from Olbia and Pantica-
           paeum. Photographed by M. Hrbas and J.
           Marco, with text by K. Dittrich. Trans.
           by I. Havlu. London, Spring Books
           [1961?].
                167p. 116 pl. 29cm.

BA80   Fulco, William J.
T4F8   Monnaies de Tell Keisan, 1971-
           1974. Extracted from the Revue
           Biblique, Tome LXXXII, 1975.
           Paris, Librairie Lecoffre, 1975.
                pp. 234-239. plate. 25cm.

BA80   Bellinger, Alfred Raymond.
T7B4   Troy. The Coins. Supplementary mono-
           graph 2. Princeton, the University Press,
           1961. Published for the University of
           Cincinnati (for their excavations, 1932-38)
                220p. 27 plates. 30cm.

COLLECTIONS

BB20   Amsterdam Kon Akademic der Wissenschaften.
A5   Beschreibung der Griechischen autonomen
              munzen im besitze der Kon Akademie der
              wissenschaften zu Amsterdam. Amsterdam,
              Johannes Muller, 1912.
                   260p. 8 pl. 28cm.

BB20   Bement, Clarence Sweet, 1843-1923.
B4   A descriptive catalogue of Greek coins,
              selected from the cabinet of Clarence S.
              Bement, esq., Philadelphia. New York, The
              American numismatic society, 1921.
                   106p. xxv pl. 28cm.

BB20   Bellinger, Alfred R.
B44   Greek coins from the Yale Numismatic
Vol.1   Collection; [Recent Additons.] Reprinted
              from Yale Classical Studies, v. 11.
              New Haven, Yale University Press, 1950.
                   pp. 307-316. plates. 24cm.

BB20   Bellinger, Alfred R.
B44   Greek coins from the Yale Numismatic
Vol.2   Collection, II; Achaean League. Reprinted
              from Yale Classical Studies, Vol. 12.
              New Haven, Yale Univ. Press, 1951.
                   pp. 253-265. plates. 24cm.

BB20   Bellinger, Alfred R.
B44   Greek coins from the Yale Numismatic
Vol.3   Collection, III; A hoard of bronze coins
              of Cyzicus. Reprinted from Yale Classical
              Studies, Vol. 13. New Haven, Yale Univ.
              Press, 1952.
                   pp. 161-169. plates. 24cm.

BB20   Boston. Museum of Fine Arts.
B6   Greek coins. 1950 to 1963. Boston,
              [1964].
                   78p. (incl. 30 pl.)

BB20   British museum. Dept. of coins & medals.
B7   ... A guide to the principal coins of
the Greeks, from circ. 700 B.C. to A.D.
270, based on the work of Barclay V. Head.
London, The Trustees, 1932, 1959, 1965,
      106p. 50 pl. 25cm.

BB20   British museum. Dept. of coins and medals.
B71   A catalogue of the Greek coins in the British
1963   museum. Italy. London, Printed by Woodfall
Vol.1   and Kinder, 1873.
                3 pl. [iii]-viii, 432p. illus. 23cm.
                Reprinted, Arnaldo Forni, Bologna, 1963.

BB20   British museum. Dept. of coins and medals.
B71   Catalogue of Greek coins. Sicily. Ed. by
1963   Reginald Stuart Poole ... London, The
v. 2   Trustees, 1876.
                xii, 292p. illus. 22 1/2cm.
           (Added t.-p.: A catalogue of the Greek
           coins in the British museum)
                Reprinted, Arnaldo Forni, Bologna, 1963.

BB20   British museum. Dept. of coins and medals.
B71   Catalogue of Greek coins. The Tauric
1963   Chersonese, Sarmatia, Dacia, Moesia, Thrace,
V. 3   etc. Ed. by Reginald Stuart Poole ...
           London, Printed by order of the Trus-
           tees, 1877.
                xii, 274p. illus. 22 1/2cm. (Added
           t.-p.: A catalogue of the Greek coins in
           the British museum ...)
           Reprinted, Arnaldo Forni, Bologna, 1963

BB20   British museum. Dept. of coins and medals.
B71   Catalogue of Greek coins. The Seleucid
1963   kings of Syria. By Percy Gardner ...
V. 4   Ed. by Reginald Stuart Poole ... London,
           The Trustees, 1878.
                xxxix, 126p. XXVIII pl. 23cm.
           (Added t.-p.: A catalogue of the Greek
           coins in the British museum ...)
           Reprinted, Arnaldo Forni, Bologna, 1963.

BB20   British museum. Dept. of coins and medals.
B71   Catalogue of Greek coins. Macedonia,
1963   etc. By Barclay V. Head. Edited by
V. 5   Reginald Stuart Poole ... With map.
           London, Printed by order of the Trustees, 1879.
                ixiii, 200 p. illus., fold. map. 22cm.
           (Added t.-p: A catalogue of the Greek
           coins in the British museum ...)
           Reprinted, Arnaldo Forni, Bologna, 1963.

BB20   British Museum. Dept. of coins and medals.
B71   Catalogue of Greek coins. Thessaly to
1963   Aetolia. By Percy Gardner. Edited by
V. 6   Reginald Stuart Poole. London, 1879.
        Reprinted, Arnaldo Forni, Bologna, 1963.
            xlix, 234p. XXXII plates. 25cm. (A
        catalogue of the Greek coins in the British
        Museum, Vol. 6.

BB20   British museum. Dept. of coins and medals.
B71   Catalogue of Greek coins. The Ptolemies,
1963   kings, of Egypt. By Reginald Stuart Poole ...
V. 7   London, The Trustees, 1883.
            ciii p., 1 l., 136p. XXXII pl. 22cm.
        (Added t.-p.: A catalogue of the Greek
        coins in the British museum...)
        Reprinted, Arnaldo Forni, Bologna, 1963.

BB20   British museum. Dept. of coins and medals.
B71   Catalogue of Greek coins. Central Greece.
1963   (Locris, Phocis, Boeotia and Euboea.)
V. 8   By Barclay V. Head ... Ed. by
        Reginald Stuart Poole ... London, The
        Trustees, 1884.
            lxix p., 1 l., 158p. XXIV pl. 23cm.
        (Added t.-p.: A catalogue of the Greek
        coins in the British museum. Central Greece)
        Reprinted, Bologna, Arnaldo Forni, 1963.

BB20   British museum. Dept. of coins and medals.
B71   Catalogue of the Greek coins of Crete and
1963   the Aegean Islands. by Warwick Wroth. Ed. by
V. 9   Reginald Stuart Poole ... London, The Trustees,
        1886. Reprinted 1963.
            L (i.e. lii), [2] 152p. XXIX pl. 23cm.
        (Half-title: A catalogue of the Greek coins in
        the British museum)

BB20   British museum. Dept of coins and medals.
B71   Catalogue of Greek coins. Peloponnesus
1963   (excluding Corinth). By Percy Gardner ...
V. 10   Ed. by Reginald Stuart Poole ... London,
        The Trustees, 1887.
            lxiv, 230p. XXXVII pl. 23cm.
        Reprinted, Arnaldo Forni, Bologna, 1963.

BB20   British Museum. Dept. of coins and medals.
B71   Catalogue of Greek coins.
1963   Attica-Megaris-Aegina. By
v.11   Barclay V. Head. Edited by
        Reginald Stuart Poole ...
        London, The Trustees, 1888.
            lxix p., 1 l., 174 p. XXVI pl. 23cm.
        (Half-title: A catalogue of the
        Greek coins in the British museum)
        Reprinted, Arnaldo Forni, Bologna, 1964.

BB20   British Museum. Dept. of coins and medals.
B71   Catalogue of Greek coins.
1963   Pontus, Paphlagonia, Bithynia, and
v.13   the kingdom of Bosporus. by Warwick Wroth.
          Ed. by Reginald Stuart Poole ... London,
          The Trustees, 1889.
               xliv, 252p. XXXIX pl. 23cm.
          (Half-title: A catalogue of the
          Greek coins in the British museum)
          Reprinted, Arnaldo Forni, Bologna, 1964.

BB20   British Museum. Dept. of coins and medals.
B71   Catalogue of the Greek coins of Mysia.
1964   By Warwick Wroth. Ed. by Reginald Stuart
v.14   Poole ... London, Printed by order of the
          Trustees, 1892.
               XXXV, 217,[1]p. XXXV pl., fold map. 23cm.
          Half-title: A catalogue of the Greek coins
          in the British museum.
          Reprinted, Arnaldo Forni, Bologna, 1964.

BB20   British Museum. Dept. of coins and
B71   medals.
1964   Catalogue of the coins of Alexandria
v. 15   and the Nomes. By Reginald Stuart
          Poole. Reprinted from the 1892 original
          (London) by Arnaldo Forni, Bologna, 1964.
               395p. XXXII plates. Charts. 25cm.
          (Half title: a Catalogue of Greek
          coins in the British Museum, Vol. 15.)

BB20   British Museum. Dept. of coins and medals.
B71   Catalogue of the Greek coins of Ionia.
1964   By Barclay V. Head ... Ed. by Reginald
v.16   Stuart Poole ... London, The Trustees, 1892.
               lvii p., 1 l., 453, [1]p. XXXIX pl., fold. map.
          23cm. (Half-title: A catalogue of the
          Greek coins in the British museum)
          Reprinted, Arnaldo Forni, Bologna, 1964.

BB20   British Museum. Dept. of coins and medals.
B71   Catalogue of the Greek coins of Troas,
1964   Aeolis, and Lesbos. By Warwick Wroth...
v.17   London, The Trustees, 1894.
               lxxxiii, 260p. XLIII pl., fold. map. 23cm.
          (Half-title: A catalogue of the Greek coins in
          the British museum)
          Reprinted, Arnaldo Forni, Bologna, 1964.

BB20   British Museum. Dept. of coins and medals.
B71   Catalogue of the Greek coins of Caria,
1964   Cos, Rhodes, & c. By Barclay V. Head ...
v.18   London, The Trustees, 1897.
                cxviii p., 1 l., 325, [1] p. XLV pl., fold.
            map. 23cm. (Half-title: A catalogue of the
            Greek coins in the British Museum)
            Blank leaf between p. xxii and [XXV]
            Reprinted, Arnaldo Forni, Bologna, 1964.

BB20   British Museum. Dept. of coins and medals.
B71   Catalogue of the Greek coins of Lycia,
1964   Pamphylia, and Pisidia. By George Francis Hill
v.19   ... With one map and forty-four plates.
            London, The Trustees, 1897.
                cxxii, [2], 353, [1] p. XLIV pl.,
            fold. map. 23cm. (Half-title: A cata-
            logue of the Greek coins in the British museum)
            Reprinted, Arnaldo Forni, Bologna, 1964.

BB20   British Museum. Dept. of coins and medals.
B71   Catalogue of the Greek coins of Galatia,
1899   Cappadocia, and Syria. By Warwick Wroth.
v.20   With one map and thirty-eight autotype
            plates. London, The Trustees, 1899.
                xci, 341p. xxxviiipl. 23cm.
                Half-title: A catalogue of the Greek
            coins in the British museum.

BB20   British Museum. Dept. of coins and medals.
B71   Catalogue of the Greek coins of Lycaonia,
1964   Isauria, and Cilicia. By G. F. Hill ...
v.21   London, The Trustees, 1900.
                cxxxi, [1], 296p. 40 pl., fold. map. 23cm.
            Reprinted, Arnaldo Forni, Bologna, 1964.

BB20   British Museum. Dept. of coins and medals.
B71   Catalogue of the Greek coins of Lydia.
1964   By Barclay V. Head ... keeper of the Depart-
v.22   ment of coins and medals. With one map
            and forty-five plates. London, The Trus-
            tees, 1901.
                cl p., 1 l., 440p. XLV pl., fold. map.
            23cm.
            Reprinted, Arnaldo Forni, Bologna, 1964.

BB20   British Museum. Dept. of coins and medals.
B71   Catalogue of the coins of Parthia.
1964   By Warwick Wroth. With a map and thirty-
v.23   seven plates. London, Printed by order of
            the Trustees, 1903.
                lxxxviii, 289, [1] p. XXXVII pl., fold.
            map, tables. 23cm. (Half-title:
            A catalogue of Greek coins in the British
            museum)
            Reprinted, Arnaldo Forni, Bologna, 1964.

BB20   British Museum. Dept. of coins and medals.
B71   Catalogue of the Greek coins of Cyprus.
v.24   By George Francis Hill, M.A. With one map,
           a table of the Cypriote syllabary and
           twenty-six plates. London, Printed
           by order of the Trustees, 1904.
               cxliv, 119, [1] p. XXVI pl., map.
           23cm. (Half-title: A catalogue of the
           Greek coins in the British museum)

BB20   British Museum. Dept. of coins and medals.
B71   Catalogue of the Greek coins of Phrygia.
1964   By Barclay V. Head ... With one map, and
v.25   fifty-three plates. London, printed by
           order of the Trustees, 1906.
               cvi p., 1 l., 491, [1] p. incl. tables.
           LIII pl., fold. map. 23cm. (Half-title:
           A catalogue of the Greek coins in the
           British museum)
           Reprinted, Arnaldo Forni, Bologna, 1964.

BB20   British Museum. Dept. of coins and medals.
B71   Catalogue of the Greek coins of Phoenicia,
1963   by George Francis Hill, M. A.; With one map,
v.26   a table of the Phoenician alphabet and
           forty-five plates. London, Printed by order of
           the Trustees, 1910.
               clii, 361 p. XLV pl., map, 2 fold. tab.
           23cm. (Half-title: A catalogue
           of the Greek coins in the British museum)
           Reprinted, Arnaldo Forni, Bologna, 1963.

BB20   British Museum. Dept. of coins and medals.
B71   Catalogue of the Greek coins of Palestine
1965   (Galilee, Samaria, and Judaea) by George
v.27   Francis Hill ... London, Printed by order
           of the Trustees, 1914.
               cxiv p., 1 l., 363 p. 42 pl., map, fold.
           tab 22 1/2cm. (Half-title: A catalogue
           of the Greek coins in the British museum)
           Reprinted, Arnaldo Forni, Bologna, 1965.

BB20   British Museum. Dept. of coins and medals.
B71   Catalogue of the Greek coins of Arabia,
v.28   Mesopotamia and Persia (Nabataea,
           Arabia Provincia, S. Arabia, Mesopotamia,
           Babylonia, Assyria, Persia, Alexandrine
           empire of the East, Persis, Elymais,
           Characene) by George Francis Hill ...
           With a map and fifty-five plates.
           London, Printed by order of the Trustees,
           1922.

          2 p. l., ccxix, 359, 7 p. 55 pl., fold. map,
22 1/2cm. (Half-title: A catalogue of the
Greek coins in the British museum)
          "Publications of the Department of coins and medals":
7 p. at end.

BB20   British Museum. Dept. of coins and medals.
B71   Catalogue of the Greek coins of Cyrenaica,
1965   by E. S. G. Robinson ... with forty-seven
v.29   plates. London, Printed by order of
          the Trustees, 1927.
               cclxxv, 154p., 1.l. xlvii pl. 22 1/2cm.
          "list of some ... books consulted":
          p. cclxxiii-cclxxiv.
          Reprinted Arnaldo Forni, Bologna, 1965.

BB20   Forrer, L.
F6   The Weber collection [of] Greek coins.
          3 vols. Unchanged reprint of London
          1922 ed. N.Y., Attic Books, 1975.
               ea. vol. separately paged. illus.
          26cm.
               Vol. 1.-Aurial find class-Hispania,
          Gallia, Brittania, Italy & Sicily; 377p.
          69 plates.-Vol. 2-Macedon, Thrace,
          Thessaly, N.W., Central and S. Greece,
          579p. 171 plates. Vol. 3-Asia
          and Africa, 996p. 317 plates.

BB20   Glasgow. University. Hunterian museum.
G5   Catalogue of Greek coins in the Hunter-
Rare   ian collection, University of Glasgow ...
Books   By George Macdonald ... Glasgow, Maclehose,
          1899-1905.
               3v. cii pl. 30cm.

BB20   Hill, George Francis, 1867-1948.
H5   Descriptive catalogue of ancient Greek
          coins belonging to John Ward. San Diego,
          Calif., Pegasus Pub. Co. [1967].
               xxxv-xxxvi, 156, 451-458, 22p. illus.,
          maps. 26cm.

BB20   Locker-Lampson, Godfrey Tennyson, 1875-
L6   Catalogue of ancient Greek coins coll-
          ected by Godfrey Locker Lampson, compiled
          by E.S.G. Robinson ... London, A. L.
          Humphreys, 1923.
               v-xx, 126p. xxvi pl. 26 x 20cm.

BB20   Naster, Paul.
N3   Catalogue des monnaies Grecques; la
        collection Lucien de Hirsch. Bruxelles,
        Bibliotheque Royale de Belgique, 1974.
            Vol. 1-text. 353p. 28cm.
        Vol. 2-plates. 104p. 28cm.

BB20   Okonomou, Georgiou P.
O4   The numismatic collection of Anastasia
        K.P. Stamoule, Given to the National
        Numismatic School. Part A. Athens,
        n.pub., 1955.
            76p. 3 plates. 29cm.
            In Greek

BB20   Pozzi, S.
P6   Monnaies Grecques antiques; provenant
        de la collection de feu le Prof. S. Pozzi.
        Zurich, Bank Leu and Co., A.G., 1966 (reprint
        ed.)
            194p. CI plates. 29cm.

BB20   Pollard, Graham.
P64   A catalogue of the Greek coins
        in the collection of Sir Stephen
        Courtauld at University College of
        Rhodesia. 1st ed. Salisbury,
        University College of Rhodesia, 1970.
            92p. plates. 24cm.

BB20   Regling, Kurt.
R4   Die griechischen munzen der sammlung
Rare   Warren. Berlin, George Reimer, 1906.
Books   2 vol. 252p. 37 pl. 28cm.

BB20   Robinson, Edward Stanley Gotch.
R6   A catalogue of the Calouste
        Gulbenkian collection of Greek coins.
        Part 1 - Italy, Sicily, Carthage;
        by E. S. G. Robinson with the
        collaboration of M. Castro Hipolito.
        Lisboa, Fundacao Calouste Gulbenkian,
        1971.
            2 v. 136p. 42 plates. 29cm.

BB20   Scholz, Josef.
S3   Collection Ernst Prinz zu
V.5   Windisch-Gratz. V Band:
        Griechische munzen...Beschrieben
        von Dr. Josef Scholz. Wien (Vienna),
        Wilhelm Trinks, 1904.
            196p. plates. 26cm.

BB20   American Numismatic Society.
S8Aa   Sylloge nummorum Graecorum, the collection
        of the ... New York, American Numismatic
        Society, 1969-75.
            3v. plates. 40cm.
            Contents: Pt.1. Etruria-Calabria. -Pt.2.
        Lucania. -Pt.3. Bruttium-Sicily I: Abacaenum-
        Eryx.

BB20   American Numismatic Society.
S8Ab   Sylloge nummorum Graecorum, the Burton
        Y. Berry collection. New York, American
        Numismatic Society, 1961-62.
            2v. plates. 40cm.
            Contents: Pt.1. Macedonia to Attica. -
        Pt.2. Megaris to Egypt.

BB20   British Academy (London).
S8B   Sylloge nummorum Graecorum, Volume 2,
V.2   the Lloyd collection. London, Oxford Univer-
        sity Press, 1933-37.
            4v. plates. 40cm.
            Contents: Pt.1-2. Etruria to Thurium. -
        Pt.3-4. Velia to Eryx. - Pt.5-6. Galaria to
        Selinus. - Pt.7-8. Syracuse to Lipara.

BB20   British Academy (London).
S8B   Sylloge nummorum Graecorum, Volume 3,
V.3   the Lockett collection. London, Oxford
        University Press, 1938-49.
            5v. plates. 40cm.
            Contents: Pt.1. Spain-Italy. - Pt.2. Sicily
        -Thrace. - Pt.3. Macedonia-Aegina. - Pt.4.
        Peloponnese-Aeolis. - Pt.5. Lesbos-Cyreniaca,
        Addenda.

BB20   British Academy (London).
S8B   Sylloge nummorum Graecorum, Volume 4,
V.4   Fitzwilliam Museum: Leake and general collec-
        tions. London, Oxford University Press,
        1965-67.
            5v. plates. 40cm.
            Contents: Pt.1. Spain (Emporiae, Rhoda)
        -Italy. - Pt.2. Sicily-Thrace. - Pt.6. Asia
        Minor-Phrygia. - Pt.7. Asia Minor: Lycia-Cappa-
        docia. - Pt.8. Syria-Nabathaea.

BB20   British Academy (London).
S8B   Sylloge nummorum Graecorum, Volume 5,
V.5   Ashmolean Museum, Oxford. London, Oxford
        University Press, 1962-69.
            2v. plates. 40cm.
            Contents: Pt.1(A). Italy, Etruria-Lucania
        (Thurium). - Pt.2. Italy, Lucania (Thurium)
        -Bruttium, Sicily, Carthage.

BB20   British Academy (London).
S8B   Sylloge nummorum Graecorum, Volume 6,
V.6   the Lewis collection in Corpus Christi
        College, Cambridge. London, Oxford Univer-
        sity Press, 1972.
             1v. plates. 39cm.
             Contents: Pt.1. Greek and Hellenistic
        coins (with Britain and Parthia).

BB20   [Deutschen Archaeologischen Instituts.]
S8D   Sylloge nummorum Graecorum Deutschland,
        sammlung von Aulock. Berlin, G. Mann,
        1957-68.
             6v. plates. 37cm.
             Contents: Pt.1-3. Pontus, Paphlagonia,
        Bythinia. - Pt.16. Mysia, Troas, Aeolis,
        Lesbos. - Pt.17. Ionia, Caria, Lydia. - Pt.18.
        Phrygia, Lyceum, Pamphylia, Pisidia, Lycaonia,
        Isauria, Cilicia, Galatia, Cappadocia, Kaiser-
        zeitl Kistophoren.

BB20   Troxell, Hyla A.
T7   The Norman Davis Collection. New York,
        A.N.S., 1969.
             53p. 28 pl. 27cm. (Greek coins in
        North American collections).

BB20   Whitehead, D. H. E.
W6   Roman coins in the McGill
Vol.1   University collection; by D. H. E.
        Whitehead. Edited by Michael
        Woloch. Amsterdam, B. R. Gruner
        Pub. Co., 1975.
             239p. XXV illus. (McGill
        University Collection of Greek
        and Roman coins, Vol. 1).

BB20   Shlosser, Franziska E.
W6   Greek gold and silver coins
Vol.2   in the McGill University Collection;
        by Franziska E. Shlosser. Edited
        by Michael Woloch. Amsterdam,
        B. R. Gruner Pub. Co., 1975.
             72p. 25 plates. 23cm. (The
        McGill University Collection
        of Greek & Roman coins, Vol. 2).

BB20   Wroth, Warwick.
W7   Greek coins acquired by the
        British Museum, 1887, 1889-1903.
        Taken from "The Numismatic Chronicle",
        London.
             variously paged. illus. 23cm.

BB20   Wroth, Warwick.
W7s   Select Greek coins in the
            British Museum. Taken from
            "The Numismatic Chronicle",
            London, n.d.
                pp. 324-341. II plates. 23cm.

CATALOGUES

BB30   Seaby, Herbert Allen.
S4   Greek coins and their values, by H.
1959   A. Seaby and J. Kozolubski. Based on
            A catalogue of Greek coins, by Gilbert
            Askew. London, B. A. Seaby, 1959, 1966.
                157p. illus. 24cm.
                Bibliography: p.[159]

GENERAL WORKS

BB40   Benson, Frank Sherman.
B4   Ancient Greek coins. Priv. printed,
            1900-1904, 1905.
                4v. 14 pl. 27 x 23cm.

BB40   Beule, Charles Ernest, 1826-1874.
B49   Les monnaies d'Athenes par
            E. Beule. Originally published in
            Paris, 1858. Reprinted-Bologna,
            A. Forni, [1975?]
                417p. illus. 33cm.

BB40   Brett, Agnes Baldwin.
B7   Catalogue of Greek coins. N.Y., Attic
            Books, 1974.
                340p. 115 plates. 29cm.
                unchanged reprint of the 1955 ed.

BB40   Davis, Norman, 1907-
D2   Greek coins & cities; illus. from the
            collection at the Seattle Art Museum.
            London, Spink, [1967].
                223p. illus., maps, diagrs. 26cm.
                Bibliography: p. 215

BB40
D22
	Davis, Norman.
	    The Hellenistic kingdoms; portrait coins and history, by Norman Davis and Colin M. Kraay. Photographs by P. Frank Purvey. London, Thames and Hudson [1973]
	    296p. illus. 26cm.
	    Bibliography: p. 289-291.

BB40
D4
	De Tabley, John Byrne Leicester Warren, 3d baron, 1835-1895.
	    An essay on Greek federal coinage. London & Cambridge, Macmillan, 1863.
	    62p. 23cm.

BB40
G3
	Gardner, Percy, 1846-1937.
	    A history of ancient coinage, 700-300 B.C., ... with eleven plates. Oxford, Clarendon press, 1918.
	    xvi, 463p. 11 pl. 23cm.

BB40
H3
	Hands, Alfred Watson.
	    Common Greek coins. London, Spink & Son, 1907.
	    xi, 170p. illus. 25cm.

BB40
H4
	Head, Barclay Vincent, 1844-1914.
	    Historia numorum; a manual of Greek numismatics, ... assisted by G. F. Hill, George Macdonald, & W. Wroth. New and enl. ed. Oxford, Clarendon Press, 1887, 1911.
	    807p. illus., 5 pl. 25cm.
	    Bibliography: p. xix-xxvi

BB40
H4s
	Svoronos, John, 1863-1922.
	    The illustrations of the Historia numorum, an atlas of Greek numismatics. Chicago, Argonaut, 1968.
	    64p. 40 pl. 25cm.

BB40
J4
	Jenkins, G. Kenneth.
	    Munzen der Griechen [by] G. K. Jenkins and Harold Kuthmann. Munich, Ernst Battenberg, 1972.
	    330p. illus. (part col.) 25cm.
	    Library also holds copy in English.

BB40
K7a
	Kraay, Colin M.
	    Archaic and classical Greek coins. Berkeley, Calif., University of California Press, 1976.
	    xxvi, 390p. maps 64 pl. 26cm.

BB40   Kraay, Colin M.
K7g   Greek coins, by Colin M. Kraay; photos
          by Max Hirmer. London, Thames & Hudson
          [1966].
              396p. 1329 illus., col. pl., 4 maps.
          31cm.
              Bibliography: p. 386-388.

BB40   Kraay, Colin M.
K7h   Greek coins and history: some current
          problems [by] Colin M. Kraay. London,
          Methuen, 1969.
              x, 81p. 8 pl., 55 illus. 23cm. (J.H.
          Gray memorial lectures, 1967-8)
              Bibliographical footnotes.

BB40   Millingen, James, 1774-1845.
M45   Ancient coins of Greek cities and kings.
Rare   From various collections principally in
Books   Great Britain; illus. & explained by James
          Millingen ... London, 1831.
              xi, 77p. v pl. 31cm.

BB40   Milne, Joseph Grafton, 1867-1951.
M5   The first stages in the development of
          Greek coinage. Oxford, Basil Blackwell,
          [1934].
              19p. 22cm.

BB40   Milne, Joseph Grafton, 1867-1951.
M5g   Greek coinage, by J. G. Milne. Oxford,
          The Clarendon Press, 1931.
              vi, 131p. xii pl. 19cm.
              "Biliographical note": p. [123]-124.

BB40   Newell, Edward T.
N4   Some rare or unpublished Greek coins.
Vert.   From American Journal of Numismatics, v.48,
File   1914, p. 62-72. New York, 1915.
              12p. 2 pl. 28cm.

BB40   Raoul-Rochette, M.
R3   Memoires de numismatique et d'antiquite.
          Paris, Imprimerie Royale, 1840.
              256p. 10 pl. 27cm.
              Extrait des memories de l'academie des
          inscrip, et Belles-lettres.

BB40   Head, Barclay V.
R5   The coins of ancient Boeotia; a
          chronological sequence. Originally
          published in London, 1891. Reprinted-
          Chicago, Ares Pub., Inc., 1974.
              99p. VI plates. 24cm.

BB40   Roberts, W. Rhys.
R5   The ancient Boeotians: their
          character and culture and their
          reputation. Originally published
          in Cambridge, 1895. Reprinted-
          Chicago, Ares Pub., Inc., 1974.
              92p. 24cm.

BB40   Robert, Louis.
R6   Hautes etudes numismatiques; monnaie
          Grecques; types, legendes, magistrats
          monetaires et geographie. Geneve,
          Librairie Droz, 1967.
              146p. IV plates. 25cm.

BB40   Seltman, Charles Theodore, 1886-
S4b   A book of Greek coins. London, Penguin
          Books [1952].
              30p. 48 pl., map. 19cm. (The King
          penguin books, 63)
              Bibliography: p. [27]

BB40   Seltman, Charles Theodore, 1886-
S4g   Greek coins; a history of metallic
          currency and coinage down to the fall of
          the Hellenistic kingdoms. London, Methuen
          [1933, 2nd ed. 1955].
              xxvi, 311p. 64 pl., maps. 23cm.
          (Methuen's handbooks of archaeology)
              Bibliography: p. xv-xxvi.

BB40   Seltman, Charles Theodore, 1886-
S4m   Masterpieces of Greek coinage. Essay
          and commentary. Oxford, B. Cassirer [1949]
              127p. illus. 25cm.

BB40   Stillman, William J.
S7   The coinage of the Greeks.
          Originally published in the Century
          Illustrated Magazine, 1887. Chicago,
          Obol Internatl., 1975.
              16p. illus. 26cm.

BB40   Ward, John, 1832-1912.
W3   Greek coins and their parent cities, ...
          accompanied by a catalogue of the author's
          collection by G.F. Hill... London, J. Murray
          1902.
              xxxvi, 464p. illus., maps. 25cm.

DICTIONARIES, BIBLIOGRAPHIES, ETC.

BB45   Florance, A.
F5   Geographic lexicon of Greek coin inscrip-
            tions. Chicago, Argonaut Publishers, 1966.
                98p. illus., maps. 24cm. (Argonaut
            library of antiquities)
                "Bibliographical note": p. [vii]

COLLECTING

BB50   Askew, Gilbert.
A8   A Catalogue of Greek coins. London,
            B.A. Seaby, 1951.
                119p. illus. 23cm.

BB50   Hill, Sir George Francis, 1867-1948.
H5   Historical Greek coins. New York,
            Macmillan, 1906. Chicago, Argonaut, 1966.
                xvii, 180p. illus, plt. 22cm.

BB50   Klawans, Zander H.
K5   An outline of ancient Greek coins.
            Racine, Wis., Whitman Pub. Co., 1959.
                208p. illus., maps. 20cm.
                Bibliography: p. 202

BB50   Klawans, Zander H.
K5   An outline of ancient Greek coins.
1964   2d ed. Racine, Wisc., Whitman Pub. Co.
            1964.
                206p. illus. maps. 20cm.
                Bibliography: p. 200

BB50   Pennington, Paul.
P4   How to read Greek coins, an adventure in
            epigraphy for those who know no Greek.
            Chicago, Hewitt Brothers, 1946.
                22p. pl. 20cm.
                Reprinted from: Numismatics scrapbook
            magazine, 1945.

BB50   Sherwood, Earle D.
S5   Ancient Greek coins: how to quickly
            identify many of them. Reprint from the
            Numismatic Scrapbook Magazine, v. xvi, no. 7
            July 1950. p. 561-566.
                6p. illus. 18cm.

BB50   Szego, Paul S.
S9   Collecting Greek coins, New York, W.
            Raymond, inc. [c1937].
                15p. illus. 23cm.

SPECIAL, TECHNICAL

BB55   Gardner, Percy, 1846-1937.
G3   Archaeology and the types of Greek coins,
1965   with an introduction by Margaret Thompson.
            Chicago, Argonaut, 1965. [1st American
            edition].
                217p. 16 pl. 28cm.
                Reprint of types of Greek coins. Cam-
            bridge, 1883.

BB55   Gardner, Percy, 1846-1937.
G3   The types of Greek coins; an archaeolo-
1883   gical essay. ... Cambridge, University
Rare   press, 1883.
Books   viii, 217p. illus., xvi pl. 35cm.

GOLD

BB56   Robinson, David Moore.
R6   Queen Mary's necklace of Greek gold
Vert.   coins of Arsinoe II.
File   Reprint from The Classical Bulletin,
            no. 32, Jan. 1956, p. 25-29.

SILVER

BB57   Kraay, Colin M.
K7   The composition of Greek silver coins.
            Analysis by neutron activation. Oxford,
            Printed for the visitors and sold at the
            Ashmolean Museum, 1962.
                38p. 12 diagrs. 24cm.

BB57   Thompson, Margaret, 1911-
T45   The new style silver coinage of Athens.
            New York, American Numismatic Society, 1961.
                2v. plates. 28cm. (Numismatic studies,
            no. 10)

BRONZE, COPPER

BB58   Caley, Earle Radcliffe, 1900-
C3   The composition of ancient Greek bronze
         coins, by Earle Radcliffe Caley ... Phil-
         adelphia, The American philosophical
         society, 1939.
            203p. iv pl. 23cm.

ICONOGRAPHY

BB60   Anson, Leo.
A5   Numismata Graeca. Greek coin-types
         classified for immediate identification by
         L. Anson ... London, Trubner, 1910-1916.
            7v. 150 plates. 29cm.

BB60   Baldwin, Agnes.
B3   Facing heads on ancient Greek coins.
         Reprinted by Charles H. McSorley, 1968.
            21p. 4 pl. 28cm.
            [Reprinted from American Journal of
         Numismatics, v. 43 in 1909.]

BB60   Cammann, Jean B.
C3   Numismatic mythology, New York, W.
         Raymond, inc. [c1936].
            39p. illus., map. 23cm.
            "List of useful books": p. 37

BB60   Forrer, Leonard.
F6   Portraits of royal ladies on Greek coins.
         Chicago, Argonaut, 1969.
            viii, 72p. illus., port. 25cm.
            Bibliographical footnotes.

BB60   Green, Benjamin Richard, 1808-1876.
G7   A numismatic atlas of ancient history...
Rare   cont. a selection of 360 Grecian coins of
Books   kings. London, Priestley & Weale, and by
         the author, 1829.
            ii, 42p. 21 pl.

BB60   Hartman, John E.
H3   Greek numismatic epigraphy, [by]...[and]
         George Macdonald. Chicago, Argonaut, 1969.
            92p. 22cm.

BB60   Houssayl, Noel de la.
H6   Les bronzes Italiotes archaiques et leur
          symbolique. Paris, Editions du Trident,
          1938.
              42p. 4 plates, charts. 25cm.

BB60   Icard, Severin.
I3   Identification des monnaies par la
          nouvelle methode des lettres-jalons et
          des legendes fragmentees . . . aux monnaies
          Greques. . . Paris, J. Florange, 1895, 1968.
              xxivp.; 563p. 26cm.
              1968 reprint in English.

BB60   Imhoof-Blumer, Friedrich, 1838-1920.
I5   Ancient coins illustrating lost master-
          pieces of Greek art; a numismatic commentary
          on Pausanias ... [and] Percy Gardner. New
          enl. ed. with introd., commentary & notes
          by Al. N. Oikonomides. [1st American ed.]
          Chicago, Argonaut, 1964.
              lxxx, 176p. illus., map, plates. 22cm.
          (Argonaut library of antiquities)
              Bibliography: p. [175]-176.

BB60   Lattimore, Steven.
L3   Lysippian sculpture on Greek coins.
Vert.   5p. Annotated
File

BB60   Newell, Edward Theodore, 1886-1941.
N4   Royal Greek portrait coins; being an
          illus. treatise on the portrait coins of
          the various kingdoms, & cont. historical
          references to their coinages, mints, &
          rulers. New York, W. Raymond, inc. 1937.
              99p. illus.(incl. double map) 23cm.

BB60   Richter, Gisela M. A.
R5   A handbook of Greek art; a survey of
1969   the visual arts of ancient Greece [by]
          Gisela M. A. Richter. 6th ed. redesigned
          and with renumbered illustrations. London,
          New York, Phaidon [1969]
              431p. illus. 25cm.
              Bibliography: p. 399-410.

BB60   Seltman, Charles Theodore, 1886-1957.
S4   The temple coins of Olympia by
          Charles T. Seltman. Originally
          published in Cambridge, 1921.
          Reprinted-N.Y., Attic books, 1975.
              117p. XII plates. 29cm.

BB60   Starr, Chester G.
S7   Naval activity in Greek imperial issues.
Vert.   Extrait de la Revue Suisse de Numismatique,
File   Tome 46, 1967. [p. 51-57].
              illus. 24cm.

BB60   Trell, Bluma L., 1903-
T7   The temple of Artemis at Ephesos, by
          Bluma L. Trell. New York, The American
          numismatic society, 1945.
              x, 71p. xxviii pl. 17cm. (Numismatic
          notes and monographs, no. 107)
              Bibliographical foot-notes.

HOARDS

BB70   Edwards, G. Roger.
E3   A hoard of gold coins of Philip and
Vert.   Alexander from Corinth. From American
File   Journal of Archaeology, October, 1970.
              8p. 4 pl.

BB70   Milne, Joseph Grafton, 1867-1951.
M5   The Melos hoard of 1907, by J. G. Milne.
          New York, The American numismatic society,
          1934.
              19p. 17cm. (Numismatic notes and mono-
          graphs. [no. 62])
              "Notes" including bibliography: p. 18-19.

BB70   Newell, Edward Theodore, 1886-
N4f   Five Greek bronze coin hoards. New
          York, The American numismatic society, 1935.
              67p. illus., 9 double plates. 17cm.
          (Numismatic notes and monographs. [no. 68])

BB70   Newell, Edward Theodore, 1886-1941.
N4k   The Kuchuk Kohne hoard. New York,
          The American Numismatic Society, 1931.
              33p. 4 pl., map. 17cm. (Numismatic
          notes and monographs, no. 46)

BB70   Newell, Edward Theodore, 1886-1941.
N4s   A hoard from Siphnos, New York, The
          American numismatic society, 1934.
              17p. illus., pl. 16cm. (Numismatic
          notes and monographs. [no. 64])

BB70   Noe, Sydney Philip.
N6   A bibliography of Greek coin hoards.
          New York, The American Numismatic Society,
          1925. 2d. ed. 1937.
              17cm. (Numismatic notes and monographs,
          [nos. 25, 78]).

BB70   Ravel, Oscar.
R3   Corinthian hoards (Corinth and Arta) by
          Oscar Ravel. New York, The American numis-
          matic society, 1932.
              27p. illus., plates. 17cm. (Numismatic
          notes and monographs. [no. 52])

BB70   Seltman, Charles Theodore.
S4   A hoard from Side, by C. T. Seltman.
          New York, The American numismatic society,
          1924.
              20p. iii pl. 16cm. (Numismatic notes
          and monographs. [no. 22])

BB70   Thompson, Margaret, 1911-
T5   The Agrinion hoard. New York, American
          Numismatic Society, 1968.
              130p. plates. 23cm. (Numismatic notes
          and monographs, no. 159)
              Includes bibliographical references.

BB70   Thompson, Margaret, ed.
T5i   An inventory of Greek coin hoards;
          editors: Margaret Thompson, Otto Morkholm
          [and] Colin M. Kraay. Published for The
          International Numismatic Commission by
          The American Numismatic Society, New York,
          1973.
              408p. 28cm.
              "... a new edition of Sydney P. Noe's...
          A bibliography of Greek coin hoards."

BY PERIOD

BB80   Bellinger, Alfred Raymond, 1893-
B4   Essays on the coinage of Alexander the
          Great, by Alfred R. Bellinger. New York,
          American Numismatic Society, 1963.
              132p. illus., maps. 28cm. (Numismatic
          studies, no. 11)
              Bibliography: p. [114]-130.

BB80   Berry, Burton Y.
B47   A numismatic biography. Lucerne,
          Bucher Ltd, 1971.
              90p. pl. 31cm.

BB80   Bompois, H. Ferdinand, b.1813.
B6   Les types monetaires de la guere
          sociale. Paris, A. Detaille, 1873.
              116p. 3 pl. 28cm.

BB80   Boehringer, Christof.
B64   Zur chronologie mittelhellenistischer
          munzserien 220-160 v. Chr. Berlin, Walter
          de Gruyter and Co., 1972.
              2 vol. text and 40 plates. tables.
          graphs. 28cm. (Deutsches Archaologisches
          Institut, Antike munzen und Geschnittene
          Steini, Bd. V)

BB80   Cahn Herbert A.
C3   Fruhellenistische munzkunst. Basel,
          Amerbach, 1948?.
              29p. pl. 18cm.

BB80   Cahn, Herbert A.
C3g   Griechische munzen archaischer zeit.
          Basel, Amerbach-verlag, 1947.
              32p. pl. 17cm.

BB80   Clerk, Malcolm George, 1836-
C5   Catalogue of the coins of the Achaean
          league, illus. by 13 plates with 311 coins;
          compiled by Major-Genl. M.G. Clerk ...
          London, B. Quaritch, 1895.
              viii, 35p. front., xiii pl. 25cm.

BB80   Crosby, Margaret.
C7   An Achaean league hoard, by Margaret
          Crosby and Emily Grace. New York, The
          American numismatic society, 1936.
              44p. iv pl. 17cm. (Numismatic notes &
          monographs. [no. 74])

BB80   Gardner, Percy.
G3   The earliest coins of Greece proper.
          London, British Academy, [1911].
              41p. 1 pl. 25cm.

BB80   Muller, Ludwig.
M8   The coinage of Alexander the
          Great; followed by a supplement
          containing the coins of Philip II,
          III and Lysimachus; plates and tables
          by L. Muller. Translated from the
          1855 and 1858 Copenhagen ed. by
          L. A. Naughton. N.Y., Attic Books,
          1976.
              XLIX tables and plates. 24cm.
          Library holds copies in French & Eng.

BB80   Newell, Edward Theodore, 1886-1941.
N4a   Alexander hoards; intro & Kyparissia
          hoard. New York, The American numismatic
          society, 1921.
              21p. plates. 17cm. (Numismatic notes
          & monographs. no. 3)

BB80   Newell, Edward Theodore, 1886-
N4c   The coinages of Demetrius Poliorcetes,
          by Edward T. Newell. London, Oxford univer-
          sity press. H. Milford, 1927.
              174p. xviii pl. ` 26cm.

BB80   Newell, Edward Theodore, 1886-1941.
N4d   Alexander hoards: II Demanhur, 1905.
          New York, The American Numismatic Society,
          1923.
              162p. 8 pl. 17cm. (Numismatic Notes &
          Monographs, no. 19)

BB80   Newell, Edward theodore, 1886-1941.
N4e   Alexander hoards: IV. Olympia. New
          York, American Numismatic Society, 1929.
              27p. 4 pl. 17cm. (Numismatic notes
          and monographs, no. 39)

BB80   Newell, Edward Theodore, 1886-1941.
N46   Alexander hoards: Andritsaena. New York.
          The American Numismatic Society, 1923.
              39p. 6 pl. 17cm. (Numismatic Notes &
          Monographs, no. 21)

BB80   Torrey, Charles Cutler.
T6   Aramaic graffiti on coins of Demanhur.
          New York, American numismatic society,
          1937.
              13p. 2 pl. 17cm. (Numismatic notes
          and monographs, no. 77)

BB80   Williams, Roderick T.
W5   The confederate coinage of the Arcadians
          in the fifth century B. C., by Roderick T.
          Williams. New York, American Numismatic
          Society, 1965.
              xix, 141p. map, 14 plates. 23cm.
          (Numismatic notes and monographs, no. 155)

BY COUNTRY - GREECE

BB90   Barron, John Penrose.
B3   The silver coins of Samos. University
          of London, Athlone Press, 1966.
              242p. 32 pl. 25cm.

BB90   Bellinger, Alfred Raymond.
B4   Two hoards of Attic bronze coins.
          New York, American numismatic society,
          1930.
              14p. II pl. 16cm. (Numismatic notes
          and monographs, no. 42)

BB90   Brett, (Mrs.) Agnes Baldwin.
B65e   The electrum coinage of Lampsakos by
          Agnes Baldwin. New York, American Numis-
          matic Society, 1914.
              34p. 2 pl. 29cm.

BB90   Brett, Mrs. Agnes Baldwin.
B651   Lampsakos; the gold staters, silver and
          bronze coinages by Agnes Baldwin. In:
          American Journal of Numismatics, vol. 53,
          part 3 (final). New York, A.N.S., 1924.
              76p. 10 pl. 29cm.

BB90   Cammann, Jean B.
C3   Symbols on staters of Corinthian type
          (a catalogue). New York, American
          numismatic society, 1932.
              130p. illus., map. pl. 17cm.
          (Numismatic notes and monographs, no. 53)
              Bibliography: p. 6-7

BB90   Dattari, Giovanni.
D3   Monte imperiali greche. Numi Augg.
          Alexandrini catalogo della collezione G.
          Dattari, compilato cal proprietario. Cairo,
          Tipografia dell'instituto francesse d'arch-
          eologia orientale, 1901.
              2v. xii, 471p. 37 pl. 33cm.

BB90
F7
Franke, Peter Robert.
    Die antiken munzen von Epirus.
Wiesbaden, Franz Steiner Verlag,
1961.
    344p. fold. map. 67 plates.
28cm.

BB90
G7
Greenwell, William.
    The electrum coinage of Cyzicus.
London, Rollin & Feuardent, 1887.
    132p. 6 pl. 22cm. (Reprinted from
Numismatic Chronicle, 1887.)

BB90
K7
Kraay, C. M.
    Coins of Ancient Athens. [Newcastle
upon Tyne, Corbitt & Hunter, 1968].
    38p. 8 pl. 22cm. (Minerva Numismatic
Handbooks)

BB90
L3
Lambros, Paul.
    Gold coins of Philippi; translated by
Betty Gardiakos. [Oak Park, Ill.] Obol
International, 1970.
    19p. illus., map. 21cm.
In Greek and English.

BB90
M3
Macdonald, George, 1862-
    The silver coinage of Crete, a metrologi-
cal note. London, Pub. for the British
Academy by H. Milford, Oxford, [1919].
    29p. pl. 25cm.
From the proceedings of the British
Academy, vol. 9.

BB90
M5
Milbank, Samuel Robbins, 1906-
    The coinage of Aegina. New York,
American numismatic society, 1924.
    66p. illus, pl. 16cm. (Numismatic
notes and monographs, no. 24)

BB90
N4
Newell, Edward Theodore, 1886-1941.
    The octobols of Histiaea. New York,
American numismatic society, 1921.
    25p. 2 pl. 17cm. (Numismatic notes
and monographs, no. 2)

BB90
N4s
Newell, Edward Theodore.
    Some Cypriate 'Alexanders'
by E. T. Newell. Chicago, Obol
International, 1974.
    29p. plates. 21cm.

BB90   Noe, Sydney.
N6   The Alexander coinage of Sicyon; arr.
          from notes of Edward T. Newell with comments
          and additions by Sydney P. Noe. New York,
          1950.
               41p.   18 pl.   28cm. (Numismatic studies,
          no. 6)
               Bibliographical footnotes.

BB90   Ravel, Oscar.
R3a   The "colts" of Ambracia. New York,
          American numismatic society, 1928.
               180p.   illus., xix pl.   17cm. (Numis-
          matic notes and monographs, no. 37)

BB90   Robinson, David Moore, 1880-
R6   A hoard of silver coins from Carystus.
          New York, American Numismatic Society, 1952.
               62p.   6 plates.   23cm. (Numismatic
          notes and monographs, no. 124)
               Bibliographical footnotes.

BB90   Rogers, Edgar, 1873-
R63   The copper coinage of Thessaly. London,
          Spink, 1932.
               iv, 190p.   illus.   24cm.

BB90   Schumacher, Carolus.
S3   De republica Rhodiorum
          commentatia...Heidelberg, Aedibus
          C. Winteri, 1886.
               64p.   24cm.

BB90   Seager, Richard B.
S4   A Cretan coin hoard. New York, The Amer-
          ican numismatic society, 1924.
               55p.   plates.   16cm. (Numismatic notes &
          monographs. [no. 23])

BB90   Sear, David R.
S42   A hoard of "double-headed" imperial
Vert.   bronzes from six mints of Moesia Inferior
File   and Thrace. Seaby's, 1969.
               16p.   6 pl.   21cm. (Seaby's coin and
          medal bulletin, September, 1969-Supplement)

BB90   Seltman, Charles Theodore, 1886-1957.
S43   Athens: its history and coinage before
          the Persian invasion by C.T. Seltman. -
          Chicago: Ares Publishers, 1974.
               xix, 228p., [12] leaves of plates: ill.
          29cm.
               Reprint of the 1924 ed. published by The
          University Press, Cambridge, England.
               Bibliography: p. [xiv]-xvi.

BB90   Starr, Chester G.
S7   Athenian coinage, 480-449 B.C. Oxford,
          Clarendon, 1970.
              95p. pl. 24cm.
              Bibliography

BB90   Svoronos, J. N., 1863-1922.
S9   Numismatique de la Crete ancienne;
          accompagne de l'histoire, la
          Geographie et la Mythologie de l'Ile.
          Bonn, Rudolf Habelt, 1972. Originally
          published 1889-1890.
              376p. 13 plates. 28cm.

BB90   Waage, Frederick Oswin.
W2   Greek bronze coins from a well at
          Megara. New York, American Numismatic
          Society, 1935.
              42p. illus, pl. 17cm. (Numismatic
          notes and monographs, no. 70)

BB90   Wallace, William P.
W3   The Euboian League and its coinage. New
          York, American Numismatic Society, 1956.
              xi, 180p. illus., 16 plates, map. 24cm.
          (Numismatic notes and monographs, no. 134)
              Bibliographical footnotes.

EUROPE

BB94   Brett, (Mrs.) Agnes (Baldwin) 1876-
B7   Victory issues of Syracuse after 413 B.C.
          New York, The American numismatic society,
          1936.
              6p. front., pl. 17cm. (Numismatic
          notes & monographs, [no. 75])

BB94   Caskey, Lacey D.
C3   Coins of Syracuse. American Numismatic
          Association, 1962. Reprint from The
          Numismatist.
              8p. illus. 22cm.

BB94   Gallatin, Albert.
G3   Syracusan dekadrachms of the Euainetos
          type. Cambridge, Harvard Univ. Press, 1930.
              53p. 12 plates. 31cm.

BB94   Gabrici, Ettore.
G32   La monetazione del bronzo nella
         Sicilia antica; con dieci tavole in
         fototipia e sette zinchi nel testo
         by E. Gabrici. Originally published
         in Palermo, 1927. Reprinted-
         Bologna, A. Forni, [1975].
             211p. X plates. 32cm.

BB94   Gabrici, Ettore.
G32t   Topografia e numismatica dell'
         antica Imera (e di Terme). Originally
         published in Naples, 1894. Reprinted
         Bologna, A. Forni, [1972].
             109p. VIII plates. 32cm.

BB94   Hands, Alfred Watson.
H3i   Italo-Greek coins of southern Italy.
         London, Spink, 1912.
             205p. illus. 24cm.

BB94   Hands, Alfred Watson.
H3m   Coins of Magna Graecia. The coinage of
         the Greek colonies of southern Italy.
         London, Spink & Son, 1909.
             xii, 337p. illus. 25cm.

BB94   Hill, George Francis, 1867-
H5   Coins of ancient Sicily. Westminster,
         A. Constable & Co., Ltd., 1903.
             256p. 15 pl., map. 27cm.

BB94   Jenkins, Kenneth.
J4   Coins of Greek Sicily. British
         Museum, 1966.
             31p. 16 pl. 22cm.
             Bibliography.

BB94   Jenkins, G. Kenneth.
J4c   The coinage of Gela. Berlin,
         Walter de Gruyter & Co., 1970.
             2 Vols. 312p. 56 plates. tables.
         28cm.

BB94   May, John Maunsell Frampton.
M3   The coinage of Damastion and the lesser
         coinages of the Illyro-Paeonian region, by
         J.M.F. May. London, Oxford University
         press, H. Milford, 1939.
             xiv, 207p. xii double pl. 23cm. (Ox-
         ford classical & philosophical monographs)
             Bibliography: p. [xiii]-xiv.

BB94   Monnaies de Tarente, collection.
M6   Claudius Cote de Lyon; la vente
        sous la direction de Rodolfo
        Ratto. Reprint of the auction
        catalogue compiled by Rodolfo Ratto
        and sold by him on 28 and 29
        January, 1929. N.Y., Attic Books,
        1975.
           42p. xix plates. 27cm.

BB94   Muller, Ludwig.
M8   Lysimachus, king of Thrace; mints and
        mint-marks by Dr. L. Muller. New York,
        Reprinted by Frederick S. Knobloch, 1966.
           IXp. 25cm.

BB94   Noe, Sydney Philip.
N6c   The coinage of Metapontum, by Sydney P.
        Noe. New York, The American numismatic
        society, 1927-1931.
           2v. illus., plates. 17cm. (Numismatic
        notes and monographs. [no. 32,47]).
           Bibliography: pl. I, p. 132-134; pt. II,
        p. 133-134.

BB94   Noe, Sydney Philip.
N6m   The Mende (Kaliandra) hoard, by Sydney P.
        Noe. New York, The American numismatic
        society, 1926.
           73p. illus., x fold. pl. 17cm. (Num-
        ismatic notes & monographs no. 27)

BB94   Noe, Sydney Philip.
N6t   The Thurian di-staters, by Sydney P.
        Noe. New York, The American numismatic
        society, 1935.
           68p. xi double pl. 16cm. (Numismatic
        notes and monographs. [no. 71])

BB94   Noehden, George Henry.
N65   Specimens of ancient coins of Magna
        Graecia and Sicily, selected from the cabinet
        of ... Lord Northwick. London, S. Prowett,
        1826.
           63p. 20 pl. 36cm.

BB94   Price, Martin.
P7   Coins of the Macedonians. London,
        British Museum Pubs., Ltd., 1974.
           47p. XVI plates. 22cm.

BB94   Raymond, Doris.
R3   Macedonian regal coinage to 413 B.C.
          New York, American Numismatic Society, 1953.
              xi, 170p. 15 pl. 23cm. (Numismatic
          notes and monographs, no. 126).
              Bibliographical footnotes.

BB94   Salinas, Di Antoino.
S2   Sul tipo de ' tetradrammi di Segesta
          e su di alcune rappresentazioni
          numismatiche di pane agreo. Firenze,
          Di M. Ricci, 1870.
              39p. plates. 24cm.

BB94   Vlasto, Michel P.
V5   Tapae Oikiethe, a contribution to
          Tarentine numismatics. New York, American
          numismatic society, 1922.
              234p. illus, xiii pl. 17cm. (Numis-
          matic notes and monographs, no. 15)

BB94   West, Allen Brown, 1886-
W4   Fifth and fourth century gold coins
          from the Thracian coast. New York,
          American numismatic society, 1929.
              183p. illus., xvi pl. 17cm. (Numis-
          matic notes and monographs, no. 40)

BB94   Work, Eunice, 1894-
W6   The earlier staters of Heraclea Lucaniae,
          by Eunice Work. New York, The American
          numismatic society, 1940.
              40p. 17cm. (Numismatic notes and
          monographs. no. 91)

BB94   Zlatkovskaya, T. D.
Z5   Early coins of the Southern Thracian
          tribes. From Numizmatika i Epigrafika,
          #VII. n.p., n.d.
              50p. 4 plates. 29cm.

ASIA, AFRICA

BB97   Babelon, Ernest Charles Francois.
B3   Les rois de Syrie d'Armenie
          et de commagene; catalogue des
          monnaies Grecques de la Bibliotheque
          Nationale par M. Ernest Babelon.
          Originally published in Paris, 1890.
          Reprinted-Bologna, A. Forni, 1971.
              2 vols. 268p. XXXII plates. Fold.
          chart. 25cm.; 31cm.
              Vol. 1-Text Vol. 2-plates.

BB97   British Museum. Dept. of coins & medals.
B7b   The coins of the Greek & Scythic kings
        of Bactria & India in the British Museum,
        by Percy Gardner. Ed. by Reginald Stuart
        Poole. Chicago, Argonaut, 1966.
            lxxvi, 193p. illus., map. 25cm.

BB97   Brett, Agnes Baldwin.
B74   The electrum and silver coins of Chios,
        issued during the 6th, 5th and 4th
        centuries B.C. Reprinted from American
        Journal of Numismatics, V. 48, 1914.
            60p. plates. 28cm.

BB97   Cunningham, Sir Alexander, 1814-1893.
C8   Coins of Alexander's successors in the
        East (Bactria, Ariana & India). [1st
        American ed.] Chicago, Argonaut, 1969.
            337p. 14 illus., map. 24cm. (The
        Argonaut library of antiquities)
            Bibliographical footnotes.

BB97   Franke, Peter Robert.
F7   Kleinasien zur Romerzeit; Griechis-
        ches leben im Spiegel der munzen.
        Munchen, C. H. Beck, 1968.
            71p. plates. 23cm.

BB97   Gardner, Percy, 1846-
G3   ...The gold coinage of Asia before Alex-
        ander the Great. London, Pub. for the
        British Academy by H. Frowde, Oxford, [1908]
            32p. 2 pl. 24cm.

BB97   Gilevich, A. M.
G5   Ancient coins of other cities from
        excavations at Chersonesus. From
        "Numizmatika i Sfragistika", #3, 1968.
            122p. charts. 29cm.

BB97   Head, Barclay V.
H4   The earliest Graeco-Bactrian and Graeco-
        Indian coins. Chicago, Argonaut, 1969.
            16p. 2 pl. 23cm.
            Reprinted from the Numismatic Chronicle,
        4th series, vol. 6.

BB97   Hill, Sir George Francis, 1867-1948.
H5   Attambelos I of Characene. New York,
        The American numismatic society, 1922.
            12p. iii pl. 16cm. (Numismatic notes
        and monographs [no. 14])

BB97   Imhoof-Blumer, Friedrich, 1838-
I5   Kleinasiatische muneen; von F. Imhoof-
            Blumer ... Wien, A. Holder, 1901-02.
                 2v. 578p. 20 pl. 29cm.

BB97   Lahiri, Amarendra Nath, 1918-
L3   Corpus of Indo-Greek coins [by] A.N.
            Lahiri. With a foreword by R. C. Majumdar.
            Calcutta, Poddar Publications [1965].
                 xviii, 287p. illus. 24cm.
                 Bibliography: p. [269]-275.

BB97   Levante, Edoardo.
L4   The coinage of Alexandreia
            Kat'isson in Cilicia. Reprinted from
            the Numismatic Chronicle, seventh
            series, Vol. XI, 1971.
                 pp. 93-102. 3 plates. 24cm.

BB97   Milne, Joseph Grafton, 1867-1951.
M5   Kolophon and its coinage: a study, by
            J.G. Milne. New York, The American
            numismatic society, 194].
                 113p. plates. 17cm. (Numismatic notes
            & monographs, no. 96)

BB97   Mitchiner, Michael.
M58   Indo-Greek and Indo-Scythian
Vol.1   coinage. Vol. 1-The early Indo-
            Greeks and their antecedants:
            Alexander the Great, the satraps of
            Egypt, Babylon, . . . the Seleucids
            circa 330 to 150 BC. London,
            Hawkins Pub., 1975.
                 102p; XXIXp. illus. 31cm.

BB97   Narain, A. K.
N3   The coin types of the Indo-Greek kings,
            by A. K. Narain. Chicago, Argonaut, 1968.
                 37p. geneal. table, map. 23cm.
                 Bibliography: p. [2]

BB97   Newell, Edward Theodore, 1886-1941.
N4s   Some unpublished coins of eastern dynasts.
            New York, The American numismatic society.
            1926.
                 21p. 2 pl. 17cm. (Numismatic notes &
            monographs. [no. 30])

BB97   Newell, Edward Theodore, 1886-1941.
N4t   Tarsos under Alexander. New York, 1919.
                 47p. 8 pl. 27cm.
                 Reprint from American Journal Numismatics.
            v. 52, 1918.

BB97   Waddington, William Henry, 1826-1894.
W3   Recueil general des monnaies grecques
         d'asie mineure commence par feu W. H.
         Waddington, continue et complete par E.
         Babelon, Th. Reinach. Paris, E. Leroux,
         1904-1912.
             4v. plates. 27cm.

BB97   Whitehead, Richard Bertram.
W5   Indo-Greek numismatics. Chicago,
         Argonaut, 1970.
             144p. illus., 8 plates. 24cm.
             Bibliographical footnotes.

COLLECTIONS

BC20   British Museum. Dept. of Coins & Medals.
B7   A guide to the exhibition of Roman coins
         in the British Museum, by Harold Mattingly.
         London, Trustees, 1927, 1963.
              80p. illus. 8 pl. 21cm.
              Bibliography: p. 73-74.

BC20   Instituto de Prehistoria y Arqueologia.
I5   Diputacion Provincial de Barcelona.
              Exposicion de numismatica Romana,
         catalogo, Palacio del Museo Arqueologico.
         Caridad, Casa Provincial de Caridad, 1964.
              62p. illus. 27cm.

BC20   Leyniers, C. J.
L4   Catalogue raisonne d'une collection
         de medailles. Bruxelles, 1774.
              162p.; 46p. illus. 25cm.

BC20   Madden, Frederic W.
M3   Account of the collection of Roman gold
         coins of the late Duke de Blacas, purchased
         ...for the British Museum. London, 1868.
              126p. pl. 22cm.

BC20   Terrace, Edward Lee.
T4   Some historical Roman coins; from the
         Henry Fairbanks collection of Greek and
         Roman coins at Dartmouth College. Hanover,
         N.H., Dartmouth Publications, 1958.
              44p. illus. 23cm.
              Includes bibliography.

BC20   Sammlung Franz Trau; munzen der
T7   Romischen Kaiser. Reprint of the
         auction catalogue compiled by
         Gilhofer and Ranschburg, May,
         1935. N.Y., Attic Books, 1976.
         130p. 53 plates. 28cm.
         -in German. Prices realized in
         Austrian shillings.

CATALOGUES

BC30   Seaby (B.A.) ltd.
S4c   A catalogue of Roman coins, compiled by
            Gilbert Askew. [New ed.] London, 1948.
                126p. illus. 24cm.
                Bibliography: p. 126

BC30   Sear, David R.
S4r   Roman coins and their values.
            2d rev. ed. London, Seaby, 1974.
                376p. 12 plates. 23cm.

BC30   Thimonier, J. L.
T5   Monnaies imperiales Romaines; lere partie
            lecons de numismatique; 2eme partie princi-
            pales abreviations de l'avers et du revers
            des monnaies imperiales Romaines. Clermont-
            Ferrand, France, [Editions Thimonier], 1976.
                76p. illus. 21cm.

GENERAL WORKS

BC40   Akerman, John Yonge, 1806-1873.
A4   A descriptive catalogue of rare and
Rare   unedited Roman coins: from the earliest
Books   period of the Roman coinage, to the extinc-
            tion of the empire under Constantinus
            Paleologos. ... London, E. Wilson, 1834.
                2v. illus., pl. 22cm.

BC40   [Boyne, William]
B6   A manual of Roman coins, from the
            earliest period to the extinction of the
            Empire, [by W.B.] London, W.H. Johnston,
            1865.
                79p. xxi pl. (1 fold.) 23cm.

BC40   [Chassepol, Francois de].
C5   A treatise of the revenue and false mon-
Rare   ey of the Romans. To which is annexed, a
Books   dissertation upon the manner of distin-
            guishing [by Guillaume Beauvais]. Trans-
            lated from the original printed at Paris,
            1740. London, Knapton, 1741.
                227p. 20cm.

BC40   Chifletio, Henrico Thoma.
C55   Dissertatio de Othonibus Aereis. Auc-
            tore Henrico Thoma Chifletio, Ioannis
            Iacobi F. Subiunctus eft Claudii Chief-
            letii de Antiquo numismate liber posthumus.
            Antwerp, ex officina Plantiniana Balthas-
            aris Moreti, 1656.
                143p. illus. 24cm.

BC40   Gnecchi, Francesco.
G6m   Monete romane. Milano, U. Hoepli,
            1907.
                418p. 25 pl.

BC40   Gnecchi, Francesco, 1847-
G6r   Roman coins, elementary manual, compiled
            by Cav. Francesco Gnecchi. 2nd ed, rev.
            corrected & amplified. Trans, by the Rev.
            Alfred Watson Hands. London, Spink, 1903.
                216p. 25 pl. 25cm.

BC40   Grant, Michael.
G7   Coins and the growth of the Roman
Vert.   Empire; three articles from the Geographi-
File   cal Magazine, v. 28, May-July, 1955.
                illus. maps. 24cm.

BC40   Harduini, Joannis.
H3   Chronologiae ex numis antiquis
Rare   restitutae. Paris, Joannem Boundot, 1697.
Books   2 vol. in 1. 150p. illus. 26cm.

BC40   Hill, George Francis, 1867-1948.
H5   Historical Roman coins. Chicago,
            Argonaut, 1966, London, Constable, 1909.
                xvi, 191p. pl. 22cm. (Argonaut
            library of antiquities).
                Bibliographical footnotes.

BC40   Instituto de Prehistoria y Arqueologia.
I5   Diputacion Provincial de Barcelona.
                Estudios de numismatica Romana ... ,
            recopilacion y edicion: Dr. Eduardo Ripoll
            Perello. Barcelona, Casa Provincial de
            Caridad, 1964.
                94p. illus. 28cm.

BC40   Kennett, Basil.
K4   Roman money; an exerpt from "The
            Antiquities of Rome." originally
            published in London, 1713. Chicago,
            Obol Internatl., 1975.
                unpaged. plate. 22cm.

BC40   Mattingly, Harold, 1884-1964.
M35   Roman coins from the earliest times to
          the fall of the Western Empire. London,
          Methuen, 1928.
              xx, 300p. 64 pl. 22cm.
              Bibliography: p. 259-272

BC40   Milne, Joseph Grafton, 1867-1951.
M5   The development of Roman coinage.
          Oxford, Basil Blackwell, 1937.
              22p. 22cm.

BC40   Reece, Richard.
R4   Roman coins. London, Ernest
          Benn Ltd., 1970.
              189p. 64 plates. 23cm.
          (Practical handbooks for collectors)

BC40   Sutherland, Carol Humphrey Vivian.
S8   Munzen der Romer [by] C. H. V.
          Sutherland. Munich, Ernst Battenberg,
          1974.
              311p. illus; part. col. 25cm.
              Library also holds a translation-
          Roman coins.

BC40   Thompson, Margaret.
T5   The Athenian Agora; results of
Vol. 2   excavations conducted by the American
          School of Classical Studies at
          Athens. Vol. 2-Coins from the Roman
          through the Venetian Period. Princeton,
          N.J., The American School of Classical
          Studies at Athens, 1954.
              122p. 4 plates. 32cm.

DICTIONARIES, BIBLIOGRAPHIES, ETC.

BC45   Stevenson, Seth William.
S7   A dictionary of Roman coins, Republican
          and Imperial, by S.W. Stevenson, C. Roach
          Smith, Frederic W. Madden. London, Bell,
          1889.
              viii, 929p. illus. 24cm.

COLLECTING

BC50   Coins of the Roman Empire; beginners' guide.
C6   No date.
              15p. illus. 23cm.

BC50   Doering, David R.
D6   Collection of Roman coins made easy.
          A dissertation on the identification of
          Roman coins from 27 B.C. to 476 A.D.,
          with a guide to the reading of inscriptions,
          recognition of the Emperors and a relative
          price guide. [Pegasus Pub. Co., 1968]
              72p. illus. 23cm.

BC50   Kankelfitz, B. Ralph.
K3   Katalog Romischer munzen; von
Vol.1   Pompejus bis Romulus; ein handbuch
          fur sammler mit vielen proktischen
          hinweisen und preistaxen nach
          erhaltungsgraden. Band I.
          Munchen, Ernst Battenberg, 1974.
              217p. illus. 25cm.

TECHNICAL ASPECTS

BC60   Akerman, John Yonge.
A4   Fourres and forgeries: general observa-
          tions on the coins and coinage of the
          Romans. New York, Numismatic communica-
          tions, 1970.
              xix p. illus. 22cm.

BC60   Boon, George C.
B6   Counterfeiting in Roman Britain.
Vert.   Taken from Scientific American. Dec.,
File   1974, Vol. 231, No. 6.
              pp. 121-130. illus. 29cm.

BC60   Buttrey, Theodore V.
B8   Halved coins, the Augustan Reform
          and Horace, Odes 1.3. n.p., n. pub.,
          n.d.
              pp. 31-48. 2 plates. 28cm.

BC60   Caley, Earle Radcliffe, 1900-
C3   Orichalcum and related ancient alloys:
        origin, composition, & manufacture, with
        special reference to the coinage of the
        Roman Empire. New York, American Numismatic
        Society, 1964.
            v, 115p. 23cm. (Numismatic notes and
        monographs, no. 151)
            Bibliographical footnotes.

BC60   Carson, R. A. G.
C37   The Geneva forgeries by R. A. G.
        Carson, MA. Reprinted from the Royal
        Numismatic Society's Numismatic Chronicle
        6th series, Vol. XVIII. Great Britain,
        1958.
            pp. 47-58. plates. 22cm.

BC60   Hill, Philip V. 1917-
H5b   Barbarous radiates; imitations of third-
        century Roman coins. New York, American
        Numismatic Society, 1949.
            44p. 4 pl., map. 23cm. (Numismatic
        notes & monographs, no. 112)

BC60   Sydenham, Edward Allen.
S9m   The mint of Lugdunum by E. A.
        Sydenham. Reprinted from The Numismatic
        Chronicle, 4th series. London, Royal
        Numismatic Society, 1917.
            44p. 2 plates. 22cm.

BC60   Sydenham, Edward Allen.
S9o   The origin of the Roman Serrati.
        Reprinted from the Numismatic Chronicle,
        5th series, Vol. XV, 1935.
            23p. 22cm.

BC60   Sydenham, Edward Allen.
S9r   The Roman monetary system by E.A.
        Sydenham. Part II. Reprinted from
        The Numismatic Chronicle, 4th series.
        London, Royal Numismatic Society,
        1919.
            91p. 22cm.

BC60   Webb, Percy H.
W4   Third-century Roman mints and marks.
        Reprinted from The Numismatic Chronicle,
        5th series, vol. 1, p. 226-293.
            69p. 22cm.

GOLD

BC63   West, Louis C.
W4   Gold and silver coin standards in the
           Roman empire. New York, American Numis-
           matic Society, 1941.
               199p. tables. 17cm. (Numismatic notes
           and monographs, no. 94)
               Bibliography: p. 27-30.

SILVER

BC65   Gronovii, Joh. Frederici.
G7   De sestertiis seu subsecivorum
Rare   pecuniae veteris Graecae & Romanae
Books   Libri IV. Accesserunt L. Volvsius
           Maecianus J.C. & Balbus Mensor...
           de foenore unciario & centefemis
           ufuris item de hyperpyro. Lyons,
           Joannis du Vivie, 1691.
               766p. 23cm.

BC65   Seaby, Herbert Allen.
S4   Roman silver coins. London, Seaby,
           1952-1971
               4v. illus., tables. 22cm.
               Contents: v.1 Republic to Augustus.
           v.2 Tiserius to Commodus. v.3 Pertinax to
           Babinus and Pupienus v.4 Gordian III to
           Postumus.

BRONZE, COPPER

BC67   Akerman, John Yonge.
A4   Roman coins; the as and its divisions.
           [New York, Numismatic Communications,
           1970].
               19p. illus. 22cm.

BC67   Bruck, Guido.
B7   Die spatromische kupferpragung. Ein
           bestimmungsbuch fur schlecht erhaltene
           munzne. Graz, Akademische Druck-U.
           Verlagsanstalt, 1961.
               101p. illus., map. 25cm.

BC67   Grant, Michael.
G7   From imperium to auctoritas; a
        historical study of aes coinage in the
        Roman empire, 49 B.C. - A.D. 14.
        Cambridge, University Press, 1946, 1969.
            xvii, 512p. illus. 12 pl. 22cm.

BC67   Hill, Philip.
H51   Late Roman bronze coinage, A.D. 324-498.
        Reprinted with additions and corrections
        from the Numismatic Circular. London, Spink
        & Son, 1965.
            114p. 4 pl. 25cm.

BC67   Seidl, Johann Gabriel.
S4   Das alt-italische schwergeld im K.K.
        Munz-und Antiken-cabinette zu wien, bes-
        chrieben vom Custos J.G. Seidl, Wien, 1854
            97p. 24cm.

BC67   Sydenham, Edward Allen, 1873-1948.
S9a   Aes grave, a study of the cast coin-
        ages of Rome and central Italy. London,
        Spink, 1926.
            145p. illus., pl. 25cm.
            Bibliography: p. 10

BC67   Sydenham, Edward Allen.
S9a3   The Aes Grave; its chronology and
        theory, by E. A. Sydenham. Reprinted
        from the Numismatic Chronicle, 5th
        series. London, Royal Numismatic
        Society, 1925.
            25p. 22cm.

ICONOGRAPHY

BC70   Brown, Donald Frederick, 1909-
B7   Temples of Rome as coin types. New
        York, American numismatic society, 1940.
            51p. ix pl. 17cm. (Numismatic notes
        and monographs, no. 90).

BC70   Burzio, Humberto F.
B8   La marina en la moneda Romana.
        Buenos Aires, 1961.
            179p. illus. 24cm.
            Bibliography

BC70   Franke, Peter Robert.
F7   Romische Kaiserportrats im
           munzbild; aufnahmen von Max Hirmer.
           Munchen, Hirmer Verlag, 1972.
                55p. 52 plates., part. col. 19cm.

BC70   Gnecchi, Francesco.
G55   The fauna and flora on the coin-types of
           ancient Rome. London, Spink & Son, 1919.
                120p. illus. 25cm.
                Reprint from Numismatic Circular, 1916-
           18.

BC70   Handler, Susan.
H3   Architecture on the Roman coins of
Vert.   Alexandria. From American Journal of
File   Archaeology, vol. 74, no. 1 (January,
           1971).
                [18]p. illus. 28cm.

BC70   Humphreys, H. Noel.
H8   Abbreviations on Roman coins, with
           their explanations and English
           translations. N.Y., Attic Books,
           1971.
                24p. 22cm.

BC70   Kahler, Heinz.
K3   The art of Rome and her empire, by
1965   Heinz Kahler. Translated by J. R. Foster.
           New York, Crown Publishers [1965].
                259p. illus. col. pl. 24cm. (Art
           of the world library, second series:
           European cultures)

BC70   Levi, Annalina Calo.
L4   Barbarians on Roman imperial coins and
           sculpture. New York, American Numismatic
           Society, 1952.
                xi, 56p. illus. 23cm. (Numismatic
           notes and monographs, no. 123)
                Bibliographical footnotes.

BC70   Stanton, Earle Kezartee.
S7   Architectura numismatica. Reprint from
           The Numismatist, v. 60, no. 7, July, 1947.
                7p. illus. 22cm.

BC70   Vergara, Ruben W.
V4   El retrato en la moneda romana.
           Montevideo, 1966.
                23p. illus. 22cm.

BC70   Westdal, Stewart J.
W4   A guidebook for the identification
            of Roman coin inscriptions. 2d. ed.
            San Diego, the author, 1973.
                 64p. 21cm.

HOARDS

BC75   Bellinger, Alfred R.
B4e   The eighth and ninth Dura hoards.
            New York, ANS, 1939.
                 92 p. 13 pl. 17 cm. (Numismatic
            notes and monographs, no. 85)

BC75   Bellinger, Alfred Raymond, 1893-
B4s   The sixth, seventh and tenth Dura hoards.
            New York, The American numismatic society,
            1935.
                 75p. plates. 16cm. (Numismatic notes
            and monographs, no. 69)

BC75   Bellinger, Alfred Raymond.
B4t   The third and fourth Dura hoards. New
            York, American numismatic society, 1932.
                 85p. xx pl. 17cm. (Numismatic notes
            and monographs, no. 55)

BC75   Bellinger, Alfred Raymond, 1893-
B4t2   Two Roman hoards from Dura-Europos. New
            York, American numismatic society, 1931.
                 66p. xvii pl. 17cm. (Numismatic notes
            and monographs, no. 49)

BC75   Christiansen, E., ed.
C5   The Roman coins of Alexandria.
Vert.   [Collection of the International
File   Numismatic Congress.] n.p., Internatl.
            Numismatic Congress, 1973.
                 unpaged. graphs. 30cm.

BC75   Eddy, Samuel K.
E3   The minting of Antoniniani A.D. 238-249
            and the Smyrna hoard. New York, American
            Numismatic society, 1967.
                 vii, 133p. vii pl. 23cm.

BC75   Karyshkovski, P. O.
K3   Finds of Roman coins in the Odessa
            Oblast. Taken from "Brief comm-
            unications on archeological field
            studies of the Odessa Archeological
            Museum." Odessa, 1963.
                 21p. 32cm.

BC75   Kropotkin, V. V.
K7   New finds of Roman coins in the
            USSR. Supplement to "Corpus of Arch-
            eological Sources". From
            Numizmatika i Epigrafika, Vol. 6,
            Moscow, 1966.
                 78p. 32cm.

BC75   Kropotkin, V. V.
K7h   Hoards of Roman coins on the
            territory of the USSR. Moscow,
            Academy of Sciences of the USSR, 1961.
                 3 Vols. pagination irregular. illus.
            maps. 29cm.
                 Vol. 1-Text, translated from the
            Ukranian
                 Vol. 2-Annex I, Maps
                 Vol. 3-Annex II, Maps

BC75   Leeds, Edward Thurlow, 1877-
L4   A hoard of Roman folles from Diocletian's
            reform (A.D. 296) to Constantine Caesar,
            found at Fyfield, Berks. ... Oxford,
            Ashmolean museum, 1946.
                 63p. viii pl. 25 x 19cm.

BC75   Lewis, Naphtali.
L45   A hoard of folles from Seltz (Alsace)
            ... with a supplement on The chemical com-
            position of the follis, by David Lewis.
            New York, American numismatic society, 1937-
                 81p. plates. 17cm. (Numismatic notes
            and monographs. no. 79)
                 Includes bibliographies.

BC75   Mattingly, Harold, 1884-1964.
M3   The Richborough hoard of 'radiates,'
            1931, by H. Mattingly and W.P.D. Stebbing.
            New York, American numismatic society,
            1938.
                 118p. pl. 17cm. (Numismatic notes and
            monographs, no. 80)

BC75   Newell, Edward Theodore, 1886-1941.
N4f   The fifth Dura hoard. New York, Amer-
            ican numismatic society, 1933.
                 14p. plates. 16cm. (Numismatic notes
            and monographs no. 58)

BC75   Newell, Edward Theodore, 1886-1941.
N4t   Two hoards from Minturno. New York,
          American numismatic society, 1933.
              38p. illus, 5 pl. 16cm. (Numismatic
          notes and monographs. no. 60).

BC75   Thirion, Marcel.
T45   Le tresor de Liberchies; aurei des
          Ier et IIe siecles, avec une introduction
          archeologique par Pierre Claes et Charles
          Leva. Bruxelles, Pro Geminiaco A.S.B.L.,
          1972.
              218p. illus. 26 pl. 25cm.

BY PERIOD - REPUBLICAN 449B.C.-A.D.31

BC80   Babelon, Ernest Charles Francois.
B3   Description historique et chronologique
          des monnaies de la Republique romaine
          vulgairement appelees monnaies consulaires.
          Bologna, A. Forni, 1963. Reprint: Paris,
          1885-86.
              2v. v.1-562p; v.2-669p. illus. 24cm.

BC80   Bahrfeldt, Max von.
B34   Sammlung Romischer munzen der
          Republik u. des West-Kaiserreichs;
          [von] Max von Bahrfeldt. Originally
          printed in 1922. Reprinted-Darmstadt,
          Scientia Verlag Aalen, 1972.
              128p. XXXIII plates. 30cm.

BC80   Bellorius, Joannis Petri.
B4   Romani adnotationes nunc primum
Rare   evulgatae in XII priorum Caesarum
Books   numismata ab aenea vico Parmensi. Rome,
          1730.
              78p. plates unpaged. 35cm.

BC80   British museum. Dept. of coins & medals.
B7   Coins of the Roman republic in the
          British museum. ... With an intro and 123
          plates ... London, Printed by order of
          the Trustees, 1910.
              3v. illus., cxxiii pl. 25cm. (A
          catalogue of the Roman coins in the British
          museum.)

BC80   Buttrey, Theodore V.
B8   The triumviral portrait gold of the
           quattuorviri monetales of 42 B.C.   New
           York, American Numismatic Society, 1956.
               x, 69p. 9 plates. 23cm. (Numismatic
           notes and monographs, no. 137)
               Bibliographical footnotes.

BC80   Crawford, M. H.
C7   Roman republican coin hoards. London,
           Royal Numismatic Society, 1969.
               170 p. 3 pl.
               Bibliography.

BC80   Crawford, Michael H.
C7r   Roman Republican coinage.
           Cambridge, Cambridge Univ. Press,
           1974.
               2v. 919p. LXX plates. 26cm.
               V. 1-Introduction Catalogue
           V. 2-Studies, plates, indices.

BC80   Fava, Anna Serena.
F3   I simboli nelle monete argentee
           Repubblicane e la vita dei Romani. Catalogo
           di Anna Serena Fava. Marzo, Museo Civico di
           Torino, 1969.
               199p. illus. 24cm.

BC80   Foy-Vaillant, Jean, 1632-1706.
F6   Nummi antiqui familiarum Roman arum
Rare   perpetuis interpretationious illustrati,
Books   per J. Vaillant. Amsterdam, G. Gallet,
           1703.
               2v. 152 pl. 34cm.

BC80   Fuchs, Gunter.
F8   Architekturdarstellung auf Romischen
           munzen der Republik und der fruhen Kaiserzeit
           Berlin, W. de Gruyter, 1969.
               2 vol. Vol. 1--text 138p. diagrs. 27cm.
           Vol. 2--plates 20p. 27cm.

BC80   Mattingly, Harold.
M3   The date of the Roman denarius and other
           landmarks in early Roman coinage by
           Mattingly and E. S. G. Robinson. Obol,
           1970.
               58p. 3 pl. 22cm.

BC80   Mattingly, Harold.
M3a   "Aes" and "Pecvnia": records of
           Roman currency down to 269 B.C.
           Reprinted from the Numismatic Chronicle,
           6th series. Chicago, Obol Internatl.,
           1972.
               19p. 22cm.

BC80   Mattingly, Harold.
M3r   Roman numismatics: miscellaneous
           notes, from the proceedings of the
           British Academy, Vol. XLIII. London,
           Oxford University Press, n.d.
               pp. 179-210. 25cm.

BC80   Mattingly, Harold.
M3v   The various styles of the
           Roman Republican coinage. Reprinted
           from the Numismatic Chronicle, 6th
           series. Oak Park, Ill., Obol Internatl.,
           1971.
               18p. 21cm.

BC80   Magnaguti, Conte Alessandro.
M33   Ex nummis historia; IV monete
           Romane. Rome, P. & P. Santamaria,
           1951.
               110p. XXI plates. 27cm.

BC80   Oiselio, Jac.
O3   Thesaurus selectorum numismatum antiquorm
Rare   ...by Jac. Oiselio, J.C. Amsterdam,
Books   Henrici & Theodori Boom, 1677.
               570p. CXII plates. 24cm.

BC80   Riccio, Gennaro.
R5   Le monete della antiche famiglie di
           Roma fino allo imperadore Augusto. ... 2nd
           ed. Napoli, Stamperia del Fibreno, 1843.
               viii, 289p. 71 pl. 26cm.

BC80   Rolland, Henri.
R6   Numismatique de la Republique Romaine.
           Catalogue general et raisonne. Paris,
           Ciani, 19--
               220p. 10 pl. 23cm.

BC80   Smyth, William Henry.
S6   Descriptive catalogue of a cabinet of
           Roman family coins belonging to ... the
           Duke of Northumberland. London, privately
           printed, 1856.
               xxxix, 323p. 30cm.

BC80
S7
	Stern, Jean.
	    Historical implications of Roman coins; a survey of Roman coinage and its role in deciphering history. La Mesa, Ca., Historia, 1975.
	    32p. illus. 21cm.

BC80
S9
	Sydenham, Edward Allen.
	    Symbols on denarii of L. Papius and L. Roscius, by Rev. Edward A. Sydenham. Reprinted from the Numismatic Chronicle, 5th series. London, Royal Numismatic Society, 1931.
	    13p. 22cm.

BC80
S9c
	Sydenham, Edward Allen, 1873-1948.
	    The coinage of the Roman Republic. Rev. with indexes by G.C. Haines. ed. by L. Forrer & C.A. Hersh. London, Spink, 1952.
	    lxix, 343p. 30 pl. 25cm.

BC80
S9d
	Sydenham, Edward Allen.
	    The date of Piso-Caepio by Rev. E. A. Sydenham. Reprinted from the Numismatic Chronicle, 5th series. London, Royal Numismatic Society, 1940.
	    16p. 22cm.

BC80
S9o
	Sydenham, Edward Allen.
	    Ornamental detail as a guide to the classification of Republican Denarii. Reprinted from the Numismatic Chronicle, 6th series, Vol. 1, 1941.
	    pp. 117-127. 1 plate. 22cm.

BC80
S9r
	Sydenham, Edward Allen.
	    The retariffing of the Denarius at sixteen asses by Rev. E. A. Sydenham and H. Mattingly. Reprinted from the Numismatic Chronicle, 5th Series. London, Royal Numismatic Society, 1934.
	    11p. 22cm.

BC80
S9v
	Sydenham, Edward Allen.
	    The Victoriate by Rev. Edward A. Sydenham. Reprinted from the Numismatic Chronicle, 5th series. London, Royal Numismatic Society, 1932.
	    23p. 2 plates. 22cm.

BC80   Vollenweider, Marie-Louise.
V6   Die portratgemmen der romischen
          Republik by Marie-Louise Vollenweider.
          Mainz am Rhein, Verlag Philipp von Zabern,
          1964.
              2 vols. plates. 30cm.
              vol. 1.- text 316p.
          vol. 2.-Katalog und tafeln 110p.   168 plates

BY PERIOD - IMPERIAL 27B.C.-A.D.476

BC85   Adelson, Howard L.
A3   A bronze hoard of the period of Zeno I,
          by H. L. Adelson & George L. Kustas. New
          York, American Numismatic Society, 1962.
              ix. 89p. illus., tables. 23cm. (Num-
          ismatic notes & monographs, no. 148)
              Bibliographical footnotes

BC85   Banduri, Anselmo.
B3   Numismata imperatorum romanorum a
Rare   Trajan decio ad palaeologos Augustos.
Books   Paris, 1718.
              2 v. pl. 38cm.

BC85   Bononiensi, Philippo Argelato.
B65   Imperatorum Romanorum numismata
Rare   a Pompejo magno ad Heraclium...
Books   Caroli VI. n.p., Ex Aedibus
          Societatis Palatine, 1730.
              624p. illus. 41cm.

BC85   Boyce, Aline Abaecherli.
B69   Festal and dated coins of the Roman
          Empire: four papers. New York, American
          Numismatic Society, 1965.
              x, 102p. 16 pl. 23cm. (Numismatic
          notes and monographs, no. 153)
              Bibliographical footnotes.

BC85   Breglia, Laura.
B7   Roman Imperial coins: their art & tech-
          nique, intro by Ranuccio Bianchi Bandinelli
          [trans from the Italian by Peter Green].
          New York, Praeger [1968].
              236p. 303 illus. 24cm.
              Bibliography: p. 232-233.

BC85   British Museum. Dept. of Coins and Medals.
B74   Coins of the Roman Empire in the British
        Museum. London, Printed by order of the
        Trustees, 1923-62, 1965-
            6v. in 7 pl. 26cm.
            Includes bibliographies.
            Contents: v. 1. Augustus to Vitellius. -
        v.2. Vespasian to Domitian. - v.3. Nerva to
        Hadrian. - v.4. Antoninus Pius to Commodus. -
        v.5. Pertinax to Elagabalus. - v.6. Severus
        Alexander to Balbinus and Pupienus.

BC85   Brown, Augustus.
B76   The financial collapse of the
        Roman coinage in the 3rd century AD.
        Kyrenia, Kent, England, the author,
        n.d.
            21p. 1 plate. charts. 20cm.

BC85   Brown, Augustus.
B76c   The coinage of Elagabulus, AD 218-
        292. Canterbury, Kent College, n.d.
            17p. 1 plate. 20cm.

BC85   Brown, Augustus.
B76m   The coinage of Maximinius, the
        Gordiani, Balbinus and Pupienus, AD
        235-238. N.Y., Attic Books, n.d.
            13p. 1 plate. charts. 20cm.

BC85   Brown, Augustus.
B76t   The coinage of Trajan Decius
        AD249-251. Kyrenia, Kent, England,
        the author, n.d.
            21p. 1 plate. charts. 20cm.

BC85   Bruun, Patrick.
B78   Studies in Constantinian chronology.
        New York, American Numismatic Society, 1961.
            xi, 116p. viii pl. 23cm. (Numismatic
        notes and monographs, no. 146)
            Includes bibliographies.

BC85   Carey, Michael.
C3   The Emperors of Rome, together with the
        usurpers or rebel emperors, illus with
        photos taken from their coins. Los Angeles.
        Wetzel, 1951.
            146p. 16 pl. 21cm.

BC85   Celis, Jesus P.
C4   Roman numismatics with reference to
         imperial coins. Philippine numismatic and
         antiquarian society. Manila, The society,
         1954.
             16p. illus. (Philippine numismatic
         monographs, no. 10)

BC85   Cohen, Henry, 1808-1880.
C6   Description historique des monnaies fra-
         ppees sous l'Empire romain communement app-
         elees medailles imperiales. ... 2nd ed.
         Graz, Akademische Druck-U. Verlagstalt,
         1955. v.3-8: continue par Feuardent
         Previously published Paris, Rollin & Feuar-
         dent, 1880-92.
             8v. plates. 24cm.

BC85   Corpus nummorum Romanorum. V.1.
C61   Da Cneo Pompeo a Marco Antonio,
V.1   con 1481 illustrazioni. Firenze,
         Editori A. Banti - L. Simonetti,
         1972.
         313p. illus. 27cm.

BC85   Corpus nummorum Romanorum, V.2.
C61   Da Marco Antonio alle Famiglia Licinia'
V.2   . . ., con 1071 illustrazioni. Firenze,
         Editori A. Banti-L. Simonetti, 1973.
         324p. illus. 27cm.

BC85   Corpus nummorum Romanorum, V.3.
C61   Dalla famiglio Livineia alla famiglia
V.3   voconia ..., con 916 illustrazioni.
         Firenze, Editori A. Banti-L. Simonetti,
         1973.
         282p. illus. 27cm.

BC85   Corpus nummorum Romanorum, V.4.
C61   Augusto . . . con 1376 illustrazioni.
V.4   Firenze, Editori A. Banti-L. Sinonetti,
         1974.
         307p. illus. 27cm.

BC85   Corpus nummorum Romanorum, V.5.
C61   Augusto; monete d'argento con 2078
V.5   illustrazioni. Firenze, Editori
         A. Banti-L. Simonetti, 1974.
         328p. illus. 27cm.

BC85   Corpus nummorum Romanorum, V.7.
C61   Augusto; monetazione coloniale con
V.7   684 illustrazioni. Firenze,
               Editori A. Banti-L. Simonetti, 1975.
               336p. illus. 27cm.

BC85   Corpus nummorum Romanorum, V.8.
C61   Da Augusto E. Livia a Tiberio;
V.8   con 1285 illustrazioni. Firenze,
               Editori: A. Banti-L. Simonetti,
               1975.
               329p. illus. 27cm.

BC85   Corpus nummorum Romanorum, V.9.
C61   Tiberio; monete d'oro, d'argento,
V.9   di bronzo e coloniali; con 1170
               illustrazioni. Firenze, A. Banti-
               L. Simonetti, 1976.
               319p. illus. 27cm.

BC85   Comparette, Thomas Louis, 1868-
C63   Debasement of the silver coinage under
Vert.   the emperor Nero. From American Journal
File   of Numismatics, v.47, 1913. New York,
           1914.
               11p. 28cm.

BC85   Eisenberg, Jerome M.
E4c   A catalog of Roman Imperial coins. New
           York, Royal-Athena coin corp. 1958.
               18p. illus. 21cm.

BC85   Eisenberg, Jerome M.
E4g   A guide to Roman imperial coins. New
           York, Royal Coin Co., 1957, 1959.
               32p. illus. 22cm.

BC85   Foy-Vaillant, Jean, 1632-1706.
F6   Numismata imperatorium Romanorum
Rare   praestantiora a Julio Caesare ad postumum
Books   usque, per Johannem Vaillant. Rome, 1743.
               3v. illus. 28cm.

BC85   Foy-Vaillant, Jean, 1632-1706.
F6i   Numismata imperatorum Roman-
Rare   orum praestantiora a Julio
Books   Caesare ad postumum et tyrannos,
           per Joannem Vaillant. ... Paris,
           Joannem Jombert, 1694.
               2v. in 1(256, 397p.) illus. 21cm.

BC85   Gillespie, J. U.
G5   A study of the coinage of the "Ionian
          League". Bruxelles, 1956.
               Reprint from Revue belge de numismati-
          que, v. 102, 1956, p. 31-52, pl. 3-8.

BC85   Grant, Michael, 1914-
G7a   Aspects of the principate of Tiberius;
          historical comments on the colonial coinage
          issued outside Spain. New York, American
          Numismatic Society, 1950.
               xviii, 199p. illus., 8 pl. 24cm.
          (Numismatic notes & monographs, no. 116)
               Bibliography: p. 173-187.

BC85   Grant, Michael.
G7r   Roman history from coins; some uses of
          imperial coinage to the historian. Cam-
          bridge, University Press, 1958, 1968.
               96p. 32 pl. 19cm.

BC85   Hill, Philip V. 1917-
H5   The coinage of Septimius Severus and his
          family of the mint of Rome, A.D. 193-217,
          London, Spink, 1964.
               56p. 2 pl., tables. 25cm.

BC85   Kestner-Museums.
K4   Kataloge der mungsammlung des Kestner-
          Museums, Hannover. Goldmunzen der
          Romischen kaiserzeit. Hannover, Schluter,
          1964.
               104p. 46 illus. 20cm.

BC85   Klawans, Zander H.
K5   Reading and dating Roman imperial
          coins. Racine, Wis., Whitman Pub. Co.,
          1953.
               125p. illus. 20cm.
          Includes bibliography.

BC85   Klawans, Zander H.
K5   Reading and dating Roman imperial
1959   coins. 2d ed. Racine, Wis., Whitman
          Pub. Co., 1959.
               128p. illus. 20cm.
          Includes bibliography.

BC85   Kraay, Colin M.
K7   The aes coinage of Galba. New York,
          American Numismatic Society, 1956.
               x, 125p. 37 pl. 23cm. (Numismatic
          notes & monographs, no. 133)
               Bibliographical footnotes.

BC85   Mattingly, Harold, 1884-1964.
M3   The imperial vota, by H. Mattingly.
          From the proceeding of the British
          Academy, Vol. XXXVI. London, Geoffrey
          Cumberlege Amen House, n.d.
              Pt. 1, pp. 154-195. Pt. 2, pp. 219-
          268. 25cm.

BC85   Mattingly, Harold, 1884-1964.
M3m   The man in the Roman street ... with an
          introduction by Thomas Ollive Mabbott.
          New York, Numismatic Review, 1947.
              xx, 116p. 22cm.

BC85   Mattingly, Harold, 1884-1964, ed.
M3r   The Roman imperial coinage, edited by
          ... and Edward A. Sydenham. London, Spink,
          1968.
              8v. in 11 illus. pl. 26cm.
              Bibliography.
              Contents: v.1. Augustus to Vitellius. -
          v.2. Vespasian to Hadrian. - v.3. Antoninus
          Pius to Commodus. - v.4. Pertinax to Geta &
          Macrinus to Pupienus & Gordian III to Uraniua
          Antoninus. - v.5. Valerian I to Florian,
          Probus to Amandus. - v.6. Diocletian's reform
          to death of Maximinus. - v.7. Constantine &
          Licinius. - v.9. Valentinian I to Theodosius I.

BC85   Patin, Charles, 1633-1693.
P3   Imperatorum romanorum numismata ex
Rare   aere, mediae et minimae formae. Argen-
Books   tinae, S. Paulli, 1671.
              537p. illus. 36cm.

BC85   Pedrusi, Paolo.
P4   I cesari, in oro, in argento, in
Rare   Medaglioni, raccolti nel Farnese Museo.
Books   Parma, 1694-1709.
              5 v. pl. 35cm.

BC85   Pearce, J. W. E.
P42   The Vota-legends on the Roman
          coinage. Reprinted from the Royal
          Numismatic Society's Numismatic
          Chronicle, London. 5th series,
          Vol. XVII, 1937.
              13p. 22cm.

BC85   Pearce, J. W. E.
P42s   Siliqua issues at Treveri from
            the death of Valens to the accession
            of Magnus Maximus. Reprinted from
            The Royal Numismatic Society's
            "Numismatic Chronicle", London.
            5th series, Vol. XV, 1935.
                28p. plates. 22cm.

BC85   Polzer, Joseph.
P6   The villa at Piazza Armerina and
            the numismatic evidence. n.p., n. pub.,
            n.d.
                pp. 139-150. illus. 28cm.

BC85   Robertson, Ann S.
R55   Roman Imperial coins in the Hunter Coin
            Cabinet, University of Glasgow. Vol. II.
            Trajan to Commodus. London, Oxford
            Univ. Press, 1971.
                692p. 124 pl. 25cm.
                Bibliography

BC85   Rohde, Theodore.
R6   Die munzen des Kaisers Aurelianus, seiner
            Frau Severina und der Funsten von Palmyra.
            Miskoloz (Hungary) Forster, 1881.
                429p. 3 folded tables 25cm.

BC85   Rodewald, Cosmo.
R63   Money in the age of Tiberius.
            Manchester, England, Manchester
            University Press, 1976.
                154p. 25cm.

BC85   Schulten, Peter N.
S3   Die Romische Munzstatte trier; von der
            Viederaufnahme ihrer tatigkeit unter
            Diocletian bis zum ende der Falles-Pragung.
            Frankfort/Main, Numismatischer Verlag PN
            Schulten, 1974.
                52p. X plates. 21cm.

BC85   Stein, Harry J.
S7   Brutus and the background of his coin-
            age. Reprinted from The Numismatist.
            March, 1940.
                8p. illus. 23cm.

BC85   Sutherland, Carol Humphrey Vivian.
S8   Coinage in Roman imperial policy 31 B.C.
            A.D. 68. London, Methuen, 1951.
                xi, 220p. 17 pl. 21cm.

BC85   Sutherland, Carol Humphrey Vivian.
S8c   The cistophori of Augustus, by C. H. V.
          Sutherland, Nekriman Olcay, and K. E.
          Merrington. London, Royal Numismatic
          Society, 1970.
               132p. illus. 36 pl. 26cm. (Royal
          Numismatic Society, special publication,
          no. 5)

BC85   Sydenham, Edward Allen, 1873-1948.
S9   Historical references on coins of the
          Roman Empire from Augustus to Gallienus,
          by Edward A. Sydenham. London, Spink &
          Son, 1917.
               155p. illus. 24cm.

BC85   Sydenham, Edward Allen, 1873-1948.
S9   Historical references on coins
1968   of the Roman Empire from Augustus to
          Gallienus, by Edward A. Sydenham.
          London, Spink & Son; San Diego, Cal.,
          Pegasus Pub. Co., 1968.
               155p. illus. 25cm.
               Reprint of 1917 ed.

BC85   Sydenham, Edward Allen.
S9a   The coinages of Augustus. Reprinted
          from the Numismatic Chronicle, 4th
          series, Vol. XX, 1920.
               40p. 2 plates. 22cm.

BC85   Sydenham, Edward A.
S9c   The coinage of Nero, an introductory
          study. Reprinted from Numismatic Chron-
          icle, 1916.
               24p. 1 pl. 22cm.

BC85   Sydenham, Edward Allen.
S9d   Divus Augustus by E. A. Sydenham.
          Reprinted from The Numismatic Chronicle.
          4th series, London, Royal Numismatic
          Society, 1918.
               22p. plate. 22cm.

BC85   Sydenham, Edward Allen.
S9v   The vicissitudes of Maximian
          after his abdication. Reprinted from
          the Numismatic Chronicle, 5th series,
          Vol. XIV, 1934.
               27p. illus. 22cm.

BC85   Webb, Percy H.
W4   The reign and coinage of Carausius.
          London, Spink, 1908.
              xi, 260p. 5 pl. 22cm.
              Reprinted from the Numismatic Chronicle.
          4th series, v. vii.

BC85   Windler, F. J., Jr.
W5   A description of late Roman Imperial
          coins (350-478A.D.) ... and the Becker
          forgeries of this period. Nashville, Tenn.
          The author, 1960.
              57p. [mimeograph] 28cm.

BY REGION - AFRICA

BC93   Boyce, Aline Abaecherli.
B6   Coins of tingi with latin legends. New
          York, American Numismatic Society, 1947.
              27p. 5 pl. 17cm. (Numismatic notes
          and monographs, no. 109)

BC93   Curtis, James W.
C8c   The coinage of Roman Egypt, a survey.
          New York, American Numismatic Association,
          1956.
              Reprint from The Numismatist, v. 69,
          no. 1 & no. 9, January-August, 1956.
              62p. 44 pl. 22cm.

BC93   Curtis, James W.
C8p   Pictorial coin types at the Roman mint
Vert.   of Alexandria; a third supplement. Reprint
File   from The Journal of Egyptian Archaeology.
          v. 41, 1955, p. 119-120, plate no. 24.

BC93   Curtis, James W.
C8t   The tetradrachms of Roman Egypt. Chicago
          Argonaut, 1969.
              xxiv, 172p. illus., map. 24cm.

BC93   Milne, Joseph Grafton, 1867-1951.
M5   Catalogue of Alexandrian coins
          [in] the Ashmolean Museum, Oxford
          University by J. G. Milne with a
          supplement by Colin M. Kraay. Oxford,
          Oxford University Press,
          1971.
              155p.; 10p. VII plates; fold.
          charts. 29cm.

BC93   West, Louis C.
W4   Currency in Roman and Byzantine Egypt.
           by West and Allan Chester Johnson.
           Amsterdam, A. M. Hakkert, 1967.
               195p. 22cm.
               Bibliography

BY REGION - ASIA

BC95   Gupta, Parmeshwari Lal.
G8   Roman coins from Andhra Pradesh.
           Hyderabad, India; Govt. of Andhra
           Pradesh, [1965].
               128p. 26 plates. 29cm.
           (Andhra Pradesh Govt. Museum Series
           #10).

BC95   Newell, Edward T.
N4   The pre-Imperial coinage of Roman
           Antioch. [Oak Park, Ill.], Obol, 1970.
               45p. 2 pl. 21cm.
               Reprint of 1919 ed.

BC95   Sydenham, Edward A.
S9   The coinage of Caesarea in Cappadocia.
           London, Spink, 1933.
               138p. illus. 24cm.

BY REGION - EUROPE

BC97   Akerman, John Yonge.
A4   Coins of the Romans relating to
           Britain. London, J. R. Smith, 1844.
               170p. 6 pl. 23cm.

BC97   Askew, Gilbert.
A8   The coinage of Roman Britain. London,
           B.A. Seaby, 1951.
               95p. illus., maps. 24cm.
               Bibliography: p. 78-80

BC97   Hill, George Francis, 1867-
H5   Notes on the ancient coinage of Hispania
           citerior. New York, The American numismatic
           society, 1931.
               196p. illus., xxxvi pl. 17cm. (Numis-
           matic notes and monographs, no. 50)

BC97   Holloway, R. Ross, 1934-
H6   The thirteen-months coinage of Hieronymos
        of Syracuse. By R. Ross Holloway. (With
        11 figures & 12 plates.) Berlin, de Gruyter
        1969.
            xxiii, 47p. 12 inserts, illus., pl. 28cm.
        (Antike Munzen und geschnittene Steine,
        Bd. 3)
            Bibliography: p. [xi]-xxi

BC97   Miller, David.
M5   Coins of Roman Britain. 1st ed.
        London, Stanley Gibbons Pub. Ltd.,
        1976.
            52p. illus. 20cm. (Stanley
        Gibbons Guides). 75p.

BC97   Robertson, Anne S.
R6   Roman coins found in Scotland. Society
        of Antiquaries of Scotland, 1949-50.
            32p. tables. 25cm.

BC97   Shortt, W. T. P.
S5   Sylva antiqua iscana, numismatica,
        quiunetiam figulina, or Roman and other
        antiquities of Exeter ... ancient coins and
        other relics. London, Nichols, 1840.
            xviii, 144p. 5 pl. 23cm.

BC97   Stukeley, William, 1687-1765.
S8   The medallic history of Marcus Aurelius
        Valerius Carausius, emperor in Britain...
        by William Stukeley. London, Printed for
        C. Corbet, 1757-1759.
            2 v. illus. 27cm.

BC97   Sutherland, Carol Humphrey Vivian.
S9c   Coinage and currency in Roman Britain.
        London, Oxford university press, H. Milford
        1937.
            xii, 184p. xiv pl. 22cm.

BC97   Sutherland, Carol Humphrey Vivian.
S9r   Romano-British imitations of bronze coins
        of Claudius I. New York, The American
        Numismatic society, 1935.
            35p. plates. 16cm. (Numismatic notes
        and monographs no. 65)

INDIA - COLLECTIONS

BD10   British Museum. Dept. of Coins and Medals.
B7   Catalogue of the coins of ancient India,
            by John Allan. London, British Museum,
            1967.
                 clxvii, 318p. illus., xlvi pl., tables.
            22cm. (Catalogue of the Indian coins in
            the British Museum)
                 Photolithographic reprint of 1936 ed.
                 Bibliographical footnotes.

BD10   British Museum. Dept. of Coins & Medals.
B7a   Catalogue of the coins of the Andhra
            dynasty, the western Ksatrapas, the Traiku-
            taka dynasty, and the "Bodhi" dynasty, by
            Edward James Rapson. London, British Mus-
            eum, 1908, 1967.
                 ccviii, 268p. illus, fold. map., xxi pl.
            tables. 22cm. (Catalogue of the Indian
            coins of the British Museum.)
                 Bibliographical footnotes

BD10   British Museum. Dept. of coins and medals.
B7g   Catalogue of the coins of the Gupta
            dynasties and of Sasanka, king of Gauda, by
            John Allan. London, British Museum, 1967.
                 cxxxviii, 184p. illus., pl., tables. 22cm.
                 Photolithographic reprint of 1914 ed.
                 Bibliographical footnotes.

BD10   Burn, Richard.
B8   Some coins of the Maukharis, and of the
            Thanesar line. From: Journal of the Royal
            Asiatic Society, Oct., 1906.
                 8p. 1 pl. 22cm.

BD10   Chakrabortty, Surendra Kisor.
C4   A study of ancient Indian numismatics
            (indigenous system) from the earliest times
            to the rise of the imperial Guptas (third
            cent. A.D.) With special reference to
            northern India. ... [Mymensingh, The
            author] 1931.
                 242p. 18cm.
                 Bibliography: p. [228]-231.

BD10   Chattopadhyay, Bhaskar.
C5   The age of the Kushanas-a numismatic
         study. Foreword by Dr. Benoy Chandra,
         Sen. Calcutta, Punthi Pustak, 1967.
             xxxiii, 289p. pl. 23cm.

BD10   Cunningham, Sir Alexander, 1814-1893.
C8   Coins of ancient India from the earliest
         times down to the seventh century A.D.
         London, B. Quaritch, 1891.
             118p. 14 pl., map. 21cm.

BD10   Madras. Government Museum.
M3   Select Satavahana coins in the govern-
         ment museum, madras by M. Rama Rao. Madras.
         1959.
             27p. 2 pl. 28cm. (Bulletin of the
         Madras Government Museum, vol. 7, no. 2)

BD10   Rama Rao, M.
R35   Satavahana coins in the Andhra Pradesh
         government museum. Hyderabad, Government
         of Andhra Pradesh, 1961.
             iii, 69p. 20 pl. 24cm. (Andhra Pradesh
         Government Museum Series, no. 2)

BD10   Rapson, Edward James, 1861-1937.
R3   The coinage of ancient and medieval
         India. [2d reprint ed.] San Diego, Calif.
         Malter-Westerfield Pub. Co. [1969]
             56p. illus. 26cm.

BD10   Sahni, Birbal.
S2   The technique of casting coins in ancient
         India. Bombay, The Numismatic Society of
         India, 1945. Memoirs of the Numismatic
         Society of India, no. 111.
             68p. 7 pl. 37cm.

BD10   Thomas, Edward.
T5   Ancient Indian weights. London, Trubner,
         1874.
             viii, 74p. pl. map. 32cm. (Marsden's
         Numismata Orientalia)

BD10   Thomas, Edward.
T5e   The epoch of the Sah kings of Surashtra.
         Illus. by their coins. A paper presented
         to the Royal Asiatic Society, 15 April,
         1948. London, Harrison, 1848.
             77p. 7 pl. 22cm.

BD10   Whitehead, Richard Bertram.
W4   The Pre-Mohammedan coinage of north-
            western India. New York, American numis-
            matic society, 1922.
                 56p. xiv pl. 17cm. (Numismatic notes
            and monographs no. 13)

INDIA - GENERAL WORKS

BD15   Mitchiner, Michael.
M5   The origins of Indian coinage.
            London, Hawkins Publications, 1973.
                 174p; 5p. IX plates. 25cm.

CEYLON

BD20   Abeywardene, T.M. DeSilva.
A2   Price catalogue of ancient coins of
            Ceylon. Colombo, Ceylon, Careem & Co. 1952.
                 41p. 10 pl. 22cm.

BD20   Rhys-Davids, T. W.
D3   On the ancient coins and measures of
            Ceylon. London, Trubner, 1877.
                 62p. pl. 31cm. (International Numis-
            mata Oriental)

PARTHIA

BD30   Allotte de la Fuye, d. 1939.
A4   Monnaies arsacides de la collection
            petrowicz. Paris, Rollin et Feuardent,
            1905.
                 Reprint: Revue Numismatique (1905)
                 43p. 1 pl. 25cm.

BD30   Caley, Earle Radcliffe, 1900-
C3   Chemical composition of Parthian coins.
            New York, American Numismatic Society, 1955-
                 v, 104p. diagrs., tables. 23cm. (Num-
            ismatic notes and monographs, no. 129)
                 Bibliographical footnotes.

BD30   Gardner, Percy, 1846-
G3   The coinage of Parthia ... Introduction
         and supplementary catalog of a recent hoard
         by Joel L. Malter. San Diego, CA, Malter-
         Westerfield, [1968]. (Reprint)
             68p. pl. 28cm.

BD30   Lindsay, John, 1789-1870.
L5   A view of the history and coinage of
         the Parthians, with descriptive catal-
         ogues and tables, illus with a complete
         set of engravings of coins, a large num-
         ber of them unpublished. Cork, Printed
         by J. Crowe, 1852.
             viii, 250p. 12 pl. 28 x 22cm.

BD30   McDowell, Robert Harbold, 1894-
M3   Coins from Seleucia on the Tigris. Ann
         Arbor, University of Michigan press, 1935.
             xiv, 248p. vi pl. 28cm. (University of
         Michigan studies. Humanistic series. vol.
         xxxvii)

BD30   Newell, Edward Theodore, 1886-1941.
N4   Mithradates of Parthia and Hyspaosines of
         Characene: a numismatic palimpsest. New
         York, American numismatic society, 1925.
             18p. illus., ii pl. 17cm. (Numismatic
         notes and monographs, no. 26)

BD30   Sellwood, David.
S4   An introduction to the coinage of
         Parthia. London, Spink, 1971.
             315p. 8 pl. 22cm.
             Bibliography

PERSIA

BD32   Drouin, Edmond.
D7   Observations sur les monnaies a
         Legendes en Pehlvi et Pehlvi-Arabe.
         [(In Revue Archeologique. Paris, 1886).]
             98p. plates. 25cm.

BD32   Frye, Richard Nelson, 1920-
F7   Sasanian remains from Qasr-i Abu Nasr; seals,
         sealings, and coins. Edited by Richard N.
         Frye. Cambridge, Harvard University Press,
         1973.
             133p. illus. 29cm. (Harvard Iranian
         series, v.1)
             Includes bibliographical references.

BD32   Gaube, Heinz.
G3   Arabosasanidische numismatik.
          Braunschweig, Klinkhardt & Biermann,
          1973.
              171p.   10 charts; 14 plates;
          fold. map. 26cm.
          (Handbucher der mittelasiatischen
          numismatik, Band II).

BD32   Gobl, Robert.
G6   Sasandische numismatik. Braunschweig,
          Klinkhardt & Biermann [c1968]
              100 [33] p. illus, map, tables, plates
          (Handbucher der Mittelasiatischen Numis-
          matik, Band 1)
              Bibliography: p. 88

BD32   Head, Barclay Vincent, 1844-1914.
H4   The coinage of Lydia and Persia. San
          Diego, Calif., Pegasus Pub. Co. [c1967].
              viii, 55p. illus. 28cm.
              Bibliographical footnotes.

BD32   Herzfeld, Ernst Emil, 1879-1948.
H45   Notes on the Achaemenid coinage and some
Vert.   Sasanian mint-names. Reprinted from the
File   Transactions of the International Numismatic
          Congress, London, June 30-July 6, 1936,
          p. 413-426.
              illus. 23cm.

BD32   Hill, George Francis.
H5   Imperial Persian coinage. Oak Park,
          Ill., Obol International, 1968.
              17p. 1 pl. 26cm.

BD32   Mitchiner, Michael.
M5   The early coinage of Central Asia.
          London, Hawkins Publication, 1973.
              77p. XIV plates. 26cm.

BD32   Newell, Edward Theodore, 1886-1941.
N4   Myriandros--Alexandria Katisson in:
          American Journal of Numismatics, vol. 53,
          part 2 (1919), New York, A.N.S. 1920.
              42p. 2 pl. 29cm.

BD32   Noe, Sydney Philip.
N6   Two hoards of Persian sigloi. New York,
          American numismatic society, 1956.
              44p. 15 pl. 23cm. (Numismatic notes
          and monographs, no. 136)

BD32   Valentine, William H.
V3   Sassanian coins. London, Spink, 1921.
                 118p. illus. 24cm.

SELEUCIA

BD34   Bellinger, Alfred Raymond.
B4   A seleucid mint at Dura-Europus, by A.R.
Vert.   Bellinger and Edward T. Newell.
File   5p. illus., 1 pl. 25, 28cm.

BD34   Newell, Edward Theodore, 1886-1941.
N4   The coinage of the eastern Seleucid
            mints, from Seleucus I to Antiochus III.
            ... New York, The American numismatic
            society, 1938.
                 307p. lvi pl. 27cm. (Numismatic
            studies, no. I)

BD34   Newell, Edward Theodore, 1886-1941.
N4c   The coinage of the western Seleucid
            mints from Seleucus I to Antiochus III.
            New York, American numismatic society,
            1941.
                 450p. map, lxiv pl. 27cm. (Numis-
            matic studies, no. 4)

BD34   Newell, Edward Theodore, 1886-1941.
N4f   First Seleucid coinage of Tyre. New
            York, American numismatic society, 1921.
                 40p. viii pl. 16cm. (Numismatic notes
            and monographs, no. 10)

BD34   Newell, Edward Theodore, 1886-1941.
N4l   Late Seleucid mints in Ake-Ptolemais
            and Damascus. New York, ANS, 1939.
                 107p. 17 pl. 17cm. (Numismatic
            notes and monographs, no. 84)

BD34   Newell, Edward Theodore, 1886-1941.
N4p   Pergamene mint under Philetaerus.
            New York, American numismatic society,
            1936.
                 34p. x pl. 17cm. (Numismatic notes
            and monographs, no. 76)

BD34   Newell, Edward Theodore, 1886-1941.
N4s   The Seleucid coinages of Tyre, a supp-
            lement. New York, American numismatic
            society, 1936.
                34p. v pl. 17cm. (Numismatic notes
            and monographs no. 73)

BD34   Rogers, Edgar, 1873-
R6   The second and third Seleucid coinage
            of Tyre, New York, American numismatic
            society, 1927.
                33p. plates. 17cm. (Numismatic notes
            and monographs, no. 34)

BD34   Seltman, E. J.
S35   Re-attribution of a Seleucid tetradrachm.
Vert.   From: American Journal of Numismatics, v. 47,
File   1913, p. 121-129.
                1 pl. 28cm.

SYRIA

BD36   LaVoix, Henri.
L3   Monnaies a legendes Arabes,
            frappees en Syria par les
            Croises. Paris, Joseph Baer et Cie,
            1877.
                62p. scattered illus. 28cm.

BD36   Seyrig, Henri.
S4   Notes on Syrian coins. New York, Amer-
            ican Numismatic Society, 1950.
                35p. 2 pl. 23cm. (Numismatic notes and
            monographs, no. 119).
                Bibliographical footnotes.

OTHER CITIES, A-Z

BD38   Malloy, Alex G.
A5M3   The coinage of Amisus. N.p., Alex G.
            Malloy, 1970.
                31p. pl. 21cm.

BD38   Hill, George Francis, 1867-1948.
A7H5   Ancient coinage of southern Arabia.
           Chicago, Argonaut, 1969.
               28p. illus. 23cm.
               Bibliographical footnotes.

BD38   Fellows, Charles.
L9F4   Coins of ancient Lycia before the
           reign of Alexander. London, J. Murray,
           1855.
               20p. 19 pl. 28cm.

BD38   Castelin, Karel O.
R5C3   The coinage of Rhesaena in Mesopotamia.
           New York, American numismatic society, 1946.
               111p. illus., xvii pl. 17cm. (Numismatic
           notes and monographs, no. 108)
               Bibliographical footnotes.

BD38   Frye, Richard Nelson, 1920-
T7F7   Notes on the early coinage of Transoxiana
           New York, American Numismatic Society, 1949.
               49p. front. 23cm. (Numismatic notes
           and monographs, no. 113)

ISRAEL - GENERAL WORKS

BD40   Hendin, David.
H4   Guide to ancient Jewish coins.
           Values by Herbert Kreindler. N.Y.,
           Attic Books, 1976.
               134p. illus.; 9 plates. 24cm.

BD40   Israel Numismatic Society.
I8   The dating and meaning of ancient Jewish
           coins and symbols; Six essays in Jewish
           numismatics. Tel-Aviv, Schochen, 1958.
               116p. pl. 24cm. (Numismatic studies
           and researches, vol. 2)

BD40   Kanael, Baruch.
K3   Ancient Jewish coins and their histori-
           cal importance. From: The Biblical Archa-
           eologist, v. xxvi, no. 2, May, 1963.
           Published by The American Schools of
           Oriental Research.
               25p. illus. 21cm.

BD40   Klimowsky, Ernst W.
K5   On ancient Palestinian and
        other coins; their symbolism
        and metrology. Tel Aviv, Israel,
        Israel Numismatic Soc., 1974.
            179p. illus.; VII plates. 24cm.
        (Numismatic studies and
        researches [of the] Israel Numismatic
        Society, Vol. VII).

BD40   Madden, Frederic William.
M3c   Coins of the Jews. ... With 279 wood-
        cuts and a plate of alphabets. Boston,
        Osgood, 1881.
            x, 329p. illus. 38 x 25cm.

BD40   Madden, Frederic William.
M3h   History of Jewish coinage, and of money
        in the Old and New Testament. ... With 254
        woodcuts and a plate of alphabets, by F.W.
        Fairholt, F.S.A. London, B. Quaritch,
        1864, San Diego, Calif, Pegasus, [1967].
            xii, 350p. illus., fold. tab. 26cm.

BD40   Reifenberg, Adolf, 1899-1953.
R4   Ancient Jewish coins. 3rd, 4th eds.
        Jerusalem, R. Mass, 1963, 1965.
            66p. 16 pl. 25cm.
        Bibliographical footnotes

BD40   Reinach, Theodore, 1860-1928
R42   Jewish coins. Translated by Mary Hill.
        With an appendix by G. F. Hill. [1st
        American ed.] Chicago, Argonaut, 1966.
            xv, 77p. illus., 12 pl. 22cm.
        Bibliographical footnotes.

BD40   Rogers, Edgar.
R6   A handy guide to Jewish coins. London,
        Spink, 1914.
            108p. 9 pl. 23cm.

BD40   Romanoff, Paul, 1898-1943.
R62   Jewish symbols on ancient Jewish coins
        ... with an introduction by Abraham A.
        Neuman ... Philadelphia, Dropsie college
        for Hebrew and cognate learning, 1944.
            xv, 79p. 7 pl. 23cm.

BD40   Wirgin, Wolf, 1902-
W5h   The history of coins and symbols in
         ancient Israel [by] W. Wirgin and Sieg-
         fried Mandel. [1st ed.] New York,
         Exposition Press [1958].
             264p. illus. 21cm. (An exposition-
         university book)
             Includes bibliography

ISRAEL - COLLECTIONS

BD45   Rosenberger, Mayer.
R6   The Rosenberger Israel collection.
         Jerusalem, n.pub., 1972.
             2 v. (68, 79p.) illus. 28cm.
             Contents: Vol. 1. Aelia Kapitolina, Akko,
         Anthedon Antipatris, and Ascalon. - Vol. 2.
         Caesarea, Diospolis, Dora, Eleutheropolis,
         Gaba, Gaza, and Joppa.

ISRAEL - SPECIAL, BY PERIOD

BD50   Gillespie, J. U.
G5   The dating of the shekel. ANA Reprint,
         1950.
             16p. illus.

BD50   Meshorer, Ya'akov.
M4   Jewish coins of the Second Temple Period
         by Ya'akov Meshorer. Translated from the
         Hebrew by I. H. Levine. Tel Aviv, Am Hassefer,
         1967.
             184p. 32 pls. 27cm.

BD50   Reifenberg, Adolf, 1899-
R4i   Israel's history in coins from the
         Maccabees to the Roman conquest. London,
         East and West Library, 1953.
             46p. illus. 20cm.

BD50   Reifenberg, Adolf, 1899-
R4p   Portrait coins of the Herodian kings.
         Reprinted from the Numismatic Circular,
         1935. London, Spink, 1935.
             12p. illus. 24cm.

BD50   Wirgin, Wolf.
W5p   Propaganda on ancient Jewish coins.
          Jewish coins are historical monuments.
          N.p, n. pub., n.d.
               6p. illus. 22cm.

REGIONAL, A-Z

BD60   Kadman, Leo.
P3K3   The Coins of Aelia Capitolina.
V.1   Jerusalem, Universitas, 1956.
               191p. 17 pl. 25cm. (Corpus nummorum
          Palaestinensium, v.1)
               Bibliography: p. 179-180.

BD60   Kadman, Leo.
P3K3   Coins of Caesarea Maritima. Jerusalem,
V.2   Schocken [1957].
               243p. pl., map. 25cm. (Corpus nummo-
          rum Palaestinensium, v.2)
               Bibliography: p. 229-230.

BD60   Kadman, Leo.
P3K3   The coins of the Jewish War of 66-73 C.E.
V.3   Tel Aviv, Schocken Pub. House [1960].
               203p. 5 pl., map, plan. 24cm. (Corpus
          nummorum Palaestinensium, 2d ser., v.3)

BD60   Kadman, Leo.
P3K3   The coins of Akko Ptolemais. Tel Aviv,
V.4   Schocken Pub. House [1961].
               240p. illus., 20 pl. 25cm. (Corpus
          nummorum Palaestinensium, 1st series, v.4)
               Bibliographical footnotes

BD60   Sperber, Daniel.
P3S6   Roman Palestine, 200-400: Money
          and prices. Jerusalem, Ahva Press;
          Ramat-Gan, Bar-Ilan Univ., 1974.
               331p. illus. charts. 25cm.
          (Bar-Ilan studies in Near
          Eastern languages and culture).

BD60   Kindler, Arie.
T5K5   The coins of Tiberias. Tiberias,
          Hamei Tiberia Co., 1961.
              118p. pl., col. map. 22cm.
              Bibliographical footnotes.

AFRICA - GENERAL, SPECIAL ASPECTS

BD70   Falbe, Christian Tuxen, 1791-1849.
F3   Numismatique de L'ancienne
          Afrique. Ouvrage prepare et
          commence par C. T. Falbe et J. Chr.
          Lindberg; refait, acheve et publie
          par L. Muller. Originally published
          in Copenhagen, 1860. Reprinted-
          Bologna, A. Forni, [1964].
              3 Vols. illus. 32cm.

CARTHAGE

BD80   Jenkins, G. Kenneth.
J4   Carthaginian gold and electrum coins, by
          G.K. Jenkins and R.B. Lewis. London,
          Royal Numismatic Society, 1963.
              140p. 38 pl. 25cm. ([Royal Numismatic
          Society] Special publication no.2)

BD80   Villaronga, Leandro.
V5   Las monedas hispano-cartaginesas. Barce-
          lona, Cooperativa Grafica Dertosense, 1973.
              189p. pl. 27cm.

EGYPT

BD83   Curtis, James W.
C8   Media of exchange in ancient Egypt by
Vert.   Colonel James W. Curtis. New York, Amer-
File   ican Numismatic Association, 1951. Reprints
          The Numismatist, v. 64, no. 5, May, 1951.
              10p. 5 pl. 23cm.

BD83   Newell, Edward Theodore, 1886-1941.
N4   ... Standard Ptolemaic silver. New
          York, Wayte Raymond, Inc. [c1941]
              16p. illus. 22cm. (The coin collector
          series, no. 7)

BD83   Newell, Edward Theodore, 1886-1941.
N42   Two recent Egyptian hoards. New York,
          American numismatic society, 1927.
              34p. iii pl. 17cm. (Numismatic notes
          and monographs, no. 33)
              Bibliography: p. 32-34

BD83   Rome, Museo Borgiano.
R6   Numi aegypti imperatorii prostantes in
Rare   Museo Borgiano velitris. Rome, 1787.
Books   404p. 22 pl. 30cm.

MAURETANIA

BD85   Mateu y Llopis, Felipe.
M3   Monedas de mauritania. Contribuciou al
          estudio de la numismatica de la Hispania
          ulterior Tingitana, segun el Monetario
          del museo Argueologico de Tetuan. Madrid,
          1949.
              56p. 31 pl. 24cm. (Publicaciones del
          Instituto "General Franco" para la In-
          vestigacion Hispano-Arabe, no. 27)

OTHER, A-Z

BD87   Rosenfield, John M.
K8R6   The dynastic arts of the Kushans
          by John M. Rosenfield. Berkeley,
          Ca., Univ. of Ca. Press, 1967.
              377p. 167 plates. 29cm.

<u>BYZANTINE</u>

COLLECTIONS

BE20   Bellinger, Alfred R., 1893-
B4   Catalogue of the Byzantine coins in the
            Dumbarton Oaks collection and in the Whitte-
            more collection, edited by ... and Philip
            Grierson. Washington, Dumbarton Oaks Center
            for Byzantine Studies, 1966-68.
                2v. in 3 (383, 728p.) pl. 30cm.
                Bibliography: V. 1, p. xxii-xxvi.
                Contents: V. 1. Anastasus I to Maurice,
            491-602. - V. 2. Phocas to Theodosius III,
            602-717.

BE20   British museum. Dept. of coins and metals.
B7b   Catalogue of the imperial Byzantine
            coins in the British museum, by Warwick
            Wroth ... In two volumes, with an intro-
            duction and 79 plates. London, the
            Trustees, 1908. Reprinted, Chicago, Argo-
            naut, 1966.
                2v. 79 pl. 26cm.

BE20   British museum. Dept. of coins & medals.
B7v   Catalogue of the coins of the Vandals,
            Ostrogoths and Lombards, and of the empires
            of Thessalonica, Nicaea and Trebizond in
            the British museum, by Warwick Wroth ...
            with an introduction & 43 plates. London,
            the Trustees, 1911, 1966.
                xciv, 344p. pl. 26cm.
                Note: Title of 1966 edition: Western
            & provincial Byzantine coins of the Vandals,
            Ostrogoths, and Lombards, and of the empires
            of Thessalonica, Nicaea, and Trebizond ...

BE20   Ratto, Rodolfo.
R3   Monnaies Byzantines et d'autres
            pays contemporaines a l'epoque.
            Byzantine...sous la direction de
            Rodolfo Ratto. Amsterdam, J. Schulman,
            1959.
                151p. LXVIII plates. 28cm.

BE20   Stearns, John Barker, 1894-
S8   Byzantine gold coins from the Dartmouth
        College collection [by] J.B. Stearns and
        Vernon Hall, Jr. Hanover, N.H., Dart-
        mouth College Library, 1953.
             18p. illus. 24cm.

CATALOGUES

BE30   Doering, David R.
D6   Standard catalogue of Byzantine coin
        values for 1967, 383 A.D. to 1503 A.D.
        [Seattle, AAA Coin Shop, n.d.].
             34p. 8 pl. 21cm.

BE30   Rynearson, Paul F.
R9   Byzantine coin values; a guide. San
        Diego, Calif., Pegasus Pub. Co. [c1967]
             103p. illus., map. 23cm.
             Bibliography: p. 102-103.

BE30   Rynearson, Paul F.
R9   Byzantine coin values; a guide.
1971   San Clemente, Calif., Malter-Westerfield
        Pub. Co. [c1971]
             112p. illus. map. 3 pl. 23cm.
             Bibliography: p. 107

BE30   Sear, David R.
S4   Byzantine coins and their values.
        London, Seaby, 1974.
             415p. illus. 23cm.

GENERAL WORKS

BE40   Bates, George Eugene.
B3   Byzantine coins [by] George E. Bates.
        Cambridge, Harvard University Press, 1971.
             x, 159p. illus. maps. 29cm.
        (Archaeological Exploration of Sardis.
        Monograph 1)

BE40   Goodacre, Hugh.
G6   A handbook of the coinage of the Byzan-
            tine empire. London, Spink, 1957. [Re-
            print of 1928-33 ed.]
                xi, 361p. illus. 23cm.

BE40   Hahn, Wolfgang.
H3   Von Anastasius I bis Justinianus I (491-
            565), einschliesslich der ostgotischen und
            vandalischen pragungen. Vienna, Osterreich-
            ischen Akademie der Wissenschaften, 1973.
                141p. illus. 42 pl. 30cm. (Moneta
            Imperii Byzantini, pt. 1)

BE40   Hendy, Michael F.
H4   Coinage and money in the Byzantine
            Empire, 1081-1261. Washington, Dumbarton
            Oaks, 1969.
                xviii, 453p. 51 pl., maps.
                Bibliography

BE40   Lhotka, John F.
L5   Introduction to East Roman Coinage.
            Reprinted from The Numismatist, 1954-55,
            American numismatic association.
                112p. illus. 5 pl. 23cm.

BE40   Longuet, Henry.
L6   Introduction a la numismatique Byzan-
            tine. London, Spink, 1961.
                158p. 24 pl. 24cm.

BE40   Sabatier, Justin.
S2   Description generale des monnaies By-
            zantines frappees sous les empereurs
            d'Orient depuis arcadius jusqu'a la prise
            de constantinople par Mahomet II. Graz,
            Akademische Druck-U. Verlagsanstalt, 1955.
                2v. 377p. 70 pl. 16, 23cm.

BE40   Saulcy, Louis Felicien de, 1807-1880.
S3   Essai de classification des suites
            monetaires Byzantines. Metz, S. Lamont,
            1836.
            2v. 33 pl. 29cm.

BE40   Whitting, Philip D.
W4   Byzantine coins, by P.D. Whitting. New
            York, Putnam [1973]
                311p. illus. 25cm. (The World of
            numismatics)
                Errata slip inserted.

BE40   Whitting, Philip D.
W4   Munzen von Byzanz [by] P. D.
            Whitting. Munchen, Ernest Battenberg
            [1973]
                319 p. illus. col. 25cm.

DICTIONARIES, BIBLIOGRAPHIES, ETC.

BE50   Malter, Joel L.
M3   Byzantine numismatic bibliography,
            1950-1965. Chicago, Argonaut, 1968.
                59p. 23cm. (Argonaut library of
            antiquities)

BE50   Mosser, Sawyer McArthur, 1905-
M6   A bibliography of Byzantine coin
            hoards. New York, American numismatic
            society, 1935.
                x, 116p. 16cm. (Numismatic notes and
            monographs, no. 67)

SPECIAL, ICONOGRAPHY

BE60   O'Hara, Michael D.
O4   Some forgeries of Byzantine gold coins
Vert.   from the "Beirut" and other "schools".
File   [Paris], International Association of Profes-
            sional Numismatists, 1974.
                14p. illus. 23cm.
                Note: "... reprint with corrections, addi-
            tions and enlarged illustrations of the article
            which first appeared in Seaby's Coin & Medal
            Bulletin in October, 1973."

TECHNICAL ASPECTS

BE70   Bellinger, Alfred Raymond, 1893-
B4   The anonymous Byzantine bronze coinage.
            New York, American numismatic society,
            1928.
                27p. illus. 17cm. (Numismatic notes
            and monographs, no. 35)

BY PERIOD

BE80   Adelson, Howard L.
A3   Light weight solidi and Byzantine trade
         during the sixth and seventh centuries.
         New York, 1957.
             187p. map, 14 pl. 23cm. (Numismatic
         notes and monographs, no. 138)

BE80   Bendall, S.
B4   The billion trachea of
         Michael VIII Palaeologos, 1258-
         1282 by S. Bendall and P. J.
         Donald. N.P., A. H. Baldwin
         and Sons, Ltd., 1974.
             44p. illus. 21cm.

BE80   Breckenridge, James Douglas.
B7   The numismatic iconography of Justinian
         II (685-695, 705-711 A.D.) New York,
         American numismatic society, 1959.
             x, 104p. 10 pl. 23cm. (Numismatic
         notes and monographs, no. 144)
             Bibliographical footnotes.

BE80   Metcalf, David Michael.
M4   The origins of the Anastasian currency
         reform. Chicago, Argonaut, 1969.
             vi, 105p. illus. 26cm.
             Bibliography: p. 103-105.

BE80   Miles, George C.
M5   A Byzantine weight validated by Al-
         Walid. New York, The American numismatic
         society, 1939. (Numismatic notes and
         monographs, no. 87)
             11p. front. 17cm.

BY PLACE

BE90   Bellinger, Alfred Raymond, 1893-
B4   Coins from Jerash, 1928-1934. New
         York, American numismatic society, 1938.
             141p. ix pl. 17cm. (Numismatic
         notes and monographs, no. 81)

BE90   Fagerlie, Joan M.
F3   Late Roman and Byzantine solidi found
        in Sweden and Denmark. New York, American
        numismatic society, 1967.
            xxv, 213p. 33 pl. 23cm. (Numismatic
        notes and monographs, no. 157)
            Bibliography: p. xiii-xviii.

BE90   Hohlfelder, Robert L.
H6   A small deposit of bronze coins from
        Kenchreai. From Hesperia, vol. 39,
        no. 1 (1970).
            [5]p. 28cm.

BE90   Newell, Edward Theodore, 1886-1941.
N4   The Byzantine hoard of Lagbe. New
        York, American numismatic society, 1945.
            22p. vii pl. 17cm. (Numismatic
        notes and monographs, no. 105)

COLLECTIONS

CC10   The Chase Manhattan Bank.
C5   Museum of moneys of the world.
Vert.   N.Y., Chase Manhattan Bank, 1959.
File   32p. illus. 16cm.

CC10   Weyl, Adolph.
F6   Die Jules Fonrobert Sammlung uberseeis-
cher Munzen und medaillen. Berlin,
1878. Reprinted 1962, 1970, 1974.
    2v. illus.
    Contents: v.2 Latin America
v.3 Asia, Africa, Oceania

CC10   Greiling munz sammlung. Dresden, Zigaretten-
G7   fabrik Greiling, N.d.
    unpaged chiefly pl. 30 x 33cm.

CC10   Teyler Fondation, Harlem
T4   Catalogue du cabinet numismatique de
la Fondation Teyler a Harlem. Th. M.
Roest, conservateur. [2nd ed, La Haye,
1909].
    516p. 24 pl. 29cm.

CC10   U.S. Mint.
U5   Catalogue of coins, tokens, and medals
in the numismatic collection of the Mint
of the United States at Philadelphia, Pa.
Prepared under the direction of the director of the Bureau of the mint. Washington, Govt. print. off., 1912-1914.
    634p. pl. 24cm.
    Bibliography: p. 21-22

CATALOGUES

CC20   Imlay & Bicknell.
I4   Coins of the world .... Philadelphia,
Imlay & Bicknell, 1859.
    55p. illus. 29cm.

CC20   Premium catalog of modern foreign
P7   coins; listing the prices paid
        for the modern coin issues of over
        125 foreign countries, states and
        cities...n.p., Hewitt, 1948.
        48p. illus. 20cm.

CC20   Thompson, J., comp.
T5   The coin chart manual. Chicago,
        Obol International, for Bank Note
        and Commercial Reporter, 1974.
        48p. illus. 26cm.

GENERAL WORKS WRITTEN BEFORE 1900

CC30   Eckfeldt, Jacob Reese, 1803-1872
E3m   A manual of gold and silver coins of
        all nations, struck within the past century
        ..., by ... and William E. Du Bois. Phila-
        delphia, Assay Office of the Mint, 1842, 1851.
        220p. xvi pl. 27cm.

CC30   Eckfeldt, Jacob Reese, 1803-1872.
E3n   New varieties of gold and silver coins,
1851   counterfeit coins, and bullion; with mint
        values, 2d ed., rearranged with numerous
        additions, ... and William E. Du Bois ... to
        which is added a brief account of the collec-
        tion of coins belonging to the mint. 2d ed.
        enl. New York, Putnam, 1851.
        72p. 5 pl. 23cm.

CC30   Engel, Arthur, 1855-
E6   Traite de numismatique modern et
1965   contemporaine, par Arthur Engel ... et
        Raymond Serrure...Paris, E. Leroux, 1897-
        99.
            2 v. in 1. illus. 25cm.
            Reprinted by Arnaldo Forni Editore,
        Bologna, 1965.

CC30   Hodges, Daniel M., Comp.
H6   Hodges' gold and silver coin chart
        manual; compiled and published by Daniel
        M. Hodges. New York, n.d.
        50p. illus. 23cm.

CC30   Rohlers, Johann David.
R6   Historischer munzbelustigung...
Rare   Nurnberg, Ben Christoph Weigels,
Books   1729-1750.
              22v. each Vol. varies. Illus.
         21cm.
              Index (2 Vols.) by Johann
         Gottfried Bernhold, 1764-65.

CC30   Scott & Company.
S3   The coin chart manual, or the
         bankers, brokers and storekeepers vade
         mecum: containing fac-similes of the gold
         and silver coins found in circulation
         throughout the world. N.Y., (1881?)
              unpaged. illus. 24cm.

CC30   Von Bergen, William.
V6   The rare coins of America, England,
         Ireland, Scotland, France, Germany, and
         Spain. Cambridge, Mass., W. Von Bergen,
         1889.
              106p. illus. 17cm.

GENERAL WRITTEN AFTER 1900

CC35   Andrews, H. Lyle
A5   Foreign coins; a descriptive
         catalog including a thumbnail sketch
         of each country. Sumner, Wash., the
         author, n.d.
              31p. 23cm.

CC35   American Bank Reporter.
A54   Moneys of the world. Annual
         research supplement, Vol. 165.
         Published in conjunction with the
         American Bankers Assn. Convention.
         N.Y., Charles Steurer Press, 1939.
              53p. illus. 29cm.

CC35   Brooklyn Coin Club.
B7   Papers presented at meetings of the ....
         N.p., Brooklyn Coin Club, 1941.
              71p. illus. 20cm.
              Reprinted from the Numismatic Scrapbook
         Magazine, 1941.

CC35   Guttag Bros.
G8   Guttag's foreign currency and exchange
         guide. New York, Guttag Bros., 1921.
             130p. 21cm.

CC35   Rittmann, Herbert.
R5   Moderne munzen. Munich, Ernst
         Battenberg, 1974.
             346p. illus.; part. col. 25cm.

CC35   U.S. Department of Commerce.
U5   Handbook of foreign currencies.
         Washington, GPO, 1936.
             232p. 23cm. (Trade Promotion
         Series, #164).

CC35   Villefaigne, J.G. de.
V5   Manual pratique du change de monnaies
         etrangeres. Billets de Banque Travellers'
         cheques, pieces d'or, d'argent, etc. 10th
         ed. Paris, 1963.
             575p. photog. 22cm.

COLLECTING, INCLUDES MINT MARKS

CC40   Baker, Lee.
B3   Foreign mints and banks. How to order
         direct. Santa Clara, Calif., the author,
         [1964, 1st ed.], 1965, 3rd ed.
             118p. 23cm
             Third edition under title: Foreign
         coins. How to order direct.

CC40   Carson, R. A. G., ed.
C3   Mints, dies and currency - essays
         in memory of Albert Baldwin. London,
         Methuen and Co., Ltd., 1971.
             336p. Pl. 25cm.

CC40   Coin world.
C6   How to order foreign coins. [Sidney,
         Ohio, 1967-1975.
             8v. 28cm.

CC40   Coin World.
C6s   A survey of mint marks; their
         development and use. n.p., Coin World,
         n.d.
             22p. 27cm.

CC40   Eisenberg, Jerome M.
E5   A guide to modern foreign coins.
         [New York? 1958] Royal coin Co.
            24p. illus. 22cm.

CC40   Firester, Lee.
F5   Foreign coins for young people.
         Roslyn Heights, N.Y., Jolie coins, 1960.
            33p. illus. 21cm.

CC40   Holzer, Hans W. 1920-
H6   Collector's guidebook to coins. New
1966   York, Maco Pub. Co. [1966].
            128p. illus., maps. 24cm.

CC40   James, Somer, Ed.
J3   Cash for your Canada, Newfoundland,
         Great Britain, U.S., Australia and New Zealand
         coins and bills ... 10th ed. vol. 10
         Winnipeg, Numismatic Guild of Canada, 1961-1966.
            104p. illus. 17cm.

CC40   Madonia, Gail.
M3   How to collect coins for profit.
         Derby, Conn., Topical Magazines, c1964.
            104p. illus. 23cm. (Topical book
         no. 42)

CC40   Raymond, Wayte, 1886-   ed.
R3w   Coins of the world. Special printing.
         New York, W. Raymond, Inc. [1955-1956].
            6v. illus. 24cm.

CC40   Rulau, Russell.
R8   World mint marks. Sidney, Ohio,
         Sidney Printing and Pub. Co., 1966.
            [20 p] 22cm.

CC40   Rulau, Russell.
R8   Modern world mint marks, by Russell
1970   Rulau and Mary Jane Hook. 2d ed.
         Sidney, Ohio, Sidney Printing and Pub. Co.,
         1970.
            [24p] 22cm.

CC40   Sten, George J.
S7   World coin and currency handbook by
         George J. Sten and Dwight L. Musser.
         Dunbar, W. Virginia, Manor Press, c1960.
            20p. 23cm.

COUNTERFEITING, PSEUDONUMIA

CC50   Bloom, Murray Teigh.
B55   Money of their own; the great counter-
           feiters. New York, Scribner, 1957.
              302p. 21cm.

CC50   Dieffenbacher, Alfred
D5   Counterfeit gold coins nineteenth and
           twentieth centuries. Fully illustrated.
           Montreal, Dieffenbacher Coin Ld., c1963.
              unpaged. illus. 29cm.

CC50   International Assoc. of Professional
I5   Numismatists.
              First International Congress for the
           study of and the defense against coin
           forgery. Paris, 1965. Analytical
           report. [c1967].
              117p. 23cm. (Publications of I.A.P.N.
           no. 2).
              In French and English.

CC50   Kenney, Richard D.
K4   Unofficial coins of the world. Amer-
           ican Numismatic Association, 1964. Re-
           printed from The Numismatist, 1962-1964.
              unpaged. illus. 23cm.
              Bibliography

EMERGENCY MONEY

CC53   Brunk, Gregory G., ed.
B7   World countermarks on medieval
           and modern coins; an anthology
           edited by Gregory G. Brunk.
           Lawrence, Mass., Quarterman Pubs.,
           1976.
              401p. illus. 24cm.

CC53   Cederlund, Ragnar.
C4   The siege coins of Landau, 1702 and
Vert.   1713. Reprinted from the Numismatist,
File   Jan., 1936.
              unpaged. illus. 22cm.

CC53   Duffield, F.G.
D8   A trial list of the countermarked
         modern coins of the world. American
         Numismatic Association, 1962. Reprinted
         from The Numismatist.
            88p. illus. 21cm.

CC53   Kisch, Guido.
K5   War prisoner money and medals. Re-
         printed from The Numismatist (v.58,
         1945), 1963.
            24p. illus. 22cm.

CC53   Lapa, Frank A.
L3   Check list of siege coins and necessity
         issues, 16th - 20th century. San Diego,
         Cal., Pegasus, 1968.
            [26]p. 21cm.
            Bibliography

CC53   Mailliet, Prosper.
M3   Atlas des monnaies obsidionales et de
         necessite. Bruxelles, Gobbaerts, 1868-
         1871.
            3v. pl. 23 x 30cm.

CC53   Slabaugh, Arlie R.
S5   Emergency monies of the world, 1914-
Vert.   1924; a catalog of the emergency monies of
File   World War I and the post-war inflation
         period. Distributed by Spotlite Publica-
         tions, Oakland, Maryland, n.d.
            54p. illus. 20cm.
            Reprinted from Numismatic Scrapbook
         July 1947-Oct. 1948.

CC53   Slabaugh, Arlie R.
S5p   Prisoner of war monies and medals;
         from the 18th century to the present,
         a priced catalog for collectors.
         [Chicago, Hewitt, 1965]
            71p. illus. 20cm. (Hewitt's
         Numismatic Information Series)

CC53   Westerfield, Wiley
W4   An introduction to siege coins. [San
         Diego, Cal. the author, 1967].
            10p. illus. 21cm.

SHIPWRECKS, HOARDS, TREASURE

CC55   Atwater, James.
A8   Spanish gold two fathoms deep.
Vert.   n.p., n. pub., n.d.
File   pp. 66-71. illus. (col) 35cm.

CC55   Hill, George Francis, 1867-
H5   Treasure trove in law and practice
            from the earliest times to the present
            day. Oxford, Clarendon, 1936.
                311p. 23cm.
                Bibliography: p. 296-300

CC55   Horn, Jeanne.
H6   Hidden treasure how and where to find
            it. New York, Arco, 1962.
                xiv, 234p. illus. pl. 24cm.

CC55   National Geographic Society, Washington, D.C.
N3   Special Publications Division.
                Undersea treasures. [Washington, National
            Geographic Society, 1974]
                199p. illus. 26cm.
                Bibliography: p. 199.

CC55   Nesmith, Robert I.
N4   Dig for pirate treasure. New York,
            Devin-Adair, 1959.
                xiv, 302p. illus., photog., maps.
            21cm.
                Bibliography: p. 275-288.

CC55   Noe, Sydney Philip.
N6   The Castine deposit: an American hoard,
            by S.P. Noe. New York, American numis-
            matic society, 1942.
                37p. pl. 17cm. (Numismatic notes
            and monographs, no. 100).

CC55   Noe, Sydney Philip.
N6c   Coin hoards, by Sydney P. Noe. New
            York, The American numismatic society,
            1920.
                47p. plates. 17cm. (Numismatic notes
            & monographs)
                Bibliography: p. 44-47

CC55   Peterson, Mendel.
P4   History under the sea; a manual for
        underwater exploration. Washington, D.
        C., Smithsonian Institution, [1969].
            208p. 56pl. 23cm.
            Bibliography: p. 193-206.

CC55   [Sadler, Jerry].
S2   Treasure tempest in Texas.
        N.p., [State of Texas], n.d.
            19p. illus. 23cm.

CC55   Stack's Coin Company.
S7   The treasure of 1715, [price list of the
        Wagner ship wreck recovery]. [New York,
        Stack's Coin Company, n.d.]
            unpaged illus. 21cm.

CC55   Sullivan, George.
S9   The modern treasure finders
        manual. 1st ed. Radnor, Pa.,
        Chilton Book Co., 1975.
            187p. illus. 27cm.

CC55   Tradewinds Evaluation System Inc.
T7   Treasure ports and forts
        of America...section I, Vol. I.
        N.Y., the author, 1952.
            14p. illus. 29cm.

CC55   Wagner, Kip.
W3   Pieces of eight; recovering the riches
        of a lost Spanish treasure fleet by Kip
        Wagner as told to L.B. Taylor, Jr. New
        York, Dutton, [1968, c1966].
            221p. col. photog. 24cm.

CC55   Wagner, Kip.
W3a   Drowned galleons yield Spanish gold.
Vert.   Photographs by Otis Imboden.
File   (In The National Geographic Magazine,
        Washington, D.C., Jan., 1965, V.127, No. 1)
            37p. illus. 26cm.

CC60   Feely, E. F.
F4   Recent trends in coinage metals.
          Reprinted from The Numismatist, July,
          1958.
               [5]p. tables. 23cm.

CC60   Hosch, Charles R.
H6   World Proof and specimen issues since
          1950. The author, 1971.
               264p. 23cm.

CC60   Hosch, Charles R.
H6o   Official guide to world proof coins.
          2d ed. Florence, Alabama, House of
          Collectibles, 1975.
               382p. illus. 23cm.

CC60   Kelley, William D.
K4   International coinage, speech of
          Hon. William D. Kelley of Pennsylvania,
          delivered in the House of Representatives,
          Apr. 13, 1870. Wash., Rives and Bailey,
          1870.
               8p. 23cm.

GOLD

CC63   Durst, Sanford J.
D8   Contemporary world gold coins,
          1934-1974/by Sanford J. Durst.
          -1st ed.-New York: Durst, [1975]
               98p.: ill.; 25cm.

CC63   Federal Coin and Currency, Inc.
F4   Gold coins. N.Y., Federal Coin
          and Currency, 1973.
               121p. col. plates. 21cm.

CC63   Florange, Charles.
F5   Catalogue general illustre des monnaies
          d'or modernes de tous les pays, par C.
          Florange et J. G. de Villefaigne. Neuilly-
          sur-Seine, Bureau de bulletin "Change."
          n.d.
               308p. illus. 21cm.

CC63   Friedberg, Robert
F7   Gold coins of the world; complete
1976   from 600 AD to the present, an
         illustrated catalogue with valuations
         by Robert Friedberg. Revised and
         edited by Jack and Arthur Friedberg.
         4th ed. N.Y., The Coin and Currency
         Inst., 1976.
            467p. illus. 28cm.

CC63   Hobson, Burton
H6   Historic gold coins of the world.
         New York, Doubleday, 1971.
            192p. illus. 28cm.

CC63   Hoppe, Donald J.
H65   How to invest in gold coins [by] Donald
         J. Hoppe. New Rochelle, N.Y., Arlington
         House [1970]
            304p. illus. 24cm.
            Bibliography: p. [293]-295.

CC63   Mason, Don Walter.
M3   Intrinsic values of gold coins; for bullion
V.1   ranges of $50-$800 per ounce. Long Beach,
         Calif., D. Mason and Associates [1973]
            165p. 28cm.
            Bibliography: p. 165.

CC63   Mason, Don Walter.
M3   Intrinsic values of gold coins; for
v.2   bullion ranges of $300-$1050 per ounce.
         Long Beach, Calif., D. Mason and Associates
         [1973]
            141p. 28cm.

CC63   Schweizerischer Bankverein, Basel.
S3   Goldmunzen. Basel, Schweizerischer
         Bankverein, 1968.
            127p. illus. (col. pl.) 21cm.

CC63   Turner, W. W.
T8   Double eagles of the world; a study
         of the U.S.A. $20.00 gold piece and its
         equivalent in other monies of the world.
         Nashville, W.W. Turner, 1967.
            47p. illus. 28cm.

CC63   Turner, W. W.
T8g   Gold coins for financial survival.
          Nashville, Turner Publ., 1971.
              240p. illus. 24cm.

CC63   Turner, W. W.
T8s   Turner's simplified pricing
          system for USA and world gold coins.
          Vol. 1-popular world gold coins and
          sets by W. W. Turner. Leesburg, Fla.,
          Turner Publications, 1976.
              51p. illus. 25cm.

CC63   Verbanec, William R.
V4   Handbook of gold coin technology;
          buyers' guide for gold coins.
          Santa Clara, Ca., Wm. R. Verbanec
          Enterprises, 1974.
              242p. looseleaf. fold. charts.
          23cm.

CC63   Wurttembergische Bank, Stuttgart,
W8   Germany.
              Goldmunzen aus aller welt. Stuttgart,
          wurttembergische Bank, 1973.
              48p. plates 21cm.

SILVER

CC65   Bachtell, Lee M.
B3   World dollars, 1471-1877; pictorial
          guide. Ludowici, Ga., the author, 1974, 1975
              606p. unpaged index and price
          guide. illus. 29cm.

CC65   Castan Ramirez, Carlos.
C3   Duros del mundo, 1831-1971.
          Madrid, 1970.
              353p. illus. 24cm.

CC65   Dollars of the world; an exhibition
D6   of coins selected from the Louis G.
              Kaufman collection of silver pieces
              of dollar size... N.Y., Chatham
              Phoenix, Natl. Bank & Trust Co., n.d.
              30p. 23cm.

CC65   Galletta, Gene.
G3   Crowns of the world; a guide for sil-
          ver coins from Afghanistan to Zanzibar.
          Edited by Eric W. Roberts. Lynbrook,
          N.Y., World-Wide Numismatic [1965].
              87p. illus. 22cm.

CC65   Garner, Paul E.
G37   A catalog of silver coins of the
          world since 1900. 1st ed. San Antonio,
          Vest Pocket Coins, 1974.
              62p. 22cm.

CC65   Hoskins, Charles R.
H6   The story of the dollar. N.p., Inter-
          national Program Development Corporation,
          1970.
              65p. illus. 18 slides 28cm. (Inter-
          national Numismatic Collector Society,
          Library 1, Volume 2.)

CC65   Schneider, William A.
S3   Evolution of the silver dollar. List-
          ing the coins in an exhibit of dollar
          size specimens from 1486-1958, owned by
          The author. Kankakee, Ill., the author,
          1958.
              unpaged 18cm.

CC65   The Silver Institute.
S5   Modern silver coinage ... Washington, D.C.,
          Silver Institute, 1969-72, 1975.
              4v. in 2 22 x 30cm.

CC65   Wesch, H. J.
W4   A selection of popular silver crowns
          of the world (20th century). San Diego,
          Malter-Westerfield, [1969].
              42p. illus. 22cm.
              Bibliography: p. 42

BRONZE, COPPER, NICKEL

CC67   Feely, Edward F.
F4   Subsidiary coinage in the Americas
          1949 and pure nickel coinage of the
          world 1881-1950. New York, Int'l Nickel,
          [1951?].
              8p. illus. 23cm.

CC67   Henderson, Kenn.
H4   World nickel coinage. N.p., Kenn
         Henderson, 1968.
              various pagings 28cm.

CC67   Hunter, John.
H9   Price catalog of pure nickel coins of
         the world. Chicago, Hewitt, [1970?].
              72p. illus. 20cm.

CC67   [International nickel Co. of Canada, Ltd.]
I5   Nickel coins. 2d ed. [New York]
         Priv. print. [The Caxton press, inc.]
         1930.
              ix, 243p. illus. 27cm.

CC67   Kortjohn, Martin F.
K6   Aluminum coins. Reprinted from the
         Numismatist, vol. lix, Feb. 1946.
              8p. illus. 23cm.

CC67   Neumann, Josef, 1815-1878.
N4   Beschreibung der bekanntesten kupfermunzen,
1965   von Josef Neumann... Prag, Eigenthum und
         verlag des verfassers, 1858-72. Reprint,
         New York, Johnson Reprint, 1965.
              7v. 79 pl. 23 1/2cm.

CC67   Scott & Company.
S3   Illustrations of copper coins.
         N.Y., n.d.
              unpaged xxiv pl. 23cm.

CC67   Stride, H. G.
S7   Nickel for coinage. London, Interna-
         tional Nickel Co., 1963.
              122p. col. photog.

CC67   Wharton, Joseph.
W5   Memorandum concerning small money with
         illustrations and descriptions of existing
         nickel alloy coins. [Camden, N.J., Amer-
         ican Nickel works, 1876]
              36p. illus. 23cm.

ICONOGRAPHY

CC70   Becker, Thomas W.
B4   Pageant of world commemorative coins;
            their meaning and symbolism. Racine,
            Whitman, 1962.
                197p. illus. 24cm.

CC70   Collectors Research Ltd., Montreal.
C6   Numismatic fish and ships of 1967.
            Montreal, [1967].
                38p. illus. 24cm.

CC70   Obojski, Robert.
O2   Ships & explorers on coins. New York,
            Sterling Pub. Co. [1970]
                48p. illus. 20cm. (Topical coin
            library)

CC70   Schon, Gunter.
S3   Animals, birds and fishes on coins.
            New York, Sterling, [1971].
                48p. illus. 19 x 19cm.

BY PERIOD - MEDIEVAL

CC80   Saulcy, Louis Felicien Joseph Caignart
S2   de, 1807-1880.
                Numismatique des Croisades [by] Louis
            Felicien de Saulcy. [Bologna], Arnaldo
            Forni, 1974. Originally published:
            Paris, M. Rollin, 1847.
                174p. XIX plates. 32cm.

BY PERIOD - EARLY MODERN - EIGHTEENTH CENTURY

CC83   Craig, William D.
C7   Coins of the world, 1750-1850. 1st
            ed. Racine, Wis., Whitman Pub. Co.
            [1966, 1971, 1976]
                756p. (754-756 blank for "Notes")
            illus., map. 20cm.

CC83   Ede, James.
E3   A view of the gold and silver coins of
            all nations ... by J. Ede, Goldsmith.
            London, J.M. Richardson, [1808?]
                74p. 34 pl. 15 x 14cm.

BY PERIOD - NINETEENTH CENTURY

CC85   Bonneville, Alphonse.
B6   Encyclopedie monetaire ou
Rare   nouveau traite des monnaies d'or et
Books   d'argent en circulation chez les
            divers peoples du monde...par
            Alphonse Bonneville. Paris, Chez
            l'auteur, 1849.
                220p. illus. 39cm.

CC85   Bonneville, Pierre-Frederic.
B65   Traite des monnaies d'or et d'
Rare   argent qui circulent chez les diff-
Books   erens peuples...Paris, l'auteur et
            Duminil-Lesueur, 1806.
                266p. illus. 37cm.

CC85   Comencini, M.
C6   Coins of the modern world, 1870-1936.
            London, Methuen & Co., Ltd. [1937].
                xii, 185p. illus. 19cm.
                Bibliography: p. 185

CC85   Raymond, Wayte, editor.
R3c   Coins of the world, nineteenth century
            issues, edited by W. Raymond. First
            edition. New York, W. Raymond, [c1947].
            2nd edition, 1953.
                252p. pl. 23cm.

CC85   Schon, Gunter.
S3   Weltmunzkatalog; 19 jahrhundert, [von]
            Gunter Schon [und] Jean-Francois Cartier.
            Munich, Ernst Battenberg, 1973.
                1045p. illus. 19cm.
                Bibliography: pp. 1042-1045.

CC85   Walrafen, Barbara C.
W3   Influencia de plata gruesa. Topeka,
          Kansas, Verne R. Walrafen, 1968.
              24p. pl. 28cm.
              Bibliography: p. 23-24

BY PERIOD - TWENTIETH CENTURY

CC87   Krause, Chester L.
K7   Standard catalog of World Coins by
          Chester L. Krause & Clifford Mishler.
          Krause Publ., 1972, 1973, 1976, 1977.
              792p. illus. 28cm.

CC87   Numismatics International. (Dallas).
N8   Report of the "Committee to Research
          World Coinage Types and varieties."
          Numismatics International and Globe Coin
          Traders Assoc. [1968].
              126p. 10 pl. 29cm.

CC87   Raymond, Wayte, editor.
R3t   Coins of the world, twentieth century
          issues, edited by W. Raymond. New York,
          W. Raymond, 1938-1955.
              256p. pl. 23cm.

CC87   Schon, Gunter.
S3   Welt-Munz-Katalog, XX Jahrhundert;
          5888 Munzen mit den neuesten Preisen,
          1775 fotos, [by] Gunter Schon. Munchen,
          Ernst Battenberg [1969]
              600p. illus. 19cm.

CC87   Schon, Gunter.
S3   World coin catalogue. Twentieth
1975   century. Translated by Ernest
          Sheridan. Munich, Ernst Battenberg,
          1975.
              1088p. illus. 19cm.
              Library also holds copy in German.

CC87   Yeoman, Richard S.
Y4c   Current coins of the world, by R.S.
          Yeoman. 1st-6th ed. Racine, Wis., West-
          ern Pub. Co., Whitman Hobby Division,
          1966-1974.
              256p. illus. 20cm.

CC87   Yeoman, Richard S.
Y4m   A catalog of modern world coins.   1st-
          11th ed.   Racine, Whitman Pub. Co., 1957-
          1974.
              v.   illus.   20cm.

COLLECTIONS, CATALOGUES

FA10   Guttag, Julius.
G8C   The Julius Guttag collection of Latin
1974   American coins/arr. by Edgar H. Adams. -
          Lawrence, Mass.: Quarterman Publications, [1974]
              527p. Illus. 24cm

FA10   Guttag bros., New York.
G9   Coins of the Americas. New York,
          Guttag bros., [c1927].
              100p. illus. 26cm.

FA10   Turner, W. W.
T8   The dramatic story of gold in the new
Vert.   world; a collection of rare and beautiful
File   gold coins telling the story of man's
          persuit (SIC) of the precious metal.
          Nashville, Tenn., the author, n.d.
              12p. illus. 28cm.

GENERAL WORKS

FA15   Almanzar, Alcedo.
A4   Latin American numismatic bibliography
          (including the Caribbean) San Antonio, Tex.,
          Almanzar's Coins of the World [1972].
              42p. 22cm.

FA15   Burzio, Humberto F.
B8d   Diccionario de la moneda hispanoameri-
          cana. Santiago de Chile, Fondo Historico
          y Bibliografico Jose Toribio Medina,
          1956-58.
              3v. 327, 453p. 116 pl. 29cm.

FA15   Coinage of the Americas. Edited by Theodore
B82   V. Buttrey, Jr. New York, American Numismatic
          Society, 1973.
              139p. illus. 22cm.

FA15   The Coinages of Latin American and the
F8   Carribbean: an anthology / edited by E. A.
         Furber: -Lawrence, Mass.: Quarterman
         Publications, c1974.
             ix, 486p. : ill. ; 24cm. - (Gleanings from the
         Numismatist; v. 5)
             "Originally published between 1911 and 1971
         in the Numismatist."

FA15   Harris, Robert P.
H3   A guide book of modern Latin American
         coins. Racine, Wis., Whitman [c1966]
             125p. illus. 20cm.
             Bibliography: p. 123-125.

FA15   Medina, Jose Toribio, 1852-1930
M4   Las monedas coloniales hispano-
Rare   americanas. Santiago, Chile, Elzeviriana,
Books   1919.
             viii, 406p. illus. 27cm.

FA15   Seppa, Dale Allan, ed.
S4   Guidebook of the rare and scarce coins of
         Latin America. San Antonio, Hemisphere
         Coin Co., [1969].
             65p. illus. 22cm.
             Bibliography: p. 65

TECHNICAL ASPECTS

FA20   Burzio, Humberto F.
B8   La ceca de la villa imperial de Potosi
         y la moneda colonial. Buenos Aires,
         Peuser, 1945.
             297p. illus. 17 pl. 27cm.
             Bibliography: p. 191-201

FA20   Sellschopp, Ernesto A.
S4   Las acunaciones de las cecas de Lima,
         La Plata y Potosi, 1568-1651. Barcelona,
         Asociacion Numismatica Espanola, [1971].
             159p. illus. 58 pl. 29cm.
             Bibliography: p. 81

FA23 Allen, W. Frank.
A5   Previously unknown Spanish gold coins.
Reprinted from The Numismatist, American
Numismatic Association, 1967.
   16p. illus. 28cm.

FA23 Harris, Robert P.
H3   Gold coins of the Americas ... 1750
to date. Alabama, ANCO, 1971.
   280p. illus. 23cm.

FA23 Lopez-Chaves y Sanchez, Leopoldo.
L6   Catalogo de las onzas de America Inde-
pendiente, by Leopoldo Lopez Chaves y
Sanchez and Jose D. Yriarte y Oliva.
Madrid, Editorial Iber-Amer., 1962.
   88p. illus. 30cm.

FA23 Raymond, Wayte, 1886-
R3   Spanish American gold coins; being a
detailed list of the gold coins struck by
the Spanish kings in America at the mints
of Mexico, Guadalaxara, Lima, Potosi,
Bogota, Popayan, Guatemala, Santiago. New
York, W. Raymond, Inc. [c1936].
   48p. illus. 23cm.

FA23 Raymond, Wayte, 1886-
R3g   The gold coins of North and South
America, an illustrated catalogue of all
the types with an indication of their
retail value. New York, W. Raymond, Inc.
[c1937].
   102p. illus. 26cm.

FA23 Williams, Harry F.
W5   The gold coinage of Latin America.
From: American Journal of Numismatics,
v. 48, 1914.
   16p. 2 pl. 28cm.

FA25   Elizondo, Carlos A., Jr.
E5   Eight reales and pesos of the new
           world. 1st ed. San Antonio, Roy's Coin
           Center, [1968], 1971 (2nd ed.).
               142p. illus. 22cm.
               Bibliography: p. 142

FA25   Harris, Robert P.
H3   Pillars & portraits, a catalogue of
           Spanish American silver coins 1732 to 1826.
           Cupertino, Calif., Bonanza Press, [1968],
           1969.
               112p. illus. 20cm.
               Bibliography.

FA25   Perez, Gilbert Somers.
P4   The "Dos mundos" pillar dollars
           by Gilbert S. Perez. Manila, P. I.,
           The Philippine Numismatic and
           Antiquarian Society, 1948.
               unpaged. illus. 24cm. (Philippine
           Numismatic Monographs, 1).

FA25   Ramsay, Robert M.
R3   A tentative checklist of Spanish-
           American bust-type silver. Chicago,
           Hewitt, 1969.
               67p. illus. 20cm.

FA25   Raymond, Wayte, 1886-
R35   The silver dollars of North and South
           America; an illustrated catalogue of all
           the types and an indication of their re-
           tail value. New York, W. Raymond, Inc.
           [c1939], c1964.
               52p. illus. 26cm. (Reprinted from
           Coin Collector's Journal, N.Y. v. 1938-39)

FA25   Raymond, Wayte.
R35s   The silver and minor coins of North
           and South America exclusive of the
           United States. N. Y., Wayte Raymond,
           n.d.
               no continuous pagination. illus.
           24cm.

FA25   Riddell, John Leonard.
R5   A monograph of the silver dollar,
            good and bad. New Orleans, Norman,
            1845, 1969.
                1 v. unpaged. illus. 23cm.

FA25   Sherwood, Earl D.
S45   Spanish American silver coins. From:
            The Numismatic Scrapbook Magazine. v. XVIII
            no. 3, March, 1952. pp. 209-211.
                3p. illus.

FA25   Smith, Samuel, Jr.
S6   The silver coins and the mints of
            Spanish America, from the intro of the
            type with bust of the King in 1772 to
            1825. Boston, private, 1895.
                16p. 24cm.

COPPER

FA27   Eklund, O. P.
E5   Copper coins of Central and South
            America. American Numismatic Association,
            1962. From: The Numismatist.
                26p. illus. 21cm.

ICONOGRAPHY

FA30   McNickle, A.J. Stanley.
M3   Los Escudos de los reyes de Espana en
            las monedas coloniales de Mexico. Medio de
            identificacion de las monedas por las
            variaciones de los escudos. Mexico City,
            Sociedad Numismatica de Mexico, 1962.
                97p. illus. 22cm. Trans. (and added
            to) by Luis Enrique Ruiz.

FA30   McNickle, A. J. Stanley.
M3e   Spanish colonial coins of North Amer-
            ica-Mexico mint. Variations in the coat-
            of-arms as an aid to identification.
            Sociedad Numismatica de Mexico, 1962.
                53p. illus. 21cm.

FA30   Nesmith, Robert I.
N4   Castles and lions on Spanish
            colonial coins; a study of details of
            design as an aid to identification.
            Reprinted from the American Numismatic
            Society Museum Notes IV, New York,
            1950.
                pp. 99-104. illus. 23cm.

SPECIAL ASPECTS

FA40   Medina, Jose Toribio, 1852-1930.
M4   Las monedas obsidionales hispano-amer-
Rare   icanas. Santiago, Chile, Elzeviriana,
Books   1919.
                viii, 240p. illus. 27cm.

<u>MEXICO</u>

COLLECTIONS

FB20   Utberg, Neil S.
U8   Numismatic sidelines of Mexico ... the
            numismatic collection of the Banco de
            Mexico. Edinburg, Texas, the author,
            1965-
                illus. 28cm.
                Contents: v.1 (1965)-Medals, hacienda
            tokens, patterns, errors, counterfeits,
            oddities, counter stamps. v.2 (1967)
            patterns, errors, counterfeits, oddities.

CATALOGUES

FB30   Raymond, Wayte, 1886-
R3   ... The coins of Mexico in silver and
            copper, 1536-1939; with estimated valua-
            tions based upon their rarity or demand,
            intro by Dr. A. F. Pradeau, compiled and
            published by W. Raymond, Inc. New York,
            [c1940].
                23p. illus. 23cm. (The coin coll-
            ector series, no. 2)

GENERAL WORKS

FB40   Academia Mexicana de Estudios.
A2   Numismaticos.
                Memorias de la Academia Mexicana
            de Estudios Numismaticos. Mexico
            City, Mexico, la Academia, 1973-1974
            (Tomo III, No. 9, July 1973-
            June, 1974)
                68p. illus. 23cm.

FB40   Artes de Mexico. (Periodical).
A7   Monedas de Mexico. Mexico City, 1968.
                111p. illus. 32cm. (v. 15, no. 103)
                In Spanish, English, French & German.

FB40   Munoz, Miguel L.
M8   Historia numismatica del estado
         de Mexico. Liminar de Mario, Colin,
         Mexico, Biblioteca Enciclopedica
         del Estado de Mexico, 1975.
             125p.; unpaged addenda. 33 plates.
         24cm.
             Bibliography.

FB40   Romero de Terreros y Vincent, Manuel, 1880-
R6   La moneda Mexicana; bosquejo historico-
         numismatico. Mexico, Banco de Mexico,
         1952.
             52p. 15 pl. 20cm.

FB40   Robles de la Torre, Jose Leon.
R62   Monedas Mexicanos; 1536-1966.
         Torreon, Coah, Mexico, n.p., 1967.
             196p. illus. 22cm.

FB40   Sobrino, Jose Manual.
S6   La moneda Mexicana su historia,
         por Jose Manuel Sobrino. Fotos de
         Roberto Reyes Bernal. Mexico City,
         Banco de Mexico, 1972.
             [344]p. illus. col. 24cm.
             Bibliography: p. 317-319.

FB40   Utberg, Neil S.
U8   Coins of Mexico, 1536-1963. The
         author, [1960, 1962, 1963, 1967]. Prices.
             illus. 23cm.

FB40   Utberg, Neil S.
U8g   A guide book of the coins of
1967   Mexico 1536-1967; with additional
         information concerning the
         Olympic games... and the Hemis-
         Fair. Edinburg, Tex., the author,
         c1966, 1967.
             80p. illus. 23cm.

SPECIAL ASPECTS

FB45   Pradeau Aviles, Alberto Francisco.
P72   Mexican patriots and their part in
         numismatics. Reprinted from The Numisma-
         tist, 1962.
             32p. illus. 21cm.

TECHNICAL ASPECTS

FB50   Donati, Robert G.
D6   Guide to the grading of the coins
            of modern Mexico. 1st ed. n.p.,
            the author, 1975.
                47p. illus. 22cm.

FB50   Martinez, Carlos T.
M3   Breves apuntes historicos sobre la casa
            de moneda. Mexico, Depto. Graficas, Secretaria
            de Hacienda y Credito Publico, 1949.
                6p. pl. 23cm.

FB50   Moreno, Alvaro J.
M6 $ el signo de pesos; cual es su
            origen y que representa? por Alvaro
            J. Moreno. Mexico [City] Edicion
            Particular, 1965.
                105p. 25cm.

FB50   Pradeau Aviles, Alberto Francisco.
P7   The Mexican mints of Alamos and
            Hermosillo. New York, A.N.S., 1934.
                73p. illus. 3 pl. 16cm. (Numismatic
            notes and monographs, no. 63)

FB50   Ulan, H. S.
U3   Condition grading of Mexico's
            modern coins. 1st ed. n.p., the
            author, 1963.
                32p. illus. 29cm.

SILVER

FB55   de Jesus, P.I.
D4h   A hoard of Mexican silver coins dis-
Vert.   covered in the Philippines. Manila,
File   Philippine Numismatic and Antiquarian
            Society, 1955.
                5p. photo. (Philippine Numismatic
            Monographs, no. 11)

FB55   de Jesus, P.I.
D4m   Mexican pillar dollar of 1772. The
Vert.   Philippine Numismatic and Antiquarian
File   Society. Manila, The Society, 1956.
                6p. illus. 22cm. (Philippine
            Numismatic monographs, no. 12)

FB55   Pitts, Edward H.
P5   The infancy of New Spain's
            ubiquitous piece of eight. Syracuse,
            New York, manuscript of the author,
            1973.
               looseleaf 18p. 30cm.

COPPER, ETC.

FB57   Eklund, O.P.
E4   Copper coins of Mexico. Reprinted from
            the Numismatist, 1962.
               20p. illus. 22cm.

BY PERIOD - TO EARLY NINETEENTH CENTURY

FB60   Betts, Benjamin.
B4   Mexican imperial coinage; the medals
1968   and coins of Augustine I (Iturbide),
            Maximilian, the French invasion, and of
            the republic during the French interven-
            tion. Priv. print. 1899. Organization
            of International Numismatists, 1968.
               48p. illus. 22cm.

FB60   Contreras Barrios, Ignacio.
C6   Historia de la moneda durante
            la epoca del General Don Jose
            Maria Morelos y Pavon, 1811-1814;
            por Ignacio Contreras Barrios. 1st
            ed. Mexico City, Mexico, the author,
            1975.
               unpaged. illus. 23cm.

FB60   Low, Lyman, Haynes.
L6   A sketch of the coinage of the Mexican
Vert.   revolutionary general, Morelos. Based up-
File   on an important find. Read before the
            Amer. numismatic & archaeological society,
            New York, June 2, 1886 ... New York,
            Privately, 1886.
               18p. illus. 24cm.

FB60   Nesmith, Robert I.
N4   The coinage of the first mint of the
       Americas at Mexico City, 1536-1572. New
       York, American Numismatic Society, 1955.
           vii, 139p. illus., pl. 23cm. (Num-
       ismatic notes and monographs, no. 131)
           Bibliographical footnotes.

FB60   Pradeau, Alberto Francisco.
P7   Numismatic history of Mexico from the
       pre-Columbian epoch to 1823. Los Angeles,
       CA, Western printing co. (Whittier),
       1938.
           146p. xxiii pl. 28cm.

FB60   Pradeau Aviles, Alberto Francisco.
P7a   Apuntes biograficos historicos de Don
       Jose Francisco Osorno por el Dr. Alberto
       Francisco Pradeau. [Edicion particular
       de 100 ejemplares]. Los Angeles, the
       author, 1932.
           13p. illus. 20cm.

FB60   Pradeau, Alberto Francisco.
P7e   Emperor Maximilian I of Mexico, the
       French intervention, its history and that
       of its coinage 1864-1867. Yuma, Ariz.,
       Maximilian Numismatic Soc., 1970.
           22p. 28cm.
           Bibliography

FB60   Utberg, Neil S.
U8   The coins of colonial Mexico, 1536-
       1821, and the empire of Iturbide, 1821-
       1823. [Edinburg, Texas], The Author,
       1966.
           104p. illus. 23cm.

FB60   Utberg, Neil S.
U8   The coins of colonial Mexico, 1536-
1970   1821, and the empire of Iturbide, 1821-
       1823. 2d ed. rev. by George W. Vogt.
       Houston, Colonial Coins, 1970.
           100p. illus. 23cm.

FB65   Garza, J. Sanchez.
G3   Historical notes on coins of the Mexi-
         can revolution 1913-1917. Trans. by A.
         Frank. Mexico, D.F., 1932.
             44p. illus. 19cm.

FB65   Gaytan, Carlos.
G32   La revolucion Mexicana y sus monedas.
         1st ed., Mexico City, editorial Diana,
         [1969].
             252p. illus. 24cm.

FB65   Guthrie, Hugh S.
G8   Mexican Revolutionary coinage,
         1913-1917; based on the Bothamley
         collection, by Hugh S. Guthrie in
         collaboration with Merrill
         Bothamley. Photography by
         Mark E. Goldberg. Beverly Hills,
         Ca., Superior Stamp & Coin Co.,
         1976.
             93p. illus. 29cm.

FB65   Leslie, Elwin C.
L4   Coinage of the Mexican revolutionist,
         Zapata; a classification guide, by Elwin
         C. Leslie and Erma C. Stevens. [n.p.,
         c1968]
             viii, 81p. illus. 23cm.

FB65   Low, Lyman Haynes.
L6   La moneda del General insurgente Don
         Jose Maria Morelos. Cuernavaca, 1897.
             38p. illus. 23cm.

FB65   Martinez del Rio, Pablo.
M3   Notas de numismatica de la epoca de la
         independencia. Mexico City, 1934.
             4p. 3 pl. 30cm.

FB65   Munoz, Miguel L.
M8   The first mint of the Mexican
         Insurgents. Mexico City, Sociedad
         Numismatica da Mexico, 1968.
             33p. map. 23cm.
             Bibliography.

FB65   Utberg, Neil S.
U8   The coins of the Mexican revolution
          1910-1917. Edinburg, Texas, The author,
          1965.
              79p. illus. 23cm. (v.4 of Utberg's
          coins of Mexico series)

FB65   Utberg, Neil S.
U8g   Gold coins of the Mexican revolution,
          1910-1917. The author, 1967.
              28p. illus. 28cm.
          In Spanish and English.

FB65   Wood, Howland, 1877-
W6c   The coinage of the Mexican revolution-
          ists. New York, American numismatic soc-
          iety, 1928.
              53p. xv pl. 17cm. (Numismatic notes
          and monograph, no. 38)
              Revised edition of Numismatic notes and
          monographs, no. 4.

FB65   Wood, Howland, 1877-
W6m   The Mexican revolutionary coinage, 1913-
          1916. New York, American numismatic
          society, 1921.
              44p. xxvi pl. 17cm. (Numismatic
          notes and monograph, no. 4)
              Revised edition: Numismatic notes and
          monographs, no. 38.

OTHER NINETEENTH, TWENTIETH CENTURY

FB67   Buttrey, Theodore V.
B8c   The coinage of Mexico since 1905.
          American Numismatic Association, 1952.
          Reprint from The Numismatist.
              21p. illus. 22cm.

FB67   Buttrey, Theodore V.
B8g   A guide book of Mexican decimal coins,
          1863-1963; a comprehensive illustrated
          valuation catalog of Mexican decimal coins
          with official reports of coinage and his-
          torical notes about each issue. Historical
          & supplementary data by Neil Shafer.
          Racine, Whitman, [1963].
              122p. illus. 20cm.
              Includes bibliography.

FB67
B82
Buttrey, Theodore V.
    Guide book of Mexican coins, 1822 to
date. Supplementary data and values com-
piled by Holland Wallace and Neil Shafer.
Cover art and maps by Robert B. Kissner.
[Racine, Wis, Western, 1969, 1971.]
    256p. illus., maps. 20cm.
    Bibliography: p. 255-256.

FB67
H3
Hanks, William Lawrence.
    The comprehensive catalog and
encyclopedia of modern Mexican coins.
Translations by Paul A. Rios; Photography
by H. S. Ulan; edited by Judith M.
Hanks. 1976 ed. [El Paso,] Tex., the
author, c1975, 1976.
    154p. illus. 23cm.

FB67
L6
Long, Richard A.
    The availability of 20th century Mexi-
can coins. [1st ed. Corpus Christi, TX.,
1969]
    viii, 116p. illus. 22cm.
    Bibliography: p. 116

FB67
P7
Pradeau, Alberto Francisco.
    Historia numismatica de Mexico de 1823
a 1950. Mexico, Sociedad Numismatica
de Mexico, 1957.
    1 v. 24cm.
Contents: v.1 Cecas de:Mexico y Tlalpam.

FB67
S5
Shlieker, Ed.
    The un peso of the Bank of Mexico
[by] Ed Shlieker, Samuel M. Paonessa
[and] William L. Spencer. 1st ed.
El Paso, Tex., the authors, 1973.
    55p. illus. 21cm.

FB67
U8
1971
Utberg, Neil S.
    Coins of Mexico, 1905-1971. 2d ed.
Revised by Geo. W. Vogt. Houston, Texas
Colonial Pub. Co. 1971.
    40p. illus. 24cm.

FB67
U8r
Utberg, Neil S.
    The coins of the Republic of Mexico,
1823-1905 and the Empire of Maximilian,
1864-1867. The author, 1966.
    92p. illus. 23cm. (v.2 of Utberg's
coins of Mexico series)

GENERAL WORKS

FC20   Raymond, Wayte, 1886-
R3   ... The coins of Central America,
          silver and copper, 1824-1940, compiled and
          published by W. Raymond, Inc. New York,
          [c1941].
              15p. illus. 23cm. (The coin coll-
          ector series. No. 5)

FC20   Robinson, Charles M.
R6   The coins of Central America, 1733-
          1965; an illus. guide to Central American
          coinage, with pricing aids. [San Benito,
          Texas, 1965].
              131p. illus., maps. 28cm.
              Bibliography: p. 127-130.

FC20   Wallace, Holland.
W3   Central American coinage since 1821.
          [Weslaco, TX] 1966 [c1965].
              123p. illus. 22cm.
              Bibliography: p. [124]-[125]

COSTA RICA

COPPER

FC50   Gurdian, Raul.
G8   Contribucion al estudio de las monedas
          de Costa Rica. San Jose, Costa Rica, 1958.
              72p. 6 pl. 23cm.

GUATEMALA

FC55   Prober, Kurt.
P7   Historia numismatica de Guatemala.
         Edicion de Aniversario del Banco de
         Guatemala. Guatemala City, Editorial
         del Ministerio de Educaion Publica,
         1954, 1957.
             270p. 18 pl. 26cm.
             Bibliography: p. 267.

FC55   Robinson, Charles M.
R6   A catalogue of the coins of Guatemala,
         1733-1963; an illus, introductory guide to
         Guatemalan coinage, with pricing aids.
         [San Benito, Texas], 1964.
             31p. illus., map. 28cm.
             Bibliography: p. 30

HONDURAS

FC60   Wood, Howland
W6   The Tegucigalpa coinage of 1823. New
         York, A.N.S., 1923.
             16p. 2 pl. 16cm. (Numismatic notes
         and monographs, no. 18)

FC60   Zelaya, Manuel A.
Z4   The history and coins of Honduras.
         Tegucigalpa, Honduras, 1965.
             34p. illus. 28cm.

FC60   Zelaya, Manual A.
Z4a   Apuntes para la historia de la
         moneda en Honduras. Tegucigalpa,
         Honduras, 1958.
             60p. illus. 24cm.

PANAMA

FC65   Burns, Jack F.
B8   The coinage of Panama, an annotated
         check list and bibliography. [Pittsburgh,
         Carnegie Museum, 1963]
             16p. 19cm.
             Reprinted from: Numisma, an occasional
         numismatic magazine, Melbourne, Australia,
         May, 1963, no. 7, p. 105-120.
             Bibliography: p. 114-120.

FC65   Diez Morales, Guillermo E.
D5   Historia completa y documentada
            de la moneda Panamena [by] Guillermo
            E. Diez Morales. 1st ed. Panama,
            the author, 1974.
                 386p. illus. 21cm.

FC65   Grigore, Julius.
G7   Coins and currency of Panama. Iola,
            Wisc., Krause Publications [1972]
                 202p. illus. 24cm.

FC65   Isthmian Numismatic Society.
I8   Grading of Panama coins, 1904-1962.
Vert.   Balboa, Canal Zone, the Society, 1965.
File   7p   29cm.

FC65   Stickney, Brian R.
S7   Numismatic history of Republic of
            Panama. San Antonio, Alamnzar's, [1971].
                 64p. illus. 22cm.
                 Bibliography

EL SALVADOR

FC75   Almanzar, Alcedo.
A4   The coins and paper money of El Salvador,
            by Alcedo F. Almanzar & Brian R. Stickney.
            San Antonio, Tex., Almanzar's Coins of the
            World [1973]
                 88p. illus. 22cm.
                 Bibliography: p. 87-88.

NICARAGUA

FC80   Stickney, Brian R.
S7   The coins and paper money of
            Nicaragua, by Brian R. Stickney and
            Alcedo F. Almanzar. [San Antonio, Texas,
            Almanzar's Coins of the World], 1974.
                 64p. illus. 22cm.
                 Bibliography: p. 59.

CATALOGUES

FD20   Raymond Wavte, 1886-   comp.
R3   ... The coins of the West Indies,
            silver and copper, including the cut and
            counterstamped pieces, compiled and pub-
            lished by W. Raymond, Inc. New York
            [1942].
                 24p. illus. 23cm. (The Coin collector
            series, no. 10)

GENERAL WORKS

FD30   Wood, Howland, 1877-1938.
W6   The coinage of the West Indies, and The
            sou marque, by H. Wood. New York, American
            Numismatic society, 1915.
                 48p. illus. 29cm.

SPECIAL ASPECTS

FD35   Caldecott, J. B.
C3   The spanish dollar as adapted for
            currency in our West Indian colonies.
            Reprinted from British Numismatic Journal,
            1904, p. 287-298, Salina, Kansas, Olympic
            Press, 1963.
                 3 pl., table. 22cm.

BERMUDA

FD40   Bermuda. Bank of Bermuda.
B3   The Bank of Bermuda coin collection;
           a short history of coins used for
           trading in Bermuda from the 16th
           century to the present date. 2d. ed.
           Bermuda, 1972.
              2 vols. 37p; 24p. illus., part.
           col. 26cm.

CUBA

FD45   Banco Nacional de Cuba, Havana.
B3   Cotizacion numismatica de
           las monedas de la Republica de
           Cuba, 1915-1970. Habana, Banco
           Nacional de Cuba, 1971.
              23p. 23cm.

FD45   Burns, Jack F.
B8   A bibliography of Cuban numismatics.
           [Pittsburgh, 1958].
              25p. 22cm.

FD45   Lismore, Thomas.
L5   Las monedas de Cuba (1870-1953) Havana,
           1955.
              84p. 3pl. 22cm.
           In Spanish and English.

FD45   Lismore, Thomas.
L5   The coinage of Cuba, 1870 to date.
1966   Miami, Roy Renderer, 1966.
              47p. illus. 23cm.
           Bibliography: p. 47

FD45   Pesant, Roberto.
P4   Birth of the Cuban souvenir pesos.
           Reprinted from Numismatic Scrapbook, 1968.
              [19]p. illus. 20cm.

FD45   Pesant, Roberto.
P4b   A bibliography of the coinage
           of Cuba. New York, Roberto Pesant,
           1972.
              8p. illus. 22cm.

DOMINICAN REPUBLIC

FD50   Prober, Kurt.
P7   Numismatic history of the Dominican
Vert.   Republic. Reproduced from Revista Numis-
File   matica. (Brazil), 1950, no. 1-4, p. 14-77.
                8 pl., map. 29cm.

FD50   Remick, Jerome H.
R4   The coinage of the Dominican Republic,
            by Jerome H. Remick, Alcedo Almanzar. San
            Antonio, TX, Almanzar's coins of the World
            1965.
                35p. illus. 21cm.

FD50   Remick, Jerome H.
R4   The coinage of the Dominican Republic,
1972   by Jerome H. Remick and Alcedo Almanzar.
            [San Antonio, Tex., Almanzar's Coins of
            the World, 1972]
                [37p] illus. 22cm.
                Bibliography: p. [37]

HAITI

FD53   Arroyo, Carmen.
A7   Coins of Haiti, 1803-1970. ... Research
            data compiled and published by Almanzar's
            coins of the world. San Antonio, [1970]
                52p. illus. 21cm.

FD53   Byrne, Ray.
B9   Hispaniola divided (The Haiti-Santo
            Domingo experiment). Reprinted from the
            Numismatist, A.N.A., c1965.
                12p. illus. 22cm.
                Bibliography.

JAMAICA

FD55   Byrne, Ray.
B9   The coinage of Jamaica by Ray Byrne and
            Jerome H. Remick. San Antonio, TX,
            Almanzar's, c1966.
                106p. illus. 21cm.
                Bibliography: p. 103-106

PUERTO RICO

FD60   Gonzalez, Jaime.
G5   A Puerto Rican counterstamp, by Jaime
            Gonzalez. New York, American numismatic
            society, 1940.
                21p. illus., II pl. 17cm. (Numis-
            matic notes and monographs, no. 88)

FD60   Gould, Maurice M.
G6   The money of Puerto Rico, by Maurice M.
            Gould and Lincoln W. Higgie. Racine,
            Wisc., Whitman, 1962.
                83p. illus. 19cm.

FD60   Puerto Rico. Banco Credito y Ahorro Ponceno.
P8   Historica monetaria de Puerto Rico,
            [The Edward Roehrs collection, 1964, the
            money of Puerto Rico, including tokens,
            coins, patterns, paper money & transpor-
            tation tokens]. n.d.
                27p. 21cm.

VIRGIN ISLANDS

FD65   Higgie, Lincoln W.
H5   The colonial coinage of the U.S. Virgin
            Islands. Racine, Wisc., Whitman, 1962.
                61p. illus. 20cm.

<u>SOUTH AMERICA</u>

GENERAL WORKS, CATALOGUES

FE20   Raymond, Wayte, 1886-   comp.
R3   ... The coins of South America, silver
           and copper ... compiled and published by
           W. Raymond, Inc. ... New York [1942].
              44p. illus. 23cm. (The Coin collec-
           tor series, no. 9)

ARGENTINA

FE30   Cunietti-Ferrando, Arnaldo Jose.
C8   Monedas de la Republica Argentina.
           Buenos Aires, Asociacion Numismatica
           Argentina, 1965, 1971-72.
              62p. illus. 26cm.

FE30   Elmezian, Jorge.
E4   Monedalandia (Manual de numismatica).
           [2nd ed. Buenos Aires, 1945].
              144p. illus. 19cm.
              Bibliography: p. 145.

FE30   Gonzalez Conde; Jose Maria.
G6   Catalogo de la moneda metalica
           Argentina, 1813-1970. Buenos Aires,
           Asociation Numismatica Argentina, 1970.
              55p. 9 pl. 27cm.

FE30   Taullard, Alfredo, 1876-
T3   ... Monedas de la Republica Argentina.
           Ed de 200 ejemplares profusamente ilus-
           troda y documentada. Buenos Aires, 1924,
              193p. illus., port. 26cm.

BOLIVIA

FE35   Seppa, Dale.
S4   The coins of Bolivia by Dale Seppa and
            Alcedo Almanzar. San Antonio, Almanzar's
            [1970].
                70p. illus. 21cm.
                Bibliography: p. 8

BRAZIL

FE40   Baumann, Charles A.
B3   Numismatica Brasilera. Fonte auxilia-
            dore aos principiantes. Alto de Theres-
            opolis, 1938.
                x, 136p. 8 pl. 17cm.

FE40   Hamilton, Peter F.
H3   The coins of Brazil; Portuguese
            colonial period 1683-1822. n.p.,
            the author, 1976.
                77p. illus. 23cm.

FE40   Moura Soares, Edgard de.
M6   Notas numismaticas. Rio de Janeiro,
            [Assoc. Atletica Banco de Brasil], 1958.
                70p. illus. 18cm. (Cadernos A.A.
            B.B., No. 43)
                Bibliography: p. 67-70.

FE40   Neto, Fernando de Carvalho.
N4   Catalogo de moedas de ouro do Brasil.
            Sao Paulo, 1966.
                113p. 15cm.

FE40   Porcher, Hermann.
P6   Catalogo de precas de moedas
            Brasileiras, 1643-1945.
            Sao Paulo, Hermann Procher, [1945].
                141p. plates. 18cm.

FE40   Prober, Kurt.
P7   Catalogo das moedas Brasileras. 2nd ed.
            rev., aug. [Sao Paulo, Grafica Canto Ltda
            1966], 1960.
                237p. illus. 27cm. (Monografias
            Numismaticas, vol. x)

FE40   Prober, Kurt.
P7c   Catalogo de moedas Brasileiras de
           cobre; com suplemento do miguel e bronze-
           alum. [Rio de Janeiro], 1957.
               168p. 12 pl. (Monografias Numismatias
           v.9)

FE40   Prober, Kurt.
P7p   Catalogo de moedas Brasileiras de prata.
           [Sao Paulo, 1947].
               201p. illus., pl. 24 x 29cm. (Mono-
           grafias numismaticas, vol. 3)

FE40   Salles Oliviera, Alvarode.
S15   Moedas do Brazil. Sao Paulo, 1944.
               508p. pl., maps. 40cm.

FE40   Santos Leitao & Co., Ltda. (Rio de Janeiro).
S2   Catalogo de moedas Brasileiras de
           1643-. Rio de Janeiro, 1948-1967.
               illus. 23cm.
               Library has: 5th, 6th, 9th, 10th, 11th eds.

CHILE

FE50   Chile. Superintendancia de la casa de.
C3   moneda y especies valoradas.
               Monedas de Chile, 1743-1944. N.p.,
           n.pub., n.d.
               unpaged illus. 28cm.

FE50   Chile. Casa de Moneda.
C5   La casa de moneda de Santiago de
           Chile, 1743-1943. Santiago, 1944.
               244p. 64 pl. 28cm.

FE50   Medina, Jose Toribio, 1852-1930.
M4   Manual ilustrado de numismatica Chilena,
           la colonia. Santiago, Chile, Elzeviriana,
           1919.
               19p. x pl. illus. 27cm.

FE50   Medina, Jose Toribio, 1852-1930.
M4m   Las monedas coloniales de Chili
           par J. T. Medina. Santiago, Chili,
           Elzeviriana, 1919.
               70p. illus. 28cm.

FE50   Medina, Jose Toribio 1852-1930.
M4o   Las monedas obsidionales de
            Chili par J. T. Medina. Santiago,
            Chili, Elzeviriana, 1919.
               37p. illus. 28cm.

COLOMBIA

FE55   Almanzar, Alcedo.
A58   Coins of Colombia, by Alcedo Almanzar and
            Dale Seppa. San Antonio, Almanzar's Coins of
            the World [1973]
               97p. illus. 22cm.
               Bibliography: p. 96.

FE55   Barriga Villalba, A. M.
B3   Historia de la casa de moneda.
            Bogota, 1969.
               3 v. illus. 23cm.

FE55   Banco de la Republica.
B35   Monedas de Colombia, 1813-1973.
            Vol. 1. Bogota, Numismaticos Colombianos,
            1973.
               98p. illus. 17cm.

FE55   Burnett, Davis.
B8   Half dollars of Colombia, 1868-
            1969. San Antonio, Almanzar's Coins
            of the World, 1971.
               27p. illus. 22cm.

FE55   Calico, F. Xavier.
C3   Aportacion a la historia monetaria de
            Santa Fe de Bogota (Colombia). (Ensayo de
            catalogo de las acunaciones de oro con
            marcas F.S. o S.F. erroneamente atribuidas
            a sevilla). Barcelona, the author, 1953.
               81p. illus. 24cm.

FE55   Temprano, Leo.
T4   Catalogo monedas de Colombia,
            1811-1975; plata - cobre - niquel
            sin variedades. 1st ed. Bogota,
            Filatelia Tematica Numismatica,
            1976.
               123p. illus. 16cm.

ECUADOR

FE60   Seppa L., Dale Allan.
S4   The coins of Ecuador, 1833-1969. Las
          monedas de la Patria, 1833-1969, by Dale
          Allan, Seppa L. Quito, Ecuador, C. Arroyo;
          U.S. distributor: A. Almanzar, San Antonio,
          TX [1969], 1973.
              39p. illus. 21cm.

PARAGUAY

FE70   Almanzar, Alcedo F.
A4   The coins of Paraguay. By Almanzar
          and D. Seppa. Texas, Almanzar's Coins
          of the World, 1971.
              22p. illus. 22cm.

FE70   Cezar, Eduardo de Oliveira.
C4   Monedas del Paraguay [by] Eduardo de
          Oliveria Cezar [and] Miguel Angel Migliarini.
          Rosario, Argentina, Circulo Numismatico
          de Rosario, 1971.
              49p. illus. 24cm.

PERU

FE75   Almanzar, Alcedo F.
A4   The coins of Peru, 1822-1972, by
          Al Almanzar and Dale A. Seppa. San
          Antonio, Almanzar's Coins of the World
          [1972]
              83p. illus. 21cm.
              Bibliography: p. 81.

FE75   Saba Sumar, Wadi.
S3   Ensayo de un catalogo de las monedas
          Peruanas Acunadas en, Cobre y Plata,
          de 1822-1856. [Lima, 1971].
              35p. 13 pl. 22cm.

URUGUAY

FE80   Academia Uruguaya de Numismatica
A2   y Bibliofilia.
             Exposicion 75 Ariversario Banco de
         Cobranzas. Montevideo, 1968.
             22p. illus. 16cm.

FE80   Almanzar, Alcedo F.
A4   The coins of Uruguay, 1840-1971, by
         Alcedo F. Almanzar and Dale Seppa. San
         Antonio, Almanzar's Coins of the World,
         1971.
             45p. illus. 22cm.
             Bibliog: p. 45

FE80   Oliveres, F. N.
O3   Apuntes sobre numismatico nacional
         [by] F. N. Oliveres. Montevideo, Uruguay,
         1923.
             225p. illus. 28cm.

FE80   San Jose. Uruguay. Banco.
S2   La patria traves de las monedas.
         Cincuentenario del Banco de San Jose.
         1959.
             40p. illus. 19cm.

VENEZUELA

FE85   Pardo, Mercedes Carlota de.
P3   Monedas Venezolanas por Mercedes
         Carlota de Pardo. Caracas, Banco
         Central de Venezuela, 1961.
             2 vols. 182p; 481p. illus. charts;
         some fold-out. 24cm.

FE85   Stohr, Tomas F.
S8   Venezuela numismatica. Maracaibo,
         Venezuela, Universidad del Zulia, [1965].
             vii, 169p. illus. 23cm.
             Bibliography: p. 165-167

FE85   Stohr, Tomas.
S8c   Catalogo de monedas, ensayos,
         fichas y resellos de Venezuela; catalog
         of coins, patterns, tokens and
         counterstamps of Venezuela. Car-
         acas, the author, 1975.
             96p. illus. 22cm.
             -in English and Spanish.

SOCIETIES

GA10   Adelson, Howard L.
A5   The American Numismatic Society,
          1858-1958. New York, ANS, 1958.
              400p. illus. 26cm.

GA10   American Numismatic Society.
A55   A colloquium in memory of George
          Carpenter Miles (1904-1975). New York,
          American Numismatic Society, 1976.
              47p. illus. 23cm.

GA10   Boston Numismatic Society.
B6   Constitution, by-laws, charters
Vert.   and list of members of Boston
File   Numismatic Society. Boston, the
          Society, 1884, 1944.
              7p. 23cm.

GA10   New York Numismatic Club.
N4   History of the New York Numismatic
          Club; 1908-1961. N.Y., 1961.
              56p. illus. 23cm.

PUBLIC COLLECTIONS

GA20   American numismatic society.
A5   ... Exhibition of United States and
          colonial coins, January 17 to February
          18, 1914. Catalogue ... New York, 1914.
              vii, 133p. front., 39pl. 23cm.

GA20   Clain-Stefanelli, Vladimir.
C5   History of the national numismatic
          collections. [Washington] Smithsonian
          [Institution; for sale by the Supt. of
          Docs., U.S. Govt. Print. Off., 1968].
              108p. illus. 28cm.
              Bibliographical footnotes.

GA20   McClure, R. A., comp.
M3   An index to the coins and medals
         of the Cabinet of the Mint of
         the United States at Philadelphia.
         2d ed. Prepared by R. A. McClure,
         Philadelphia, Avil Printing and
         Lithograph Co., 1895.
             45p. 19cm.

GA20   New York. State Library.
N4   Catalogue of the medals, coins,
         paper money etc. in the New York
         State Library. Albany, the
         Library, 1854, 1857.
             212p. 24cm.

PRIVATE COLLECTIONS

GA25   Baltimore National Bank.
B3   An exhibition of the world's
         greatest collection of United States
         coins; including coins of other
         countries. Baltimore, Maryland,
         the Baltimore Natl. Bank, n.d.
             20p. illus. 23cm.

GA25   Life Magazine.
E4   Gems from the greatest collection of
         U.S. coins. [Louis Eliasberg collection],
         April 27, 1953.
             [9]p. col. illus. 20cm.

CATALOGUES

GA30   Brown, Martin R.
B7   Market value index for circulated United
         States coins, by M. T. Brown and John W.
         Dunn. 1962-63. Oklahoma City, 1961-1962.
             vii, 103p. illus. 19cm.

GA30   Dellquest, Augustus Wilfrid.
D4   Burt's United States coin book...
         3rd, 6th ed. N.Y., Blue Ribbon
         Books, 1935, 1940.
             73p. scattered illus. 16cm.

GA30   Guttag Bros.
G8r   Rare coins of the United States.
          New York, [1924].
               40p. illus.

GA30   Liebers, Arthur.
L5   The guide to North American coins.
          N.Y., Arco Publishing Co., 1961.
               107p. illus. 25cm.

GA30   Raymond, Wayte, 1886- comp.
R3b   Standard price list of United States
          silver and copper coins, 1931, compiled
          by W. Raymond, inc. New York, Scott stamp
          & coin co. [c1931].
               7p. illus. 23cm.

GA30   Raymond, Wayte, 1886-   comp.
R3c   Standard price list of United States
          coins, listing and illustrating some
          early American coins. New York, W.
          Raymond, inc. c1933-1950.
               v. illus. 23cm.

GA30   Raymond, Wayte, 1886-
R3p   Premium values of rare U.S. coins. ...
Vert.   W. Raymond, inc. New York, Distributed by
File   Scott stamp & coin co., 1935.
               16p. illus. 23cm.

GA30   Raymond, Wayte, 1886-
R3r   Standard premium list of all rare
          United States coins, including early col-
          onial, experimental pieces and private
          gold issues, together with a supplement
          illustrating all United States commemora-
          tive coins; listing all coins the pub-
          lisher will buy and the prices paid for
          them. New York, 1930 [c1932], [c1938]
               35p. 23cm.

GA30   Raymond, Wayte, 1886- comp.
R3s   Standard catalogue of early American
          coins, 1652-1796 ... compiled by W. Ray-
          mond ... New York, Scott stamp & coin co.
          [c1933-]
               v. illus. 23cm.

GA30   Raymond, Wayte, 1886-   comp.
R3t   Standard type list of United States
         coins, 1947. The author, 1947.
             16p. illus. 23cm.

GA30   The Standard catalogue of United States.
R3u   coins from 1652 to present day. [1st]
             18th ed.; 1935-1957. New York.
             18v. illus. 24cm.

GA30   Schnelling, L. W., comp.
S3   Illustrated catalogue of U.S.
         gold, silver and copper coins; giving
         the dates, conditions and prices of
         coins most desirable to collectors.
         Also showing some of the very rare
         private gold coins minted in Calif.
         between 1849 and 1861. New York,
         Colonial Coin & Stamp, 1933.
             23p. illus. 26cm.

GA30   Standard U.S. coin catalogue.
S4   1976 ed. N.Y., Scott Publishing
1976   Co., 1975.
             191p. illus. 14cm.

GA30   Shinkle, C. H.
S5   U.S. coin values and lists; an exhibit
         of prices paid for U.S. coins at auction
         sales, 1907-10. Pittsburgh, c1905.
             23p. illus. 25cm.

GA30   Stack, Norman.
S7   U.S. coins of value. [New ed. New
         York, Dell Pub. Co., 1966], 1974, 1975.
             223p. illus. 18cm.

GA30   Stack's Coin Company.
S72   Stack's numismatic guide, containing
         current prices and general information of
         the colonial coins of America, continental
         and colonial paper currency, U.S. gold,
         silver and copper coins ... from 1609 to
         the present. New York, Stack's, n.d.
             158p. illus. 23cm.

GA30   Steigerwalt, Chas.
S75   ... Illustrated history of United
         States and colonial coins. Lancaster, Pa.
         [1884].
             40p. illus. 24cm.

GA30   Taxay, Don, ed.
T3   1971; the comprehensive catalogue and
        encyclopedia of United States coins.
        1st ed. Prepared and edited by Don
        Taxay. New York, Scott, [1970].
            397p. illus. 24cm.

GA30   Texas Coin Exchange.
T4   U.S. coins (numismatic values), price
        trends, 1951-1958, as per R.S. Yeoman
        guide (Red Book), 5th through 12th editions.
        Dallas, Texas Coin Exchange, [1958].
            36p. 23cm.

GA30   Wallis, Edward T.
W3   The national catalog of U.S.
        coins. 1st, 4th ed. Los Angeles,
        Calif. Stamp Co., 1933, 1941.
            199p. illus. 16cm.

GA30   Wilson, R. A.
W54   American coin book and standard
        retail premium list of all United States
        coins. Los Angeles, American Numismatic
        Co., 1958, 1960, 1948.
            128p. illus. 21cm.

GENERAL WORKS

GA40   Albany [New York] Numismatic Society.
A4   Papers presented at meetings of
        the Albany Numismatic Society,
        1941. Reprinted from the Numismatic
        Scrapbook Magazine, n.p., 1941.
            44p. illus. 20cm.

GA40   American Numismatic Association.
A5   Selections from the Numismatist: United
        States coins. Racine, Wisc., Whitman, 1960.
            301p. illus. 24cm. (The Numismatist
        reprint series)

GA40   Browin, Frances (Williams) 1898-
B7   Coins have tales to tell; the story of
        American coins. [1st ed.] Philadelphia,
        Lippincott [1966].
            152p. illus. 26cm.

GA40   Coffin, Joseph.
C6   Our American money; a collector's
            story, illus. with photos. New York,
            Coward-McCann, 1940.
                xi, 153p. front. plates 19cm.
                Bibliography: p. 151-153.

GA40   Davis, Holland A., comp.
D3   The Davis Rocky Mountain
            Coin encyclopaedia. 3rd ed.
            Denver, the compiler, 1935.
                73p. 18cm.

GA40   Dickeson, Montroville Wilson.
D5   The American numismatical manual of
            the currency or money of the aborigines,
            and colonial, state, and United States
            coins. With historical and descriptive
            notices of each coin or series. Philade-
            lphia, Lippincott, 1859, 1860.
                x, 256p. tables., xix col. pl. 29 x
            22cm.

GA40   Dickinson, Willard Edward.
D55   Old United States coins ... written and
            published by W. E. Dickinson ... [Win-
            sted, Conn., Winsted,] 1933.
                18p. 23cm.

GA40   Fletcher, W. A.
F5   United States and foreign
            coin catalogue. 4th ed. Chicago,
            Fletcher, n.d.
                16p. illus. 21cm.

GA40   Fox Emmet.
F6   The historical destiny of the
            United States; the mystery of the
            American money, being the substance of
            a lecture delivered by Mr. Fox
            in New York City and in Denver,
            Colorado. N.Y., Church of the
            Healing Christ, 1934.
                37p. 22cm.

GA40   Frost, Harwood.
F7   Evolution of the dollar. Chicago,
            author, 1927.
                64p. 20cm.

GA40   Green, Charles Elmore.
G7   Mint record and type table, United
            States coins; listing the major varieties
            of all regular issues of U.S. coins as well
            as private gold, encased postage, and frac-
            tional currency. [Chicago, John S. Swift
            co., inc. c1936].
                252p. illus. 18cm.

GA40   Johnson, James B., ed.
J6   Auction prices, U. S. coins...,
            1942-1944. 3rd ed. Cincinnati,
            the editor, 1944, 1942.
                165p. illus. 22cm.

GA40   Kosoff, A.
K6   An illustrated history of U.S. coins,
            depicting the proposed designs as well as
            the accepted types. Encino, Calif., 1962.
                76p. illus. 28cm.

GA40   Majer, Frederic.
M2   Our country's money. New York,
            Crowell, 1939.
                121p. photog. 23cm.

GA40   Martin, Lee.
M3   Coin columns, Anaheim, Cal., Clarke
            Printing, c1966.
                160p. illus. 21cm.

GA40   Massey, J. Earl.
M32   America's money; the story of our coins
            and currency. New York, Crowell, [1968].
                278p. illus. 21cm.

GA40   Mickley, Joseph J.
M5   Dates of United States coins
Vert.   and their degrees of rarity.
File   Philadelphia, the author, 1858.
                4p. 25cm.

GA40   Reinfeld, Fred.
R4   A treasury of American coins. Garden
            City, N.Y., Hanover House, 1961.
                123p. illus. 27cm.

GA40   U.S. Treasury Department.
U5   Facts about United States money.
Vert.   Washington DC, 1966.
File   Looseleaf, 16pp. 27cm.

GA40   Webb, E. O.
W4   A history of our metallic money from
           the earliest period to the present time,
           and the coins of the United States ...
           including a description and history of
           each one of the gold & silver commemor-
           ative coins. [San Jose, 1936].
               79p. illus. 23cm.

GA40   Weissbuch, Ted N.
W42   United States numismatic dictionary,
           by Ted N. Weissbuch and Lee F. Hewitt.
           [Chicago, Hewitt Bros., 1967]
               39p. illus., map. 20cm. (Hewitt's
           numismatic information series)

COLLECTING

GA50   Andrews, Charles J.
A6   Fell's United States coin book., 3rd, 4th,
           7th, ed. New York, F. Fell, 1955 [1958, 1970]
               illus. 20cm.

GA50   Bowers, Q. David.
B6   Coins and collectors. [Johnson City,
           N.Y., Windsor Research Pub., 1964].
               213p. illus. 23cm.

GA50   Bowers, Q. David.
B6h   How to start a coin collection.
           Los Angeles, Petersen Publishing Co., c1973.
               64p. illus. 16cm.

GA50   Brown, Martin R.
B72   A guide to the grading of United States
           coins, by M.R. Brown and John W. Dunn.
           Illus. by Arthur Mueller. Racine, Wis,
           Western, 1958-1975.
               206p. illus. 20cm.

GA50   Coin world, Sidney, Ohio.
C6g   Coin world; guide to coins, by the
           editors of Coin world. New York, Arco
           [1965, c1964]. [1974]
               110p. illus., ports. 24cm. (Arco
           hobby library)

GA50   Coins; questions and answers: what, when,
C65   why. Iola, Wis., Krause Pub. 1964.
            127p. illus. 22cm.

GA50   Allenbaugh, Carl.
C65   Coins; questions and answers
1976   by Carl Allenbaugh. Edited by
        Robert M. Poeschl. 2d ed. Iola,
        Wisc., Krause Publ., 1976.
            128p. illus. 21cm.

GA50   Davis, Norman M.
D3   The complete book of United States
        coin collecting. New York, Macmillan,
        [1971], 1976.
            336p. illus. 21cm.
            Bibliography

GA50   The Official black book of United States
D4   coins. Ralph DeVincenzo, co-ordinating
            editor. New York, HC Publishers
            1965-1976.
            v. illus. 18cm.

GA50   Dunham, William F.
D8   Easy finding list Canadian and United
        States; U.S. Colonial and territorial
        coins; hard times tokens; encased U.S.
        postage stamps. [Los Angeles, Carl A.
        Bundy Quill, n.d.].
            47p. 22cm.

GA50   French, Charles F.
F7   American guide to U.S. coins. New
        York, Cornerstone Library [1964].
            176p. illus. 21cm.

GA50   Gettys, Loyd B.
G4   "AU" or "BU", [a new approach to scien-
        tific grading, by Loyd B. Gettys & Ed-
        ward M. Catich. A.N.A., 1965]
            16p. illus. 22cm.
            Reprinted from The Numismatist, May,
        June, July, 1956.

GA50   Guiton, Harold H.
G9   Guiton's coin grading guide for grading
        United States coins. Terre Haute, Ind.
        [Moore-Langen, Print. and Pub. Co.] 1966.
            105p. illus. 23cm.

GA50   Hobson, Burton.
H55   Coin collecting for beginners, by ...
            Hobson and Fred Reinfeld. No. Hollywood,
            Wilshire, 1970.
                160p. illus. 21cm.

GA50   Hood, Clyde.
H6   Numistic authority. [Mattoon, Ill.]
            Numistic Authority Pub. Co. [1965].
                61p. illus. 20cm.

GA50   Jones, George F., comp.
J6   The coin collectors manual,
            containing a description of the gold,
            silver, copper and other coins of
            the United States, together with an
            account of actual sales in Philadelphia
            and New York, designed as a guide book
            for coin collectors. Philadelphia,
            Edward Cogan, 1860.
                41p. 30cm.

GA50   Knight, Hugh McCown.
K5   A simplified guide to collecting Amer-
            ican coins. Introd. by Richard S. Yeoman.
            New rev. and enl. ed. Garden City, N.Y.
            Doubleday [1963, c1962]
                187p. illus. 27cm.

GA50   Masters, Robert V.
M3   Coin collecting by Robert V. Masters
            and Fred Reinfeld. New York, Sterling
            Publishing Co., 1960.
                128p. illus. 20cm.

GA50   Neuce, Ed.
N4   Basic knowledge for the coin collector.
            Coin World, 1964-
                68p. illus. 22cm.

GA50   Reed, Fred Morton.
R4   Cowles complete encyclopedia of U.S.
            coins. Foreward by Gilroy Roberts.
            [1st ed.] New York, Cowles Book Co.,
            [1969, 1972].
                xx, 300p. illus. 24cm.
                Bibliography: pp. 293-294.

GA50   Reed, Fred Morton.
R4c   The complete coin collector. Chicago,
         Henry Regnery Co., 1976.
             xii, 330p. illus. 24cm.

GA50   Reinfeld, Fred, 1910-1964.
R45h   Coin collectors' handbook. N.Y.
         President Coin Corp., 1966, 67.
             153p. illus. 20cm.

GA50   Ruddy, James F.
R8   Photograde; a photographic grading guide
         for United States coins. Hollywood,
         Ruddy Investments, 1970, 1974, 1975
             208p. photog. 22cm.

GA50   Smedley, Glenn B., comp.
S6   Type list of regular U. S. Coins.
Vert.   Taken from The Numismatic Scrapbook,
File   Vol. XIII, #8. Chicago, 1947.
             pp. 889-896. illus. 20cm.

GA50   Titus, Wright.
T5   Collecting U.S. coins for pleasure
         and profit by Wright Titus and others.
         Dallas, Texas Coin Exchange, n.d.
             44p. illus. 28cm.

GA50   A Guide book of United States coins: fully
W5   illus. catalog & price list, 1616 to
             date; incl. a brief history of Amer.
             coinage, early Amer. coins & tokens,
             early mint issues, regular mint issues,
             private, state & territorial gold, sil-
             ver & gold commemorative issues, proofs.
             [1st]-3d ed; 1947-1977. Racine, Wis,
             Whitman.
             v. 20cm.

GA50   Yeoman, R. S.
Y4   Handbook of United States coins, with
         premium list. Racine, Wis., Whitman,
         1942-1977.
             34v. illus. 20cm.

GA50   Yeoman, R. S.
Y42   Handbook of United States type coins,
         regular issues, copper, nickel, silver.
         Racine, Wis., Whitman, 1943, 1948

GA55   Appraising and selling your coins ...,
A6   edited by Robert Friedberg. New York,
       Coin and Currency Institute, 1960-73.
       v. ill. 20cm.

GA55   Bale, Don.
B3   Complete guide for profitable coin
      investing. 1st ed. Hills, Minn.,
      Crescent Pub. Co., 1963, 1969
       208p. illus., tables. 22cm.
       Bibliography: p. 200

GA55   Berson, Fred.
B4   Secrets of a professional coin
      dealer, by Fred Berson and Abner
      Berson. N.Y., Frederick Fell, Inc.,
      1967.
       153p. illus. 22cm.

GA55   Bieler, James.
B54   Coin charts of United States coins. 1st
      ed. Lanham, Maryland, Coin Charts, 1977.
       viii, 96p. 23cm.

GA55   Bilinski, Robert.
B55   A guide to coin investment. 1st-3rd
      ed. 1957-1962.
       28cm.

GA55   Bowers, Q. David.
B6   High profits from rare coin in-
      vestment / by Q. David Bowers.
      -Los Angeles: Bowers and Ruddy
      Galleries, 1974.
       208p.: ill.; 22cm.
       Includes index.

GA55   Bowers, Q. David.
B6c   Collecting rare coins for
      profit; [by] Q. David Bowers. N.Y.,
      Harper and Row, 1975.
       326p. illus. 24cm.

GA55   Bressett, Kenneth.
B65   Buying and selling United States coins
         by Ken Bressett and R. S. Yeoman. Racine,
         Western, 1970, 1971, 1972, 1974, 1975, 1976.
             7v. illus. 18cm.

GA55   Coin investors manual. Data compiled from
C5   Coin Dealer Newsletter. Ed. by Geo. W.
             Haylings, James G. Miladin, Allen
             Harriman. Gardena, Cal., Payne, 1965.
             250p. charts. 22cm.

GA55   Coen, Joel B.
C6   What your coins are worth, 1972, [by]
         Coen & Messer. New York, Bantam Books,
         1972.
             91p. illus. 14cm.

GA55   Coin world, Sidney, Ohio.
C6c   Coin collecting for fun and profit, by
         the editors of Coin World. [Greenwich,
         Conn., Fawcett Publications, 1964.]
             112p. illus., ports. 24cm.

GA55   Coins Gallery.
C64   United States rare coin value guide.
         Beverly Hills, Ca., Coin Gallery, n.d.
             48p. illus. 20cm.

GA55   Deutch, Howard E.
D4   High profits without risk; how you can
         earn more than 50% on your investment with
         absolute safety. Monroeville, Penn., Jefren,
         1976.
             223p. ill. 24cm.

GA55   Haylings, George W.
H3pb   The profit march of the Buffalos and
         the Indians from 1935 to 1970. Carlsbad,
         Calif., Publico Publishers, 1961.
             96p. 22cm.

GA55   Haylings, George W.
H3pm   The profit march of your Buffalos, Indians
         and early Lincoln cents, 1935-1972. Gardena,
         Calif., Payne Publishing Co., 1964.
             viii, 229p. illus. 23cm.

GA55   Haylings, George W.
H3po   The profit march of your coin investment,
        1935-1971. Gardena, Calif., Payne Publishing
        Co., 1964.
            xiv, 224p. 23cm.

GA55   Haylings, George W.
H3py   The profit march of your coins from 1935
        to 1968. Carlsbad, Calif., Publico Publishers,
        1960.
            96p. 23cm.

GA55   Hobson, Burton.
H55   Manual for coin collectors and inves-
        tors, by B. Hobson and Fred Reinfeld.
        New York, Sterling, [1963].
            160p. illus. 20cm. (Worthwhile how-
        to paperbacks, 402)

GA55   Jones, Ernest R.
J6   Simplified inventory system for
        investors, collectors & dealers.
        1st ed. Virginia, Beach, Va.,
        the author, 1975.
            128p. charts, forms. 29cm.

GA55   Mehl, B. Max.
M4b   A brief history of the Mehl numis-
        matic establishment. Ft. Worth, Tex.,
        the author, [1939.]
            unpaged. illus. 19cm.

GA55   Mehl, B. Max, [ed.]
M4r   Recognition of fifty years of numismatic
        service. Fort Worth, Texas, n.pub., 1950.
            32p. ill. 22cm.

GA55   Mills, Brad.
M5   Coin collecting for all its worth; a
        guide to coin collecting for fun and
        profit. New York, H C Publishers,
        [c1970].
            192p. illus. 14 x 11 cm.

GA55   Molyneaux, Peter J.
M6   A Texas master of coins.
        Reprinted from the Magazine of
        Texas. n.d.
            32p. illus. 18cm.
            Cover title: The romance of
        money.

GA55   Numismatic Times and Trends, comp.
N8   Investing in coins; complete with
            charts. New Orleans, the author, 1961.
                 32p. tables, charts. 21cm.

GA55   Pollack, Irving.
P6   Profit with proof coins. 1st ed.
            The author, 1957.
                 24p. 25cm.

GA55   Reinfeld, Fred, 1910-1964.
R45c   Cash for your coins. [Rev. ed.] New
            York, Sterling Pub. Co., [1963].
                 128p. illus. 16cm.

GA55   Spotz, Michael J., III.
S6   A proof set investment primer. The
            author, 1966.
                 52p. tables. 17cm.

GA55   Sternfeld, Bernard.
S7   How to grow money. Brooklyn. N.Y.,
            How-to Pub., [1961].
                 124p. 28cm.

GA55   Stack, Harvey G.
S8   Coins as an estate asset.
Vert.   Reprinted by Stacks from Trusts
File   and Estates. N.Y., Communication
            Channels, 1976.
                 6p. illus. 29cm.

GA55   West, R. W.
W3   Coins for profit. Charlotte, N.C.,
            Imperial Pub. Co., 1962.
                 56p. 21cm.

GA55   Weiss, Wilfred.
W4   Want $3750 for a nickel?;
            [B. Max Mehl], the dean of American
            numismatics. Reprinted...
            from the Saturday Evening Post. N.p.
            Curtis Pub., Co., 1949.
                 unpaged. 22cm.

GA55   Wright, Glenn.
W7   Standard guide to U. S. coin and
            paper money valuations by Glenn
            Wright and Clifford Mishler.
            Iola, Wisc., Krause, 1975.
                 194p. illus. 18cm.

GA55   Zegarowicz, Edward.
Z4   Inflation-proof your future. New
         York, Walker, [1971].
             216p. 22cm.

SPECIAL ASPECTS

GA70   Bradfield, Elston G., ed.
B7f   Franklin and numismatics. Colorado
         Springs, American Numismatic Association,
         1966.
             84p. ill. 23cm.
             Reprinted from the Numismatist, Decem-
         ber 1956.

GA70   Bradfield, Elston G., ed.
B7r   Theordore Roosevelt and numismatics.
         American Numismatic Assoc., c1958, c1966.
             Reprinted from The Numismatist, Novem-
         ber-December, 1958.
             56p. pl. 23cm.

GA70   Glaser, Lynn.
G5   Counterfeiting in America, the history
         of an American way to wealth. Clarkson,
         N. Potter, 1968.
             274p. illus. 22cm.

GA70   Harsche, Bert.
H3   Detecting altered coins. Bismarck,
         N.D., the author, 1962-64.
             26p. illus. 21cm.

GA70   Kenney, Richard D.
K4   Struck copies of early American coins
         New York, W. Raymond, 1952.
             16p. illus. 23cm. (Coin collector's
         Journal)

GA70   Spanbauer, Larry
S6   Counterfeits of United States coins.
         [Oshkosh, Wisc.,] the author, 1975.
             75p. illus. 22cm.

GA70   Taxay, Don.
T3   Counterfeit, mis-struck, and unofficial
         U.S. coins, a guide for the detection of
         cast and struck counterfeits, electro-
         types, and altered coins. Introd. by John
         J. Ford, Jr. New York, Arco Pub. Co.
         [1963].
             221p. illus. 25cm.

GA80 Altz, Charles G.
A5   Foreign coins struck at United States
mints, by C. G. Altz and E. H. Barton.
Racine, Wis., Whitman [1965]
   63p. illus. 20cm.
   Bibliography: p. 63
   Supplement, 1970, by Numismatic
Scrapbook Magazine and World Coins.

GA80 Amos, John O.
A6   The worthy line, [Reprint of a series
Vert. from Coin World on U.S. Mint Engravers].
File   [6]p. illus. 44 x 28cm.

GA80 Belden, Bauman L.
B4   A mint in New York. New York, ANS,
1930.
   40p. 5 pl. 17cm.

GA80 Breen, Walter.
B7d   Dies and coinage. [New York, R.
Bashtow, 1962].
   38p. 22cm.

GA80 Breen, Walter.
B7m   The minting process, how coins are made
and mismade. Beverly Hills, Cal.,
American Institute of Professional Numismatists, [1970].
   162p. illus. 22cm.

GA80 Breen, Walter H.
B7p   Proof coins struck by the United States
mint, 1817-1921. New York, Wayte Raymond, 1953.
   48p. 23cm. (Coin collector's journal
nos. 148-149)

GA80 Coin World
C6   A collection of United States mint
photographs. [Sidney, Ohio, Sidney,
1969].
   13p. of illus. 15 x 24cm.

GA80   The story of the U. S. mint at
D4   Denver. Prepared through the
            Denver Convention and Visitors
            Bureau by the Miller-Stockman
            Supply Co. Denver, n.d.
            unpaged. illus. 23cm.

GA80   Evans, George G., pub.
E9   Illustrated history of the United States
        mint with a complete description of Amer-
        ican coinage. Philadelphia, Evans, 1886-
        1893.
            illus., 24 pl. 23cm.

GA80   Ferguson, Eugene S., ed.
F4   Early engineering reminiscences (1815-40)
        of George Escol Sellers. Washington D.C.,
        Smithsonian Institution, 1965.
            203p. illus. 29cm. (Smithsonian Institu-
        tion Bulletin 238)

GA80   Franklin Mint.
F7   A tour of the Franklin Mint.
        Franklin Center, Pa., The Franklin Mint,
        n.d.
            20p. illus. 28cm.

GA80   Heaton, A. G.
H4   A treatise on the coinage of the U.S.
        branch mints. Washington, 1893.
            54p. 23cm.

GA80   Hickson, Howard.
H5   Mint mark: "CC"; the story of the
        United States mint at Carson City,
        Nevada. Edited by Guy Shipler.
        Carson City, Nevada State Museum [1972].
            124p. illus. charts, photos. 26cm.
        (Nevada State Museum popular series,
        no. 4)

GA80   Making money at the Philadelphia
M3   mint and the American Bank Note
            Company. A reprint of articles
            originally appearing in the Harper's
            New Monthly Magazine 1861-1862.
            Babylon, N.Y., Geo. A. Flanagan, nd.
            36p. illus. 26cm.

GA80   Sellers, George Escol.
S4   Early engineering reminiscences;
         the United States Mint. Taken from
         the American Machinist, N.Y., 1893.
              26p. 28cm.

GA80   Smith, Andrew Madsen, 1841-1915, pub.
S6c   Coins and coinage, the United States
         mint. Philadelphia, A.M. Smith, [1881;
         1884?].
              illus. 29cm.

GA80   Smith, Andrew Madsen, 1841-1915.
S6v   Visitor's guide and history of the
         United States mint, Philadelphia, Pa. ...
         with over 1600 fine engravings and full
         descriptions. Philadelphia, A.M. Smith,
         1885.
              175p. illus. 24cm.

GA80   Snowden, James Ross.
S66   Communication from the director of the
         mint to the Secretary of the Treasury,
         relative to a proposed branch mint at New
         York. Philadelphia, Board of Trade, 1860.
              12p. 24cm.

GA80   Steiner, Phillip.
S7   Foreign coins struck at mints in
         the United States, by Phillip Steiner
         and Michael Zimpfer. Wanatah, Ind.,
         the authors, 1974.
              unpaged. 28cm.

GA80   Stewart, Frank H.
S7f   History of the first United States
         mint; its people and its operations.
         Priv. printed, 1924, 1974.
              209p. illus. 23cm.

GA80   Stewart, Frank H.
S7y   Ye olde mint; being a brief description
         of the first U.S. mint, established ... in
         1792, at ... Philadelphia. Philadelphia,
         Stewart Electric Co., [1909].
              24p. 6pl. 23cm.

GA80   Stautzenberger, Anthony Joseph.
S8   The establishment of the
         Charlotte branch mint: a documented
         history. 1st ed. Austin, Tx., the
         author, 1976.
              186p. illus. 29cm.

GA80   Taxay, Don.
T3   The U.S. mint and coinage; an illus.
          history from 1776 to the present. Foreword
          by Gilroy Roberts. New York, Arco Publ.,
          1966.
              400p. illus., plates. 26cm.

GA80   Thompson, Walter.
T5   How United States coins are made. Chi-
          cago, Numismatic scrapbook. [1962].
              48p. illus. 19cm.

GA80   Thompson, Walter.
T52   [Articles on U.S. coins and mints from
Vert.   Numismatic Scrapbook, 1959-1961].
File   illus. 20cm.

GA80   U.S. Bureau of the Mint.
U5d   Domestic and foreign coins manufactured
          by mints of the United States, 1792-1965.
          Washington D.C., Government Printing Office,
          1966.
              119p. 24cm.

GA80   U.S. Bureau of the Mint.
U5do   Domestic coin manufactured by
          mints of the United States. Washington,
          GPO, 1936, 1950, 1958, 1961, 1963.
              29p. 24cm.

GA80   U.S. Bureau of the Mint.
U5f   Final report on a study of alloys suit-
          able for use as United States coinage to
          U.S. Dept. of the Treasury, Bureau of the
          mint. Columbus, Ohio, Battelle Memorial
          Institute, 1965.
              44p. illus., tables. 27cm.

GA80   U.S. Bureau of the Mint. Office of the
U5i   Director.
              Instructions relative to the transaction
          of business at the mint of the United States
          and its branches. Philadelphia, Benjamin
          F. Mifflin, 1858, 1908, 1917.
              22p. 24cm.
              Title varies slightly. 1908 edition also
          contains coinage laws.

GA80   U.S. Bureau of the Mint.
U51   The laws relating to the mint of the
            United States and its branches. Philadelphia,
            B.F. Mifflin, 1859.
                59p. 23cm.

GA80   U.S. Bureau of the Mint.
U5m   The mint story. Washington [1967].
                40p. illus. 20cm.

GA80   Young, James Rankin.
Y6   The United states mint at
            Philadelphia. Philadelphia,
            the author, 1903.
                87p. illus. 26cm.

GOVERNMENT REPORTS

GA85   Bowen, Thomas M.
B6   Coinage of silver dollars;
Vert.   speech of Hon. Thos. M. Bowen of
File   Colorado, in the Senate of the
            United States. Wash., 1885.
                13p. 23cm.

GA85   U.S. Congress. House.
U41   Laws authorizing issuance of medals and
            commemorative coins. Washington D.C., G.P.O.
            1938.
                168p. 23cm.

GA85   U.S. Congress. House.
U412   Laws of the United States relating to
            the coinage, 1792-1903. Washington D.C.,
            G.P.O., 1904.
                121p. 23cm.

GA85   U.S. Congress. House. Committee on Banking
U42c   and Currency.
                Coinage act of 1965; hearings before
            the ... 89th Congress, 1st session. Washing-
            ton D.C., GPO, 1965.
                418p. charts 23cm.

GA85   U.S. Congress. House. Committee on Banking
U42s   and Currency.
                Sale of standard silver dollars held by
            the Treasury; hearings before the ... 89th
            Congress, 2d session on H.R. 13150. Wash-
            ington, D.C., GPO, 1966.
                165p. 23cm.

GA85   U.S. Congress. House. Committee on Coinage,
U43c   Weights, and Measures.
            Circulation of silver; notes of a confer-
         ence between the committee on coinage, weights
         and measures, the Secretary of the Treasury
         and the Treasurer of the U.S. ... . Wash-
         ington, D.C., GPO. 1880.
            36p. 23cm.

GA85   U.S. Congress. House. Committee on Govern-
U44c   ment Operations.
            Coin shortage; hearings before a sub-
         committee of the ... 88th Congress, 2d
         session. Washington, D.C., GPO, 1964.
            various pagings. 24cm.

GA85   U.S. Congress. Senate. Committee on Banking
U72a   and Currency.
            Additional mint facilities; hearing before
         a subcommittee of the ... 88th Congress, 1st
         session on S. 874. Washington, D.C., GPO,
         1963.
            193p. 23cm.

GA85   U.S. Congress. Senate. Committee on Banking
U72r   and Currency.
            Retention of "1964" on all coins; hearings
         before the ... 88th Congress, 2d session on
         S. 2950, a bill to authorize the mint to
         inscribe the figure 1964 on all coins minted
         until adequate supplies of coins are
         available. Washington, D.C., GPO, 1964.
            104p. 23cm.

GA85   U.S. Congress. Senate. Committee on Finance.
U73c   Coinage laws of the United States, 1792-
         1894 with an appendix of statistics relating
         to coins and currency. 4th ed. Washington,
         D.C., GPO, 1894.
            847p. 23cm.

GA85   U.S. Supreme Court.
U79g   Gold clauses in obligation; opinions of
         the ... and the dissenting opinions ... .
         Washington, D.C., GPO, 1935.
            42p. 22cm.

GA85   U.S. Treasury Dept.
U8b   A brief history of coinage legislation in
         the United States. Washington, D.C., GPO,
         1891.
            20p. 24cm.

GA85   U.S. Treasury Dept.
U8g   Gold regulations. Washington, D.C.,
Vert.   GPO, 1954.
File   16p.   23cm.

GA85   U.S. Treasury Dept.
U8i   Information respecting U.S. bonds, paper
           currency, coin, production of precious
           metals etc. Washington, D.C., GPO, 1915.
               106p.   charts.   24cm.

GA85   U.S. Treasury Dept.
U8j   The joint commission on the coinage,
           transcript of the proceedings, Dec. 5, 1968.
           Washington, D.C., Treasury Dept., 1968.
               128p.   27cm.

GA85   U.S. Treasury Dept.
U8p   Provisional regulations issued under
Vert.   the Gold Reserve Act of 1934. Washington,
File   D.C., GPO, 1935.
               33p.   23cm.

GA85   U.S. Treasury Dept.
U8t   Treasury staff study of silver and
           coinage. Washington, D.C., GPO, 1965.
               91p.   charts.   24cm.

GA85   U.S. Treasury Dept.
U8w   The world's monetary stocks of gold, silver
           and coins (from annual report of the director
           of the Mint). Washington, D.C., GPO, 1968.
               88p.   23cm.

GA85   U.S. Treasury Dept. Bureau of the Mint.
U82c   Coinage act of 1965; a legislative history.
           Washington, D.C., GPO, 1965.
               various pagings.   25cm.

GA85   U.S. Treasury Dept. Bureau of the Mint.
U82i   Information relating to United States
           coins and medals. Washington, D.C., GPO,
           1930.
               8p.   24cm.

GA85   U.S. Treasury Dept. Bureau of the Mint.
U82l   Laws of the United States relating to
Supp.   the coinage, supplement. Washington, D.C.,
           GPO, 1912.
               36p.   23cm.

GA85   U.S. Treasury Dept. Bureau of the Mint.
U82p   Proceedings of the assay commission of
          1899 and text of coinage executed and
          reserved during the calendar year 1898 ... .
          Washington, D.C., GPO, 1899.
              33p. 24cm.

PATTERNS, MINT ERRORS, ODDITIES

GA90   Adams, Edgar Holmes, 1868-
A4   United States pattern, trial, and experi-
          mental pieces, ... by Edgar H. Adams and
          William H. Woodin. New York, American
          Numismatic Society, 1913.
              196p. illus. 24cm. (American numismatic
          series no. 1)

GA90   Barker, F. B.
B3   Cracked dies and flaws in the
          Lincoln cent. Sebring, Fla., the
          author, 1966.
              50p. illus. 22cm.

GA90   Bausher, Jess.
B39   "It's only money" (a comedy of
          errors); an illustrated reference
          and price guide for major mint errors,
          token errors, Canadian errors, foreign
          errors; by Jess Bausher and Charles
          Dolan. Birdsboro, Pa., Numismatic
          Enterprises, Inc., 1966.
              291p. illus. 24cm.

GA90   Breen, Walter.
B7s   The secret history of the Gobrecht
          coinages, 1836-1840.
              28p. illus. (Vol. 21, nos 5/6 Sept-
          Dec 1954), of Coin Collectors Journal.

GA90   Breen, Walter.
B7u   The United States patterns of 1792.
          New York, Wayte Raymond, 1954.
              16p. illus. 23cm. (Coin Collector's
          Journal, no 154, March-April, 1954)

GA90   Cohen, Jean, 1930-
C6   The classification and value of errors
         on the Lincoln cent; the encyclopedia of
         fidology. Written, compiled, and illus-
         trated by Jean Cohen. Lincoln cent
         imprint by Margood. Photography by
         Ganar Brown. [1st ed.] Bonita Springs,
         Fla. [1969]
              600p. illus. 29cm.

GA90   Cohen, Jean.
C6s   The spiked head; a study of
         head to rim die cracks on the Lincoln
         cent, their identification and value.
         1st ed. Bonita Springs, Florida,
         the author, 1967.
              28p. illus. 28cm.

GA90   Collectors of Numismatic errors (C.O.N.E.)
C63   Register of numismatic errors.
         1st ed. Dresden, Ohio, C.O.N.E., Inc.,
         1966.
              Sections separately paged. 22cm.

GA90   Curtis, James W.
C8   United States pattern coin handbook.
         Reprinted with additions from the Numis-
         matic Scrapbook Magazine, [1949].
              48p. illus. 20cm.

GA90   Curtis, James W.
C8u   United States pattern coin prices; 1946-
         1947 by Col. James W. Curtis. Reprinted from
         The Numismatic Scrapbook Magazine, [1948], 1955.
              16p. illus. 20cm.

GA90   Ford, Delmas.
F6   United States major and minor mint error
         types. Del City, Okla, The author, 1964.
              51p. illus. 21cm.

GA90   Goodman, Mort.
G6   The "Cud" error (and related items).
Vert.   The Author, n.d.
File   12p. illus. 28cm.

GA90   Goodman, Mort.
G6d   The design cud (and related items)
         Santa Ana, Calif, Mort Goodman,
         1969.
              135p. illus. 23cm.

GA90   Hardy, Howard O., ed.
H3   BIE handbook; best in errors. Ft. Lauder-
          dale, Fla., BIE Guild, 1972.
              42, cix p. ill. 28cm.
              Contains: The Gedko Catalog.

GA90   Herbert, Alan.
H4   The official guide to mint errors Alan Herbert.
          - New York: House of Collectibles, [1974]
              176p. ill. 22cm.
              Bibliography: p. 43-44.

GA90   Hewitt, Lee F.
H48   Price catalogue of United States
          pattern coins. Chicago, Hewitt,
          1936, 1940.
              44p. 23cm.

GA90   Jewett, E. G.
J4   Mistrikes and oddities in the Lincoln
          cent. Fresno, Cal., the author, 1960-
          1966.
              35p. illus. 21cm.

GA90   Judd, J. Hewitt, 1899-
J8   United States pattern, experimental
          and trial pieces. With the collaboration
          of Walter H. Breen and Abe Kosoff.
          Racine, Wis., Whitman Pub. Co., 1959.
              253p. illus. 24cm.

GA90   Kolman, Michael, Jr.
K6   The numismatic Lincoln cent errors.
          Cleveland, Ohio, Sunrise Printing Co.,
          1961.
              39p. illus. 21cm.

GA90   Kolman, Michael.
K6f   The numismatic flying eagle, Indian and
          Lincoln cent errors. Cleveland, Ohio,
          Federal Brand Enterprises, 1963.
              61p. illus. plates. 21cm.

GA90   Kramer, Albert.
K7   Identification and classification of
          the double "D" Lincoln cent varieties.
          Reprinted with additions from The
          Numismatic Scrapbook Magazine, 1965-1966.
          Supplements, 1968.
              87p. illus. 19cm.

GA90
M3c
    Margolis, Arnold.
      The error collector's handbook. [New York, Error Trends Coin Magazine], c1969.
      48p. illus. 21cm.

GA90
M3n
    Margolis, Arnold.
      The numismatic error primer. n.p., 1968-72.
      131p. illus. 22cm.

GA90
M6
    Morgan, Carl E.
      Lincoln cent oddities and valuable coins of other denominations. 2d. ed. n.p., C. E. Morgan, [1964].
      63p. illus. 22cm.

GA90
O4
    Olson, Warren L.
      A study of United States overdate coins copper and silver. Reprinted from The Numismatic Scrapbook Magazine, v. 32 (1966).
      26p. illus. 19cm.

GA90
S2
    Sams, Jack E.
      Primary die varieties of the 1960-D Lincoln cent; vols. 1-4 combined; a descriptive study and collector's guide. Wheeling, West Va., the author, c1961-1962.
      38p. 21cm.

GA90
S6m
    Spadone, Frank G.
      Major variety-oddity guide of United States coins, listing all U.S. coins from half cents through gold coins. Fully illus., with values. 1st-6th ed. Iola, Wis., Krause Pub., 1962-1974.
      illus. 22cm.

GA90
S6v
    Spadone, Frank G.
      Variety-oddity checklist record book of United States coins, 1st ed. East Orange, N.J., The author, 1965.
      83p. illus. 22cm.

GA90
S7
    Steiner, Phillip.
      Modern mint mistakes, by Phillip Steiner and Michael Zimpfer. La Porte, Indiana, Ideal Printing Co., [1972]
      149p. illus. 22cm.

GA90   Swalwell, Irving V.
S9   Research variety and oddity collection
        reference list of U.S. coins. Honolulu,
        The author, 1964.
            124p. 21cm.

GA90   Walker, Gerald E.
W3   Collector's guide and index to errors.
        [Hayward, Cal.?], 1967.
            51p. illus. 21cm.

GB10   Akers, David W.
A3   United States gold patterns;
         a photographic study of the gold
         patterns struck at the United States
         Mint from 1836 to 1907. Racine,
         Wisc., Western Pub. Co.; Paramount
         Internatl. Coin Corp., 1975.
             115p. illus. (part. col.) 27cm.
             -bibliography

GB10   Akers, David W.
A3g   United States gold coins; an
Vol.1   analysis of auction records. Vol.
         1-gold dollars, 1849-1889 by David
         W. Akers. Photography by Thomas
         A. Mulvaney. Englewood, Ohio,
         Paramount Publ., 1975.
             110p. illus. 26cm.

GB10   Akers, David W.
A3g   United States gold coins,
Vol.2   an analysis of auction records.
         Vol. 2-Quarter eagles, 1796-1929,
         by David W. Akers. Photography
         by Larry Stevens and Thomas A.
         Mulvaney. Englewood, Ohio, Paramount
         Publ., 1975.
             248p. illus. 26cm.

GB10   Baxter, William J.
B3   Gold is going higher; these shares
         should be bought. New York, Internatl.
         Economic Research Bureau, 1959.
             91p. illus. 28cm.

GB10   Breen, Walter.
B7e   Early United States half eagles, 1795-
         1838. [Chicago], Hewitt Bros., 1966.
             72p. ill. 20cm.

GB10   Breen, Walter.
B7mg   Major varieties of U.S. gold dollars.
         Chicago, Hewitt Bros., 1964.
             24p. ill. 19cm.

GB10   Breen, Walter.
B7mt   Major varieties of the United States
         three dollar gold pieces. Chicago, Hewitt
         Bros., n.d.
             19p. ill. 19cm.

GB10   Breen, Walter.
B7u   United States eagles. Chicago, Hewitt
         Bros., n.d.
             59p. ill. 20cm.

GB10   Breen, Walter.
B7vh   Varieties of United States half eagles,
         1839-1929. Chicago, Hewitt Bros., n.d.
             45p. ill. 20cm.
             Reprinted from Numismatic Scrapbook
         Magazine.

GB10   Breen, Walter.
B7vq   Varieties of United States quarter
         eagles. Chicago, Hewitt Bros., n.d.
             32p. ill. 19cm.

GB10   Carabini, Louis E., ed.
C3   Everything you need to know now
         about gold and silver. New Rochelle,
         N.Y., Arlington House, 1974.
             175p. 24cm.
             -bibliography, pp. 159-175.

GB10   Dryfhout, John H.
D7   The 1907 United States gold
         coinage. Cornish, N.H., Eastern
         Natl. Park & Monument Assn., 1972.
             12p. illus. 28cm.

GB10   Kaplan, Sol.
K3   History of Augustus Humbert and
Vert.   fifty dollar slug. Cincinnati, the
File   author, n.d.
             unpaged. 23cm.

GB10   Mason, Don Walter.
M3   Annual evaluation of U. S. gold coin
         prices, 1974-75. 2d. ed. The author,
         Long Beach, Ca., c1974; 1973.
             100p. 28cm.

GB10   Raymond, Wayte, 1886-   comp.
R3u   United States gold coins of the Phila-
            delphia and branch mints; listing all the
            dates and principal varieties and giving
            the average retail values with illustra-
            tions of all the types and rare dates,
            compiled & pub. by W. Raymond. New York,
            1928, 1933.
                24p. illus. 23cm.

GB10   Sinclair, James E.
S5   How the experts buy and sell gold
            bullion, gold stocks and gold coins
            [by] James E. Sinclair and Harry D.
            Schultz. New Rochelle, N.Y.,
            Arlington House, 1975.
                143p. 24cm.

GB10   Timmons, William L.
T5   The gold trial of Ercell and
            Paul Slone. El Paso, Timmons
            Pub., 1971.
                120p. illus. 18cm.

GB10   Turner, W. W.
T8   A study of popular U.S. gold sets ...
            The author, 1967.
                30p. illus. 28cm.

GB10   Wood, Howland.
W6   The gold dollars of 1858 with notes of
            the other issues. New York, A.N.S., 1922.
                7p. 2 pl. 16cm. (Numismatic notes and
            monographs, no. 12)

PRIVATE AND TERRITORIAL GOLD

GB15   Adams, Edgar H.
A3   Adam's official premium list of United
            States private and territorial gold coins;
            indicated by prices brought at public
            coin sales. New York, Willett, 1909.
                72p. illus. 18cm.

GB15   Kimmell's analysis of Pioneer gold.
K5   n.p., n. place, n.d.
                44p. 27cm.

GB15   Kosoff, Abraham.
K65   Pioneer gold coinage of the west. Sol
         Kaplan, c1964.
             24p. illus. 28cm.

GB15   Raymond, Wayte, comp.
R3   Private gold coins struck in the United
         States, 1830-1861. A complete illustrated
         list of the various coins issued by private
         assayers in Georgia, Carolina, Colorado,
         Utah, Oregon & California. W. Raymond,
         New York, 1931.
             32p. illus. 23cm.

GB15   Renz, Russell H.
R4   Private gold coinage of the United
         States. Detroit, Heath, [1938].
             23p. 24cm.

GB15   Seymour, Dexter C.
S4   Templeton Reid, first of the
         pioneer coiners. Reprinted from
         The American Numismatic Society
         Museum Notes, #19. (New York),
         1974.
             pp. 225-266. I plate. 23cm.

SILVER

GB20   American Numismatic Association.
A5   A proposal for the equitable
         distribution of silver dollars now
         held by the Treasury Dept. Colorado
         Springs, Co., American Numismatic
         Assn. [1967].
             sections variously paged. 28cm.

GB20   Beistle, Martin Luthur.
B4   A register of half dollar die varieties
         and sub-varieties; being a description of
         each die variety used in the coinage of
         U.S. half dollars as far as the issues are
         known, covering the U.S. mint at Philad-
         elphia, and branches at New Orleans, San
         Francisco, Carson City & Denver. Shippens-
         burg, Pa., The Beistle Co., 1929.
             261p. pl. 23cm. Biblio: p. 261

GB20   Behn-Miller Publishers, Inc.
B44   New silver coin boom. No. 1
         Encino, Calif, Behn-Miller Publ.,
         1968.
             66p. illus. 20cm.

GB20   Bolender, M. H.
B6   The United States early silver dollars
         from 1794-1803. Freeport, Ill., 1950.
             75p. 9 pl. 30cm.

GB20   Breen, Walter.
B7s   Silver coinages of the Philadelphia
         mint, 1794-1916. Coin Collector's Journal,
         1958, no. 159. New York, Wayte Raymond,
         1958.
             28p. 22cm.

GB20   Breen, Walter.
B7u   United States half dimes: a supplement.
         New York, Wayte Raymond, 1958.
             16p. 22cm. (The coin collector's
         Journal)

GB20   Browning, A. W.
B8   The early quarter dollars of the
         United States, 1796-1838. New York,
         Wayte Raymond, 1925.
             36p. 8 pl. 22cm.

GB20   Cline, J. H.
C5   Standing liberty quarters. [Dayton,
         Ohio, J.H. Cline, 1976.]
             135p. illus. 22cm.

GB20   Duphorne, R.
D9   The early quarter dollars of the
         United States; 1796-1838. Albuquerque,
         the author; Windsor Group, 1975.
             73p. illus. 23cm.

GB20   Hammer, Ted.
H3   U.S. dimes and their designers. From
Vert.   Numismatic Scrapbook, July 1952.
File   5p. illus.

GB20   Haseltine, John W.
H4c   Catalogue of John W. Haseltine's type
         table of U.S. dollars, half dollars and
         quarter dollars, also, many other rare and
         fine coins ... to be sold at auction by
         Messrs. Bangs & co., ... Nov. 29-30, 1881.
         Philadelphia, 1881.
             130p. 24cm.

GB20   Hazeltine, John W.
H4e   The early United States silver dollars,
         half dollars and quarter dollars; an
         arrangement of the different die varieties
         as described in "Hazeltine type table
         catalog" to which is added a list of the
         1804 dollars and other varieties not for-
         merly listed. Reprinted by B. Max Mehl,
         Fort Worth, 1927.
             76p. 23cm.

GB20   Hazeltine, John W.
H4h   Hazeltine type table catalog of early
         U.S. half dollars. Originally published
         in 1881 by John W. Hazeltine. Additional
         varieties by B. Max Mehl, 1927. Chicago,
         Hewitt Bros.
             55p. 19cm. (Numismatic Information
         Series)

GB20   Hazeltine, John W., comp.
H4t   Type table of United States silver
         dollars as compiled by John W.
         Hazeltine. A reprint. n.p., n. pub.,
         n. d.
             XIIp. 22cm.
             -xerox copy

GB20   Jones, John P.
J6   Money; speech of Hon. John P.
         Jones...on the free coinage of silver
         in the U.S. Senate. Washington, 1890.
             111p. 23cm.

GB20   Kelman, Keith N.
K4   Standing liberty quarters.
         Nashua, N.H., International
         Numismatica Corp., 1976.
             98p. illus. 22cm.
         (Numismatica Information Series)
             -bibliography

GB20   Klaes, F. X.
K5   Die varieties of Morgan silver dollars.
         Northampton, Mass.; the author, 1963.
             26p. illus. 27cm.

GB20   Kosoff, A.
K6   United States dimes from 1796. New
         York, Numismatic Gallery, 1945.
             25p. pl. 25cm.

GB20   McIlvaine, Arthur D.
M3   The silver dollars of the United States
       of America, with a short sketch of the
       1804 dollars. New York, A.N.S., 1941.
           35p. pl. 17cm. (Numismatic notes
       and monographs, no. 95)
           Bibliography: p. 35

GB20   Mallis, A. George.
M35   List of die varieties of Morgan head
       silver dollars. [2nd ed.] The author,
       c1966.
           120p. 28cm.

GB20   Margolis, Arnold.
M37   Mint errors on Carson City silver dollars
       offered for sale in auctions conducted by
       the General Services Administration of the
       U.S. government. Error Trends Coin
       Magazine. 1973.
           50p. illus. 21cm.

GB20   Newlin, Harold P.
N4   The early half dimes of the United
       States. 1883. Reprint, 1933.
           12p. 21cm.

GB20   Newman, Eric P.
N42   The fantastic 1804 dollar by Eric P.
       Newman and Kenneth E. Bressett. Racine,
       Whitman, [c1962].
           144p. illus. 23cm.

GB20   Overton, Al C.
O8   Early half dollar die varieties, 1794-
       1836. Colorado Springs, the author, 1967,
       1970.
           349p. illus. 23cm.

GB20   Osbon, James B.
O82   Jim Osbon's silver dollar
       encyclopedia. Richmond, Va.,
       Headquarters Pub. Co., 1976.
           271p. illus.; charts, graphs.
       26cm.

GB20   Patton, Pat.
P3   Bust half dollar, major die varieties.
       [Bethel Park, Pa., the author, 1967].
           unpaged ill. 21cm.

GB20   Piper, Richard.
P5   The elusive 1836 reeded half
          dollar by Richard Piper; foreword
          by Edward Rochette. n.p., Piper
          Publ., 1976.
               61p. illus. 22cm.

GB20   Raymond, Wayte, 1886-   comp.
R3   Silver coins of the United States mints,
          Philadelphia, New Orleans, Carson City,
          Denver, San Francisco, listing all the
          dates and principal varieties and giving
          the average retail values. Compiled &
          pub. by W. Raymond. New York, 1933.
               49p. illus. 23cm.

GB20   Rupp, Robert O.
R8   The silver twenty-cent piece.
          Ft. Collins, Co., the author, 1967.
               unpaged. 30cm.

GB20   Sheldon, John.
S4   Secretary Windom's plan concerning silver.
          N.p., n. pub., March 1890.
               pp. 205-223 24cm.
               Reprinted from the New Englander and Yale
          Review.

GB20   The silver question, memorial to Congress,
S5   January 1878. New York, Arthur & Bonnell,
               1878.
               49p. 23cm.

GB20   Stewart, William M.
S7   Silver and the science of money.
          Washington, 1894.
               97p. 23cm.

GB20   Valentine, Daniel Webster, 1863-
V3   The United States half dimes. New
          York, American numismatic society, 1931.
               79p. 47 pl. 17cm. (Numismatic notes
          and monographs, no. 48).

GB20   Valentine, Daniel Webster, 1863-
V3   The United States half dimes. Reprint.
1975   Lawrence, Mass., Qu rterman, 1975.
               273p. illus. 24cm.

GB20   Van Allen, Leroy C.
V35   Morgan and peace dollar varieties; a
              comprehensive guide and reference book on
              U.S. silver dollars. Baltimore, The
              author, 1965.
                  183p. illus. 21cm.
                  1971 edition: Guide to Morgan and
              Peace dollars, by ... and George A. Mallis.

COPPER, NICKEL

GB30   Andrews, Frank D.
A5   An arrangement of United States copper
              cents, 1816-1857. ... Vineland, New
              Jersey, 1883.
                  42p. 15cm.

GB30   Bowers, Q. David.
B6   United States half cents 1793-1857,
              by Q.D. Bowers and James F. Ruddy.
              Johnson City, N.Y., Empire Enterprises,
              1962.
                  47p. illus. 21cm.

GB30   Breen, Walter.
B7   The United States minor coinages 1793-
              1916. New York, Wayte Raymond, [1954].
                  16p. illus. 22cm. (Coin collectors
              journal, May-June, 1954)

GB30   Chapman, Samuel Hudson.
C45   The United States cents of the year
              1794. Philadelphia, 1926.
                  29p. 4 pl. 31cm.

GB30   Clapp, George H.
C55a   The United States cents of the years
              1798-1799. Sewickley, Pa., 1931.
                  64p. illus., pl. 31cm.

GB30   Clapp, George H.
C55b   The United States cents of the years
              1795, 1796, 1797, and 1800, by G. H.
              Clapp and Howard R. Newcomb. New York,
              A.N.S., 1947.
                  vi, 74p. 4 pl. 31cm.

GB30   Clapp, George H.
C55c   The United States cents, 1804-1814.
          New York, Wayte Raymond, [c1941].
              12p. illus. 23cm. (Coin collector
          series, no. 8)

GB30   Cohen, Roger S., Jr.
C6   American half cents, the "little
          half sisters". author, 1971.
              105p. illus. 29cm.

GB30   Crosby, Sylvester Sage, d. 1914.
C7   The United States coinage of 1793, cents
          and half-cents ... Boston, author, 1897.
              36p. 3 pl. 25cm.

GB30   Doughty, Francis Worcester.
D6   The cents of the United States, a
          numismatic study. New York, Scott, 1890.
              115p. 6 pl. 22cm.
              Reprinted by Holland A. Davis, 1934.

GB30   Frossard, Edouard.
F7m   Monograph of United States cents and
          half cents issued between the years 1793
          and 1857. Irvington, N.Y., The author,
          1879.
              58p. ix pl. 25cm.

GB30   Frossard, Edouard.
F7v   Varieties of United States cents of
          the year 1794 ... by Ed. Frossard ... and
          W. W. Hays ... New York, Priv. print.,
          1893.
              18p. 2 pl. 29cm.

GB30   Gilbert, Ebenezer.
G5   The United States half cents, from ...
          1793 to ... 1857. New York, Elder,
          [1916].
              43p. 6 pl. 25, 22cm.

GB30   Gilbert, Ebenezer.
G5v   The varieties of the United States
          cents of 1796, an arrangement by E.
          Gilbert and Thomas L. Elder. New York,
          Elder, 1909.
              [15]p. 2 pl. 30cm.

GB30   Hewitt, Lee F.
H4p   Price catalog of Andrews varieties
          of United States large cents; compiled
          from public and mail auction sales
          held in 1940 and 1941. Chicago,
          Lee F. Hewitt, n.d.
              40p. 19cm.

GB30   Hewitt, Lee F., comp.
H4u   United States large cents;
Rare   prices realized at 1933-34 auction
Books   sales. Chicago, Lee F. Hewitt,
          1934.
              79p. 15cm.

GB30   Kessler, Alan.
K4   The fugio coppers; a simple method
          for identifying die varieties with
          rarity listing and price guide.
          Newtonville, Mass., Colony Coin Co.,
          1976.
              84p. illus. 25cm.

GB30   Lapp, A. Warren, ed.
L3   United States large cents, 1793-
          1857; an anthology edited by
          Warren A. Lapp and Herbert A.
          Silberman. Lawrence, Mass.,
          Quarterman Pub. Inc., 1975.
              647p. illus. 24cm. (Gleanings
          from The Numismatist,7).

GB30   Loring, Denis W., ed.
L6   Monographs on varieties of United States
          large cents, 1795-1803. Lawrence, Mass.,
          Quarterman Publications, Inc., 1976.
              ix, 233p. illus. 29cm.

GB30   Newcomb, Howard R.
N4   The United States cents of the years
          1801-1802-1803. Detroit, 1925.
              85p. 5 pl. 30cm.

GB30   Newcomb, Howard R.
N4c   United States copper cents, 1816-
          1857. [New York, Numismatic Review,
          1944], 1956, 1963.
              284p. 11 pl. 31cm.

GB30   Raymond, Wayte, comp.
R3   The United States copper coins; an
        illus. catalogue of all the types and
        principal varieties of the copper cents and
        half cents, 1793 to 1857, ... description
        of the copper-nickel, bronze and nickel
        coins to date. W. Raymond, New York, 1931.
            21p. illus. 23cm.

GB30   Raymond, Wayte, comp.
R3s   Standard catalogue of minor coins
        of the United States...1st ed.
        N.Y., Scott Stamp & Coin Co.,
        1930.
            16p. illus. 23cm.

GB30   Sheldon, William Herbert, 1899-
S5e   Early American cents, 1793-1814; an
        exercise in descriptive classification with
        tables of rarity and value. With the coll-
        aboration of H. K. Downing and M. H.
        Sheldon. [1st ed]. New York, Harper
        [1949].
            xvi, 339p. 51 pl. 23cm.
            Bibliography: p. 26-27

GB30   Sheldon, William Herbert, 1899-
S5p   Penny whimsy, a revision of Early
        American cents, 1793-1814; an exercise in
        descriptive classification with tables of
        rarity and value. With the collaboration of
        Dorothy I. Paschal and Walter Breen. New
        York, Harper [1958].
            xii, 340p. illus. 24cm. (The John J.
        Ford, Jr. Numisco Series)
            Bibliography: p. 26-27.

GB30   Snow, Warren B., Comp.
S6   Large proof cents, 1817-1857;
        auction record and data over the
        last 14 years, 1946-1960. n.p.,
        W. B. Snow, 1960.
            unpaged. 29cm.

GB30   Steinberger, Otto C.
S75   Indian cent date varieties. Reprinted
        from Numismatic Scrapbook, [1962].
            15p. illus. 20cm.

GB30   Wallace, E. V.
W3   A numismatography of the Lincoln head
            cent. Reprinted from the Numismatic
            Scrapbook, [v. 18- v. 20, 1952-1954].
                87p. 20cm.

GB35   Hammer, Ted R.
H3   Types of U.S. nickel coins. From
Vert.   Numismatic Scrapbook, 1943.
File   [9]p. illus. 20cm.

ICONOGRAPHY, COMMEMORATIVES

GB40   American Numismatic Association.
A5   The story of the first coinage in America
            and the proposed commemorative coin to be
            minted in 1952 "the Pine Tree shilling ter-
            centenary quarter dollar". Prepared and pub-
            lished by the Pine Tree Shilling Tercentenary
            Commemorative Committee of the ... Philadel-
            phia, Magee, n.d.
                unpaged ill. 23cm.

GB40   Baker, Harold E.
B3   48 vs 73; a humorous touch on
Vert.   commemorative half dollars. Cincinnati,
File   Sol Kaplan, n.d.
                4p. 23cm.

GB40   Becker, Thomas W.
B4   Eisenhower, the man, the dollar, and
            the stamps. Edited by Ernest R. Lilley.
            [1st ed.] [Philadelphia] American Mint
            and Postal Society [1971].
                viii, 81[1]p. illus. port. 25cm.

GB40   Beware the Buy-Centennial; a candid
B49   report on investment opportunities
            for the collector of limited
            edition, commmemorative memorabilia.
            Rye, N.Y., Reymont Assn., 1974.
                unpaged. 22cm.

GB40   Bullowa, David M.
B8   The commemorative coinage of the United
            States, 1892-1938. New York, A.N.S., 1938.
                192p. ix pl. 17cm. (Numismatic notes
            and monographs, no. 83)

GB40   Daniel Boone Bicentennial Commission.
D3   Report ... to the 1936 General
            Assembly of Kentucky and appendix ...
            [1936?].
                62p. illus. 23cm.

GB40   Foster, Charles W.
F6   Historical arrangement of United States
            commemorative coins. Rochester, Museum of
            Arts & Sciences, 1936.
                73p. illus. 23cm.

GB40   Ganz, David L.
G3   14 bits; the story of America's
            Bicentennial coinage, 1976.
            Washington DC, Three Continents
            Press, 1976.
                102p. illus. 23cm.

GB40   Gettys, Loyd B.
G4   "AU" or "BU"; U.S. commemorative half
            dollars by Loyd B. Gettys and Edward M.
            Catich. A.N.A., 1958.
                17p. illus. 23cm.

GB40   Hobson, Burton.
H6   U.S. commemorative coins and stamps,
            by B. Hobson and Fred Reinfeld. New
            York, Stesling Pub. Co., 1964.
                64p. illus. 25cm. (Visual History
            Series).

GB40   King, Robert.
K5   Lincoln in numismatics. N.p., Token and
            Medal Society, 1966.
                variously paged ill. 23cm.
                Reprint of articles published in the
            Numismatist.

GB40   Krakel, Dean Fenton, 1923-
K7   End of the trail; the odyssey of
            a statue [by] Dean Krakel. [1st ed.]
            Norman, University of Oklahoma Press
            [1973].
                xvii, 196p. illus. 26cm.
                Includes bibliographical references.

GB40   McKinney, Willis J.
M3   U.S. commemorative half-dollars. From
Vert.   Numismatic scrapbook, [1943].
File   16p. illus. 20cm.

GB40   Mehl, B. Max, comp. & pub.
M4   The commemorative coins of the United
          States; a chronological and historical
          arrangement ... Fort Worth, [1937].
              59p. illus. 18cm.

GB40   Mosher, Stuart.
M6   United States commemorative coins
          1892-1939. New York, Wayte Raymond,
          [c1940].
              52p. illus. (Coin collector series,
          no. 1)

GB40   National Portrait Gallery, Washington, D.C.
N3   A nineteenth-century gallery of distin-
          guished Americans. Washington, Smithsonian
          Institution Press, 1969.
              93p. ports. 27cm. (Smithsonian publi-
          cation no. 4762)
              Bibliography: p. 93

GB40   Pettit, William A.
P4   The resurrection of the first
          Columbian half dollars. Chicago,
          the author, [1967].
              15p. 8 plates. 28cm.

GB40   Reed, Fred Morton.
R4   United States commemoratives, 1892-
          1954, by Mort Reed. 1st ed. Sidney, Ohio,
          Sidney Print. and Pub. Co., 1972.
              1 v. unpaged. illus. 26cm.
              Bibliography compiled by Frank Katen.

GB40   Ruby, Warren A.
R8   Commemorative coins of the United
          States (gold and silver). Lake Mills,
          Iowa, Graphic Pub. co., 1961.
              128p. illus. 22cm.

GB40   Skipton, Amy C.
S4   One fatt calfe, being an account of the
          New Rochelle half-dollar and of the cele-
          bration marking the 250th anniversary of
          the founding and settlement of the city of
          New Rochelle, New York. N.R. Commemorative
          coin committee, 1939.
              123p. pl. 22cm.

GB40   Slabaugh, Arlie R.
S5   United States commemorative coins; the
        drama of America as told by our coins.
        Racine, Wis., Whitman, [1962], 1975.
            144p. illus. 20cm.

GB40   Taxay, Don.
T3   An illustrated history of U.S. commemorative
        coinage. New York, Arco Pub. Co. [1967]
            viii,256p. illus., ports. 27cm.

GB40   Vermeule, Cornelius Clarkson, 1925-
V4   Numismatic art in America; aesthetics
        of the United States coinage, by Cornelius
        Vermeule. Cambridge, Mass., Belknap
        Press of Harvard University Press, 1971.
            xix, 266p. illus. 27cm.
            Bibliography

GB40   Weber, Charles E.
W4   Let's have new commemorative coins.
        American Numismatic Association, 1961.
        Reprinted from The Numismatist, Jan., 1961.
            3p. illus. 22cm.

GB40   Wood, Howland.
W6   The commemorative coinage of the United
        States. New York, A.N.S., 1922.
            62p. 6 pl. 17cm. (Numismatic notes
        and monographs, no. 16)

COLONIAL

GB50   Betts, Wyllys.
B4   Counterfeit half pence current in the
        American colonies, and their issue from
        the mints of Connecticut and Vermont.
        Address ... before the Amer. Numismatic
        and Archaeological Society. New York,
        1886.
            17p. illus. 23cm.

GB50   Crosby, Sylvester Sage, d. 1914
C7   The early coins of America; and the
        laws governing their issue. Comprising
        also descriptions of the Washington
        pieces, the Anglo-American tokens, many
        pieces of unknown origin, of the seventeenth
        and eighteenth centuries, and the first
        patterns of the United States mint. By
        Sylvester S. Crosby. Boston, The author,
        1875, 1945, 1965, 1974.
            2p. l., iii-v, 3p., 1l., 11-381p.
        illus. x pl. 31cm.

GB50   Del Mar, Alexander.
D4   The history of money in America;
         from the earliest times to the
         establishment of the Constitution.
         N.Y., The Cambridge Encyclopedia Co.,
         1899.
             121p.   24cm.

GB50   Durst, Sanford J.
D8   Comprehensive guide to American
         colonial coinage; its origins, history,
         and value. Bicentennial 1st ed.
         N.Y., the author, 1976.
             153p.   illus.   24cm.

GB50   Hickcox, John H.
H5   An historical account of American
         coinage. Albany, Munsell, 1858.
             151p.   5 pl.   21cm.

GB50   Newman, Eric P., ed.
N4   Studies on money in early America.
         Eric P. Newman, ed; Richard G. Doty,
         Assoc. ed. N.Y., ANS, 1976.
             216p.   illus.   23cm.

GB50   Newman, Eric P.
N4c   The 1776 Continental currency coinage,
         Varieties of the Fugio cent. New York,
         Wayte Raymond, 1952.
             20p.   6 pl.   23cm. (Coin Collector's
         Journal, July-August, 1952)

GB50   Newman, Eric P.
N4f   First documentary evidence on the
Vert.   American colonial pewter 1/24th real.
File   Reprinted from The Numismatist, July,
         1955.
             7p.   illus.   23cm.

GB50   Newman, Eric P.
N4j   The James II 1/24th real for the
Vert.   American plantations. Reprinted from the
File   A.N.S. Museum Notes XI, p. 319-332. New
         York, [1964].
             1 pl.   23cm.

GB50   Newman, Eric P.
N4s   The secret of the Good Samaritan shil-
          ling, supplemented with notes on other
          genuine and counterfeit Massachusetts sil-
          ver coins. New York, American Numismatic
          Society, 1959.
              xi, 71p. 9 pl. 23cm. (Numismatic notes
          and monographs, no. 142)

GB50   Scott, Kenneth.
S3   Counterfeiting in colonial America.
          New York, Oxford University Press, 1957.
              283p. 8 pl. 20cm.
              Bibliography: p. 265-266.

GB50   Tatman, Charles T.
T3   The beginnings of United States coinage.
          Reprinted from American Journal of Numis-
          matics, January, 1895.
              16p. illus. 18cm.

GB50   Vlack, Robert A.
V5   A catalog of early American coins, ...
          a comprehensive listing with valuations of
          early American coins and tokens used in the
          American Colonies and early America prior to
          the establishment of the United States mint
          issue of 1793 including the Washington issue
          up to 1796. Anaheim, Calif., Ovolon, 1963,
          1965.
              17p. 23cm.

POST COLONIAL TO 1860

GB60   Schilke, Oscar G.
S3   America's foreign coins; an illus
          standard catalogue with valuations of
          foreign coins with legal tender status in
          the U.S., 1793-1857, by O. Schilke and
          Raphael E. Solomon. [1st ed.] New York,
          Coin and Currency Institute [c1964]
              xvii, 211p. illus. 24cm.
              Bibliography: p. 203-205.

GB70
B6
    Boosel, Harry X.
       1873-1873. Rev. and edited from orig-
inal publication in Numismatic scrapbook
magazine, Mar. 1957 through Dec. 1958.
[Chicago] c1960.
      64p. illus. 21cm.

GB70
V4
    Venn, Theodore Joseph, 1860-
       U.S. three dollar gold pieces, large
U.S. cents, U.S. half cents, U.S. bronze
two-cent pieces; a series of four mono-
graphs on obsolete U.S. coinage. Chicago,
R. Thomas [c1919]
      72p. 20cm.

GB70
W5
    Willem, John M., Jr.
       The United States trade dollar; Amer-
ica's only unwanted, unhonored coin. New
York, Priv. printing, 1959. Racine, Wis.,
Whitman, [rev. ed. 1965].
      194p. illus. 23cm.
      Bibliography: p. 181-186.

LOCAL, A-Z

GB80
C3A3
    Adams, Edgar H.
      Private gold coinage of California,
1849-55, its history and its issues.
Brooklyn, 1913.
      xxviii, 110p. pl. 27cm.
      Reprinted from the American Journal of
Numismatics, 1911-1912.

GB80
C3B8
    Burnie, Robert Harry, 1916-
      Small California and territorial gold
coins: quarter dollars, half dollars,
dollars. [Pascagoula? Miss., 1955].
      96p. 30cm.

GB80
C3L4
    Lee, Edward Melvin, 1871-
      California gold, quarters-halves-
dollars; a descriptive list of privately
issued, interesting and historical coins of
small denominations. [Los Angeles, Tower-
Lee Co., c1932].
      94p. pl. 22cm.

GB80   Lee, Kenneth W.
C3L42   California gold dollars, half dollars,
           quarter dollars; a descriptive listing of
           the varieties of fractional issues in the
           personal collection of the author, plus a
           few additions noted and examined by the
           author. [Los Angeles, University Press,
           1970]
               xii, 138p. 23cm.

GB80   Yeoman, R. S.
C3Y4   The emergency coinage of the California
           gold rush. From: The Numismatist, v.57
           (1944).
               [9]p. illus. 23cm.

GB80   Mumey, Nolie.
C5M8   Clark, Gruber and company (1860-1865)
           a pioneer Denver mint. History of their
           operation and coinage. Denver, Artcraft
           Press, 1950.
               93p. illus. 25cm.

GB80   Miller, Henry C.
C6M5   The state coinage of Connecticut.
           Reprinted from: American Journal of Numis-
           matics, vol. 53, part 1 (1919). New York,
           A.N.S., 1920.
               62p. 5 pl. 29cm.
           Reprinted 1962, Ovolon, Wayland, Mass.

GB80   Adler, Jacob.
H3A3   Coinage of Hawaii by J. Adler and
           A. Kosoff. Reprinted from The Numismatist
           1960.
               28p. illus. 23cm.

GB80   Arndt, John P.
H3A7   The coins of Hawaii.
Vert.   4p. illus.
File   Photocopy of Coin Collector's Journal,
           n.s., v. 9, no. 2, March-April, 1942,
           pp. 36-39.

GB80   Gould, Maurice M.
H3G6   Hawaiian coins, tokens, and paper
           money, by Maurice M. Gould and Kenneth
           Bressett. Racine, Whitman, [1960, 1961].
               48p. illus. 19cm.
               Bibliography

GB80   Medcalf, Gordon G.
H3M4   Hawaiian money and medals; an illus
          price catalog of Hawaiian money, medals,
          orders, and tokens, 1837 to 1967 by G.
          Medcalf and Robert Fong. 1st ed. Kailua,
          Numismatics Hawaii [1967].
              43p. illus. 22cm.
              Bibliography: p. 43

GB80   Noe, Sydney Philip.
M4N6n   The New England and willow tree coin-
          ages of Massachusetts. New York, Ameri-
          can numismatic society, 1943.
              55p. xvi pl. 17cm. (Numismatic notes
          and monographs, no. 102)

GB80   Noe, Sydney Philip.
M4N6o   The Oak Tree coinage of Massachusetts.
          New York, American Numismatic Society,
          1947.
              viii, 23p. 10 pl. 29cm. (Numismatic
          notes and monographs, no. 110)

GB80   Noe, Sydney Philip.
M4N6p   The pine tree coinage of Massachusetts.
          New York, American Numismatic Society,
          1952.
              ix, 48p. 11 pl. 23cm. (Numismatic
          notes and monographs, no. 125)
              Bibliographical footnotes

GB80   Noe, Sydney Philip.
M4N6s   The silver coinage of Massachusetts.
          Lawrence, Mass., Quarterman Publications
          [1974, c1973]
              xiv, 246p. illus. 24cm.
              Includes bibliographical references.

GB80   Ryder, Hillyer.
M4R9   The copper coins of Massachusetts.
Vert.   From American Journal of Numismatics.
File   Vol. 53, pt. 1 (1919)
              [7]p. pl. 28cm.

GB80   Wild, William J.
M4W5   Six over twelve (Oak tree sixpence
          struck over oak tree shilling). The
          author, 1966.
              10p. illus. (Mimeograph) 21cm.

GB80   Wurtzbach, Carl.
M4W8   Catalogue of collection of Massachusetts
         colonial silver. Lee, Mass., 1937.
             8p. 8 pl. 28 x 22cm.

GB80   Guttag Bros., New York.
N4G8   New Jersey cents. New York, [1925?].
         59p. illus. 25cm.

GB80   Maris, Edward.
N4M3   A historic sketch of the coins of New
         Jersey, with a plate containing specimens
         of the Mark Newbie coppers, & issues of
         1786-7-8: with the obverses, reverses &
         combinations of the different varieties
         of the latter; and a detailed description
         of the distinctive differences and rarity.
         Philadelphia, W. K. Bellows, 1881, 1962.
             16p. front. 48cm.

GB80   American Numismatic Society.
N44a   The state coinages of New England.
         New York, 1920.
             77p. illus. 29cm.

GB80   Griffin, Clarence, 1904-
N6G7   The Bechtlers and Bechtler coinage, and
Vert.   gold mining in North Carolina 1814-1830.
File   Forest City, N.C., 1929.
             15p. illus. 22cm.

GB80   Roberts, Bruce.
N6R6   The Carolina gold rush.
         Charlotte, McNally and Loftin, 1971.
             80p. illus. 22cm.

GB80   Schultz, William J., Comp.
03S3   An historical sketch of Cincinnati.
Vert.   Presented in four papers from The
File   ANA convention program, 1931.
             Variously paged. illus. 23cm.

GB80   Newman, Eric P.
V4N4   A recently discovered coin solves a
Vert.   Vermont numismatic enigma. Reprinted
File   from Centennial Volume of the American
         Numismatic Society, New York, [1958].
             [12]p. 2 pl. 27cm.

GB80   Richardson, John M.
V4R5   The copper coins of Vermont. Re-
          printed from the Numismatist, vol. lx,
          May, 1947.
              24p. illus. 23cm.

GB80   Ryder, Hillyer.
V4R9   The colonial coins of Vermont. From
Vert.   American Journal of Numismatics, vol. 53,
File   pt. 1 (1919).
              [6]p. pl. 28cm.

GB80   Newman, Eric P.
V5N4   Coinage for colonial Virginia. New
          York, American Numismatic Society, 1956.
              57p. illus. 23cm. (Numismatic notes
          and monographs, no. 135)
              Bibliographical footnotes.

GB80   Tatman, Charles T., d. 1946.
V5T3   The Virginia coinage: proof that it
          was by legislative and royal authority.
          Worcester, Mass., the author, 1894.
              12p. illus. 18cm. (American Numis-
          matic Series, no. 2)

<u>CANADA</u>

CATALOGUES

HA30
C3
    Carmichael, Neil.
        Canada coin catalogue. Pt. 1:
    Decimal coinage. 3rd. ed., 6th ed.
    Toronto, the author, 1957, 1959.
        22p. illus. 24cm.

HA30
G8
    The guide book of Canadian coins, currency and
        tokens. Winnipeg, Canadian Numismatic
        Publishing Institute, 1958-70.
        10v. ill. 20cm. annual.
        1963-1966 includes modern British coins.
    1966 includes Australia and New Zealand.

HA30
H3
    Haxby, J.A.
        Coins of Canada by J. A. Haxby and R.
    C. Willey. Racine, Western, 1971, 1973.
        160p. ill. 20cm.
        Bibliography: p. 159

HA30
P32
    Park Coin Catalogue, 1936; The greatest
        numismatic guide of Canadian rare
        tokens, coins, and currency. [Winnipeg
        Park coin shop], 1936.
        182p. illus. 20cm.

HA30
S7
    Standard catalogue of Canadian coins, tok-
        ens, and paper money.
        Racine, Wis., Whitman Pub. Co.
        v. illus. 20-24cm. annual.

HA30
Z6
    Zoell, Hans.
        Canada, major and minor coin varieties
    including Newfoundland. Regina, Hobby Pub-
    lishing, 1961-1965.
        v. ill. 20cm.

HA30
Z6p
    Zoell, Hans.
        Premium catalogue; a complete and
    fully illustrated listing of Canadian
    and Newfoundland coins; fractional
    and paper currency plus...tokens.-
    including...U.S. coins. 8th, 10th ed.
    Regina, Saskatchewan, Hobby Pub.
    Co., [1967], 1963.
        48p. illus. 21cm.

HA30   Zoell, Hans.
Z6s   Simplified catalog of Canadian, New-
         foundland coins and paper money. 1st ed.
         4th ed. Canada, Hobby Pub. Co., 1962, c.
         1961; 1965, c.1962.
             40p. illus. 21cm.

COLLECTING

HA35   Breton, Pierre Napoleon, 1858-
B7   Popular illustrated guide to Canadian
         coins, medals, etc. Guide populaire
         illustre des monnaies et medailles Canad-
         iennes, etc. Montreal, [L'Imprimerie
         Modele, 1912]
             195p. illus. 27cm.
             English and French.

HA35   Charlton, James Edward, 1911-
C4   Standard grading guide to Canadian
         decimal coins, by J. E. Charlton and Robert
         C. Willey. Racine, Wis., Whitman Pub.
         Co. [1965]
             157p. illus. 20cm.

HA35   Paul, Cecil S.
P3   A guide for the grading of Canadian
         coins, by C.S. Paul and Gerald B. Parker.
         Watertown, N.Y., Hungerford-Holbrook Co.,
         1964.
             42p. illus. 22cm.

HA35   Raymond, Wayte, 1886-   ed.
R3   The coins and tokens of Canada; an
         illus list of all types of Canadian coins
         and tokens from 1670 to date, including
         official mint reports from 1858 to 1950.
         New York, W. Raymond, inc., 1937, 1947,
         1952.
             32p. illus. 23cm. (The Coin collector
         series, no. 12)

HA40
A5
    Allen, Harold Don.
        Canadian numismatic digest. Published
by Robert Verity for National coin week,
1960.
        73p. illus. 24cm.

HA40
B6c
    Bowman, Fred.
        Canadian numismatic research index.
Canadian Numismatic Research Society, 1969.
        177p. 20cm.

HA40
B6d
    Bowman, Fred.
        The decimal coinage of Canada and
Newfoundland. Reprinted from The Numis-
matist, 1962.
        24p. illus. 22cm.

HA40
B7
    Breton, Pierre Napoleon.
        Histoire illustre de monnaies et jetons
du Canada ... illus history of coins and
tokens relating to Canada. Montreal,
Breton & Co., [1894].
        239p. illus, 11 port. 28cm.
        French and English

HA40
L4a
    Leroux, Joseph.
        Atlas numismatique du Canada; par Jos.
Le Roux ... Numismatic atlas for Canada ...
[Montreal, Beauchemin & Valois, 1883].
        vi, 40p. illus. 23cm.

HA40
L4m
    Leroux, Joseph.
        Le medaillier du Canada ... The
Canadian coin cabinet ... Montreal,
Beauchemin, [1888].
        308p. illus. 25cm.
        French and English.

HA40
L4s
Rare
Books
    Leroux Joseph.
        Supplement du medaillier du Canada;
supplement to the Canadian coin cabinet.
Montreal, Beauchemin, [1890].
        illus. 24cm.
        French and English.

HA40   McLachlan, Robert Wallace.
M2   Presidential address ... ["The money
          of Canada from the historical standpoint"].
          Ottawa, Printed for the Royal Society of
          Canada, 1915.
               p. [51]-63. 8 pl. 25cm.

HA40   McLachlan, Robert Wallace.
M3   Canadian numismatics; a descriptive
          catalogue of coins, tokens, and medals.
          Montreal, 1886.
               127p. illus. 23cm.

HA40   Sandham, Alfred, 1838-
S2   Coins, tokens and medals of the
          Dominion of Canada; ... Montreal, D. Rose,
          Printer, 1869. Reprinted by Canadian
          Numismatic Pub. Inst., Winnipeg, 1962.
               72p. illus. viii pl. 20cm.

HA40   Vancouver Numismatic Society.
V3   Selected articles from the
          Vancouver Numismatic Society News
          Bulletin. Vol. 1,3. Vancouver,
          BC, 1963, 1964.
               2v. 23cm.

SPECIAL, TECHNICAL ASPECTS

HA50   Bowman, Fred.
B6   Canadian patterns. Ottawa, Canadian
          Numismatic Association, 1957.
               11p. illus. 23cm.

HA50   Heads and tales; a 60th anniversary
C3   souvenir of minting in Canada-
               the Royal Canadian Mint, Ottawa,
               Canada, 1908-1968. Toronto,
               Hunter Straker Templeton, Ltd.,
               1968.
          unpaged. illus. 25cm.

SILVER

HA55
C6
Vert.
File

Coin World.
     The fantastic story of the 1965
Canadian dollar varieties. Taken
from Coin World, Oct. 6, 1965.
     unpaged. illus. 25cm.

HA55
G5

Gilmore, Starr.
     Canadian silver dollars; voyageurs
and commemoratives. Edited by H. C. Taylor and Somer James. Photos. by H. C.
Taylor. Winnipeg, Canadian Numismatic
Pub. Institute, c1961.
     96p. illus. 20cm.

HA55
P3

Paterson, Donald D.
     How to make a dollar. [Don Mills,
Ontario, Canada, Studio Graphics,
1975.]
     unpaged. illus. 20cm.

COPPER

HA57
C7

Croghan, James R.
     Canadian cent varieties. [1st ed.]
Montreal, 1963.
     55p. illus. 23cm.

HA57
K8

Kurth, Howard H.
     Canadian coppers. A paper presented
to the Albany Numismatic Society.
Reprinted from the Numismatic Scrapbook
Magazine., n.d.
     unpaged. illus. 20cm.

HA57
P3

Park coin shop, Winnipeg.
     Canadian Provincial Copper Cents, 1858-
1859. Bert Kopen, Proprietor, Winnipeg,
1944.
     8p. illus. 23cm.

HISTORY

HA70   Bank of Canada.
B3   Pre-Confederation currency in
            Canada. Reprinted from Annual Report
            for the year 1966.
                 unpaged. illus. 23cm.
                 Contains also 1967 Centennial coins.

HA70   McLachlan, Robert Wallace.
M2   Coins struck in Canada previous 1840.
            Bruxelles, J. Goemaere, 1892.
                 15p. 23cm.

HA70   McLachlan, Robert Wallace.
M25   The money and medals of Canada under
Rare   the old regime. n.p., c.1890.
Books   27p. 24cm.

NOVA SCOTIA

HA85   Becker, J. Richard.
B4   The decimal coinage of
            Nova Scotia, New Brunswick and
            Prince Edward Island. 1st ed.
            Acton Center, Mass. the author,
            1975.
                 72p. illus. 23cm.

HA85   Courteau, Eugene Gaspard, 1868-
C6   The coins and tokens of Nova Scotia.
            St. Jacques, Que., 1910.
                 30p. vii pl. 24 x 20cm.

HA85   McLachlan, Robert Wallace.
M3   Annals of the Nova Scotia Currency.
            Transactions of the Royal Society of
            Canada, Section II, 1892, p. 33-68.
                 [36]p. 30cm.

COLLECTIONS

JA20
E7   Erbstein, Julius, d. 1907.
       Die Ritter von Schulthess-Rechberg'sche Munz-u Medaillen-Sammlung [von] Julius and Albert Erbstein. Lawrence, Mass., Quarterman Publications [1974]
       xvi, 435, 20, xiii, 603, 17p. illus. 23cm.
       A continuation of K.G. v Schulthess Rechberg's Thaler-Cabinet. Reprint of the 1868-69 ed. published in Dresden.

JA20
M3   Madai, David Samuel von.
       Vollstandiges Thaler-Cabinet. Konigsberg, 1765-1767. Supplement, 1768-
       4v. 19cm.

JA20
R4
Rare
Books   Reimmann, Johann Friedrich Christian, 1804-1891.
       Munzen- und medaillen: cabinet des Justitzraths Reimmann in Hannover. Frankfurt, Adolph Hess, 1891.
       3 vols. plates. 23cm.

JA20
S3
Rare
Books   Schultess-Rechberg, K.G. Ritter von
       Thaler-cabinet. Beschreibung aller bekannt gewordenen Thaler der Kaiser und Konige. Vienna, 1840-1867.
       4v. 24cm.

JA20
V6
Rare
Books   Vollstandiges Thaler-Cabinet, das ist:
       Historische-critische Beschreibung derjenigen zweylothigen Silver-Munzen, welche unter dem Namen der Reichs-Thaler bekannt sind, und seit drittehalbhundert Jahren her. Konigsberg und Leipzig, J.H. Hartung, 1747.
       868p. illus. 18cm.

JA40
H35
    Hazlitt, William Carew.
      The coinage of the European continent
with catalogues of mints, denominations,
and rulers ... London, Swan Sonneyschein,
1893, supp. 1897.
      xviii, 554p. illus. 21cm.

GOLD

JA63
H4
    Hewitt Brothers.
      Price catalog of modern European
gold coins. Chicago, Hewitt Bros., 1969.
      32p. illus. 20cm. (Hewitt's
Numismatic Information Series.)

JA63
H45
    Henze, Adolf.
      Das geld aller Volker; funfte
lieferung diese lieferung enthalt die
munzen und das papiergeld der Republik
Frankreich. Liepsig, Adolf Henze,
n.d.
      58p. illus. 27cm.

JA63
I8
    Ives, Herbert Eugene, 1882-
      Foreign imitations of the English noble,
New York, American numismatic society,
1941.
      36p. pl. 17cm. (Numismatic notes
and monographs, no. 93)

JA63
S3
    Schlumberger, Hans.
      Gold coins of Europe since 1800; a catalog
with variations. New York, Sterling, [1968].
      352p. ill. 26cm.
      Copies in English and German. German title:
Goldmunzen katalog; Europa seit 1800.

JA63
S3e
    Schlumberger, Hans.
      European gold coins guide book.
Iola, Wisc, Krause Pub.; Munich,
Ernst Battenberg, 1975.
      490p. illus. 26cm.

SILVER

JA65   Mey, Jean de.
M4   European crown size coins and
Vol. 1   their multiples; vol. 1 Germany
          1486-1599. Amsterdam, Mevius &
          Hirschhorn, 1975.
               331p. illus. 30cm.

COPPER, ETC.

JA67   Higgins, Frank C.
H5   An introduction to the copper coins of
          modern Europe, 3rd ed. London, Swan Sonn-
          enschein, 1892, 1910.
               95p. illus. 19cm. (The young
          collector series)

ICONOGRAPHY, INSCRIPTIONS, COMMEMORATIVES

JA70   Fassbender, Dieter.
F3   Spezialkatalog der gedenk-munzen
          Deutschlands, Osterreichs und der
          Schweiz seit 1918 mit bewertungstrend
          nach erhaltungsgraden. Munchen,
          Ernst Battenberg, 1973.
               311p. illus. 20cm.

JA70   Flamig, Otto.
F5   Monogramme auf munzen, medaillen, marken
          zeichen und urkunden. 2nd ed., rev., enl.
          Braunschweig, Germ., Klinkhardt & Bierman,
          [1968].
               184p. illus.
               Contents: 1. Medieval migrations 700-
          1500 AD 2. Cyrillic monograms 3. Prin-
          cely monograms.

JA70   Molnar, Imre.
M6   The commemoration of music on coins.
          [Reprinted with additions from Numis-
          matic Scrapbook, Chicago, 1956].
               26p. 20cm.

ANCIENT

JA79   Blanchet, Adrien.
B5   Recherches sur les monnaies celtiques
         de l'Europe centrale. Paris, Extrait
         de la Revue Numismatique, 1902.
             35p. illus. 24cm.

JA79   Gobl, Robert.
G6   Ostkeltischer typenatlas; mit
         52 tafeln. Braunschweig, Klink-
         hardt & Biermann, 1973.
             43p. 52 plates. 30cm.

JA79   Koenig, Marie E. P.
K6   Celtic coins: A new interpretation.
Vert.   From Archaeology, vol. 19, no. 1 (January
File   1966).
             [7]p. illus. 27cm.

JA79   LaBaume, Peter.
L3   Keltische munzen. Braunschweig,
         Klinkhardt and Biermann, [1960].
             52p. 20 pl., map. 19cm.

JA79   Pink, Karl.
P5   Die munzpragung der ostkelten
         und ihrer nachbarn...erganzte
         und verbesserte auflage...von Robert
         Gobl. Originally pub. in 1939.
         Reprinted- Braunschweig, Klinkhardt
         & Biermann, 1974.
             136p. XXX plates. fold. map.
         30cm.

MEDIEVAL

JA80   Albrecht, Gunther.
A5   Das munzwesen im niederlothringischen
         und friesischen Raum vom 10. bis zum
         beginnenden 12. jahrhundert. Hamburg,
         Museum fur Hamburgische geschichte, 1959.
             2v. xv, 208p. illus, atlas. 26cm.
         (Numismatische Studeen, Heft 6)
             Bibliography: p. vi-xv.

JA80   Cipolla, Carlo M.
C5   Money, prices and civilization in
       the Mediterranean world, fifth to seven-
       teenth century. Princeton University
       Press, 1956.
           75p. 4 pl. 22cm.
           Bibliography.

JA80   Chautard, Jules Marie Augustin,
C53   1825-1901.
           Les imitation des monnaies au type
       esterlin frappees en Europe pendant
       le XIII et le XIV siecle [par] J.
       Chautard. Originally pub. in Nancy,
       Imprimerie d'Academie de Stanislas,
       1871. Reprinted-Bologna, Studio
       Numismatico-Gamberini di Scarfea,
       1963.
           36 plates. 25cm.

JA80   Cox, Dorothy Hannah, 1893-
C6c   The Caperelli hoard. New York, Amer.
       Numismatic Society, 1930.
           17p. illus. 17cm. (Numismatic notes
       and monographs, no. 43)

JA80   Cox, Dorothy Hannah, 1893-
C6t   The Tripolis hoard of French seignorial
       and crusader's coins. New York, Amer.
       Numismatic society, 1933.
           61p. illus. viii pl. 17cm. (Numis-
       matic notes and monographs, no. 59)
           Bibliography: p. 60-61

JA80   Engel, Arthur, 1855-
E5   Traite de numismatique du moyen age,
       par Arthur Engel ... et Raymond Serrure ...
       Paris, E. Leroux, 1891-1905.
           3v. illus. 25cm.

JA80   Frey, Albert Tomer, 1858-
F7   The dated European coinage prior to
       1501. New York, 1914.
           92p. illus. 28cm.

JA80   Lelewel, Joachim, 1786-1861.
L4   Numismatique de moyen-age consideree
       sous le rapport du type. Paris, 1835.
           331p. illus. 21cm.

JA80
L5
Lhotka, John F.
    Medieval bracteates: an empirical
guide. Reprinted from The Numismatist,
v. 71 (1958).
    47p. illus., map. 23cm.
    Bibliography: p. 47

JA80
M4
Vert.
File
Merrick, J. M.
    Milliprobe analyses of some problematic
Burgundian and other gold coins of the
early middle ages, by Merrick and D. M.
Metcalf. From Archaeometry, vol. ii,
1969.
    [5]p. illus. 25cm.
    Bibliography

JA80
M58
Morris, Robert.
    Coins of the Grand Masters of the
order of Malta, or knights hospitallers
of St. John of Jerusalem; with a chapter
on the money of the crusaders. Boston,
Marvin & Son, 1884.
    70p. 6 pl. 23cm.
    Reprinted from the American Journal of
Numismatics, v. 17, v. 18.

JA80
M6
Morrison, Karl F.
    Carolingian coinage of Karl F.
Morrison and Henry Grunthal. New York,
A.N.S., 1967.
    465p. 48 pl., maps. 23cm. (Numis-
matic notes and monographs, no. 158)

JA80
P4
Plantijin, Christoffel, pub.
    Dongheualueerde gouden ... Antwerp,
1575.
    mostly illus. 16cm.
    Contents: Manual of medieval crowns
and money.

JA80
R3
Rackus, Alexander M.
    Guthones (the Goths), kinsmen of the
Lithuanian people. Chicago, Draugas,
1929.
    432p. illus. 20cm.

JA80
S28
Schembri, H. Calleja.
    Coins and medals of the Knights of
Malta. London, Spink, 1966.
    xii, 262p. 84 pl. 25cm.
    Reprint of 1908 ed.

JA80   Schlumberger, Gustave Leon, 1844-1929.
S3   Numismatique de l'Orient Latin.
        Graz, Akademische Druck-U. Verlagsanstalt,
        1954.
            2v. xii, 563p. 21 pl. 23, 30cm.
            Reprint of Paris ed., 1878-1882
            Bibliography: p. vii-xii

JA80   Schlumberger, Gustave Leon, 1844-1929.
S3   Numismatique de l'orient Latin. Paris,
Rare   Leroux, 1878-1882.
Books   2v. in 1, xii, 504, 22, 37p. 21 pl.
        32cm.

JA80   Tomasini, Wallace J.
T6   The barbaric tremissis in Spain and
        Southern France, Anastasius to Leovigild.
        New York, A.N.S., 1964.
            xxv, 302p. illus, [46] pl. 23cm.
        (Numismatic notes and monographs, no. 152)
            Bibliography: p. xiii-xxv

EARLY MODERN

JA83   Beeldenaer ofte Figuer-boeck, dienende op
B4   de nieuwe Ordonnantie vander Munte. ...
            Graven-Haghe, Hillebrandt Jacobsz, 1606.
            72p. illus. 19cm.

JA83   Caerte oft lyste inhoudende den prijs.
C3   (coins and mintmasters up to 1619)
            Antwerpen, Verdussen, 1620.
            132p. illus. 19 x 15cm.

JA83   Davenport, John S.
D3   European crowns; 1600-1700.
        Galesburg, Ill., the author, 1974.
            634p. illus. 24cm.

JA83   (Fliessbach, Ferdinand).
F5   Munzsammlung der wichtigsten seit dem
Rare   Westphalischen Frieden bis zum Jahre
Books   1800 ... Leipzig, M. Schafen, 1885.
            2v. viii, 444p. 120 pl. 27cm.

JA83   Spiess, Johann Jacob.
S6   Kleine beitrage zur aufname und aus-
        breitung der munzwissenschaft. Anspach,
        J.C. Posch, 1765-68.
            4v. in 1. illus., 7 pl. 17cm.

EIGHTEENTH CENTURY

JA85   Davenport, John Stewart, 1907-
D3   European crowns, 1700-1800.
        Galesburg, Ill., 1961, 1964, 1971.
            334p. illus. 24cm.
            Bibliography: p. 332-334.

NINETEENTH AND TWENTIETH CENTURIES

JA87   Davenport, John Stewart, 1907-
D3   European crowns since 1800, excluding
        the German states. Buffalo, Foster &
        Stewart [1947], 1964.
            v, 193p. illus. 24cm.
            Bibliography: p. 190-192
            2d edition title: European crowns and
        talers since 1800.

JA87   Dietzel, Heinz.
D5   Die munzen Europas ab 1945. Berlin,
        E. Proh, 1970.
            83p. illus. 17cm.

JA87   Harris, Robert P.
H3   A guide book of modern European coins,
        Racine, Wis., Whitman, [1965].
            202p. 20cm.

COLLECTIONS

JB20
B6
No.1
British Academy (London).
        Sylloge of coins of the British Isles;
Fitzwilliam Museum, Cambridge, Part I, ancient
British and Anglo-Saxon coins, by Philip
Grierson. London, Oxford University Press,
1958.
        xxii, 70p. 32 pl. 25cm. (Sylloge of coins
of the British Isles, No. 1)

JB20
B6
No.2
British Academy (London).
        Sylloge of coins of the British Isles;
Hunterian and Coats collections, University
of Glasgow, Part I, Anglo-Saxon coins, by
Anne S. Robertson. London, Oxford Univer-
sity Press, 1961.
        xviii, 88p. xlii pl. 25cm. (Sylloge of
coins of the British Isles, No. 2)

JB20
B6
No.3
British Academy (London).
        Sylloge of coins of the British Isles;
the coins of the Coritani, by D.F. Allen.
London, Oxford University Press, 1963.
        44p. 8 pl. 25cm. (Sylloge of coins
of the British Isles, No. 3)

JB20
B6
No.4
British Academy (London).
        Sylloge of coins of the British Isles;
royal collection of coins and medals, National
Museum, Copenhagen, Part I, ancient British
and Anglo-Saxon coins before Aethelred II,
by Georg Galster. London, Oxford University
Press, 1964.
        viii, 116p. 30 pl. map 25cm. (Sylloge
of coins of the British Isles, No. 4)

JB20
B6
No.5
British Academy (London).
        Sylloge of coins of the British Isles;
Grosvenor Museum, Chester, Part I, the
Willoughby Gardner collection of coins with
the Chester mint-signature, by Elizabeth
J.E. Pirie. London, Oxford University Press,
1964.
        xx, 43p. 16 pl. 25cm. (Sylloge of coins
of the British Isles, No. 5)

JB20
B6
No.7
British Academy (London).
    Sylloge of coins of the British Isles;
royal collection of coins and medals, National
Museum, Copenhagen, Part II, Anglo-Saxon
coins, Aethelraed II, by George Galster.
London, Oxford University Press, 1966.
    xiv, 148p. 71 pl. 25cm. (Sylloge of coins
of the British Isles, No. 7)

JB20
B6
No.10
British Academy (London).
    Sylloge of coins of the British Isles;
Ulster Museum, Belfast, Part I, Anglo-Irish
coins: John-Edward III, by Michael Dolley
and Wilfred Seaby. London, Oxford University
Press, 1968.
    lvii p. 16 pl. 25cm. (Sylloge of coins
of the British Isles, No. 10)

JB20
B6
No.12
British Academy (London).
    Sylloge of coins of the British Isles, 12;
Ashmolean Museum, Oxford, Part II, English
coins 1066-1279, by D.M. Metcalf. London,
Oxford University Press, 1969.
    xviii, 76p. 36 pl. 25cm. (Sylloge of
coins of the British Isles, No. 12)

JB20
B6
No.13
British Academy (London).
    Sylloge of coins of the British Isles, 13;
royal collection of coins and medals, National
Museum, Copenhagen, Part IIIA, Anglo-Saxon
coins: Cnut mints Axbridge-Lymne, by Georg
Galster. London, Oxford University Press,
1970.
    xxiii p. 54 pl. 25cm. (Sylloge of coins
of the British Isles, No. 13)

JB20
B6
No.14
British Academy (London).
    Sylloge of coins of the British Isles, 14;
royal collection of coins and medals, National
Museum, Copenhagen, Part IIIB, Anglo-Saxon
coins: Cnut mints Lincoln and London, by Georg
Galster. London, Oxford University Press, 1970.
    55-111 pl. 25cm. (Sylloge of coins of
the British Isles, No. 14)

JB20
B6
No.15
British Academy (London).
    Sylloge of coins of the British Isles, 15;
royal collection of coins and medals, National
Museum, Copenhagen, Part IIIC, Anglo-Saxon
coins: Cnut mints Lydford to the end, by
Georg Galster. London, Oxford University
Press, 1970.
    317-326p. 112-158 pl. 25cm. (Sylloge of
coins of the British Isles, No. 15)

JB20   British Academy (London).
B6   Sylloge of coins of the British Isles, 16;
No.16   collection of ancient British, Romano-British
           and English coins formed by Mrs. Emery May
           Norweb ... Part I, Ancient British, Romano-
           British, Anglo-Saxon and post-conquest coins
           to 1180, by C.E. Blunt, F. Elmore Jones and
           Commander R.P. Mack. London, Spink & Son,
           1971.
               ix, 87p. 17pl. 25cm. (Sylloge of coins
           of the British Isles, No. 16)

JB20   British Academy (London).
B6   Sylloge of coins of the British Isles, 17;
No.17   ancient British, Anglo-Saxon and Norman coins
           in Midlands Museums, by A.J.H. Gunstone.
           London, Oxford University Press, 1971.
               xxvi, 66p. 30 pl. 25cm. (Sylloge of coins
           of the British Isles, No. 17)

JB20   British, Academy (London).
B6   Sylloge of coins of the British Isles, 18;
No.18   royal collection of coins and medals, National
           Museum, Copenhagen, Part IV, Anglo-Saxon coins
           from Harold I and Anglo-Norman coins, by
           Georg Galster. London, Oxford University
           Press, 1972.
               xv, 116p. 54 pl. 25cm. (Sylloge, of
           coins of the British Isles, No. 18)

JB20   British Academy (London).
B6   Sylloge of coins of the British Isles, 19;
No.19   Bristol and Gloucester Museums, ancient British
           coins and coins of the Bristol and Gloucester-
           shire mints, by L.V. Grinsell, C.E. Blunt, and
           Michael Dolley. London, Oxford University
           Press, 1973.
               119p. 18, 9 pl. 25cm. (Sylloge
           of coins of the British Isles, No. 19)

JB20   British Academy (London).
B6   Sylloge of coins of the British Isles, 22;
No.22   royal collection of coins and medals, National
           Museum, Copenhagen, Part V, Hiberno-Norse and
           Anglo-Irish coins, by Georg Galster with
           Michael Dolley and Jorgen Steen Jensen. London,
           Oxford University Press, 1975.
               xxx p. 22pl. 25cm. (Sylloge of
           coins of the British Isles, No. 22).

JB20   British Academy (London).
B6   Sylloge of coins of the British 23;
No. 23   Ashmolean Museum, Oxford, Part III, coins of
          Henry VII, by D.M. Metcalf. London, Oxford
          University Press, 1976.
              xlviii p. 53pl. 25cm. (Sylloge
          of coins of the British Isles, No. 23)

JB20   British museum. Dept. of coins and medals.
B7   Handbook of the coins of Great Britain
          and Ireland in the British museum. By
          Herbert A. Grueber, F.S.A., assistant
          keeper of coins. London, The Trustees,
          1899, 1970.
              lxiii, 272p. lxiv pl. 23cm.

JB20   Great Britain. Royal Mint.
G7   Catalogue of the coins, tokens, medals,
          dies, and seals in the museum of the Royal
          Mint, by William John Hocking. London,
          Printed for H. M. Stationery Off. by
          Darling, 1906-10.
              2v. 26cm.
              Contents: v. 1 Coins and tokens
          v.2 Dies, medals, and seals

JB20   Nummi Anglici et Scotici cum aliquot
P4   Numismatibus recentioribus collegit
Rare   Thomas Pembrochiae et Montis Gomerici
Books   comes. [London, 1746].
              41pl. 37cm.

JB20   Spink and Son, London.
S6   Catalogue with numerous illus of a
          collection of milled English coins dating
          from the reign of George I to that of her
          present Majesty, and incl. patterns &
          proofs of coins of that period in gold,
          silver, bronze, etc. formed by H. Montagu
          London, 1891.
              175p. illus. 25cm.

JB20   Spink and son, London.
S6s   Some rare coins and medals illus-
          trating several centuries of English
          history from the past and present
          collections of Messrs. Spink & Son
          Ltd. London, 1910.
              11p. illus. 28cm.

CATALOGUES

JB30   Coin Monthly
C6   Coin year book. Brentwood, England,
            Numismatic Pub., 1969-1974-76.
                225p. illus. 21cm.

JB30   Friedberg, Robert, 1912-
F7   Coins of the British world; complete
            from 500 AD to the present. An illus
            standard catalogue with valuations of the
            coinage of the British Isles from 500 AD,
            the British Empire from 1600 AD [1st ed]
            New York, Coin and Currency Institute
            [1962].
                xii, 210p. illus. 29cm.

JB30   Standard catalogue of the coins of Great
S8   Britain and Ireland.
                London, B. A. Seaby. 1934-1960.
                v. illus. 24cm.

JB30   Standard catalog of British coins, I.
S82   England and United Kingdom that is,
                excluding Scottish, Irish and the Island
                coinages, Herbert Allen Seaby, editor.
                London, B.A. Seaby, 1962-1972.
                v. illus. 19cm. annual
                Note: Beginning with 1969 edition, part
            2 bound in.

JB30   Standard catalogue of British coins, part II,
S82   British coins 1816-1968, a catalogue of
Pt.2   modern coins with prices for each date.
1969   London, B.A. Seaby, Ltd., 1969.
                211-279p. illus. 19cm.

JB30   Seaby's standard catalogue, part 3, coins
S82   and tokens of Ireland, compiled by Peter
Pt.3   Seaby. London, B.A. Seaby Ltd., 1970.
                167p. illus. 20cm.

JB30   Seaby's standard catalogue of British coins,
S82   part 4, coins and tokens of Scotland,
Pt.4   compiled by P. Frank Purvey. London,
            B.A. Seaby Ltd., 1972.
                160p. illus. 20cm.

JB40   Avebury, John Lubbock, baron, 1834-1913.
A8   A short history of coins and currency,
in two parts. ... London, J. Murray, 1902.
   x, 138p. illus. 17cm. (Murray's
home and school library).

JB40   English, Scotch, and Irish coins; a
E5   manual for collectors, being a history
Rare   and description of the coinage of
Books   Great Britain, from the earliest ages
to the present time. London, Gill,
1883.
  160p. illus. 20cm.

JB40   Henfrey, Henry William, 1852-1881.
H4   A guide to the study of English coins,
from the conquest to the present time.
London, Smith; Bell, 1870, 1885, 1891.
   323p. front., illus. 19cm.

JB40   Humphreys, Henry Noel, 1810-1879.
H8   The coinage of the British empire: an
outline of the progress of the coinage in
Great Britain and her dependencies, from the
earliest period to the present time. By
Henry Noel Humphreys ... Illustrated by facsimiles of the coins of each period, worked
in gold, silver, and copper. London, N. Cook
1854, 1861.
   160p. XXIII (i.e. 24) pl. (incl. front,
partly col.) 24cm.

JB40   [Humphreys, Henry Noel], 1810-1879.
H8c   The coins of England. London, William
Rare   Smith, 1846.
Books   vi, xii, 120p. 23 pl. 20cm.

JB40   Jewitt, Llewellynn.
J4e   English coins and tokens...with a
chapter on Greek and Roman coins by Barclay V. Head. London, Swan Sonnenscheim,
1894, 1910.
   128p. illus. 18cm. (The Young
Collector series)

JB40   Jewitt, Llewellynn Frederick William,
J4h   1816-1886.
Rare   Handbook of English coins. ...
Books   London, W. Tegg, 1879.
   xvi, 77p. 10 p . 1 cm.

JB40   Leake, Stephen Martin, 1702-1773.
L4h   An historical account of English
Rare   money, from the conquest to the present
Books   time. ... London, Printed for W.
          Meadows, 1745., 3rd ed., 1793.
              428p. 13 pl. 20cm.

JB40   Morrieson, H. W.
M6   The influence of war on the
          coinage of England. Reprinted from
          the British Numismatic Journal. Vol.
          4. London, Harrison and Sons, 1908.
              15p. plates. 25cm.

JB40   Rawlings, Gertrude Burford.
R3   The story of the British coinage.
          London, George Newnes, 1898.
              224p. illus. 15cm.

JB40   Ruding, Rogers, 1751-1820.
R8   Annals of the coinage of Great Britain,
          and its dependencies; from the earliest
          period of authentic history to the reign
          of Victoria. London, Printed for J.
          Hearne, 1840.
              3v. pl. 29cm.

JB40   Thorburn, William Stewart, 1838-
T5   A guide to the coins of Great Britain
          & Ireland, in gold, silver, and copper,
          from the earliest period to the present
          time, with their value. London, L. U.
          Gill; New York, Scribner's [1884], 1898,
          1905.
              283p. illus., pl. 20cm.

JB40   Till, William.
T55   An essay on the Roman denarius and
          English Silver penny ... London, 1837.
              230p. illus. 20cm.

GENERAL WORKS WRITTEN SINCE 1910

JB45   Amstell, Margaret.
A5   A start to coin collecting; English
          coins, Elizabeth II to Charles II. London
          W. Foulsham and Co., Ltd., 1966.
              78p. illus. 22cm.

JB45   Berry, George, 1928-
B4   Discovering coins. Tring, Shire
        Publications, 1968.
            56p. illus. 18cm.
            Bibliography: p. 46

JB45   Brooke, George Cyril, 1884-
B7   English coins, from the seventh
        century to the present day. London,
        Methuen, [1932, 1950, 1952].
            xii, 300p. illus. 22cm. (Methuen's
        handbooks of archaeology)
            Bibliography: p. 243-247, 267-268.

JB45   Edge, Brian.
E4   Coins and all about them, a numismatic
        quiz; 600 questions and answers devised
        and compiled by Brian Edge. London, Faber
        and Faber; distributed by Transatlantic
        Arts, Levittown, New York [1973]
            143p. 21cm.
            Bibliography: p. 143.

JB45   Henshall, John M., Ed.
H4   Dealers in coins; the directory of
        dealers in coins and medals in the
        British Isles. Richmond, England,
        Numismatic Directories, Inc., 1969.
            120p. 21cm.

JB45   Josset, C. R.
J6   Money in Britain, a history of the
        currencies of the British Isles. London,
        New York, Frederick Warne, [1962].
            214p. 8 pl. 21cm.

JB45   Josset, C. R.
J6m   Money in Great Britain and Ireland;
        a history of coins and notes of the
        British Isles. Rutland, Vermont,
        Charles E. Tuttle Co., 1971.
            390p. illus. 23cm.

JB45   Linecar, Howard.
L5   An advanced guide to coin collecting
        [by] Howard Linecar. London, Pelham Books,
        1970.
            287p. illus. 23cm.

JB45   Oman, Sir Charles William Chadwick, 1860-
O5   The coinage of England. ... Oxford,
           Clarendon press, 1931.
                xii, 395p. xlv pl. 24cm.

JB45   Seaby, Peter.
S4   The story of the English coinage.
           London, Seaby, 1952.
                110p. illus., maps. 23cm.

JB45   Spink and Son, Ltd., London.
S6   The milled coinage of England, 1662-
           1946. [2nd ed.] London, 1950.
                145p. illus. 23cm.

JB45   Sutherland, Carol Humphrey Vivian.
S9   English coinage 600-1900 [by] C. H.
           V. Sutherland. London, B. T. Batsford
           [1973]
                viii, 232p. illus. 108 pl.
                Bibliography: pp. 214-219.

SPECIAL ASPECTS

JB50   Engstrom, John Eric.
E6   Coins in Shakespeare; a numismatic
           guide. Hanover, N.H., Dartmouth College
           Museum Publications, 1964.
                67p. illus. 22cm.

JB50   Ratcliffe, E. E.
R3   The royal maundy, a brief outline of
           its history and ceremonial, by E.E. Rat-
           cliffe & Peter A. Wright. [London, The
           Royal Almonry, 1960].
                32p. illus. 22cm.

JB50   Trowbridge, Richard J.
T7   Maundy coins of Great Britain. [1st
           ed. Long Beach, Cal., Coins of the
           British World, 1969]. 1972 2d ed.
                iv, 48p. illus. 22cm.

JB55   Brown, I. D.
B7   Coin hoards of Great Britain and Ireland
           1500-1967, by I.D. Brown and Michael
           Dolley. Lond., Royal Numis. Society,
           1971.
                88p. 26cm.

JB60   Craig, John.
C7m   The mint; a history of the London
          mint from A.D. 287 to 1948. Cambridge,
          University Press, 1953.
             xviii, 450p. 16 pl.
             Bibliography: 430-434.

JB60   Craig, John.
C7n   Newton at the mint. Cambridge, Univ-
          ersity Press, 1946.
             128p. front., illus. 19cm.

JB60   Crowther, G. F.
C75   A guide to English pattern coins in
          gold, silver, copper, and pewter from
          Edward I to Victoria. London, Gill, 1887.
             57p. illus. 20cm.

JB60   Folkes, Martin, 1690-1754.
F6   Tables of English silver and gold coins;
          first published by Martin Folkes, Esq.,
          and now reprinted with plates and explan-
          ations, by the Society of Antiquaries.
          London, 1763.
             216p. 67 pl. 29cm.

JB60   Grinsell, L. V.
G7   The Bath mint; an historical outline;
          by L. V. Grinsell; with a section on the
          Moneyers' names by Mrs. V. J.
          Smart. London, Spink & Son, 1973.
             47p. IV plates. 22cm.

JB60   Hocking, W. J.
H6   Simon's dies in the Royal Mint Museum
          with some notes on the early history of
          coinage by machinery. Numismatic Chronicle,
          1909.
             65p. 4 pl. 22cm.

JB60   Linecar, Howard W. A.
L5   English proof and pattern crown-size
          pieces, 1658-1960 [by] H. Linecar and Alex
          G. Stone. London, Spink, 1968.
             116p. illus. 26cm.

JB60   Nathanson, Alan J.
N3   Thomas Simon; his life and
            work, 1618-1665. Photographs
            by P. Frank Purvey. London,
            Seaby Publications, 1975.
                60p. illus. 25cm.

JB60   Newman, E. G. V.
N4   The gold metallurgy of Isaac
Vert.   Newton. Taken from the Gold
File   Bulletin, Vol. 8, #3, 1975.
                94p. illus. 30cm.

JB60   Newman, W. A. C.
N48   British coinage. London, Royal
            Institute of Chemistry, 1953.
                37p. 5 pl. 24cm.

JB60   Rayner, Peter Alan.
R3   The designers & engravers of the English
            milled coinage, 1662-1953. London, B.A.
            Seaby, 1954.
                26p. illus. 23cm. (Seaby's numismatic
            publications)

JB60   Great Britain. Royal Mint.
R6r   The Royal Mint, an outline history.
            London, Her Majesty's Stationery Office,
            1970.
                35p. illus. 22cm.

GOLD

JB63   Allen, J. J. Cullimore.
A4   Sovereigns of the British Empire.
            London, Spink, 1965.
                60p. illus. 21cm.

JB63   Cleveland Museum of Art.
C5   English gold coins, ancient to modern
            times; on loan to the Cleveland Museum of
            Art from the Norweb collection. [Cleveland
            1968].
                82p. illus. 25cm.

JB63   Duveen, Sir Geoffrey.
D8   The history of the gold sovereign, by
        Sir Geoffrey Duveen and H. G. Stride.
        London, Oxford University Press, 1962.
            112p. illus. 18 pl. 23cm.
            Bibliography: p. [107]

JB63   Kenyon, Robert Lloyd, 1848-1931.
K4   The gold coins of England, arranged and
        described: being a sequel to Mr. Hawkins'
        Silver coins of England, by his grandson,
        Robert Lloyd Kenyon ... London, B. Quaritch
        1884.
            217p. xxiii pl. 22cm.

JB63   Turner, W. W.
T8   Britain's 5 pound gold and the
        golden age. Leesburg, Fla., the
        author, 1975.
            15p. illus. 24cm.

SILVER

JB65   Hawkins, Edward, 1780-1867.
H3   The silver coins of England, arranged
        and described; with remarks on British
        money, previous to the Saxon dynasties.
        ... with alterations and additions by R.
        L. Kenyon. London, B. Quaritch, 1876,
        1887.
            vi, 504p. 54 pl. 23cm.

JB65   Hearn, G.
H42   Collection of milled silver crowns to
        sixpences. London, Hearn, 1973.
            36p. 25cm.

JB65   Henry, J.
H45   English silver coins issued since the
        conquest and their values with illus
        engravings, compiled by J. Henry. London,
        1889, 4th ed.
            64p. illus. 18cm.

JB65   Linecar, Howard W. A.
L5   The crown pieces of Great Britain and
        the British Commonwealth of Nations,
        1551-1961. London, Benn, 1962.
            94p. illus. 26cm.

JB65   Raymond, Wayte.
R3   The silver crowns of Great Britain
            and Ireland. New York, 1941.
                12p. 12 pl. 23cm. (The Coin collector
            series, no. 6)

JB65   Seaby, Herbert Allen, ed.
S4b   The British imperial silver coinage;
            or, The English silver coinage from 1649.
            Joint-editor: Peter Alan Rayner. London,
            B.A. Seaby, 1949, 1957, 1968.
                136p. illus. 23cm.
                Bibliography: 1968 ed; p. 201

JB65   Seaby, Herbert Allen, ed.
S4n   Notes on English silver coins, 1066-
            1648, to help collectors in their
            classification. London, Seaby, 1948.
                82p. illus. 23cm.

JB65   Spink & Son, Ltd., London.
S6   The milled silver coinage of England,
            from Charles II to the present day,
            including patterns and proofs, with a
            chapter on Maundy money ... London,
            Spink, 1925.
                134p. illus. 24cm.
                Reprinted from the Numismatic circular,
            1924, with revisions and additions.

JB65   Trowbridge, Richard J.
T7   Crowns of the British Empire.
            [Long Beach, Cal., 1970], 1971.
                vi, 164p. illus. 23cm.
                Bibliography: p. 160-164.

COPPER, ETC.

JB67   British Museum.
B7   English copper, tin, and bronze coins
            in the British Museum, 1558-1958. London,
            Trustees, 1960, 1964.
                xx, 648p. illus., 50 pl. 27cm.
                Bibliography: p. [xvii]-xviii.

JB67   Christmas, Henry, 1811-1868.
C5   [Papers on copper coinage, 1862-1863]
          12, 24, 24, 12, 16p. 22cm.

JB67   Crowther, D. J., Ltd., Pub.
C7   British copper and bronze coins issued
          from 1837 to 1952. London, [1966].
              36p. illus. 18cm. (Coin collectors'
          Pocket Guides, no. 1)

JB67   Henry, J.
H4   The series of English coins, in
          copper, tin, and bronze. London, 1879.
              27p. 22cm.

JB67   Montagu, Hyman.
M6   The copper, tin and bronze coinage and
          patterns for coins of England, from the
          reign of Elizabeth to that of Her present
          Majesty. London, 1885, 1893.
              xxiii, 150p. illus. 23cm.

JB67   Seaby, Peter John.
S4b   British copper coins and their values,
          ed. by P. J. Seaby & Monica Bussell.
          London, Seaby, 1961, 1963, 1968, 1969.
              112p. illus. 19cm.

JB67   Seaby (B.A.) Ltd.
S4c   A catalogue of the copper coins and tok-
          ens of the British Isles, compiled by
          Herbert Allen Seaby and Peter John Seaby.
          London [1949], 1952.
              142p. illus. 23cm.

ICONOGRAPHY, INSCRIPTIONS, COMMEMORATIVES

JB70   Trowbridge, Richard J.
T7   Latin legends on British coins,
          translated. [Long Beach, Cal., 1970].
              14p. 22cm.

JB80
B4
    Brown, Augustus.
        Coins of the first British
Empire, AD 287-296. N.Y., Attic
Books, n.d.
        12p. 1 plate. 20cm.

JB80
B4r
    Brown, Augustus.
        Romano-British coins. New York,
Attic Books, n.d.
        28p. plate. 20cm.

JB80
B7
    British museum. Dept. of coins & medals.
        A catalogue of English coins in the
British museum. Anglo-Saxon series ... By
Charles Francis Keary ... London, The
Trustees, 1887-93.
        2v. illus., 62 pl. 24cm.

JB80
C7
    Creeke, A. B.
        The regal sceatta and styca series of
Northumbria. Reprinted from the British
Numismatic Journal, v.1, 1905.
        32p. 2 pl. 25cm.

JB80
D6c
    Dolley, R. H. Michael, ed.
        Anglo-Saxon coins. Studies presented
to F.M. Stenton on the occasion of his
80th birthday, 17 May 1960. London,
Methuen, [1961].
        xv, 296p. 16 pl. 24cm.

JB80
D6p
    Dolley, Reginald Hugh Michael.
        Anglo-Saxon pennies. London, Trustees
of the British Museum, 1964.
        32p. pl. 22cm.
        Bibliography: p. 31-32

JB80
D6v
    Dolley, Reginald Hugh Michael.
        Viking coins of the Danelaw and of
Dublin. London, Trustees of the British
Museum, 1965.
        32p. map, 16 pl. 22cm.
        Bibliography: p. 31-32.

JB80
E9
    Evans, Sir John, 1823-1908.
        The coins of the ancient Britons.
With plates engr. by F. W. Fairholt ...
London, B. Quaritch, 1864.
        424p. illus., 26 pl. 24cm.

JB80   Hildebrand, Bror Emil.
H4   Anglosachsiska mynt svenska kongliga
        myntkabinettet, funna i Sveriges jord.
        2nd ed. Stockholm, 1881.
            viii, 502p. 14pl. 24cm.

JB80   Hildebrand, Bror Emil.
H5   Numismata Anglo-Saxonica Musei
        Academiae Lundensis ordinata & descripta
        Venia ampl. ord. philos. Lund. (In
        Lycio Carolino, 1829).
            48p. 20cm.

JB80   Lockett, R. Cyril.
L6   The coinage of Offa. Taken from
        the Numismatic Chronicle, 4th series,
        Vol. XX. London, Royal Numismatic
        Society, n.d.
            89p. plates. 23cm.

JB80   Mack, Richard Paston.
M3   The coinage of ancient Britain. London,
        Spink, 1953.
            x, 151p. 29 pl., maps. 22cm.

JB80   Mossop, Henry Richard.
M6   The Lincoln mint; c890-1279 by H.R.
        Mossop, D.F.C. Edited by Veronica Smart,
        M.A. Newcastle-Upon-Tyne, Corbitt & Hunter,
        Ltd., 1970.
            CIIp. plates; CIp. appendices;
        analytical appendices unpaged. illus. 25cm.

JB80   Pegge, Samuel, 1704-1796.
P4   A series of dissertations on some ...
        Anglo-Saxon remains ... also the coins
        engraved on a copper-plate. London, J.
        Whiston and B. White, 1756.
            xi, 42p. front. 28 x 22cm.

JB80   Petersson, H. Bertil A.
P42   Anglo-Saxon currency. King Edgar's
        reform to the Norman conquest. Lund,
        Gleerup, 1969.
            294p. pl., illus. 24cm. (Bibliotheca
        historica Lundensis 22)
            Bibliography: p. 274-280

JB80   Snelling, Thomas, 1712-1773.
S6   A descriptive catalogue of the ancient
Rare   British and British Roman coins...
Books   extracted from volume 1 of Materials for
          the history of Britain.
               20p.   17 pl.   34cm.

JB80   Stainer, Charles Lewis, 1871-
S7   Oxford silver pennies from A.D. 925-
          A.D. 1272, described by C. L. Stainer,
          M.A. Oxford, Printed for the Oxford
          historical society at the Clarendon press,
          1904.
               xiv, 93p.   14 pl.   22cm.   (Oxford
          historical society)

JB80   Sutherland, Carol Humphrey Vivian.
S8   Anglo-Saxon gold coinage in the light
          of the Crondall hoard.   London, Pub. on
          behalf of the visitors of the Ashmolean
          Museum, Oxford, by Oxford Univ. Press,
          1948.
               106p.   5 pl., maps.   26cm.
          Bibliographical footnotes.

JB80   Thompson, J. D. A.
T5   Inventory of British coin hoards
          AD 600-1500. [London].   Royal Numismatic
          Society, 1956.
               xlix, 165p.   24pl., maps.   25cm.
          Bibliography: p. ix-xi.

MEDIEVAL, ANGLO-GALLIC (1066-1485)

JB83   [Ainslie, George Robert], 1776-1839.
A4   Illustrations of the Anglo-French
Rare   coinage.   London, Hearne, 1830.
Books   x, 168p.   7 pl.   30 x 26cm.

JB83   Beresford-Jones, R. D.
B4   A manual of Anglo-Gallic gold coins.
          London, Spink & Son, 1964.
               90p.   4 pl.   tables, map.

JB83   British Museum. Dept. of coins and medals.
B7c   A catalogue of English coins in the
          British Museum.   The cross and crosslets
          (Tealby) type of Henry II. ... London,
          The Trustees, 1951.
               clxxiv, 216p.   25 pl.   23cm.

JB83
B7n
British museum. Dept. of coins & medals.
A catalogue of English coins in the
British museum. The Norman kings, by
George Cyril Brooke ... with an intro
and 62 plates ... London, The Trustees,
1916.
2v. lxii pl., tables. 24cm.

JB83
C6
Cox, J. Stevens.
The Ilchester mint and Ilchester trade
tokens. Ilchester, the author, 1948.
68p. illus. 19cm. (Ilchester historical monographs, no. 3)

JB83
D6
Dolley, Reginald Hugh Michael.
The Norman conquest and the English
coinage. London, Spink, 1966.
40p. illus. 22cm.

JB83
H4
Hewlett, Lionel Mowbray.
Anglo-Gallic coins. ... London, A.H.
Baldwin and Sons [ltd.] 1920.
xvi, 278p. illus., xvii pl. 22cm.

JB83
N6
North, Jeffrey James.
English hammered coinage. London,
Spink, 1960.
2v. illus. 26cm.
Bibliography
Contents: v.1 Early Anglo-saxon to Henry
III, c650-1272. v.2 Edward I-Charles II,
1272-1662.

JB83
N6c
North, J. J.
The coinages of Edward I & II.
London, Spink & Son, 1968.
39p. illus. 22cm.

JB83
O4
Ogden, William Sharp.
Concerning the evolution of some
reverse types of the Anglo-Norman coinage.
British Numismatic Journal, 1906.
29p. illus. 25cm.

JB83
O9
Owens, T.
The bishops of Durham and their
coinage. Taken from the Numismatic
Gazette. Newcastle Upon Tyne,
Corbitt & Hunter, Ltd., 1965.
sections variously paged. 21cm.

JB85   Cooper, G.O. White, ed.
C6   Nicholas Tyery's proposals to Henry the
Rare   Eighth for an Irish coinage ... ed. by
Books G.O. White Cooper and F.J.H. Jenkinson.
Cambridge, Deighton, Bell, 1886.
   51p. illus. 24cm. (Cambridge Anti-
quarian Society, Octavo publications, no.
22)

JB85   Farquhar, Helen.
F3   Portraiture of our Stuart monarchs on
their coins and medals. Reprinted from
the British Numismatic Journal, vol. v,
1909.
   262p. illus. 25cm.

JB85   Ferguson, W. D.
F4   The coinage of Henry VII of England.
Vert. From the Numismatist, July, 1947.
File   [5]p. illus. 22cm.

JB85   Henfrey, Henry William, 1852-1881.
H4   Numismata Cromwelliana: or, The medallic history of Oliver Cromwell, illus by
his coins, medals, and seals. ... London,
J. R. Smith, 1877.
   ix, 230p. illus., viii pl. 29cm.

JB85   Humphreys, Henry Noel, 1810-1879.
H8   The gold, silver, and copper coins of
Rare   England, 6th ed. London, H.G. Bohn, 1849.
Books   xviii, 136p. pl. 19cm.

JB85   Kent, E. R. Jackson.
K4   The silver coinage of William III,
1695-1701. London, Spink, 1961.
   10p. illus., 3 pl. 24cm. Reprinted
from the Numismatic Circular, May, 1961.

JB85   McLachlan, Robert Wallace.
M3   A touch piece of Henry IX. Reprinted
from The Numismatist, March, 1912.
   [6]p. illus. 23cm.

JB85   Marshall, George.
M37   A view of the silver coin and coinage
          of Great Britain from the year 1662 to 1837,
          containing . . . also an account of the silver
          coins struck in Scotland . . . London, John
          Hearne, 1838.
              161p. 26cm.

JB85   Nelson, Philip.
N4a   The coinage of William Wood for the
          American colonies. Amer. Numismatic
          Association, 1962.
              [16]p. illus. 22cm.

JB85   Nelson, Philip.
N4c   The coinage of William Wood, 1722-1733.
          By Philip Nelson ... Brighton, W. C.
          Weight, 1903.
              44p. illus., iii pl. 22cm.

JB85   Nelson, Philip.
N4g   The obsidional money of the Great
          Rebellion, 1642-1649. San Diego, Malter-
          Westerfield, n.d.
              66p. illus. 23cm.
              [Reprinted from: British Numismatic
          Journal, vol. 2, 1906.]

JB85   Nesmith, Robert I.
N42   The Lima pieces of George II of Eng-
          land. New York, W. Raymond, 1954.
              16p. illus. 23cm. (Coin collector's
          Journal, v. 21, no. 4).

JB85   Pegge, Samuel, 1704-1796.
P4   An assemblage of coins,
          fabricated by authority of the
          Archbishops of Canterbury. Chicago,
          Obol Internatl., 1975.
              125p. 1 plate. 26cm.

JB85   Schneider, Herbert.
S3   The five guinea and two guinea pieces
          of George II. London, Spink, 1957.
              7p. illus. 25cm.
              Reprinted from Numismatic Circular,
          v. 65.

JB85   Symonds, Henry.
S9   The Pyx trials of the Commonwealth,
Vert.   Charles II and James II. Reprinted
File   from the Numismatic Chronicle, 4th
          series. London, Royal Numismatic
          Society, 1915.
              6p. 22cm.

JB85   Symonds, Henry.
S9s   Some light coins of Charles I.
Vert.   Reprinted from the Numismatic Chronicle,
File   4th series. London, Royal Numismatic
              Society, 1916.
                   5p. 22cm.

JB85   Theobald, Ormond E. C.
T5   A short numismatic history of King
              Charles the First, 1625-1647; a talk given
              to the London Numismatic Club in February,
              1948. London, L.S. Forrer [1950]
                   16p. 19cm.

JB85   Trowbridge, Richard J.
T7   Queen Anne, 1702-1714; mystery farthings.
              [Long Beach, Cal., 1970].
                   19p. illus. 22cm.
                   Bibliography: p. 19.

JB85   Watson, J. H.
W3   Ancient trial plates; a des-
              cription of the ancient gold and
              silver trial plates deposited in
              the Pyx stronghold of the Royal
              Mint. London, Her Majesty's
              Stationery Office, 1962.
                   104p. illus. 22cm.

NINETEENTH, TWENTIETH CENTURIES

JB87   Bell, R. C.
B4   Unofficial farthings, 1820-1870.
              London, Seaby Publ., 1975.
                   248p. illus. 23cm.

JB87   Bressett, Kenneth E.
B7   A guide book of English coins, nine-
              teenth and twentieth centuries; a com-
              plete, illus valuation catalogue of mod-
              ern English coins with official reports
              of coinage figures for each year & his-
              torical notes about each issue. Racine,
              Whitman, [1962, 1964, 1965, 1966], 1968, 1975.
                   126p. illus. 20cm.
                   Bibliography: p. 124

JB87   Dyer, G. P.
D89   The proposed coinage of King Edward
          VIII, by G. P. Dyer. London, published
          for the Deputy Master and Comptroller
          of the Royal Mint by Her Majesty's
          Stationery Office, 1973.
              31p. illus. 22cm.

JB87   Freeman, Michael J.
F7b   The bronze coinage of Great Britain,
          (1860-1971). Glasgow, H.B. Langman, 1970.
              154p. illus. 28 pls. 22cm.

JB87   Freeman, Michael J.
F7v   The Victorian bronze penny (1860-1901).
          n.d.
              38p. illus. 21cm.

JB87   Raymond, Wayte.
R3   The coins of King George the Sixth.
          New York, 1952.
              32p. illus. 23cm. (Coin collector's
          journal, March-April, 1952)

JB87   Spink & Son, London.
S6   The development of English coinage.
          Elizabeth I - Elizabeth II. [London],
          The Midland Bank in collaboration with
          Spink & Son, [1963].
              31p. illus. 17 x 20cm.

JB87   Taylor, H.C.
T3   The guide book of Great Britain's
          modern coins 1860 to 1960 A.D. [by] H.C.
          Taylor and Somer James ... Price list in
          dollars. 1st ed ... Winnipeg, Canadian
          Numismatic Publishing Institute, 1961.
              88p. illus. 19cm.

JB87   Trowbridge, Richard J.
T7   History, coinage, paper notes and
          medals of Edward VIII of Great Britain.
          [Long Beach, Cal., 1970].
              56p. illus. 21cm.

JB90 Coffey, G.
C6   Guide to the collection of Irish antiquities,
(Royal Irish Academy collection); Anglo Irish
coins. Dublin, National Museum of Science and
art, 1911.
    105p. 21cm.

JB90 Dolley, Reginald Hugh Michael.
D551   Medieval Anglo-Irish coins by
Michael Dolley. London, B. A.
Seaby, 1972.
    90p. illus. 26cm.

JB90 Dowle, Anthony.
D6   The guide book to the coinage of Ireland
from 995 AD to the present day, by A. Dowle
& Patrick Finn; foreword by Michael Dolley.
London, Spink, 1969.
    127p. illus., map. 19cm.
    Bibliography: p. 119-125

JB90 Lindsay, John, 1789-1870.
L5   A view of the coinage of Ireland, from
the invasion of the Danes to the reign of
George IV.; with some account of the ring
money; also, copious tables, etc.
Cork, Printed by L. H. Bolster, 1839.
    143p. 14 pl. 27cm.

JB90 Nelson, Philip.
N4   The coinage of Ireland in copper, tin,
and pewter, 1460-1826. London, Spink,
1905.
    98p. 6 pl. 25cm.

JB90 O'Sullivan, William.
O8   The earliest Anglo-Irish coinage, by
William O'Sullivan. Dublin, The
Stationery Office, 1964.
    88p. illus. 10 pl. 25cm.

JB90 Remick, Jerome H.
R4   The coinage of the Republic of Ireland.
1928-1968. San Antonio, Almanzar's
[1967], 1968.
    59p. illus. 21cm.
    Bibliography: p. 59

JB90   Simon, James, 18th cent.
S5   Simon's Essay on Irish coins, and of
            the currency of foreign monies in Ireland.
            Dublin, Printed for the editors, by G. A.
            Procter, 1810.
                x, 180, 13p. 12 pl. 27 x 22cm.

JB90   Westropp, M. S. Dudley.
W4   Notes on Irish money weights and
Vert.   foreign coin current in Ireland. Dublin,
File   Hodges Figgis, 1916.
                31p. 1 pl.

JB90   Young, Derek.
Y6   Coin catalogue of Ireland; 1722-1968.
            3rd ed. Dublin, Stagecast Pub., 1968.
                72p. illus. 22cm. (Coin record series
            #1)

SCOTLAND

JB93   Burns, Edward, d. 1886.
B8   The coinage of Scotland, illus from the
            cabinet of Thomas Coats of Ferguslie and
            other collections. ... Edinburgh, A. and
            C. Black, 1887.
                3v. illus., lxxviii pl. 31cm.

JB93   Cardonnel-Lawson, Adam Mansfeldt de, d. 1820.
C3   Numismata Scotiae, or A series of the
Rare   Scottish coinage, from the reign of
Books   William the Lion to the union. Edinburgh,
            Printed for G. Nicol, 1786.
                157, 33p. 20 pl. 30 x 24cm.

JB93   Cochran Patrich, Robert William, 1842-1897.
C6n   Notes on the annals of the Scottish
            coinage. Communicated to The Numismatic
            Society of London, London, 1872.
                17, 21, 24, 13p. 22cm.

JB93   Cochran-Patrick, Robert William, 1842-1897.
C6r   Records of the coinage of Scotland,
Rare   from the earliest period to the union;
Books   collected by R. W. Cochran-Patrick ...
            Edinburgh, 1876.
                2v. xvi pl. 29cm.

JB93   Lindsay, John, 1786-1870.
L5   A view of the coinage of Scotland, with
          copious tables, lists, descriptions, and
          extracts from acts of Parliament; and an
          account of numerous hoards or parcels of
          coins discovered in Scotland, and of Scot-
          tish coins found in Ireland. Cork, Printed
          by Messrs. Bolster, 1845.
              viii, 291p. 18 pl. 28cm.

              ---- A supplement to the coinage of Scotland,
          ... Cork, Philip John Crowe, 1859.
              64p. 3 pl. 28cm.

              ---- A second supplement to the coinage of
          Scotland, ... Cork, Philip John Crowe, 1868.
              48p. 2 pl. 28cm.

JB93   Robertson, John Drummond.
R6   A handbook to the coinage of Scotland.
          London, Bell, 1878.
              xxvi, 146p. 22cm.

JB93   Stewart, Ian Halley.
S7   The Scottish coinage. London, Spink,
          1955, 1967.
              181p. illus. 22cm.

ISLE OF MAN, LUNDY

JB94   Becker, Thomas W.
B4   The puffin coins of Lundy [1961].
              16p. illus. 19cm.
              Reprinted from Numismatic Scrapbook,
          v. 26.

JB94   Boundy, Wyndham S.
B6   Bushell and Harman of Lundy.
          Grenville, Gazette Printing Service, [1961].
              95p. illus. 19cm.

JB94   Nelson, Philip.
N4   The coinage of the Isle of Man. London
          Spink, 1899.
              51p. 4pl. 22cm.
              Reprinted from Numismatic Chronicle,
          v. 19 (1899).

JB94   Parsons, H. Alexander.
P3   The earliest coinage of the Isle of
Vert.   Man, London, Spink, 1935.
File   19p. illus. 23cm.
                 Reprinted from the Numismatic Circular.

CHANNEL ISLANDS

JB95   Almanzar, Alcedo.
A3   Coins of Guernsey and Jersey (the
            British Channel Islands). San
            Antonio, Almanzar's Coins of the World,
            1965.
                 19p. illus. 22cm.

JB95   Exley, W.
E9   Guernsey coinage; a historical &
            numismatic monograph. [Guernsey Press,
            1968].
                 40p. illus. 19cm.

JB95   Howlett, C. J.
H6   History and catalogue of Channel
            Islands coinages. St. Martins, Guernsey,
            Le Mont Durand, 1968.
                 20p. pl. 22cm.

BRITISH COMMONWEALTH

JB96   Atkins, James.
A8   The coins and tokens of the possessions
            and colonies of the British empire. Lon-
            don, B. Quaritch, 1889.
                 vi, 402p. illus. 23cm.

JB96   Clark, James W., comp.
C5   The colonial coinage of Great Britain
Vert.   during the reign of Edward VII, (1902-10).
File   With mintage figures. Alexandria, VA,
            the author, 1964.
                 5 typewritten p. 28cm.

JB96   Guide Book and catalogue of British Common-
G8   wealth coins, 1750-1967 ... by Jerome
        Remick and Somer James. Winnipeg, Regency,
        1967, 1969, 1971.
        310p. ill. 20cm.
        Contents: Canadian coins, 9th ed. - British
        Commonwealth, 1st ed. - Great Britain's modern
        coins, 6th ed. - Australian and New Zealand
        coins, 2d ed.

JB96   Harris, Robert P.
H3   A guide book of modern British Common-
        wealth coins. Racine, Western, [1970].
        128p. illus. 20cm.
        Bibliography: p. 124-125.

JB96   Howorth, Daniel F.
H6   Coins and tokens of the English
        colonies ... with an intro chapter by
        Samuel Smith. London, Swan Sonnenschein,
        1890.
            93p. illus. 19cm. (Young Collector
        Series)

JB96   Linecar, Howard W. A.
L5   British commonwealth coinage. London,
        Ernest Benn, 1959.
            291p. 26 pl., maps. 22cm.

JB96   Pridmore, F.
P7   The coins of the British Commonwealth
        of Nations to the end of the reign of
        George VI, 1952. [London] Spink, 1960-
        1965, 1975.
            4v. illus. 25cm.

JB96   Raymond, Wayte, ed.
R3   Great Britain & Ireland and
        British Colonies in Europe. N.Y.,
        Wayte Raymond, 1955.
            24p. illus. 23cm.
        (Coins of the world).

JB96   Raymond, Wayte, Ed.
R3b   British colonies and dominions
        in Asia and the Pacific (except
        India.) Special printing. N.Y.,
        W. Raymond, 1955.
            28p. illus. 23cm.
        (Coins of the world.)

JB96   Scaife, J. Verner.
S3   British colonial coins and tokens.
          Reprinted from The Numismatist, 1962.
              87p. illus. 22cm.

JB96   Wright, Laurence Victor Ward.
W7   Colonial and Commonwealth coins; a
          practical guide to the series. London,
          G. G. Harrap [1959].
              236p. illus. 23cm.

GENERAL WORKS

JC10   Galster, Georg.
G3   Unionstidens Udmontninger;
          Danmark og Norge 1397-1540,
          Sverige 1363-1521. With a
          summary in English. Kobenhavn,
          Dansk Numismatisk Forening, 1972.
                119p. illus. 32cm.

JC10   Hede, Holger.
H4   Danmarks og Norges monter, 1541, 1814,
          1970, [by] Holger Hede. Copenhagen, Selskabet
          Den kgl. Mont-og Medaillesamlings Venner,
          1971.
                223p. illus. 32cm.

JC10   Hobson, Burton.
H6   Catalogue of Scandinavian coins; gold,
          silver, and minor coins since 1534 with
          their valuations. New York, Sterling
          Pub. Co. [c.1970], 1972.
                128p. illus. 27cm.

JC10   Holm, Johan Christian.
H64   Nordiske Monter efter 1808. Copenhagen
          Politikens forlag, 1969.
                302p. illus. 17cm.

JC10   Schou, H. H.
S3   Beskrivelse af Danske og Norske monter,
          1448-1814 og Danske monter, 1815-1923.
          Copenhagen, Numismatisk Forening, 1926.
                2v. 380p. 51 pl. 31cm.

JC10   Sieg, Frovin.
S5   Sieg' montkatalog, with English
          summary, [by] Frovin Sieg. Denmark, 1971-75.
                222p. illus. 21cm.

DENMARK - GENERAL

JC20   Bendixen, Kirsten.
B4   Denmark's money. N.p., National Museum of
          Denmark, 1967.
              116p. ill. 21cm.

JC20   Galster, Georg, 1889-
G2   Coins and history, selected numismatic
          essays. Denmark, Aarhus, 1959.
              149p. ill. 28cm.
              Bibliography: p. 7-13.

JC20   Galster, Georg.
G3c   Christiern II's Danske monter.
          Taken from Norsk Numismatisk
          Forening, 1928.
              16p. 23cm. (Norsk numismatisk
          forenings smaskrifter, #3)

JC20   Galster, Georg.
G3m   Die Munzen Danemarks (bis etwa 1625).
          Halle (Saale) A. Riechman, 1939.
              60p. illus. 23cm.
              Reprinted from Blatter fur Munzfreunde,
          v. 72-73 (1937-38)

JC20   Holm, Johan Chr.
H6   Danske monter, 1848-1947. 2nd ed.
          Copenhagen, J. Holm, 1960.
              57p. illus. 17cm.

JC20   Somod, Jorgen.
S6   Danmarks monter fra middelalder til
          nutid, by Jorgen Somod. Ulbjerg, Denmark,
          Sieg's Forlag, 1971, 1973, 1975.
              53pp. 21cm.

DENMARK - SPECIAL, TECHNICAL ASPECTS

JC30   Eklund, O. P.
E4   Copper coins of Denmark and her
          possessions. Reprinted from The Numis-
          matist, v. 58 (1945), 1962.
              14p. illus. 22cm.

JC40   Becker, Thomas William.
B4   The althing coins of Iceland.
Vert.   Reprinted from The Numismatic Scrapbook,
File   v. 24 (1958).
               5p. illus. 23cm.

JC40   Carlson, O. B.
C3   The coinage of Iceland and Greenland.
           Reprinted from The Numismatist, 1962.
               8p. illus. 21cm.

JC40   Kolbeinsson, Finnur.
K6   Islenzkar Myntir. 1969, 1970.
           Raykjavik, Frimerkjamidstodin.
               illus. 21cm.

NORWAY - GENERAL, HISTORICAL

JC50   Aamlid, Jan Olav.
A2   Norges mynter 1628-1814 med
           verderingspriser [by] Jan Olav
           Aamlid and Petter Christensen.
           Oslo, Oslo Mynthandel, 1976.
               30p. 15cm.

JC50   Ahlstrom, Bjarne.
A4   Norges mynter, the coinages of Norway,
1976   [by] ... Bernhard F. Brekke [and] Bengt
           Hemmingsson. Stockholm, Numismatiska Bokfor-
           laget AB, 1976.
               165p. illus. 31cm.
               Note: Text in Norwegian and English.

JC50   Andersin, Olaf J.
A5   Norska mynt handboken standardupp-
           lagan artalsforleckning med var-
           deringspriser, 1974. Huddinge,
           Lembit Forlags, 1974.
               88p. illus. 21cm.

JC50   Bjornstad, Ole Christian.
B5   Norges mynter efter 1814 (by) O. Chr.
           Bjornstad og Hans Holst. Oslo, 1927.
           Supplement, 1954.
               38p. 6 pl. 26cm. (Publikas joner fra
           universitetes myntkabinett, no. 2)

JC50   Brekke, Bernhard F.
B7   Norges mynter, 1483-1969 av ... Brekke
          og Bjarne N. A. Ahlstrom. Stockholm,
          B. Ahlstrom, 1970.
              129p. 20cm.

JC50   Parsons, H. Alexander.
P3   The earliest coins of Norway. New
          York, American Numismatic Society, 1926.
              41p. front., illus. 17cm. (Numis-
          matic notes and monographs, no. 29).

JC50   Schive, C. I.
S3   Norges mynter i middelalderen.
          Aalborg, Pilegaards Forlag, 1974.
              6p. XVIII plates. 39cm.

JC50   Sorensen, Terje.
S6   Norges mynter, 1814-1974 [by]
          Terje Sorensen [and] Tore Sorensen.
          Oslo, Utgave, 1975.
              48p. illus. 15cm.

NORWAY - SPECIAL, TECHNICAL ASPECTS

JC60   Eklund, O. P.
E5   Copper coins of Norway. Reprinted
          from The Numismatist, v. 58 (1945).
              5p. (Incl 2 pl.) 23cm.

SWEDEN - GENERAL

JC70   Ahlstrom, Bjarne.
A4   Sveriges mynt, 1521-1977; the coinage of
          Sweden, [by] Bjarne Ahlstrom, Yngve Almer,
          [and] Bengt Hemmingsson. Stockholm, Numis-
          matiska Bokforlaget Ab, 1976.
              325p. illus. 30cm.
              Note: Text in Swedish and English.

JC70   Brandt, Tage.
B7   Svenska provinsmynt. Stockholm,
          1963.
              41p. pl. 20cm.

JC70   Gluck, Harry.
G5   Artals forteckning over Svenska mynt
        med varderingspriser. Gustav vasa-
        Gustav VI Adolf, 1521-1968. Stockholm,
        Numismatiska Bokforlaget, 1953, 1961,
        1969, 1970, 1971, 1975.
            135p. ill. 21cm.
            Bibliography

JC70   Holmberg, Daniel.
H6   Mynt af guld, silfver och koppar
        proglade i Sverige och dess utlandska
        besittningar 1478-1892. Stockholm, 1894.
        Supplement, 1899.
            ii, 59p. 20cm.

JC70   Kosoff, A.
K6   The coinage of Sweden. [Encino?
        Calif., 1961]
            28p. illus. 28cm.

JC70   Lagerqvist, Lars O.
L3   A thousand-year history of Swedish coins.
Vert.   From Sweden Illustrated. Stockholm, 1961-
File   62.
            misc. paging. illus. 34cm.

JC70   Oldenburgs, J. F.
O5   Beskrifning ofver J.F.H. Oldenburgs
        samling af Svenska, Svenska besittnin-
        garnes och landtgrefven Fredriks
        (Konung Fredrik I) Hessiska mynt.
        Stockholm, 1883.
            406p. 20cm.

JC70   Stockholm. Statens historiska museum.
S7   Kungl. Myntkabinett.
            Sveriges mynthistoria. Vagledning vid
        studiet av Kungl Myntkabinett. (Av Eli
        F. Heckscher och Nils Ludvig Rasmusson).
        Stockholm, 1961.
            56p. 8 pl. 18cm.

JC70   Tingstrom, Bertel.
T5   Svensk numismatisk uppslagebok. Mynt i
        ord och bild 1521-1962. Stockholm, M.C.
        Hirsch, (1963).
            260p. illus. 23cm.
            Bibliography: p. 259-260.

JC70   Tingstrom, Bertel.
T5s   Swedish coins, 1521-1968. Stockholm,
              Numismatiska Bokforlaget, 1969.
                  271p. illus. 24cm.
                  Bibliog: p. 268-271
                   Heraldry maps: p. 266-267
                  Swedish numismatic terms: p. 255-264

JC70   Tonkin, A. B.
T6   Mynt guide 1971. Stockholm, Svenska
Vert.   Numismatiska foreningen, 1972.
File   64p. illus. 11cm.

SWEDEN - CATALOGUES

JC75   Andersin, Olaf J.
A5   Svenska mynthandboken standard-
              dupplagan, med varderingspriser,
              1973-74. Lembit Forlags, [1974?]
                  192p. illus. 21cm.

JC75   Cordry, Scott Eric.
C6   The modern coinage of Sweden.
              San Clemente, Malter-Westerfield Publ. Co.,
              1971.
                  75p. illus. 24cm.

JC75   Corpus nummorum saeculorum IX-XI qui in
C66   Suecia reperti sunt; Gotland, Akeback-
No.1   Atlingbo, ediderunt Brita Malmer, Nils
                  Ludvig Rasmusson. Stockholm, Almquist
                  & Wiksell International, 1975.
                  198p. maps pl. 26cm.
                  Note: Text in English

JC75   Ortendahl, Raouhl.
O7   Mynt kalender 1975; katalog over
              Sveriges mynt, 1872-1975 med
              aktuella varderingspriser. Enkoping,
              Sweden, the author, 1974.
                  96p. illus. 15cm.

JC75   Tonkin, W. A. R.
T6   Myntboken, 1971 [by] Archie
              Tonkin. Sodertalje, Sweden, The
              Author, 1971.
                  190p. illus. 21cm.

JC80
A5
    Andersin, Olaf J.
       Coinlex ficklexikon; med
varderingspriser 1976. Huddinge,
Lembit Forlags, [1976.]
       128p. illus. 15cm.

JC80
A6
    Applegren, T. G.
       Konung Gustaf's mynt. Stockholm,
Norstedt & Soner, 1905.
       145p. illus. 23cm. (Numismatiska
Meddelanden, no. xvi; pub. by Svenska
Numismatiska Foreningen)

JC80
E5
    Eklund, O. P.
       Copper coins of Sweden ... Coinage of
Swedish plate money by ... Berta Holmberg.
Reprinted from The Numismatist, 1962.
       36p. illus. 22cm.

JC80
H6
    Holmberg, Berta.
       Beskrivning over Isidor Adolf Bonniers
Samling Carl XI's mynt. Stockholm, 1931.
       326p. illus. 25cm.

JC80
W3
    Wahlstedt, Axel.
       The history of Swedish plate-money.
Reprinted from the Numismatic Circular,
London, Spink, 1933.
       13p.

SWEDISH POSSESSIONS

JC85
A5
    Ahlstrom, Bjarne.
       Sveriges besittningsmynt ... Coins
of the Swedish possessions, 1561-1878.
Stockholm, B. Ahlstrom Mynthandel, 1967.
       xi, 172p. ill. 26cm.
       In Swedish, German and English.

JC85
R3
    Stockholm. Statens historiska museum.
    Kungl myntkabinett.
       Svenska besittningsmynt. Vagledning
vid studiet av Kungl Myntkabinettets
utstallning. (Av Nils Ludwig Rasmusson).
Stockholm, 1950.
       66p. 8 pl. 18cm.

FINLAND

JC90   Borg, Erkki.
B6   Suomi-Finland, Rahat, Setelit varianttej
            Kortshoy, 1860-1971. Helsinki, Merkki
            Borg, 1971, 1975.
                32p. illus. 15cm.

JC90   Finland. Bank.
F5   Monnaies metalliques de Finlande et la
            frappe des monnaies, 1864-1938. Helsinki,
            1939.
                11p. 1 pl. 23cm.

SPAIN - COLLECTIONS, CATALOGUES

JD10
A5
    Anderson, P. K.
       [Collection of Spanish coins.] No imprint.
    3v. 28cm.
       Contents: v.1. Ancient and medieval Spain. -
    v.2. Spain, 1474-1968. - v.3. Colonial Spanish
    mints and cut and counter-marked coins.

JD10
N3
    Navascues, Joaquin M. de.
       Las monedas Hispanicas del
    Museo Arqueologico Nacional de
    Madrid. Barcelona, Asociacion
    Numismatica Espanola 1969, 1971.
       2v. 124p.; 59p. LXXXII plates;
    LXII plates. 29cm.
       Vol. 1- Ciclos Griegos e Ibero-
    Romano, 1969.
       Vol. 2-Ciclo Andaluz: grupo-
    Bastulo-Turdetano Tesoros de
    Azaila, Salva Canete y Cerro de la
    Miranda, 1971.

JD10
V5
    Vicenti, Jose A.
       Catalogo neto espana. Duros espanoles,
    Felipe V-Alfonso XIIII, 1701-1899.
    Madrid, 1968.
       87p. illus. 21cm.

JD10
V5b
    Vicenti, Jose A.
       Catalogo neto espana; monedas y billetes,
    1869-1968. [Madrid, 1967], 1976.
       47p. illus. 22cm.
       Title, 1976 edition: Catalogo general
    de la moneda Espanola.

SPAIN - SOCIETIES

JD15
A4
    Almirall, Juan, comp.
       Acta numismatica, I, editada bajo
    ed patrocinio de la Seccion Numismatico
    del circulo Filatelico y Numismatico.
    Barcelona, 1971.
       235p. illus. 25cm.

JD20   The Andorra story; the beautiful
A5   Andorra crowns. New York, Hans
Vert.   M.F. Schulman, n.d.
File   unpaged. illus. 24cm.

JD20   Beals, Gary.
B4   Numismatic terms of Spain and Spanish
          America. San Diego, Ca. [1966].
              ii, 88p. illus. 22cm.
              Bibliography: p. 84-85.

JD20   Castan, Carlo.
C39   Las monedas Espanolas desde los Reyes
          Catolicos al [present], [by] Carlos Castan
          [and] Juan R. Cayon. Madrid, G. Cristobal,
          1973, 1974, 1975, 1976.
              4v. ill. 24cm.

JD20   Vicenti, Jose A.
V5   Catalogo general de la moneda
          Espanola, Espana peninsular y
          provincias de ultramar; reyes
          Catolicos 1475-Isabel II, 1868.
          8th ed. Madrid, the author, 1976.
              431p. illus. 24cm.

SPAIN - SPECIAL, TECHNICAL ASPECTS

JD30   Pellicer i Bru, J.
P4   Glosario de maestros de ceca y
          ensayadores; ensayo de ordenacion
          alfabetico-cronologica [por] J.
          Pellicer i Bru. Barcelona,
          Asociacion Numismatica Espanola, 1975.
              206p. 29cm.

JD33   Calico, F. Xavier.
C3   Florines de Aragon. Barcelona, X. & F.
        Calico, 1966.
            113p. 25cm.

JD33   Guinovart, Jorge.
G8   El oro Espanol. Acunaciones a partir
        de Fernando VI. Barcelona, 1968.
            111p. illus. 22cm.

JD33   Lopez-Chaves y Sanchez, Leopoldo.
L6   Catalogo de la onza espanola. ... con la
        colaboracion de Jose de Yriarte y Oliva.
        Madrid, [1961]
            168p. illus. 30cm.
            Bibliography: p. 167-8.

JD33   Lopez-Chaves y Sanchez, Leopoldo.
L6d   Catalogo del doblon de a dos escudos
        [por] Leopoldo Lopez-Chaves y Sanchez con
        la colaboracion de Jose de Yriarte y Oliva.
        Madrid, Editorial Iber-Amer [1964]
            172p. (chiefly illus., port.) 31cm.
            Spanish and English.
            Bibliography: p. 171-172.

JD33   Lopez-Chaves y Sanchez, Leopoldo.
L61   Catalogo general de la onza (doblon
        de a ocho) de Espana y America, por
        Leopoldo Lopez-Chaves Sanchez y Jose
        de Yriarte Oliva. Madrid, The Authors,
        1968.
            75pp. illus. 28cm.

JD33   Lopez-Chaves y Sanchez, Leopoldo.
L6m   Catalogo de la media onza o doblon
        de a cuatro [por] Leopoldo Lopez-Chaves
        y Sanchez [by] Jose de Yriarte y Oliva.
        Madrid, Editorial Iber-Amer. [1963].
            140p. col. illus. 30cm.
            Bibliography: p. 137-138.

JD35 Badia i Torres, Antoni.
B3   Cataleg dels Croats de Barcelona,
       1285-1706. Barcelona, 1969.
          211p. 65 pl. 27cm.
          Bibliography

JD35 Calbeto de Grau, Gabriel.
C3   Compendio de las piezas de ocho reales.
       San Juan, P. R., Ediciones Juan Ponce de
       Leon, 1970.
          2 v (733p.) illus., maps. 31cm.
          English and Spanish.
          Bibliography: p. 729-730.

JD35 Dasi, Tomas.
D3   Estudio de los reales de a ocho,
       tambien llamados pesos, dolares, piastras,
       patacones o duros espanoles. Valencia,
       1950-51.
          5v. illus. 24cm.
          Covers the period 1474-1899.

JD35 Guinovart, Jorge.
G8   La plata Espanola, acunaciones a partir
       de Felipe V [by] Jorge Guinovart. 2d ed.
       Barcelona, 1972 [c1971].
          133p. illus. 22cm.

JD35 Herrera, Adolfo.
H4   El duro ... estudio de los reales de a
       ocho espanoles y de los monedas de igual o
       aproximado valor labradas en los dominios
       de la corona de Espana. Madrid, J. Lac-
       oste, 1914.
          2v. 54 pl. 33cm. (Real Academice de
       la Historia, Madrid)
          Bibliography: p. 503-523.

JD35 Pellicer i Bru, J.
P4   El medio duro; Espana, Provincias de
       America e Imperio por J. Pellicer i Bru,
       con la colaboracion y direccion de X. & F.
       Calico. [1st ed.]. Barcelona, 1971.
          429p. illus. 26cm.
          Bibliography: pp. 17-24.

JD35   Rodriquez Lorente, J.J.
R6   Catalogo de los reales de a dos
            espanoles. Madrid, Altamira Talleres
            Graficos, S.A., 1965.
                122p. illus. 27cm.
                In Spanish and English.
                Bibliography

JD35   Yriarte y Oliva, Jose de.
Y7   Catalogo de los reales de a ocho
            espanoles [por] Jose de Yriarte.
            Madrid, Editorial Tecnos [1955]
                207p. illus. (part col.) 27cm.
                Bibliography: p. 13-[15]

SPAIN - COPPER

JD37   Eklund, O. P.
E5   The copper coins of Spain. Reprinted
            from The Numismatist, v. 41, 1928, 1962.
                21p. illus. 23cm.

SPAIN - ANCIENT

JD40   Boudard, P. Andre
B6   Essai sur la numismatique iberienne
            precede de recherches sur l'alphabet et la
            langue des iberes. Paris, A. Leleux
            [etc.], 1859.
                vii, 319p. 39 pl., map. 28cm.

JD40   Guadan, Antonio Manuel de.
G81   Las leyendas ibericas en las dracmas
            de imitacion emporitana. Estudio de
            epigrafia numismatica iberica. Madrid,
            [Blass], 1956.
                129p. 7 pl. 21cm.

JD40   Guadan, Antonio Manuel de.
G8m   Las monedas de Gades. Asociation
            Numismatica Espanola, 1963.
                95p. 13 pl. 24cm. (Monografias
            sobre numismatica antiqua, no. 2)

JD40   Heiss, Aloiss, 1820-
H4   Description generale des monnaies
            antiques de l'espagne. Chicago, Argonaut,
            1967. [1st Amer. ed.]
                 548p. 68 pl. 30cm.
                 "Bibliographie Basque": p. 539

JD40   Ortega Galindo, Julio.
O7   La espana primitiva, a traves de las
            monedas ibericas. Bilbao, 1947.
                 19p. 35 pl. 21cm.

JD40   Trapero, Maria Ruiz.
T7   Las acunaciones Hispano-Romanas de
            calagurris; su ordernacion cronologica
            y su trascendencia historica. Barcelona,
            Asociacion Numismatica Espanola, 1968.
                 149p. plates. 25cm.

JD40   Vives y Escudero, Antonio.
V5   La moneda hispanica, ... Madrid, 1926.
                 4v. in 1 various pagings, illus. 28cm.

JD40   Villaronga Garriga, Leandro.
V54   Las monedas de Arse-Saguntum. Barcelona,
            Asociacion Numismatica Espanola, 1967.
                 179p. X plates. 25cm.

SPAIN - MEDIEVAL

JD43   Cabre, Aguilo, Juan.
C3   El tesorillo visigodo de trientes de
            las excavaciones del plan nacional de
            1944-45 en zorita de los canes (Guadal-
            ajara). Madrid, 1946.
                 56p. 15 pl. 25cm.

JD43   Heiss, Aloiss, 1820-
H41   Descripcion general de las monedas
            hispano-cristianas des de la invasion de
            los arabes. Madrid, R.N. Milangro, 1865-
            1869. [Reprinted, Zaragoza, 1962].
                 2v. illus. 30cm.
                 Lacking v.2.

JD43   Heiss, Aloiss.
H4r   Description generale des monnaies des
          rois wisigoths d'Espagne. Paris,
          Imprimerie Nationale, 1872.
             185p. illus., 13 pl. 32cm.

JD43   Lhotka, John F.
L5   Survey of medieval Iberian coinages,
          by J.F. Lhotka and P. K. Anderson. The
          American Numismatic Association, 1963.
          Reprint from The Numismatist.
             123p. illus. 22cm.

JD43   Mateu y Llopis, Felipe.
M3   Las monedas visigodas del Museo
          arqueologico nacional. Madrid, 1936.
             432p. illus., maps., 40 pl. 24cm.
             Bibliography: p. 43-54.

JD43   Mateu y Llopes, Felipe.
M3r   Les relacions del principat de
          Catalunya i els regnes de Valencia
          i Mallorca amb. Anglaterra i el
          paral lelisme monetari d' aquests
          paisos durant els segles XIII, XIV,
          i XV. [Spain,] Castello de la Plana, 1934.
             125p. plates. 22cm.

JD43   Miles, George Carpenter, 1904-
M5u   The coinage of the Umayyads of Spain.
          Published in cooperation with the Hispanic
          Society of America. New York, American
          Numismatic Society, 1950.
             2v. (xi, 591 p.) pl. 23cm. (His-
          panic numsimatic series, monograph no. 1)

JD43   Miles, George Carpenter, 1904-
M5v   The coinage of the Visigoths of Spain,
          Leovigild to Achila II. Pub. in co-
          operation with the Hispanic Society of
          America. New York, American Numismatic
          Society, 1952.
             xv, 519p. illus., map. 23cm. (His-
          panic numismatic series, monograph no. 2)
             Bibliography: p. [1]-20

JD43   Miles, George C.
M55   Coins of the Spanish Muluk al-Tawa'if.
          Published in co-operation with the His-
          panic Society of America. New York
          American Numismatic Society, 1954.
             xi, 168p. 15 pl. 23cm. (Hispanic
          numismatic series, no. 3)

JD43   Rada y Delgado, Juan de Dois de la.
R3   Catalogo de monedas arabigas espanolas
Rare   que se conservan en el Museo Arqueologico
Books   nacional. Madrid, Fortanet, 1892.
                xxiv, 264p. 23cm.

SPAIN - POST MEDIEVAL THROUGH EIGHTEENTH CENTURY

JD44   Castan, Carlos.
C3   Las monedas del imperio-Espanol;
            1479-1713 [by] Carlos-Castan [and] Juan
            R. Cayon. Madrid, G. Cristobal, 1974, 1976.
                280p. illus. 24cm.

JD44   Vicenti, Jose A.
V5   Catalogo general de la moneda
            Espanola; imperio Espanol (Europa),
            Fernando II-Fernando I 1475-1825.
            1st ed. Madrid, Jose Vicenti, 1976.
                255p. illus. 24cm.

JD44   Vicenti, Jose A.
V5c   Catalogo general de la moneda Espanola;
            Felipe V (1700) - Isabel II (1868). Madrid,
            Salinero, 1969.
                404p. illus. 22cm.

SPAIN - MODERN

JD45   Nathan, S.
N3   Small change in Spain, 1931-
            1941. Brighton, England, Spanish
            Philatelic Society, 1974.
                20p. illus. 30cm.

JD45   Noel, James A., Jr.
N6   Spain: the coinage of Joseph Napoleon,
            the "Intruder King", 1808-1814. The
            Author, [1968].
                24p. illus. 22cm.

JD45   Raymond, Wayte.
R3   Spain; Spanish American mints;
            Filipinas. N.Y., the author, 1956.
                24p. illus. 23cm. (Coins
            of the world)

JD45   Rodriguez Lorente, Juan Jose.
R6   Las monedas de Isabel II;
            by Juan Jose Rodriguiz Lorente.
            Madrid, Par. Artes Graficas,
            1967.
                89p. illus. 24cm.

JD45   Scott, Michael N.
S3   Guidebook of Spanish coins (since
            the monetary reform of 1868 to date)
            by Michael N. Scott. [Madrid, Artes
            Graficas, 1972]
                121p. illus. 22cm.

SPAIN - LOCAL, A-Z

JD50   Rua, Fernando Gimeno.
C3R8   Aportacion al estudio de las
            monedas de Laie; par Fernando
            Gimeno Rua. Barcelona, Gabinete
            Numismatico de Cataluna, 1950.
                82p. VIII plates. 23cm.

PORTUGAL - COLLECTIONS, CATALOGUES

JD60   Almeida, Basto & Piombino & Ca. (Lisbon).
A4   Guia duma notavel coleccao de moedas
            Portuguesas. Lisbon, Palacio Foz, 1948.
                17p. 14 pl. 25cm.

PORTUGAL - GENERAL WORKS

JD70   Almeida Ribeiro, Fernando.
A4   Uma hipotese ... uma tese ... Porto,
            1959.
                47, 20p. illus. 23cm. (Publicacoes
            da sociedade Portuguesa de Numismatica,
            no. 86)

JD70   Batalha Reis, Pedro.
B3   Precario das moedas Portuguesas de 1140-
          1940. Lisbon, 1956-1958.
             2v. pl. 25cm.

JD70   Brazao, Arnaldo.
B7   Numismatolos contemporaneas
          e a sua actividade cultural.
          Lisboa, Portugal, Editorial
          Imperio, 1963.
             332p. 26cm.

JD70   Ferraro Vaz, J.
F4   Catalogo das moedas Portuguesas ...
          Portugal continental, 1640-1948. Lisbon,
          1948.
             246p. illus. 24cm.

JD70   Ferraro Vaz, J.
F4m   Livro das moedas de Portugal. Book of
          the coins of Portugal-Braga, 1969.
             2v. 863p. illus. 23cm.
             In Portuguese & English.

JD70   Leite de Vasconcellos, Jose.
L4   Nomenclatura numismatica. Porto, 1958.
             36p. 36cm. (Publicacoes da Sociedade
          Portuguesa de Numismatica, no. 79)

JD70   Lestro, Carlos Antonio.
L48   Catalogo de Numismatica Precario.
          I Moedas; Portugal Continental, 1816-1972;
          Ultramar, 1921-1972. 2d ed. Lisbon, n.p.
          1972.
             141p. illus. 21cm.

JD70   Teixeira de Aragao, Augusto C., 1823-1903.
T4   Descripcao geral e historica das
          moedas cunhadas em nome dos reis,
          regentes e governadores de Portugal.
          Porto, Livraria Fernando Machado, [1964].
             3v. 62, 15 pl. 30cm.
             Reprint of 1874-1880 ed.

PORTUGAL - SPECIAL, TECHNICAL ASPECTS

JD80   Lisbon, Portugal. Casa da Moeda.
L5   Estatistica das moedas de ouro,
            prata, cobre e bronze que se
            cunharam na casa da Moeda de
            Lisboa; desde 1752...-1871,
            segundo consta das respectivas
            libros que existem na mesma
            reparticao. Lisboa, Casa da Moeda,
            1873.
                22p. charts. 35cm.

PORTUGAL - COPPER

JD87   Eklund, O. P.
E4   Copper coins of Portugal. Reprinted
            from The Numismatist, v. 42, 1929.
                54p. illus. 21cm.

PORTUGAL PRIOR TO 1640

JD90   Ferraro Vaz, J.
F4   Numaria medieval Portuguesa, 1128-
            1383. Lisboa, 1960.
                2v. 448p. xvi. illus. pl.
                Bibliography: p. iii-xvi

JD90   Porto, E. J.
P6   Dinheiros e mealhas Portuguesas.
            Lisboa, 1949.
                36p. illus. 17cm. Covers period
            1112-1383.

PORTUGAL SINCE 1900

JD95   Raymond, Wayte.
R3   The coins of Portugal and colonies,
            1901-1951. New York, Wayte Raymond, 1952.
                16p. illus. 23cm. (The Coin collec-
            tor's journal, v. 19, no. 3, May-June,
            1952)

SOCIETIES

```
JE10      Societe Francoise de Numismatique;
S6            reconnue comme etablissement d'
              utilite publique; statuts et re-
              glement interieur.  Paris,
              Edmond Dubois, 1924.
              20p.  21cm.
```

COLLECTIONS

```
JE20      DeWitte, Alphonse.
D4            Le mouton du Roi Jean Le Bon et ses
          imitations, [by] Alphonse DeWitte.  Chalon-
          Sur-Saone, France, Emile Bertrand, 1900.
              40p.  illus.  29cm.

JE20      Monnaie de Paris.  Musee Monetaire.
M6            Deuxiene concours-exposition
Vert.     de numismatique.  Mai-Jun, 1951.
File      reglement.  Paris, 1951.
              7p.  25cm.
```

CATALOGUES

```
JE30      Thimonier, Argus.
T5            Monnaies-Assignats billets;
          France 1792-1974; tirages et
          cotes actuelles.  10th ed.
          Clermont-Ferrand, France, Argus
          Thimonier, [1974].
              159p.  illus.  22cm.
```

GENERAL WORKS

JE40   Gadoury, Victor.
G3   Monnaies Francaises, 1795-1973
            par Victor Gadoury. 1st ed. [Baden-
            Baden, Germany, The Author, 1973], 1975.
                240p. illus. 21cm.

JE40   Guilloteau, Victor.
G8   Monnaies francaises. Colonies 1670-
            1942; metropole, 1774-1942, y compris:
            republiques, royaunes, souverainetes,
            principantes, sieges et occupations sous
            demination francaise, dresse par V.G.
            numismate, Versailles, 1937-1942.
            [Paris, A. Barry, 1943]
                829p. illus. 19cm.

JE40   Letellier, Eugene.
L4   Description historique des monnaies
Rare   francaises, gauloises, royales et seig-
Books   neuriales; donnant un apercu desprix a
            chaque numero. Paris, Letellier, 1888-
            1890.
                4v. in 2. illus., 52 pl. 19cm.

JE40   Mazard, Jean.
M32   Histoire monetaire et numismatique
            contemporaire 1790-1963. Tome 1: 1790-
            1848. Paris, E. Bourgey, 1965.
                297p. illus. 28cm.

TECHNICAL ASPECTS

JE60   France. Administration des monnaies et
F7   medailles.
                La monnaie de Paris, [Paris, 1964?]
                81p. 26cm.

JE60   Mazerolle, Fernand.
M3   L'hotel des monnaies, les batiments,
            le musee, les at eliers. Paris, 1907.
                180p. illus. 23cm.

SILVER

JE65   Kelpsh, A. E.
K4   Silver dollar-size coins of French
          provinces. Reprinted from The Numismatist
          v. LX, 1947.
               18p. illus. 23cm.

JE65   Kirby, Norman H.
K5   Crowns of France: Louis XVI, DeGaulle.
          [Chicago, Ill., Printed by Hewitt Bros.,
          1968]
               vii, 64p. illus. 24cm.

JE65   Raymond, Wayte.
R3   The silver ecus of France from Louis
          XIII to the third republic, 1642-1936, with
          estimated valuations based upon their
          rarity or demand; intro by Shepard Pond.
          New York, Wayte, Raymond, [1940].
               23p. pl. (The coin collector series,
          no. 3)

JE65   Sobin, George.
S6   The silver crowns of France;
          1641-1973. Teaneck, N. J., Richard
          Margolis, 1974.
               260p. illus. 26cm.

COPPER, ETC.

JE67   Eklund, O. P.
E5   Copper coins of France. Reprinted
          from the Numismatist, (1931-32), 1962.
               40p. illus. 22cm.

BY PERIOD - ANCIENT

JE79   Prou, M. Maurice.
P7   ...Les monnaies Merovingiennes
          par M. Maurice Prou. Graz,
          Austria, Akademische Druck, 1969.
          Reprinted from Catalogue des Monnaies
          Francaises de la Bibliotheque
          Nationale, 1896.
               628p. xxxvi plates. map. 28cm.

GAUL (ANCIENT)

JE80   Blanchet, Jules Adrien, 1866-
B55   Traite des monnaies gauloises.
Rare   Paris, E. Leroux, 1905.
Books   650p. illus., iv pl., map. 25cm.
               List of finds, p. 539-611.

JE80   Boudeau, E.
B6   Monnaies Gauloises. Maastricht,
           Nederland, Herdruck, 1970.
               42p. illus. map.

JE80   Ciani, Louis.
C5   Les monnaies Royales Francaises
           de Hugues Capet a Louis XVI avec
           indication de leur valeur actuelle.
           Maastricht, Holland, Van Der Dussen,
           n.d. Originally published: Paris,
           1926.
               502p. illus. 25cm.

JE80   Hill, Sir George Francis, 1867-
H5   On the coins of Narbonensis with
           Iberian inscriptions. New York, Amer-
           ican numismatic society, 1930.
               39p. illus., vi pl. 17cm. (Numis-
           matic notes and monographs, no. 44)

JE80   LaTour, Henri de, 1855-1913.
L3   Atlas de monnaies gauloises prepare
           par le commission de topographie des
           gaules. Lund Humphries for Spink, 1965.
               12p. 55 pl., map. 34cm.
               Reprint of 1892 ed.

MEDIEVAL

JE82   Bigot, Alexis.
B5   Essai sur les monnaies du royaume et
           duche de Bretagne, par Alexis Bigot.
           Paris, Rollin, 1857.
               iv, 422p. 40 pl. 24cm.
               Covers the period 550-1539 A.D.

JE82   Boudeau, E.
B6   Catalogue general illustre et a
          prix marques en francs or de monnaies
          Francaises (provinciales). Nouvelle ed.
          Reprint. Maastricht, Netherlands,
          A. G. Van Der Dussen, 1970.
               313p. illus. maps. 22cm.

JE82   Boudeau, E.
B6c   Catalogue general illustre et a
          prix marques de monnaies Francaises
          (nationales). Nouvelle ed. Paris,
          Cabinet de Numismatique, n.d.
               394p. illus. 21cm.

JE82   Cerexhe, Michel.
C4   Les monnaies de Charlemagne. Gand,
Rare   Typ. S. Leliaert, A. Siffer & co., 1887.
Books   174p. 4 pl. 23cm.

JE82   D'avant, Faustin Poey.
D3   Monnaies feodales de France. Graz,
          Austria, Akademische Druck-U. Verlagsan-
          stalt, 1961.
               3v. 163 pl. 27cm.

JE82   Engel, Arthur, 1855-
E5   Numismatique de L'Alsace, par Arthur
1973   Engel [and] Ernest Lehr. Paris, Ernest
          Leroux, 1887. [Liege, Belgium, Guy
          Genard; Distribution in France by
          Bernard Poindessault, Paris, 1973?]
               xxviii, 272p. illus. 46 pl. 33cm.

JE82   Lhotka, John F., Jr.
L5   Medieval feudal French coinage.
          Reprinted from The Numismatist, 1965.
          American Numismatic Association, c1966.
               36p. illus. 22cm.

JE82   Mey, Jean de.
M4   Les monnaies de Bretagne (781-1547)
          par Jean de Mey. Bruxelles, J. De
          Mey; Paris, B. Poindessault, 1970.
               157p. illus. 20cm. (Numismatic
          Pocket)

JE82   Ponton d'Amecourt, Gustave, Vicomte de,
P6d   1825-
               Description raisonne des monnaies
          merouingiennes de Chalon-sur. Saone, par
          le Vte G. de Ponton d'Amecourt ...
          Paris, La Societe, 1874.
               116p. 5 pl. 27cm.

JE82   Ponton d'Amecourt, Gustave, Vicomte de,
P6r   1825.
               Recherche des monnaies merovingiennes
           di Cenomannicum, par le Vte de Ponton
           D'Amecourt ... Mamers, Fleury & Dangin,
           1883.
               284p. illus. 28cm.

JE82   Saulcy, F. de.
S2c   Recherches sur les monnaies des comtes
           et ducs de Bar pour faire suite aux recherches
           sur les monnaies des ducs hereditaires de
           Lorraine. Paris, Didot Freres, 1843.
               44p. 7 pl. 31cm.

JE82   Saulcy, F. de.
S2d   Rescherches sur les monnaies des ducs
           hereditaires de Lorraine. Metz, S. Lamort,
           1841.
               247p. 36 pl. 31cm.

EARLY MODERN TO NAPOLEON

JE83   Rollin et Feuardent. Paris.
R6   Monnaies royales et seigneuriales de France,
           planches. Paris, Rollin et Feuardent, 1891.
               8p. 28 pl. 31cm.

NAPOLEONIC ERA

JE85   Ernst, Barbara.
E7   Les Monnaies Francaises au systeme
           decimal, 1795-1848.
           Braunschweig, Klinkhardt & Biermann, 1970.
               148p. illus. 24cm.
               (text in French and German)

JE85   Myers, Robert J.
M8   Napoleon and his family; coins
           and medals; 1796-1840 by Robert J.
           Myers and Frances M. Schwartz.
           Lennox Hill Station, N.Y., Robt. J.
           Myers, n.d.
               unpaged. illus. 31cm.

JE85   Parsons, George M.
P3   The French revolution of 1789 illus-
            trated by coins and medals of the period.
            Colombus, Ohio, priv. print., 1886.
                 40p. 1 pl. 29cm.

JE85   Pipito, F. F.
P5   Napoleon and his family. A
Vert.   paper presented to the Albany (N.Y.)
File   Numismatic Society, n.d.
                 5p. 28cm.

JE85   Pond, Shepard.
P6   Napoleon Emperor of the French Republic
            [Reprinted from the Numismatist, 1942]
                 8p. illus. 23cm.

JE85   Pond, Shepard.
P6p   The piastre decaen 1810. Reprinted
            from the Numismatist, January, 1940.
                 9p. illus. 23cm.

TO PRESENT

JE87   Ciani, Louis.
C5   Catalogue illustre des monnaies
            Francaises de la guerre, 1914-1919 ...
            Paris, n.d.
                 39p. illus. 21cm.

JE87   Dietzel, Heinz.
D5   Die munzen Frankreichs ab 1848.
            Berlin, E. Proh, 1970.
                 21p. illus. 17cm.

JE87   Ernst, Barbara.
E7   Les monnaies Francaises depuis 1848.
            Braunschweig, Klinkhardt & Biermann, 1968.
                 78p. illus. 24cm.
                 (text in French & German)

JE87   Mey, Jean de.
M4   Repertoire de la numismatique
            Francaise contemporaine 1793-1968.
            Par Jean de Mey et Bernard
            Poindessault. Bruxelles, Imprimerie
            Cultura, 1969.
                 252p. illus. 25cm.

JE87   Thimonier, J. L.
T5   Essais monnaies Francaises, monnaies
            et medailles de visite, monnaies Francaises
            dites de necessite emises de 1914 a 1931.
            3d ed. Clermont-Ferrand, France, [Editions
            Thimonier], 1976.
                128p. illus. 21cm.

LOCAL, A-Z

JE90   Mey, Jean de
B8M4   Les monnaies de Bourgogne.
            Bruxelles, J. de Mey, 1973.
                128p. illus. 21cm.

JE90   Mey, Jean de.
C6M4   Les monnaies du Comtat Venaissin.
            Bruxelles, Jean de Mey, 1975.
                168p. illus. 21cm.

JE90   Saulcy, Louis Felicien Joseph
M4S2   Caignart de, 1807-1880.
                Les monnaies de la cite de
            metz; les monnaies des eveques
            de Metz par F. de Saulcy. Originally
            published Metz, S. Lamort, 1835.
            Reprinted, Luxembourg, Numa Revue
            Internationale de Numismatique,
            1974.
                unpaged. fold. plates. 22cm.

JE90   Levrault, Louis.
S7L4   Essai sur l'ancienne monnaie de
            Strasbourg. Strasbourg, Paris, 1842.
                462p. 22cm.

COLONIES

JE95   Mazard, Jean.
M3   Histoire monetaire et numismatique
            des colonies et de l'union Francaise,
            1670-1952. Paris, Emile Bourgey, 1953.
                202p. 17 pl. 29cm.

JE95   Mazard, Jean.
M3m   Monetary and numismatic history of
          the colonies and of the French Union,
          1670-1952. Paris, Emile Bourgey, 1953.
              96p. 29cm.

JE95   Raymond, Wayte, ed.
R3   France and colonies. Special
          printing. N.Y., W. Raymond,
          1956.
              40p. illus. 23cm.

JE95   Zay, Ernest, 1830-1909.
Z3   Histoire monetaire des colonies
          francaises d'apres les documents officiels
          avec 278 figures. Paris, J. Montorier,
          1892.
              380p. illus. 25cm.

MONACO

JE97   Jolivot, C.
J6   Medailles et monnaies de Monaco.
          Bologna, Forni, Reprint of 1885 ed.
              98p. illus. 21cm.

SOCIETIES

JF10   Societe Royale de Numismatique.
S6   Vingt-cinquiene election a la
          presidence. Assemblee Generale
          du 6 Juillet 1873. Bruxelles,
          Fr. Gobbaerts, 1873.
               75p. II plates. 24cm.

COLLECTIONS

JF20   Societe Royal de Numismatique de
S6   Belgique.
               Exposition numismatique [a] Bruxelles
          Bibliotheque Albert I, 30 Avril-
          29 Mai 1966. Bruxelles,
          Secretariat [de Belgium], [1966?]
               197p. XVIII plates. 26cm.
          -Written in French and Dutch.

CATALOGUES

JF30   Agence Numismatique Interphilatelie.
A3   Catalogue des monnaies Luxembourgeoises
          1740-1967. Luxembourg, Agence Numismatique
          Interphilatelie, [1964], [1976].
               unpaged ill. pl. 20cm.

JF30   Frans, Morin.
F7   Katalogus der Belgische munten van 1832
          tot heden ... prijzen der munten aangepast
          door Renie Van Bergen. Antwerpen, Numis,
          n.d.
               96p. illus. 18cm.

JF30   Mevius, Johan.
M4   Speciale catalogus van
          de nederlandse munten van 1795
          tot heden; met Ned. West-Indie,
          Suriname-Curacao - Ned. Antillen.
          Amsterdam, Mevius & Hirschhorn,
          1976, 1975, 1972, 1971, 1969.
               96p. illus. 20cm.

JF30   L'union des Timbrophiles de Luxembourg.
U4   La Section Numismatique.
         Catalogue des monnaies Luxembourgeoises
de Henri II (1026) a Charlotte (1939)
et de celles des fiefs, by Maurice Campill
and Jean Harpes. Luxembourg, 1945, 1952.
         32p. 18cm.

GENERAL WORKS

JF40   Gelder, Hendrik Ennovan.
G4   De Nederlandse munten. Utrecht,
Antwerp, Aula-Bocken, [1965].
            272p. illus. 18cm.

JF40   Heylen, Adrianus.
H4   Antword ... [Treatise on Dutch and
Belgian mintages between 1300 and 1500]
Brussels, 1787.
            128p. 26cm.

JF40   Mey, Jean de.
M4   Les monnaies de Belgique, (1790-
1973), [by] J. De Mey & G. Pauwels.
Wetteren, Belgium, Editions Cultura,
1974, 1973, 1968.
            32p. illus. 21cm.

JF40   Morin, Francois.
M6   Catalogus Belgische munten van 1832 tot
1970, met perfekte cliche 's van voor- en
keerzijde van ieder munttype; Congolese
munten van 1887 tot 1970 (Congo, Katanga,
Burundi, Rwanda). Boom, Belgium, The
author, 1971.
            120p. illus. 18cm.

JF40   Probst, Romain.
P7   Catalogue illustre des monnaies
Luxembourgeoises, 984-1976. ...Prifix 1976;
par Romain Probst et Andre Ungeheuer. Luxem-
bourg, [Chambre Syndicate des Experts et
Negocients en Numismatique de Belgique, 1975.]
            176p. illus. 19cm.

JF40   Raymond, Wayte.
R3   Modern coins of Belgium and Belgian
         Congo. New York, Wayte Raymond, 1953.
             16p. illus. 23cm. (The Coin
         collector's journal, v. 20, no. 5)

JF40   Schulman, Jacques.
S3   Handboek van de Nederlandsche munten
         van 1795- [date]. Amsterdam, the author,
         1946, 1962.
             178p. illus. 24cm.

JF40   Van Keymeulen, Andre.
V3   Les tresors monetaires modernes trouves
         en Belgigue, 1434-1970 [par] Andre Van Keymeulen
         Bruxelles, Cercle d'Etudes Numismatique
         Travaux, 1973.
             286p. 24cm.

JF40   Zonnebloem, Uitgave van Uitgeverij.
Z6   Catalogus van de zilveran munten
         geslagen door de Zeven Provincien der
         Verenigde Nederlanden, 1606-1795.
         Amsterdam, [1971], 1974, 1976.
             152p. illus. 19cm.

GOLD

JF63   Delmonte, A.
D4   Le benelux d'or; repertoire du
         monnayage d'or des territoires composant
         les anciennes Pays-Bas. Amsterdam,
         J. Schulman, 1964.
             207p. maps, 33 pl. 26cm.
             In French and Dutch
             Bibliography: p. 12-13

SILVER

JF65   Delmonte, A.
D4   The silver benelux. Amsterdam,
         Jacques Schulman, 1967.
             320p. 52 plates. maps. 27cm.

COPPER, ETC.

JF67   Eklund, O. P.
E4   Copper coins of Luxembourg. Reprinted
            from the Numismatist, [1962?].
                6p. illus. 22cm.

JF67   Zonnebloem, Uitgave van Uitgeverij.
Z6   Catalogus van de koperen
            munten geslagen door de zeven
            provincien de verenigde nederlanden,
            1546-1795. Amsterdam, the author,
            n.d., 1975.
                64p. illus. 19cm.

BY PERIOD - ANCIENT

JF79   Pauwels, G.
P3   Les monnaies de la Gaule Belgique.
            Bruxelles, J. De Mey, 1971.
                100p. 5 plates. 21cm.
                (Numismatic Pocket series #12.)

JF79   Thirion, Marcel.
T5   Les tresors monetaires
            Gaulois et Romains trouves en
            Belgique. Bruxelles, Cercle
            d'Etudes Numismatiques, 1967.
                208p. map. 24cm.
            (Cercle d'Etudes Numismatiques,
            Travaux 3).

BY PERIOD - MEDIEVAL

JF80   den Duyts, Francois, 1790-1848.
D85   Notice sur les anciennes monnaies des
            comtes de Flandre, ducs de Brabant,
            comtes de Hainaut ... faisant partie de
            la collection des Medailles de l'univ-
            ersite de Gand. Nouvelle edition, Gand,
            Impr. de C. Annoot-Braeckman, 1847.
                128p. 48 pl. 22cm.

JF80   Gaillard, Victor Louis Maria, 1825-1856.
G3   Recherches sur les monnaies des comtes
        de Flandre depuis les temps les plus
        recules, jusqu'au regne de Robert de
        Bethune inclusivement par Victor Gaillard
        ... Gand, H. Hoste, 1852.
            144, 30p. illus, 23 pl. 27cm.

JF80   Ghyssens, Joseph.
G5   Les petits deniers de Flandre des
        XII et XIII siecles; [par] Joseph
        Ghyssens. Bruxelles, Cercle d'
        Etudes Numismatiques Travaux, 1971.
            184p. XVI plates. 24cm.
        (Cercle d'Etudes Numismatiques
        Travaux #5.)

JF80   Haeck, Aime.
H3   De munten van de graven van Vlaan-
        deren, deel 1. Brussel, J. de Mey,
        1973.
            108p. 2 plates. 21cm.
        (Numismatic pocket book, #16).

JF80   Liege, Loos, Heinsberg et quelques
L5   particularites; [coins from the
            collection of Renesse-Briedbach.]
        n.p., n. pub., n.d.
        40p. illus. 21cm.

JF80   Mey, Jean de.
M4   Les monnaies des ducs de Brabant. (1106-
        1598). Amsterdam, Mevius, 1966.
            2v. 62, 87p. illus. pl. 20cm.

JF80   Serrure, Raymond.
S4   L'imitation des types monetaires
        Flamands [au moyen age;] depuis
        Marguerite de Constantinople jusqu'
        a l'avenement de la maison de
        Bourgogne. Deuxieme ed. [Originally
        published] Bruxelles, Alfred Vromant
        & Cie, 1899. Reprinted-Liege, Guy
        Genard, 1972.
            65p. ill. 22cm. (Materiaux
        pour l'histoire du commerce de la Flandre
        au moyen age.)

EARLY MODERN

JF83   Gelder, Hendrik Enno Van.
G4   Les monnaies des pays-bas Bourguignons
         et espagnols, 1434-1713, ... par H.
         Enno van Gelder et Marcel Hoc. Amsterdam,
         J. Schulman, 1960-1964.
             210, 11p. 34 pl. 27cm.

JF83   Loon, Gerard van.
L6   Beschrijving van Nederlandsche historie-
         penningen. 1731-1806. Amsterdam, 1821-
         1869.
             2v. 88 pl. 40cm.

JF83   Mey, Jean de.
M4   Les monnaies des souverains Luxem-
         bourgeois (984-1790). Amsterdam,
         Mevius, 1966.
             74p. 2 pl. 20cm.

JF83   Mey, Jean de.
M4m   De munten van Benelux 1790-
         1967; door J. de Mey en G.
         Pauwels. Brussel, the author, 1968.
             143p. illus. 20cm.

JF83   Serrure, Raymond.
S4   Dictionnaire geographique de
         l'histoire monetaire Belge.
         Originally published in Brussels,
         1880. Reprinted-Bologna, A. Forni,
         1969.
             340p. scattered illus. 22cm.

EIGHTEENTH CENTURY

JF85   Dirks, Jacob.
D5   Beschrijving der Nederlandsche of op
         Nederland en Nederlanders betrekking
         hebbende penningen, geslagen tusschen
         November 1813 en November 1863. Haarlem,
         Bohn, 1889-1894.
             3v. 24cm. Atlas of 130 pl.

JF85   Mevius, Johan.
M4   Speciale catalogus van de munten van het
            koninkrijk der Nederlanden. Amsterdam,
            1969, 1974.
                 45p. illus. 20cm.

JF85   Nahuys, Maurin.
N3   Histoire numismatique de la hollande,
            pendant la reunion a l'empire Francais ...
            Utrecht, Bosch & Zoon, 1863.
                 224p. 15 pl. 30cm.

JF85   Van Keymeulen, Andre.
V3   De munten van Maria-Theresia uit de
            oostenrykse Nederlanden, 1744-1780.
            Brussels, Jos. Philippen, [1973.]
                 70p. illus. 19cm.

NINETEENTH AND TWENTIETH CENTURIES

JF87   Dietzel, Heinz.
D5   Die munzen Belgiens ab 1831. Die
            munzen Luxemburgs. .Berlin, E. Proh, 1970.
                 30p. illus. 17cm.

JF87   Dietzel, Heinz.
D5m   Die munzen der Niederlande ab
            1815 mit den uberseeprovinzen.
            Berlin, Erich Proh, 1970.
                 16p. illus. 17cm.

JF87   Jaeger, Kurt.
J3   Die munzpragungen der letzten
            uberlebenden Monarchien des "Teutschen
            Bundes" von 1815; furstentum Liechtenstein
            ... und Grossherzogtum Luxemburg. Basel,
            Switzerland, Munzen und Medaillen A.G.
            Basel, 1963.
                 67p. illus. looseleaf plate. 22cm.

JF87   Raymond, Wayte, 1886-   comp.
R3   Coins of the Netherlands and colonies
            from 1890-1953. New York, Wayte Raymond,
            1953.
                 16p. illus. 23cm. (The Coin
            collector's journal)

JF87   Thirion, Marcel.
T5   Monnaies conventionnelles (depuis
         1816) et monnaies de necessite (1914-
         1918)-Belges, par M. Thirion et F.J.
         Bingen. Bruxelles, J. DeMay, 1970.
              74p. illus. 20cm.

REGIONAL, A-Z

JF90   Bibliotheque Alberti, Brussels.
B7B5   Mille ans de monnayage Bruxellois,
         965-1965. 1965.
              108p. illus. photos. 26cm.

JF90   Chalon, Renier.
H3C5   Recherches sur les monnaies des
         comtes de Hainaut. Originally
         pub. in Bruxelles, A la Librarie
         Scientifique et Litteraire, 1848.
         Reprinted-Liege, Guy Genard, 1972.
              variously paged. 6 plates. 29cm.

JF90   Chestret de Haneffe, J. de, Baron.
L5C5   Numismatique de la Principaute
         de Liege et de ses dependances
         (Bouillon, Looz) depuis leurs annex-
         ions; par le Baron J. de Chestret de
         Haneffe. Originally pub. in 1887.
         Reprinted-Liege, Guy Genard, 1972.
              466p. 11 plates. 29cm.

JF90   Magain, Pierre.
L5M3   Les monnaies de Jean-
         Theodore de Baviere Prince-
         Eveque de Liege, 1744-1763.
         Bruxelles, Cercle d'Etudes
         Numismatiques, 1964.
              64p. IV plates 24cm.
         (Cercles d'Etudes Numismatiques,
         Travaux I).

JF90   Mey, Jean de.
L5M4   Les monnaies de cuivre liegeoises 1378-
         1763. Brussels, 1968.
              56p. illus. 20cm.
              Bibliography

JF90   Mignolet, Andre.
L5M5   Les monnaies de la principaute
            de Liege 1482-1792. Tome II.
            Bruxelles, J. de Mey, 1973.
                133p. illus. 20cm.

JF90   Perreau, A.
M3P4   Recherches sur la ville de Maestricht
            et sur ses monnaies. Brussels, A. Van
            Dale, 1846.
                70p. 9 pl. 20cm.

JF90   Chalon, Renier, 1802-1889.
N3C5   Recherches sur les monnaies des comtes
            de Namur. Bruxelles, M. Hayez, Academie
            Royale de Belgique, 1860.
                172p. 24 pl. 28cm.

JF90   Mey, Jean de.
N3M4   Les monnaies de Namur, 946-
            1714; par Jean de Mey. Bruxelles,
            J. de Mey, 1971.
                104p. illus. 2 plates. 21cm.

JF90   Kiezebrink, Th H. R.
09K5   De munten van Overijssel (1578-
            1796). Brussels, J. de Mey, 1971.
                53p. illus. 20cm.
            (Numismatic pocket book, #13).

JF90   Mey, Jean de.
R4M4   Les monnaies de Reckheim (1340?-1720).
            Brussels, 1968.
                99p. illus. pl. 20cm.

JF90   Hoc, Marcel.
T6H6   Histoire monetaire de Tournai, [by]
            Marcel Hoc. Bruxelles, Societe Royale de
            Numismatique de Belgique, 1970.
                220p. illus. 48 pl. 28cm.
                Bibliography: p. [6]

JF90   Mieris, Frans van, 1689-1763.
U8M6   Beschryving der bisschoplyke munten en
            zegelen van Utrecht. (Money and medals of
            the Bishops of Utrecht). Leyden, S.
            Luchtmans, 1726.
                296p. xi pl. 20cm.

JF90   Mey, Jean de.
Z4M4   De Zeeuwse munten door Jean de
          Mey. Brussel, J. De Mey, 1969.
              44p. plates. fold. charts. 21cm.

COLONIES

JF95   Bucknill, (Sir) John.
B8   The coins of the Dutch East Indies,
          an introduction to the study of the series.
          London, Spink, 1931.
              xii, 291p. illus. 25cm.
              Bibliography: p. vii-ix

JF95   Harpes, Jean.
H3   Monnaies frappees a l'etranger
          par les princes regnants Lux-
          embourgeois, les seigneurs et
          Prelats de la Maison de Lux-
          embourg. Essai de classification
          et de compilation. Luxembourg,
          P. Linden, 1950.
              74p. illus. 22cm.

JF95   Netscher, E.
N4   De munten van Nederlandsch Indie,
          door E. Netscher en J.A. Vander Chijs.
          Batavia, Lange En co., 1863.
              x, 230p. 33 pl. 27cm.

JF95   Scholten, C.
S3   The coins of the Dutch overseas
          territories, 1601-1948. Amsterdam,
          J. Schulman, 1953.
              176p. 20 pl. 26cm.

JF95   Zonnebloem, Uitgave van Uitgeverij.
Z6c   Catalogus munten van de Verenigde
          Oostindishe Compagnie en van Nederlands
          Indie, 1594-1949. Amsterdam, the author,
          [1972], 1975.
              128p. illus. 19cm.

JF95   Zonnebloem, Uitgave van Uitgeverij.
Z6v   Catalogus van de munten van het
          koninkrijk der Nederlanden met
          Curacao, Nederlandse Antillen en Suriname,
          1795-1972. [5th] ed. Amsterdam, [1971].
              117p. illus. 19cm.

SOCIETIES

JG10   Berlin Numismatic Society.
B4   100 jahre Numismatische Gesell-
        Schaft zu Berlin; 1843-1943.
        Berlin, [1943?].
            87p. III tables. 31cm.

JG10   Numismatischen Gesellschaft (Berlin).
N8   Sitzungsberichte der ... From Zeitschrift
        fur Numismatik, 1896.
            32p. 23cm.

COLLECTIONS

JG20   Frankfurt, Main. Historisches Museum.
F7   Das munzkabinett; munzen und medaillen.
        [Exhibition], 1964.
            50 pl. 22cm. (Heft 5 der Kleinen
        Schriften des Historischen Museums).
            Bibliography: p. [15].

JG20   Friedlaender, Julius, 1813-1884.
F75   Das konligliche munzkabinet, geschichte
        und ubersicht der sammlung nebst erklar-
        ender beschreibung der auf schautischen
        ausgelegten auswahl. Von Dr. Julius
        Friedlaender und Dr. Alfred Von Sallet.
        Berlin, S. Calvary, 1873.
            251p. 9 pl. 23cm.

JG20   Nuremberg. Germanischen Nationalmuesum
N8   Munze und medaille in Franken.
        Austellung ... von 31 Marz bis 15 June,
        1963. [Nuremberg, 1963].
            48p. 16 pl. 20cm.

CATALOGUES

JG30   Berliner Numismatische Zeitschrift.
B4   BNZ-Katalog der deutschen munzen von
            1806 bis 1918. Berlin, 1958.
                91p. 21cm.

JG30   Klenau, Tyra Grafin.
K5   Deutsches munzpreis-jahrbuch
            1976; 30,000 auktionssergebnisse
            Deutscher munzen im jahr 1975.
            Munchen, Ernst Battenberg, 1976.
                714p. 22cm.

GENERAL WORKS

JG40   Craig, William D.
C7   Germanic coinages (Charlemagne through
            Wilhelm II). [The author, 1954].
                242p. illus. 25cm.
                Supplement.

JG40   Halke, Heinrich.
H3   Einleitung in das studium der numis-
            matik. 3rd ed. Berlin, Reimer, 1905.
                219p. 8 pl. 24cm.

JG40   Suhle, Arthur.
S9   Deutsche munz- und geldgeschichte
            von den anfangen bis zum 15 jahr-
            hundert. Munchen, Ernst Battenberg,
            1970.
                258p. illus. 22cm.

SPECIAL ASPECTS

JG50   Wormser, Moritz.
W6   German siege pieces from the sixteenth
            to the eighteenth century. Reprinted
            from The Numismatist, 1962.
                12p. illus. 22cm.

JG65   Davenport, John Stewart, 1907-
D3c   German church and city talers, 1600-
       1700. Galesburg, Ill., 1967. Estimated
       prices.
           349p. illus. 23cm.
           Bibliography: p. 345-348.

JG65   Davenport, John Stewart, 1907-
D3g   German talers, 1700-1800.
       Galesburg, Ill., 1958. London,
       Spink, 1965.
           416p. illus. 23cm.
           Bibliography: 414-416

JG65   Davenport, John Stewart, 1907-
D3g2   German talers since 1800. Galesburg,
       Ill. [1949]
           xii, 207p. illus., maps. 24cm.
           Bibliography: p. 206-207.

JG65   Davenport, John Stewart, comp, 1907-
D3o   Oversize multiple talers of the
       Brunswick duchies and Saxe-Lauenburg,
       [The author, 1956]
           73p. illus. 28cm.
           Second edition: Large size silver coins
       of the world. (CC65.D3)

JG65   Deutschen Bundesbank.
D4   Deutsche taler, von den anfangen der
       talerpragung bis zum dreisig jahrigen
       Krieg. Aus der munzensammlung der Deutsche
       Bundesbank. Munchen, Deutsche Bundesbank,
       [1974].
           unpaged. 60 plates. 29cm.

JG65   Hierinn verden Verganchent und abgerissen-
H5   befunden/ verinn und ausserhalb des Reichs/
Ref.   gemunzten Thalergroschen/ ... N.p., n.
       pub., 1567.
           122p. ill. 22cm.

JG65   Kittelmann, E.
K5   Beschreibung der neusten Deutschen
       thaler. Neustrelitz, E. Germany,
       Emil Frehse, 1897.
           79p. illus. 22cm.

JG65   Schwalback, Carl.
S3   Die neuesten Deutschen thaler, doppel-
          thaler und doppelgulden. Leipzig,
          Zschiesche & Koder, 1895.
              39p. 4 pl. 29cm.

JG65   Schulten, Wolfgang.
S38   Deutsche munzen aus der zeit
          Karls V.; typenkatalog der geprage
          zwischen dem beginn der talerpragung
          (1484) und der dritten Reichsmunzordnung
          (1559)... Frankfurt/Main, P. N. Schultez
          1974.
              503p. 115 plates. 24cm.

COPPER, PORCELAIN, ETC.

JG67   Eklund, O. P.
E4   Copper coins of German states. A.N.A.,
          1962.
              126p. illus. 22cm.
              Reprinted from The Numismatist, v.48,
          (1935).

JG67   Eklund, O. P.
E4c   Copper coins of the German Empire and
          republic, 1871-1924. Reprinted from The
          Numismatist, [1962?].
              5p. illus. 22cm.

JG67   Funck, Walter.
F8   German porcelain coins. 2nd ed.
          German-English ed. Nevenburg, 1964.
              12p. 26cm.

JG67   Horn, Otto.
H48   Die Munzen und Medaillen aus der
          Staatlichen Porzellan-Manufactur zu
          Meissen, von Otto Horn. Leipzig,
          Karl W. Hiersemann, 1923.
              x, [40]p. illus. 24 pl. 30cm.

JG67   Roosbroech, Adelbert Van.
R6   Die munzen aus der Staatlichen
          Porzellan manufactur zu meissen.
          Jette-Bruxelles, The author, 1951.
              unp. illus. 30cm.

JG67   Scheuch, Karl.
S3   Munzen aus porzellan und ton der
            staatlichen Porzellan-manufaktur meissen
            und anderen Keramischen Fabriken des In-
            und Auslandes. 2nd ed. Ober-Eschbach,
            The author, 1965.
                176p. illus. 20cm.
                Supp. 1971-Price list.

JG67   Schwalbach, Carl.
S35   Die neuesten Deutschen munzen unter
            thalergrosse vor einfuhrung des reichs-
            geldes. ... Leipzig, Zschiesche & Koder,
            1904.
                51p. 14 pl. 29cm.

ICONOGRAPHY, INSCRIPTIONS, COMMEMORATIVES

JG70   Kuhn, Hermann.
K8   Gepragte form, Goethes morphologie und
            die munzkunst. Weimar, Hermann Boklaus,
            1949.
                62p. front., 24 pl. 25cm.

JG70   Wormser, Moritz.
W6   Luther and the Reformation, illus on
            coins and medals. Priv. print., 1918.
                16p. illus. 24cm.

BY PERIOD - ANCIENT

JG79   Forrer, Robert.
F6   Keltische numismatik der Rhein-
            und Donaulande; erganzte neu-
            ausgabe; ed. by Karel Castelin.
            Originally pub. in 1908. Reprinted-
            Graz, Austria, Akademische Druck,
            1968-69.
                2 vols. illus. 25cm.

JG79   Salmo, Helmer.
S2   Deutsche munzen in vorgeschicht-
            lichen funden Finnlands. Helsinki,
            K.F. Puromichen, 1948.
                432p. 77 plates. 27cm.
            (Suomen miustoyhdristyksen aikakaus-
            kirja, XLVII).

JG80   Bahrfeldt, Emil.
B3   Munzfund von Aschersleben; ein beitrag
          zur denarkunde des XIII. und XIV. Jahrhun-
          derts. Berlin, 1890.
              66p. illus., 4 pl. 22cm.

JG80   Cappe, Heinrich Philipp.
C3   Die munzen der deutschen kaiser und
          Konige des mittelalters. ... Dresden,
          Auf kosten des verfassers, 1848-57.
              3v. in 1. 54 pl. 22cm.

JG80   Dannenberg, Hermann.
D3   Die Deutschen munzen der
          Sachsischen und Frankischen
          Kaiserzeit. 4 vols. with
          addendum. Originally pub. in
          Berlin, 1876. Reprinted-Aalen,
          Scientia Verlag Aalen, 1967.
              Vol. 1-4. 1019p.p adden. 109p.
          121 plates; XV plates. 28cm.

JG80   Heusinger, Friedrich.
H4   Versuch einer abhandlung. ... [Trea-
Rare   tise of practical applications of German
Books   numismatic science of the middle ages;
          its grammar, history, geography, heraldry;
          as well as the German feudal states and
          church law.] Nuremberg, Lochuers, 1750.
              246p. 2 pl. 17cm.

JG80   Jesse, Wilhelm.
J4   Der wendische munzverein.
          Braunschweig, Klinkharat & Biermann,
          1927. Reprint edition., 1967.
              322p. plates. 24cm.

JG80   Krusy, Hans.
K7   Gegenstempel auf munzen des
          spotmittelalters. Frankfurt/Main
          P. N. Schulten, 1974.
              422p. 19 plates. 24cm.

JG80   Lange, Kurt.
L3   Munzkunst des mittelalters.
          Liepzig, Dieterichschen verlags-
          buchhandlung, 1942.
              94p. 64 plates. 29cm.

JG80
M4

Metcalf, David Michael.
     The coinage of South Germany in the
thirteenth century. London, Spink, 1961.
     79p. illus. 24cm.

JG80
M8

Muller, Johannes Heinrich.
     Deutsche munzgeschichte bis zu der
Ottonenzeit, von Dr. Johannes Heinrich.
Leipzig, Weigel, 1860.
     376p. 21cm.

JG80
S2

Die saurmasche munzsammlung.
     Deutscher, Schweizerischer und
     Polnischer geprage von etwa dem
     beginn er graschenzeit bis zur
     kipperperiode. Berlin, Adolph
     Weyl, 1892. Reprint by Gesell-
     schaft fur internationale geld-
     geschichte, Frankfurt/Main, nd.
     151p. civ plates. 30cm.

JG80
S3

Schlumberger, Gustave Leon.
     Des bracteates d'Allemagne, considera-
tions generales et classification des
types principaux, par G. L. Schlumberger.
Paris, 1875.
     xvi, 429p. 8 pl. 28cm.

NINETEENTH AND TWENTIETH CENTURIES

JG87
A7

Arnold, P.
     Catalogue of German coins; gold,
silver & minor coins since 1800 with
their valuations., by P. Arnold, D.
Steinhilber & H. Kuthmann. N.Y. Sterling
Publ. Co., 1972.
     320p. illus. 26cm.

JG87
A7g

Arnold, Paul.
     Grosser Deutscher munz katalog;
von 1800 bis heute [von] Dr. Paul
Arnold, Dr. Harold Kuthmann #[und]
Dr. Dirk Steinhilber. Munchen,
Ernst Battenberg, c1970, 1974.
     431p. illus. 25cm.

JG87   Beckenbauer, Egon.
B4   Standard - munzkatalog Deutschland,
         1871-1969. Munchen, Beckenbauer, 1968, 1954.
              152p. illus. 21cm.

JG87   Bericht uber die thatigkeit des K. K. Haupr-
B45   munzamtes in den jahren 1892 und 1893;
Rare   seit einfuhrung der kronenwahrung.
Books   Vienna, Kaiserlich-Koniglichen Hof-
              und Staatsdruckerei, 1894.
              85p. illus. 27cm.

JG87   Dietzel, Heinz.
D5   Die munzen des deutschen reiches ab
         1871. Berlin, E. Proh, 1970.
              53p. illus. 17cm.

JG87   Fassbender, Dieter.
F3   Gedenkmunzen; Deutschlands und
         Osterreichs seit 1918. Munchen,
         Ernst Battenberg, 1969.
              158p. illus. 21cm. (Kleine
         Numismatische Bibliothek, #4).

JG87   Grasser, Walter.
G7   Deutsche munz gesetze, 1871-
         1971. Munchen, Ernst Battenberg,
         1971.
              431p. 21cm.

JG87   Jaeger, Kurt.
J3   Die deutschen reichsmunzen seit 1871.
         Basel, Munzen und medaillen, 1948-1976.
              6v. ill. 14cm.
              Title beginning 1970: Die deutschen Munzen
         seit 1871.

JG87   Jaeger, Kurt.
J3b   Bewertungstabellen der deutschen Reichs-
         munzen seit 1871, [by] ... [and] Erich B. Cahn.
         Basel, Munzen und Medaillen, 1957-1968.
              6v. 15cm.

JG87   Schon, Gunter.
S3   Kleiner Deutscher munzkatalog;
         mit Liechtenstein, Osterreich
         und Schweiz-von 1871 bis heute.
         Munchen, Ernst Battenberg, 1975.
              174p. illus. 19cm.

JG87   Thun, Norbert.
T5   Deutsche Taler-doppelgulden-
         doppeltaler von 1800-1871 [von]
         Norbert Thun. Frankfurt am Main,
         Norbert Thun, 1976.
             272p. illus. 21cm.

BAVARIA

JG90   Beierlein, J. B.
B4   Die Bayerischen munzen des Hauses
         Mittelsbach, 1180-1550. Munchen, C. Wolf
         & Sohn, 1868. Reprinted Oakdale, N.Y.,
         Alfred Szego, 1972.
             66p. IX plates. 21cm.

JG90   Cappe, Heinrich Philipp.
C3   Die munzen der Herzoge von Baiern, ber
         Burggrafen von Regensburg und der Bifchdfe
         von Augsburg aus dem zehnten und eilften
         Jahrhunderte. Dresden, 1850.
             56p. 8 pl. 22cm.

JG90   Gebhart, Hans.
G4   Die munzen und medaillen der stadt
         donauworth. Halle (Saale), A. Riechmann,
         1924.
             55p. 8 pl. 29cm. (Reichmann's
         munzstudien)

JG90   Hecht, E.
H35   The ducal talers and multiples of
         Bavaria prior to 1800. Baltimore,
         Hesperia Art, 1954.
             36p. pl., map. 24cm. (Hesperia Art
         monograph no. 1)

JG90   Heller, Joseph.
H4   Die bambergischen munzen chronologisch
         geordnet und beschrieben. Bamberg, 1839.
             139p. illus. 18cm.

JG90   Jaeger, Kurt.
J3   Die neueren Munzpragungen der deutschen
V.5   Staaten vor Einfuhrung der Reichswahrung;
         5 [th] Heft, Konigreich Bayern 1806-1871 mit
         Grossherzogtum Berg und Wurzburg. Basel,
         Munzen und Medaillen A.G., 1957, 1968.
             80p. illus. 21cm. (Die neueren Munzpra-
         gungen der deutschen Staaten, V. 5)

JG90   Kellner, Hans-Jorg.
K4   Die munzen der niederbayerischen
         munzstatten. Grunwald bei munchen,
         H. Geiger, 1958.
             150p. illus. 24cm. (Bayerische
         munzkataloge, v.2)

JG90   Och, Friedrich.
O2   Munzen bayerischen klaster, kirchen,
         Wollfahrsorte und anderer geistlichen
         institute...beschrieben von Friedrich
         Och. From the Oberbayarischen archive
         des hist. Vereins von oberbayern, S.13
         Bd. 50. Munich, 1897.
             102p. 2 plates. 25cm.

BRANDENBURG-PRUSSIA

JG92   Jaeger, Kurt.
J3   Die Munzpragungen der deutschen Staaten
V.9   vor Einfuhrung der Reichswahrung; Band 9,
         Konigreich Preussen, 1786-1873. 2d erweit-
         erte auflage. Basel, Munzen und Medaillen,
         1970.
             127p. ill. 21cm. (Die Munzpragungen
         der deutschen Staaten, V. 9)

JG92   Meyer, Adolf.
M4   Pragungen Brandenburg-Preussens, be-
         treffend dessen Afrikanische Besitzungen und
         Aussenhandle, 1681-1810. Berlin, Mittler
         und Sohn, 1885.
             27p. 3 pl. 26cm.

JG92   Schrotter, Friedrich Freiherr von, ed.
S3   Die munzen Friedrich Wilhelms des
         Grossen Kurfursten und Friedrichs III,
         Von Brandenburg. Berlin, Paul Parey,
         1913.
             311p. 53p. 30cm.

JG92   Weyl, Adolph.
W4   Die Paul Henckel'sche Sammlung; Brand-
         enburg-Preussischer munzen und medaillen.
         Berlin, 1876.
             4 v. in 1 ill. 24cm.

SAXONY

JG94 Dorfmann, Bruno.
D6   Munzen und medaillen der Herzoge von
      Sachsen-Lauenburg, eine volkstumliche
      Darstellung des lauenburgischen munzwesens,
      Ratzeburg, H.H.C. Freystatzky, 1940.
          51p. 8 pl. 23cm.

JG94 Jaeger, Kurt.
J3   Die Munzpragungen der deutschen Staaten
V.10 vom Ausgang des alten Reiches bis zur Ein-
      fuhrung der Reichswahrung (Anfang des 19.
      Jahrhunderts bis 1871/73; Band 10, Konigreich
      Sachsen 1806-1873 und Herzogtum Warschau
      1810-1815. Basel, Munzen und Medaillen A.G.,
      1969.
          88p. illus. 22cm. (Die Munzpragungen
      der deutschen Staaten, V.10)

JG94 Jaeger, Kurt.
J3m   Die Munzpragungen der deutschen Staaten
V.11 vom Ausgang des alten Reiches bis zur Ein-
      fuhrung der Reichswahrung (Anfang des 19.
      Jahrhunderts bis 1871/73); Band 11, die
      Sachsischen Herzogtumer. Basel, Munzen und
      Medaillen A.G., 1970.
          128p. illus. 22cm.

WURTEMBURG

JG96 Binder, Christian, 1775-1850.
B5   Wurttembergische Munz-und medaillen
      Kunde, von Christian Binder, neu bearbeit-
      et von Julius Ebner. Unter mitwirkung der
      Stuttgarter Numismatischen Vereinigung
      herausgegeben von der Wurttembergischen
      Kommission fur Landesgeschichte. Stuttgart
      W. Kohlhammer, 1910-1915.
          2v. xxvii pl. 29cm.

JG96 Jaeger, Kurt.
J3   Die neueren Munzpragungen der deutschen
V.1   staaten vor Einfuhrung der Reichswahrung
      (etwa 1806-1873); 1st Heft, Wurttemberg
      und Hohenzollern. Stuttgart, Kurt Jaeger,
      1951, 1966.
          32p. 8 pl. 21cm. (Die neueren Munzpra-
      gungen der deutschen Staaten, Vol. 1).

JG98   Jaeger, Kurt.
A5J3   Die neueren Munzpragungen der deutschen
V.2   Staaten vor Einfuhrung der Reichswahrung
        (etwa 1806-1873); 2[d] Heft, Anhalt, Baden.
        Basel, Munzen und Medaillen A.G., 1954, 1969.
            40p. illus. 21cm. (Die neueren Munzpra-
        gungen der deutschen Staaten. V.2)

JG98   Berstett, Adrian, Freiherr von, 1814-1867.
B3B4   Munzgeschichte des Zahringen-Badischen
        furstenhauses und der unter seinem
        scepter vereinigten stadte und landschaften
        Freiburg im Breisgau, Herder'sche ver-
        lagshandlung, 1846.
            viii, 278p. xlix pl., map. 28 x 22cm.

JG98   Wielandt, Friedrich.
B3W5   Die anfange des landesherslichen
        munzwesens der markgrafen von Baden.
        Karlsruhe, G. Braun, 1949.
            176p. plates. 25cm.

JG98   Jungk, Hermann, 1834-1902.
B7J8   Die bremischen munzen. Bremen, C.E.
Rare   Muller, 1875.
Books   x, 408p. 39 pl. 26cm.

JG98   Duve, Gebhard.
B78D8   Dicktaler-pragungen, 1544-1679;
        geschichte der Braunschweig-
        Luneburgischen, Mehrfachtaler.
        Frankfurt am Main, P. N. Schulten, 1974.
            138p. illus. 24cm.

JG98   Pilartz, Heinrich.
C6P5   Heinrich Pilartz, ein leben im
        dienste der numismatik. Cologne,
        Munzhandlung Heinrich Pilartz,
        1967.
            31p. illus. 21cm.

JG98   Berghaus, Peter.
D6B4   Munzgeschichte der Stadt Dortmund.
        Stadtsparkasse Dortmund, 1958.
            83p. 6 pl., maps. 21cm.

JG98
D6M4
Meyer, Adolf, 1829-1895.
    Die munzen der stadt Dortmund.
Wien, [1884] Supplement 1888.
    138p. 7 pl. 23cm.
    Bibliography

JG98
F7J3
V.6
Jaeger, Kurt.
    Die neueren Munzpragungen der deutschen
Staaten vor Einfuhrung der Reichswahrung;
6 [th] Heft, Frankfurt, Hessen und Isenburg.
Basel, Munzen und Medaillen A.G., 1959.
    83p. illus. 21cm. (Die neueren Munzpra-
gungen der deutschen Staaten, V.6)

JG98
H3J3
V.8
Jaeger, Kurt.
    Die Munzpragungen der deutschen Staaten
vor Einfuhrung der Reichswahrung; 8 [th] Heft,
Hannover und Braunschweig nach 1813. Basel,
Munzen und Medaillen A.G., 1964, 1971.
    104p. illus. 21cm. (Die Munzpragungen
der deutschen Staaten, V.8)

JG98
H3K4
Kennepohl, Karl.
    Die Hammer munzen. Aus 700 jahre stadt
Hamm (Westf.). Festschriff zur erinnerung
an das 700 jahrige bestehen der stadt.
Hamm, Breer & Thiemann, 1927.
    26p. 4 pl. 32cm.

JG98
H34D4
Erstes jahrbuch des Deutschen
    hortgeldsammlerbundes sitz
    Hamburg, 1923-1924. Harburg,
    F. C. Bertram, [1924?]
    45p. 23cm.

JG98
H4B4
Berghaus, Peter.
    Munzgeschichte Herfords [by] Professor
Dr. Peter Berghaus. Herford, Germany
Kreissparkasse, [1971?]
    31p. plates. map. 21cm.

JG98
M4J3
V.4
Jaeger, Kurt.
    Die Munzpragungen der deutschen Staaten
vom Ausgang des alten Reiches bis zur Ein-
fuhrung der Reichswahrung (Anfang des 19.
Jahrhunderts bis 1871/73); [4th Band],
Mecklenburg-Schwerin 1763-1872, Stadte in
Mecklenburg (Rostock und Wismar), Mecklen-
burg-Strelitz im 19. Jahrhundert. 2 [d]
uberarbeitete Auflage. Basel, Munzen und
Medaillin A.G., 1969, 1971.
    48p. illus. map 21cm. (Die Munzpra-
gungen der deutschen Staaten, V. 4)

JG98   Trippe, Anton.
M41T7   Die munzen von Medebach, by Anton
          Trippe. Braunschweig, Klinkhardt &
          Biermann [1967]
              88p. illus. pl. 25cm.
              Bibliography: p. 77-78.

JG98   Jaeger, Kurt.
N3J3   Die Munzpragungen der deutschen Staaten
V.7   vom Ausgang des alten Reiches bis zur Ein-
1969   fuhrung der Reichswahrung Anfang des 19.
          Jahrhunderts bis 1871/73; 7 [th] Band, Herzog-
          tum Nassau 1808-1866, Konigreich Westfalen
          1807-1815, Furstentumer Waldeck und Pyrmont,
          sowie Lippe-Detmold und Schaumburg-Lippe
          mit Wallmoden-Gimborn 1802-1866. [2d erganzte
          Auflage]. Basel, Munzen und Medaillen A.G.,
          1969.
              86p. illus. 22cm. (Die Munzpra-
          gungen der deutschen Staaten, V.7)

JG98   Jaeger, Kurt.
N6J3   Die Munzpragungen der deutschen Staaten
V.6   vor Einfuhrung der Reichswahrung; Band 6,
1971   ... und Jens-Uwe Rixen, Nordwestdeutschland,
          Ostfriesland, Oldenburg, Jever, Kniphausen,
          Bremen, Hamburg, Lubeck, Schleswig-Holstein,
          Laurenburg. Basel, Munzen und Medaillen
          A.G., 1971.
              204p. illus. maps 22cm. (Die Munzpra-
          gungen der deutschen Staaten, V.6)

JG98   Saurma-Jeltsch, Hugo von.
S5S3   Schlesische munzen und medaillen.
          Breslau, 1883.
              79p. 55 pl. 30cm.

JG98   Nau, Elisabeth.
S9N3   Die munzen und medaillen der
          Oberschwabischen stadte. Freiburg,
          Kricheldorf Verlag, 1964.
              186p. XXXV plates. 28cm.

JG98   Noss, Alfred.
T7N6   Die munzen von Trier. Beschreibung
          der munzen 1307-1556. Bonn, Peter
          Harnsteins, 1916.
              364p. 32 pl. 28cm.

COLLECTIONS

JH20   South Kensington museum, London.
P6   ... A descriptive catalogue of Swiss
        coins in the South Kensington museum;
        bequeathed by the Rev. Chauncy Hare
        Townshend. With intro and historical
        notices by Reginald Stuart Poole ...
        London, G. E. Eyre & W. Spottiswoode,
        1878.
            xix, 673p. 25cm.

JH20   Reinhardt, Hans.
R4   Basler munzsammler. Historisches
        museum, Basel, 1946.
            12p. 29cm.

JH20   Collections numismatiques de feu
S7   Dr. Paul=Ch. Stroehlin. Geneva,
            L. Forrer, 1911.
            3rd part. 434p. illus. LIV
            plates. 25cm.

CATALOGUES

JH30   Catalogue des monnaies edite par "Helvetische
C3   Munzenzeitung", Suisse Leichtenstein, 1798-
            1968. Hilterfinger, Albert Meier, 1968,
            1971.
            unpaged ill. 15cm.

GENERAL WORKS

JH40   Clarke, Robert L.
C5   The coinage of Switzerland, 1850 to
            date; an up-to-date pricing guide
            [1st ed.] San Diego, Cal., Malter-
            Westerfield Pub. Co. [1968].
                64p. illus. 24cm.

JH40   Coraggioni, Leodegar.
C6   Munzgeschichte der Schweiz. Geneva,
            Paul Stroehlin & co., 1896.
                xi, 184p. 50 pl. 29cm.

JH40   Weissenrieder, F. X.
W4   100 jahre schweizerisches munzwesen,
            1850-1950. Ein querschnitt durch ein
            jahrhundert eidgenossischer munzges-
            chichte und wahrungspolitik. [Bern,
            1950, rep. 1964].
                101p. illus., 12 pl. 30cm.

SILVER

JH65   Divo, Jean-Paul.
D5   Die taler der Schweiz. Zurich,
            Bank Leu & Co., Lucerne, Adolf Hess, 1966.
                94p. 36 pl. 23cm.
                Bibliography: p. 93-94.

BY PERIOD - MEDIEVAL

JH80   Meyer, H.
M4   Die altesten munzen von Zurich
            oder Zurichs munz geschichte im mittel-
            alter. Zurich, Meyer und Zeller, 1840.
                65p. 2 plates. 18cm.

EIGHTEENTH CENTURY

JH85   Divo, Jean-Paul.
D5m   Die munzen der Schweiz im 18 jahrhundert
            [by] Jean-Paul Divo and Edwin Tobler. Zurich,
            Bank Leu AG, 1974.
                437p. illus. 23cm.

JH85   Hofer, Paul F.
H6   Die munzpragungen der Helvetischen
            republik. Bern, 1936.
                20p. 2 pl. 23cm. (Einfuhrung in die
            schweizerische munzkunde, Heft 1.)

NINETEENTH AND TWENTIETH CENTURIES

JH87   Dietzel, Heinz.
D5   Die munzen der Schweiz ab 1848. Die
            munzen Liechtensteins ab 1858. Berlin,
            E. Proh, 1969.
                28p. illus. 17cm.

JH87   Divo, Jean-Paul.
D51   Die neueren munzen der Schweiz und
1968   des Furstentums Liechtenstein, 1850-
            1967 [by] Jean-Paul Divo. 3d rev. and
            enl. ed. Freiburg im Breisgau,
            Kricheldorf Verlag, 1968.
                126p. illus. 21cm.
                Includes bibliographies

JH87   Divo, Jean-Paul.
D51m   Die Munzen der Schweiz im 19. und
            20. jahrhundert, von ... Divo und Edwin
            Tobler. Zurich, Hess-Leu, 1967.
                212p. illus. 23cm.
                Bibliography: p. 211-212.

JH87   Jaeger, Kurt.
J3   ... Die munzpragungen des Kantons
            Appenzell-Ausserrhoden und der "Neuen
            Kantone" der Schweiz von 1803. Bern,
            1963.
                63p. 15 pl. 24cm. (Schweizrische
            munzkataloge, no. 3)

JH90   Lohner, Carl.
B4L6   Die munzen der Republik Bern;
          beschrieben von Carl Lohner.
          Zurich, Meyer & Zeller, 1846.
              269p; 55p. tables. 23cm.

JH90   Cahn, Erich B.
F7C3   Les monnaies du canton de Fribourg.
          Berne, Societe Suisse de Numismatique,
          1959.
              65p. Viii plates. 24cm. (Catalogue
          des monnaies Suisses, #1)
              In French and German

JH90   [Mildenberg, Leo.]
Z8M5   Zurcher munzen und medaillen. Zurich,
          Haus zum Rechberg, 1969.
              62p. ill. 21cm.

COLLECTIONS

JI20
C3
Catalogo della collezione Sambon di.
monete dell'Italia Meridionale
in oro, argento e bronzo, dal
VII al XIX secolo. Originally
publ. in Milan, 1897. Reprinted-
Bologna, A. Forni, 1967.
125p. X plates. 22cm.

JI20
H3
Hamburger, Leo.
Catalog sammlung des Herrn cav.
E. Gnecchi in Mailand- Italienische
munzen; abtheilung munzstatten acqui
bis Lucca. Auction...7 Januar 1902,
...von L. & L. Hamburger. Originally
publ. in Frankfurt Am Main, 1901.
Reprinted-Oakdale, N.Y., Alfred
Szego, n.d.
290p. XLII plates. 23cm.
Contains prices realized.

CATALOGUES

JI30
B6
Bobba, Cesare.
Super manuale del collezionista di monete
decimali italiane, 1798-1970, con valutazioni
numero dei pezzi coniati e ritirati. Asti,
Bobba, 1970, 1972, 1973.
3v. ill. 17cm.

JI30
C6
Rare
Books
Corpus nummorum Italicorum. Primo
tentativo di un catalogo generale
delle monete medievali e moderne
coniate in Italia o da Italiani in
altri paesi. Rome, 1910-1943.
20v. pl. 35cm.

JI30
G3
Gaudenzi, Luciano.
Prezzario delle monete. Italia-
Vaticano-San Marino. Anno 1966. Bologna,
Arnaldo Forni, [1966].
74p. mostly illus. 17cm.

JI30   Investimenti Trust Finanziario Numismatica.
I5   Catalogo-Prezzario. Rarita monete,
          Casa Savoia, Stato Pontificio, Vaticano,
          San Marino (Dal 1796 al 1963). Florence
          [1964].
              xiv, 252p. 20cm.
              Bibliography: p. xi, xii

JI30   Misul, Marcello.
M5   Le monete d'italia, catalogo delle
          monete emesse da governi provvisori,
          Sardegnia, regno, repubblica, colonie,
          Albania, San Marina, Vaticano. Firenze,
          "La Moneta", [1964-1965].
              90p. illus. 21cm.

JI30   Varesi, Clelio.
V3   Monete decimali Italiane. Pavia, Italy,
          Varesi e Grossule, 1973.
              313p. illus. 17cm.

JI30   Orfino, Vincenzo.
V5   Monete Italiane, from the Venitian sequins
          to the coins of the actual republic; evalua-
          tion for collectors, numismatists, museums,
          exchange banks, goldsmiths, and antiquaries.
          Vienna, n. pub., [ca. 1967].
              301p. illus. 17cm.

GENERAL WORKS

JI40   Bobba, Cesare.
B6   Regioni d'Italia; dal 1730 alla caduta
          del regime Napoleonico by Cesare Bobba. Asti,
          Italy, the author, 1970.
              2 vol., consecutively paged. 622p.
          illus. 17cm.
              Vol. 1-Piemonte e Sardegna; Liguria;
          Lombardia; Veneto; Emilia.
              Vol. 2-Toscana; Lazio; Campania; Sicili

JI40   Dotti, Enrico.
D6   Le monete decimali coniate in Italia da
          Napoleone console a Vittorio Emanuele III
          [by] Enrico Dotti e Mario Rolla. Torino,
          1927.
              138p. illus. 24cm.

JI40   Pagani, Antonio.
P28   Monete Italiane moderne a sistema
        decimale da Napoleone console a Vittorio
        Emanuele III (1800-1946). Milan, M.
        Ratto, 1947, 1953.
            83p. illus. 28cm.
            Bibliography: p. 4-5.

JI40   Pagani, Antonio.
P32   Monete Italiane. Dall'invasione napol-
        eonica ai giorni nostri (1796-1963).
        2nd ed. rev. & corr. Milan, Mario Ratro,
        1965.
            381p. illus. 27cm.

JI40   Rinaldi, Oscar.
R5   Le monete coniate in Italia dalla
        Rivoluzione Francese ai nostri giorni.
        [Mantova, 1954].
            127p. illus. 28cm.

SPECIAL ASPECTS

JI50   Spaziani Testa, Girolamo.
S6   Ducatoni, piastre scudi, talleri e loro
        multipli battuti in zecche Italiane e da
        Italiani all'estero. Rome, Santamaria, 1951.
            2v. ill. 25cm.
            Contents: v.1. Casa savoia da Filiberto II
        a Vittorio Emanuele III (1497-1946), - v.2. I
        romani pontefici interregni e occupazioni
        degli stati pontifici (1523-1870).
            Price supplement.

TECHNICAL ASPECTS

JI60   Clain-Stefanelli, Elvira Eliza.
C5   Italian coin engravers since 1800.
        [Washington, For sale by the Superinten-
        dent of Documents, U.S. Govt. Print.
        Off., 1965]
            67p. illus., ports. 28cm. (Contri-
        butions from the Museum of History and
        Technology, paper 33)
            Bibliography: p. 63-67.

GOLD

JI63   [Vettori, Francesco].
V4   Il fiorino d'oro; antico illustrato
Rare   discorso di un accademico etrusco indiri-
Books   zzato al sig dottore Antonio Francesco
            Gori. Florence, 1738.
                xxviii, 540p. illus. 26cm.

COPPER, ETC.

JI67   Eklund, O. P.
E5   Copper coins of Italy, excluding the
            coins of Papal States. American Numis-
            matic Association, 1963.
                65p. illus. 22cm. Reprinted from
            The Numismatist.

ICONOGRAPHY, INSCRIPTIONS, COMMEMORATIVES

JI70   Bernareggi, Ernesto.
B4   Monete d'oro con ritratto del
            rinascimento Italiano, 1450-1515.
            Milano, Mario Ratto, 1954.
                200p. illus. 30cm.

BY PERIOD - ANCIENT

JI79   Kraus, Franz Ferdinand.
K7   Die munze Odovacars und
            des Ostgotenreiches in Italien
            von Dr. Phil. Franz Ferdinand
            Kraus. Originally pub. in
            Halle, 1928. Reprinted-
            Bologna, A. Forni, [1967].
                227p. XV plates. 25cm.

JI79   Sambon, L.
S2   Recherches sur les anciennes
            monnaies de L'Italie meridionale.
            Naples, Joseph Catango Pub., 1863.
                244p. 28cm.

JI80
B4
Bernardi, Giulio.
    Monetazione del patriarcato
di Aquileia. Trieste,
Italy, Edizioni Lint, 1975.
    212p. illus. 25cm.

JI80
C3
Cagiati, Memmo.
    I tipi monetali della zecca di Salerno.
Atlante-Prezzario, [Napoli, 1925].
    101p. illus. 25cm.

JI80
C35
Cairola, Aldo.
    Le antiche zecche d'Italia [by] Aldo
Cairola. Rome, Edizioni d'Italia, 1971.
    270p. col. plates. illus. 31cm.

JI80
M8
Murari, Ottorino.
    La monetazioni dell'Italia
settentrionale nel passaggio
dal comune alla signoria. Taken
from Nova Historia, no. 2. Verona,
1961.
    45p. illus. 25cm.

JI80
S5m
Simonetti, Luigi.
    Manuale di numismatica Italiana
medioevale e moderna; dalla caduta
dell, impero Romano alla Rivoluzione
Francese. 2 vols. Firenze, Luigi
Simonetti, [1965].
    625p; 616p. 25cm.
    vol. 1.-Acaia-Avisan
    Vol. 2.-Banias-Bologna

JI80
S5mo
V.1
Simonetti, Luigi.
    Monete Italiane medioevali e moderne, volume
I, casa savoia, parte I, da Oddone-Conte (1056)
a Carlo Emanuele, I Duca (1630). Firenze,
Luigi Simonetti, 1967.
    485p. ill. 24cm.

EARLY MODERN

JI83   Kelpsh, A. E.
K4   Silver dollars of Tuscany during the
            rule of the House of Medici. Reprinted
            from The Numismatist, v. lix, 1946.
               19p. 41 illus. 23cm.

EIGHTEENTH CENTURY

JI85   Gamberini, Cesare.
G3   Prontuario-Prezziario della monete
            correnti di Napoleone I (1802-1815).
            Bologna, 1952.
               167p. illus. 17cm.

NINETEENTH AND TWENTIETH CENTURIES

JI87   Cermentini, Cav. Gino.
C4   Prezzario delle monete coniate in Italia
            dal 1800 ab 1966. [by] Cav. Gino Cermentini
            [and] Dr. Giuseppe Toderi. Firenze, A. Gari,
            1966, 1971.
               199p. illus. 17cm.

PAPAL COINS

JI93   Bobba, Cesare.
B6   Le monete dello stato pontificio
            e della citta' del Vaticano da
            Pio VI a Paolo VI. Asti, Italy,
            C. Bobba, n.d.
               270p. illus. 17cm.

JI93   Cinagli, Angelo.
C5   Le monete dei Papi con supplemento di
            Ortensio Vitalini. Reprint. Bologna,
            Forni Editore, [1848].
               480p. plates. 25cm.

JI93   Coffin, Joseph.
C6   Coins of the popes. New York, Coward-
            McCann, [c1946].
                vi, 169p. 17 pl. 22cm.

JI93   Eklund, O. P.
E5   The copper coinage of the Papal States.
            Amer. Numis. Assoc., 1962.
                37p. illus. 22cm. Reprinted from
            The Numismatist.

JI93   Lapa, Frank A.
L3   Vatican City, 1929-; Malter Wester-
            field [1st ed, 1969].
                unpg. illus. 20cm.

JI93   Le Loux, S.A.M.
L4   The coinage of the Republic of San
            Marino (1864-1938) and the state of
            Vatican City (1929-1966). Amsterdam,
            Numismatica Nederland, [1967].
                107p. 6pl.
                Bibliography: p. 107.
                In Dutch and English.

JI93   Low, Lyman Haynes.
L6   The coinage of the popes, showing in
            a tabulated form the papal issues of
            money, together with their rarity, the
            metals used and the provinces and towns
            for which coins were struck. Boston,
            Marvin, 1886.
                8p. 22cm.

COLONIES

JI95   Lambros, Paul
L3   Monete inedite dei gran maestri
            dell'ordine di S. Giovanni di Geru-
            salemme in Rodi. Venice, n.p., 1865;
            Bologna, A. Forni, 1967; Chicago,
            Argonaut Inc., [1975?]
                20p. illus. 22cm.

JI97   Lenzi, Luciano.
L5L4   Le monete Medicee di Livorno nel
          Museo Nazionale di San Matteo in
          Pisa. Estratto da Soldi Numismatica
          1972-1973.
              24p. illus. 30cm.

JI97   Promis, Domenico.
M6P7   Monete dei Paleologi marchesi
          de Monferrato; pubblicate da
          Domenico Promis. Torino,
          Stamperia Reale, 1858.
              39p. VII plates. 27cm.

JI97   Brunatii, Joannis.
P3B7   De re nummaria patavinorum.
Rare   Venice, Jo. Baptistae Pasquali,
Books   n.d.
              80p. 18cm.
              -in Latin.

JI97   Lenzi, Luciano.
P5L4   Sulle Tracce di una sconosciuta
Vert.   moneta di Pisa del II secola A.C.
File   Extracted from "Soldi" numero 2
          anno VII 1972., n.p., n.d.
              unpaged. illus. 32cm.
              contains summary in English by
          William E. Wilson.

JI97   Murari, Ottorino.
P5M8   Tirolino dei conti di valperga
          moneta Piemontese del primo decennio
          del XIV secolo. Taken from Riv. It.
          di Numismatica, vol. IX, serie
          quinta, LXIII, [Perugia, di Salvi
          & Co.,] 1961.
              11p. 25cm.

JI97   Barzan, Rino.
S2B3   Prezzario generale delle monete, prove-
          progetti - esperimenti - saggi coniati
          nelle varie zecche per conti duchi principa
          e sovrani di Casa Savoia [by] Rino Barzan.
          Florence, Editore Luigi Simonetti, 1970.
              314p. illus. 25cm.

JI97   Bobba, Cesare.
S2B6   Monete di Casa Savoia [by] Cesare Bobba.
            Asti, Italy, the author, 1971.
                283p. illus. 17cm.

JI97   Aravamuthan, T. G.
V4A7   Catalogue of Venetian coins in the
            Madras government museum. Madras,
            Gov't. Press, 1938.
                59p. pl. 28cm.

JI97   Gamberini, Cesare di Scarfea.
V4G3   Prontuario prezzario delle monete, osell
            bolle di Venezia; monete dei possedimenti ed
            oselle di Murano, monete battute a Venezia
            ed ossidionali di Napoleone; monete degli
            Absburgo e del Risorgimento, 814-1912, [by]
            Cesare Gamberini di Scarfea. Bologna, La
            Grafica Emiliana, 1960.
                279p. 18cm.

JI97   Ives, Herbert Eugene, 1882-1953.
V4I9   The Venetial gold ducat and its
            imitations. Edited and annotated by
            Philip Grierson. New York, A.N.S., 1954.
                viii, 37p. 16 pl. 23cm. (Numismatic
            notes and monographs, no. 128)

JI97   Murari, Ottorino.
V5M8   Il denaro aquilino grasso di Vicenza.
            Taken from Nova Historia, Verona,
            1956.
                15p. 25cm.

<u>POLAND</u>, <u>CZECHOSLOVAKIA</u>, <u>HUNGRY</u>, <u>RUMANIA</u>, <u>YUGOSLAVIA</u>

POLAND - GENERAL WORKS

JJ20   Czapski, Emeric Hutten.
C9   Catalogue de la collection des
            medailles et monnaies Polonaises. Graz,
            Akademische Druck - U. verlagsanstalt,
            1957.
                5v. in 3 29 pl. 25cm.
                Reprint of 1871-1916 ed.

JJ20   Dietzel, Heinz.
D5   Die munzen polens ab 1916. Berlin,
            E. Proh., 1969.
                16p. illus. 17cm.

JJ20   Gumowski, Marian.
G8   Handbuch der Polnischen numismatik.
            Graz, Akademische Druck-U. Verlagsanstalt,
            1960.
                226p. illus., 56 pl. 27cm.

JJ20   Gumowski, Marian.
G8h   Hebraische munzen im mittel-
            alterlichen Polen. Graz, Austria,
            Akademische Druck, 1975.
                136p. X plates. 28cm.

JJ20   Kalkowski, Tadeusz.
K3   Tysiac lat monety polskiej. Krakow,
            1963.
                261p. illus. 29cm.
                (English summary in back. Thousand
            years of Polish coins).

JJ20   Kaminski, Czeslaw.
K34   Ilustrowany katalog monet Polskich;
            1916-1972. Warsaw, Agencia Wydawnicza, 1973.
                157p. illus. 22cm.

JJ20   Szwagrzyk, Jozef Andrzej.
S9   Pieniadz na ziemiach Polskich
            X-XXw. Warsaw, Zaklad Narodowy
            Imienia Ossolinskich, 1973.
                36p. 137 plates. 30cm.
                Bibliography-pp. 330-339.
                Introductions and lists of tables
            in both Polish and English.

JJ20   Terlecki, Wladyslaw.
T4   Katalog monet polskich 1916-1958.
        Warsaw, 1960.
            71p. illus. 15cm.

POLAND - SPECIAL ASPECTS

JJ30   Gumowski, Marian.
G8   Monety Sasko-Polskie. Krakow, 1920.
            23p. 7 pl. 26cm.

YUGOSLAVIA

JJ40   Colich, Jerome.
C6   Coins of Dubrovnik. Taken from the
Vert.   Journal of Croatian Studies. N.Y. Vol.
File   IX-X, 1968-1969.
            pp. 160-173. illus. 23cm.

JJ40   Mihailovic, Vojislav.
M5   Katalog novca Srbije i Crne Gore
        1868-1918, by Vojislav Mihailovic [and]
        Dragoslav Glogonjac. Beograd,
        Republickog Sekrelarijata Za Kulturu
        SR Srbye, 1973.
            72p. ill. 25cm.
            Book is written in both English and
        Yugoslavian.

CZECHOSLOVAKIA - GENERAL WORKS

JJ50   Artia Foreign trade corporation, Prague.
A7   A catalog of Czechoslovak coins. 2nd ed
        Praha, 1968.
            [40]p. illus. 19 x 20cm.

JJ50   Czechoslovakia State Bank. Prague.
C8   A catalog of Czechoslovak coins.
        Praha, 1968.
            22p. illus. 21cm.

JJ50   Davis, Dolores H.
D3   Czechoslovak coins. [Dallas, Numismatics
          International, 1972]
              112p. illus. 22cm.

JJ50   Dietzel, Heinz.
D5   Die munzen der Tschechoslowakei ab
          1919. Berlin, E. Proh, 1969.
              16p. illus. 17cm.

JJ50   Janovsky, Hubert.
J3   Katalog Knihovny; numismaticke
          spolecnosti ceskoslovenske v praze.
          Praha, 1967.
              201p. 24cm.

JJ50   Nohejlova-Pratova, Emanuela.
N6   Dve stoleti vedecke numismatiky
          v ceskych zemich, 1771-1971; [by]
          Emanuela Nohejlova-Pratova [and]
          Eduard Simek. Praha (Prague),
          Numismaticka Komise, 1971.
              271p. 20cm.

JJ50   Polivka, Eduard.
P6   Mince ceskoslovenske, 1918-1968.
          Hradec kralove, 1969.
              71p. illus. 17cm.
              Bibliography: p. 65-68.

CZECHOSLOVAKIA - SPECIAL ASPECTS

JJ60   Klaasesz, Paul F.
K5   The coinage of the Slovak republic
          1939-1944. Amer. Numismatic Association,
          [1971].
              4p. illus. 22cm.

JJ60   Nemeskal, Lubomir.
N4   Ceskobudejovicka mincovna v letech,
          1569-1611. Budejovice, Jihoceske muzeum,
          1969.
              138p. 16 pl. 21cm.
              Bibliography: p. 120-123.

JJ50   Davis, Dolores H.
D3   Czechoslovak coins. [Dallas, Numismatics
            International, 1972]
                112p. illus. 22cm.

JJ50   Dietzel, Heinz.
D5   Die munzen der Tschechoslowakei ab
            1919. Berlin, E. Proh, 1969.
                16p. illus. 17cm.

JJ50   Janovsky, Hubert.
J3   Katalog Knihovny; numismaticke
            spolecnosti ceskoslovenske v praze.
            Praha, 1967.
                201p. 24cm.

JJ50   Nohejlova-Pratova, Emanuela.
N6   Dve stoleti vedecke numismatiky
            v ceskych zemich, 1771-1971; [by]
            Emanuela Nohejlova-Pratova [and]
            Eduard Simek. Praha (Prague),
            Numismaticka Komise, 1971.
                271p. 20cm.

JJ50   Polivka, Eduard.
P6   Mince ceskoslovenske, 1918-1968.
            Hradec kralove, 1969.
                71p. illus. 17cm.
                Bibliography: p. 65-68.

CZECHOSLOVAKIA - SPECIAL ASPECTS

JJ60   Klaasesz, Paul F.
K5   The coinage of the Slovak republic
            1939-1944. Amer. Numismatic Association,
            [1971].
                4p. illus. 22cm.

JJ60   Nemeskal, Lubomir.
N4   Ceskobudejovicka mincovna v letech,
            1569-1611. Budejovice, Jihoceske muzeum,
            1969.
                138p. 16 pl. 21cm.
                Bibliography: p. 120-123.

JJ60   Polivka, Eduard.
P6   Mince Frantiska Josefa I, 1848-1916.
          Praha, Czech. Numis. Society, 1968.
              67p. 18pl. 17cm.
              Bibliography: p. 57-63.

JJ60   Posvar, Jaroslav.
P69   Moravske mincovny. Brne, Numismaticka
          Spolicnost, 1970.
              175p. pl. 25cm.

JJ60   Sbornik, I. Numismatickeho symposia.
S3   1964. Brno, Moravske museum, 1966.
              244p. 43 pl. map. 25cm. (Numismatica
          moravica, no. 2)

JJ60   Sejbal, Jiri.
S4   Moravska mince doby husitske. Brno,
          Moravske museum, 1965.
              354p. 36 pl. 24cm. (Numismatica
          moravica, no. 1)

JJ60   Zaloha, Jiri.
Z3   Soupis eggenberskych minci. (Coins of
          the Princes von Eggenberg, 17th century).
          Budejouccich, 1969.
              65p. pl. 20cm.
              Resume in German.

HUNGARY - GENERAL WORKS

JJ70   Dietzel, Heinz.
D5   Die munzen Ungarns ab 1848. Berlin,
          E. Proh, 1970.
              24p. illus. 17cm.

JJ70   Huszar, Lajos.
H8   The art of coinage in Hungary.
          [Translated by Susanna Horn. Budapest]
          Corvina Press [c1963]
              50p. 99 plates. 19cm.

JJ70   Pohl, Artur.
P6   Die Grenzlandpragung, Munzpragung
          in Osterreich und Ungarn im funfzehnten
          Jahrhundert. Graz, Austria,
          Akademische Druck-und Verlagsanstalt,
          1972.
              188p. illus. 8 pl. maps. 28cm.
              bibliography: pp. 183-184.

JJ70   Rethy, Ladislaus.
R4   Corpus nummorum Hungariae. Graz,
         Akademische Druck-U. Verlagsanstalt, 1958.
             128p. map, 49 pl. 26cm.

HUNGARY - SPECIAL ASPECTS

JJ80   Kelemen, G. Bela.
K4   The commemorative coins of Hungary.
         1965. Reprinted from The Numismatic
         Scrapbook, v. 29 (1963)
             13p. illus. 20cm.

JJ80   Miklos, Grof Dessewffy.
M5   Barbar Penzei. Budapest,
         Harnyanszky Viktor, 1910.
             72p. 42 plates. 30cm.

JJ80   Molnar, Imre.
M6   The commemoration of 1848. Reprinted
         from The Numismatic Scrapbook, v. 15,
         (1949).
             13p. illus. 20cm.

JJ80   Pohl, Artur.
P6   Ungarische goldgulden des
         mittelalters (1325-1540); mit 4
         abbildungen in farbe und 59 doppel-
         seitigen munztabellen. Graz, Austria,
         Akademische Druck, 1974.
             50p. 59 plates; map. 28cm.

RUMANIA

JJ85   Rauta, Aurelio.
R3   Modern Romanian coins, 1867-1966; a
         detailed and historical description of
         every Romanian coin from the first until
         the present time, patterns included.
         Salamanca, Spain, Asociacion Cultural
         Hispano-Rumana de Salamanca, 1974.
             167p. illus. maps. 25cm.

SOCIETIES

JK10
N8
      Numismatischen Gesellschaft (Vienna).
         Jahresbericht 1910 der ... Wien, K.K.
      Hof, 1911.
         28p. 27cm.

JK10
N8s
Vert.
File
      Numismatischen Gesellschaft (Vienna).
         Statuten der ... Wien, Paul Gerin, 1909.
         8p. 23cm.

JK10
O8
      Osterreichischen Numismatischen
      Gesellschaft.
         Numismatische zeitschrift. Wien,
      the society, 1959.
         83p. V plates. 30cm.

COLLECTIONS

JK20
D8
      Dudik, Beda.
         Des hohen Deutschen Ritterordens
      munz-sammlung in Wien...von
      Dr. B. Dudik. Band 6. Bonn,
      Wissenschaft-liches archio, 1966.
         267p. XXII plates 23cm. (Quellen
      und studien zur geschichte des Deutschen
      ordens. Band 6).

JK20
H6
Vert.
File
      Holzmair, Eduard.
         Das wiedergefundene inventar der
      munzsammlung Ferdinands I. Vienna, 1961.
         11p. 2pl. 29cm.
         Reprinted from Numismatischen Zeit-
      schrift, v. 79, 1961, p. 79-89.

CATALOGUES

JK30   Cejnek, R. Josef.
C4   Osterreichische munzpragungen von
            1705 bis 1935...von R. Josef Cejnek.
            Wien, 1935.
                93p. 23cm.

GENERAL WORKS

JK40   Aichholz, V. Miller zu.
A5   Osterreichische munzpragungen 1519-1938
Rare   ... A. Loehr - E. Holzmair. 2nd ed.
Books   Wien, 1948.
                2v. 56 pl. 27 x 36cm.

JK40   Corpus nummorum Austriacorum.
C6   Band V. Leopold I-Karl VI,
Vol. 5   1657-1740. Neu gestaltet und
            bearbeitet von Helmut Jungwirth
            nach dem werk [von] V. Miller zu
            Aichholz, A. Loehr, E. Holzmair:
            Osterreichische munzpragungen 1519-1938
            1938. Wien, Kunst-historisches
            Museum, 1975.
                232p. 42 plates. 30cm.

JK40   Jaeckel, Peter.
J3   Die munzpragungen des hauses Habsburg
            1780-1918 und der bundesrepublic Osterreich
            1918-[date]. Basel, Munzen und medaillen
            A. G., 1956, 1965, 1970.
                183p. illus. 21cm. (Die Munzpragun-
            gen der deutschen Staaten, v.3)

JK40   Mort, Selwyn, R.
M6   Coins of the Hapsburg emperors and
            related issues, 1619 to 1919. Melbourne,
            Hawthorn Press, 1959.
                179p. front. 22cm.

JK40   Probszt, Gunther.
P7   Quellenkunde der munz-und geldges-
            chichte der ehemaligen Osterreichisch-
            Ungarischen monarchie. Graz, Akademische
            Druck-U. Verlagsanstalt, 1954.
                xii, 134p. 24cm.

SPECIAL ASPECTS

JK50   Davenport, John Stewart, 1907-
D3   The talers of the Austrian noble houses,
            by John S. Davenport. Organization of
            International Numismatists [1972]
                vi, 64p. illus. 23cm.
                bibliography: p. 63

JK50   Hans, J.
H3   Maria-Theresien-Taler, zwei jahr-
            hunderte, 1751-1951. Klagenfurt, 1950, 1961.
                60p. 21cm.

SILVER

JK65   Voglhuber, Rudolf.
V6   Taler und Schautaler des erzhauses
            Habsburg, 1484-1896. Frankfurt am Main,
            Numismatischer verlag Pr. Busso Peus
            Nachf, 1971.
                415p. 191 plates. 24cm.

COPPER, ETC.

JK67   Eklund, O. P.
E4   Copper coins of Austria-Hungary.
            Reprinted from the Numismatist, 1962.
                16p. illus. 22cm.

BY PERIOD - ANCIENT

JK79   Archaeologia Austriaca; beitrage.
A7   zur Palaanthropologie ur-und
                fruhgeschichte Osterreichs. Heft
                6. Wien, Franz Deuticke, 1950.
                    55p. VIII plates. map. 26cm.

BY PERIOD - MEDIEVAL

JK80   Egg, Erich.
E35   Die munzen Kaiser Maximilians I.
Rare   Tiroler Numismatische Gesellschaft, 1970.
Books   229p. illus. 28cm.

JK80   Moeser, Karl.
M6   Die grosse munzreform unter Erzhoerzog
            Sigmund von Tirol (Die ersten grossen
            silver und deutschen bildnismunzen aus
            der munzstatte hall im Inntal) by Karl
            Moeser und Fritz Dworschak. Vienna,
            Edward Stepan, 1936.
                176p. 24 pl. 25cm. (Osterreichisches
            munz und geldwesen im mittelalter, vol 7).
                Bibliography: p. 164-170.

JK80   Szego, Alfred.
S9   The coinage of medieval Austria, 1156-
            1521, a basic outline. The author, 1970.
                56p. illus. 21cm.

EARLY MODERN

JK83   Cejnek, R. Josef.
C4   Osterreichische, Ungarische, Bohmische
            und Schlesische Munzpragungen v. 1519-
            1705... von R. Josef Cejnek. Wien [1937]
                144p. 23cm.

JK83   Koch, Bernhard.
K6   Ein beitrag zum munzwesen der osterr-
Vert.   eichischen Schinderlingszeit. Vienna,
File   1961.
                [7]p. illus. 29cm.
                Reprinted from Numismatische Zeit-
            schrift, v. 79 (1961)

NINETEENTH AND TWENTIETH CENTURIES

JK87   Dietzel, Heinz.
D5   Die munzen Osterreichs ab 1848.
            Berlin, Buchdruckerei Erich Proh, 1969.
               26p. illus. 17cm.

JK87   Holzmair, Eduard.
H6   Munzgeschichte der osterreichischen
            Neufursten. ... Vienna, 1946.
               73p. 1 pl. 29cm.
               Reprinted from Numismatische Zeit-
            schrift, v.71, 1946, p. 6-74)

REGIONAL, A-Z

JK90   Posvar, Jaroslav.
B6P6   Die wahrung in den landern der
            Bohmischen krone; eine ubersicht der
            zahlungsmittel vom neunten bis zum
            anfang des zwanzigsten jahrhunderts.
            Austria, Akademische Druck, 1970.
               129p. XII plates. 28cm.

JK90   Koch, Bernhard.
S2K6   Der Salzburger pfennig. Munz-und
            geldgeschichte Salzburgs im mittelalter.
            Vienna, 1953.
               38p. 2 pl. 29cm.
               Reprinted from Numismatische Zeit-
            schrift, v. 75 (1953)

JK90   Probszt, Gunther.
S2P7   Die munzen Salzburgs. Graz,
            Akademische Druck-und Verlagsanstalt,
            1959.
               289p. 27 pl. 23cm.

JK90   Luschin, Arnold.
S7L8   Steirische munzfunde; fund-
            tabellen und ergebnisse. Graz,
            Austria, Akademische Druck, 1971.
               148p. illus. 28cm.

JK90   Modrijan, Walter.
S7M3   Schild von Steier; beitrage
          zur Steirischen vor-und
          fruhgeschichte und munzkunde. Graz,
          Steirischen Landesmuseum, 1954.
              47p. illus. 23cm.

JK90   Resch, Adolf.
T7R4   Siebenburgische munzen und medaillen
1965   von 1538 bis zur gegenwart; herausgegeben
          von ausschuss des vereines fur siebenbur-
          gische landeskunde, by Adolf Resch.
          Hermannstadt, 1901.
              [259]p. illus. 86 pl. 25cm.
              "Reprinted in 1,000 copies, 1965."

JK90   Wormser, Moritz.
T7W6   Coins and medals of Transylvania in
          New York collections. From Amer.
          Journal of Numismatics, v. 48, 1914.
              42p. 10 pl. 28cm.

<u>GREECE</u> <u>AND</u> <u>BALKAN</u> <u>STATES</u>

BALKANS - SPECIAL ASPECTS

JL40   Gardiakos, Soterios.
G3   A catalogue of the coins of Dalmatia et
         Albania (1410-1797). [Oak Park, Ill.],
         Obol International, 1970.
             31p. illus., map. 21cm.
             Bibliography: p. 28

JL40   Metcalf, David Michael.
M4   Coinage in the Balkans, 820-1355.
         Institute for Balkan Studies. Chicago,
         Argonaut, 1966.
             xix, 286p. 16 pl., maps. 25cm.
             Bibliographical footnotes.

JL40   Rengjeo, Ivan.
R4   Corpus der mittelalterlichen
         munzen von Kroatien, Slavonien,
         Dalmatien und Bosnien [by] Ivan
         Rengjeo. Graz, Austria, Akademische
         Druck- u. Verlagsanstalt, 1959.
             142p. illus. 26 pl. 28cm.
             Includes bibliographies

GREECE - GENERAL WORKS

JL70   Divo, Jean Paul.
D5   Modern Greek coins, 1828-1968; a
         detailed description of every known Greek
         and Cretan coin from the time of
         Capodistrias until the present time.
         Zurich, Bank Leu; Amsterdam, Jacques
         Schulman, 1969.
             100p. illus. 26cm.
             Bibliography: p. 100

JL70   Gardiakos, S.
G3   The coinage of modern Greece, Crete,
         the Ionian Islands & Cyprus. Chicago,
         Argonaut, 1969.
             96p. illus., maps, 16pl. 22cm.

JL70   Katsouros, Floros.
K3   Die numismatische situation...
          wahrend der Revolution von 1821 und
          die ersten neugriechischen munzen
          des I. A. Kapodistrios. Hamburg,
          Auktionshaus Tietjen & Co., 1975.
               76p. illus. 24cm.

GREECE - SPECIAL ASPECTS

JL80   Lambros, Paulos, 1819-1887.
L3c   Coins and medals of the Ionian Islands.
          Coins issued under Venetian rule ca.
          1730-1797. Coins and medals of the
          republic of the Ionian Islands 1801-1807.
          Coins and medals issued under the provi-
          sional occupation by Britain 1809-1815.
          Trans & ed. by Aloisius Barozzie. Amster-
          dam, B.R. Gruner, 1968.
               80p. with illus. 22cm.

JL80   Lambros, Paul, 1819-1887.
L3g   The coins of the Genoese rulers of
          Chios (1314-1329). Trans by Aloisius
          Barozzi. Oak Park, Ill., Obol Interna-
          tional, 1968.
               29p. pl. 21cm. (In Greek & English)

JL80   Lambros, Paul, 1819-1887.
L3u   Unpublished coins struck at Glarentza
          in imitation of Venetian by Robert of
          Taranto Sovereign of the Peloponnesus
          (1346-1364). Trans by Betty Gardiakos.
          Oak Park, Ill. Obol International, 1969.
               31p. 2 pl. 21cm.
               Contains: Greek text & English trans.

CYPRUS - GENERAL WORKS

JL90   Fitikides, T. J.
F5   Collect Cyprus coins; a handbook for
          collectors of modern coins of Cyprus.
          San Diego, Malter-Westerfield, [1969].
               34p. illus. 21cm.

JL90   Gardiakos, Soterios.
G3   The coins of Cyprus, 1489-1571.
          [Oak Park, Ill.], Obol International,
          [1969]; 1975.
              36p. illus. 21cm.
              Bibliography: p. 36

JL90   Lambros, Paul.
L3   Monnaies inedites du royaume de
1967   Chypre au moyen age, par P. Lambros.
          Bologna, Forni, 1967.
              2 v. in 1, illus. 9pl. 22cm.
              In Greek and French.
              Reprint of 1876 ed.

JL90   Pridmore, F.
P7   Modern coins and notes of Cyprus
          by Major F. Pridmore. Nocosia,
          Cyprus, Central Bank of Cyprus, 1974.
              323p. illus. 25cm.

CYPRUS - SOCIETIES

JL92   Santamas, M. L., ed.
S2   Cyprus Numismatic Society, Numismatic
          Report, 1973-75 (vol. IV-VI). [Larnace,] Cyprus,
          Cyprus Numismatic Society, 1973.
              71p. 29cm.

<u>SOVIET UNION</u>, <u>LATVIA</u>, <u>LITHUANIA</u>, <u>ESTONIA</u>

COLLECTIONS

JM20 Kosoff, A., ed.
K6   The Mikhailovitch collection: Russian
coins and medals. [Encino, Calif.]
c1958.
  24p. illus. 28cm.

JM20 Patchkoff, O. G., et. al.
P3   World collection. Alma-
Ata, USSR, "Kazakstan", 1967.
  223p. illus. 21cm.
In Russian.

JM20 Zograf, A. N.
Z6   Gallery of coins. Moscow,
Russian Academy of Science, 1957.
  129p. X tables. 23cm.
In Russian.

GENERAL WORKS

JM40 Bekish, John I.
B4   Numismatic notes; collection of articles about Russian numismatics. Sydney,
the author, 1960.
  64p. illus. 26cm.
In Russian.

JM40 Harris, Robert P.
H3   A guidebook of Russian coins, 1725-
1970. Santa Cruz, Cal., Bonanza, 1971, 1974.
  160p. illus. 20cm.
Bibliography: p. 158-160

JM40 Kratchkofski, V. A.
K7   Eastern epigraphs. Moscow,
Science Academy of the USSR, 1953.
  124p. illus. 26cm.
In Russian.

JM40   Georgii Mikhailovich, Grand Duke of Russia, 1863-1919.
M5   Monnaies de l'empire de Russie,
       1725-1894 [par] Georges Michailovitch.
       Traduction francaise par Nadine Tacke
       nee Lenivova. Boston, Quartermann
       Publications [1973]
            xxxvi, 657p. illus. 32cm.
            Reprint of the 1916 ed. published in
       Paris.

JM40   Petrov, V.I.
P4   Catalogue des monnaies russes de tous
       les princes, tsars et empereurs depuis
       980 jusqu'a 1899. Graz, Akademische
       Druck-U. Verlagsanstalt, 1964.
            86p. 46 pl. 29cm. Reprint of 1899 ed.

JM40   Shelloff, D. B.
S5   Coin works from 2d century BC
       to present. Moscow, Russian
       Academy of Science, 1956.
            221p. IX plates. 23cm.
            In Russian.

JM40   Soohodolsky, Anatol.
S6   Rare copper, silver, gold and platinum,
       coins of Russia. San Francisco, 1944.
            40p. 15cm.

JM40   Spassky, I. G.
S65   The Russian monetary system. Amster-
       dam, J. Schulman, 1967.
            253p. illus. 27cm.

TECHNICAL ASPECTS

JM60   Yahnin, V. L.
Y3   Medieval Russian monetary
       weighing system. Moscow,
       Moscow University, 1956.
            205p. fold-out charts. 22cm.
            In Russian.

GOLD

JM63   Clain-Stefanelli, Elvira Eliza.
C5   Russian gold coins. London, Spink,
    1962.
       39p. illus. 19cm.

JM63   Severin, H. M.
S4   Gold and platinum coinage of Imperial
    Russia from 1701 to 1911; a compilation
    of all known types and varieties. New
    York, Crown and Taler, 1958.
       77p. 17 pl. 23cm.

SILVER

JM65   Holmasto, Thure R.
H6   Venajan Hopearahat 1700-
    1917. Helsinki, the author, 1968.
       77p. 21cm.

JM65   Severin, H. M.
S4   The silver coinage of Imperial Russia,
    1682 to 1917: a compilation of all known
    types and varieties. Basel, Munzen &
    Medaillen; Amsterdam, Schulman; London,
    Spink, 1965.
       276p. 48 pl., tables, diagrs. 23cm.

COPPER, ETC.

JM67   Eklund, O. P.
E5   Copper coins of Russia and Poland.
    Reprinted from The Numismatist, 1962.
       22p. illus. 21cm.

ICONOGRAPHY, INSCRIPTIONS, COMMEMORATIVES

JM70   Becker, Thomas Wm.
B4   The defeat of Napoleon in Russia.
Vert.   Reprinted from Numismatic Scrapbook,
File   v. 25, no. 5, (May, 1959).
              [6]p. illus. 20cm.

BY PERIOD - MEDIEVAL

JM80   Alef, Gustave.
A5   The political significance of the
Vert.   inscriptions on Muscovite coinage in the
File   reign of Vasili II. In: Speculum a
          journal of medieval studies, vol. 35,
          no. 1 (January, 1959).
              19p. xi pl. 25cm.

EARLY MODERN

JM83   Kelpsh, A. E.
K4   Rubles of Peter the Great. Reprinted
          from The Numismatist, 1962.
              32p. illus. 22cm.

JM83   Lapa, Frank A.
L3   Russian wire money. [1st ed. n.p.,
          1967]
              16p. illus. 23cm.

EIGHTEENTH CENTURY

JM85   Antoshevski, I. K.
A5   The Konstantine rouble 1825. Trans.
          by V. Arefiev. St. Petersburg, 1904.
              28p. illus. 21cm.
          In Russian and English.

NINETEENTH AND TWENTIETH CENTURIES

JM87   Arefiev, Vsevolod.
A7   Russian coins, 1802-1917, guidebook of
          coin types. Santa Barbara, Cal., 1971.
              26p. illus. 24cm.
              Bibliography

RUSSIA, PROVINCES, A-Z

JM90   Pakomof, E. A.
A9P3   Monetary treasures of Azerbaijan and
          other Republican fundamental and
          regional Caucasus pieces. USSR,
          Science Academy of Azerbaijan,
          1954.
              91p. 25cm.
              -in Russian.

JM90   Lang, David Marshall.
G4L3   Studies in the numismatic history of
          Georgia in Transcaucasia, based on the
          collection of the Amer. Numis. Society.
          New York, American Numismatic Soc., 1955.
              x, 138p. illus., map, xv pl. (Numis-
          matic notes and monographs, no. 130)
              Bibliography: p. 126-131.

UZBEK SSR

JM91   Yernazarova, Tamara S.
Y4   The monetary circulation of Sam-
          arkand in the light of numismatic
          data (up to the beginning of the
          IXth century AD). From "Afrasiab",
          "Fan" Pub. House, Tashkent, 1974.
              144p. plates. 29cm.

JM92   Bertier de la Garde, A. L.
B4   Coins of rulers of the Cimmerican
            Bosporus who are identified by
            monograms. From "Sovietskaya Ark-
            heologiya", Moscow, 1971.
                259p. V plates. 29cm.

JM92   Frolova, N. A.
F7b   The Bosporus and Rome at the end
            of the 1st century AD and the
            beginning of the 2nd, in the light of
            numismatic data. From "Vestnik
            Drevnei Istorii," #2, Moscow, 1968.
                26p. 1 plate. 29cm.

JM92   Frolova, N. A.
F7c   The coinage of the Bosporus king Eupator
            (154-170A.D.). From "Numizmatika i Epigra-
            fika," 1971.
                41p. pl. 30cm.

JM92   Frolova, N. A.
F7c2   The coins of Sauromates III
            (229-231 AD). From "Brief
            communications of the Institute of
            Archeology in the USSR Academy of
            Sciences", #133, 1973.
                20p. 3 plates. 29cm.

JM92   Frolova, N. A.
F7c3   The coins of the Scythian King
            Seilurus. From "Sovietskaya
            Arkheologrya", 1964.
                32p. illus. 30cm.

JM92   Frolova, N. A.
F7c4   The currency of the Bosporus
            during the reign of Cotys III
            (227-233AD). From "Sovietskaya
            Arkheologiya", #3, Moscow, 1973.
                29p. 6 plates. 29cm.

JM92   Frolova, N. A.
F7c5   The currency of the Bosporus under
            Rhescuporis IV (233-234AD) and
            Ininthimeus (234-238 AD). From
            "Sovietskaya Arkheologiya, #1.
            Moscow, 1974.
                34p. 6 plates. 29cm.

JM92   Frolova, N. A.
F7i   An item from the history of the
          Bosporus at the middle of the 2nd.
          cent. AD. From "Vestnik Drevnei
          Istorii," #1. Moscow, 1972.
              16p. 1 plate. 29cm.

JM92   Frolova, N. A.
F7o   On the dates of the reigns of the Bosporus
          kings Rhadamsades and Rhescuporis VI. From
          "Sovietskaya Arkheologiya", 1975.
              33p. ill. 30cm.
              Bound with JM92.F7c3.

JM92   Frolova, N. A.
F7o2   On the monetary circulation of the
          Bosporus in the 3rd cent. BC. From
          "Sovietskaya Arkheologiya", #4,
          Moscow, 1970.
              16p. 1 plate. 29cm.

JM92   Karyshkovski, P. O.
K3b   The Bosporus and Rome in the first century
          A.D. in the light of numismatic data. From
          "Vestnik Drevnii Istorii", 1953.
              35p. 2 pl. 29cm.

JM92   Karyshkovski, P. O.
K3c   Comments on coins of Olbia.
          Taken from "Sovietskaya Arkheologiya",
          #3, 1960.
              29p. illus. 29cm.

JM92   Karyshkovski, P. O.
K3c2   Concerning inscriptions on
          early coins of Olbia. From
          "Materialy po arkheologii
          Severnogo Prichernomorya", Odessa,
          1962.
              29p. illus. 29cm.

JM92   Karyshkovski, P. O.
K3f   From the history of the
          currency of Olbia in the 1st-
          2nd centuries AD. From
          "Numizmatika i Epigrafika", Vol. 9,
          1971.
              26p. 2 plates. 29cm.

JM92   Karyshkovski, P. O.
K3i   Items from the history of the currency in
            the Bosporus in the IIIrd century A.D. N.p.,
            Odessa State Archeological Museum, 1959.
                33p. ill. 30cm. (Materials on the Archae-
            ology of the Northern Black Sea Littoral,
            no. 2)

JM92   Karyshkovski, P. O.
K3i2   Items from the history of the Olbia coinage
            in the Hellenistic period. N.p., Odessa State
            Archeological Museum, 1962.
                59p. 30cm. (Materials for the Archaeology
            of the Northern Black Sea Littorial, no. 4)

JM92   Karyshkovski, P. O.
K3m   The monetary circulation of Olbia
            at the end of the 2nd century BC
            and during the 1st half of the 1st
            century. From "Numizmatika i
            Epigrafika", Vol. 5, 1965.
                23p. 29cm.

JM92   Karyshkovski, P. O.
K3o   Olbia and Chersonesus in the light of
            numismatic data. From "Kratkiye Soobsch-
            cheniya Odesskogo Arkheologicheskogo Muzeya",
            1963.
                17p. 30cm.

JM92   Karyshkovski, P. O.
K3o2   Olbia ases with an owl type. From "Soviet-
            skaya Arkheologiya", 1962.
                16p. ill. 29cm.

JM92   Karyshkovski, P. O.
K3o3   Olbia coins found near Odessa.
            From "Studies of the Mechnikov Odessa
            State Univ." Vol. 149, 1959.
                13p. illus. 30cm.

JM92   Karyshkovski, P. O.
K3o4   On the circulation of Cyzicenes
            at Olbia. From "Numizmatika i
            Epigrafika", Vol. 2. Moscow, 1960.
                28p. 29cm.

JM92   Karyshkovski, P. O.
K3v   The value of the coin metals in the Olbia
            and in the Bosporus state during the IVth
            century B.C. From "Vestnik Drevnii Istorii",
            1958.
                59p. 30cm.

JM92   The Olbia Ases; items from the
O4   history of the currency and the
            monetary circulation at Olbia.
            From "Studies of the Metchnikov
            Odessa State Univ.", V. 149, 1959.
            75p. 2 plates. 30cm.
            -translated from the Ukranian.

LATVIA

JM93   Holmasto, Thure R.
H6   Latvia - Lettland; metallirahat ja
            setelit; mynt och sedlar; munzen und
            banknoten; coins and notes, by Thure R.
            Holmasto. Helsinki, The Author, 1969.
            12p. 21cm.

LITHUANIA

JM95   Holmasto, Thure R.
H6   Liettua - Litauen, Lithuania;
            metallirahat ja setelit; mynt och sedlar;
            munzen und banknoten; coins and notes,
            by Thure R. Holmasto. Helsinki, The
            Author, 1969.
            12p. 20cm.

JM95   Karys, Jonas K.
K3   Senoves lietuviu pinigai; istoriga
            ir numizmatika. (Ancient Lithuania
            currencies; history and numismatics)
            Bridgeport, Conn., 1959.
            396p. ill. 24cm.
            English summary: p. 364-374.
            Bibliography: p. 375-382

OTHER

JM97   Andersin, Olof J.
A5   Estniska mynthandboken; Estnisches
            munz-handbuch, med varderingspriser,
            1975. Huddinge, Lembit Forlags, [1975].
            23p. illus. 21cm.

JM97   Holmasto, Thure R.
H6   Viron metallirahat ja setelit; Estlands
         mynt och sedlar; die Estnische munzen und
         banknoten; coins and notes of Esthonia.
             23p. 21cm.

JM97   Platbarzdis, Aleksandrs.
P5   Coins and notes of Estonia, Latvia,
         Lithuania. Stockholm, Numismatiska
         Bokforlaget, 1968.
             123p. pl. 26cm.

CATALOGUES

JN30   Said, Emmanuel.
S2   Said Malta stamp and coin
          catalogue. 7th ed. Valletta,
          Malta, the author, 1976, 1977.
              271p. illus. 22cm.

GENERAL WORKS

KA10   Allan, John.
A4   A brief survey of the coinages of Asia
Vert.   from the earliest times to the present
File   day. In: Bartholomew, J.G., A literary
          and historical atlas of Asia, p. 129-144.
            x pl.

KA10   Bartholomew, John George, 1860-
B3   A literary and historical atlas of Asia.
          London, J.M. Dent, n.d.
            xi, 226p. maps. 17cm.
            Partial Contents: Allan, J., A brief
          survey of the coinages of Asia, from the
          earliest times to the present day.

KA10   Kouymjian, Dickran K., Ed.
K6   Near Eastern numismatics, iconography
          epigraphy and history; studies in honor of
          George C. Miles. Beirut, American University
          of Beirut, 1974.
            478p. illus. 30cm.

KA10   Robinson, John, Comp.
R6   Oriental numismatics; a catalog of the
          collection of books relating to the coin-
          age of the East presented to the Essex
          Institute, Salem, Massachusetts by John
          Robinson. Compiled by the donor. Salem,
          compiler, 1913.
            102p. 24cm.

REGIONAL, A-Z

KA20   Hamidi, Hakim.
A3H3   A catalog of modern coins of Afghani-
          stan. [1st English ed.] Kabul, Ministry
          of Finance, 1967.
            vii, 43p. 19 pl, illus. 26cm.

KA20
A3M5
Mitchiner, Michael.
    The multiple dirhems of medieval
Afghanistan. London. Hawkins Publica-
tions, 1973.
    137; 11p. illus. 31cm.

KA20
A7B3
Basmadjian, K. J.
    Numismatique generale de l'Armenie
(Monnaies Armeniennes et autres monnaies
frappees en armenia) Venice, 1936.
    226p. illus. 24cm.
    In Armenian

KA20
A7B4
Bedoukian, Paul Z.
    Coinage of Cilician Armenia. New
York, A.N.S., 1962.
    xxxi, 494p. illus, map. 23cm.
(Numismatic notes and monographs, no. 147)
    Bibliography: p. xi-xxi.

KA20
A7B4m
Bedoukian, Paul Z.
    Medieval Armenian coins. Reprinted
from Revue des Etudes Armenennes, Tome VIII.
Paris, n.p., 1971.
    69p. illus. 24cm.

KA20
K5T6
Torrey, Charles Cutler, 1863-
    Gold coins of Khokand and Bukhara.
New York, A.N.S., 1950.
    37p. illus. 24cm. (Numismatic
notes and monographs, no. 117)

KA20
T8A7
Artuk, Ibrahim.
    Fatih'in sikke ve Madalyalari
[by] Ibrahim Artuk and Cevriye Artuk.
Istanbul, Belediye Matbaasi, 1946.
    40p. IX plates, 24cm.

KA20
T8B8
Butak, Behzad.
    Resimli Turk Paralari (Turkish coins
in pictures); 11th, 12th & 13th centuries.
Istanbul, Pulhan Matbaasi, 1947 (1948).
    140p. illus. 24cm.

KA20
T8B8c
Butak, Behzad.
    Cumhuriyet devrinde madeni paralar,
1923-1955 [by] Behzad Butak. Istanbul,
Pulhan Matbaasi, 1955.
    [74p.] illus. 25cm.

KA20
T8B8g

Butak, Behzad.
    Giyas Ud-din Keyhusrev II bin
Keykubad'in; Gorulememis iki Sikkesi;
Resimli Turk Paralarina (Turkish coins
in Pictures) 11th, 12th & 13th centuries.
Istanbul, Pulhan Matbaasi, 1950.
    pp. 129-136. illus. 25cm.

KA20
T8C6

Constantinople. Musee imperial Ottoman.
    Catalogue des monnaies turcomanes ...
Beni Ortok, Beni Zengui, Frou' Atabeq-
veli et Meliks eyoubites de Meiyafarikin
par I. Ghalib Edhem ... Bologna, Forni,
[1894].
    175p. 8 pl. 21cm.

KA20
T8H3

Hadziotis, Costas Chr.
    Greek counterstamps on Turkish
coins. Reprinted from the Numismatist,
Oct., 1970.
    pp. 1417-1428. illus. 24cm.

KA20
T8K6

Kocaer, Remzi.
    Osmanli altinlari; gold coins of the
Ottoman Empire. Istanbul, 1967.
    191p. illus. 16cm.
In Turkish and English

KA20
T8M3

MacKenzie, Kenneth M.
    Countermarks of the Ottoman Empire,
1880-1922 [by] Kenneth M. MacKenzie
and Samuel Lachman. London, Hawkins
Publications, 1974.
    56p. illus. 29cm.

KA20
T8O3

Olcer, Cuneyt.
    Sovyet Rusya Muzelerindeki
(Moskova ve Leningrad) nadir Osmanli
Madeni Paralari. Istanbul, Yenilik
Basimeri, 1972.
    64p. 5 plates. 24cm.

KA20
T8S2

Santamas, M. L.
    Turkish coins in British Cyprus,
Larnaca, Cyprus, 1973.
    pp. 163-173. charts. 24cm.

KA20
T8S7
Vert.
File

Stepkova, Jarmila.
    Coins of the Osmanli Sultans in the
coin-hoards found on Czechoslovak territory. Annals of the Naprstek Museum,
Prague, 1963.
    [50]p. 5 pl. map. 24cm.

KA20   Wood, Howland.
T8W6   The toughra as found upon coins.
            Printed from The Numismatist for July, 1905
            (v.18).
                13p. illus. 22cm.

IRAN, MEDIEVAL PERSIA

KA30   British Museum. Dept. of coins & medals.
B7   The coins of the shahs of Persia,
            Safavis, Afghans, Efsharis, Zands, and
            Kajars, by Reginald Stuart Poole. London,
            British Museum, 1887.
                xcv, 336p. 24 pl. 23cm.

KA30   Rabino, Hyacinth Louis, 1877-
R3   ... Coins, medals, and seals of the
            shahs of Iran, 1500-1941 ... [Hertford,
            Eng., S. Austin and Sons, Ltd., oriental
            and general printers] 1945, 1973 (reprinted).
                xv, 108p. 4 pl., tables. 25cm.

KA30   Walker, John.
W3   The coinage of the second Saffarid
            dynasty in Sistan. New York, A.N.S., 1936.
                46p. map, tables, 5 pl. 17cm.
            (Numismatic notes & monographs, no. 72)

MODERN ISRAEL

KA40   Bertram, Fred.
B4   Israel's 20-year catalog of coins and
            currency including Palestine Mandate and
            state medals by Fred Bertram & Robert
            Weber. New York, Louis Denberg Founda-
            tion, [c1968].
                127p. illus. 22 x 20cm.

KA40   Bertram, Fred.
B4c   Catalog of Israel's coins, currency and
            medals, including Palestine mandate. 1st ed.
            Jerusalem, Israel-American Coin Co. Ltd., c1966.
                56p. illus. 22cm.

KA40   Gould, Maurice M.
G67   Israel numismatics and its bright future.
         New York, American Israel Numismatic Assoc.,
         n.d.
             16p. ill. 23cm.

KA40   Gould, Jean.
G68   The story of Israel in coins, by Jean
         & Maurice Gould. Hollywood, Wilshire
         Book Co., 1971.
             137 p.

KA40   Haffner, Sylvia.
H3   . The history of modern Israel's money,
         1917 to 1967, including state medals
         and Palestine mandate. 1st ed. [La Mesa,
         Calif., 1967] 2nd ed, 1970.
             196p. illus. 23cm.

KA40   Israel Numismatic Society.
I8   Thirteen years of the Israel
         Numismatic Society, 1945-1959. Jerusalem,
         1959.
             28p. 24cm.

KA40   Israel Government Coins and Medals
I86   Corporation.
             Catalogue [of commemorative
         coins and State medals.] Jerusalem,
         1969.
             40p. illus. 27cm.

KA40   Kadman, Leo.
K3   Israel's money; a catalogue of the coins,
         commemorative coins, medals, and bank-
         notes issued by the State of Israel, 1948-
         1963. Tel-Aviv, Schocken Pub. House, 1963.
             98p. illus. 24cm. (Pub. of the
         Israel Numismatic Society. Numismatic
         studies and researches, v.4)

KA40   Kagan, Arnold H., comp.
K33   Israel's money and medals 1948-
         1973. 1st ed. Valley Stream,
         N.Y., A. H. Kagan; Tel Aviv, Israel
         Numismatic Publications, Ltd., 1974.
             V. 1 314p. illus. 23cm.

KA40   Nurock, Max.
N8   The ceremonial coins and medals of
           Israel. Published in Ariel; a
           review of the arts and sciences
           of Israel. Jersulem, Cultural
           Relations Dept., 1965.
                38p. illus. 23cm.

KA40   Orient Publishing House of stamps
O7   and Coins, Inc., comp.
                Israel coin and state medals
           catalog, 1975-76. Tel-Aviv, [1975].
                127p. illus. 17cm.

KA40   Trowbridge, Richard J.
T7   Coinage of the Palestine mandate.
           [1st ed. Long Beach, Cal., Coins of the
           British world, 1969], 1971.
                14p. illus. 21cm.

LEBANON

KA45   Hulse, Granvyl G.
H8   Modern Lebanese coinage. Dallas,
           Numismatics International, 1974.
           Reprint from the Numismatic International
           Bulletin.
                18p. illus. 22cm.

MOHAMMEDAN EMPIRE

KA50   Balog, Paul.
B3   Umayyad, Abbasid and Tulunid
           glass weights and vessel stamps.
           N.Y., A.N.S., 1976.
                322p. LV plates. 28cm.
           (Numismatic Studies, #13).

KA50   British Museum, Dept. of Coins & Medals.
B7   A catalogue of the Muhammadan coins in
           the British Museum by John Walker. London,
           British Museum, the Trustees, 1941-1956.
                2v. illus, pl, map. 25cm.
                Contents: I. Cat of the Arab-Sassanian
           coins. II Arab-Byzantine & post-reform
           Umaiyad coins.

KA50   Codrington, Oliver.
C6   A manual of Musalman numismatics.
          Chicago, Argonaut, 1970.
              230p. 24cm.
              Reprint of London, 1904 ed.
              Bibliography: p. 233-239

KA50   Hodivala, Shahpurshan Hormasji.
H6   ... Historical studies in Mughal
          numismatics. Calcutta, The Numismatic
          society of India, 1923.
              376p. 24cm. (Occasional memoirs of
          the Numismatic society of India, II)

KA50   Lane-Poole, Stanley.
L3   The coins of the Eastern khaleefehs
Vol.1   in the British Museum by Stanley Lane
          Poole; edited by Reginald Stuart Poole.
          Originally published in London, 1875.
          1st reprinting: Bologna, A. Forni, 1967.
              263p. VIII plates. 22cm.
          (Catalogue of Oriental coins in the
          British Museum, Vol. 1.)

KA50   Lane-Poole, Stanley.
L3   The coins of the Mohammedan
Vol.2   dynasties. Classes III-X, by
          Stanley Lane Poole; edited by Reginald
          Stuart Poole. Originally pub-
          lished in London, 1876. 1st
          reprinting: Bologna, A. Forni, 1967.
              279p. VIII plates. 22cm.
          (Catalogue of Oriental coins
          in the British Museum, Vol. 2.)

KA50   Lane-Poole, Stanley.
L3   The coins of the Turkuman Houses
Vol.3   of Seljook, Urtuk, Zengee etc. in the
          British Museum. Classes X-XIV, by
          Stanley Lane Poole; edited by Reginald
          Stuart Poole. Originally published in
          London, 1877. 1st reprinting: Bologna,
          A. Forni, 1967.
              305p. XII plates. 22cm.
          (Catalogue of Oriental coins
          in the British Museum, Vol. 3).

KA50   Lane-Poole, Stanley.
L3   The coinage of Egypt, (A.H. 358-922) under
V.4   the Fatimee Khaleefehs, the Ayyoobees, and
          the Memlook Sultans, classes XIVa, XV, XVI,
          by Stanley Lane Poole; edited by Reginald
          Stuart Poole. Originally published in London,
          1879. Reprinted: Bologna, A. Forni, 1967.
              279p. viii pl. 22cm.
          (Catalogue of Oriental coins in the British
          Museum, vol. 4)

KA50   Lane-Poole, Stanley.
L3   The coins of the Moors of Africa
Vol.5   and Spain; and the Kings and Imams of
          the Yemen in the British Museum.
          Classes XIVI-XXVII, by Stanley Lane
          Poole; edited by Reginald Stuart Poole.
          Originally published in London, 1880.
          1st reprinting: Bologna, A. Forni,
          1967.
             175p. VII plates. 22cm.
          (Catalogue of Oriental coins in the
          British Museum, Vol. 5).

KA50   Lane-Poole, Stanley.
L3   The coins of the Mongols in the
Vol.6   British Museum, by Stanley Lane Poole;
          edited by Reginald Stuart Poole.
          Originally published in London, 1881.
          1st reprinting: Bologna, A. Forni,
          1967.
             300p. IX plates. 22cm.
          (Catalogue of Oriental coins in the
          British Museum, Vol. 6).

KA50   Lane-Poole, Stanley.
L3   The coinage of Bukhara (Transoxiana)
Vol.7   in the British Museum from the time
          of Timur to the present day, classes
          XXII, XXIII, by Stanley Lane Poole;
          edited by Reginald Stuart Poole.
          Originally published in London, 1882.
          1st reprinting: Bologna, A. Forni,
          1967.
             131p. V Plates. 22cm.
          (Catalogue of Oriental coins in the
          British Museum, Vol. 7).

KA50   Lane-Poole, Stanley.
L3   The coins of the Turks in the
Vol.8   British Museum. Class XXVI, by Stanley
          Lane Poole. Originally published in
          London, 1883. 1st reprinting: Bologna,
          A. Forni, 1967.
             431p. XII plates. 22cm.
          (Catalogue of Oriental coins
          in the British Museum, Vol. 8)

KA50   Lane-Poole, Stanley.
L3   Additions to the Oriental Collection
Vol.9   1876-1888. Part I: Additions to Vols.
         I-IV, by Stanley Lane Poole; edited
         by Reginald Stuart Poole. Originally
         published in London, 1889. 1st
         reprinting: Bologna, A. Forni, 1967.
             405p. XX plates. 22cm.
         (Catalogue of Oriental coins in the
         British Museum, Vol. 9).

KA50   Lane-Poole, Stanley.
L3   Additions to the Oriental
Vol.10   collection 1876-1888. Part II.
         Additions to Vols. V-VIII, by Stanley
         Lane Poole; edited by Reginald Stuart
         Poole. Originally published in London,
         1890. 1st reprinting: Bologna, A.
         Forni, 1967.
             206p; cclxxi XXXIII plates. 22cm.
         (Catalogue of Oriental
         coins in the British Museum, Vol. 10.)

KA50   Lane-Poole, Stanley.
L3a   The coins of the Amawi Khalifehs.
         (Catalogue of the collection of Oriental
         coins belonging to Col. C. Seton Guthrie)
         Chicago, Argonaut, 1968.
             38p. 5 pl. 21cm.
         Reprint of 1874 ed.

KA50   Lane-Poole, Stanley.
L3m   The Muhammadan dynasties; chronological
         and genealogical tables with historical
         introductions. Paris, Paul Geuthner,
         1925.
             361p.

KA50   Lane-Poole, Stanley.
L3u   Coins of the Urtuki Turkumans.
         London, Trubner, 1875. Reprinted [196-].
             x, 44p. 6 pl. 32cm.

KA50   Mayer, Leo Ary, 1895-
M3   Bibliography of Moslem numismatics,
         India excepted. 2d, considerably enl.
         ed. London, Royal Asiatic Scoiety,
         1954.
             ix, 283p. 25cm. (Oriental translation
         Fund [London]. Publications, new ser, v.35)

KA50   Miles, George C.
M5c   Contributions to Arabic metrology, I.
V.1   Early Arabic glass weights and measure
          stamps acquired by the A.N.S., 1951-1956.
          New York, A.N.S., 1958.
              124p. 13 pl. 23cm. (Numismatic notes
          and monographs, no.141)

KA50   Miles, George C.
M5c   Contributions to Arabic metrology, II.
V.2   Early Arabic glass weights & measure
          stamps in the Benaki Museum, Athens &
          the Peter Ruthven Collection, Ann Arbor,
          New York, A.N.S., 1963.
              64p. 11 pl. 23cm. (Numismatic notes
          and monographs, no. 150)

KA50   Miles, George Carpenter.
M5e   Early Arabic glass weights and stamps.
          With a study of the manufacture of eighth-
          century Egyptian glass weights and stamps,
          by Frederick R. Matson. New York, A.N.S.,
          1948.
              168p. 14 pl. 23cm. (Numismatic notes
          and monographs, no. 111)

KA50   Miles, George Carpenter.
M5f   Early Arabic glass weights and stamps,
          a supplement. New York, A.N.S., 1957.
              60p. 4 pl. 23cm. (Numismatic notes
          and monographs, no. 120)

KA50   Miles, George Carpenter, 1904-
M5r   Rare Islamic coins. New York, A.N.S.,
          1950.
              xi, 138p. 10 pl. 23cm. (Numismatic
          notes and monographs, no. 118)

KA50   Plant, Richard J.
P4   Arabic coins and how to read them. 1st
          ed. London, B. A. Seaby Ltd., 1973.
              147p. illus. 22cm.

KA50   Stockholm. Statens historiska museum och
T6   myntkabinet.
              Numi cufici Regii numophylacii holm-
          iensis, quos omnes in terra sueciae
          repertos, (by) Carolus Johannes Tornberg
          ... Upsaliae, Leffler, 1848.
              88, 315p. 14 pl. 28cm.

KA50   Valentine, William H.
V3   Modern copper coins of the Muhammadan
              states of Turkey, Persia, Egypt, Afghani-
              stan, Morocco, Tripoli, Tunis, etc., by
              W.H. Valentine. London, Spink & Son,
              Ltd., 1911.
                   203p. front., illus., maps. 25cm.

MOHAMMEDAN EMPIRE - REGIONAL, A-Z

KA55   Miles, George C.
C7M5   The coinage of the Arab Amirs of
              Crete. New York, A.N.S., 1970.
                   86p. 9 pl. 23cm. (Numismatic notes
              and monographs, no. 160).

KA55   Balog, Paul.
E3B3   The coinage of the Mamluk Sultans of
              Egypt and Syria. New York, A.N.S., 1964.
                   444p. illus, 44pl. 26cm. (Numis-
              matic studies no. 12)

KA55   Adler, Jacob Georg Christian, 1756-1834.
K8A3   Museum cuficum borgianum Velitris,
V.1   Rome, A. Fulgonium, 1782.
Rare   172p. 12 pl. 26cm.
Books

KA55   Sanchez-Giron Blasco, Jose Maria.
M6S2   Monedas de Marruecos; Moroccan coins,
              1879-1971, 1298-1390 [by] Jose Maria
              Sanchez Giron Blasco. Ceuta, Spain, The
              Author, 1972.
                   [79]p. illus. 22cm.
              In Spanish and English

KA55   Miles, George Carpenter, 1904-
P4M5   Excavation coins from the Persepolis
              region. New York, A.N.S., 1959.
                   124p. 21 pl, map. 23cm. (Numismatic
              notes and monographs, no. 143)

KA55   Miles, George Carpenter.
R3M5   The numismatic history of Rayy. New
              York, A.N.S., 1938.
                   xii, 240p. 6 pl. 27cm. (Numismatic
              studies, no. 2)

KA60   Andhra Pradesh Govt. Museum, Hyderabad,
A5b   India.
          Bahmani coins in the Andhra Pradesh
     Government Museum, Hyderabad; [catalogue]
     by Md. Abdul Wali Khan, keeper of coins.
     Hyderabad, Govt. of Andhra Pradesh, 1964.
          xv, 183p. illus, 35 pl. 28cm.

KA60   Andhra Pradesh Govt. Museum, Hyderabad,
A5q   India.
          Qutub Shahi coins in the Andhra Pradesh
     Government Museum; [catalogue] by Md.
     Abdul Wali Khan, keeper of the coins.
     General ed.: N. Ramesan. Hyderabad,
     Govt. of Andhra Pradesh, 1961.
          vii, 50p. illus, 14 pl., map. 33cm.

KA60   Andhra Pradesh Government Museum, Hydera-
A5s   bad, India.
          Select gold and silver coins in the
     Andhra Pradesh Government Museum, Hydera-
     bad, by M. Rama Rao. General editor:
     Md. Abdul Waheed Khan. Hyderabad, Govt. of
     Andhra Pradesh, 1963.
          13p. illus. 28cm. (Andhra Pradesh
     Govt. archaeological series, no. 13)

KA60   Andhra Pradesh Govt. Museum, India.
A5v   A catalogue of the Vijayanagar coins
     of the Andhra Pradesh Govt. museum by
     Sri N. Ramesan. Hyderabad, 1962.
          156p. 21 pl. 28cm.

KA60   Assam. Provincial Coin Cabinet.
A7   Catalogue. 2d ed. by A. W. Botham.
     Allahabad, The Superintendent, Govt. Press
     United Provinces, 1930.
          viii, 577p. illus. 25cm.

KA60   Bombay. Prince of Wales Museum of Western
B6   India.
          Catalogue of the coins in the Prince of
     Wales Museum of Western India. The sultans
     of Gujarat, comp. by C.R. Singhal; ed. by
     G. V. Acharya. Bombay, Pub. for the
     Trustees, 1935.
          xxxii, 154p. pl, map. 26cm.
          Bibliography: p. 151-152.

KA60   British museum. Dept. of coins & medals.
B7m   Catalogue of Indian coins in the British
         museum; the Moghul Emperors. [by Stanley
         Lane-Poole; ed. by Reginald Stuart Poole]
         London, the Trustees, 1892.
             clii, 140(ie 401)p. 33 pl. 23cm.

KA60   British Museum. Dept. of coins and medals.
B7s   Catalogue of Indian coins in the
         British museum. The Sultans of Dehli.
         [By Stanley Lane-Poole ... ed. by Regin-
         ald Stuart Poole]. London, the Trustees,
         1884.
             xliv, 199p. map, 9 pl. 21cm.

KA60   Indian Museum, Calcutta.
I5   Catalogue of the coins in the Indian Museum,
         Calcutta, including the cabinet of the Asiatic
         Society of Bengal. Oxford, Clarendon, 1906-
         1928.
             4v. pl. maps 25cm.

KA60   Indian museum, Calcutta.
I5   Catalogue of coins in the Indian mus-
Supp.   eum, Calcutta. Supplement to vols. II,
         III. by Shamsuddin Ahmad. Delhi,
         Archaeological Survey of India, 1939.
             2v. pl. 25cm.

KA60   Lahore, Central Museum.
L3r   Catalogue of the coins in the Govt.
         Museum, Lahore, comp. by Chas. J. Rodgers.
         Pub. by orders of the Panjab Govt.
         Calcutta, Baptist Mission Press, 1891.
             xix, 149, 29p. 28cm.

KA60   Lahore. Central Museum.
L3w   Catalogue of coins in the Panjab
         museum, Lahore, by R. B. Whitehead ...
         Published for the Panjab government.
         Oxford, Clarendon press, 1914-1934.
             3v. illus, pl, tables. 25cm.
             Contents: I. Indo-Greek coins II.
         Mughal emperors III. Nadir Shah, Durrani
         dynasty.

KA60   Peres, Damiao.
P4   Catalogo das moedas Indo-portuguesas do
         Museu Numismatico Portugues. N.p., Casa da
         moeda, 1963-1975.
             4v. pl. 24cm.
             Contents: Tomo 1. 1511-1657. - Tomo 2.
         1657-1778. - Tomo 3. 1778-1829. - Tomo 4.
         1826-1961.

KA60   Rebello, Fenelon.
R4   Some of the rarer specimens in early
            Indo-Portuguese coinage, by Fenelon Rebello
            [Margao-Goa, India, The Author, 1970]
                [49p.] illus. 4 pl. 18cm.
                Bibliography: p. 9.

KA60   Subrahmanyam, R.
S9   A catalogue of the Ikshvaku coins
            in the Andhra Pradesh Govt. Museum.
            General editor: Iri N. Ramesan.
            Hyderabad, India, the Govt. of
            Andhra Pradesh, 1962.
                48p. map. XV plates. 29cm.
            Rs.3-00 (Andhra Pradesh Govt. Museum
            Series, #5).

INDIA AND CEYLON - GENERAL WORKS

KA70   Brown, C. J.
B7   The coins of India. With twelve
            plates. London, Oxford U., 1922.
                120p. pl. 21cm. (Heritage of India
            series)

KA70   Elliot, (Sir) Walter.
E4   Coins of Southern India. London,
            Trubner, 1886.
                xi, 159p. 4 pl., map. 29cm. (The
            International Numismata Orientalia)

KA70   Gupta, Parmeshwari Lal.
G8   Coins [by] Parmeshwari Lal Gupta. New
            Delhi, Natl. Book Trust, 1969.
                241p. XXXIV plates. 21cm. (India-
            the Land and People)

KA70   Madras, Government Museum.
M3   Coin of India through the ages. Madras,
            1960.
                17p. 3 pl. 25cm.

KA70   Maity, Sachindra Kumar.
M35   Early Indian coins and currency
            system. New Delhi, Munshiram Manoharlal,
            1970.
                136p. 21cm.
                Bibl. p. 119-127

KA70   Prakash, Vidya.
P7   Coinage of South India, an
         introductory survey. Edited by
         A. K. Narain. Varanasi, India,
         The Numismatic Society of India, 1968.
             103p. Vii plates. 24cm.
         (Numismatic Society of India.
         Numismatic notes and monographs, No. 14)

KA70   Singhal, C. R., comp.
S5   Bibliography of Indian coins. Compiled
         by C.R. Singhal, ed by A.S. Altekar.
         Bombay, Numismatic Society of India, 1950-
         52.
             2v. 25cm.
             Contents: 1. Non-Muhammadan series
         2. Muhammadan and later series.

KA70   Sircar, D. C.
S55   Studies in Indian coins. Delhi,
         Motilal Banarsidass, [1968].
             405p. 26 pl. 22cm.

KA70   Tufnell, R. H. C.
T8   Hints to coin-collectors in southern
         India. (From Madras Journal of Literature
         and Science for the Session 1886-87.
             25p. pl. 22cm.

INDIA AND CEYLON - SPECIAL, TECHNICAL ASPECTS

KA75   Valentine, William H.
V3   The copper coins of India ... London,
         Spink & Son, Ltd., 1914-
             2v. maps, illus. 25cm.
             Contents: pt. 1 Bengal & the United
         provinces. pt. 2 The Panjan and contiguous
         native states.

INDIA AND CEYLON - MEDIEVAL

KA80   Cunningham, Sir Alexander.
C8   Coins of medieval India from the
         seventh century down to the Muhammadan
         conquests. London, B. Quaritch, 1894.
             108p. 11 pl., map. 22cm.

KA80   Sivaramamurti, C.
S5   Numismatic parallels of Kalidasa.
           With a foreword by Sir C. P. Ramaswami
           Aiyar. Madras, Shahti Karyalayam [1945].
                xvi, 40p. illus. 20cm.

INDIA AND CEYLON - EARLY MODERN

KA83   Taylor, George P.
T3   The coins of Tipu Sultan. Oxford,
           Numismatic Society of India, 1914.
                32p. II plates. 24cm. (Occasional
           memoirs of the Numismatic Society
           of India).

KA83   Whitehead, R. B.
W5   Some notable coins of the Mughal
           Emperors of India. Reprinted from Numis-
           matic Chronicle, 1923-1930.
                113p. 8 pl. 22cm.

KA83   Whitehead, Richard Benjamin.
W5m   The mint towns of the Mughal
           emperors of India; by R. B.
           Whitehead. Taken from the
           Journal and Proceedings, Asiatic
           Society of Bangal (New Series), Vol.
           VIII, No. 11, 1912.
                531p. charts. 25cm.

INDIA AND CEYLON - MODERN

KA85   Falcke, George.
F3   India's 1862 rupees by George Falcke
           and Robert L. Clarke. [Iola, Wis, Krause,
           1971].
                34p. illus. 23cm.

KA85   India. Ministry of Finance.
I5   Decimal coinage in India. Delhi, Ministry
           of Finance, 1957.
                30p. ill. 21cm.

KA85   Raymond, Wayte, ed.
R3   East India Co; British India;
            native Indian states. Special
            printing. N.Y., Wayte Raymond,
            1955.
                 24p. illus. 23cm.
            (Coins of the World)

INDIA AND CEYLON - REGIONAL, A-Z

KA90   Colombo museum, Colombi, Ceylon.
C4C6   Catalogue of coins in the Colombo
            museum. Part I ... By H.W. Codrington ...
            Hertford, Printed for the Ceylon govern-
            ment by S. Austin & Sons, Ltd., 1914.
                 61p. 4pl. 22cm.

KA90   Codrington, Humphrey William, 1879-
C4C6c   ... Ceylon coins and currency. ...
            Colombo, A. C. Richards, 1924.
                 vii, 290p. 7 pl. 30cm. (Memoirs of
            the Colombo museum, ed. by Joseph Pearson
            ... ser.A, no. 3)

KA90   Lapa, Frank A.
C4L3   Kandy kings of Ceylon, 1055-1295 A.D.
            [Beverly Hills, the author, 1968].
                 44p. illus. 21cm.

KA90   Still, John.
C4S7   Catalogue of coins exhibited in the
            Colombo Museum. Colombo, Ceylon, H.C. Cottle,
            1908.
                 51p. 21cm.

KA90   Still, John.
C4S7f   Notes on a find of eldlings made in
            Anuradhapura. From the Journal of the Royal
            Asiatic Society, Ceylon Branch, 1907.
                 191-198p. pl. 21cm.

KA90   Still, John.
C4S7n   Notes on the variations of the copper
            massas of six Sinhalese rulers. From the
            Journal of the Royal Asiatic Society, Ceylon
            Branch, 1905.
                 398-405p. pl. 21cm.

KA90   Still, John.
C4S7r   Roman coins found in Ceylon. From the
          Journal of the Royal Asiatic Society, Ceylon
          Branch, 1907.
             161-190p. pl. map 21cm.

KA90   Still, John.
C4S7s   Some early copper coins of Ceylon. From
          the Journal of the Royal Asiatic Society,
          Ceylon Branch, 1907.
             199-214p. pl. 21cm.

KA90   Wood, Howland, 1877-1938.
C4W6   The Gampola larin hoard. New York,
          A.N.S., 1934.
             84p. illus, pl. 17cm. (Numismatic
          notes and monographs, no. 61)

KA90   Hull, Donald B.
D4H8   Collectors' guide to Muhammadan coins
          of India, 1200 A. D. to 1860 A. D.
          [Alhambra, Calif., Cunningham Press,
          1972]
             789p. illus. 29cm.
          Includes bibliographies

KA90   Wright, Henry Nelson.
D4W7   The coinage and metrology of the sul-
          tans of Dehli, incorporating a catalogue
          of the coins in the author's cabinet now
          in the Dehli museum. ... pub. for the
          govt. of India. Delhi, Manager of pub-
          lications, 1936.
             xx, 432p. xxiv pl., map. 24cm.

KA90   Clark, William L.
K8C5   The modern coinage of Kutch. New
          York, Wayte Raymond, 1952.
             16p. illus. 23cm. (Coin collector's
          journal, Sept-Oct, 1952)

KA90   Codrington, O.
K8C6   The coinages of Cutch and Kathiawar.
Vert.   Numismatic Chronicle, ..., p. 59-88.
File

KA90   Browder, Tim J.
M3B7   Maldive Islands money. [San Diego,
          Malter-Westerfield, c1969 by The Society
          for International Numismatics].
             48p. illus. 21cm.

KA90   Henderson, John Robertson, 1863-
M8H4   The coins of Haidar Ali and Tipu
            Sultan. ... Madras, Printed by the
            superintendent, Government press, 1921.
                x, 123p. front. (map) ix pl. 24cm.
                Bibliography: p. 117-118

KA90   Tracy, James E.
P3T7   Pandyan coins. From the Madras
Vert.   Journal of literature and science, 1887-
File   88.
                7p. illus. 22cm.

KA90   Webb, William Wilfred.
R3W4   The currencies of the Hindu states of
            Rajputana. Westminster, A. Constable and
            Co., 1893.
                xxi, 135p. 12 pl, map. 25cm.

KA90   Gray, John C. F.
T7G7   Tranquebar: a guide to the coins of
            Danish India, circa 1620 to 1845/John
            C.F. Gray.-Lawrence, Mass.: Quarterman
            Publications, c1974.
                83p. ill. 24cm.
                Bibliography: p. [34]-35.

KA90   Holm, Johan Christian.
T7H6   Trankebar-monter. Copenhagen, 1956.
                14p. illus. 22cm.

FAR EAST - GENERAL WORKS

KB10   Bowker, Howard Franklin.
B6   A numismatic bibliography of the Far
          East: a check list of titles in European
          languages. New York, American numismatic
          society, 1943.
               144p. 17cm. (Numismatic notes and
          monographs, no. 101)

KB10   Coole, Arthur Braddan, 1900-
C6   A bibliography on far eastern numis-
          matics and an union index of the currency,
          charms & amulets of the Far East. ...
          Peking, Calif. college in China, College
          of Chinese studies, 1940.
               421p. 23cm.

KB10   International Numismatic Company.
I5   Value of Ancient Oriental coins.
          Tokyo, International Numismatic Co., 1953.
               unpaged. illus. 26cm.

KB10   Oka, M.
O38   Silver crowns of the far east, by M.
          Oka. Tokyo, Taisei Stamps & Coins, 1966.
               115p. illus. 22cm.
          In Japanese and English.

INDONESIA, MALAYSIA - GENERAL WORKS

KB20   International Stamp and Coin
I5   Agency.
               Coin & paper money catalogue
          of Malaysia-Singapore-Brunei
          (1845 to date). 1st ed. Kuala
          Lumpur, Malaysia, Internatl. Stamp
          & Coin Agency, 1976.
               72p. illus. 22cm.

KB20   Kavanagh, Kevin F.
K3   The coins of Malaysia, 1845-1967,
          including Straits Settlements, Malaya,
          British North Borneo, Sarawak, Brunei,
          Singapore, British trade dollars; compiled
          by Kevin F. Kavanagh. Adelaide, 1969.
               96p. illus., maps. 23cm.
               Bibliography: p. 89

KB20   Millies, Henricus Christiaan, 1810-1868.
M5   Recherches sur les monnaies des
          indigenes de l'archipel indien et de la
          peninsule Malaie. Ouvrage posthume,
          publie par l'institut royal pour la phil-
          ologie et l'ethnographie de l'inde neer-
          landaise. La Haye, M. Nijhoff, 1871.
               viii, 179p. 26pl. 28cm.

KB20   Shaw, William.
S4   Coins of North Malaya by Wm. Shaw and
          Md. Kassim Haji Ali. Kuala Lumpur,
          Muzium Negara, [1971].
               62p. 10pl. 22cm.
               Bibliography

KB20   Singh, Saran, Comp.
S5   The catalogue of Malaysia,
          Singapore and Brunei coins, (1700-1974).
          1st ed. Kuala Lumpur, Malaysia
          Numis. Soc., 1974.
               92p. illus. 27cm.

INDONESIA - LOCAL, A-Z

KB25   Pridmore, F.
P7   Coins and coinages of the Straits
          settlements and British Malaya, 1786 to
          1951. Singapore, Government Printing
          Office, 1955.
               177p. 12pl. 24cm. (Memoirs of the
          Raffles museum, no. 2, June, 1955)
               Bibliography: p. 173-174

KB25   Shaw, William.
S5   Mallacca coins by ... Shaw and Mohd
          Kassim Haji Ali. Kuala Lumpur, Muzium
          Negara, [1970].
               20p. illus. 22cm.
               Bibliography

KB25   Ferraro Vaz, J.
V3   Moeda de Timor. Centenario do Banco
          Nacional Ultramarino, 1864-1964. Lisbon,
          1964.
               171p. 22pl. 28cm.
               Bibliographia: p. 169-171.

PHILIPPINES - GENERAL WORKS

KB30   Allen, Lyman L.
A5   A catalog of Philippine coins, 1828
           to date. 2nd ed., 1968.
                30p. illus. 21cm.

KB30   Bantug, J. P.
B3   The three duros, a chat about Philippine
           numismatics. Manila, Philippine Numismatic
           and Antiquarian Society, 1967.
                17-26p. 23cm. (Philippine numismatic
           monographs, no. 17)

KB30   Basso, Aldo P.
B37   Coins, medals, and tokens of the
           Philippines. Menlo Park, Calif., Chenby
           Publishers, 1968, 1975.
                136p. illus. 24cm.
                Bibliography: p. 136

KB30   De Jesus, Pablo I.
D4   Further report on the Manila hoard. Manila,
           Philippine Numismatic and Antiquarian Society,
           1953.
                5p. ill. 23cm. (Philippine Numismatic
           monographs, no. 9)

KB30   Font, Gregnio S.
F6   Central bank of the Philippines coin issues,
           (1958-1966). Manila, Philippine Numismatic
           and Antiquarian Society, 1967.
                13-16p. 23cm. (Philippine numismatic
           monographs, no. 17)

KB30   Garcia, Mauro, comp.
G3   Philippine numismatic literature, a
           bibliography. Manila, Philippine Numis-
           matic and Antiquarian Society.
                54p. 23cm. (Philippine Numismatic
           monographs, no. 14)

KB30   Huie, Byron S., Jr.
H9   Why the overstrike? Manila, Philippine
           Numismatic and Antiquarian Society, 1967.
                11-12p. ill. 23cm. (Philippine numismatic
           monographs, no. 17)

KB30   Perez, G. S.
P4   The founding of the Philippine Numismatic
            and Antiquarian Society. Manila, Philippine
            Numismatic and Antiquarian Society, 1953.
                6-8p. ill. 23cm. (Philippine numismatic
            monographs, no. 9)

KB30   Perez, Gilbert S.
P4m   The mint of the Philippine Islands.
            New York, American Numismatic Society,
            1921.
                8p. illus. 16cm. (Numismatic notes
            and monographs, no. 8)

PHILIPPINES - SPECIAL ASPECTS

KB40   Ciriaco, Conrado F.
C5   Notes on recent finds of the piloncito.
            Manila, Philippine Numismatic and Antiquarian
            Society, 1973.
                28-30p. 23cm. (Philippine numismatic
            monographs, no. 18)

KB40   De Jesus, Pablo I.
D4   Counterstamped coins of the Philippines.
            Manila, Philippine Numismatic and Anti-
            quarian society, 1966.
                26p. 8pl. 23cm. (Philippine Numis-
            matic monographs, no. 16)

KB40   De Jesus, Pablo I.
D4a   A catalog of the countermarked coins of
            the Philippines from 1828 to 1837. Manila,
            Philippine Numismatic and Antiquarian
            Society, 1950.
                20p. illus. 23cm. (Philippine
            Numismatic monographs, no. 6)

KB40   De Jesus, Pablo I.
D4s   Supplement to the "Catalog of counter-
            marked coins of the Philippines from 1828-1837.
            Manila, Philippine Numismatic and Antiquarian
            Society, 1953.
                9-11p. 23cm. (Philippine numismatic
            monographs, no. 9)

KB50 Bantug, Jose P.
B3   The gold coin of the ancient Maniolas.
Manila, Philippine Numismatic and Antiquarian
Society, 1973.
     27p. ill. 23cm. (Philippine numismatic
monographs, no. 18)

KB50 Bantug, Jose P.
B3m   Monetario de las islas Filipinas durante
Vert. el regimen espanol. Manila, Philippine
File   Numismatic and Antiquarian Society, 1951.
     30p. illus. 22cm. (Philippine Numis-
matic Monographs, no. 8)

KB50 De Jesus, Pablo I.
D4   Early coins of the Philippines.
Reprinted from The Numismatist [v.60,
1947], 1962.
     16p. illus. 23cm.

KB50 Ganzon de Legarda, Angelita.
G3   Piloncitos to pesos; a brief history of
coinage in the Philippines. Manila, Bancom
Development Corp., 1976.
     84p. illus. 24cm.

KB50 Perez, Gilbert S.
P4   Foreign coins related to Philippine
Vert. history. Manila, Philippine Numis. &
File   Ant. Society, 1954.
     5p. 22cm. (Philippine numismatic
monographs, no. 10)

KB50 Santos, Ildefonso.
S2   Tagalog terminology for monetary values
Vert. during the Spanish regime. Manila,
File   Philippine Numis. & Antiquarian Society,
1954.
     9p. 22cm. (Philippine Numismatic
Monographs, no. 10)
     Bibliography

KB50 Shafer, Neil.
S5   United States territorial coinage for
the Philippine Islands; an illus history
and price list of coins, tokens, & medals
issued for the Philippine Islands as a
United States Territory. Racine, Wis.,
Whitman, [1961].
     63p. illus. 20cm.

KB50   Vanderwende, George S.
V3   United States-Filipinas coinage from
           1903 to 1946. The Philippine numismatic
           and antiquarian society. Manila, The
           society, 1958.
               23p. illus. 22cm. (Philippine
           numis. monographs, no. 13)

INDOCHINA, A-Z

KB70   Novak, John A.
A5N6   A working aid for collectors of
           Annamese coins. [Longview, Wash.,
           Olmsted, 1966].
               115p. illus. 21cm.

KB70   Permar, Bernard J.
A5P4   Catalogue of Annam coins, 968-1955.
           [Saigon, the author, 1963].
               71p. 73pl. 24cm.

KB70   Schroeder, Albert, 1851-
A5S3a   ... Annam. Etudes numismatiques.
           Paris, Imprimerie nationale, F. Lerous,
           1905.
               2v. 651p. tab. 28cm.
               Bibliography: p. 639-648

KB70   Schroeder, Albert, 1861-
A5S3g   ... Gold and silver coins of Annam
           edited by J. Permar and John A. Novak.
           Based on ... Annam, etudes numismatiques,
           ... Paris, 1905. Original plates, basic
           index numbers retained. Okinawa, Louis
           King, 1968.
               80p. illus. 21cm.

KB70   Daniel, Howard A., III.
C3D3   The catalog and guidebook of
Vol.1   Southeast Asian coins and
           currency. 1st ed. Reston, Va.,
           the author, 1975.
               110p. illus. 28cm.
               -Vol. 1-French Colonial

KB70   de Sousa, Antonio B., Comp.
H6D4   Standard catalogue--Hong Kong coins
           and currency notes [and] British trade
           dollars, 1863-   . Hong Kong, the
           compiler, 1967.
               47p. illus. 19cm.

KB70   Hamson, Ray.
H6H3   Regal coinage of Hong Kong. Hong
          Kong, Govt., [1960?].
              26, 15p. illus. 19cm.
              In English and Chinese.

KB70   Joshi, Satya Mohan, comp.
N4J6   Catalogue of the coins of Nepal.
          [Nepal, His Majesty's Govt.; Dept.
          of Archaeology & Culture, 1961.
          Reprinted 1963].
              39p. 22cm.

KB70   Bencharit, Phairot.
T5B4   Garuda bird on Thai coins. Bankok, Thailand,
          Treasury Dept., Ministry of Finance, 1976.
              41-56p. ill. 21cm.
              In English and Thai.

KB70   Le May, Reginald Stuart, 1885-
T5L4   The coinage of Siam. ... Bangkok,
          The Siam society, 1961, 1962, 1975.
              xi, 136p. illus., xxxii pl. 25 x 20cm.

KB70   Piromya, Sompop, Comp.
T5P5   Coins in Thailand [by] Capt. Sompop Piromya
          R.T.N. Bangkok, Bangkok Natl. Museum, 1975.
              183p. illus. 21cm.
              Written in both Thai and English

KB70   Siam Society Journal.
T5S5   Studies of old Siamese coins; selected
          articles from The Siam society journal.
          Volume X, Bangkok, 1961.
              148p. pl. 25cm.
              Bibliography: p. 148

KB70   Sonakul, M.R. Ayumongol.
T5S6   The legend of Garuda. Bangkok,
          Thailand, Treasury Dept. Ministry
          of Finance, 1976.
              6-8p. ill. 21cm.
              -in English and Thai
              -Bound with: "Garuda bird on
          Thai coins"-by Phairot Bencharit.

KB70   Kempf, Fred.
T6K4   A primary report on native Tibetan
          coins. 1st ed. [Seattle], the author,
          c1969.
              [14p] illus. 28cm.

<u>CHINA</u>

GENERAL WORKS

KC20   Chun-Po, Chang.
C5   Chinese coins and their history. From
Vert.   China Reconstructs, v. VII, no. 4, April,
File   1958.
                [4]p. illus. 28cm.

KC20   Coole, Arthur Braddan.
C6c   Coins in China's history. ... Tientsin,
           Hopeh, China, Student work department of
           the Tientsin Hui wen academy, 1937. Kan-
           sas, Inter-Collegiate Press, 1963, 1965.
                158p. illus. 24 x 31cm.
                Bibliography: p. 158.

KC20   Coole, Arthur Braddan, 1900-
C6e   A bibliography on Far Eastern numismatology
V.1   and a coin index, by A. B. Coole assisted by
           Hitoshi Kozono (and) Howard F. Bowker.
           (1st ed. Denver, 1967.)
                581p. 24cm. (His An Encyclopedia of
           Chinese coins, v.1)

KC20   Coole, Arthur Braddan, 1900-
C6e   The early coins of the Chou dynasty.
V.2   Boston, Quarterman Publications [1973].
                557p. illus. 24cm. (His
           An encyclopedia of Chinese coins, v.2).

KC20   Coole, Arthur Braddan, 1900-
C6e   Spade coin types of the Chou dynasty.
V.3   Boston, Quarterman Publications [1973,
           c1972].
                513p. illus. 24cm. (His An
           encyclopedia of Chinese coins, v.3)

KC20   Coole, Arthur Braddan.
C6e   Pointed spade coins of the
Vol.4   Chou dynasty. Lawrence, Mass.,
           Quarterman Inc., 1975.
                450p. illus. 24cm.
           (Encyclopedia of Chinese coins,
           Vol. 4).

KC20
C6e
Vol.5

Coole, Arthur Braddan.
     Ch'i heavy sword coins and debatable
pieces of the Chou era. Lawrence, Mass.,
Quarterman Pub., 1976.
     574p. illus. 24cm.
(Encyclopedia of Chinese coins, Vol. 5).

KC20
C6e
V.6

Coole, Arthur Braddan, 1900-
     State of Ming knife coins and minor knife
coins. Lawrence, Mass., Quarterman, 1976.
     512p. ill. 24cm. (An Encyclopedia
of Chinese Coins, v.6)

KC20
H3

Hang Seng Bank Ltd, Hong Kong.
     An introduction to Chinese coinage.
[1965].
     16p. illus. 19 x 18cm.

KC20
K3

Kann, Edward, 1880-1962.
     Illustrated catalog of Chinese coins,
[gold, silver, nickel and aluminum].
Los Angeles, 1954, 1966.
     476p. 224 pl. map, 24cm.

KC20
R4

Remmelts, A. A., comp.
     Chinesische kaschmunzen; [618-1912.]
Zusammengestellt von A. A. Remmelts.
Amsterdam, J. Mevius, n.d.
     77p. illus. 20cm.

KC20
S3

Schjoth, Fredrik.
     Chinese currency (currency of the Far
East.) ... Chou dynasty (1122B.C.-255B.C.)
through Ch'ing dynasty (1644 A.D.-1911
A.D.) Rev. & ed. by Virgil Hancock.
Iola, Wis., Krause, 1965.
     xviii, 88p. 146 pl. 34cm.

KC20
T7

Tsiang, C. C.
     Illustrations of Chinese gold silver
and nickel coins. Shanghai, Universal
Stamp & Coin Co., 1939.
     257p. illus. 19cm.
     In Chinese and English.

KC20
W3

[Wang, Shou-ch'ien].
     Rare Chinese coins. [Shanghai, China,
Universal coins & stamps co., 1935]
     104p. 20cm.

KC20   Watson, John G.
W32   Common Chinese coins. London, Spink,
                  1924.
                      26p. illus. 24cm.
                      Reprinted from the Numismatic Circular.

SPECIAL ASPECTS

KC30   Gibbs, Howard D.
G5   Chinese imperial names, a finding list
                  of era and personal names on Chinese
                  imperial coins. Pub. under direction of
                  Numismatic review ... New York. Stack,
                  c1944.
                      [56]p. 28 x 22cm.

KC30   Higgins, Francis Carlos, 1867-
H5   The Chinese numismatic riddle. ... an
                  address delivered before the A.N.A. in
                  convention. New York, The Elder numis-
                  matic press, 1910.
                      34p. illus. 23cm.

KC30   Raeburn, G. Duncan.
R3   Coins that never were. Shanghai,
Vert.   Reprinted from the China Journal, 1938.
File   [6]p. illus. 25cm. (Bulletin of the
                  Numismatic Society of China, no. 4)

KC30   Wood, Howland.
W6   Recent faking of Chinese coins at the
Vert.   Chinese mints. From The Numismatist,
File   v. XLV, 1932.
                      [5]p. illus. 22cm.

TECHNICAL ASPECTS

KC40   China, Republic of.
C5   Coins minted by the Central Mint of
                  China. Tapei, Taiwan, 1964.
                      22p. illus. 19cm.

KC40   Kann, Edward, 1880-1962.
K3   The currencies of China; an investiga-
            tion of gold and silver transactions
            affecting China, with a section on copper.
            Shanghai, Kelly & Walsh, 1926.
                xviii, 540p.,xlviii. illus. 26cm.

GOLD

KC43   Kann, Edward, 1880-
K3   The coinage of gold in China. Bulletin
Vert.   of the Numismatic Society of China, no. 7,
File   Shanghai, 1941.
                24p. 2 pl. 24cm.
                Reprinted from the Central Bank of
            China's Bulletin, vol. 7, no. 3.

SILVER

KC45   Chang, Nai-chi.
C5   An inscribed Chinese ingot of the XII
            Century A.D. New York, American numis-
            matic society, 1944.
                9p. pl. 17cm. (Numismatic notes and
            monographs, no. 103)

KC45   Kann, Edward, 1880-1962.
K3   Early Chinese silver coinage.
Vert.   Shanghai, Reprinted from The Asia Stamp
File   Journal, v.1, (1939)
                8p. illus. 19cm. (Bulletin of the
            Numismatic Society of China, no. 6)

KC45   Sigler, Phares O.
S5   Sycee silver. New York, The American
            numismatic society, 1943.
                37p. pl. 17cm. (Numismatic notes and
            monographs, no. 99)
                Bibliography: p. 29-31.

COPPER

KC47   Lockhart, Sir James Haldane Stewart,
L6   1858-1937.
               ... The Stewart Lockhart collection of
          Chinese copper coins. ... Shanghai,
          Kelly & Walsh, 1915, 1975.
               174, 36p. illus. 31cm. (Royal Asiatic
          Society, North China branch. Extra volume
          no. 1)

KC47   Mandel, Edgar J.
M3   The copper and brass coins of Kirin.
Vert.   The author, no date.
File   10p. illus. 28cm.

KC47   Ramsden, Henry A.
R3   Modern Chinese copper coins. Reprinted
          from The Numismatist, v. 23-24 (1910-
          1912), 1962.
               28p. illus. 22cm.

ANCIENT

KC50   Jorgensen, Holger.
J6   Old coins of China, a guide to their
          identification, arranged chronologically.
          Los Angeles, 1944, Reprinted 1962.
               [27]p. (incl. 20 pl.) 27, 22cm.

KC50   Li Shih Ch'uan, Pi Tu Pu K'ao.
L5   Historical coin illustrations.
          Taipei, Taiwan, Four Seas Book Room, 1954.
               70p. illus. 25cm.

KC50   Ramsden, H. A.
R3   Chinese early barter and uninscribed
          money. Yokohama, Japan, 1912.
               34p. 3pl. 22cm.

KC50   Terrien de Lacouperie, Albert Etienne
T4   Jean Baptiste, d. 1894.
               Catalogue of Chinese coins from the
          7th cent. B.C., to A.D. 621 including the
          series in the British museum. ed. by
          Reginald Stuart Poole ... London, The
          Trustees; 1892.
               lxxi, 443p. illus. 29cm.

KC50   Ting Fu-Pao.
T5   A catalog of ancient Chinese coins
            (including Japan, Korea & Annam).
            [Shanghai, 1938].
                 illus. 26cm.
                 In Chinese.

KC50   Wang, Yu-Ch'uan.
W3d   The distribution of coin types in
Vert.   ancient China. From The American Numis-
File   matic Society, Museum Notes, no. 3, 1948.
                 [20]p. 3pl. 23cm.

KC50   Wang, Yu-Ch'uan.
W3e   Early Chinese coinage. New York,
            A.N.S., 1951.
                 viii, 254p. maps, 55 pl. 23cm.
            (Numismatic notes & Monographs, no. 122)

EARLY MODERN

KC55   Brudin, J. A.
B7   China, coins of Wang Mang and the
            Mantchu dynasty. [Colorado Springs],
            A.N.A., [1963?].
                 20p. illus. 23cm.
                 "A reprint from The Numismatist"

KC55   Cresswell, O. D.
C7   Chinese cash. London, Spink, 1971.
                 110p. pl. 22cm.

KC55   Mowery, Thomas E.
M6   One cash coins of China's Manchu
            dynasty, 1644-1911; values in five
            grades. 1st ed. St. Paul, Minn.,
            Fortmeyer and Lang, c1972.
                 32p. illus. 22cm.

KC55   Petrie, Alfred E. H.
P4   An illustrated guide to Chinese cash
            pieces of the Manchu mints, A.D., 1662-
            1796. Ottawa, 1964.
                 31p. illus. 21cm. (Collectors
            Research Monograph)

KC55   Woodward, Alphonse Marie Tracey.
W6   The minted ten-cash coins of China,
1971   by A. M. Tracey Woodward. Rev. ed.
          Oakland, Calif., M. R. Fried, c1971.
                151p. illus. 24cm.
                Includes bibliographical references.

MODERN

KC60   Kann, Edward.
K3   Coinage of the Chinese Emigre govern-
          ment, 1949-1957 by David Graham and E.
          Kann. Reprinted from The Numismatist
          vol. 70 (1957).
                12p. illus. 22cm.

KC60   Raeburn, G. Duncan.
R3   Chinese Soviet coins and notes [Shang-
Vert.   hai] Reprinted from The China Journal,
File   1937.
                [6]p. illus. 24cm. (Bulletin of the
          Numismatic Society of China, no. 2)

KC60   Ros, Giuseppe.
R6   Coins of the Republic of China. From
Vert.   Journal of the North-China Branch of the
File   Royal Asiatic Society, vol. 48 (1917).
                [27]p. 17 pl. 24cm.

KC60   Shih, Kalgan.
S5   ... Modern coins of China. 1st ed.
          Shanghai, 1949.
                2v. 147 pl. 23cm.
                Contents: v.1 Chinese v.2 English

REGIONAL, A-Z

KC70   Dorfman, Ben.
M3D6   Manchurian currencies. From "Asia",
Vert.   May, 1934.
File   8p. illus. 29cm.

JAPAN - CATALOGUES, COLLECTIONS

KD10
A5

Andre, Babette, ed.
An exhibit of Oriental coins;
a centennial-Bicentennial gift from
Japan to the city of Denver 1976.
Coin display created and donated
by Kimpo Hanaya. Denver, Commission
on Community Relations, 1976.
12p. illus. 28cm.

KD10
D3

Osaka. Daiwa Bank Ltd.
A glimpse of moneys in Japan. [Osaka,
Japan, 1960]
12p. illus. 18cm.

KD10
H3

Hartshorn, Derick S., III.
Modern Japanese coins with prices by
date and grade; complete with latest
available mintage figures. Springfield,
Mass., [196-?].
20p. 21cm.

KD10
S6

Spadone, John G.
Catalog of modern Japanese, Korean,
Manchukuo coins. 1st ed. Tokyo, Phoenix
Pub. Co. [1960]
88p. illus. 19cm.

JAPAN - GENERAL WORKS

KD20
A7

Art and Coin Publication Co.
Values of ancient Japanese gold
and silver money. Tokyo, Art and
Coin Publication Co., 1951.
48p. illus. 26cm.

KD20
C8

Cummings, Michael L.
Modern Japanese coinage, 1870 to
date. Tokyo, the author, 1975.
112p. illus. 23cm.

KD20   Encyclopedia of Japanese coins and
E5   paper money, including Korea, Manchuria
          ancient gold and silver coins and
          modern paper money. Tokyo, Numismatic
          Dealers Assn., 1970-71, 1973-1976.
          132p. illus. 21cm.

KD20   International Numismatic Co.
I5   International ancient coins and
          medals. Tokyo, International Numismatic
          Co., 1959.
              118p. illus. 18cm.
          Contains lists of mint sets.

KD20   International Numismatic Co.
I5c   A catalog of modern Japanese coins.
          Tokyo, 1966.
              91p. illus. 19cm.
          In Japanese

KD20   Jacobs, Norman, 1924-
J3   Japanese coinage [by] N. Jacobs [and]
          Cornelius C. Vermeule III. New York,
          Numismatic Review, 1953, 1972.
              142p. illus. 26cm.

KD20   Japan, Bank of Economic Research Dept.
J35   A brief history of money in Japan.
          [1964].
              32p. illus. 18cm.

KD20   Kikusen, Nakahashi.
K5   Esen Tsenshu. Tokyo, Ch'ao Yang
          She Shu Tieng, 1916.
              unpaged. illus. 23cm.
              In Japanese.

KD20   Kozono, Hitoshi, ed.
K6   Money history [of Japan]. Translation
          [by] Yong-Joon Kim [and] Reiko Hayashi.
          Editing and notes [by] Hitoshi Kozono
          [and] Alan D. Craig. [1st ed.] Berkeley,
          1964.
              2v. illus. 25cm.
              Contents: v.1 English text v.2 Illus-
          trations, Japanese notes.

KD20   Munro, Neil Gordon.
M8   Coins of Japan. 1st ed. Yokohama,
          1904. Reprinted, 1962.
              xx, 281p. illus, pl (part col.)
          19, 21cm.

KD20   Tsukamoto, Toyojiro.
T8   The old and new coins of Japan. ...
            trans. by Saichiro Itami. Tokyo, Toyo
            Kahei kyo-kai, 1930.
                205p. incl pl. 26cm.

JAPAN - TECHNICAL ASPECTS

KD40   Japan. Osaka mint.
J3   A guidebook of the mint. October,
            1963, 1965.
                26p. illus. 24cm.

KD40   Japan. Osaka Mint. Personnel Dept.
J3b   [Brochure] from the Personnel Dept.
            of the Osaka Mint. Osaka, Osaka &
            Tokyo Mints, 1965.
                15p. illus., part. col., 26cm.
                In Japanese

KD40   The Imperial Mint, Osaka.
J3g   A glimpse of the Imperial Mint, Osaka.
            Osaka, Japan, The Imperial Mint, 1923.
                34p. illus. 19cm.

KD40   Japan. Imperial Mint. Osaka.
J3h   [History of the Imperial Mint
            at Osaka, Japan and its coinages,
            1871-1971]. Japan, the Osaka Mint,
            [n.d.]
                125p. illus. 26cm.

JAPAN - GOLD

KD43   Sarazin, Francois.
S3   Traite des monnaies d'or au Japan.
Rare   Traduit ... du Japonais. Paris, 1874.
Books   16p. pl., front. 24cm.
                [From Congres international oriental-
            istes, 1873].

396

JAPAN - SILVER

KD45   Yamaga, Yos Ninori.
Y3   The history of the one yen silver coins.
            Tokyo, [1927].
                117p. illus. 19 x 27cm.
                In Japanese. Foreword in English.

JAPAN - COPPER

KD47   Bramsen, William.
B7   The coins of Japan; part I-the copper,
            lead and iron coins issued by the Central
            Govt. Reprinted, with modifications, from
            the Mittheilungen der Deutschen gesellschaf
            fur Natur-und volkerkunde ostasiens. Aug.,
            1880. Yokohama, Kelly & Co., 1880.
                10p. unpaged plates. 30cm.

JAPAN - HISTORICAL

KD50   Tokai Bank, Ltd.
T6   A story of Japanese currency-from
            olden times to the Meiji Era. No date.
                21p. illus. 21cm.

KOREA - GENERAL WORKS

KD70   Craig, Alan David, 1930-
C7   The coins of Korea, and an outline of
            early Chinese coinage. Berkeley, Cal.,
            c1955.
                96p. illus. 22cm.

KD70   Gardner, C. T.
G3   The coinage of Corea. From Journal of
            the China Branch of the Royal Asiatic
            Society. [v.27 (1892-93)] Reprinted
            1963.
                60p. illus. 22cm.

KD70   Korea, Bank.
K6   The money of Korea. Seoul, 1960,
         1963.
             246p. illus. 26cm.
             In Korean.

KD70   Mandel, Edgar J.
M3   Cast coinage of Korea [by]
         Edgar J. Mandel. Racine, Wisc.,
         Western Pub. Co., 1972.
             160p. illus. 22cm.
             Bibliography: pp. 154-155.
             Includes numismatic dictionary.

GENERAL WORKS

LA10 Davenport, John Stewart, 1907-
D3d   The dollars of Africa, Asia & Oceania.
    Galesburg, Ill., 1969.
     208p. illus. 24cm.
     Bibliography: p. 208.

LA10 Davenport, John S.
D3s   The silver dollars of Africa. Racine,
    Whitman Pub. Co., 1959.
     42p. illus. 20cm. Reprint from The
    Numismatic Scrapbook, Jan.-Aug, 1958.

BRITISH POSSESSIONS, FORMER AND CURRENT

LA20 Almanzar, Alcedo F.
A4   The coinage of British West Africa.
    San Antonio, Almanzar's, [1970].
     45p. illus. 21cm.
     Bibliography: p. 44-45.

LA20 Parsons, H. Alexander.
P3   The colonial coinages of British
    Africa with the adjacent islands. London,
    Spink, 1950.
     94p. illus. 18cm.

LA20 Raymond, Wayte.
R3   British colonies in Africa; Union
    of South Africa; Independent African
    countries. Special printing.
    N.Y., the author, 1955.
     24p. illus. 23cm.
     (Coins of the world).

LA30   Arndt, E. H. D.
A7   The South African mints. Pretoria,
         1939.
             115p. 25cm. (Publications of the Univ-
         ersity of Pretoria, Series no. III: Arts
         and Social Sciences, no. 9)

LA30   Becklake, J. T.
B4   Notes on the coinage of the South
         African Republic. Reprinted from the
         Numismatic Chronicle, 15th ser, v. 14,
         1934.
             33p. illus. 22cm.

LA30   Becklake, J. T.
B44   From real to rand; the story of money,
         medals and mints in South Africa, by J.
         T. Becklake. South Africa, Central News
         Agency, [n.d.]
             83p. illus. 22cm.
             Bibliography: pp. 82-83.

LA30   Jaffe, Allen.
J3   The South African coin
         collectors' handbook. 2d ed.
         Cape Town, Howard Timmons, 1974.
             94p. illus. fold. chart. 19cm.

LA30   Kaplan, Alec.
K3   Catalogue of the coins of South Africa.
         Rev. and edited by Stan Kaplan. [Johannes-
         burg, South Africa, Printed by A.M. & I.
         Abrahams Print. Ltd., 1950, 1964, 1969, 1972, 74.
             illus. 25cm.

LA30   Levine, Elias.
L4   The coinage and counterfeits of the
         Zuid-Afrikaansche Republiek;
         published 100 years after the advent
         of the first coinage of the South
         African Republic. Capetown, S. A.,
         Purnell, 1974.
             127p. illus. 25cm.

LA30   Parsons, H. Alexander.
P3g   The coinage of Griqualand. London,
         Spink, 1927.
             11p. illus. 22cm.
             Reprinted from the Numismatic Circular.

LA30   Shaw, E. M.
S4   A history of currency in South Africa.
          Capetown, South African Museum, 1956.
              27p. 28 pl. 22cm.

LA30   The South African Gold Coin Exchange.
S6   How to evaluate your proof
          krugerrands. [South Africa,]
          n.d.
              24p. illus. 21cm.

LA30   [South African Gold Coin Exchange].
S6s   S100, the simplified system for evalua-
          tion of proof Krugerrands. [Johannesburg,
          South Africa], South African Gold Coin Ex-
          change, Ltd., [1976].
              26p. illus. 21cm.

LA30   South African Numismatic Society.
S65   Van Riebeeck tercentenary numismatic exhibi-
          tion, 1952, an introduction to the exhibition
          of the coins, medals and notes of our country's
          first three hundred years, especially arranged
          at the S.A. museum, Cape Town, by the S.A.
          Numismatic Society on behalf of the festival
          committee. Cape Town, South African Numisma-
          tic Society, 1952.
              34, 34p. ill. 22cm.

PORTUGUESE POSSESSIONS, FORMER AND CURRENT

LA40   Azevedo, Vasco.
A9   Catalogo das moedas de Mocambique.
          Porto, F. Nachado, 1969.
              78p. illus. 24cm.

LA40   Eads, Ora W.
E2   St. Thomas and Prince Islands;
          Numismatic analysis of a developing
          political system. Nashville, Tenn.,
          Practical Behavioral Studies Institute,
          1974.
              69p. illus. 22cm.

LA40   Ferreira, Virgilio.
F4   Prontvario de moeda de Angola.
          Luands, Angola [Centro de informacao e
          turismo, 1967.
              200p. illus., col. photog. 22cm.

LA40   Folgosa, Jose Maria.
F6m   A moeda de Mocambique. [From no. 48
           of tri-yearly "Mocambique" of December,
           1946].
              [19]p. illus. 27cm.

LA40   Folgosa, Jose Maria.
F6mo   As moedas da Africa oriental Portuguesa,
           Mocambique. Porto, 1956.
              160p. 26cm. (Publicacoes da sociedade
           Portuguesa de numimsatic, xlviii)

LA40   Garcia, Luis Pinto.
G3   Descricao das moedas de Angola e
           S. Tome e Principe. Castelo Branco,
           1941.
              30p. 21cm.

ETHIOPIA

LA50   Kohl, Melvin J.
K6   Ethiopia-treasure house of Africa; a
           review of Ethiopian currency and related
           history. Santa Monica, Society for
           International Numismatics, [1969].
              50p. illus. 21cm.
              Bibliography

LA50   Wood, Howland, 1877-
W6   The coinage of Ethiopia. New York,
           W. Raymond, Inc. [c1937]
              12p. illus. 23cm.

EGYPT

LA60   Grabar, Oleg.
G7   The coinage of the Tulunids. New
           York, A.N.S., 1957.
              x, 78p. pl. 23cm. (Numismatic notes
           and monographs, no. 139)
              Bibliographical footnotes.

LA60   Miles, George Carpenter, 1904-
M5   Fatimid coins in the collections of
         the University Museum, Philadelphia, and
         the A.N.S.   New York, A.N.S., 1951.
             51p. illus. 23cm. (Numismatic notes
         and monographs, no. 121)

LA60   Rogers, Edward Thomas, 1830 or 1-1884.
R6   The coinage of the Tuluni dynasty.
         San Diego, Cal., Malter-Westerfield,
         [196-?]
             21p. illus. 28cm.

FRENCH POSSESSIONS - FORMER AND CURRENT

LA70   Schweikert, Helmut.
S3   Les monnaies Tunisiennes depuis
         1859; de l'avenement de Mohamed
         Sadak Pacha Bey a la Republique
         Tunisienne [par] H. Schwikert.
         Munich, Ernst Battenberg, 1973.
             80p. illus. 24cm.

AUSTRALIA, NEW ZEALAND - GENERAL WORKS

MA20
C5a
    Clarke, Robert L.
       ... Catalog of modern Australian and
New Zealand coins. 1st ed. Venice, Cal.,
Dansco, 1962.
      45p. illus. 17cm.

MA20
C5b
    Clarke, Robert L.
      Catalog of the coins of British Oceania.
[Australia, Fiji, New Guinea, New Zealand].
2nd ed. Venice, Cal., Dansco, 1964, 1967, 1968.
      77p. illus. 17cm.

MA20
C5c
    Clarke, Robert L.
      The coins and tokens of British
Oceania. San Clemente, Malter-Westerfield
1971.
      162p. illus.

MA20
G3
    Gartner, John, ed.
      The Australian coin catalogue; the
complete coinage of Australia, New Zeal-
and, New Guinea, Fiji. Melbourne,
Hawthorn Press, 1964-67.
      4v. 22cm.

AUSTRALIA - GENERAL WORKS

MA40
A5
    Andrews, Arthur.
      Australasian tokens and coins, a handbook.
Sydney, Australia, W.A. Guillick, 1921.
      163p. ill. 61 pl. 26cm.
      Bibliography: pl. 149-160.

MA40
D4
    Deacon, James Hunt.
      Catalogue of the Australian Common-
wealth coinage, 1910-1960, compiled by J.
H. Deacon and Kenneth J. Irons. [Adelaide]
Numismatic Society of South Australia,
1961.
      23p. illus. 22cm. (N.S.S.A. publi-
cation no. 1).

MA40   Dean, John.
D45   ... Australian coin varieties catalogue.
          1st ed., 1965. Melbourne, Hawthorn,
          [1964].
              61p. illus. 21cm.

MA40   Gartner, John.
G3   The standard Australian coin
          catalogue. Melbourne, the Hawthorne
          Press, [1965], 1966.
              16p. 22cm.

MA40   Hanley, Tom.
H3   Collecting Australian coins by Tom
          Hanley and Bill James. Sydney, Murray,
          1966.
              223p. illus. 24cm.

MA40   McNeice, Roger V.
M3   Coins and tokens of Tasmania, 1803-
          1910, by Roger V. McNeice. Hobart,
          Platypus Publication [1969]
              xii, 112p. illus., tables. 22cm.
              Bibliography: p. 103-104.

MA40   Skinner, Dion Hickson.
S5   Renniks Australian commonwealth coinage
          guide. Unley, South Australia, Renniks, 1964,
          1965, 1970, 1974.
              v. ill. 25cm.
              Later editions expanded to include paper
          money.

MA40   Sydney. Bank of New South Wales.
S9s   The story of currency in Australia;
Vert.   from George III to Elizabeth II. [Sydney,
File   1954].
              18p. illus. 24cm.

AUSTRALIA - SPECIAL ASPECTS

MA50   Deacon, J. Hunt.
D4   The "ingots" and "assay office pieces"
          of South Australia. Melbourne, Hawthorne,
          [1952].
              iv, 70p. illus. 22cm.
              Bibliography: p. 66-67.

MA50   The Royal Australian mint; impressive establish-
R6   ment at Canberra. Reprinted from the
                Australasian Engineer, February 1965.
                32p. ill. 29cm.

AUSTRALIA - EARLY HISTORY

MA60   Bank of New South Wales.
B3   The early history of currency in
Vert.   Australia. Sydney, Waite and Bull, 1949.
File   unpaged. illus. 24cm.

MA60   Chitty, Alfred.
C45   Early Australian coinage. Reprinted
Vert.   from British Numismatic Journal, 1907,
File   p. 179-187. Salina, Kansas, Olympic
                Press, 1963.
                [6]p. pl. 22cm.

NEW ZEALAND - GENERAL WORKS

MA70   Cresswell, John C. M.
C7   Collecting coins and medals [by] John
            C. M. Cresswell. Christchurch, New Zealand.
            Whitcombe and Tombs, 1973.
                50p. illus. 21cm. (New Zealand
            Practical Guides.)

MA70   Hargreaves, R. P.
H3   From beads to bank notes. Dunedin
            [New Zealand] John McIndoe [1972]
                197p. illus. 22cm.
                Bibliography: p. [192]

MA70   Robb, Alistair F.
R6   Profitable coin collecting in
            New Zealand. New Zealand, the
            author, 1974.
                61p. illus. 21cm.

MA70   Skinner, Dion H.
S5   Renniks New Zealand coinage guide;
            1965-1966 [by] Dion H. Skinner. Unley,
            South Australia, Renniks and Co., 1966.
                56p. illus. 25cm.

MA70   Sutherland, Allan.
S8   Numismatic history of New Zealand,
         history reflected in money and medals.
         Wellington, N.Z. Numismatic Society, 1941.
            310p. illus. 8 pl. 25cm.

PART II

Exonumia

Tokens
Politicana
Primitive Money
Seals and Scarabs
Medals
Orders and Decorations

TOKENS - SPECIAL USES

COMMERCIAL

NB20   Feisel, Duane H., comp.
F4   Feisel's catalogue of parking tokens of
            the world, 1966. Boston, American Vec-
            turist Assoc., [1966].
               142p. illus. 23cm.
               Supplement, n.d.

NB20   Schwartz, Max M.
S3   Trial list of die varieties.
Vert.   n.p., n. pub., n.d.
File   27p. 28cm.

NB20   Smith, Kenneth E.
S6   Catalogue of world transportation tokens
            and passes except North America. 1st ed.
            [Boston] American Vecturist Association;
            distributed through K. E. Smith, Redonda
            Beach, Cal., 1967.
               xviii, 268p. illus. 24cm.

NB20   Smith, Kenneth E., comp.
S6c   Checklists of foreign transportation tokens.
            Redondo Beach, Calif., American Vecturists
            Assoc., n.d.
               variously paged 30cm.
               Includes Africa, Asia, Australia, Belgium,
            Denmark, Finland, France, Germany, Great
            Britain, Ireland, the Netherlands, New Zealand,
            Norway, South America, Sweden, and the West
            Indies.

NB20   Targonsky, Paul.
T3   A catalog of telephone tokens of the
            world. 1st ed. Meriden, Conn., 1968.
               23p. 5 pl. 28cm.

NB40   Beverley, James Andrew.
B4   A history of the communion token ...
         and the story of the formation of the
         token collection ... by Oliver Keith
         Rumbel. Austin, Tex., Austin Presbyterian
         Theological Seminary, 1961.
             20p. illus. 23cm.
             Bibliography: p. 19

NB40   Burns, Thomas.
B8   "Communion tokens", chapter four
         from Old Scottish communion plate.
         Edinburgh, R. & R. Clark, 1892.
             pp. 435-468. 5 plates. 28cm.

NB40   Grieg, R. M.
G7   Communion tokens, the Australian, New Zealand
         and miscellaneous series, by ..., Harry Robin-
         son and W.W. Woodside. Melbourne, Australia,
         Hawthorn Press, 1964.
             viii, 36p. xix pl. 22cm.
             Bibliography: p. viii.

NB40   Kisch, Bruno.
K5   Jewish community tokens, a neglected
         field in Jewish numismatics. New York,
         [1953].
             16p. 4 pl. 23cm.

NB40   Lapa, Frank.
L3   Jewish shekel tokens, compiled by
         Frank Lapa. Translations by Ruth
         Ruchlemer. The Author, 1972.
             7p. illus. 8 pl. 19cm.

NB40   Shiells, Robert.
S4   The story of the token as belonging to
         the sacrament of the Lord's Supper.
         Philadelphia, 1902.
             196p. 9 pl. 19cm.

NB40   Woodside, William W.
W6   Communion tokens-a bibliography.
         [Pittsburgh Carnegie Museum, 1958].
             26p. 21cm.

JETONS, COUNTERS

NB60   Barnard, Francis Pierrepont, 1854-
B3   The casting-counter and the counting-
          board; a chapter in the history of numis-
          matics and early arithmetic. Oxford,
          Clarendon, 1916.
              357p. 63 pl. 30cm.
              Bibliography: p. 11-24

NB60   Berry, George.
B4   Medieval English jetons. London, Spink
          & Son, Ltd., 1974.
              83p. illus. 24cm.

NB60   Smith, David Eugene, 1860-
S5   Computing jetons. New York, The
          American Numismatic Society, 1921.
              70p. front., illus, 4 pl. 16cm.
          (Numismatic notes and monographs, no. 9)

NB60   Snelling, Thomas, 1712-1773.
S6   A view of the origin, nature, and use of
Rare   jettons or counters, especially those
Books   commonly known by the name of black money
          and abbey pieces. London, 1769.
              16p. 7 pl. 34cm.

OTHER USES

NB80   Acworth, R. W. H.
A3   Love tokens; read at the meeting of the
Vert.   Kent Numismatic Society, August 22, 1941.
File   8p.

NB80   Bowers, Q. David.
B6   A tune for a token; a catalogue
          of tokens and medals relating to
          automatic musical instruments circa
          1850-1930. 1st ed. Thiensville,
          Wisc., Token and Medal Soc., Inc., 1975.
              79p. illus. 28cm.

NB80   Lowande, Joseph H.
L5   Analecta of rationing; 10th
          anniversary special edition--
          collected articles on rationing.
          N.p., Society of Ration Token
          Collectors, 1975.
              unpaged. 28cm.

<u>UNITED</u> <u>STATES</u>

GENERAL WORKS

PA30   Baum, J. W.
B3   A primer of American exonumia
          [by] J. W. Baum. Chicago, Hewitt Bros.,
          1973.
              45p. 20cm.

PA30   Barnard, B. W.
B37   The use of private tokens for money
Vert.   in the United States by B. W. Barnard.
File   (In the Quarterly Journal of Economics,
          Princeton, N.J., Aug., 1917. pp. 600-634.)
          21cm.

PA30   Fuld, George.
F8   Token collector's pages [by] George and
          Melvin Fuld. Boston, Quarterman Publications
          [c1972].
              253p. illus. 24cm. (Gleanings from the
          Numismatist, v. 3)
              "Originally published in 87 issues of the
          Numismatist between February 1948 and October
          1971, principally under the title Token
          collector's page."

PA30   Token and Medal Society.
T6   Selected articles on the subject of Ameri-
          can tokens reprinted from The Numismatist,
          1904-1938. N.p., Token and Medal Society, 1969.
              228p. ill. 24cm.

SPECIAL USES OR FORMS

PA40   American Vecturists Assn.
A4   Personal tokens of vecturists.
          Jamaica, New York, Northeastern
          Vecturists Assn., 1972, 1975.
              unpaged. 22cm.

PA40   Atwood, Roland C.
A8a   Atwood's checklist of American
1952   transportation tokens. Edited by Max
            M. Schwartz. 1952 edition. Boston,
            American Vecturists Assn., 1952.
                30p; 260p. 29cm.
                Also contains supplements - 1952-1955.

PA40   Atwood, Roland C.
A8c   Atwood's catalogue of United States and
            Canadian transportation tokens. Comp. &
            edited by the Catalogue Committee of the
            Amer. Vecturist Assoc. Boston, American
            Vecturist Assoc, 1958, 1963, 1970, 1973.
                450p. illus. 24cm.

PA40   Atwood, Roland C., comp.
A8n   National check and premium list of all
1948   U.S. transportation tokens. 1st ed. Los
            Angeles, American Numismatic Company,
            1948.
                432p. 22cm.

PA40   Baum, J. W., comp.
B3   Baum's checklist & album of Office of
            Price Administration tokens. [Wichita,
            Kans, 196-].
                12p. 21cm.

PA40   Burns, Jack F.
B8   Media of exchange used in state and
            Federal penitentiaries. Pittsburgh,
            Carnegie Museum, [1960].
                [38]p. illus. 23cm. (Annals of
            Carnegie Museum, v.35)

PA40   Cabot, George D.
C3   Priced catalogue of the state and
            city revenue and tax stamps of the
            United States. Weehawken, N.J., the
            author, 1940.
                138p. illus. 24cm.

PA40   Coffee, John M.
C6   Real estate tokens, by John M. Coffee.
            Boston, American Vecturist Assn., 1973.
                64p. illus. 23cm.

PA40   Dennis, Virginia H.
D4   A check list for Sambo coffee chips,
         by Virginia H. Dennis. 1st ed. The
         author, 1972.
             vi, 70p. 22cm.

PA40   DiBella, Emil.
D5g   A guide to wooden money. New York,
         Royal Coin Co., 1958, 1966.
             24p. 22cm.
             1966 edition: Guide book of wooden
         money, by Thomas Hudson.

PA40   DiBella, Emil.
D5h   A history and checklist of wooden money.
         [Reprinted from Numismatic Scrapbook, 1964].
             83p. 20cm.

PA40   DiBella, Emil.
D5r   Revised check-list of wooden money.
         [Numismatic Scrapbook, 1948?].
             30p. 20cm.

PA40   DiBella, Emil.
D5s   Sales tax tokens [Numismatic Scrapbook,
         1944, 1961], 1971.
             12p. 19cm.

PA40   Ford, Harold V.
F6   Car wash tokens; by Harold V.
         Ford and John M. Coffee, Jr.
         Boston, American Vecturist Assn.,
         1974.
             107p. 10 plates. 24cm.

PA40   Fuld, Melvin.
F8   Put another token in; amusement and
         vending tokens in America. [Reprinted from
         Numismatic Scrapbook, 1969].
             17p. illus. 21cm.

PA40   Dennis, M. Wayne.
H8s   Wooden money for United States (1966-
1972   1972 official and semi-official issues)
         and Canada (all known issues); first
         supplement, 1972, by M. Wayne Dennis and
         Thomas B. Hudson. The authors, 1972.
             62p. 22cm.
             Supplement to Guide book of wooden
         money, by Thomas Hudson, 1966.

PA40   Hunt, Inez.
H88   Otto Mears, the little giant, by
          Inez Hunt. Illustrated by Jack Frost.
          Colorado Springs, Colo., Colorado Springs
          Public Schools, 1973.
              38p. illus. 26cm.

PA40   King, Edward A., 1877-, ed.
K5   Masonic chapter pennies, the Albert M.
          Hanauer collection. Pittsburgh, Pa., 1926.
              465p. pl. 27cm.

PA40   Kurth, Howard H.
K8   American game counters. From Numismatic
          Scrapbook, 1943. Revised 1952.
              24p. illus. 20cm.

PA40   Logsdon, Clyde A.
L6   The American transportation token
          catalog of United States fare tokens;
          arranged "alphabetically" by the stamping
          on the tokens. Omaha, 1953.
              338p. 23cm.

PA40   Mazzulla, Fred.
M3   Brass checks and red lights, being a
          pictorial pot pourri of (historical) pros-
          titutes, parlor houses, professors, procuresses
          and pimps, by Fred and Jo Mazzulla. Denver,
          Fred and Jo Mazzulla, 1966.
              56p. ill. 22cm.

PA40   Morgenthau, Bernard.
M6c   Check list of U.S. transportation
          tokens, Chicago, Hewitt brothers, 1944.
              70p. 24cm.
              Reprinted from the Numismatic Scrap-
          book, Jan. 1943-Sept. 1944.

PA40   Morgenthau, Bernard.
M6e   Early numismatic highways and byways.
          Early United States transportation tokens.
          Reprinted from The Numismatist, vol. LX,
          1947.
              11p. illus. 23cm.

PA40   Morganthau, Bernard.
M6k   Key to unidentified U.S.
          Transportation tokens. Chicago,
          Hewitt Bros., n.d.
              21p. 20cm.

PA40   O'Cathey, Earl R.
02   The story of wooden money. N.p., n.
         pub., n.d.
           53p. illus. 27cm.

PA40   Orr, M. B.
07   Warner's "Communion tokens of the
         United States" simplified. N.P.,
         the author, n.d.
           13p. 28cm.

PA40   Rickenbacker, William F.
R5   Wooden nickels or, the decline and
         fall of silver coins. New Rochelle,
         N.Y., Arlington House, 1966.
           191p. 21cm.

PA40   Schimmel, Jerry F.
S3   U.S. state issued sales tax tokens.
         Photographs by Syd Joseph and Duane Feisel.
         Azusa, California, American Tax Token Society,
         1973.
           19p. illus. 22cm.

PA40   Society of Ration Token Collectors.
S6   U.S. Ration currency and tokens,
         1942-1945. Author n.d.
           loose leaf no pagination
           Addenda and supplements-1971.

PA40   Warner, Thomas.
W3   Communion tokens of the
         United States. Taken from the
         American Journal of Numismatics,
         Vol. XXII, #1. Boston, 1887.
           2 vols. 89p. plates. 30cm.

PA40   Wright, B. P.
W7   The mark penny; Masonic pieces. Salina,
         Kansas, Olympic Press, 1963.
           89p. ill. 22cm.
           Reprinted from The Numismatist, 1901-1904.

COLONIAL

PA50   Schmall, Charles N.
S3   Check list of the American colonial
            coins commonly called Bungtown halfpence.
            Reprinted from Numismatic Scrapbook, 1945.
                 11p. 20cm.

EARLY NATIONAL (EIGHTEENTH CENTURY)

PA60   Fuld, Melvin.
F8   The Talbot, Album and Lee cents.
            Reprinted from the Numismatic Scrapbook,
            [1956].
                 11p. illus. 20cm.

NINETEENTH - TWENTIETH CENTURIES

PA70   Adams, Edgar Holmes.
A3   United States store cards; a list of
            merchants' advertising checks, restaurant
            checks, and kindred pieces issued from
            1789 up to recent years, including many
            of the tokens which passed as money and
            known as hard times tokens, by Edgar H.
            Adams. New York, Adams & Raymond, 1920.
                 75p. illus. 23cm.

PA70   Bushnell, Charles Ira, 1826-1883.
B8   An arrangement of tradesmen's cards,
            political tokens, also, election medals,
            medalets, etc. ... New York, 1858.
                 118p. 4 pl. 23cm.

PA70   Caldwell, Walter.
C3   Coal company scrip. [Fayetteville,
            W. Va.] 1969.
                 81p. illus., map. 28cm.

PA70   Curto, James J.
C8i   Indian and post trader tokens.
            Reprinted from The Numismatist, 1951, 1962.
                 2 v. illus. 22cm.

PA70   Curto, James J.
C8m   Military tokens of the United States,
         1866-1969. Iola, Wis., Krause, 1970.
             304p. illus. 24cm.
             Bibliography: p. 298.

PA70   Curto, James J.
C8p   Post exchange canteen and other
         military tokens. Reprinted from The
         Numismatist, 1954.
             41p. 14 pl. 22cm.

PA70   Cuttle, Cole S., ed.
C82   The company store; a bulletin for coll-
         ectors, traders, and dealers, containing
         miscellaneous information mainly related
         to coal mine scrip. Bristol, Tennesse,
         November 1966 - June 1967.
             illus. 28cm.

PA70   Dodrill, Gordon.
D6   20,000 coal company stores in the
         United States, Mexico and Canada.
         The author, 1971.
             287p. illus. 28cm.

PA70   Gould, Maurice M.
G6   Merchant counterstamps on American
         silver coins. Wayland, Mass., Ovolon
         Pub. Co., [1962].
             16p. illus. 21cm.

PA70   Hallenbeck, Kenneth, Jr.
H3   Counterstamped U.S. large cents.
         Reprinted from The Numismatist, 1965.
             7p. illus. 22cm.

PA70   Miller, Donald M.
M5   A catalogue of U.S. store cards or
         merchants tokens. Indiana, Pa., [1962].
             100p. 1 pl. 23cm.

PA70   Orrahood, David.
O7   Checklist U.S. coal tokens. Owensboro,
         Ky, [1966].
             44p. 28cm.

PA70   Philadelphia. Numismatic Society.
P5   Catalogue of American store cards, etc.
         n.d.
             [29]p. 27cm.

PA70   Pollack, Foster B.
P6   Pollack's catalogue of Hickey brothers
            trade checks. New York, the author, 1967.
                27p. 18 pl. 28cm.

PA70   Schenkman, David E., ed.
S3   A survey of American trade
            tokens. Lawrence, Mass., Quarterman
            1975.
                493p. illus. 24cm.

PA70   Wright, Benjamin P.
W7   The American store or business cards. N.p.,
            Token and Medal Society, 1963.
                unpaged ill. 23cm.
                Originally published in The Numismatist,
            1898-1901.
                Reprinted in 1972 by Quarterman as: Ameri-
            can Business Tokens.

HARD TIMES TOKENS

PA73   Guttag Bros.
G8   Hard times tokens. New York, n.d.
                33p. illus. 27cm.

PA73   Low, Lyman Haynes.
L6   Hard times tokens. 2nd ed., rev. &
            enl. New York, the author, 1899.
            Supplement, 1906. Reprint, 1955.
                78p. illus. 25cm.

PA73   Numismatic Scrapbook.
N8   Hard times tokens. Chicago, Hewitt
            Bros., n.d.
                illus. 20cm. (Hewitt's numismatic
            information series)

CIVIL WAR

PA75   Curto, James J.
C8   Sutlers and their tokens, 1861-1866;
            (the rebellion tokens of the U.S.) Reprinted
            from The Numismatist, 1962.
                37p. illus. 22cm.

PA75   Curto, James J.
C8s   Sutler issues of the Civil War; a
           supplemental listing with other related
           issues. Reprinted from The Numismatist,
           1959.
               27p. illus. 23cm.

PA75   Fuld, George.
F8a   Antislavery tokens. From The Numisma-
           tist, April, 1957.
               [14]p. illus. 23cm.

PA75   Fuld, George.
F8g   A guide to Civil War store card tokens;
           a descriptive and price guide to various
           types of Civil War store card tokens,
           advertising pieces used as a money substi-
           tute during the American Civil War.
           Racine, Whitman, [1962].
               96p. illus. 20cm.

PA75   Fuld, George.
F8p   Patriotic Civil War tokens. Racine,
           Whitman, [1960].
               77p. 22 pl. 20cm.

PA75   Fuld, George.
F8u   U. S. Civil War store cards, by
           George and Melvin Fuld. 1st ed.
           [The Civil War Token Society, 1972].
               xxxviii, 615p. illus. 29cm.
               Bibliography: p. vi

PA75   Hallenbeck, Kenneth L.
H3   Empty till; coin shortages in
Vert.   Civil War America--money and its
File   circulation during Civil War
           times. Taken from Old Fort News,
           Fort Wayne, Ind., 1973.
               unpaged. illus. 28cm.

PA75   Hetrich, George.
H4   Civil War tokens and tradesmen's store
           cards; a tentative list of the Civil War
           tokens, and store cards issued by the mer-
           chants of the United States, and used as
           money during the period from 1861 to 1864,
           by Hetrich & Julius Guttag. The authors,
           1924.
               289p. illus., 16 pl. 26cm.

PA75   Wismer, David Cassel, 1857-
W5   Varieties of Dix civil war tokens of the
            year 1863, described by D. C. Wismer ...
            Hatfield, Penna., 1922.
                 [11]p. 20cm.

LOCAL, A-Z

PA80   Fernald, Kay.
A4F4   Rubles to statehood by Kay Fernald and
            Kay McDowell; a catalog of Alaskan numis-
            matic items. ... Anchorage, K&K, [1965].
                 134p. illus. 28cm.
                 Bibliography: p. 133

PA80   Gould, Maurice M.
A4G6   Alaska's coinage through the years by
            Maurice M. Gould and Kenneth Bressett.
            Racine, Whitman, [1960], 1965.
                 46p. illus. 20cm.
                 Bibliography

PA80   Birt, Hal.
A7B5a   Arizona Indian trade tokens. [n.p.]
            1970.
                 [19]p. (Chiefly illus) 28cm.
                 Bibliography: p. [2]

PA80   Birt, Hal.
A7B5t   Tokens of Arizona territory. [n.p.]
            1970.
                 [12]p. (Chiefly illus.) 21cm.
                 Bibliography: p. [3]

PA80   Album, Stephen.
C3A4   Catalogue of California merchants
            tokens. Berkeley, Calif., The author,
            1971 [c1972]-1974.
                 2v. illus. 24cm.
                 Contents: v.1-Northern California.
            v.2-S. Calif. & San Francisco County.

PA80   Feisel, Duane H.
C3F4   California trade token place names,
            by Feisel and Stephen Album. Palo Alto,
            CA, 1971, 1973.
                 42p. 3 pl. 22cm.

PA80   Abbott, Morris W.
C6A2   The Silverton railroad metallic
Vert.   passes. n.p., n. pub., n.d.
File   3p. illus. 29cm.

PA80   Cerny, Ernest.
C6C4   "Buy-an-ounce-of-silver" movement;
          Colorado silver token slugs. From the
          Numismatist, 1933.
              [7]p. illus. 22cm.

PA80   Hargett, J. L.
C6H3   Colorado merchant trade tokens. The
          author, 1968.
              unpaged. 24cm.

PA80   Whiteley, Philip W.
C6W5   The Lesher story. Reprinted from
          Numismatic Scrapbook. n.d.
              31p. illus. 20cm.

PA80   Schell, Frank R.
I3S2   Idaho merchants' tokens, 1865-1967. 1st ed.
          Twin Falls, Idaho, Frank R. Schell, 1967.
              unpaged chiefly ill. 28cm.

PA80   Slabaugh, Arlie R.
I4S5   Catalog of 19th century Chicago
          tokens. Taken from the Catamount,
          official organ of the Chicago area Token
          and Medal Society, Vol. III, #2,
          1965.
              14p. illus. 28cm.

PA80   Vacketta, Ore H.
I4V3   Catalogue of Illinois trade tokens.
V.1   V. Westville, Illinois, 1973.
              330p. illus. 23cm.
              Contents.--V.1, comprising a detailed
          list of merchants trade tokens.

PA80   Haggenjos, Raymond.
I5H3   Indiana Civil War tokens. Reprinted
          from Numismatic Scrapbook, n.d.
              29p. illus. 20cm.

PA80   Chinitz, Phillip.
I6C49   Birthday tokens of Iowa towns and
Vert.   counties, by Phillip Chinitz. 1st. ed.
File   Atlantic, Iowa, The author, 1972.
              31p. 13cm.

PA80   Ferguson, Lewis K.
I8F4   The trade tokens of Iowa. Ames,
            Iowa, the author, 1972.
                394p. 28cm.
                -Also contains 1973 and 1974 supple-
            ments.

PA80   Coinage Magazine.
N4C6   Gaming tokens. Reprint from Coinage
Vert.   v.4, no.2, February 1968.
File   6p. mostly illus. 28cm.

PA80   Dunn, Hal V.
N4D8   Nevada; trade token place names by
            Hal V. Dunn and Duane H. Feisel. 1st ed.
            Carson City, Nev., 1973.
                37p. illus. 22cm.

PA80   Hewitt, Lee F., comp.
N4H4   Nevada gaming tokens. [Chicago,
            Hewitt Bros, 1968].
                20p. illus. 20cm.

PA80   Kurth, Howard H.
N42K8   The Albany Church pennies. Reprinted
            from Numismatic Scrapbook.
                [6]. illus. 20cm.

PA80   Raymond, Wayte, 1886-
N42R3   Early New York city and state merchants'
            tokens, 1789-1850. New York, W. Raymond,
            Inc. [c1936].
                24p. illus. 23cm.

PA80   Anderson, P. K.
O4A5   [Collection of Oklahoma trade tokens.]
            N.p., n.pub., n.d.
                variously paged 28cm.

PA80   Vaia, D.
P6V3   The tokens of Puerto Rico; reference
            listing of haciendas and tokens ... years
            1800-1900. Aguadilla, Puerto Rico, n. pub.,
            1976.
                48p. 21cm.
                Note: Text in Spanish and English.

PA80   Fowler, William E.
T4F6   The trade tokens of Texas; with
            a brief historical comment by
            William E. Fowler, Travis L.
            Roberts and Harry 1. Strough.
            Part II of Tams Journal, April 1973.
                106p. illus. 28cm.

PA80   Johnson, Gerald Eugene, 1928-
W5J6   Trade tokens of Wisconsin. [Wisconsin
         Rapids, Wis., 1967].
             unp. illus. 22cm.

PA80   Watson, Doug.
W5W3   Illustrated guide to Wisconsin Civil
         War tokens. Iola, Wis., Krause, [1968].
             51p. illus. 23cm.

<u>CANADA</u>

GENERAL WORKS

PB30   Allen, Harold Don.
A4   Glimpses of the uncatalogued: modern
            numismatic byways for sharing and enjoy-
            ment. New Brunswick, Atlantic Provinces
            Numismatic Association, 1970.
                26p. 28cm.

PB30   Hoch, A. D., comp.
H6   Canadian tokens and medals; an anthology
            edited by A. D. Hoch. Lawrence, Mass.,
            Quarterman Publications [1974]
                ix, 333p. illus. 24cm. (Gleanings
            from the Numismatist, v.4)
                "Originally published between 1895 and
            1968 in the Numismatist."

PB30   McLachlan, Robert Wallace.
M3   The copper tokens of upper Canada. New
            York, American Numismatic Society, 1916.
                16p. pl. 24cm.
                Reprinted from the American Journal of
            Numismatics.

SPECIAL ASPECTS

PB40   Bowman, Fred.
B5   Communion tokens of the Presbyterian
            Church in Canada. [n.p.] Canadian
            Numismatic Association [c1965].
                xiii, 92p. illus. 23cm.
                Bibliography: p. 88

PB40   Canada revenue catalog; Federal issues.
C3   Toronto, Marks Stamp Co., n.d.
                12p. illus. 23cm.

PB40   Burke, Kenneth W., ed.
C3s   Standard Canadian revenue
            catalog. Toronto, Marks Stamp
            Co., Ltd., 1943.
                41p. illus. 23cm.

PB40   Kotler, Joseph Mark.
K6   Alphabetical index of Canadian trans-
            portation tokens. [Glencoe, Ill., 1963].
                 3 pl. 29cm.

PB40   McLachlan, Robert Wallace.
M3c   Canadian communion tokens, a catalogue
Rare   of metal sacramental tokens used in the
Books   different Presbyterian churches in Canada.
            Montreal, W. Drysdale, 1891.
                 62p. 22cm.
                 Reprinted from the Canadian Antiquarian.

PB40   McLachlan, Robert Wallace.
M3m   A catalog of the metallic tokens of the
            Presbyterian church in Canada. Montreal,
            [1912?].
                 [20]p. 28cm.

PB40   MacLennan, George A.
M32   The story of the old time communion
            service and worship; also the metallic
            communion token of the Presbyterian church
            in Canada, 1772-Montreal, 1924.
                 67p. 4 pl. 23cm.

NINETEENTH - TWENTIETH CENTURIES

PB70   Courteau, Eugene Gaspard.
C6c   Canadian bouquet-sous. St. Jacques,
            Quebec, 1908.
                 22p. illus. 23cm.

PB70   Courteau, Eugene Gaspard.
C6w   The Wellington tokens relating to
            Canada. New York, American Numismatic
            Society, 1915.
                 10p. 4 pl. 28cm.
                 Reprinted from The American Journal of
            Numismatics, vol. 48.

PB70   [Lees, W. A. D.]
L4   The ships, colonies and commerce tokens
            of Canada; a revision of W. A. D. Lees'
            classifications. London, Ont., W.G.
            Holmes, 1961.
                 16p. illus. 22cm.

PB70   McLachlan, R. W.
M3   Copper currency of the Canadian Banks,
        1837-1857. Reprinted from Transactions of
        the Royal Society of Canada, 1903.
            [56]p. 4 pl. 24cm.

PB70   Wood, Howland.
W6   The Canadian blacksmith coppers.
        Reprinted from The Numismatist, vol. 23.
        Philadelphia, 1910.
            15p. illus. 24cm.

LOCAL, A-Z

PB80   Vancouver Numismatic Society.
B7V3r   [Reports on tokens of British Columbia.
        1964-1965].
            unpaged 28cm.

PB80   Vancouver Numismatic Society.
B7V3t   The tokens of British Columbia and the
Pt.1   Yukon. Vancouver, B.C., 1969.
            88p. 22cm.
            Supplement, 1973.

PB80   Bowman, Fred.
O5B6   Trade tokens of Ontario. [n.p.] Pub.
        under the auspices of the Canadian Numis-
        matic Research Society, 1966.
            109p. 21cm. (Hobby publications)

PB80   Courteau, Eugene Gaspard.
O5C6   The St. George copper tokens of the
        Bank of upper Canada. St. Jacques, Quebec,
        1934.
            32p. illus. 25cm.

PB80   Courteau, Eugene Gaspard.
Q4C6c   The copper tokens of the Bank of
        Montreal. St. Jacques, Quebec, 1919.
            25p. illus. 25cm.

PB80   Courteau, Eugene Gaspard.
Q4C6h   The habitant tokens of lower Canada
        (province of Quebec). St. Jacques,
        Quebec, 1927.
            24p. illus. 24cm.

PB80   Tannahill, Cecil Clifton, 1912-
S3T3   Trade tokens of Saskatchewan and their
          history. [Regina] Published under the
          auspices of the Canadian Numismatic
          Research Society, 1965.
             52p. illus. 27cm.

MEXICO

PC20
E4
Eklund, O. P.
Hacienda tokens of Mexico, by O. P.
Eklund and Sydney P. Noe. New York,
American Numismatic Society, 1949.
46p. 22pl. 23cm. (Numismatic notes
and monographs, no. 115)

PC20
L4
Leslie, Elwin C.
Henequen plantation tokens of the
Yucatan Peninsula, Mexico (with an
addenda of other tokens of the area)
by Elwin C. Leslie and A. F. Pradeau.
Organization of International Numismatics
[c1972]
138p. illus. map. 25cm.

PC20
S7
Stevens, Erma C.
Privately issued store cards and tokens,
state of Sonora, Mexico. Azteca Numismatic
Society, 1970.
8p. illus. 28cm.

PANAMA AND CANAL ZONE

PC35
P5
Plumer, Warren Lloyd.
Panama and C. Z. tokens. 2d ed.
revised. Doswell, Va., the author,
1975.
10p. 28cm.

GUATEMALA

PC37
G8C5
Clark, Odis H.
The token coinage of Guatemala/by Odis
H. Clark, Jr.; research data compiled by
Almanzar's Coins of the World. - San
Antonio: Almanzar's Coins of the World,
[1974]
78p. ill. 22cm.
Bibliography: p. 78

PC37   Jason, Charles L.
G8J3   Plantation & merchant tokens of
         Guatemala by Charles L. Jason.
         [Shalimar, Fla.] The Author [1973]
              86p. illus. 28cm.

GENERAL WORKS

PD30
G3
    Gamberini, Cesare di Scarfea.
       Quando mancano gli spiccioli...
il francoballo, la marca da ballo,
il gettone e gli altri succedanei
della moneta divisionale...Brescia,
La Numismatica, 1974.
       109p. illus. 25cm.

<u>GREAT</u> <u>BRITAIN</u>

CATALOGUES

PE20   Batty, D. T.
B3   Batty's catalogue of the copper coinage of
          Great Britain, Ireland, British Isles and
          colonies, local and private tokens, jettons,
          etc. ... Manchester, Printed by J. Forsyth,
          1868-1898.
              4v. pl. 22 x 18cm.

PE20   [Batty, D. T.]
B3i   Index of first two volumes (tokens) of
          D.T. Batty's work on "Copper coinage of
          Great Britain, Ireland, British Isles and
          colonies.
              118p. 28cm.

PE20   British museum. Dept. of British and
B7   medieval antiquities.
              Catalogue of the Montague Guest coll-
          ection of badges, tokens and passes ...
          London, British museum, Printed by order
          of the Trustees, 1930.
              viii, 206p. viii pl. 25cm.

GENERAL WORKS

PE30   Berry, George.
B4   Discovering trade tokens. Tring,
          Herts, Shire, 1969.
              56p. illus. 18cm.

PE30   Kent, G. C.
K4   British metallic coins and tradesmen's
          tokens with their value from 1600-1912.
          1st ed. Chickester, 1912.
              352p. 21cm.

PE30   Lowe, Geoffrey J.
L6   An introduction to British
          tokens. Vancouver, Canada, B.C.
          Numismatic Assn., 1975.
              55p. illus. 21cm.

PE30   Mathias, Peter.
M3   English trade tokens; the Industrial
          Revolution illustrated. Photos. by A.C.
          Barrington-Brown. London, New York,
          Abelard-Schuman [1962].
              64p. 16 pl. 23cm. (Collecting coins)

PE30   Seaby, H. A., ed.
S4   British copper coins and their values.
          Part II-Tokens. [London, Seaby, 1961].
              [112-236]p. illus. 18cm.
              Bibliography: p. 112

PE30   Seaby, Peter, ed.
S43   British tokens and their values, ed. by
          Seaby & Monica Bussell. London, Audley
          House, 1970.
              199p. illus. 19cm.
              Bibliography

SPECIAL ASPECTS

PE40   Parsons, H. Alexander.
P3   The mail coach and its
          halfpennies. n.p., n. pub.,
          n.d.
              pp. 359-368. illus. 25cm.

SEVENTEENTH CENTURY

PE55   Wetton, J. L.
W4   Seventeenth century tradesmen's
          tokens. [Newcastle, Corbitt & Hunter,
          1969].
              70p. incl. 15 pl. 22cm.
              Bibliography

PE55   Williamson, George Charles, 1858-
W5   Trade tokens issued in the seventeenth
          century in England, Wales, and Ireland, by
          corporations, merchants, tradesmen, etc.
          A new and rev. ed. of William Boyne's work,
          by George C. Williamson ... London, E.
          Stock, 1889-91. [Reprinted, Seaby's], 1967.
              3v. illus., pl. 23cm.

PE60   Atkins, James, numismatist.
A8   The tradesmen's tokens of the eighteenth
          century. ... London, W.S. Lincoln & Son,
          1892.
              vi, 415p. 23cm.

PE60   Bell, Robert Charles, 1917-
B4   Commercial coins, 1787-1804. New-
          castle upon Tyne, Corbitt & Hunter, 1963.
              319p. illus., map. 23cm.
              Bibliography: p. 307

PE60   Bell, R. C.
B4s   Specious tokens and those struck for
          general circulation, 1784-1804. New-
          castel, Corbitt & Hunter, 1968.
              257p. illus.

PE60   Bell, R. C.
B4t   Tradesmen's tickets and private tokens,
          1785-1819. Newcastle, Corbitt & Hunter,
          1966.
              xii, 315p. illus.
              Bibliography.

PE60   Dalton, Richard.
D3   The provincial token-coinage of the
          18th century . . . by R. Dalton and S. H.
          Hammer. Bristol 1910. Reprinted, 1967.
              567p. illus. 26cm.

PE60   Longman, W.
L6   Tokens of the eighteenth century con-
          nected with booksellers & bookmakers
          (authors, printers, publishers, engravers
          and paper makers). ... London, New York,
          Longmans, Green and Co., 1916.
              90p. illus., pl. 23cm.

PE60   Pye, Charles.
P9   Provincial copper coins or tokens
          issued between the years 1787 and 1796,
          engraved by Charles Pye. Birmingham,
          London, [1795].
              36 pl. 23cm.

PE60   Pye, Charles.
P9r   A representation of provincial copper
Rare   tokens, tokens of trade and cards of
Books   address circulated between 1787 and 1801.
          Engraved by Charles Pye. Leamington,
          Birmingham Spa, "Privately printed at
          the Courier Press for Arthur W. Waters",
          1916.
               52p. plates. 29cm.

PE60   Waters, Arthur W.
W3   Notes on eighteenth century tokens;
          being supplementary and explanatory notes on
          the provincial token coinage of the eigh-
          teenth century, by Richard Dalton. London
          B. A. Seaby, 1954.
               x, 53p. 25cm.

NINETEENTH - TWENTIETH CENTURIES

PE70   Bell, Robert Charles, 1917-
B4   Copper commercial coins, 1811-1819,
          [by] R. C. Bell. Newcastle upon Tyne,
          Corbitt & Hunter, 1964.
               xvi, 238p. illus., map. 28cm.
               Bibliography: p. 229

PE70   Dalton, Richard.
D3   The silver token-coinage mainly issued
          between 1811 and 1812. Leamington Spa:
          A. W. Waters, 1922.
               63p. illus. 25cm.

PE70   Davis, William John, b. 1848.
D32   The nineteenth century token coinage of
          Great Britain, Ireland, the Channel Is-
          lands and the Isle of Man, to which are
          added tokens of over one penny value of any
          period. [1st ed.] reprinted. London,
          Seaby, 1969.
               xlviii, 284p. 34 pl., illus. 29cm.
               Bibliography: p. 261

PE70   Herdman, Edward F.
H4   Transport tokens, tickets, passes
Rare   and badges of Great Britain and Ireland.
Books   Bishop Auckland, Herdman, 1932.
               33p. illus. 21cm.

PE70   Todd, Neil B.
T6   British tokens, advertising
tickets, checks, passes, etc., ca.
1830 to 1920. Newtonville, Mass.,
Colony Coin Co., 1974.
             47p. 28cm.

PE70   Waters, Arthur W.
W3   Notes on the silver tokens of the
nineteenth century. London, B. A. Seaby,
1957.
             21p. 25cm.

LONDON

PE80   Burn, Jacob Henry, d. 1869.
B8   A descriptive catalogue of the London
traders, tavern, and coffee-house tokens
current in the seventeenth century; presented to the Corporation library by Henry
Benjamin Hanbury Beaufoy ... 2d ed.
[London], 1855.
             xcv, 287p. illus., 3 pl. 22cm.

PE80   Waters, Arthur W.
W3   The token coinage of South London issued
in the 18th and 19th centuries. ...
Leamington spa, Simmons & Waters, 1904.
             xiv, 33p. 22cm.
             Bibliography

IRELAND

PE85   Macalister, R. A. S.
M3   A catalogue of the Irish trader's
tokens in the collection of the Royal
Irish Academy. Dublin, Hodges, Figgis,
1931.
             19-185p. 27cm.

PE90   Campbell, Montagu.
C3   Communion tokens of the Church of
         Scotland. ... Presented to the Church of
         Scotland by Lord Balfour of Burleigh and
         other friends. N.p., n.pub., n.d.
             40, [10]p. 22cm.

PE90   Dick, Robert.
D5   Scottish communion tokens other than
         those of the established church. Edinburgh,
         Elliot, 1902.
             95p. 22cm.

PE90   Kerr, R.
K4   Scottish Episcopal communion tokens
         by R. Kerr and J. A. Lamb. [From: Society
         of Antiquaries of Scotland, Proceedings,
         v. 81, 1946-47]
             [16]p. illus. 26cm.

PE90   Orr, M. B.
O7   Brook's "Communion tokens of the
         Church of Scotland," simplified.
         Mesa, AZ, the author, 1968.
             35p. 23cm.

PE90   Orr, M. B.
O7c   Communion tokens, simplified.
         N.P., The author, 1968.
             26p. 28cm.
             -a simplified attribution of
         1342 Scottish and English communion
         tokens.

PE90   Orr, M. B.
O7s   Scottish communion tokens:
         three keys revealing the secrets
         for attribution. n.p., the author,
         1967.
             45p. 23cm.

PE90   Orr, M. B.
O7sp   Special gazeteer (sic) of Scotland
         relating the names of communion
         tokens to their shires. n.p.
         the author, n.d.
             42p. 22cm.

PE95   Oxford. University. Ashmolean museum.
O8M5   ... Catalogue of Oxfordshire seventeenth
century tokens, edited by J. G. Milne.
London, 1935.
      xx, 48p. illus., 16 pl. 21cm.

PE95   Davis, W. J.
W3D3   The token coinage of Warwickshire
with descriptive and historical notes.
Birmingham, Hudson & Son, 1895.
      132p. 24 pl. 26cm.

PE95   Boyne, William, d. 1893.
Y6B6   Tokens issued in the seventeenth,
Rare   eighteenth, and nineteenth centuries in
Books   Yorkshire by tradesmen, overseers of the
poor, etc., in gold, silver, brass and
copper. Also the seals of all the cor-
porations in that county. Headingley,
priv. print., 1858.
      viii, 62p. ill. pl. 26cm.

<u>FRANCE</u>

SIXTEENTH - EIGHTEENTH CENTURIES

PF60   Frossard, Edouard.
F7   Franco-American jetons. New York, priv.
          pub., 1899.
              15p. 2 pl. 23cm.

PF60   Robert, Charles.
R6   Recherches sur les monnaies et les
          jetons des maitres-echevins et description
          de jetons divers. Metz, Imprimerie de
          Nouvian, 1853.
              88p. 6 pl. 32cm.

NINETEENTH - TWENTIETH CENTURIES

PF70   Forbin, A.
F6   Catalogue des billets; emis
          pendant la guerre, 1914-1920.
          Amiens, Yvert & Tellier, 1920.
              110p. 29cm.

PF70   Lamb, Robert A.
L3   A catalogue of French emergency tokens
          of 1914-1922. The author, 1967.
              51p. illus. 20cm.

PF70   Rochesnard, Jean-Georges Forien de.
R6   Les monnaies de prisonniers
          de guerre en France pendant la
          guerre 1914-1918. Auxerre,
          Imprimerie moderne, 1950.
              47p. scattered illus. 29cm.

CITIES, TOWNS, AND PROVINCES, A-Z

PF90   Tricou, J.
L8T7   Jetons et medailles offerts
          par la ville de Lyon au XVIII siecle.
          Trevoux, J. Jeannin, 1912.
              43p. illus. 22cm.

PF90   Chautard, M. Jules.
V4C5   Jetons des Princes de Vendome; de la
          deuxieme maison de Bourbon. Vendome,
          Lemercier et Fils, 1882.
              57p. plates. 26cm.

MEDIEVAL

PG50   Braun von Stumm, Gustaf, 1890-1963.
B7   Die munzen der Abtei Hornbach nebst
           Beitragen zur munzkunde vom Speyergau und
           Elsass in 12.-14. jahrhundert. Halle,
           A. Riechmann, 1926.
                53p. 6 pl. 28cm.

NINETEENTH - TWENTIETH CENTURIES, INCLUDES NOTGELD

PG70   Bodenschatz, Herbert.
B6   Die gefangenenlagermunzen
           weltkrieg 1915-1918 von Deutschland
           amtlich. Dahlenburg, Germany, 1948.
                unpaged. 29cm.

PG70   Budd, Robert C.
B8   European "notgeld" issues:
Vert.   a bibliography of English language
File   articles. n.p., the author, 1976.
                6p. 29cm.

PG70   Das Deutsche notgeld, 1915-1923.
D3   Heft 1, Rheinprovinz und provinz Westfalen,
Pt.1   [by] Heinz Jansen. 2d ed. Berlin, Erich
1971   Proh, 1971.
                22p. ill. 21cm. (Die Munze, band 2)

PG70   Das Deutsche notgeld, 1915-1923.
D3   Heft 2, offizielle notmunzen, Pfalz, Hessen
Pt.2   mit Hessen-Nassau, Lothringen unt Elsass
           [by] Heinz Jansen. 1st ed. Berlin, Erich
           Proh, 1971.
                15p. ill. 21cm. (Die Munze, band 3)

PG70   Das Deutsche notgeld, 1915-1923.
D3   Heft 3, offizielle notmunzen, Baden,
Pt.3   Hohenzollern, Wurttemberg, [by] Heinz Jansen.
           1st ed. Berlin, Erich Proh, 1971.
                20p. ill. 21cm. (Die Munze, band 4)

PG70   Das Deutsche notgeld, 1915-1923.
D3   Heft 4, offizielle notmunzen, Bayern, [by]
Pt.4   Heinz Jansen. 1st ed. Berlin, Erich Proh,
            1971.
            28p. ill. 21cm. (Die Munze, band 5)

PG70   Das Deutsche notgeld 1915-1923.
D3   Offizielle notmunzen. Heft 5-
Pt.5   Anhalt, Sachsen, Thuringen und
            Provinz Sachen; [von] Heinz
            Jansen. Berlin, Erich Proh, 1972.
            16p. illus. 21cm.
        (Die Munze, band 6)

PG70   Das Deutsche notgeld, 1915-1923.
D3   Offizielle notmunzen. Nord-
Pt.6   deutschland, Hannover, Braunschweig,
            Bremen, Oldenburg, Hamburg und
            Schleswig-Holstein, Mecklenburg,
            Pommern; von Heinz Jansen. Berlin,
            Erich Proh, 1972.
            16p. illus. 21cm.
        (Die Munze, band 7)

PG70   Das Deutsche notgeld, 1915-1923.
D3   Offizielle notmunzen-Brandenberg,
Pt.7   Posen, Preussen und Schlesien
            [von] Heinz Jansen. Berlin,
            Erich Proh, 1972.
            21p. illus. 21cm.
        (Die Munze, band 8)

PG70   Das Deutsche notgeld, 1915-1923.
D3   Heft 8, private notmunzen, West- und
Pt.8   Suddeutschland (Nordrhein-Westgalen, Hessen,
            Pfalz, Saarland, Baden, Wurttemberg, Elsass,
            Lothringen und Bayern), [by] Hans Meyer.
            1st ed. Berlin, Erich Proh, 1971.
            41p. ill. 21cm. (Die Munze, band 9)

PG70   Das Deutsche notgeld, 1915-1923.
D3   Heft 9. Strassenbahngeld und
Pt.9   gasmarken von Heinz Jansen.
            Berlin, Verlag Proh, 1974.
            13p. illus. 21cm.
        (Die Munze, band 10)

PG70   Eklund, O. P.
E4   German war tokens "notgeld", with
        supplement by Helen Woodburn. American
        Numismatic Association, [c1948, 1960?]
            185p. illus. 23cm.
            Reprinted from the Numismatist, 1948-1960

PG70   Franke, Otto.
F7   Munzen aus porzellan steinzeug
        und ton. Berlin, Verlag Proh, 1975.
            42p. illus. 21cm.
        (Schriftenreihe die Munze band 20).

PG70   Funck, Walter.
F8d   Deutsche privatnotmunzen ab
        1916 sowie munzen und marken der
        Konsumvereine. Neuenburg,
        Funck, 1964.
            106p. 29cm.

PG70   Funck, Walter.
F8m   Munzen und marken der Deutschen
        strassenbahnen und der Niederlande.
        Neuenburg, Funck, 1965.
            19p. 29cm.

PG70   Funck, Walter.
F8n   Die notmunzen der Deutschen
        kriegsgefangenenlager, 1914-
        1918. II private ausgeben.
        Neuenburg, Funck, 1964.
            44p. map. 29cm.

PG70   Funck, Walter.
F8no   Die notmunzen der Deutschen
        und Osterreichisch-Ungarischen
        kriegsgefangenenlager, 1914-
        1918. I. Amtliche ausgaben.
        Neuenburg, Funck, 1964.
            10p. 29cm.

PG70   Keller, Arnold.
K4   Notgeldscheine und munzen
        aus ungewohnlichem material.
        Neuenburg, Germany, Funck,
        1933.
            unpaged. 29cm.

PG70   Lamb, Robert A.
L3   Catalogue of German war tokens;
1966   the municipal issues, 1914-1921.
        [Rev. ed.] Tucson, Ariz., 1966.
            143p. illus. 20cm.
        Includes bibliography.

PG70   Notmunzen der Deutschen gefang-
N6   enenlager. n.p., n. pub., n.d.
        unpaged. 29cm.

PG70   Ohm, Wilhelm.
O3   Gefangenlager munzen und
        marken von Rheinland-Westfalen.
        Wilhelmshaven, Funck, 1930.
            unpaged. 29cm.

PG70   Peisker, Albert.
P4   Das Berliner notgeld; 1914-1924.
        Berlin, Erich Proh, 1972.
            106p. illus. 21cm. (Schriftenreihe
        die munze, band 16)

PG70   Pick, Monika.
P5   Der notgeld-Mufti; verzeichnis
        aller ausgabeorte der Deutschen
        notgeldscheine nach den Dr.-Keller-
        katalogen alphabetisch und
        nach zeitspannen geordnet von
        Monika Pick. Schwabach, Dieter
        Hoffman, 1975.
            76p. 30cm.

PG70   Rottinger, Bruno.
R6   Das Deutsche gefangenenlagergeld
        sowie gruben und zechengeld,
        1914-1918. Frankfurt, A. Cahn,
        1922.
            unpaged. 29cm.

PG70   Emergency Money Society.
U6   Emergency coins of Germany: metal and
        porcelain. Arranged and edited by Richard
        Upton. 1st ed. [n.p.] Printed by
        the Sidney Print. and Pub. Co. [1970]
            viii, 200p. illus. 22cm.

PG90   Landau notmunzen, die wahrend der
L3R5   belagerung 1702 und 1713 geschlagen
     wurden; zusammengestellt von "Rigo"
     Nurnberg. Nurnberg, n.p., 1961.
     126p. illus. 15cm. (Rigo-
   Katalog, #3)

PG90   Eklund, O. P.
N8E4   The counters of Nuremberg. From the
   Numismatist, 1926.
     [25]p. illus. 23cm.

PG90   Hyman, Arthur.
N8H8   Nurnberg-Furth; strassenbahngeld;
   Nurnberg transportation tokens;
   illustrated. N.P., the author, 1965.
     unpaged. illus. 21cm.

SPECIAL ASPECTS

PH40   Eklund O. P.
E4   Charity tokens of the Netherlands.
          Reprinted from The Numismatist, v. 61,
          1947-48.
              20p. illus. 23cm.

PH40   Minard, Louis Francois Martial, 1801-1875.
M5   Description de mereaux et autres objets
Rare   ancients des gildes et corps de metiers
Books   eglises, etc. par L. Minard-van Hoorebeke.
          Gand, Van Doosselaere, 1877-79.
              3 vol in 2 illus. 35 x 27cm.
          Text in French and Dutch.

IBERIA

PI30   Barnard, Francis Pierrepont.
B3   Portuguese jettons. From Numismatic
            Chronicle, Ser 5, v.3, 1923.
                [39]p. 1 pl. 22cm.

ITALY

PI50   Barnard, Francis Pierrepont.
B3   Italian jettons. From Numismatic
            Chronicle, v. 20.
                [57]p. 2 pl.

SWEDEN

PI62   Ehnbom, Ingvar.
E3   Svenska polletter, genem tiderna
            med avbildningar av Ingvar Ehnbom.
            Malmo, Sweden, Malmo Mynthandel,
            1975.
                120p. illus. 21cm.
                -price list included. Covers years
            1600-1900.

DENMARK

PI66   Somod, Jorgen.
S6   Busmaerker & sporvognspoletter
            Danmark, 1863-1972. Roslev, Denmark,
            Siegs Forlag, 1972.
                41p. illus. 21cm.
                -summary and glossary in English

<u>ASIA</u>

CHINA

PL20
W6
     Woodward, A. M. Tracey.
        The coins of Shanghai ... Reprinted
from the China Journal, 1937.
        15p. 5 pl. 25cm. (Bulletin of the
Numismatic Society of China, no. 3)

DUTCH EAST INDIES

PL30
W6
     Woodside, W. W.
        Catalogue of East Indies estate
tokens. [Pittsburg, Carnegie Museum],
1963.
        84p. illus. 28cm.
        Bibliography: p. 4

INDIA AND CEYLON

PL40
B7
     Brotman, Irwin F.
        A guide to the temple tokens of India.
Los Angeles, Shamrock, 1970.
        208p. illus., map. 22cm.
        Bibliography: p. 204

PL40
S3
     Scaife, J. Verner.
        Assamese tea garden tokens. London,
Spink & Son, 1952.
        116p. illus. 26cm. (Reprinted from
the Numismatic Circular, v.60, no. 1,2,
Jan. & Feb., 1952.)

KOREA

PL50   Mandel, Edgar J.
M3   Trial listing Korean charms and
          amulets. [Coral Gables, 1968].
              144p. illus. 28cm.

PL50   Ramsden, Henry A.
R3   Corean coin charms and amulets. Yokohama,
          Jun Kobayagawa Co., 1910. Reprint. Salina,
          Kansas, Olympic Press, 1963.
              40p. ill. pl. 23cm.

THAILAND

PL60   Ramsden, H. A.
R3   Siamese procelain and other tokens.
          Yokohama, Jun Kobayagawa Co., 1911.
              37p. 20 pl. 21cm.

PHILIPPINES

PL70   Perez, Gilbert Somers.
P4   The leper colony currency of Culion.
          New York, A.N.S., 1929.
              10p. 3 pl. (Numismatic notes and
          monographs)

PL70   Snider, D. M.
S6   Culion leper colony coinage and die varieties.
          Manila, Philippine Numismatic and Antiquarian
          Society, 1967.
              10p. ill. 23cm. (Philippine numismatic
          monographs, no. 17)

<u>AUSTRALIA</u>, <u>NEW ZEALAND</u>

AUSTRALIA

PN20
S7
Stainsfield, C. W.
    Descriptive catalogue of Australian
tradesmen's tokens, illus with woodcuts;
also some account of the early silver
pieces, and gold coinage of Australia.
London, C. W. Stainsfield, 1883.
    iii, 74p. 21cm.

NEW ZEALAND

PN40
M4
Meek, W. F. W.
    An authentic record of the currency
tokens of New Zealand, issued from 1857
to 1881. Dunedin, New Zealand, 1951.
    69p. illus. 25cm.

PN40
N4
New Zealand. Royal Numismatic Society,
    Canterbury Branch.
    They made their own money, the story of
early Canterbury traders & their tokens.
E. R. Thomas, L. J. Dale, associate edi-
tors. Christchurch, 1950.
    94p. ill. 23cm.

PN40
R6
Robinson, H. A.
    Auckland tradesmen's tokens. [Auck-
land, N.Z.] Numismatic Society of Auckland
1960.
    25p. 18 x 22cm.

PN40
S8
Sutherland, Allan.
    New Zealand tokens. Wellington, N.Z.
Numismatic society, 1960.
    6p. 23cm.

<u>US</u> <u>POLITICANA</u> (<u>TOKENS</u>, <u>MEDALS</u>, <u>BUTTONS</u>)

GENERAL WORKS

QA20   Albert, Alphaeus H.
A4   Political campaign and commemorative
          buttons. Hightstown, N.J., 1966.
              76p. illus. 22cm.
              Bibliography

QA20   Dewitt, J. Doyle.
D4   America goes to the polls; highlights
          of the presidential campaigns, 1789-1960.
          Hartford, Conn., Travelers Insurance, 1952,
          1960, 1964.
              [64]p. illus. 31cm.

QA20   Wearin, Otha D.
W4   Political campaign buttons in color.
          Leon, Iowa, Mid-America Book Co., 1969.
              50p. (incl. 24 pl.) 23cm.

EIGHTEENTH - NINETEENTH CENTURIES

QA40   Albert, Alphaeus H.
A5   Washington historical buttons.
          Hightstown, N.J., 1949.
              75p. illus. 24cm.

QA40   Dewitt, J. Doyle.
D4c   A century of campaign buttons, 1789-
          1889. The author, 1959.
              420p. illus. 23cm.
              Bibliography

QA40   Dewitt, J. Doyle.
D4e   Election medals of the campaign of
          1844. Reprinted from the Numismatist,
          1943.
              30p. 23cm.

QA40   Dewitt, J. Doyle.
D4m   Medalets of the presidential campaigns
          of 1852. Reprinted from The Numismatist,
          n.d.
              18p. illus. 23cm.

QA40   Dewitt, J. Doyle.
D4p   Medalets of the presidential campaign
        of 1848. Reprinted from The Numismatist,
        1948.
             28p. illus. 23cm.

QA40   Kobbe, Gustav.
K6   Presidential campaign medals. Reprinted
        from: Scribner's Magazine, Sept, 1888,
        p. 332-343.
             12p. illus. 24cm.

QA40   Zerbe, Farran.
Z4   Bryan money; tokens of the presidential
        campaigns of 1896 and 1900, comparative
        and satirical. Reprinted from The Numis-
        matist of 1926, 1961.
             70p. illus. 22cm.

TWENTIETH CENTURY

QA60   Bristow, Dick.
B7   The illustrated political button
        book. Santa Cruz, the author, 1971.
             129p. illus. 28cm.

QA60   Lee, Warren G.
L4   The 1944 campaign. From the APIC
        Keynoter, Spring 1970.
             pp. 5-21. illus. 28cm.

<u>PRIMITIVE MONEY</u>

COLLECTIONS

QB20   Mosher, Stuart.
M6   The story of money as told by the Knox
            Collection. Buffalo, 1936.
                 77p. illus. 24cm. (Bulletin of
            the Buffalo Society of Natural Science,
            vol. xvii, no. 2)
                 Bibliography

QB20   Wieschhoff, H. A.
W5   Primitive money. Philadelphia, University
            of Pennsylvania, 1945.
                 43p. ill. 21cm.
                 Bibliography.

GENERAL WORKS

QB30   DuPuy, William Atherton.
D8   The geography of money. From National
            Geographic, December, 1927.
                 [24]p. illus. 25cm.

QB30   Gibbs, Howard D.
G5   Odd and curious money of the world, a
            complete register. New York, Schulman,
            1946, 1956.
                 39p. illus. 23cm.

QB30   Perez, Gilbert.
P4   The lure of "odd money". From The
            Numismatist, August, 1946.
                 6p. illus. 22cm.

QB30   Reed, F. Morton.
R4   Odd and curious. Coin World, 1963.
                 120p. illus. 21cm.

QB30   Sigler, Phares O.
S5   Strange money of the world. Reprinted
            from The Numismatist, n.d.
                 36p. illus. 23cm.

QB40   Dalton, George, ed.
D3   Tribal and peasant economics. Readings
         in economic anthropology. Garden City,
         N.Y., Natural History Press, 1967.
             584p.   21cm.
             Bibliography

QB40   Desmonde, William H.
D4   Magic, myth, and money; the origin of
         money in religious ritual. New York,
         Free Press of Glencoe, 1962.
             208p.   22cm.

QB40   Einzig, Paul.
E3   Primitive money in its ethnological,
         historical and economic aspects. London,
         Eyre & Spottiswood, [1948].
             517p.   22cm.
             Bibliography

QB40   Quiggin, Alison Hingston.
Q5   A survey of primitive money; the
         beginnings of currency. London, Methuen,
         [1949, 1963].
             xxii, 344p.   32 pl., maps.   22cm.
             Bibliography

AFRICA

QB50   Johansson, Sven-Olof.
J6c   Nigerian currencies, manillas, cowries
         and others. 1st ed. [Sweden, 1967].
             57p.   tables, map, illus.   21cm.

QB50   Johansson, Sven-Olof.
J6p   Nigerian primitive currency values with
         supplement to Nigerian Currencies. 1st
         ed. The author, 1968.
             14p.   illus.   21cm.

QB60   Gillilland, Cora Lee C.
G5   The stone money of Yap; a
numismatic survey. Washington
D.C., Smithsonian Institution Press,
1975.
       75p. illus. 28cm. (Smithsonian
Studies in History & Technology, #23).

QB60   Lewis, Albert B.
L4   Melanesian shell money in Field Museum
collections. Chicago, 1929.
       36p. 25 pl.
       Bibliog. p. 35-36.

QB60   Ritzenthaler, Robert E.
R5   Native money of Palau. Milwaukee,
Milwaukee Public Museum, 1954.
       46p. 26cm. (Milwaukee Public
Museum Publications in Anthropology,
#1).

QB60   Shaw, William.
S5   Tin 'hat' and animal money by ... Shaw
and Mohd. Kassim Haji Ali. Kuala Lumpur,
Malaysia, Muzium Negara, [1970].
       17p. 9 pl. 22cm.
       Bibliography

AMERICAS

QB70   Carter, William Harry.
C3   North American Indian trade silver.
[London, Ont., 1971]
       2 v. illus. 21cm. (A fur trade
series)

QB70   Taxay, Don.
T3   Money of the American Indians and
other primitive currencies of the Americas. New York, Nummus, [1970].
       158p. illus. 24cm.
       Bibliography

QB70   Vreeland, Nehemiah.
V7   Wampum; the native substitute for
Vert.   currency in North America. From The
File   Numismatist, 1914.
               [8]p. illus.

QB70   Weeden, William B.
W4   Indian money as a factor in New
          England civilization. Baltimore, Johns
          Hopkins, 1884.
               51p. 24cm.

<u>SEALS</u> <u>AND</u> <u>SCARABS</u>

ANCIENT ASIA

QC20   Jitta, Annie N. Zadoks - Josephus.
J5   Catalogue sommaire des cylindres
              orientaux au cabinet royal des medailles
              a la haye. La Haye, 1952.
                   39p. 5 pl. 22cm.

QC20   Middleton, J. Henry.
M5   Ancient gems, the engraved gems of
              classical times. Chicago, Argonaut, 1969.
                   157, 36p. 2 pl. 23cm.

QC20   Corpus of ancient near Eastern seals in
P6   North American collections. Edited for
                   the committee of ancient near Eastern
                   seals. Morgan library. Catalogued
                   and edited by Edith Porada. Bollinger
                   Foundation, Pantheon, 1948.
                   2v. 187p. 176 pl., map. 31cm.

QC20   Ravn, O. E.
R3   A catalogue of Oriental cylinder seals
              and seal impressions in the Danish
              National Museum. Kobenhaven, 1960.
                   135p. pl. 30cm.

QC20   Von der Osten, Hans Henning.
V6b   Ancient Oriental seals in the
              collection of Mrs. Agnes Baldwin Brett.
              Chicago, Univ. of Chicago Press, 1936.
                   76p. 12 pl. 30cm.
                   Bibliography

QC20   Von der Osten, Hans Henning.
V6n   Ancient Oriental seals in the col-
              lection of Mr. Edward T. Newell. Chicago,
              Univ. of Chicago, 1934.
                   204p. 41 pl. 30cm.
                   Bibliography

QC20   Wiseman, D. J.
W5   Cylinder seals of Western Asia.
              Photog. by Werner and Bedrich Forman.
              London, Batchworth Press, n.d.
                   47, 240p. Chiefly illus., map.
              21 x 21cm.
                   Bibliography

ANCIENT EGYPT

QC30   Blanchard, R. H.
B5   Handbook of Egyptian gods and
            mummy amulets. Originally pub. in
            Cairo, 1909. Reprinted-N.Y.,
            Attic Books, [1976].
                 28p. LIV plates. 23cm.

QC30   Elder, Thomas L.
E4   The ancient Egyptian scarab. New
            York, n.d.
                 16p. illus. 14cm.

QC30   Petrie, W. M. Flinders.
P4   Historical scarabs: a series of drawings
            from the principal collections. Reprinted
            from the 1889 original. New York, Attic
            Books, 1974.
                 14p. plates unpaged. 17cm.

QC30   Ward, John.
W3   The sacred beetle; Egyptian scarabs
            in art and history. Five hundred examples
            of Scarabs and cylinders. Translations
            by F. Llewellyn Griffith. San Diego, CA,
            Malter-Westerfield, n.d.
                 122p. 16 pl. 21cm.

QC30   Williams, Caroline Ransom.
W5   Material bearing on the new discourses
Vert.   in Egypt.
File   In: The New York Historical Society
            Quarterly Bulletin, vol. vii, no. 1
            (April, 1923).

EUROPE

QC40   Gumowski, Marian.
G8   Handbuch der Polnischen
            Siegelkunde mit 129 textabbildungen
            und 76 kunstdrucktafeln. Graz,
            Austria, Akedemische Druck, 1966.
                 176p. 75 plates. 28cm.

GREAT BRITAIN

QC50   Brindley, H. H.
B7   Impressions and casts of seals, coins,
            tokens, medals and other objects of art
            exhibited in the Seal Room, National
            Maritime Museum. Greenwich, 1938.
                44p. 8 pl. 24cm.

QC50   Vertue, George.
V4   Medals, coins, great seals, and other
Rare   works of Thomas Simon. London, 1780.
Books   96p. 38 pl. 30cm.

UNITED STATES

QC60   Walker, Edwin Robert.
W3   The great seal of the state of New
            Jersey.
                21p. 1 pl. 23cm.

MODERN WORLD

COLLECTIONS

RA10   American numismatic society.
A5c   Catalogue of the international exhibi-
            tion of contemporary medals. The American
            Numismatic Society, March, 1910. New and
            rev. ed. New York, 1911.
                412p. pl. 29cm.

RA10   American Numismatic Society.
A5i   International medallic exhibition of the
            American Numismatic Society, opening on the
            twelfth of March, 1910; catalogue. New York,
            American Numismatic Society, 1910.
                3v. pl. 24cm.
                Contents: v.1 Contemporary medalists.-
            v.2. Medals. - v.3. Coins.

RA10   Bowdoin College. Museum of Art.
B6   The Salton collection. Renaissance and
            baroque medals and plaquettes. Brunswick,
            Maine, 1965, 1969.
                [78]p. illus. 29cm.

RA10   Brown, M. D.
B7   David Salomons house; catalogue of medals
            relating to the history of transport. N.p.,
            "printed privately", 1968.
                37p. v pl. 22cm.

RA10   Catalogue of the exhibition of medallic
C3   art; models for medals, commemorative,
                naval and military, and for tablets
                and other memorials...from the
                Renaissance to the present day.
                Under the patronage of H.M., the
                Queen. London, the Georgian Hall,
                Waring and Gillow Ltd., 1917.
                    74p. 20cm.

RA10   Ciechanowiecki, Andrew S.
C5   Sculpture in miniature. The Andrew S.
         Ciechanowiecki collection of gilt and gold
         medals and plaquettes. Louisville, J.
         B. Speed Art Museum, 1969.
             222p. (incl. 118 pl.) 30cm.

RA10   Esposizione internazionale della medaglia
E8   contemporanea. Rome, Palazzo Braschi,
             1961, 1963.
             2v. ill. 21cm.

RA10   Hill, George Francis.
H5   Renaissance medals from the Samuel
         H. Kress collection at the National
         Gallery of Art; based on the catalogue
         of Renaissance medals in the Gustave
         Dreyfus collection. Rev. and enlarged
         by Graham Pollard. London, Phaidon Press
         [1967].
             307p. illus. pl. 31cm.

RA10   Marx, Roger.
M3   The medallist's art, as seen at the Paris
         exhibition. Excerpt from The Studio, 1901(?).
             221-232p. pl. 31cm.

RA10   Middeldorf, Ulrich.
M5   Medals and plaquettes from the Sigmund
         Morgenroth collection by Ulrich Middeldorf
         and Oswald Goetz. Chicago, Art Institute,
         1944.
             64p. 32 pl. 28cm.
             Bibliography: p. 61-62

RA10   Norris, Andrea S.
N6   Medals and plaquettes from the
         Molinari collection at Bowdoin
         College, by Andrea S. Norris and
         Ingrid Weber. With an introduction
         to the medals catalogue by Graham
         Pollard. Brunswick, Maine, Bowdoin
         College Museum of Art, 1976.
             292p. plates. 29cm.

RA10   Pope-Hennessy, John.
P6   Renaissance bronzes from the Samuel
         H. Kress collection; reliefs, plaquettes,
         statuettes, utensils and mortars.
         London, Phaidon Press [1965]
             333p. illus. 30cm.

CATALOGUES

RA20   Nebraska Numismatics, Inc.
N4   Imported medals. [Omaha, 1967].
                107p. illus. 22cm.

RA20   Nebraska Numismatics, Inc.
N4w   World medals 1971. Omaha, [1971].
                92p. illus. 28cm.

GENERAL WORKS

RA30   Babelon, Jean.
B3   The medal in art and society. From:
Vert.   Journal of the Royal Society of Arts,
File   September, 1955.
                [11]p. 4 pl. 24cm.

RA30   Barcelona. Circulo filatelico y numismatico.
B35   Medallas. Zaragoza, La Academica,
            1957.
                197p. plates. 22cm.

RA30   Brenner, Victor D.
B7   The art of the medal. New York, 1910.
                [43]p. (incl. pl.) 24cm.

RA30   DeKay, Charles.
D4   A brief word on medals. New York,
            1910.
                24p. 24cm.

RA30   Forrer, Leonard.
F6   Biographical dictionary of medallists.
Rare   London, Spink, 1904-1930.
Books   8v. illus. 24cm.

RA30   Jobert, Louis.
J6   Einleitung zur medaillen, oder
Rare   munzwissonschaft. Leipzig, 1718.
Books   488p. pls. 17cm.

RA30   Pinkerton, John, 1758-1826.
P5   An essay on medals: or, An introduction
            to the knowledge of ancient and modern
            coins and medals; especially those of
            Greece, Rome, and Britain. 3d ed. Lon-
            don, Printed for T. Cadell and W. Davies,
            [etc.] 1808.
                2v. 6 pl. 22cm.

RA30   Spicer-Simson, T.
S6   Portrait reliefs, medals and coins in
           their relation to life and art. New York,
           American Numismatic Society, 1918.
                11p. 29cm.
                Reprinted from the American Journal of
           Numismatics.

RA30   Sutherland, Carol Humphrey Vivian.
S8   The art of the modern medal. From
Vert.   Journal of the Royal Society of Arts,
File   June, 1955.
                [14]p. 4 pl. 24cm.

SPECIAL ASPECTS

RA40   Kisch, Guido.
K5   Studien zur medaillengeschichte.
           Aalen, W. Germany, Scientia Verlag,
           1975.
                222p. illus. 23cm.

RA40   Linecar, Howard W. A.
L5   The commemorative medal; its
           appreciation and collection. Detroit,
           Gale Research Co., 1974.
                154p. illus. 23cm.

ARTISTS, A-Z

RA50   Henseler, Antoine.
B6H4   Antoine Bovy, artiste-graveur en
           medailles; sa vie et ses principales
           oeuvres; par Ant. Henseler. Fribourg,
           Switzerland, 1881.
                100p. VIIp. VI plates. 27cm.

ICONOGRAPHY - PERSONS, FAMILIES, A-Z

RA60   Demole, Eugene.
C3D4   Description des medailles concernant
           Jean Calvin. Extrait de l'Iconographic
           Calvinienne par E. Doumerque. Lausanne,
           n.d.
               18p. plates. 32cm.

RA60   Hill, George Francis.
J4H5   The medallic portraits of Christ; The
           false shekels; the thirty pieces of silver.
           Oxford, Clarendon Press, 1920.
               123p. illus. 26cm.

RA60   Mayhew, Aubrey.
K4M3   The world's tribute to John F. Kennedy
           in medallic art. New York, Morrow, 1966.
               197p. illus. 29cm.

RA60   Rochette, Edward C.
K4R6   The medallic portraits of John F.
           Kennedy. ... A descriptive catalogue of
           the coins, medals, tokens and store cards
           struck in his name. Iola, Wisc., Krause,
           1966.
               188p. illus. 22cm.

RA60   Westervelt, Leonidas.
L5W4   The Jenny Lind medals and tokens.
           New York, American Numismatic Society,
           1921.
               25p. 9 pl. 17cm. (Numismatic
           notes and monographs, no. 5)

ICONOGRAPHY - SUBJECTS, A-Z

RA80   Svarstad, Carsten.
A2S9   Medals of actors, singers and
           dancers. London, Spink & Son, Ltd.,
           1963.
               26p. illus. 24cm.

RA80   Van Keymeulen, A.
A5V8   L'art animalier dans la medaille par A.
           Van Keymeulen avec la collaboration de A.
           Gijzen. Antwerp, Societe Royale de Zoologie,
           1973.
               100p. ill. 40 pl. 23cm.

RA80   Eidlitz, Robert James.
A7E5   Medals and medallions relating to
           architects. Compiled ... from the col-
           lection of Robert James Eidlitz. New York,
           The author, 1927.
              190p. 125 pl. 41 x 30cm.

RA80   Walter, David L.
C6W3   Medallic memorials of the great comets
           and the popular superstitions connected
           with their appearance. New York, Scott,
           1893.
              55p. 5 pl. 25cm.

RA80   Hamburg. Zirkel-correspondenz.
F7H3   Abbildungen freimauer denkmunzen und
           medaillen. Hamburg, Rademacher, 1898-
           1906.
              2v. pl. 28cm.
              Library has: v.7 North & South America.
           v.8 Germany.

RA80   Friedenberg, Daniel M. ed.
J4F7   Great Jewish portraits in metal,
           selected plaques and medals from the Samuel
           Friedenberg collection of the Jewish
           museum. New York, Schocken Books, 1963.
              143p. illus. 27cm.

RA80   Friedenberg, Daniel M.
J4F7j   Jewish medals, from the Renaissance to
           the fall of Napoleon (1503-1815) by Daniel
           M. Friedenberg. [1st ed.] New York,
           Published for the Jewish Museum [by] C. N.
           Potter; distributed by Crown Publishers [1970]
              152p. illus., ports. 26cm.
              Bibliography: p. 146-148.

RA80   Friedenberg, Daniel M.
J4F7m   Jewish minters and medalists. Philadel-
           phia, Jewish Publication Society of America,
           1976.
              x, 131p. illus. 24cm.

RA80   Kisch, Guido.
L3K5   Recht und gerechtigkeit in der medail-
           lenkunst. Heidelberg, C. Winter, 1955.
              170p. pl. 26cm.

RA80   Medailles d'amour.
L6M6   Paris, Monnaie de Paris, n.d.
              31p. illus. 24cm.

RA80   Hodes, Alfred L.
M3H6   Collecting marriage medals. Reprinted
         from The Numismatist, 1959.
              6p. illus. 23cm.

RA80   Freeman, Sarah Elizabeth.
M4F7   Medals relating to medicine and allied
         sciences in the numismatic collection of
         the Johns Hopkins University. Baltimore,
         Evergreen House Foundation, 1964.
              430p. 32 pl. 30cm.

RA80   Holzmair, Eduard.
M4H6   Medicina in nummis; katalog der sammlung
         Dr. Josef Brettauer. Vienna, [Published
         by Trustees of Brettauer Foundation],
         1937.
              384p. 25 pl. 29cm.

RA80   Levinson, Abraham.
M4L4   Medical medallions. Taken from
         The Bulletin of the Medical Library
         Assn., Washington D.C., Jan. 1943
         (Vol. 31, #1).
              pp. 5-34. illus. 26cm.

RA80   Storer, Haratio Robinson.
M4S7   Medicina in nummis; a descriptive list
         of the coins, medals, jetons relating to
         medicine, surgery, and the allied
         sciences. Ed. by Malcolm Storer.
         [Boston, 1931].
              1146p. 16 pl. 25cm.
              Bibliography: p. 1135-1140

RA80   Milford Haven, Louis Marquees of.
N3M5   Naval medals ... of foreign countries.
         London, J. Murray, 1921-
              2v. illus. 41cm.
              Vol 1: France, Netherlands, Spain,
         Portugal.
              Vol 2: Europe, N., S. Amer., Japan,
         China.

RA80   Sandwich, George Charles.
N3S3   British and foreign medals relating to
          naval and maritime affairs. Greenwich,
          National Maritime Museum, 1937.
               308p. 27 pl. 25cm.

RA80   Storer, Malcolm.
N3S7   Catalogue of the Malcolm Storer
          collection of naval medals bequeathed
          to the U.S. Naval Academy, 1936.
               38p. 20cm.

RA80   Durand, Anthony.
N8D8   Medailles et jetons des numismates.
Rare   Geneva, 1865.
Books   246p. 20 pl. 29cm.
               Bibliography: p. ix-xiv.

RA80   Schulman, Jacques.
P4S3   Pax in nummis. Collection Le Maistre.
          Medailles, jetons et monnaies ... depuis
          le xvie siecle jusqu'a nos jours.
          Amsterdam, [1912].
               277p. illus. 12 pl. 25cm.

RA80   Dudley, Mayo.
W3D8   The war told in medals. From Munsey's
Vert.   Magazine, April 1918.
File   11p. illus. 23cm.

RA80   Frankenhuis, M.
W3F7   Catalogue of medals, medalets, and
          plaques relative to the world war, 1914-
          1918, The Hague, n.d.
               198p. 24 pl. 21cm.

<u>ANCIENT</u>

COLLECTIONS

RB10   Bartolo, Pietro Santas.
B3   Medailles de grand et moyen bronze
Rare   du cabinet de la Reine Christine,
Books   frappees...que par les colonies
            Romaines, et...les villes Grecques...
            Traduit du Latin de Sigebert Havercamp.
            Friburg, Pierre de Hondt, 1792.
            464p. illus. 39cm.
            In French and Latin

GENERAL WORKS

RB20   Evelyn, J.
E9   Numismata, a discourse of medals,
Rare   ancient and modern...London, Benj.
Books   Tooke, 1697.
            342p. illus. 32cm.

SPECIAL ASPECTS

RB30   Clarke, Edward Daniel.
C5   The tomb of Alexander. A dissertation
            on the sarcophagus brought from Alexandria
            and now in The British Museum. Cambridge
            University Press, 1805.
            161p. illus. 32cm.

ROMAN - COLLECTIONS, GENERAL WORKS

RB50   Boston. Museum of Fine Arts.
B6   Roman medallions. 1962.
            [20]p. 10 pl.

RB50   Cooke, William.
C6   The medallic history of imperial Rome
         from the first triumvirate, ... to ...
         Constantine the Great ... London, Dodsley,
         1781.
             2v. 61 pl. 28cm.

RB50   Dressel, Heinrich.
D7   Die Romischen medaillone;
         des munzkabinetts der staatlichen
         Museen zu Berlin. Zurich, Weidman,
         1973.
             2 vols. 484p. XXXIV plates.
         22cm; 30cm.

RB50   Smyth, William Henry.
S6   Descriptive catalogue of a cabinet of
         Roman imperial large-brass medals, by
         William Henry Smyth. Bedford [England].
         James Webb, 1834.
             [xxiv] 352p. 29cm.

RB50   Toynbee, Jocelyn M. C.
T6   Roman medallions. New York, ANS, 1944.
             268p. 49 pl. 27cm. (Numismatic
         Studies, no. 5)

ROMAN - BY PLACE OR PERIOD

RB60   Baldwin, Agnes, 1876-
B3i   Five Roman gold medallions or multiple
         solidi of the late empire. New York, ANS,
         1921.
             103p. illus. 17cm. (Numismatic
         notes and monographs, no. 6)
             Bibliography: p. 93-97.

RB60   Baldwin, Agnes, 1876-
B3o   Four medallions from the Arras hoard.
         New York, ANS, 1926.
             36p. illus., 4 pl. 17cm. (Numis-
         matic notes and monographs, no. 28)

RB60   Baldwin, Agnes, 1876-
B3s   Six Roman bronze medallions. New
         York, ANS, 1923.
             39p. 6 pl. 16cm. (Numismatic
         notes and monographs, no. 17)

RB60   Wirgin, Wolf.
W5   A metrological inquiry into the
           cistophoric medallions of the Emperor
           Hadrian. Bronxville, N.Y., Variety
           Books, [1966].
                44p. tables. 23cm.

ICONOGRAPHY

RB70   Babelon, Jean.
B3   Portraits en medaille. Introduction
           de Jean Babelon-Photos de Jean Raubier.
           Paris, Encyclopedia Alpina Illustree,
           c1946.
                4p. XL plates. 35cm.

OTHER COUNTRIES, A-Z

RB90   Goudard, A. C.
E3G6   Notice sur les medailles dites pieds
Rare   de sanglier. Toulouse, E. Privat,
Books   1880-1884.
                2 vol. 7 pl. 24cm.

RB90   Tochon d'Annecy, Joseph Francois.
E3T6   Recherches historiques et geographiques
           sur les medailles des nomes ou prefectures
           de l'egypte. Paris, Imprimerie Royale,
           1822.
                256p. illus. 27cm.

RB90   Ouseley, William.
P409   Observations on some medals and gems,
           bearing inscriptions in the Pahlovi or
           ancient Persick character. London, Wil-
           son & co., 1801.
                47p. illus. 32cm.

NETHERLANDS

RD20 Bizot, Pierre, 1630-1696.
B5   Medalische historie der republyk van
Holland. Amsterdam, Pieter Mortier,
1690.
   364, 40p. illus. 22cm.

RD20 Guioth, M.
G8   Histoire numismatique de la revolution
Belge, ou description raisonnee des
medailles, des jetons et des monnaies ...
Hasselt, 1844-45.
   2v. 406p., 62pl. 32cm.

RD20 LaLoire, Edouard.
L3   Souvenirs numismatiques des fetes
Jubilaires de 1905. Bruxelles,
G. Van Oest and Co., 1907.
   68p. X plates. 31cm.

RD20 Nahuys, Maurin.
N3h   Histoire numismatique du royaume de
Rare Hollande sous le regne de Louis-Napoleon.
Books 111 Amsterdam, Muller, 1858.
   181p. 13 pl. 29cm.

RD20 Nahuys, Maurin.
N3m   Medailles et jetons inedits relatifs
Rare a l'histoire des dix sept anciennes
Books provinces des Pays-Bas. Bruxelles,
Fr. Gobbaerts, 1873.
   89p. 14 pl. 24cm.

RD20 Orden, Gerrit van.
O7   Bijdragen voor de penningkunde.
Gravenhage, A. D. Schinkel, 1841.
   44p. 2 pl. 24cm.

RD20 Polak, Arthur.
P6   Joodse penningen in de nederlanden;
Jewish medals in the Netherlands.
Amsterdam, J. Schulman, 1958.
   80p. 17 pl. 27cm.
   In Dutch. Summaries in English.

RD20   Snoek, Jhr. M. W.
S6   Penningen en munten van de stad en
           de markiezen Van Bergen op zoom.
                [Pt. 1], 54p. illus. [Pt. 2],   12p.   24cm.
                Reprinted from "Taxandria", Tijdschnf
           voor noordbrabantshe geschiedenis da
           volkakunde. XXXI; XXXIII.

DENMARK

RD45   Holm, Johan Christian.
H6   Danmarks Krigsmedailler (with English
           summary) Copenhagen, Hohan Chr. Holm's
           Forlag, 1964.
                32p. illus. 18cm.

SWEDEN

RD50   Hildebrand, Bror Emil, 1806-1884.
H5m   Minnespenningar ofver enskilda Svenska
           man och quinnor. Stockholm, 1860.
                xii, 454p. pl. 24cm.

RD50   Hildebrand, Bror Emil, 1806-1884.
H5s   Sveriges och Svenska konungahusets
           minnespenningar praktmynt och belonings-
           medaljer. Stockholm, 1874-75.
                2v. 24cm.

RD50   Ossbahr, C. A.
07   Mynt och medaljer; slagna for
           frammande makter i anledning av krig mot
           sverige. Uppsala, 1927.
                265p. 48 pl. 24cm.

RD50   Skade-penningor ofver de
S5   fornamfta handelfer fom tillhorn.
Rare   Konung Gustof IIIs Historia.
Books   Stockholm, P.A. Norstedt & Soner,
                1858.
                93p. illus. 56cm.

RD60   Demole, Eugene.
D4   Visite au cabinet de numismatique
           ou coup d'oeil sur l'histoire de Geneve.
           Geneve, H. Jarrys, 1914.
               95p. illus. 19cm.

RD60   Kisch, Guido.
K5   Die schaumunzen der Universitat
           Basel und medaillen auf ihre
           professoren. Sigmaringen, W. Germany,
           Jan Thorbecke, 1975.
               63p. XIII plates. 24cm.

RD60   Krause, Delbert Ray.
K7   Swiss shooting talers and medals by
           Delbert Ray Krause with the assistance of
           Lawrence Block. Racine, Whitman, 1965.
               160p. illus. 20cm.

RD60   Martin, Jean L.
M3   Les medailles de tir suisses; Die
           Schutzenmedaillen der Schweiz; Le medaglie
           di tiro della Svizzera; Swiss shooting
           medals, 1612-1939, by Jean L. Martin.
           Lausanne, The Author, 1972; [Distributed
           by Galerie des Monnaies S. A., Lausanne]
               254p. illus. 31cm.
               Bibliography: p. 253-254.

RD60   [Societe suisse des Carbiners].
S6   Gedenkschrift zum 100 jahrigen jubilaum
           des schweizerisschen Schutzenvereins, 1824-
           1924. Zurich, W. Coradi-Maag, [1924].
               448p. illus. 28cm.

RD60   Widmer, Hans.
W5   Schweizer medaillen, 1934-1967;
           pragetabelle mit richtpreisen.
           Zurich, Erwin Dietrich, n.d.
               unpaged. 17cm.

COLLECTIONS

RE10
B7   British Museum. Dept. of Coins & Medals.
         A guide to the English medals exhibited
in the King's library. 1st ed. By
Herbert A. Grueber, London, 1881.
      170p. 21cm.

CATALOGUES

RE15
J6   John Pinches Ltd. (Medallists).
         Medallic craftmanship. London, n.d.
      8 pl. 25cm.

GENERAL WORKS

RE20
B7
Rare
Books   British Museum.
         Medallic illustrations of the history
of Great Britain and Ireland. London,
the Trustees, 1904-1910.
      19v. 130 pl. 42cm.

SPECIAL ASPECTS

RE30
C6   Cole, Howard N.
         Coronation and commemorative medals
1887-1953. Aldershot, Gale & Polden,
1953.
      52p. illus. 18cm.

RE30
E3   Edmundson, Joseph.
         Collecting modern commemorative medals.
London, Pelham Books, 1972.
      247p. illus. 22cm.

RE30   Till, William.
T5   Descriptive particulars of English
         coronation medals from the inauguration of
         King Edward the Sixth to Queen Victoria.
         London, Longmans, 1838.
             xix, 112p. front. 19cm.

RE30   Whiting, J. R. S.
W5   British commemorative medals; a medallic
         history of Britain from Tudor times to the
         present day. N.Y., Drake Pub., Inc., 1972.
             236p. illus. 23cm.

INDIVIDUAL ARTISTS, A-Z

RE35   Gray, John M.
T3G7   James and William Tassie; ... with a
         catalogue of their portrait medallions of
         modern personages. Edinburgh, W. G.
         Patterson, 1894.
             174p. 18 pl. 20cm.

RE35   A notable medallist; the work of
V5M6   Paul Vincze. Reprinted from the
            Monumental Journal and
            Commemorative Art, Vol. XXIX, No. 11.
            N.P., N. Pub., 1962.
            pp. 302-315. illus. 23cm.

RE35   [Carlisle, Nicholas].
W9C3   A memoir of the life and works of
         William Wyon, esq., A.R.A., Chief
         Engraver of the Royal mint. [London,
         1837].
             213p. 23cm.

RE35   Forrer, Leonard.
W9F6   The Wyons. London, Spink, 1917.
            119p. illus. 25cm.
            Reprinted from the Biographical
         Dictionary of Medallists, v. VI.

NINETEENTH - TWENTIETH CENTURIES

RE70   Grant, M. H.
G7   Catalogue of British medals since 1760.
            Reprinted from British numismatic jour-
            nal, 1936-41.
               [153]p. 25cm.

ICONOGRAPHY - PERSONS, FAMILIES, A-Z

RE80   Eidlitz, Robert James.
B6E4   Medallic portraits of Matthew Boulton
            and James Watt. New York, Priv. Print,
            1928.
               13p. 7 pl. 31cm.

RE80   Engstrom, J. Eric.
C4E5   The medallic portraits of Sir
            Winston Churchill, by J. Eric Engstrom.
            With a foreword by the Marquess of Bath.
            London, Spink & Son [1972]
               52p. illus. 26cm.

RE80   Hill, Leslie C.
C6H5   Captain Cook's resolution &
            adventure medal dated 1772; a paper
            prepared for the Vancouver
            Symposium in conjunction with
            the annual coin show of the
            Vancouver Numismatic Society.
            Vancouver, Canadian Numismatic
            Research Society, 1973.
               5p. 1 plate. 30cm.

RE80   Robinson, H.
C6R6   'A cook's tour' (Captain James
            Cook); navigator and explorer.
            Auckland, N.Z., Numis. Society of
            Auckland, Inc., n.d.
               28p. illus. 26cm.

RE80   McCormick-Goodhart, Leander.
V4M3   Admiral Vernon medals. New York,
            Numismatic Review, 1945.
               42p. 3 pl. 28cm.

RE85   Thomason, Edward.
B5T5   Enamelled impressions struck off from the
Rare   spendid series of medal dies, illustrative
Books   of the Holy Scriptures, engraved by British
            artists in the employ of the author. N.p.,
            n. pub., ca. 1832.
                2v. unpaged illus. 29cm.

RE85   Milford Haven, Louis Marquess of.
N3M5   British naval medals ... London,
            J. Murray, 1919.
                499p. illus. 41cm.

RE85   Poulsom, Neville W.
P6P6   The white ribbon, a medallic record of
            British polar expeditions. London,
            Seaby's [1968].
                216p. 8 pl. 25cm.

LOCAL, A-Z

RE90   Welch, Charles.
L6W4   Numismata Londinensia. Medals struck
            by the corporation of London to commemorate
            important municipal events, 1831 to 1893.
            London, 1894.
                169p. 14 pl. 32cm.

RE90   Peate, Iorwerth C.
W3P4   Welsh society and Eisteddfod medals
            and relics. Cardiff, National Museum of
            Wales, 1938.
                46p. 5 pl. 22cm.

COLLECTIONS

RF10   Le Breton, M. Gaston.
L4   Les medaillons des mois du musee de
          Rouen. Tours, P. Bousrez, 1881.
              16p. 2pl. 28cm.

RF10   Paris. Administration des monnaies et
P3   medailles.
              Les medailles de l'ancienne collection
          royale. Paris, 1900.
              10p. 20pl. 30cm.

CATALOGUES

RF15   Paris. Administration des monnaies et
P3c   medailles.
              Catalogue illustre des medailles en
          vente. Paris, 1908, 1912, 1926, 1928,
          1968, 1971.
              illus. 23cm.

RF15   Paris. Administration des monnaies et
P3m   medailles.
              Medailles France-Amerique. Paris,
          [1968], 1972.
              60p. (mainly illus.) 22cm.

GENERAL WORKS

RF20   Babelon, Jean.
B3   La medaille en France. Paris,
          Librarie Larousse, [1948].
              146p. 48pl. 17cm.

RF30
A3
Vert.
File
Paris. Administration des
Monnaies et Medailles.
Service commercial tarif courant
medailles et plaquettes. Paris,
1969.
unpaged. 24cm.

RF30
A3s
Vert.
File
Paris. Administration des Monnaies et
Medailles.
Service des medailles tarif courant
medailles et plaquettes. Paris, 1974.
12p. 24cm.

RF30
A3t
Vert.
File
Paris. Administration des
Monnaies et Medailles.
Tarif des medailles d'or de
petite modules. Paris, 1972.
11p. 24cm.

RF30
P6
Pond, Shepard.
Pretenders to the French throne in
numismatics. From Mass. Historical
Society, Proceedings, v. 67 (1942).
17p. 4pl. 24cm.

RF30
R3
Richebe, R.
Medaille's Francaises, inedites ou peu
connues. Paris, Raymond Serrure, 1898.
12p. illus. 28cm.

INDIVIDUAL ARTISTS, A-Z

RF35
B3M3
Mazerolle, F.
Manifestation en l'honneur de E. Babelon
..., biographie et bibliographie. Paris,
Ernest Leroux, 1912.
32p. pl. 29cm.

RF35
D4W5
Witte, Alphonse de.
Biographie et catalogue de l'oeuvre de
Godefroid Devreese, medailleur. Paris, E.
Leroux, 1912.
33-94p. ill. pl. 29cm.

RF35   Kunz, George Frederick.
R6K8   The late Louis Oscar Roty; ... his
          influence on ... medallic art. From
          American Journal of Numismatics, v. 47,
          1913.
              27p. 5pl. 28cm.

MEDIEVAL

RF40   Paris. Bibliotheque nationale. Department
D8   des medailles et antiques.
              Description des medailles gauloises
          faisant partie des collections de la
          Bibliotheque royale, accompagnee de notes
          explicatives, par Adolphe Duchalais.
          Paris, Chez Rollin, etc., 1846.
              x, 487p. 4pl. 21cm.

EIGHTEENTH CENTURY

RF60   Kortenbach, C. J.
K6   De fransche revolutie; de medailles en
          decoraties betreffende de verovering
          van de Bastille 1789-1792.
              35p. 6pl.

RF60   Millin de Grandmais ou, Aubin Louis, 1759-
M5   1818.
              Histoire metallique de la revolution
          francaise ... Paris, Imprimerie imperiale,
          1806.
              74p. 26pl. 30cm.

NINETEENTH - TWENTIETH CENTURIES

RF70   Florange, Charles.
F5   Le siege d'Anvers, 1832. Paris,
          J. Florange, 1932.
              156p. front., illus. 19cm.

RF80   Olivier, P.
L204   Iconographie metallique du General
          Lafayette ... medailles ... et jetons
          frappes a son nom ou a son effigie tant
          en France qu'en Amerique. Baltimore,
          Johns Hopkins, 1933.
              85p. illus. 5pl. 27cm.
          (Institut Francais de Washington,
          Cahier 6)

RF80   Betts, Benjamin.
L3B4   A descriptive list of the medals re-
          lating to John Law and the Mississippi
          system. Priv. print., 1907.
              77p. pl. 26cm.
              Reprinted from American Journal of
          Numismatics.

RF80   Academia Royale des medailles & des
L6F7   inscriptions.
Rare   Medailles sur les principaux evenements
Books   du regne de Louis le Grand, Paris,
          Imprimerie Royale, 1702.
              292p. illus. 29cm.

RF80   Babelon, Ernest.
N3B3   Les medailles historiques du
          regne de Napoleon Le Grand, empereur
          et roi. Publiees sous les auspices
          de la Societe de Numismatique de
          New-York. Paris, Ernest Leroux, 1912.
              430p. illus. 46cm.

RF80   Bramsen, Ludwig Ernst.
N3B7   Medaillier Napoleon le Grand. Paris,
          Copenhagen, 1904-13.
              3v. 27cm.
              Covers period 1799-1869.

RF80   Millin, Chevalier.
N3M5   Medallic history of Napoleon; a
          collection of all the medals, coins and
          jettons relating to his actions and
          reign from the year 1796 to 1815.
          Originally printed in London,
          Rodwell & Martin, 1819; supplement,
          1821.
              LXXIV plates. 28cm.
              -xerox copy of original

RF85   Lannois, M.
M4L3   Medailles medicales, par le
            Dr. M. Lannois. A supplement to
            Albums du Crocodile; premiere
            annee, numero IV, Lyon, 1933.
                unpaged. illus. 26cm.

RF85   [Saulcy, Louis Felicien Joseph Caignart
R4S2   de] 1807-1880.
                Souvenirs numismatiques de la revolution
            de 1848; recueil complet des medailles,
            monnaies et jetons qui ont paru en France
            depuis le 22 fevrier jusqu'au 20 decembre 1848.
            Paris, J. Rousseau [1848-50] Reprinted 1973-R.
            Lobel, London.
                2p. 1., 111p. 60pl. 28cm.

LOCAL, A-Z

RF90   Van Peteghem, C.
A4V3   De la valeur des medailles et monnaies
Rare   d'Alsace avec leur description d'apres
Books   les planches du Baron Berstett. Paris,
            1885.
                42p. 16pl. 28cm.

COLLECTIONS

RG10 Kirschner, Bruno.
K5   Deutsche spottmedaillen auf Juden,
bearbeitet und herausgegeben von
Arie Kindler. Munchen, Ernst
Battenberg, 1968.
   92p. illus. 25cm.

SPECIAL ASPECTS

RG30 Scheuch, Karl.
S3   Medaillen aus porzellan de Staatlichen
porzellan-manufaktur Meissen. Ober-
Eschbach, 1967-.
   100p. illus. 21cm.
   Library has: v. 1, 2: A-E.

RG30 Scheuch, Karl.
S3s   Spenden-medaillen aus porzellan und
ton der staatlichen porzellan-manufaktur
Meissen und anderen keramischen fabriken
des inlandes, by Karl Scheuch. Ober-
Eschbach, The author, 1966.
   [109]p. illus. 21cm.

INDIVIDUAL ARTISTS, A-Z

RG35 Sallet, Alfred von.
D8S3   Untersuchungen uber Albrecht Durer.
Berlin, Weidmann, 1874.
   50p. illus. 22cm.

RG35 Kienast, Gunter W.
G6K5   The medals of Karl Goetz. Cleveland,
Artus, 1967.
   284p. (incl. 154 pl.) 28cm.

```
RG50        Braun, Edmund Wilhelm, ed.
B7              Die deutschen renaissance plaketten
            der sammlung Alfred Walcher ritter von
            Moltheim in Wien.  Wien, Schroll & Co.,
            1918.
                2v.  ill.  pl.  32cm.

RG50        Ebner, J.
E2              Deutsche renaissance medaillen.  Aus
            dem Stuttgarter K. Munzkabinett und privat-
            vesitz.  Esslingen, P. Neff, 1909.
                44p.  3 pl.  26cm.

RG50        Habich, Georg.
H3m             Die deutschen medailleure des XVI,
            jahrhunderts; Halle A. D. Saale, A.
            Riechmann & Co., 1916.
                xx, 290p.  illus., 12 pl.  28cm.

RG50        Habich, George, 1868-
H3s             Die deutschen schaumunzen des XVI
            jahrhunderts, ... Munchen, F. Bruchmann,
            [1929-33].
                illus.  pl.  40cm.
                Library has v. 2, pt. 1 only.
```

NINETEENTH - TWENTIETH CENTURIES

```
RG70        Beard, Edward L., comp.
B4              Nazi medals; compiled and edited
            by Edward L. Beard.  Norwood, Ohio,
            Pioneer Guns, [1970].
                50p.  illus.  22cm.
```

ICONOGRAPHY - PERSONS, FAMILIES, A-Z

```
RG80        Fromery & Fils, Berlin, Publishers.
F7F7            Receuil de medailles pour servir a
Rare        l'histoire de Frederic le Grand dedie
Books       a son altesse Royale Monseigneur le
            Prince de Prusse par les tres humbles et
            tres obeissans serviteurs.  Berlin,
            Fromery & Fils, 1764.
                119 pl.  20cm.
```

RG80   Schreiber, Otto Louis.
L8S3   Martin Luther and the Reformation
           numismatic art during four and one-half
           centuries. The Mount Airy Evangelical
           Lutheran Theological Seminary Collection.
           Philadelphia, [1951].
               44p. 22cm.

LOCAL, A-Z

RG90   Hauser, Josef.
M8H3   Die munzen und medaillen der im
           Jahre 1156 gegrundeten Haupt-und
           residenzstadt munchen. Munich, 1905.
               xxxii, 318p. 32 pl. 25cm.

<u>SPAIN</u>, <u>PORTUGAL</u>, <u>ANDORRA</u>

EARLY MODERN, SIXTEENTH - EIGHTEENTH CENTURIES

RH65   Garcia, D. Valentin Gil Y.
G3   Valuador de las medallas de
           proclamacion de los reyes de Espana...
           Madrid, R. Velasco, 1883.
               unpaged. 25cm.

<u>ITALY</u>

COLLECTIONS

RI10   British Museum. Dept. of Coins and Medals.
B7i   A guide to the exhibition of Italian
            medals by C. F. Keary. 2nd ed., London,
            the trustees, 1893.
                99p. 7 pl. 23cm.

RI10   British Museum.
B7m   A guide to the exhibition of medals of
            the Renaissance in the British Museum, by
            G. F. Hill. London, 1923.
                84p. illus. 22cm.

RI10   British Museum.
B7s   Select Italian medals of the Renaissance
            in the British Museum. Printed by order
            of the Trustees, 1915.
                16p. 50 pl. 29cm.

RI10   Imp. et Royale Galerie de Florence
G3   dessinee par le Professeur Gozzini
Rare   et gravee par le Chevalier P. Lasini
Books   Cinqueme Serie. Florence, n.p.,
                n.d.
                54 plates. 32cm.

CATALOGUES

RI15   Johnson, Stefano.
J6   Medaglie per raccolta. Milan, n.d.
                4p. 9 pl. 28cm.

INDIVIDUAL ARTISTS, A-Z

RI35   Lawrence, Richard Hoe.
C3L3   The Paduans; medals by Giovanni Cavino.
            Hewitt, N. J., Hellenic-Roman Coins,
            [1964].
                31p. illus. 22cm.
                Originally published 1883.

RI35   Hill, George Francis.
P4H5   Pisanello. New York, Scribner, 1905.
              263p. 74 pl. 20cm.

RI35   Forrer, Leonard.
P5F6   Benedetto Pistrucci; Italian medalist
          and gem-engraver, 1784-1855. London,
          Spink, 1906.
              40p. illus. 25cm.
              Extract from the Biographical
          dictionary of medallists.

RENAISSANCE

RI50   Comparette, T. L.
C6   A brief study of the medal; its origin
Vert.   and early development. Reprinted from
File   the Proceedings of the Numismatic and
          Antiquarian Society of Philadelphia, 1910.
              [91-113]p. 3 pl. 22cm.

RI50   Fabriczy, Cornelius von.
F3m   Medaillen der Italienischen Renaissance
          Leipsig, H. Seemann Nachfolger, [1902], 1904.
              108p. illus. 26cm.
              1904 edition in English.

RI50   Goethe, Johann Wolfgang, 1749-1832.
G6   Goethe's Italian medals; first republica-
          tion of an essay in the Jenaische Allgemeine
          Literatur-Zeitung, 1810, by J.W. Goethe and
          Heinrich Meyor. Introduction and comments
          by Edward Gans. Trans. by Max Knight. San
          Diego, Malter-Westerfield, 1969.
              ix, 12p. 16 pl. 29cm.

RI50   Hill, George Francis.
H5c   A corpus of Italian medals of the
          Renaissance before Cellini. London,
          British Museum, 1930.
              2v. 201 pl. 40cm.

RI50   Hill, George F.
H5p   Portrait medals of Italian artists of
          the renaissance, with an introductory essay
          on the Italian medal. London, Philip
          Lee Warner, 1912.
              92p. 32 pl. 27cm.

RI50   Mercante, Luciano, 1902-
M4M4   Scultore e medaglista. Prefazione
          di Giuseppe Mesirca. Testi critici
          di Luigi Mattei e Laura Miceli.
          Rebellato Editore [1970].
              253p. illus. 32cm.

NINETEENTH - TWENTIETH CENTURIES

RI70   Johnson, Stefano Carlo.
J6   La conquista della libia nelle medaglie,
          1911-1914. Milan, Alfieri & Lacroix,
          1914.
              95p. illus. 24cm.

ICONOGRAPHY - PERSONS, FAMILIES, A-Z

RI80   Bartolotti, Franco.
P6B3   La medaglia annuale dei Romani
          Pontefici da Paolo V a Paolo VI, 1605-
          1967. [Rimini, Italy, Cosmi Editore]
          1967.
              xxii, 478p. illus. 32cm.

RI80   Papal States. Zecca pontificia.
P6M3   Serie dei conj di medaglie pontificie
          da Martino V. fino a tutto il pontificato
          della san. Mem. di Pio VII. esistenti
          nella Pontificia zegga di Roma. Roma,
          V. Poggioli, 1824.
              ix, 166p. 21cm.

RI80   Rinaldi, Alfio.
P6R5   Catalogo delle medaglie Papali
          annuali da Pio VII a Paolo VI. Verona,
          1967.
              xiii, 113p. illus. 24cm.
              Bibliography: p. XI

RI80   Spink & Son, Ltd. London.
P6S6   A descriptive catalogue of Papal
          medals. London, Spink & Son, 1962.
              123p. illus. 21cm.
              Originally published in 1898.

ICONOGRAPHY - PERSONS, FAMILIES, A-Z

```
RJ80      Spassky, I., Comp.
P4S6         Medals and coins of the age of
          Peter the Great; from the
          Hermitage Collection, compiled
          and introduced by I. Spassky and
          E. Shchukina.  Leningrad, Aurora
          Art Publishers, 1974.
             40p.  35 col. plates. fold. facs-
          ims.  30cm.
                -in Russian and English
```

AUSTRIA

RK20   Austria. State Printing Office.
A9   Die medaillen und plaketten des
Vert. osterreichischen Hauptmunzamtes. Wien,
File   1925.
       12p. pl. 17 x 22cm.

RK20   Kenner, Friedrich.
K4   Die munze und die medaille der Kaiserin
Maria Theresia. Fest-Vortrag zur Maria
Theresia-Feier der Numismatischen Gesellschaft
in Wien ... am 10. Mai 1888. Katalog der
ausgestellten medaillen. Vienna, 1888.
     72p. 23cm.

RK20   Loehr, August O.
L6   Die medaille in Osterreich von A. O.
Loehr und F. Dworschak, Wien, Eduard
Holzel & Co., [1951].
     15p. 13 pl. 18cm. (Kunsthistoris-
ches Museum, Wien.)

RK20   Probszt, Gunther.
P7k   Die Kartner medaillen abzeichen und
ehrenzeichen. Klagenfurt, Landes museum
fur Karnten, 1964.
     214p. 41 pl. 28cm.
     Bibliography

RK20   Probszt, Gunther.
P7s   Schau-und-Denkmunzen Maria Theresias.
Graz, Akademische Dr., 1970.
     xlii, 416p. illus. 28cm.
     Bibliography

RK20   Roll, Karl.
R6   Die Schaumunzen auf die Salzburger
emigration. Halle, A. Riechmann, 1925.
     24p. 9 pl. 24cm.

CZECHOSLOVAKIA

RK40   Ceska a slovenska medaile 1508-1968.
C4   [Exhibition at Prague, Narodna Galeria,
            1969].
                104p. 60 pl. 24cm.
                Bibliography: p. 96-102.
                Text in French and Czech.

RK40   Nohejlova-Pratova, Emanuela.
N6   Katalog vystavni sbirky medaili.
            Prague, Narodni Muzeum, 1963.
                160p. 16 pl. 21cm.
            (Introd. in Czechoslovakian, French,
            English, Russian, German)

RK40   Obermajer, Jaroslav.
O2   Jan Evangelista Purkyne v reliefni
            plastice. Brne, Moravske museum, 1970.
                96p. illus. 22 x 25cm.

RK40   Prague. Numismaticke Spolecnost Ceskoslo-
P7   venske.
                Medaile v zemich Ceskych ... (exhibition
            at the Art and Industry Museum, May 15,
            to June 9, 1924) Praha, 1924.
                71p. 20 pl. 27cm.

HUNGARY

RK60   Hungary. National Gallery.
H8f   Fulop Beck O., 1873-1945, retrospec-
            tive. Budapest, 1970.
                46p. 32 pl. 23 x 20cm.
                Text in French and Hungarian.

RK60   Hungary. National Gallery.
H8m   Magyar muveszet, 1896-1945; Art
            hongrois, 1896-1945. Exposition de la
            galerie nationale hongroise au musee ernst.
            Septembre-Octobre, 1969.
                76p. 40 pl. 23 x 20cm.
                Text in French and Hungarian.

RK60   Hungary. National Gallery.
H8me   Medailles hongroises aux XIXe et XXe
         siecles. Budapest, 1959.
              51p. 32 pl. 28cm.

RK60   Odon, Gohl.
O3   Budapest Ujabb Emlekermei.
         Budapest, 1905.
              98p. pl. 28cm.

RUMANIA

RK70   Groner, Egon.
G7   Rumanische medaillen vom jahre
         1600 bis einschliesslich 1900.
         Bucarest, Gobl, 1905.
              143p. 8cm.

<u>UNITED STATES</u>

COLLECTIONS

RM10   Morello, Theodore, ed.
M6   The Hall of Fame for great
          Americans at the N.Y. University;
          official handbook. Rev. ed. N.Y.,
          N.Y. University, 1967.
              210p. illus. 22cm.

RM10   National Sculpture Society.
N3a   Annual exhibition; sculpture, bas-
          reliefs, medals. New York, 1966, 1967,
          1968, 1969.
              Chiefly photog. 24cm.

RM10   National Sculpture Society.
N3c   Catalogue of the exhibition of Ameri-
          can Sculpture. New York, 1923.
              372p. illus. 28cm.

RM10   Norton (R.W.) Art Gallery.
N6   Medallic art of the United States, 1800-1972.
          [Exhibition] August 8 to September 17, 1972.
          [Shreveport, La., 1972]
              40p. illus. (part col.) 28cm.
              Bibliography: p. 39.

CATALOGUES

RM15   Baron, Herman, comp.
B3   The Franklin Mint index of
          sculptors; covering issues from
          1965-1971. n.p. n.pub., [1971?]
              unpaged. 28cm.
              The work is to be used as a
          supplement and index to Numismatic
          Issues of the Franklin Mint.

RM15   Culver, Virginia.
C8   Guidebook of Franklin Mint issues by
          Virginia Culver and Chester I. Krause.
          Iola, Wisc., Krause Pub., 1974, 1976.
              222p. illus. 28cm.

RM15   Darrow, Rex.
D3   Franklin mint issues - identifications and
          valuations; ... includes facts pertinent to
          the proper identification and a guide to fair
          market value ... Scotia, New York, Regent
          Graphics, 1970, 1971.
               v. ill. 28cm.

RM15   Franklin Mint.
F7   Numismatic issues. Franklin Center,
          Pa., 1967-1975.
               (mainly illus.) 28cm.
               Beginning 1973, compiled by Arlie R.
          Slabaugh, Herman Baron, and Edwin S. Traut-
          man.
               1975 title: Limited editions of the
          Franklin Mint.

RM15   Kovel, Ralph M.
K6   The Kovels' collector's guide to limited
          editions, by Ralph M. and Terry H. Kovel.
          New York, Crown Publishers, [1974].
               250p. pl. ill. 28cm.

RM15   Mishler, Clifford.
M5   ... United States and Canadian commem-
          orative medals and tokens. [Vandalia,
          Mich?, the author, 1958-1962.
               illus. 22cm.

RM15   National Commemorative Society and its
N3   first fifty issues. [Philadelphia,
               1969].
               166p. illus. 31cm.

RM15   U.S. Bureau of the Mint.
U5   Medals of the United States mint, prepared
          under the direction of ... Eva Adams, Director
          of the mint, by Captain Kenneth M. Failor ...
          Washington, D.C., 1969, 1972.
               274p. ill. 28cm.

RM15   Young, Edward.
Y6   America's United States; silver dollar
          size medals produced by the United States
          Coinage Corporation commemorating the
          entrance of the States into the Union.
          [Boston, U.S. Coinage Corp., 1970].
               127p. ill. 24cm.

GENERAL WORKS

RM20   Belden, Bauman L.
B4   Medals and publications of the Ameri-
          can Numismatic Society with an historical
          sketch. New York, 1915.
              81p. illus. 24cm.

RM20   Chamberlain, Georgia Stamm.
C5   American medals and medalists.
          [Annandale, Va., Turnpike, 1963].
              146p. 24 pl.

RM20   Furst, Moritz.
F8   Medals made in America. Reprinted from
          the Numismatist, 1954.
              [16]p. illus. 24cm.

RM20   The annual of modern medals.
M4   1974-75 library ed. 1st ed.
          Kermit, Tx., FBG Enterprises,
          1975.
              114p. illus. 28cm.

SPECIAL ASPECTS

RM30   Babin, Lenard L., comp.
B3   Elongated-rolled-out-cents. Illustrated
          check list, volume 1. New York, the
          author, [1961].
              [12]p. illus. 21cm.

RM30   Dow, Dottie.
D6   The elongated collector; an illustrated
          check list of elongated coins. Phoenix,
          Ariz, 1965.
              209p. illus. 22cm.

RM30   Greathouse, Thomas R.
G7   A guidebook of 1-ounce .999
          fine silver art bars, produced by
          Thomas R. Greathouse and J.A. Kidd.
          1st ed. Plantation, Florida, the
          author, 1975.
              100p. illus. 27cm.

RM30   Hibler, Harold E.
H5   So-called dollars; an illus. standard
          catalog with valuations by Harold E.
          Hibler and Charles V. Kappan. New York,
          Coin and Currency Institute [1963].
              156p. illus. 28cm.

RM30   Kenney, Richard D.
K4   So-clled dollars. New York, Wayte
          Raymond, 1953.
              20p. 7 pl. 23cm. (The Coin Coll-
          ector's Journal, July-August, 1953).

RM30   Martin, Lee, Comp.
M3   Today's elongateds; listing the roller
          of elongated coins. Santa Ana, Cal.,
          the author, 1974.
              205p. illus. 29cm.

RM30   Wagaman, Lloyd E.
W3   The elongated coins, by Lloyd E.
          Wagaman. Camby, Indiana, The author,
          1973.
              44p. illus. 23cm.
              Contains: supplement-1975

INDIVIDUAL ARTISTS, A-Z

RM35   Johnson, Edwin L.
B6J6   J. A. Bolen's medals, cards and
          fac-similes, an accurate and comphrehensive
          descriptive catalogue of Bolen's works...
          Springfield, Mass, Numismatic Printing
          and binding Co., 1882.
              18p. 25cm.

RM35   American Numismatic Society.
B7A5   Catalogue of the international exhibi-
          tion of contemporary medals: Victor David
          Brenner. New York, 1911.
              7p. 5 pl. 25cm.

RM35   Chamberlain, Georgia Stamm.
C4C4   Studies on John Gadsby Chapman, Ameri-
          can artist, 1808-1889. [Virginia, 1963].
              40p. illus. 25cm.

RM35   Zigrosser, Carl.
D8Z5   Medallic sketches of Augustin Dupre.
            Reprinted by the Bureau of the Mint,
            1957.
                14p. illus.

RM35   Domit, Moussa M.
E2D6   The sculpture of Thomas Eakins. [Washing-
            ton D.C.], Corcoran Gallery of Art, 1969.
                66p. illus. 21cm.

RM35   Saint-Gaudens, Homer, ed.
S2S2   The reminiscences of Augustus
            Saint-Gaudens; edited and amplified
            by Homer Saint-Gaudens. N.Y.,
            Century Co., 1913.
                2 vols. 383; 381p. plates. 23cm.

RM35   Jockers, Ernst.
S3J6   J. Otto Schweizer, the man and his
            work. Philadelphia, International,
            [c1953].
                164p. incl. 73 pl.

RM35   Noe, Sydney P.
W4N6   The medallic work of A. A. Weinman.
            New York, A.N.S., 1921.
                47p. illus. 17cm.

COLONIAL

RM50   Betts, C. Wyllys.
B4   American colonial history illustrated by
            contemporary medals. New York, Scott Stamp
            & Coin Co., 1894, 1964, 1972.
                332p. ill. 25cm.

EARLY NATIONAL

RM60   Kenney, Richard D.
K4   Early American medalists and die-
            sinkers, prior to the Civil War. New
            York, Wayte Raymond, 1954.
                24p. illus. 23cm. (Coin collector's
            Journal, Jan-Feb, 1954)

RM60   Loubat, Joseph Florimond, 1831-
L6   The medallic history of the United
            States of America, 1776-1876. New York,
            the author, 1878. Reprinted New Milford,
            Conn. N. Flayderman, [1967].
                 2v. 86 pl. 47cm.

RM60   Sattarlee, Alfred H.
S3   An arrangement of medals and tokens
            struck in honor of the presidents of the
            United States, and of the presidential
            candidates, from the administration of
            John Adams to that of Abraham Lincoln.
            New York, Printed for the author, 1862.
                 84p. 23cm.

NINETEENTH - TWENTIETH CENTURIES

RM70   [Comparette, Thomas Louis].
C6   Coins and medals in the United States
            in 1913, 1914. American Journal of
            Numismatics, 1913-14.
                 31p. 11 pl. 28cm.

ICONOGRAPHY - PERSONS, FAMILIES, A-Z

RM80   Elder, Thomas L.
C5E4   The medals and tokens of Henry Clay.
            An address delivered before the American
            Numismatic Society, 1918.
                 15p. illus. 22cm.

RM80   Eglit, Nathan N.
C6E4   Columbiana; the medallic history of
            Christopher Columbus and the Columbian
            Exposition of 1893. Chicago, Hewitt
            Bros., 1965.
                 143p. illus. 19cm.
                 Bibliography

RM80   John Fritz Medal Fund Corporation.
F7   Presentation of the John Fritz gold
            medal to Herbert Hoover. ... April 25,
            1929. [New York], 1929.
                 61p. pl. 25cm.

RM80   [Eidlitz, Robert James].
J4E4   Medals and medallions of Thomas Jeffer-
           son. Reprintd from The Numismatist,
           1924.
               [10]p. illus. 25cm.

RM80   Rosato, Angelo A.
K4R6   A tribute to John F. Kennedy in a
           series of elongated United States half
           dollars. [New Milford, the author,
           1968].
               28p. illus. 16cm.

RM80   Bartle, Dorothy Budd.
N4B3   Black heroes in history; medals
           honoring Black Americans. Newark,
           Newark Museum Assn., c1973.
               20p. illus. 26cm. (Museum
           New Series, Vol. 23, #4)

RM80   Appleton, W. S.
W3A6   Description of medals of Washington
Rare   in the collection of W. S. Appleton.
Books   Boston, T. R. Marvin, 1873.
               24p. 28cm.

RM80   Baker, William S.
W3B3   Medallic portraits of Washington, with
           historical and critical notes and a de-
           scriptive catalogue of the coins, medals,
           tokens, and cards, by W. S. Baker.
           Philadelphia, Lindsay, 1885. [Reprinted
           by Krause, 1965].
               [288]p. pl. 26cm.

RM80   Douglas, Susan H.
W3D6   George Washington medals of 1889.
           Reprinted from The Numismatist, 1949.
               32p. illus. 23cm.

RM80   Hume, Edgar Erskine.
W3H8   George Washington and the Society of
           the Cincinnati. Washington, U.S. George
           Washington Bicentennial Commission, 1933.
               32p. illus. 23cm.

RM80   Raymond, Wayte.
W3R3   The early medals of Washington, 1776-
           1834. New York, 1941.
               16p. illus. 23cm. (Coin collector
           Series, no. 4).

RM80   Snowden, James Ross.
W3S6   A description of the medals of Wash-
           ington. ... Philadelphia, B. Lippincott,
           1861.
              203p. 26cm.

ICONOGRAPHY - EVENTS, SUBJECTS, A-Z

RM85   American Numismatic Association.
A5H3   A catalogue of convention badges and
           medals, 1908-1968, by N. Neil Harris.
           [Lafayette, Ind., 1969].
              64p. 22cm.

RM85   Slabaugh, Arlie R.
C5S5   Christmas tokens and medals. [Chicago,
           the author, 1966].
              31p. illus. 20cm.

RM85   Belden, Bauman L.
I5B4   Indian peace medals issued in the
           United States. New York, American Numis.
           Society, 1927. Reprinted New Milford,
           Conn., Flayderman, [1966].
              46p. 22 pl. 28cm.

RM85   Gillingham, Harrold E.
I5G5   Indian and military medals from
           colonial times to date. Pennsylvania
           Historical Society, 1927.
              97-125p. 2 pl. 24cm.

RM85   Gillingham, Harrold E.
I5G5s   Indian silver ornaments. From Penn-
           sylvania magazine of history and bio-
           graphy, vol. 58, 1934.
              97-126p. 4 pl. 25cm.

RM85   Jamieson, Melvill Allan.
I5J3   Medals awarded to North American
           Indian chiefs, 1714-1922 and to loyal
           African and other chiefs in various
           territories within the British Empire.
           London, Spink, 1936.
              122p. illus.

RM85   Morin, Victor.
I5M6   Les medailles decernees aux
            Indiens d'Amerique. Ottawa, Societe
            Royale du Canada, 1915.
                pp. 277-353. plates. 25cm.
            (Memoires de la Societe Royale du
            Canada, series III, Tome IX)

RM85   Prucha, Francis Paul.
I5P7   Indian peace medals in American
            history. Madison, The State Historical
            Society of Wisconsin, 1971.
                xiv, 186p. illus. 27cm.
                Bibliography: p. 165.

RM85   Apelman, J.S., Comp.
M3A6   New Orleans Mardi Gras Parade Doubloon
            price guide, 1960-1969. Madisonville,
            Louisiana, 1969.
                60p. illus. 22cm.

RM85   Guren, Jay.
M3G8   Carnival panorama, New Orleans Mardi
            Gras medals and krewes, 1884-1965, by Jay
            Guren and Richard Ugan. New Orleans,
            Anderson, 1966.
                201p. illus. 22cm.

RM85   Guren, Jay.
M3G8a   Catalog of 1966 Mardi Gras Medals.
Vert.   TAMS Journal reprint, May-July 1966.
File   14p. illus. 28cm.

RM85   Kearney, W. L.
M3K4   Mardi Gras Dubloons--Guide
            book of prices, 1960-1969.
            Metairie, La., the author, n.d.
                43p. 22cm.

RM85   McLaughlin, Lloyd A., Jr.
M3M3   Mardi Gras doubloons and medaillions.
            New Orleans, 1965.
                64p. illus. 21cm.

RM85   Ross, Thomas B.
N4R6   A catalogue of NENA medals; a fully
            illustrated guide to the various medals
            issued by the New England Numismatic
            Association in conjunction with their
            Annual Conference and Convention, by
            Thomas B. Ross. Enfield, Conn., The
            Author [1972].
                31p. illus. 22cm.

RM85   Weidhaas, Ernest.
N7W4   New York world's fair medals, 1939-
          1940. Reprinted from the Numismatist, 1966.
              73p. (incl. 39 pl). 23cm.

RM85   Dusterberg, Richard B.
P7D8   The official inaugural medals of the
          Presidents of the United States. Cincinnati,
          Medallion Press, 1971, 1976.
              107p. pls. 24cm.

RM85   MacNeil, Neil.
P7M3   The president's medal, 1789-1977. New York,
          Clarkson N. Potter, 1977.
              160p. ill. pl. 31cm.

RM85   Clain-Stefanelli, Vladimir.
R4C5   Medals commemorating battles of the
          American Revolution by Vladimir and
          Elvira Clain-Stefanelli. Washington,
          D.C., Smithsonian Inst., 1973.
              44p. illus. 26cm.

LOCAL, A-Z

RM90   Heath, Robert R.
M4H4   Commemorative medals of Massachusetts cities
1977   and towns, compiled and edited by Robert R.
          Heath. Rev. ed. Burlington, Mass., Robert
          R. Heath, 1977.
              351p. ill. 23cm.

RM90   Pond, Shepard.
M4P6   Medals of Massachusetts Bay tercente-
          nary, 1930. Reprinted from The Numis-
          matist, v. 44, 1931.
              36p. illus. 22cm.

RM90   Storer, Malcolm, 1862-
M4S7   Numismatics of Massachusetts. ...
          [Boston] The Massachusetts historical
          society, 1923.
              xi, 318p. 38 pl. 25cm. (Massa-
          chusetts historical society... Collec-
          tions, v. 76)

RM90   Storer, Horatio R.
R4S7   The medals and tokens of Rhode Island
          Reprinted from the American Journal of
          Numismatics, 1895.
              14p.   24 x 21cm.

GENERAL WORKS

RN10   Betts, Benjamin.
B4   Some undescribed Spanish-American
        proclamation pieces. Private, 1898.
            25p. 6 pls. 24cm.
            [Reprinted from the American Journal
        of Numismatics.]

RN10   Langdon, William Chauncy.
L3   The international diplomacy of the
        medallic art. Reprinted from the Hispanic
        American Historical Review, vol. 8, no. 3,
        August, 1927.
            375-380p. 26cm.

RN10   Medina, Jose Toribio, 1852-1930.
M4   Medallas de Proclamaciones y
        juras de los Reyes de Espana en
        America. Reprint of 1917 ed. with
        foreword and prices by Alcedo
        Almanzar. Boston, Quarterman
        Pub., 1973.
            340p. illus. 26cm.

MEXICO

RN20   Gama, Antonio Diez Soto y.
G3   Commemorative medal in honour of
        General Emiliano Zapata. Data extracted
        from Antonio Diaz Soto y Gama's book La
        Revolucion Agraria del Sur y Emiliano
        Zapata, Su Caudillo. Mexico City,
        Cincuentenario del Plan deAyala, 1961.
            31p. 23cm.

RN20   Grove, Frank W.
G7   Medals of Mexico. San Jose, Prune Tree
        Graphics, 1970-1974.
            3v. illus. 27cm.
            Contents: I. Medals of the Spanish kings,
        [1701-1821]. - II. 1821-1871. - III. Orders,
        awards, and military decorations.

RN20   Mexico. Cincuenta aniversario de la in
M38   inciacion de la revolucion Mexicana.
           Medalla conmemorativa de homenaje al
General Francisco Villa. Mexico City,
1960.
               24p. 23cm.

RN20   Mexico. Patronato de homenaje al heroico
M4   batallon de San Patricio.
           Medalla commemorativa de homenaje
al heroico batallon de San Patricio.
Mexico City, 1960.
               16p. 23cm.

RN20   Mexico. Sociedad numismatica de Puebla.
M42   Medalla commemorativa de la heroica
batalla del 5 de Mayo de 1862. Puebla,
1962.
               28p. 23cm.

RN20   Perez-Maldonado, Carlos.
P4   Medallas de Mexico, commemorativas,
Monterrey, Mexico, Impresora Monterrey,
1945.
               484p. illus. 23cm.
           Bibliography

SOUTH AMERICA, A-Z

RN50   Almanzar, Alcedo F.
E2A4   The medals of Ecuador, by Al
Almanzar and Dale Seppa. San Antonio,
Tex., Almanzar's Coins of the World
[1972].
               55p. illus. 22cm.
           Bibliography: p. 55.

RN50   Illingworth Baquerizo, Gustavo.
E2I4   Medallas commemorativas
Ecuatorianas de bautizo, de
matrimonio, de bodas de plata
matrimoniales varios; [por] Gustavo
Illingworth Baquerizo. Segunda
ed...Guayas, Ecuador, Benemerita
Sociedad Filantropica del Guyas,
1974.
               114p. 20cm.

BRAZIL

RN60   Banco Economico da Bahia S. A. Museu de
B3   numismatica.
              Medalhas, Brasil-colonia; Brazil,
          imperio. Catalogo - Inventario. Salvador,
          Bahia, BEB, 1969.
              208p. 21cm.
              Bibliography: p. 207.

RN60   Banco Economico S.A., Museu de Numismatica.
B3m   Medalhas da Brasil-Republica; catalogo-
          inventario. Salvador, Brazil, Grafica da
          Besa, 1974.
              2 vol. 483p. 21cm.

RN60   Prober, Kurt.
P7   Catalogo das medalhas da Republica.
          Contribucao aos festejos de 4. Centenario
          do Rio de Janeiro. Rio de Janeiro,
          Banco economico da Bahia, [1965].
              211p. 28cm. (Monografias numismati-
          cas, v. XI)

CHILE

RN70   Avila Martel, Alamiro de.
A9   El arte de Rene Thenot en la medallis-
          tica chilena. Santiago, La Casa de Moneda
          de Chile, 1965.
              51p. illus. 25cm.

<u>CANADA</u>

SPECIAL ASPECTS

RO30   Craig, Hamilton.
C7   The loyal and patriotic society of
          upper Canada and its still-born child the
          "upper Canada preserved" medal. [From:
          Ontario History, vol. 52 (1960)].
              [22]p. illus. 25cm.

EIGHTEENTH CENTURY

RO60   McLachlan, Robert W.
M3   The Louisbourg medals. [From Canadian
          Antiquarian and numismatic journal, v.13,
          1886].
              14p. 22cm.

NINETEENTH - TWENTIETH CENTURIES

RO70   Roberts, Jack.
R6   Medals issued during 1967 including
          centennial with symbol, special
          projects, wooden tokens, commercial
          issues and other related events.
          1st printing. n.p., the author,
          [1974].
              141p. illus. 23cm.

<u>ASIA</u>

PHILIPPINES

RP20   Bantug, Jose P.
B3   Recuerdos de D. Alfonso XIII en Filipina
          (Ilustrados numismaticamente). Manila,
          Universidad de Sto. Tomas, 1947.
              29p. illus. 23cm.

CHINA

RP50   Brudin, J. A.
B7   The medals of China (1900). American,
          Numismatic Association, [196-].
              13p. 5 pl. 22cm.
              Reprinted from The Numismatist, 1899.

INDIVIDUAL ARTISTS, A-Z

RR35   Chitty, Alfred.
C6C6   Report of lecture entitled incidents in
         the life of E. W. Cole and a collectors'
         guide and catalogue to his medals by
         Alfred Chitty and Henry Williams. ...
         Melbourne, Southland, 1924.
            114p. 18cm.

ICONOGRAPHY - PERSONS, FAMILIES, A-Z

RR80   O'Shea, Philip P.
C6O8   Captain James Cook, R.N., F.R.S. and
         his numismatic associations. In: The New
         Zealand Numismatic Journal, Supplement to
         Vol. 12, no. 5 (47), Wellington, 1970.
            51p. 19 pl. 24cm. (The Sutherland
         Memorial Lecture, 1969.)

CATALOGUES

SA20
A5
    Allen and Ginter, Richmond, Va, pub.
        Decorations of the principal orders of
    Knighthood and chivalry of the world.
    n.d.
        10p.   10 pl.   24cm.

SA20
B3
    Babin, Gregory.
        Foreign-war medals, orders and dec-
    orations, illustrated catalogue. Comp.
    by ... and Lenard L. Babin.
        24p. of illus.   23cm.

GENERAL WORKS

SA30
B3
    Batson, Alfred B. C.
        Orders and decorations. Reprinted
    from the Encyclopedia Americana.
        11p.   2 pl.   28cm.

SA30
D6b
    Dorling, Henry Taprell.
        British and foreign ribbons; naval,
    military, air force and civil by
    Captain H. Taprell Dorling, D.S.O., R.N.
    London, Geo. Philip & Son, Ltd., 1946.

SA30
D6r
    Dorling, Henry Taprell.
        Ribbons and medals, naval, military,
    air force, and civil. London, George
    Philip, 1916-1960.
        7v.   ill.   22cm.
        Library has: 1916, 1919, 1920, 1944, 1946,
    1956, 1960.

SA30
P8c
    Purves, Alec A.
        Collecting medals and decorations.
    London, Seaby, 1968.
        192p.   15 pl.   22cm.
        Bibliography

SA30   Purves, Alec A., ed.
P8o   Orders, decorations and medals; a
         select bibliography. Compiled by the
         Orders, Decorations and medals research
         society of Great Britain. London,
         Spink, 1958.
             11p. 25cm.

SA30   Werlich, Robert.
W4   Orders and decorations of all nations,
         ancient and modern, civil and military.
         Washington D.C., Quaker Press, 1965, 1974.
             336p. illus. 29cm.
             Bibliography

SA30   Wyllie, Robert E.
W9   Orders, decorations and insignia
         military and civil. New York, Putnams,
         1921.
             290p. 29 pl. 24cm.

SPECIFIC ORDERS, GROUPS, ETC.

SA40   Gillingham, Harrold Edgar.
G5   Ephemeral decorations. New York,
         ANS, 1935.
             45p. pl. 16cm. (Numismatic notes
         and monographs, no. 66)

SA40   Luscomb, Sally C.
L8   The collector's encyclopedia of
         buttons. New York, Crown, 1967.
             242p. illus. 26cm.

EIGHTEENTH - NINETEENTH CENTURIES

SA50   Gritzner, Maximilian.
G7   Handbuch der ritter-und verdienstorden.
         (Orders of Knighthood and merit of the
         world, 19th century). Graz, Austria,
         Akademische, 1962.
             618p. illus. 17cm.
             Reprint of 1893 ed.

SA60   Pownall, Henry.
P6   Korean campaign medals, 1950-53.
          N.p., n. pub., 1954.
             10p. illus. 25cm.

EUROPE

GENERAL WORKS

SB10   Hieronymussen, Poul Ohm.
H5   Orders and decorations of Europe in
            color, by Paul Hieronymussen. Photographed
            by Aage Struwing. [Translated into English
            by Christine Crowley] New York, Macmillan
            [1967]
                256p. illus. (part col.) 19cm.
                Translation of Europaeiske ordner i farver.
                Bibliography: p. 252.

WESTERN, A-Z

SB20   Jorgensen, Peter J.
D4J6   Danish orders and medals. Copenhagen,
            1964.
                124p. illus. 24cm.

SB20   Gillingham, Harrold Edgar, 1864-
S6G5   Spanish orders of chivalry and
            decorations of honour. New York, ANS,
            1926.
                165p. front., 39 pl. 16cm.
                Bibliography

EASTERN, A-Z

SB60   Prochazka, Roman Freiherr von.
A8P7   Osterreichisches ordens-
            handbuch [von] Roman Freiherr von
            Prochazka. Munchen, Graf Klenau,
            1974.
                160p. unpaged plates. 25cm.

SB60   Schmidt, Gunter Erik.
A8S3   Ehrenzeichen und medaillen der
            Republik Osterreich und der Bundeslander
            ab dem Jahre 1945. Vienna, 1960.
                44p. 34 pl. 29cm.

Mathis, Rene.
    Les nouveaux etats europeens et leurs
decorations; preface de M. Louis Villat.
... Nancy, 1929.
    317p.   5 pl.   25cm.

<u>FRANCE</u>

GENERAL WORKS

SC30   Gillingham, Harrold Edgar, 1864-
G5   French orders and decorations.
            New York, ANS, 1922.
                110p. 35 pl. 16cm. (Numismatic
            notes and monographs, no. 11)
                Bibliography

SPECIFIC ORDERS, GROUPS, ETC.

SC40   Aspect, M. D.
A7   Histoire de l'ordre royal et militaire
            de Saint-Louis. Paris, 1780.
                3 v. 20cm.

SC40   Florange, Charles.
F6   Les decorations et insignes des
            Chapitres nobles de France avant 1789.
            Paris, Florange, 1925.
                32p. illus. 25cm.

SC40   Taurignac, Jean Joseph.
T3   L'ordre Imperial des trois
            toisons d'or par commandant
            Taurignac. Paris, J. Leroy, 1907.
                2 pts. 198p. facims (part.
            fold) 25cm.

COLONIES

SC70   Gillingham, Harrold Edgar.
G5   Notes on the decorations and medals of
            the French colonies and protectorates.
            New York, ANS, 1928.
                62p. 30 pl. 16cm. (Numismatic
            notes and monographs, no. 36)
                Bibliography

<u>GERMANY</u>

SPECIFIC ORDERS, GROUPS, ETC.

SD40   Prowse, A. E.
P7   The Iron Cross of Prussia and Germany
Vert.   1813-1945. From New Zealand Numismatic
File   Journal, Dec. 1969.
                 25p. 1 pl. 24cm.

SD40   Tantum, W. H., ed.
T3   German army, navy uniforms and insig-
             nia, 1871-1918. Ed. by Tantum and E. J.
             Hoffschmidt. Old Greenwich, Conn.,
             WE, 1968.
                 195p. (chiefly illus) 27cm.

TWENTIETH CENTURY

SD60   German military uniforms and insignia, 1933-
G4   1945. Old Greenwich, Conn., We, 1967.
                 227p. ill. 23cm.

SD60   Klenau, Arnhard Graf.
K54   Grober Deutscher ordens-
             katalog; orden und ehrenzeichen
             bis 1918. Munchen, Ernst
             Battenberg, 1974.
                 225p. illus. 25cm.

SD60   Klietmann, K. G.
K55f   Fur tapferkeit und verdienst.
             (Decorations of Germany and her allies in
             World War I and II. Munich) Schild-
             Verlag, 1955.
                 59p. 4 pl.

SD60   Klietmann, K. G.
K55p   Pour le merite und tapferkeitsmedaille.
             Berlin, "Die Ordenssammlung," 1966.
                 104p. 19 pl. 21cm.

SD60   Ross, Shelby C., Jr.
R6   Collectors' guide to the military
          badges, medals and decorations of
          the Third Reich. n.p., S. & R.
          Ross, 1969.
               57p. illus. 25cm.

SD60   Uniforms and insignia of the National
U5   Socialist German Workers party.
               NSGWP. (no other information given)
               71 pl.

LOCAL, A-Z

SD70   Schreiber, Georg.
B3S3   Die Bayerischen orden und ehrenzeichen.
          Herausgegehen und eingeleitet von
          Alexander Freiherr von Reitzenstein.
          Munich, Prestal-Verlag, 1964.
               200p. illus. 18cm.

SD70   Gebert, Carl Friedrich.
N8G4   Die marken und zeichen Nurnberg's.
          Commissioned by Nurnberg Numismatic
          Association. Nurnberg, 1901.
               31p. 14 pl. 27cm.

CATALOGUES

SE20   Baldwin, A. H., pub.
B3   Catalogue of orders, decorations
         and medals. London, 1948.
            38p. 22cm.

SE20   Gould, Robert.
G6   Campaign medals of the British Army,
         1815-1972, by Robert W. Gould. London
         Arms and Armour Press [1972]
            72p. illus. 23cm.
            Bibliography: p. 15

SE20   Joslin, E. C.
J6   Standard catalogue of British orders,
         decorations and medals, with valuations.
         London, Spink, 1969, 1972.
            2v. ill. 23cm.

SE20   Seaby, B. A.
S4   Catalogue of war medals and decorations.
         London, n.d.
            19p. 22cm.

GENERAL WORKS

SE30   Abbott, P. E.
A2   British gallantry awards [by] P. E.
         Abbott [and] J. M. A. Tamplin.
         Middlesex, England, Guinness Superlatives;
         London, B. A. Seaby [1971]
            359p. illus. col. 25cm.

SE30   Carter, Thomas.
C3   War medals of the British Army,
         1650-1891, by Thomas Carter and W. H.
         Long. London, Arms and Armour Press;
         London, J. B. Hayward and Son [1972]
            656p. illus. 23cm.
            Reprint of 1893 ed.

SE30   Gordon, Lawrence L.
G6b   British battles and medals. Alder-
         shot Gale and Polden, 1947.
             294p. illus. 25cm.

SE30   Gordon, Lawrence L.
G6o   British orders and awards. W. H.
         Smith, 1959.
             166p. 25cm.

SE30   Honours and awards of the old con-
H6   temptibles; the officers and men of
             the British Army and Navy mentioned
             in despatches, 1914-1915. London,
             Arms and Armour Press, 1971.
             58p. 26cm.

SE30   Johnson, Stanley C.
J6c   The medal collector; a guide to naval,
         military, air-force and civil medals and
         ribbons. New York, Dodd, Mead, 1921.
             320p. 24 pl. 20cm.
             Bibliography

SE30   Johnson, Stanley C.
J6m   The medals of our fighting men. London,
         Black, 193-.
             120p. 16 pl. 20cm.

SE30   Joslin, Edward C.
J68   The observer's book of British
         awards and medals. London,
         Frederick Warne & Co., Ltd., 1974.
             191p. illus., part. col. 15cm.

SE30   Payne, Algernon Archibald.
P3   A handbook of British and foreign
         orders, war medals and decorations awarded
         to the Army and Navy. Sheffield, Northend,
         1911.
             881p. illus. 25cm.

SE30   Philip, George, pub.
P4   Regimental badges and service caps.
         London, Philip, 1941.
             32p. (chiefly illus) 18cm.

SE30   Power, James R.
P6   Identification data on British war
         medals and their interpretation. The
         author, 1960.
             56p. 19cm.
             Bibliography

SE30   Risk, James Charles.
R5   British orders and decorations. New
         York, ANS, 1945.
             124p. 76 pl. 17cm. (Numismatic
         notes and monographs, no. 106)
             Bibliography

SE30   Talbot-Booth, E. C., ed.
T3   Rank and badges in the Navy, Army,
         R.A.F. and auxiliaries. London, G.
         Philip, 1940.
             40p. (Chiefly illus.) 19cm.

SPECIFIC ORDERS, GROUPS, ETC.

SE40   Bisset, Ian.
B5   The George Cross. London, Macgibbon
         and Kee, 1961.
             260p. 22cm.
             Bibliography

SE40   Creagh, (Sir) O'Moore, ed.
C7   The V.C. and D.S.O; a complete record
         of all those officers, (etc) ... who have
         been awarded these decorations ...
         London, 1923.
             3 v. photog. 28cm.

SE40   Dalton, Charles.
D3   The Waterloo roll call, by Charles
         Dalton. London, Arms and Armour;
         Hayward and Hall [1971].
             296p. 22cm.

SE40   De la Bere, Ivan.
D4   The Queen's orders of chivalry.
         London, Kimber, 1961, 1964.
             222p. photog. 23cm.

SE40   Great Britain. Order of the Bath.
G7   Statutes of the most honourable Order
Rare   of the Bath. London, 1725, rep. 1787.
Books   67p. 25cm.

SE40   Risk, James C.
R5   The history of the Order of the Bath
         and its insignia, by James C. Risk.
         London, Spink & Son, 1972.
             214p. illus. pl. col. port. 26cm.
             Bibliography: pp. 148-150.

SE40   Smyth, John.
S6   The story of the Victoria Cross, 1856-
           1963. London, Muller, 1963.
               496p. illus. 22cm.
               Bibliography

SE40   South African War honours and
S69   awards, 1899-1902; the officers
           and men of the British army and
           navy mentioned in dispatches.
           London, Arms and Armour Press,
           1971.
               132p. II plates. 26cm.

SE40   Von Allendorfer, Frederic.
V6   The Kearny cross. N.p., n. pub.,
           n.d.
               4p. illus. 26cm.

EIGHTEENTH - NINETEENTH CENTURIES

SE50   Calver, William L.
C3   The British Army button in the Ameri-
Vert.   can Revolution.
File   In: The New York Historical Society
           Quarterly Bulletin, vol. VII, no. 1
           (April, 1923).
               10-23p. ill. 25cm.

SE50   Fothergill, George A.
F6   British fire-marks from 1680.
           Edinburgh, W. Green, 1911.
               180p. 49 pl. 26cm.

LOCAL, A-Z

SE80   O'Toole, E. H.
O6   Decorations and medals of the Republic
           of Ireland, by E. H. O'Toole. London,
           B. A. Seaby [1972]
               42p. illus. 22cm.

GENERAL WORKS

SF30   Gillingham, Harrold Edgar.
G5   Italian orders of chivalry and medals
          of honour. New York, ANS, 1923.
              146p. 33 pl. 16cm. (Numismatic
          notes and monographs, no. 20)
              Bibliography

SPECIFIC ORDERS, GROUPS, ETC.

SF40   Bascape, G. C., introd.
B3   L'insigne reale ordine di San Gennaro,
          1738-1963; storia e decumenti a cura del
          Gran Magistero dell'Ordine. Naples, 1963.
              105p. col. pl. 30cm.

SF40   Galbreath, Donald Lindsay.
G3   Papal heraldry. 2d ed.
          revised by Geoffrey Briggs.
          London, Heraldry Today, 1972.
              135p. illus. 29cm.

SF40   L'ordine supremo della SS. Annunziata.
L6   Seicento anni di storia 1362-1962.
              Milan, 1963.
              44p. 14 pl. 32cm.

LOCAL, A-Z

SF70   Ordine militare di Savoia;
S207   Statuto. Rome, [Vittorio
              Emanuele Mussolini], (1943?)
              20p. 30cm.

RUSSIA

GENERAL WORKS

SG30   Andolenko, Serge.
A5   Badges of Imperial Russia, military,
          civil, religious. Translated, edited
          and enlarged by Robert Werlich. Limited
          first edition. [Washington, Quaker Press,
          1972]
              212p. illus. (col.) 30cm.
              Bibliography: p. 211

SG30   Hazelton, Alan W.
H3   The Russian imperial orders. New
          York, ANS, 1932.
              101p. 20 pl. 17cm. (Numismatic
          notes and monographs, no. 51)
              Bibliography

SG30   Walther, Ferdinand.
W3   Soviet decorations. Montreal, The
          author, 1964.
              106p. 52 pl. 21cm.
              In English and French

SG30   Werlich, Robert.
W4   Russian orders, decorations and medals
          including those of Imperial Russia, the
          provisional government and the Soviet
          Union.
              139p. illus. 28cm.
              Bibliography

EIGHTEENTH - NINETEENTH CENTURIES

SG50   Spassky, I. G.
S6   Inostrannie i russkie ordena do 1917
          goda [Foreign and Russian orders up to
          1917]. Leningrad, 1963.
              195p. 42 pl.
              Bibliography: p. 139
              In Russian, English summary-p. 134-138.

<u>UNITED STATES</u>

CATALOGUES

SH20 Irons, Charles F.
I7   Illustrated catalogue of solid gold society
      emblems, pins, and charms, ... 1885. Reprint.
      Detroit, Gale, 1966.
           194p. ill. 23cm.

SH20 Studley, George W.
S7   Regulation war medals. Rochester, N.Y.,
      George W. Studley, n.d.
           various pagings ill. 16cm.

GENERAL WORKS

SH30 Albert, Alphaeus H.
A5   Record of American uniform and
      historical buttons, a definitive
      listing of the buttons depicting
      the insignia... and relative values,
      1775-1968. Hightstown, New Jersey,
      The Author [1969]
           448p. illus. 22cm.
           ______Supplement, 1973.

SH30 Belden, Bauman L.
B4   United States war medals. New York,
      American Numismatic Society, 1916.
      Reprinted 1962.
           72p. 10 pl. 29cm.

SH30 Crouch, Kenneth E.
C7   Awards of honor in the United States.
      No imprint.
           unpaged ill. 30cm.

SH30 Hood, Jennings.
H6   American orders and societies and their
      decorations, the objects of the military and
      naval orders, commemorative and patriotic
      societies of the United States and the re-
      quirements for membership therein ..., com-
      piled by ... and Charles J. Young. Philadel-
      phia, Bailey, Banks & Biddle, 1917.
           107p. 18 pl. 25cm.

SH30   Hopper, James.
H66   Medals of honor. New York, J. Day,
         1929.
             281p. 21cm.

SH30   Kerrigan, Evans E.
K4   American war medals and decorations.
         New York, Viking Press, 1964.
             149p. illus. 23cm.
             Bibliography

SH30   Morgan, J. McDowell.
M6   Military medals and insignia of the
         United States. Glendale, Cal., Griffin-
         Patterson, 1941.
             141p. illus. 23cm.

SH30   U.S. Congress. Senate. Committee on Labor and
U5   Public Welfare.
             Medal of honor recipients, 1863-1963.
         Washington, D.C., GPO, 1964.
             1058p. 24cm.

SH30   Williams, Dion.
W5   War decorations by Colonel Dion
         Williams. United States Naval
         Institute. Proceedings, Annapolis,
         Vol. 45, #4. 1919.
             pp. 495-535. illus. (part. col.)
         23cm.

SH30   Wyllie, Robert E.
W9   The romance of military insignia.
         American decorations and insignia of
         honor and service. From National Geo-
         graphic, Dec., 1919.
             56p. illus. 26cm.

SPECIFIC ORDERS, GROUPS, ETC.

SH40   Abraham, Irwin R.
A2   U.S. Merchant Marine decorations and
         awards. The author, 1966.
             48p. illus. 23cm.

SH40   Friederich, Rudolf J.
F7   Medal of honor citation supplements.
          Chicago, Orders and Medals Society of
          America, [1968].
              [100]p. illus. 28cm.

SH40   Hume, Edgar Erskine.
H8   The medals of the United States Army
          medical department and medals honoring
          army medical officers. New York, ANS,
          1942.
              145p. 23 pl. 17cm.

EIGHTEENTH - NINETEENTH CENTURIES

SH50   Belden, Bauman L.
B4   War medals of the Confederacy. New
          York, The American Numismatic Society,
          1915. Reprinted, 1957.
              12p. 1 pl. 28cm.

SH50   Campbell, J. Duncan.
C3   American military insignia, 1800-1851,
          By J. Duncan Campbell and Edgar M.
          Howell. Washington, Smithsonian Institu-
          tion, 1963.
              126p. photog., front. 28cm. (U.S.
          National Museum of History and Technology,
          Bulletin 235).

TWENTIETH CENTURY

SH60   DeBaene, Antoine.
D4   Glory and honor to the Armies of the
          United States of America, liberators of
          Belgium 1944-1945. Brussels, J. Rosez,
          [1948].
              274p. photog. 25cm.

SH60   DuBois, Arthur E.
D8   The heraldry of heroism. Decorations,
          medals, service ribbons, badges and
          women's insignia. From: The National
          Geographic Magazine, Oct., 1943.
              35p. illus. 25cm.

SH60 Grosvenor, Gilbert.
G7   Insignia of the United States Armed
       forces. From National Geographic, June
       1943.
           illus., part. col.

SH60 Kerrigan, Evans E.
K4   Current American war medals and decora-
       tions, 1963-69. Noroton Heights, Conn.,
       Medallic, 1969.
           23p. ill. 22cm.

SH60 King, Elizabeth W.
K5   Heroes of wartime science and mercy.
       From National Geographic, June 1943.
           715-748p. ill. 26cm.

SH60 U.S. Army.
U5e   Army regulation AR 672-8, decorations,
       awards, and honors, manufacture, sale,
       wearing, and quality control of heraldic
       items. Washington, D.C., Dept. of the Army,
       July 1970.
           6p. 26cm.

SH60 U.S. Army.
U5f   Army regulation AR 672-5-1, awards.
       Washington, D.C., Dept. of the Army, May 1961.
           108p. ill. 26cm.

SH60 U.S. Army.
U5t   Army regulation AR 672-5-2, decorations
       and awards, illustrations of awards. Washing-
       ton, D.C., Dept. of the Army, July 1967.
           19p. ill. 26cm.

SH60 U.S. Navy.
U52   Summary of regulations governing the
       issuance and wearing of decorations, medals
       and ribbons now designated for naval per-
       sonnel. Washington, D.C., GPO, 1943.
           11p. ill. pl. 27cm.

SH60 Wasserman, Paul, ed.
W3   Awards, honors and prizes, a directory
       and source book. Detroit, Gale Research,
       1969, 1972.
           307p. 28cm.

CANADA

SI20   Babin, Lenard L.
B3   Cap badges of the Canadian expedition-
         ary forces 1914-1919. Rochester, N.Y.,
         n.d.
             15p. 21 pl. 21cm.

MEXICO

SI40   Gillingham, Harrold Edgar, 1864-
G5   Mexican decorations of honour. New
         York, ANS, 1940.
             53p. 17 pl. (Numismatic notes and
         monographs, no. 89)
             Bibliography

SI40   Perez-Maldonado, Carlos.
P4   Condecoraciones mexicanas y su historia.
         Monterrey, 1942.
             212p. illus. 23cm.
             Bibliography

SOUTH AMERICA

SI60   Gillingham, Harrold Edgar, 1864-
G5   South American decorations and war
         medals. New York, ANS, 1932.
             178p. map, pl. 17cm. (Numismatic
         notes and monographs, no. 56)
             Bibliography

SI60   Pardo, Oscar.
P3   "Condecoraciones Argentinas",
         la orden del libertador San Martin.
         Buenas Aires, Ano Internacional del
         Libro, 1972.
             133p. illus. 27cm.

SI80   Etienne, Francis Ed.
H3E8   Les decorations Haitiennes a travers
          l'histoire. Port-au-Prince, 1954.
              120p. col. pl. 31cm.

<u>ASIA</u>

CHINA

SJ20   Peterson, James W.
P4   Chinese nationalist medals and awards.
Vert.   Lyons, Ill., Award Publications, 1962.
File   4p. 26 pl. 28cm.

JAPAN

SJ40   Babin, Lenard L.
B3   Japanese war medals - orders -
          decorations ... Illustrations by John
          E. Snitzel. Rochester, N.Y., Babin,
          n.d.
              8p. illus. 23cm.

SJ40   Peterson, James W.
P4   Orders and medals of Japan and associa-
          ted states. Chicago, Orders and Medals
          Society, [1967].
              110p. illus. 28cm.

SJ40   Wilkinson, James.
W5   Court ranks, decorations, commemora-
          tion medals and medals of honor of Japan.
          Orders and Medals Society, 1962.
              11p. illus. 28cm.

NEAR EAST, A-Z

SJ85   Artuk, Ibrahim.
T8A7   Osmanli Nisanlari--the Ottoman orders
          [by] Ibrahim Artuk and Cevriye Artuk.
          Istanbul, Istanbul Matbaase, 1967.
              48p. XII plates. 23cm.
          In English and Turkish.

PART III

WORLD

CATALOGUES

UA20   Loeb, Walter M.
L6   Catalog of paper money around the world
        Ed. by Lee Firester. Port Washington,
        N.Y., Universal, 1961.
            75p. 12 pl. 27cm.
            Bibliography

GENERAL WORKS

UA30   Angus, Ian.
A5   Paper money. N.Y., St. Martin's
        Press, c1974, 1975.
            128p. illus. part. col. 27cm.

UA30   Beresiner, Yasha.
B4   The story of paper money [by]
        Yasha Beresiner and Colin Narbeth.
        New York, Arco Pub. Co. [1973].
            112p. illus. 25cm.

UA30   Deutsche Bundesbank, Frankfurt am Main.
D4   Fruhzeit des papiergeldes; beispiele
        aus der geldscheinsammlung der Deutsche
        Bundesbank. [1970?].
            [xxii] illus. 50 col. pl, with text
        29cm.
            Bibliography.

UA30   Lawrence, Jimmie N., comp.
L3   The foreign paper money story and
        encyclopedia; compiled and published by
        Jimmie N. Lawrence. Johannesburg, Republic
        of South Africa, [1974].
            72p. illus. 22cm.

UA30   Musser, Dwight L.
M8   Subject paper money; consisting
            of forty-three issues of
            Paper Money publications together with
            an index. Edited and published by
            Dwight L. Musser. Indian Rocks Beach,
            Florida, the author, n.d.
                unpaged. illus. 29cm.

UA30   Pick, Albert.
P5   Papiergeld. Braunschweig, Klinkhardt
            and Biermann, 1967.
                455p. illus. 24cm.

UA30   Sten, George J.
S7b   Banknotes of the world, 1368-1966.
            Menlo Park, Cal., Shirjieh, 1967.
                2v. illus. 28cm.
                Contents. v.1 Aden to China. v.2
            Colombia-Kuwait.

UA30   Sten, George J.
S7e   Encyclopedia of world paper money ...
            1661-1964. Port Washington, N.Y., Univ-
            ersal, 1965.
                152p. illus. 28cm.

TWENTIETH CENTURY

UA33   Keller, Arnold.
K4   Paper money of the world. Pt. 1.
            Modern Issues of Europe. New York, Royal
            Coin, 1956.
                88p. illus. 22cm.

UA33   Keller, Arnold.
K4p   Paper money of the 20th century based
            on a manuscript by Dr. Arnold Keller.
            Dallas, Tex., International Banknote
            Society, 1973.
                Vol. 1 no continuous pagination.
            illus. 30cm.

UA33   Pick, Albert.
P5c   Catalogue of Eropean paper money since
            1900. New York, Sterling, 1970, 1971, 1974.
                320p. ill. 27cm.

UA33   Pick, Albert.
P5s   Standard catalog of world paper
          money. Senior editor: Clifford
          Mishler; coordinating editor,
          Russell Rulau. [Iola, Wisc.], Krause
          Publications. Jointly published,
          Munich, Ernst Battenberg, 1975.
               720p. illus. 28cm.

SPECIAL ASPECTS

UA40   International Criminal Police Organization.
I5   Counterfeits and forgeries. Second
          part. 1960-.
               looseleaf. illus. 27cm.

UA40   Pick, Albert.
P5   Briefmarkengeld. Braunschweig, Klink-
          hardt & Biermann, [1970].
               xi, 66p. illus.
               Bibliography.

COLLECTING

UA50   Curto, J. J.
C8   Paper money restoration and preservation
          Reprinted from The Numismatist, 1971.
               7p. 22cm.

UA50   Lake, Kenneth R.
L3   Investing in paper money. London,
          Pelham Books, 1972.
               158p. illus. 23cm.

UA50   Musser, Dwight L.
M8   World paper money collectors guide.
          N.p., Dwight L. Musser, 1959.
               28p. 28cm.

UA50   Narbeth, Colin.
N3   Collecting paper money; a beginner's
          guide. Chicago, H. Regnery Co. [1973,
          c1968].
               134p. facsims. 21cm.
               Bibliography: p. 122-124.

UA50   Pick, Albert.
P5   Papiergeld sammeln. Munchen,
         Ernst Battenberg, 1971.
             149p. illus. 21cm. (Kleine
         Numismatische Bibliothek, #9).

MILITARY CURRENCY

UA60   Rutlader, James.
R8   Allied military currency ... from
         World War II to date and emergency issues
         caused by a war. The author, 1968.
             91p. illus. 21cm.

UA60   Swails, Alfred J.
S9   Military currency, W. W. II, U.S. and
         allies. Tucson, 1961.
             63p. illus. 21cm.

UA60   Toy, Ramond S.
T6a   Axis military currency by Raymond
         Toy and Bob Meyer. Tucson, 1967.
             98p. illus. 22cm.

UA60   Toy, Raymond S.
T6w   World War II allied military currency.
         Tucson, 1964, 1965, 1969, 1974.
             86p. illus. 22cm.

GENERAL WORKS

UB20   White, Benjamin.
W5   The currency of the Great War.
          London, Waterlow, 1921.
              104p. illus. 24cm.

GREAT BRITAIN

UB30   Bevan, David.
B4   A guide to collecting English bank-
          notes. The author, 1970.
              72p. illus. 23cm.

UB30   Douglas, James.
D6   Scottish banknotes [by] James
          Douglas. London, Stanley Gibbons,
          1975.
              257p. illus. 23cm.

UB30   Duggleby, Vincent.
D8   English paper money [by]
          Vincent Duggleby. London, Stanley
          Gibbons, 1975.
              107p. illus. 22cm.
              -bibliography

UB30   Le Marchant, R.
L4   Paper treasure of the Channel Islands; an
          illustrated reference guide describing the
          paper currency notes issued by the states of
          Jersey ... and Guernsey during the German
          occupation of the islands 1940-1945. St.
          Peter Port, Guernsey, R. Le Marchant, n.d.
              28p. ill. 22cm.

UB30   Muscalus, John A.
M8   British empire bank note proofs;
          one hundred bank note proofs of
          England, Scotland, Wales, Ireland
          and Australia of the early 1800's.
          Bridgeport, Pa., the author, 1971.
              34p. illus. 28cm.

UB30   Narbeth, Colin, ed.
N3   Collect British bank notes;
          a Stanley Gibbons priced catalogue
          of British Treasury and Bank of
          England notes. 1st ed. London,
          Stanley Gibbons, 1970.
              53p. illus. 21cm.

UB30   Quarmby, Ernest.
Q3   Banknotes and banking in the Isle of
          Man, 1788-1970; a guide for historians
          and collectors. London, Spink & Son,
          1971.
              124p. illus. 23cm.

UB30   Young, Derek.
Y6   Guide to the currency of Ireland;
          legal tender notes, 1928-1972, by
          Derek Young. Dublin, Stagecast
          Publications [1972]
              88p. illus. 22cm.
              Bibliography: p. 88.

FRANCE

UB40   Muszynski, Maurice.
M8   Les billets de la Banque
          de France. Villiers sur Marne,
          Societe numismatique de Paris,
          1975.
              120p. illus. 25cm.

UB40   Pond, Shepard.
P6   The assignats, the depreciation of a
          paper currency. Boston, Jacques and
          Melanson, 1943.
              13p. illus. 23cm.

ITALY

UB50   Banca Populare di Novara.
B3   La moneta Italiana, un secolo dal 1870.
          Novara, Italy, c1971.
              558p. illus. col. plates. 35cm.

UB50   Bobba, Cesare.
B6   Cartamoneta italiana; catalogo
1971   universal dal 1746 ai giorni nostri,
          con valutazioni. Asti [1971].
              352p. illus. 17cm.
              Bibliography: p. 351-352.

UB50   Mancini, Libero.
M3   La cartamoneta Italiana antica e
          fuori corso. Bologna, 1964.
              27p. illus. 23cm.

UB50   Marcon, Alfredo.
M32   La cartamoneta nello Stato Pontifico.
          Rome, Marte, 1965.
              53p. 22 pl. 28cm.
              Contents: v.1 1785-1798.

UB50   Sollner, Gastone.
S6   Catalogo della carta-moneta d'
          occupazione e di liberazione dei
          partiginai e dei campi di
          prigionia (seconda guerra mondiale).
          seconda ed, 1975. Asti, Italy,
          Cesare Bobba, 1974.
              185p. illus. 17cm.

SPAIN

UB53   Vicenti, Jose A.
V5   Catalogo neto; billetes espanoles, 1808-
          1969. Madrid, Salinero, 1969, 1970.
              104p. illus. 21cm.

PORTUGAL

UB55   Rebelo, Luis Manuel de Sousa.
R4   O papel-moeda em Angola; (subsidios
          para o seu estudo) [by] Luis Manuel Rebelo
          de Sousa. Luanda, Angola, Banco de Angola,
          [1970].
              157p. illus. 22cm.
              Contains English summary--pp. 147-154.

UB55   Siemsen, Carl.
S5   Das notgeld Portugals 1917-1922.
        Berlin, Erich Proh, 1973.
            69p. illus. 21cm.
        (Band 41 der schriftenreihe, "Die
        Munze".)

SCANDINAVIA

UB60   Finland, Bank.
F5   Suomen kotimaiset setelityypit, 1809-
        1951 (Paper money of Finland). Helsinki,
        1952.
            66p. 24 pl. 30cm.
        Companion volume in Swedish under title
        Inhemska sedeltyper i Finland.

UB60   Holmasto, Thure R.
H6   Suomen setelit; Finlands sedlar;
        av Th. R. Holmasto. Helsinki, the
        author, 1971.
            54p. 21cm.

UB60   Platbarzdis, Aleksandrs.
P5   Sveriges forsta banksedlar, Stockholms
        Bancos sedelutgivning, 1661-1668.
        (Earliest Swedish bank notes). Stockholm,
        Sveriges Riksbank, 1960.
            234p. 89pl. 27cm.
            English summary.
            Bibliography

NETHERLANDS, LOW COUNTRIES

UB70   Luxembourg paper money catalogue.
L8   Luxembourg, Numa Revue
            Internationale de Numismatique,
            1976.
            unpaged. illus. 18cm.
            -in English, French and German.

GENERAL WORKS

UC20
B3
    Bayerische Hypotheken-und Wechsel-Bank.
       Monetare Kostbarkeiten; ein blick
in die geldscheinsammlung der Bayerischen
Hypotheken-und Wechsel-Bank; geldscheine
aller zeiten und aller lander. Munich,
Bayerische Hypotheken-und Wechsel-Bank,
n.d.
       unpaged. illus. 20cm.

UC20
J3
    Jaeger, Kurt.
       Die Deutschen banknotes seit 1871
[by] Kurt Jaeger und Ulrich Haevecker.
Wurttenburg, Numismatischen Fachverlag
G. Speidel-Nubling, 1963, 1969.
       171p. illus. 21cm.

NOTGELD

UC40
G4
    Grasser, Walter.
       Das bielefelder stoffgeld, 1917-1923,
[by] Walter Grasser [and] Albert Pick. Berlin,
Buchdruckerei Erich Proh, 1972.
       61p. illus. 21cm.

UC40
K4
    Keller, Arnold.
       Das Deutsche notgeld; kleingeld-
scheine 1916-1922...zusammengestellt
von Dr. Arnold Keller; new bearbeitel
von Albert Pick und Carl Siemsen.
Munchen, Ernst Battenberg, 1975.
       294p. illus. 30cm.

UC40
K4d
    Keller, Arnold.
       Das notgeld der Deutschen
inflation 1923. Teil 1 (Band
1-4); Teil II, (Band 5-8)
katalog von Dr. Arnold Keller.
Vorvort von Albert Pick. Munchen,
Battenberg Verlag, 1975.
       1131p. 92 plates. 29cm.

UC40   Keller, Arnold.
K4n   Das notgeld der Deutschen in-
         flation, 1922; katalog von Dr.
         Arnold Keller. Forward by Albert
         Pick. Munchen, Ernst Battenberg,
         1975.
             106p. 13 plates. 30cm.

UC40   Lund, Karl.
L8   Das papiernotgeld von Schleswig-
         Holstein und Hamburg, 1914-1923;
         bewertet und mit einem vorwort verschen
         Berlin, Erich Proh, [1971?].
             83p. illus. 21cm. (Schriftenreihe
         die munze, band 28)

UC40   Mehl, Manfred.
M4   Das papiernotgeld von Mecklenburg
         und Vorpommern, 1914-1923; bewerte
         und mit einem vorwort versehen. Berlin
         Erich Proh, [1972?].
             40p. illus. 21cm. (Schriftenreihe
         die Munze, band 29)

UC40   Mehl, Manfred.
M4p   Das papiernotgeld von Ostpreussen,
         Westpreussen und Posen, 1914-1923;
         bewertet und mit einem vorwort
         versehen, auflage. Berlin, Erich
         Proh, 1975.
             126p. illus. map. 21cm.

UC40   Meyer, Hans.
M49d   Deutsches papiernotgeld, 1914 bis zu beginn
Pt.1   der hochinflation; heft 1, offizielle ausgaben
         Rheinprovinz. Berlin, Erich Proh, [1971].
             33p. ill. 21cm. (Schriftenreihe die Munze,
         band 21)

UC40   Meyer, Hans.
M49d   Deutsches papiernotgeld, 1914 bis
Pt.2   zu beginn der hochinflation; offizielle
         ausgeben. Heft 2. Westfalen. Berlin,
         Erich Proh, [1971?].
             32p. illus. 21cm. (Schriftenreihe
         die munzen, band 22.)

UC40   Meyer, Hans.
M49d   Deutsches papiernotgeld, 1914 bis
Pt.3   zu beginn der hochinflation; offizielle
         ausgeben. Heft 3. Sudwestdeutschland-
         hessen mit Nassau, Pfalz, Elsab und
         Lothringen. Berlin, Erich Proh, [1972?].
             31p. illus. 21cm. (Schriftenreihe
         die munze, band 23.)

UC40   Meyer, Hans.
M49p   Das papiernotgeld von Schlesien
         1914-1924. Berlin, Verlag Proh,
         1975.
             124p. illus. 21cm.
         (Schriftenreihe die Munze, band 27).

UC40   Schmitz, Hubert.
S3   Die bewertschaftung der
         nahrungsmittel und verbrauchsguter,
         1939-1950. Essen, W. Germany,
         R. Bacht Gmbh, 1956.
             603p. illus. 25cm.

UC40   Schulze, Wolfgang.
S38   Das notgeld von Essen/Ruhr
         (einschlieslich der bis 1974 ein-
         gemeindeten gebiete). Essen,
         West Germany, the author, 1976.
             56p. 29cm. (Schriften-
         reihe der munzfreunde essen, Heft 1).

UC40   Silbermann, Reinhardt.
S5   Das deutsche papiernotgeld nach 1945,
         privatausgaben aller 4 besatzungszonen.
         Hamburg, Gehard Muller, 1975.
             unpaged illus. 17cm.

EIGHTEENTH - NINETEEN CENTURIES

UC55   Deutsche Bundesbank, Frankfurt am Main.
D4d   Deutsches papiergeld, 1772-1870.
         [1963?].
             [xi] illus. 51 col. pl. 29cm.

UC55   Deutsche Bundesbank, Frankfurt am Main.
D4p   Das papiergeld im Deutschen Reich,
         1871-1948. [1965?].
             [198]p. illus. col. pl. 29cm.
         Contains bibliographies.

UC55   Pick, Albert.
P5   Deutsche lander-und privat-
         banknoten; geldscheine der
         Landesregierungen, provinzialver-
         waltungen und bezirksregierungen,
         1872-1948. Berlin, E. Proh, 1975.
             141p. illus. 21cm.
         (Der Schriftenreihe "die Munze", #50).

TWENTIETH CENTURY

UC60   Deutsche Bundesbank, Frankfurt am Main.
D4   Die noten der Deutschen Bundesbank.
          [1964?]
             132p. illus. col. 29cm.

UC60   Pirie, Anthony.
P5   Operation Bernhard; the plot to ruin
          Britain by massive counterfeiting.
          New York, Grove Press, 1961.
             254p. 18cm.

UC60   Sieg, Frovin.
S5   Sieg's seddelkatalog Slesvig Plebiscit
          zone I og II. Samt nodpengesedler fra
          Sonderjylland. 1970.
             86p. illus. 22cm.

UC60   Slabaugh, Arlie R.
S6   The German inflation. Reprinted from
          Numismatic Scrapbook, n.d.
             40p. illus. 20cm.

COLONIES

UC80   Keller, Arnold.
K4   Das papiergeld der Deutchen Kolonien.
          Munster, Westf., Dombrowski, 1967.
             142p. illus. 22cm.

SOVIET UNION

UF30   Johanson, Erik.
J6   Katalog uber banknoten der Sowjetunion,
            Helsinki, 1970.
                2 v. illus. 21cm.

UF30   Muller-Wandau, August V.
M8   "Kriegsgefangenen-lagergeld
            im rahmen Russischer und Siberischer
            papiergeld-Emissionen 1915-1919."
            Vienna, Numismatischen gesellschaft
            in Wien, 1930.
                pp. 150-154. 29cm.

UF30   Olund, Karin.
O4   Samla penpar, from Allsvensk Samling,
            December 1947. Translated by N. E.
            Rydberg.
                4p. illus. 28cm.

BALTIC STATES

UF40   Berzins, Edgars.
B4   Paper money of the Baltic States,
            Latvia, Estonia, Lithuania by Berzins
            and Dwight L. Musser, Dunbar, W. Va,
            Manor, 1961.
                14p. 28cm.

UF40   Karys, Jonas K.
K3   Currency of independent Lithuania
            New York, 1953.
                255p. illus. 23cm.
                In Lithuanian. English Summary.

BALKAN STATES

UF50   Coman, V.
C6   Catalogue of the banknotes of Roumania.
          From the foundation of the Roumanian
          state (1859) to the last issue (1966).
          Dombrowski, 1967.
               43p. illus. 21cm.

HUNGARY, AUSTRIA

UF60   Banyai, Richard A.
B3   The legal and monetary aspects of the
          Hungarian hyper-inflation, 1945-46.
          Phoenix, the author, 1971.
               28p. illus. 28cm.

UF60   Jaksch, Karl.
J3   Katalog des Osterreichischen
          notgeldes, 1916-1921. Wien,
          A. Schendl, 1971.
               263p. 21cm.

UF60   Kunz, Josef.
K8   Osterreichischer notgeld-
          katalog. Vienna, Kunz, 1925.
               23p. 29cm.
               -- Supplement, 1926.

UF60   Pick, Albert.
P5   Osterreich banknoten und staats-
          papiergeld ab 1759, [by] Pick-Richter.
          Berlin, Buchdruckerei Erich Proh abt.
          Verlag, [1972].
               79p. illus. 21cm.

UF60   Trelde, F. von der.
T7   Geschichte des Osterreich-
          ischen notgeldes, 1914-1921.
          Vienna, Trelde Verlag, 1921.
               pp. 5-46. illus. 29cm.

UF60   Trelde, F. von der.
T7n   Das notgeld des landes
          Salzburg, 1914-1921. Vienna,
          Trelde, 1921.
               8p. 29cm.

UF70   Jablonski, Tadensz.
J3   Polski pieniadz papierowy, 1794-1948.
         Warsaw, Nakladem Kola Numizmatycznego,
         1964.
            65p. illus. 20cm.

UF70   Jaeger, Kurt.
J34   Die munzen und banknoten der
         Tschechoslowakei [by] Kurt Jaeger und
         Albert Pick. Basel, Munzen und Medaillen,
         1970.
            96p. illus. 22cm. (Mitteleuropaische
         Munzkataloge, no. 14).

UF70   Sem, Julius.
S4   Papirove penize na uzemi
         Ceskoslovenksa 1762-1967. Prague,
         Numismaticka spolecnost Ceskoslovenkska,
         1967.
            86p. illus. 23cm.

UF70   Spajic, Dimitri.
S6   Paper money of the Yugoslavian
         states, [edited by] William Ittel.
         New and rev. ed. [Pittsburgh,
         Wm. Ittel, 1969.]
            35p. illus. 28cm.

CATALOGUES

```
UH20      Pick, Albert.
P5            Papermoney; catalogue of the Americas,
          [by] Albert Pick.  Munich, Ernst Battenberg
          Verlag [1973].
              335p.  illus.  25cm.
              Bibliography:  p. 335.
```

<u>CANADA</u>

GENERAL WORKS

UI30   Canada, Bank of.
C3   The story of Canada's currency, 1955, 1966.
            23p. illus. 20cm.

UI30   Charlton, J. E.
C5   Canada and Newfoundland paper money,
            1866-1935. Toronto Canada Coin Exchange,
            n.d.
                19p. illus. 22cm.

UI30   Elliot, J. A., Jr.
E4   Canadian and Newfoundland currency.
            1954.
                72p. 9 pl. 28cm.

UI30   Howard, C. S.
H6   Canadian banks and bank-notes--a
            record. Reprinted from The Canadian
            Banker, n.d.
                46p. illus. 24cm.

SPECIAL ASPECTS

UI40   Canada. Royal Mounted Police.
C3   The counterfeit detector. Ottawa,
            1966.
                16p. illus. 20cm.

UI40   Canadian Paper Money Society.
C35   Official terminology dictionary
            and grading guide. Toronto,
            Canadian Paper Money Society, 1971.
                16p. 23cm.

EIGHTEENTH - NINETEENTH CENTURIES

UI50   Greene, Ronald A.
G7   Macdonald and Company. Bankers
            Victoria, Vancouver Island, 1859 to 1864.
                12p. illus. 21cm.

UI50   McLachlan, Robert Wallace.
M3   Canadian card money. Montreal, 1911.
                33p. ill. 24cm.

UI50   Stevenson, James.
S7   The card money of Canada. Reprinted
Vert.   from the Transactions of the Literary
File   Historical Society, Quebec, 1874-1875.
                pp. 167-192. illus. 23cm.

TWENTIETH CENTURY

UI60   Allen, Harold Don.
A4   Canada rationing, 1942-1947; a
            numismatic record. Montreal, 1956.
                26p. illus. 28cm.

UI60   Shafer, Neil.
S5   Canadian World War II POW Scrip.
Vert.   Taken from the Canadian Paper Money
File   Journal, Vol. 7, No. 4., 1971.
                pp. 103-105; 115-118. illus. 25cm.

<u>MEXICO</u>

GENERAL WORKS

UJ30   Gaytan, Carlos.
G3b   Billetes de Mexico. Mexico City,
          Editorial Diana, 1965.
              150p. 138 pl. 28cm.

UJ30   Gaytan, Carlos.
G3p   The paper money of Mexico, 1822-1964
          by Gaytan and Neil S. Utberg. Edinburg,
          Tex, Eckhart, 1963.
              168p. illus. 28cm.

UJ30   Gaytan, Carlos.
G3p2   Paper currency of Mexico. Translated
          by Gabriel Navaroo. [Calexico, Calif.,
          Don Gabriel International, c1972]
              140[140]p. illus. 29cm.
              Covers period 1822-1971.

UJ30   Long, Richard Arthur.
L6   A checklist of Mexican currency.
          Corpus Christi, Texas, The author [1967]
              24p. 15cm.

SPECIAL ASPECTS

UJ40   Moreno, Alvaro J.
M6   La efigie de las damas en los billetes
          mexicanos. Mexico City, Priv. print, 1971.
              28p. illus. 24cm.

TWENTIETH CENTURY

UJ60   Banyai, Richard A.
B3   Money and finance in Mexico during the
          Constitutionalist Revolution 1913-1917.
          Taipei, Republic of China, Tai Wan Enter-
          prises Co. Ltd., 1976.
              126p. illus. 21cm.

UJ60   Brown, M. Ralph.
B7   Mexican revolutionary bills, 1913-17.
         Reprinted from The Numismatist, December,
         1950.
             26p. illus. 23cm.

UJ60   Slabaugh, Arlie R.
S5   Paper money of the Mexican revolution.
         Numismatic Scrapbook reprint, 1956.
             71p. illus. 21cm.

<u>LATIN AMERICA</u>

SOUTH AMERICA, A-Z

UK10   Seppa, Dale Allen.
B6S4   The paper money of Bolivia, by
            Dale A. Seppa and Al Almanzar. San
            Antonio, Tex., Almanzar's Coins of the
            World [1972]
                50pp. illus. 22cm.
                Bibliography: p. 50.

UK10   Galetovic, Jose M., ed.
C5G3   Billetes de Chili; catalogo
            ilustrado [par] Jose Galetovic M.
            y Hector R. Benavides T., Santiago,
            Chili, Jose Galetovic M., 1973.
                67p. illus. 26cm.

UK10   Banco de la Republica, Bogota, Colombia.
C6B3   Catalogo de Billetes, 1923-1973.
            Bogota, the author, 1973.
                unpaged, illus. 22cm.

UK10   Beresiner, Yasha L.
C6B4   Catalogue of the paper money of Columbia
            and Peru, by Yasha L. Beresiner and Eduardo
            C. Dargent. 1st ed. London, Stanley Gibbons,
            1973.
                126p. ill. 21cm.
                In Spanish and English.

CENTRAL AMERICA

UK20   Castillero, E. J.
C3   The paper money of Panama. Indian
            Rocks Beach, Fla, Musser, n.d.
                5p. 26cm.

UK20   Clark, Odis H., Jr.
C6   Paper money of Guatemala. San Antonio,
            Almanzar's, 1971.
                64p. illus. 22cm.

UK20   Franke, Enrique.
F7   The banknotes of the Republica of
         El Salvador; Banco central do
         reserva, 1934-1974; Private banks
         1867-1934. n.p.; the author, 1974.
             55p. illus. 22cm.
             -in English and Spanish.

BRAZIL

UK40   Banco Central do Brasil. Rio de
B3   Janeiro, Brazil.
             Iconografia do meio circulante
         do Brasil. Brasilia, Brasil,
         Banco Central do Brasil, 1972.
             317p. illus., part. col. 36cm.

UK40   Brasil, Banco do. Museu e Arquivo Historio.
B7   Cedulas Bra sileiras de republica
         Rio de Janeiro, 1964.
             110p. illus. 31cm.

UK40   Seppa, Dale A.
S4   The paper money of Brasil.
         Oak Park, Obol International, 1971, 1975.
             44p. illus. 21cm.

PARAGUAY, URUGUAY

UK50   Paraguay. Banco Central.
P3   Primera exposicion nacional de numis-
         matica a la inauguracion del perio do
         presidencial 1963-1968 del ... Don Alfredo
         Stroessner, Presidente ... Asuncion, 1963.
             144p. 35 col. pl. 19cm.

UK50   Seppa, Dale.
S4   Paper money of Paraguay and Uruguay.
         San Antonio, Almanzar's, 1970.
             34p. illus. 22cm.

UK50   Seppa, Dale Allan.
S4p   Paraguayan paper money, by Dale A. Seppa.
         [Chicago, Ill.] Obol International [1973,
         c1974]
             50p. illus. 21cm.

Seppa, Dale A.
    Uruguayan paper money.
Chicago, Obol Internatl., 1974.
    60p. illus. 21cm.

NEAR EAST, A-Z

UM20   Erol, Mine.
E7   Osmanli imparatorlugunda; Kagit para
            (Kaime). Ankara, 1970.
                 255p. illus. 24cm.
                 (Paper money of the Ottoman Empire)

UM20   Olcer, Cuneyt.
O4   50 yilin Turk kagit paralari;
            1923-1973. Istanbul, Is Bankasi
            Kultur yayinlari, 1973.
                 96p. illus. 25cm.
                 Contains summary in English.

PHILIPPINES

UM40   Perez, Gilbert S.
P47   Philippine guerrilla currency.
            Taken from The Numismatist, Vol. LX,
            No. 6, 1947.
                 pp. 393-399; 504-507. illus. 22cm.

UM40   Peterson, Mendel L.
P48   The emergency currency of Leyte,
            commonwealth of the Philippines. Reprinted
            from The Numismatist, 1947.
                 19p. illus. 23cm.

UM40   Philippine Islands. Emergency Currency
P5e   Board.
                 Rules and regulations of the
            registration and deposit of emergency
            currency. Manila, the author, 1946.
                 13p. 22cm.

UM40   Philippine Islands. Department of
P5f   Finance.
                 Rules and regulations covering the
            redemption of registered emergency
            and guerrila currency notes...
            Manila, the author, 1949.
                 17p. 22cm.

UM40   Shafer, Neil.
S5   Guidebook of Philippine paper money.
           Racine, Wis., Whitman, 1964.
                128p. illus. 20cm.

UM40   Shafer, Neil.
S5p   Philippine emergency and guerrilla
           currency of World War II, by Neil
           Shafer, with special support of
           Maurice M. Gould. Racine, Wis.,
           Western Pub. Co. [1974]
                464p. illus. 24cm.
                Bibliography: p. 455-456.

SOUTHEAST ASIA - CAMBODIA, LAOS, THAILAND, VIETNAM, ETC.

UM45   Shaw, William.
M3S5   Paper currency of Malaysia,
           Singapore and Brunei (1849-1970)
           by William Shaw and Md. Kassim
           Haji Ali. Kuala Lumpur, Malaysia,
           Muzium Negara, 1971.
                124p. illus. 25cm.

UM45   Little, Silas.
T5L5   Banknotes of Thailand. 1st ed.
           Falls Church, Va., the author, 1973.
                12p. illus. 28cm.

CHINA - GENERAL WORKS

UN20
R3
    Ramsden, Henry A.
        Chinese paper money. Yokohama,
Jun Kobayagawa Co., 1911.
        37p. illus. 23cm.

UN20
S6
    Smith, Ward D.
        Chinese banknotes, by Ward D. Smith
and Brian Matravers. Menlo Park, Calif.,
Shirjieh Publishers, 1970.
        225p. illus. 29cm.

SPECIAL, ANCIENT

UN30
D3a
    Davis, Andrew McFarland.
        Ancient Chinese paper money as described
in a Chinese work on numismatics. From
Proceedings of the American Academy of
Arts and Sciences. June, 1918.
        180p. incl. 158 pl. 24cm.

UN30
D3c
    Davis, Andrew McFarland.
        Certain old Chinese notes. Boston,
G. E. Littlefield, 1915.
        60p. illus. 24cm.
        From Proceedings of the Amer. Academy
of Arts and Sciences, June 1915.

UN30
F4
    Fernandez, R. I.
        Counterfeit Chinese paper money.
Reprinted from The China Journal, Sep-
tember, 1938.
        7p. 8 pl. 24cm.

UN30
K3
    Kann, Eduard.
        History of Chinese paper money, pt. 1.
(Ancient). International Banknote
Society, 196-.
        37p. 33cm.

TWENTIETH CENTURY

UN40   Mao, King O.
M3c   History of Chinese paper currency, volume 1,
V.1   illustrated catalogue of bank notes issued by
            the Central Bank of China from 1923-1949.
            Hong Kong, Chap Yau, 1968.
                793p. ill. 29cm.

UN40   Mao, King-On, comp.
M3p   History of paper currency as issued
            by the people's Republic of China from
            1921-1965. Compiled by King-On Mao. 1st
            ed. Hong Kong, 1972.
                296p. illus. 24cm.

JAPAN - GENERAL

UN50   [International Currency Society.]
I5   Catalogue of Japanese paper money.
            Tokyo, 1957.
                64p. illus. 21cm.
                In Japanese

UN50   Takaki, Masayoshi.
T3   The history of Japanese paper
            currency (1868-1890). Baltimore, Johns
            Hopkins Press, 1903.
                59p. 24cm.
                Bibliography

TWENTIETH CENTURY

UN60   Musser, Dwight L.
M8   Japanese paper money, Japanese inva-
            sion money. Reprinted from Numismatic
            Scrapbook, and from World Paper Money
            collector's Guide, 1959.
                15p. illus. 21cm.

UN60   Slabaugh, Arlie R.
S5   Japanese invasion money. Chicago,
            Hewitt, 1963, 1965, 1977.
                30p. illus. 20cm.

<u>AFRICA</u>

SOUTH AFRICA

UP30   Bergman, W.
B4   A history of the regular and emergency
          paper money issues of South Africa.
          Capetown, 1968.
              61p. illus. 22cm.

UP30   Levius, Harold P.
L4   Catalogue of South African paper
          money since 1900; including emergency
          issues of the Anglo-Boer War (1899-
          1902) & South West African notes.
          1st ed. [Houghton, Johannesburg, South
          Africa, the author, 1972]
              72p. illus. 21cm.

FRENCH POSSESSIONS, CURRENT AND FORMER

UP70   Muszynski, Maurice.
M8   Le papier-monnaie du Maroc;
Vol.2   catalogue illustre et cote par
          M. Muszynski et H. Schweikert.
          2d. vol. de "la numismatique
          d'Afrique du Nord". Maisons-
          Alfort, France, H. Schweikert, 1974.
              63p. illus. 24cm.
              -introduction in French, German
          and English. Text in French.

GENERAL WORKS

UQ30   Gill, Thomas.
G5   A brief sketch of the coinage and
           paper currency of South Australia. Adelaide
           Australia, Vardon & Sons, 1912.
               101p. scattered illus. 22cm.

UQ30   Tomlinson, Geoffrey William.
T6   Australian bank notes, 1817-1963.
           Melbourne, Hawthorn, 1963.
               143p. illus. 22cm.

BY STATE, A-Z

UQ38   McNeice, Roger V.
T3M3   Tasmanian promissory notes.
           Melbourne, Hawthorne Press, 1971.
               25cm. illus. 23cm.

UNITED STATES

SOCIETIES

US10   Anton, William T.
A5   The Albert A. Grinnell collection of
1971   United States paper money; a complete
          reprint in one volume of the seven sales
          which comprised the most complete
          collection of United States paper money
          ever assembled by an individual, by
          William T. Anton and Morey Perlmutter.
          The Authors, 1971.
              651p. 24cm.
              Reprint of Barney Bluestone catalogues.

US10   U.S. Congress. Senate. Committee on Banking
U5   and Currency.
              Silver certificates, hearing before the...
          90th congress, first session on S. 1352, a
          bill to authorize adjustments in the amount
          of outstanding silver certificates, and for
          other purposes. Washington, D.C., GPO, 1967.
              143p. 23cm.

US10   Wilson, George.
W5   The Greenbackers and their doctrines.
          Lexington, Mo., Intelligencer News,
          1878.
              116p. 24cm.

CATALOGUES

US15   Klander, Charles.
K5   Illustrated price list, paper money.
          Cincinnati, n.d.
              58p. illus. 24cm.

US15   Quaker Currency Co.
Q8   United States paper currency.
          Washington, D. C., n.d.
              unp. illus. 24cm.

US15   Raymond, Wayte.
R3sc   Scott's paper money price
            list. 1st ed. N.Y., Scott Stamp
            & Coin Co., 1932.
                12p. illus. 23cm.

US15   Raymond, Wayte.
R3st   Standard paper money catalogues.
            New York, 1940-55.
                illus. 23cm.
                Contents: pt. 1 Colonial and continental
            currency. pt. 2-U.S. Notes and fractional
            currency.

US15   Scott Stamp and Coin.
S3   Standard paper money catalogue.
            New York, 1892, 1894.
                136p. illus. 24cm.

US15   Standard U.S. paper money catalogue.
S4   1976 ed. N.Y., Scott Pub. Co.,
1976   1975.
                189p. illus. 14cm.

US15   Werlich, Robert.
W4   Catalogue of United States, Canadian
            and confederate currency. Distrib. by
            Quaker Currency, Washington, D. C.,
            1963-69, 1974-75.
                114p. illus. 24cm.

GENERAL WORKS

US20   American Numismatic Association.
A5   Selections from The Numismatist.
            United States paper money, tokens,
            medals and miscellaneous. Racine,
            Whitman, 1960.
                317p. illus. 23cm.

US20   Atlanta, Georgia. Federal
A8   Reserve Bank. Research Dept.
                Fundamental facts about United
            States money - of importance to every-
            one who handles cash. Atlanta,
            Federal Reserve Bank, 1967.
                16p. illus. 22cm.

US20   Blake, George Herbert.
B5   United States paper money. New York,
          1908.
              55p. 26cm.

US20   Criswell, Grover C., Jr.
C7   North American currency. Ida, Wis,
          Krause, 1965, 1969.
              910p. illus. 23cm.

US20   Draper, Paul E.
D7   United States paper currency. Detroit,
Vert.   n.p., n.d.
File   unpaged. 23cm.

US20   Friedberg, Robert.
F7   Paper money of the United States. New
          York, Coin and Currency, 1953-75.
              8v. ill. 28cm.

US20   Grinnell, A. A.
G7   United States paper money from
Vert.   a collector's viewpoint. Reprinted
File   from The Numismatist, 1937.
              unpaged. 23cm.

US20   Hoffman, Lyle.
H6   History and money, 1660-1870;
          by Lyle Hoffman and Will Martin.
          Cloquet, Minn, Potlatch Corp.,
          1975.
              unpaged. 6 col. plates in pocket.
          32cm. (Quality and Quintessence
          Series, #4.)

US20   Kemm, Theodore.
K4   The official guide of United States paper
          money. 1st-9th ed. New York, H.C. Publishers,
          1968-77.
              7v. ill. 18cm.

US20   Knox, John Jay.
K6   United States notes. New York,
          Scribner's 1884-85.
              247p. illus. 23cm.

US20   Muscalus, John A.
M8   Dictionary of paper money with his-
          torical specimens illustrated. The
          author, 1947, 1965.
              18p. 14 pl. 23cm.

US20   Muscalus, John A.
M8p   Paper money in sheets. Norristown,
          Pa., Lenhart Press, 1949.
             106p. illus. 26cm.

US20   O'Donnell, Chuck.
O3   The standard handbook of modern U.S.
          paper money. 4th ed, 5th Williamstown, N.J.,
          1974, 1975.
             257p. illus. 27cm.

US20   Reinfeld, Fred.
R4   The story of paper money. New York,
          Sterling, 1957, 1960.
             128p. illus. 26cm.
             1960 edition title: A simplified guide
          to collecting American paper money.

US20   Shafer, Neil.
S5   Let's collect paper money!; an
          introduction to the exciting hobby
          of collecting paper money of the
          world. Racine, Wisc., Western
          Pub. Co. 1976.
             64p. illus. 20cm.

ENGRAVING AND PRINTING

US25   Allen, Harold Don.
A3   100 years of security printing;
Vert.   American Bank Note Company, 1858-
File   1958. Reprinted from the Numismatic
          Scrapbook, Dwight Musser, n.d.
             4p. 1 photo. 22cm.

US25   Boggs, Winthrop S.
B6   Ten decades ago, 1840-1850. A study
          of the work of Rawdon, Wright, Hatch and
          Edson of New York City. American Phila-
          telic Society, 1949.
             100p. illus. 25cm.

US25   Disraeli, Robert.
D5   Uncle Sam's treasury. Boston,
          Little, Brown and Co., 1941.
             121p. illus. 22cm.

US25
G7
Griffiths, William H.
     The story of the American Bank Note
Company. New York, 1959.
     86p. illus. 27cm.

US25
M6
Morris, Thomas F.
     Felix O. C. Darley, bank note
artist, 1822-1888. Reprinted from
The Essay-Proof Journal, 1961.
     8p. illus. 26cm.

US25
O7
Ormsby, Waterman Lily.
     Description of the present system of
bank note engraving showing its tendency
to facilitate counterfeiting. Reprinted
by Essay-Proof Journal, 1957.
     pl. 24cm.

US25
R5
Rice, Foster Wild.
     Antecedents of the American Bank Note
Company of 1858. Reprinted from Essay-
Proof Journal, 1961.
     27p. illus. 25cm.

US25
U5
U. S. Treasury.
     History of the Bureau of Engraving and
Printing 1862-1962. Washington D. C.
1964.
     199p. illus. 25cm.

US27
N4
Neuce, Ed.
     Price guide for the collector of U.S.
paper money errors. Ohio, Coin World,
1971, 1973.
     38p. illus. 22cm.

COUNTERFEITING

US30
A5
Rare
Books
American Bond Detector and complete
     history of the U.S. government
     securities. Washington, American
     Bond and Currency Detector Co.,
     1869.
     80p. 30 pl. 24 x 33cm.

US30   Daniel, Russell.
D3   Counterfeiters' nemesis. Washington,
          the author, 1961.
             10p. 26cm.

US30   Dill, Earl, comp.
D53   How to detect counterfeit money;
          ready reference on genuine and
          spurious money. El Monte, Ca.,
          the comp., 1940.
             14p. 21cm.

US30   Dillistin, William H.
D55   Bank note reporters and counterfeit
          detectors, 1826-1866. New York, ANS,
          1949.
             175p. 19 pl. 23cm.

US30   Heath's greatly improved and enlarged
H4   infallible government counterfeit
             detector ... applicable to all banks
             in the United States and Canadas, ...
             By authority of the United States
             Treasury Dept. ... Boston, Heath,
             1866-77.
             47p. 10 pl. 25cm.

US30   Hodges, J. Tyler, comp.
H6   Hodges' American bank note safeguard;
Rare   giving fac-simile descriptions of upwards of
Books   ten thousand bank notes embracing every gen-
          uine note issued in the United States and
          Canada; the most effectual detector of spu-
          rious, altered and counterfeit bills ever
          published, arranged and published by J.
          Tyler Hodges. New York, Hodges, 1858, 1859,
          1860, 1861, 1861 rev., 1865.
             353p. 34cm.

US30   Peyton, George.
P4   How to detect counterfeit bank notes.
          New York, 1861.
             54p. 4 pl. 23cm.

US30   Smith, Laurence Dwight.
S6   Counterfeiting, crime against the
          people. New York, Norton, 1944.
             254p. 22cm.

US30   Thompson, J.
T5   The autographical counterfeit detector,
Vert.   5th ed. New York, 1832.
File   75p. 23cm.

US30   U.S. Secret Service.
U5   Know your money. Washington, GPO,
           1955.
               29p. ill. 23cm.

US30   Wilber, E. J.
W5   A treatise on counterfeit, altered,
           and spurious bank notes, by E. J. Wilber
           and E. P. Eastman. Poughkeepsie, 1865.
               51p. 4 pl. 24cm.

SCRIP, EMERGENCY MONEY

US35   Curto, J. J.
C8c   The copper and iron dollars of the
           U. P. ANA Reprint, 1947.
               18p. illus. 22cm.

US35   Curto, J. J.
C8m   Michigan depression scrip of the
           1930's Reprinted from The Numismatist,
           1949.
               35p. illus. 23cm.

US35   Donn, Albert I.
D6   World War II prisoner of war scrip of
           the U.S. Iola, Wis., Krause, 1970.
               111p. illus. 24cm.

US35   Kappen, Charles V.
K3   Depression scrip of the United States,
           period of the 1930's states A thru I,
           by Kappen and Ralph A. Mitchell. San
           Jose, Globe, 1961.
               89p. 51 pl. 22cm.

US35   Muscalus, John A.
M8   Kinds of scrip issues by school dis-
           tricts in financial emergencies. Bridge-
           port, Pa., The author, 1971.
               11p. illus. 23cm.

COLONIAL, CONTINENTAL

US40   Breck, Samuel.
B7   Historical sketch of continental
Vert.   paper money. Philadelphia, 1863.
File   33p. 23cm.

US40   Davis, Andrew McFarland.
D3   Colonial currency reprints, 1682-
            1751. Boston, Prince Society, 1910-11.
                 4v. illus. 22cm.

US40   Harper's Magazine.
H3   Continental money. From Harper's
            New Monthly Magazine, March, 1863.
                 36p. illus. 24cm.

US40   Hart, A. M.
H32   History of the issues of paper-money
            in the American colonies, anterior to the
            revolution. St. Louis, 1851.
                 20p. 23cm.

US40   Hessler, Gene, 1928-
H4   The comprehensive catalog of U.S.
            paper money. Chicago, H. Regnery Co.,
            [1974].
                 xiv, 456p. illus. 24cm
                 Bibliography: p. [455]-456.

US40   Hoober, Richard T.
H6   Snapshots of colonial note signers.
            Reprinted from The Numismatist, 1946.
                 24p. illus. 23cm.

US40   McKay, George L.
M3   Early American currency, New York,
            ANS, 1944.
                 85p. illus. 17cm.

US40   Newman, Eric P.
N4c   Counterfeit continental currency goes
            to war. Reprinted from The Numismatist,
            1957.
                 23p. illus. 23cm.

US40   Newman, Eric P.
N4e   The early paper money of America.
            Racine, Whitman, 1967, 1976.
                 359p. illus. 29cm.

US40   Newman, Eric P.
N4f   Franklin making money more plentiful.
           Reprinted from Proceedings of the
           American Philosophical Society, Vol.
           115., #5, Philadelphia, 1971.
               pp. 341-149. illus. 27cm.

US40   Newman, Eric P.
N4n   Nature printing on Colonial and conti-
           nental currency. Reprinted from The Numis-
           matist, 1964.
               34p. illus. 23cm.

US40   Phillips, Henry.
P5a   Historical sketches of American paper
           currency, 2nd series. Roxbury, Mass.,
           1866.
               264p. 28cm.

US40   Phillips, Henry.
P5p   Historical sketches of the paper
           currency of the American colonies, 1st
           series. Roxbury, Mass., 1865.
               233p. 28cm.

US40   Weissbuch, Ted N.
W4   Price catalogue of U.S. colonial
           and continental currency by Weissbuch and
           Richard T. Hoober. Chicago, Hewitt,
           1965.
               56p. illus. 20cm.

COLONIAL, BY STATE, A-Z

US45   Bronson, Henry.
C6B7   A historical account of Connecticut
           currency, continental money, and the
           finances of the revolution. N.p., n.
           pub., n.d.
               192p. 24cm.

US45   Scott, Kenneth.
C6S3   Counterfeiting in Colonial Connecticut.
           New York, American Numismatic Society,
           1957.
               243p. 46 pl. 23cm. (Numismatic
           notes and monographs, no. 140.)

US45
D4R6
Rodney, Richard S.
    Colonial finances in Delaware.
Wilimington, Del., 1928.
    68p. illus. 23cm.

US45
M2B4
Behrens, Kathryn L.
    Paper money in Maryland, 1727-1789.
Baltimore, Johns Hopkins, 1923.
    98p. 24cm.
    Bibliography

US45
M2G6
Gould, Clarence Pembroke.
    Money and transportation in Maryland
1720-1765. Baltimore, Johns Hopkins
Press, 1915.
    176p. 24cm.

US45
M2H6
Hoober, Richard T.
    Financial history of colonial Mary-
land. ANA Reprint, 1962.
    14p. illus. 23cm.

US45
M3D3c
Davis, Andrew McFarland.
    Currency and banking in the Province
of the Massachusetts-Bay, by Andrew
McFarland Davis. New York, Macmillan Co.;
London, Swan Sonneschein, 1901.
    332p. illus. 17 pl. 24cm. (Publi-
cations of the American Economic Assn.,
3d series, v.2, no. 2, pt. 2)

US45
M3D3t
Davis, Andrew McFarland, ed.
    Tracts relating to the currency of the
Massachusetts Bay, 1682-1720. Boston,
Houghton Mifflin, 1902.
    404p. 18 pl. 22cm.

US45
M3F4
Rare
Books
Felt, Joseph B.
    An historical account of Massachusetts
currency. Boston, Perkins and Marvin,
1839.
    259p. illus. 24cm.

US45
N3H6
Hoober, Richard T.
    Financial history of colonial New
Hampshire. ANA Reprint, 1964.
    15p. illus. 23cm.

US45
N4H6
Hoober, Richard T.
    Finances of colonial New Jersey.
Reprinted from The Numismatist, 1950.
    43p.   illus.   23cm.

US45
N5H5
Hickcox, John Howard.
    A history of the bills of credit or
paper money issued by New York, from 1709
to 1789.   Albany, 1866.
    103p.   29cm.

US45
N5S3
Scott, Kenneth.
    Counterfeiting in colonial New York.
New York, ANS, 1953.
    222p.   13 pl.   23cm.   (Numismatic
notes and monographs, no. 127)

US45
N6P3
Parker, Mattie Erma.
    Money problems of early Tar Heels.
Raleigh, 1951.
    14p.   illus.   22cm.

US45
N6S3
Vert.
File
Scott, Kenneth.
    Counterfeiting in colonial North
Carolina.   From North Carolina historical
review, October, 1947.
    16p.   23cm.

US45
P4G5
Gillingham, Harrold Edgar, 1864-
    Counterfeiting in colonial Pennsylvania,
New York, ANS, 1939.
    52p.   illus.   17cm.   (Numismatic
notes and monographs, no. 86)

US45
P4S3
Scott, Kenneth.
    Counterfeiting in colonial Pennsyl-
vania.   New York, ANS, 1955.
    168p.   23cm.   (Numismatic notes and
monographs, no. 132)

US45
R5B6
Bowen, Richard LeBaron.
    Rhode Island colonial money and its
counterfeiting, 1647-1726.   Providence,
1942.
    112p.   illus.   23cm.

US45
V4W4
Vert.
File
Weissbuch, Ted N.
    A chapter in Vermont's revolutionary
war finance.   From Vermont History,
January 1961.
    12p.   1 pl.   23cm.

US45   Hoober, Richard T.
V5H6   Financial history of Colonial Virginia.
           ANA Reprint, 1953.
               32p. illus. 23cm.

FRACTIONAL CURRENCY, ENCASED POSTAGE STAMPS, POSTAL
NOTES

US50   Carothers, Neil, 1884-
C3   Fractional money; a history of the
           small coins and fractional paper currency
           of the United States. New York,
           J. Wiley, 1930.
               372p. 22cm.

US50   Christoph, Art.
C5   United States postage and fractional
           currency, 1862-1876 by Art Christoph and
           Chet Krause. Reprinted from Numismatic
           News, 1958.
               40p. illus. 28cm.

US50   Cunningham, Thomas.
C8   Postal and fractional currency.
           Reprinted from American Journal of Numis-
           matics, n.d.
               8p. 27cm.

US50   Drowne, Henry Russell.
D7   U.S. postage stamps as necessity war
Vert.   money. From Amer. Journal of Numismatics,
File   1918.
               6p. 2 pl.

US50   Limpert, Frank Alvin.
L5c   Classified list of U.S. postage and
           fractional currency, August 1862-
           February 1876. Royal Oak, Mich, 1947.
               32p. 23cm.

US50   Limpert, Frank Alvin.
L5u   United States postage currency,
           August 1862-May 1863 and fractional
           currency, October 1863-February 1876.
           N.p., n. pub., 1946.
               36p. illus. 23cm.

US50   Muscalus, John A.
M8   Odd bank note and scrip
         denominations in American monetary
         history. Bridgeport, Pa., the
         author, 1967.
             34p. illus. 23cm.

US50   Muscalus, John A.
M8p   Paper money of the 6 1/4 cent and
         12 1/2 cent denominations. Numismatic
         Scrapbook Reprint, [1949].
             24p. illus. 20cm.

US50   Noll, James E., comp.
N6   Index of articles on U.S.
Vert.   postal notes and related
File   topics. 1st ed. L.A.,
         the comp., 1975, 1976.
             unpaged. 22cm.

US50   Noll, James E., comp.
N6i   Index of U.S. postal
Vert.   notes in collectors' hands.
File   1st ed. with updates. L.A.,
         the comp., 1975-1976.
             22p. illus. 22cm.

US50   Rothert, Matt.
R6   A guidebook of United States frac-
         tional currency. Racine, Wis., Whitman
         1963.
             81p. illus. 20cm.
             Bibliography

US50   Schultz, Walter F.
S3   Schultz's checking list of fractional
         currency. Dallas, Tex., the author, 1935.
             20p. 23cm.

US50   Slabaugh, Arlie R.
S5   U.S. and foreign encased postage stamps;
         the use of stamps as money. Chicago,
         Hewitt Bros., 1967.
             34p. illus. 20cm. (Hewitt's
         Numismatic Information Series.)

US50   Types of postage and fractional
T8   currency. Reprinted from the
             Numismatic Scrapbook Magazine.
         Chicago, Ill., [Hewitt,] n.d.
             16p. illus. 20cm.

US50   Valentine, D. W.
V3   "Fractional currency" of the United
           States. New York, Boyd, 1924.
                2v. in 1 53, 48p. 24cm.

CIVIL WAR, CONFEDERACY

US60   Affleck, Charles J.
A3   Confederate bonds and certificates, by
           ... and B.M. Douglas. Winchester, Va., the
           author, 1960.
                38p. ill. 23cm.

US60   Ball, Douglas B.
B3   Confederate interim depositary receipts
           and funding certificates issued in the
           Commonwealth of Virginia, 1861-1865, by
           Douglas B. Ball. Designed by Frank R.
           Hannah. Virginia Numismatic Association,
           1972.
                46pp. illus. 29cm.

US60   Bradbeer, William West.
B7   Confederate and southern state
           currency. Mt. Vernon, N.Y., 1915,
           reprinted, 1945, 1956.
                277p. illus. 26cm.

US60   Chase, Philip H.
C5c   CSA issues of 1861 in panorama.
           Reprinted from The Numismatist, 1962.
                23p. illus. 23cm.

US60   Chase, Philip H.
C5cs   Confederate States of America paper
           money, 1861-1865. Bala-Cynwyd, Pa., 1936.
                31p. 21cm.

US60   Chase, Philip H.
C5ct   Confederate treasury notes. The
           paper money of the Confederate States of
           America, 1861-1865. Philadelphia, 1947.
                148p. illus. 23cm.

US60   Chase, Philip H.
C5m   The mysterious chemicograph backs
Vert.   for confederate currency. Reprinted
File   from the Numismatist, Aug., 1946.
                8p. 22cm.

US60
C5p
Vert.
File
Chase, Philip H.
    Paper money of the Confederate
states of America: summary and cross
index of types. n.p., the author,
1961.
    2p. 22cm.

US60
C7
V.1
Criswell, Grover C.
    Confederate and southern state currency;
a descriptive listing including rarity and
prices. Criswell's currency series, Vol. 1.
Pass-a-Grille Beach, Florida, Criswell's
Publications, 1957, 1964, 1976.
    277p. ill. 26cm. (Criswell's Currency
Series, vol. 1)

US60
C7
V.2
Criswell, Grover C.
    Confederate and soutern state bonds; a
descriptive listing, including rarity. St.
Petersburg Beach, Florida, Criswell's Publi-
cations, 1961.
    310p. ill. 26cm. (Criswell's Currency
Series, vol. 2)

US60
C7o
Criswell, Grover C.
    The official guide to Confederate
money & Civil War tokens, tradesmen &
patriotic, by Grover Criswell & Herb
Romerstien [sic]. Hal L. Cohen, design
& editorial. [1st ed.]. [New York]
HC Publishers [1971].
    144p. illus. 15cm.

US60
D6
Douglas, B. M.
    Catalogue of confederate and southern
states currency. Comp. and pub. by
B. M. Douglas and B. H. Hughes.
Washington, 1955.
    31 p. 23 cm.

US60
F8
Fuller, Claud E.
    Confederate currency and stamps,
1861-1865. Nashville, United Daughters
of the Confederacy, 1949.
    236p. illus. 31cm.

US60
H3
Haseltine, John W.
    Descriptive catalogue of Confederate
notes and bonds for sale by John W.
Haseltine. Philadelphia, 1876.
    36p. 24cm.

US60   Massamore, George W.
M3   Descriptive and chronological
        catalogue of confederate currency.
        Baltimore, 1889.
            24p. 24cm.

US60   Reinfeld, Fred.
R4   The story of Civil war money. New
        York, Sterling, 1959.
            93p. illus. 26cm.

US60   Slabaugh, Arlie R.
S5   Confederate states paper money.
        Racine, Wis., Whitman, 1959, 1961, 1971.
            80p. illus. 20cm.

US60   Thian, Raphael P.
T5   Register of the Confederate dept. Boston,
        Quarterman Publications, 1972.
            xix, 190p. tables 24cm.

US60   Todd, Richard Cecil.
T6   Confederate finance. Athens, Univ-
        ersity of Georgia Press, 1954.
            258p. 24cm.
            Bibliography

NATIONAL BANK NOTES, 1860-1930

US70   Dillistin, William H.
D5d   A descriptive history of national
        bank notes, 1863-1935. Paterson, N.J.
        1956.
            55p. 23cm.

US70   Dillistin, William H.
D5n   National bank notes in the early
        years. Reprinting from the Numismatist,
        1948.
            24p. 23cm.

US70   Donlop, William P.
D6   United States large size paper money,
        1861 to 1923. Utica, N.Y., 1968, 1970, 1973-74.
            176p. illus. 23cm.

US70
L5
Limpert, Frank Alvin.
    United States paper money, old series,
1861-1923. Royal Oak, Mich., 1948-1950.
    110p. illus. 28cm.

US70
L6
Lloyd, Robert H.
    A type set of $1.00 and $2.00 United
States currency notes. Reprinted from
Numismatic Scrapbook.
    28p. illus. 20cm.

US70
R3
Raymond, Wayte, 1886-
    United States notes, 1861-1923.
New York, 1933.
    24p. 24cm.

US70
R8
Vert.
File
Russett, F. R.
    Large size U.S. notes. A paper
presented to the Albany Numismatic
Society. Reprinted from the
Numismatic Scrapbook Magazine. n.d.
    unpaged. 20cm.

STATE BANK NOTES, COUNTY SCRIP

US75
M3
McGarry, Sheridan L.
    Mormon money. Reprinted from the
Numismatist.
    48p. illus. 23cm.

US75
M8a
Muscalus, John A.
    Album of Georgia county and
city scrip. Bridgeport, Pa.,
John Muscalus, 1975.
    23p. illus. 23cm.

US75
M8c
Muscalus, John A.
    Characters and events illustrated on
state bank notes.
    12p. 23cm.

US75
M8d
Muscalus, John A.
    County scrip issued in the United
States.
    21p. 22cm.

US75   Muscalus, John A.
M8f   Famous paintings reproduced on paper
          money of state banks, 1800-1866.
               8p. illus. 23cm.

US75   Muscalus, John A.
M8il   Illustrations of county scrip
          issued in Mississippi, North Carolina,
          Tennessee and Pennsylvania.
          Bridgeport, Pa., the author, 1967.
               23p. illus. 23cm.

US75   Muscalus, John A.
M8inc   An index of state bank notes that
          illustrate characters and events. The
          author, 1938.
               55p. 23cm.

US75   Muscalus, John A.
M8inp   An index of state bank notes that
          illustrate presidents. The author, 1939.
               24p. 23cm.

US75   Muscalus, John A.
M8inw   An index of state bank notes that illustrate
          Washington and Franklin. Bridgeport, Pa.,
          John A. Muscalus, 1938.
               18p. 23cm.

US75   Muscalus, John A.
M8l   Locomotive engravings on state bank
          notes and scrip, 1832-1875. Bridgeport,
          Pa., 1964.
               40p. illus. 22 x 28cm.

US75   Muscalus, John A.
M8p   Parish scrip issued in Louisiana.
          Bridgeport, Pa., the author, 1966.
               32p. illus. 23cm.

US75   Muscalus, John A.
M8s   State bank note facsimiles and the
          publications that contain them. Reprinted
          from Numismatic Scrapbook, 1944.
               24p. 20cm.

US75   Muscalus, John A.
M8s2   State bank notes. New York,
          Raymond, 1942.
               144p. 23cm.

US75   Muscalus, John A.
M8u   State-owned banks, the pet banks, and
           their bank notes. Bridgeport, Pa., 1940.
              12p. 23cm.

US75   Smedley, Glenn B.
S6   Landseer paintings used on paper
           money. Reprinted from Essay-Proof
           Journal, Spring, 1959.
              61p. illus. 23cm.

US75   Sprinkle, Frank F.
S65   Master list of uncut sheets of
           obsolete bills and old bank checks. The
           author, 1964.
              61p. 21cm.

US75   Wismer, David C.
W5   The obsolete bank notes of New England.
           Boston, Quarterman Publications, 1972.
              311p. ill. 24cm. (Gleanings from The
           Numismatist, v. 2)
              Reprinted from The Numismatist, original
           title: Descriptive list of obsolete paper
           money.

SUBJECTS AND EVENTS ON NOTES, A-Z

US77   Muscalus, John A.
B8M8   Early business college bank notes.
           The author, 1942.
              12p. 23cm.

US77   Muscalus, John A.
C3M8   The Capitol; its developmental
           aspects and the Crawford Statue of
           Freedon on paper money. Bridgeport,
           Pa., the author, 1971.
              unpaged. illus. 22cm.

US77   Muscalus, John A.
C6M8   Renault's painting of the
Vert.   surrender of Cornwallis at
File   Yorktown on state bank notes.
           Bridgeport, Pa., the author, 1966.
              unpaged. illus. 23cm.

US77   Muscalus, John A.
D5M8   The Dismal Swamp Canal and Lake
          Drummond Hotel on paper money, 1838-1865.
          Bridgeport, Pa., 1965.
              6p. illus. 23cm.

US77   Muscalus, John A.
E3M8   Paper money of early educational
          institutions and organizations. The
          author, 1946.
              23p. front. 23cm.

US77   Muscalus, John A.
L3M8   The views of towns, cities, falls
          and buildings illustrated on 1800-1866
          bank paper money. Bridgeport, Pa., 1939.
              10p. illus. 23cm.

US77   Muscalus, John A.
M4M8   Paper money pertaining to druggists,
          medicines and medical practitioners.
          Bridgeport, Pa., 1969.
              37p. illus. 23cm.

US77   Muscalus, John A.
M6M8   Popularity of Wm. S. Mount's
Vert.   art work on paper money, 1838-1865.
File   Bridgeport, Pa., the author, 1965.
              unpaged. illus. 23cm.

US77   Muscalus, John A.
P5M8   Bank notes commemorating
          the landing of the pilgrims at
          Plymouth. Bridgeport, Pa.,
          Historical Paper Money Research
          Inst., 1973.
              7p. illus. 28cm.

US77   Muscalus, John A.
P6M8   Album of types of paintings and por-
          traits of Penn, Franklin and Buchanan on
          paper money. Bridgeport, Pa., 1969.
              15p. illus. 23cm.

US77   Muscalus, John A.
P7M8   Wilkie's Princess Doria of Rome on bank
          notes used in the United States. Bridge-
          port, Pa., 1971.
              7p. illus.

US77   Muscalus, John A.
R3M8   Railroad currency: bank notes
          and scrip representative of over
          one hundred railroads, 1830's
          to 1900's. Bridgeport, Pa., the
          author, 1971.
              43p. illus. 28cm.

US77   Muscalus, John A.
R4M8   The Oxford paintings of
Vert.   Reynolds virtues in the West
File   window on paper money. Bridgeport,
          Pa., the author, 1965.
              unpaged. illus. 23cm.

US77   Muscalus, John A.
R6M8   The beautiful view of the Rockville
Vert.   Bridge across the Susquehanna above
File   Harrisburg on State bank notes.
          Bridgeport, Pa., the author, 1967.
              7p. illus. 23cm.

US77   Muscalus, John A.
S5M8   Early ships and shipbuilding on paper
          money. Bridgeport, Penn., Historical
          Paper Money Research Institute, 1976.
              9p. 35 pl. 28cm.

US77   Muscalus, John A.
W5M8   Whaling art by Garneray, Stewart
Vert.   and Page on state bank notes.
File   Bridgeport, Pa., the author, 1966.
              unpaged. illus. 23cm.

BY STATE, A-Z

US80   Mumey, Nolie.
C6M8   Colorado territorial scrip; their
          history and biographies of the men who
          issued them. Boulder, Colo., Johnson,
          1966.
              129p. illus. 25cm.

US80   Muscalus, John A.
D5M8   Paper money of the District of
          Columbia. From Coin Collector's Journal
          Jan.-Feb., 1944.
              17p. illus. 23cm.

US80   Freeman, Harley L.
F5F7   Florida obsolete notes and scrip.
          Society of Paper Money Collectors, 1967.
              103p. illus. 29cm.

US80   Pfeiffer, Philip A.
F5P4   Pensacola's currency issuing
          banks and their bank notes, 1833-
          1935, by Philip A. Pfeiffer
          Edited by Marguerite Pfeiffer
          Romond. 1st ed. Pensacola, Fla.,
          Pfeiffer Printing Co., 1975.
              87p. illus. 28cm.

US80   Atlanta [Georgia] Public Library.
G4A8   Georgia banks and banking; series
          13 from Georgia, 1800-1900; a series
          of selections from the Georgiana
          Library of a private collector,
          public exhibition. Atlanta,
          the Atlanta Public Library,
          1955.
              pp. 267-295. 1 plate. 22cm.

US80   Cornely, Robert W.
G4C6   Georgia obsolete currency; a checklist
          by Cornely and Claud Murphy, Jr.
          The author, 1962.
              36p. illus. 21cm.

US80   Dillistin, William H.
G4D5   Altered notes of the Southern Bank of
          Georgia at Bainbridge. Reprinted from
          the Numismatist, 1959.
              16p. (incl. 4 pl.) 23cm.

US80   Medcalf, Gordon.
H3M4   Paper money of the kingdom and the
          Republic of Hawaii, 1859-1905.
              23p. illus. 25cm.

US80   Davis, R. Edward.
I4D3   Early Illinois paper money. Chicago,
          Hewitt, n.d.
              32p. illus. 20cm.

US80   Marckhoff, Fred R.
I4M3c   Currency and banking in Illinois
Vert.   before 1865. From Journal of the Illinois
File   State Historical Society, Autumn 1959.
              54p. illus. 24cm.

US80   Marckhoff, Fred R.
I4M3s   A summary listing of known Illinois
Vert.   obsolete notes.   Reprinted from Numismatic
File   Scrapbook.
               16p. illus. 20cm.

US80   Bowen, Harold L.
M5B6   State bank notes of Michigan.   The
          author, 1956.
               196p. illus. 26cm.
               Bibliography

US80   Rockholt, R. H.
M6R6   Minnesota obsolete notes and
          scrip. Published for the Society
          of Paper Money Collectors, Inc.,
          Iola, Wisc., Krause Publ., 1973.
               76p. illus. 29cm.

US80   Leggett, L. Candler.
M7L4   Mississippi obsolete paper
          money and scrip. Iola, Wisc.,
          Krause Publ., Society of Paper
          Money Collectors, Inc., 1975.
               141p. illus. 29cm.

US80   McKee, James L.
N3M3   The wildcat bank notes, scrip and
          currencies of Nebraska prior to 1900.
          The author, 1970.
               60p. illus. 29cm.

US80   Wismer, D. C.
N4W5   Descriptive list of obsolete paper
          money issued in New Jersey.   1928.
               56p. illus. 23cm.

US80   Muscalus, John A.
N5M8   National bank notes of Buffalo and
          vicinity 1865-1929. Bridgeport,
          Pa., the author, 1973.
               26p. illus. 23cm.

US80   Wismer, D. C.
N5W5   New York descriptive list of obsolete
          paper money. Federalsburg, Md., 1931.
               216p. illus. 23cm.

US80
O4W5
    Wismer, D. C.
        Descriptive list of old paper
money issued in Ohio. Federalsburg, Md.
1932.
        58p. illus. 23cm.

US80
P4W5
    Wismer, D. C.
        Pennsylvania descriptive list of
obsolete state bank notes, 1782-1866.
Federalsburg, Md., 1933.
        108p. illus. 23cm.

US80
S6S5
    Sheheen, Austin M.
        South Carolina obsolete notes.
1960.
        77p. illus. 20cm.

US80
T4B5
    Bieciuk, Hank.
        Texas confederate county notes and
private scrip by Bieciuk and H.G. "Bill"
Corbin. The authors, 1961.
        112p. illus. 23cm.

US80
T4M4
    Medlar, Bob.
        Texas obsolete notes and scrip.
Published by Society of Paper Money
Collectors, 1968.
        204p. illus. 29cm.

US80
V4C6
    Coulter, Mayre Burns.
        Vermont obsolete notes and scrip. Iola,
Wis., Published for the Society of Paper
Money Collectors, by Krause Publications
[1972].
        xvii, 151p. illus. 29cm.

US80
V4H3
    Harper, Terrence G.
        Historical account of Vermont paper
currency and banks. Reprinted from
Numismatic Scrapbook Magazine, n.d.
        48p. illus. 20cm.

US80
V5A4
    Affleck, Charles J.
        The obsolete paper money of Virginia.
Hampton, Va., Virginia Numismatic Assoc-
iation, 1968-1969.
        2 v. illus. 28cm.

US80   Muscalus, John A.
V5M8   Historic Jamestown and Pocahontas on
          paper money and Chapman Art. Bridgeport,
          Pa., 1971.
              11p. illus. 23cm.

PERSONS ON NOTES, A-Z

US85   American heritage: portraits of
A5A5   famous Americans appearing on
Vert.   U.S. paper money, 1861-1928.
File   n.p., n. pub., n.d.
              unpaged. illus. 22cm.

US85   Muscalus, John A.
L5M8   Lincoln portraits on state bank
Vert.   notes, college currency and scrip.
File   Bridgeport, Pa., the author, 1967.
              11p. illus. 23cm.

US85   Muscalus, John A.
M3M8   General George B. McClellan
          on paper money. n.p., the author,
          1972.
              7p. illus. 28cm.

US85   Muscalus, John A.
M4M8   The use of paper money of Peale's
Vert.   painting of the wounded General
File   Mercer. Bridgeport, Pa., the author,
          1967.
              7p illus. 2cm.

US85   Muscalus, John A.
M5M8   Portraits of the first three
Vert.   directors of the United States
File   mint on paper money. Bridgeport,
          Pa., the author, 1969.
              unpaged. illus. 23cm.

US85   Muscalus, John A.
N5M8   Saint Nicholas on early State
Vert.   bank notes. n.p., the author, 1959.
File   unpaged illus. 23cm.

US85   Muscalus, John A.
O3M8   Oglethorpe at [Christi's] (sic)
Vert.   sale of Dr. Johnson's library on
File   paper money. Bridgeport, Pa.,
          the author, 1965.
             unpaged. illus. 23cm.

US85   Muscalus, John A.
P8M8   Banknotes honoring Pulaski
          and the Pulaski monuments.
          Bridgeport, Pa., the author, 1971.
             11p. illus. 23cm.

TWENTIETH CENTURY (SMALL SIZE)

US90   Donlon, William P.
D6   Price catalog of United States
          small size paper money, by William
          P. Donlon, with additional material
          by Robert H. Lloyd and Lee F. Hewitt.
          Chicago, Hewitt, 1964-1976.
             10v. ill. 20cm. (Hewitt's
          Numismatic Information Series).

US90   Goodman, Leon J., Jr.
G6   Standard handbook of modern U.S. paper
          money, by ..., John L. Schwartz, Chuck
          O'Donnell. N.p., Fleetwood Letter Service,
          1968-1971.
             3v. ill. 21cm.

US90   Lloyd, Robert H.
L5   National bank notes, Federal Reserve
          bank notes, Federal Reserve notes, 1928-
          1950. New York, Raymond, 1953.
             16p. 23cm. (Coin collector's
          Journal, Jan-Feb, 1953).

US90   Philpott, William A. Jr.
P5   Replacement (star) Notes used in
          connection with issuance of U.S. Paper
          Currency. Reprinted from the Numismatist,
          1967.
             8p. illus. 23cm.

US90
S5
    Shafer, Neil.
       A guidebook of modern United States
currency. 1st-7th ed. Racine, Wis.,
Whitman, 1965-1975.
       160p. illus. 20cm.

US90
S55
    Slabaugh, Arlie R., ed.
       Specialized catalog of small size
national bank notes. Chicago, Hewitt,
1967.
       48p. illus. 20cm.

US90
V4
    Vero, Andrew J.
       Those incredible B2FDC/B2J4C's! a book
on bicentennial $2 cancellations, varieties,
how to collect, values. Bicentennial
edition. Annapolis, Maryland, B2FDC Adven-
tures, 1976.
       xii, 122p. illus. 22cm.

US90
W3
    Warns, M. Owen, ed.
       The National bank note issues of
1929-1935, edited by M. Owen Warns.
Authors-Peter Huntoon and Louis Van
Belkum. n.p., Society of Paper Money
Collectors, 1970.
       212p. illus. 28cm.

<u>BANKS AND BANKING</u>

UNITED STATES

GENERAL WORKS

VA30   American Institute of Banking.
A5   Principles of bank operation. n.p.,
            the author, 1966.
                 372p. 24cm.

VA30   Carson, Deane, ed.
C3   Banking and monetary studies. Home-
            wood, Ill., Irwin, 1963.
                 441p. 23cm.

VA30   Robertson, Ross M.
R62   The comptroller and bank
            supervision; a historical appraisal.
            Washington D. C., Office of the
            Comptroller of the Currency, 1968.
                 262p. illus. 24cm.

VA30   Roosa, Robert V.
R66   Federal reserve operations in the
            money and government securities markets.
            Federal Reserve Bank of New York, 1956.
                 107p. 23cm.

VA30   Thompson, Thomas William.
T5   Checks and balances; a study of the
            dual banking system in America. Washing-
            ton, 1962.

VA30   U.S. Federal Reserve System.
U5   The Federal Reserve Systems, purposes and
            functions. Washington, Federal Reserve
            System, 1954, 1961.
                 238p. tables 21cm.

GOVERNMENT REPORTS, LAWS, ETC.

VA35   U.S. Comptroller of the Currency.
U5   The National Bank Act as amended, and
            other laws relating to national banks.
            Washington, D.C., GPO, 1933.
                243p.   24cm.

SPECIFIC BANKS AND BANKERS

VA40   Bank of New York.
B3   Short stories on money and banking. New
            York, Bank of New York, n.d.
                variously paged ill.   25cm.   (Short stories
            on money and banking, no. 1-12)

VA40   Daughters of Utah Pioneers.
D3   [Banking history of the Church of
            Jesus Christ of Latter-Day Saints], compiled
            by Kate B. Carter. n.p., n.d.
                no continuous pagination. 22cm.

VA40   Lewis, Lawrence.
L4   A history of the Bank of North
            America. Philadelphia, Lippincott, 1882.
                153p.   illus.   27cm.

VA40   Rink, Paul.
R5   A. P. Giannini; building the Bank of
            America. Chicago, Encyclopedia Brit-
            annica, [1963].
                192p.   illus.   22cm.

VA40   Scates, Shelby.
S3   First bank; the story of Seattle-
            First National Bank, by Shelby Scates.
            Seattle, First National Bank [1970]
                130p.   illus.   29cm.
                Bibliography: p. 129-130.

VA40   Smith, Alice E.
S6   George Smith's money. A Scottish
            investor in America. Madison, Wis.,
            1966.
                197p.   8 pl.   22cm.

VA45   Crissey, Forrest.
C7   Moving money, 1859-1929. Chicago,
          Brinks Express Company, n.d.
               49p. illus. 21cm.

VA45   Muscalus, John Anthony.
M8   The use of banking enterprises in
          the financing of public education;
          1796-1866. Philadelphia, U. of Pa.,
          1945.

VA45   National bank organization, 1812-1904.
N3   N.Y., Natl. City Bank of N.Y., 1904.
               203p. 20cm.

VA45   Westrup, Alfred B.
W4   The financial problem; its
          relation to labor reform and pros-
          perity, the principles of monetary
          science, demonstrating the
          abolition of interest to be un-
          avoidable. Chicago, Mutual Bank
          Propaganda Headquarters, 1891.
               30p. 32cm.

NINETEENTH CENTURY

VA50   Henkels, Stan V.
H4   Andrew Jackson and the Bank of the United
Rare   States, an interesting bit of history con-
Books   cerning "Old Hickory". Philadelphia, privately
          printed, 1928.
               unpaged ill. 22cm.

VA50   Muscalus, John A.
M8   Bibliography of histories of specific
          banks. The author, 1942.
               16p. 23cm.

VA50   VanBelkum, Louis.
V3   National banks of the note issuing
          period, 1863-1935. [Chicago, Hewitt,
          1968].
               400p. illus. 22cm.

VA60
C6B8
    Burpee, Charles W.
       First century of the Phoenix National
    Bank of Hartford. Hartford, 1914.
       150p. illus. 25cm.

VA60
M3B6
    Boston. State Street Trust Co.
       The log of the State Street Trust
    Co. Boston, 1926.
       87p. illus. 24cm.

VA60
N4D5
    Dillistin, William H.
       Directory of New Jersey banks, 1804-
    1942. New Jersey Bankers Assn., 1942.
       98p. 23cm.

VA60
N4K5
    Kleinhaus, Philip L., comp.
       Down through the years, the story of
    the National State Bank of Elizabeth,
    New Jersey, 1812-1937. Compiled by
    Philip L. Kleinhaus. [Elizabeth, 1937].
       164p. photog. 23cm.

VA60
N7D5
    Dillistin, William H.
       Historical directory of the banks of
    the state of New York. New York, State
    Bankers Assn., 1946.
       383p. 24cm.

VA60
N7G5
    Gibbons, J. S.
       The banks of New York; their dealer
    the clearing house and the panic of 1850
    New York, D. Appleton & Co., 1858.
       399p. 19cm.

VA60
N7L3
    Lanier, Henry Wysham.
       A century of banking in New
    York, 1822-1922. New York, The
    Gilliss Press, 1922.
       335p. maps, charts. 24cm.

VA60
N7P4
    Peterson, Jaffray.
       Sixty-five years of progress and a
    record of New York City banks. New
    York, [Continental Bank & Trust], 1935.
       135p. illus. 24cm.

VA60   Wainwright, Nicholas B.
P4W3   History of the Philadelphia National
        Bank. ... 1803-1953. Philadelphia, 1953.
        263p. illus. 24cm.

MIDWEST, A-Z

VA70   Anderson, George L.
K3A6   Some phases of currency and banking in
Vert.   territorial Kansas. From Territorial
File   Kansas, Lawrence, 1954.
        [44]p. 23cm.

VA70   James, F. Cyril.
I3J3   The growth of Chicago banks. New
        York, Harper, 1938.
        2 vol. illus. 24cm.

VA70   Fort Wayne (Indiana) Public Library.
I5F6   Early banking in Indiana. Fort Wayne,
        Ind., n. pub., 1954.
        62p. ill. 20cm.

VA70   Erickson, Erling A.
I8E7   Banking in frontier Iowa; 1836-1865
        [by] Erling A. Erickson. 1st ed. Ames,
        the Iowa State University Press, 1971.
        183p. illus. 24cm.

VA70   Woodford, Arthur M.
M5W6   Detroit and its banks; the story of
        Detroit Bank and Trust. Detroit, Wayne
        State University, 1974.
        299p. illus. 24cm.

VA70   Rule, W. G.
M6R8   "The means of wealth, peace, and
        happiness," the story of the oldest bank
        west of the Mississippi. ... The Boat-
        men's National Bank of Saint Louis,
        1847-1947. [St. Louis, 1947].
        90p. pl. 22cm.

VA70   Bellevue, Ohio. The First National
O3B4   Bank.
             First one hundred years of
        banking, 1875-1975. Sandusky,
        Ohio, Gull Press, 1975.
        unpaged. illus. 28cm.

VA70   [Huntington, C. C.]
O3H8   A history of banking and currency in
          Ohio before the Civil War. From Ohio
          Archaeological and historical Quarterly,
          July 1915.
              304p. 23cm.

VA70   Driscoll, R. E.
S6D7   Seventy years of banking in the Black
          Hills. Rapid City, Gate City Guide, n.d.
              87p. 23cm.

VA70   Andersen, Theodore A.
W6A5   A century of banking in Wisconsin.
          Madison, State Historical Society of
          Wisconsin, 1954.
              226p. 22cm.

VA70   Krueger, Leonard Bayliss.
W6K7   History of commercial banking
          in Wisconsin (with certain sections
          applicable to the Mid-west). Madison,
          Wis., University of Wisconsin,
          1933.
              232p. charts. 25cm. (University
          of Wisc. studies in the Social Sciences
          and History, #18.)

WEST, A-Z

VA80   Armstrong, Leroy.
C3A7   Financial California. San Francisco,
          Coast Banker, 1916.
              191, xcv p. illus. 26cm.

VA80   Wilson, Neil C.
C3W5   400 California street; a century plus
1969   five, by Neil C. Wilson. 2d ed.
          San Francisco, The Bank of California,
          1969.
              106p. illus. 27cm.

VA80   Niehaus, Fred R.
C6N5d   Development of banking in Colorado.
          Denver, Mountain States Pub., 1942.
              122p. 24cm.
              Bibliography

VA80   Niehaus, Fred R.
C6N5s   Seventy years of progress. History of
         banking in Colorado, 1876-1946. Federal
         Deposit Insurance Corp., 1948.
             100p. tables. 23cm.
             Bibliography

VA80   Spring, Agnes Wright.
C6S6   The First National Bank of Denver.
         The formative years 1860-1865. Denver,
         [196-.]
             48p. ill. 28cm.

VA80   Warns, Melvin Owen.
N3W3   The Nevada "Sixteen" national banks
         and their mining camps. Washington D.C.,
         Society of Paper Money Collectors Inc., c1974.
             390p. illus. 29cm.

VA80   McFarland, Cara Lee.
O6M3   The United States National Bank of
         Portland, Oregon; a historical sketch,
         by Cara Lee McFarland. Portland, Ore.,
         Binfords & Mort [1940]
             [151]p. Tables. 24cm.

VA80   Marple, Elliot.
W3M4   The National Bank of Commerce of
         Seattle, 1889-1969; territorial to world-
         wide banking in eighty years, including
         the story of the Marine Bancorporation [by]
         Elliot Marple & Bruce H. Olson. Palo Alto,
         Calif., Pacific Books [1972].
             x, 277p. illus. 25cm.
             Bibliography: p. 267-270.

SOUTH, A-Z

VA90   Lesesne, J. Mauldin.
S6L4   The bank of the state of South Carolina.
         Columbia, S.C., [1970].
             211p.
             Bibliography

VA90   South Carolina. Legislature.
S6S6   A compilation of all the acts, resolutions,
         reports, and other documents, in relation to
         the Bank of the State of South Carolina,
         affording full information concerning that
         institution. Columbia, S.C., South Carolina
         Legislature, 1848.
             753p. 24cm.

VA90   List of National bank notes...
T4L5   issued by Texas banks from 1865 to
            1928; more than 1000 notes shown,
            representing more than 700 different
            banks. Display prepared for the
            Republic National Bank of Dallas,
            Nov.,-Dec., 1954.
            unpaged. 29cm.

CANADA

VB30   The Bank of Nova Scotia, 1832-1932.
N6   [Toronto, 1932].
              166p. illus. 24cm.

SOUTH AMERICA

VB50   El banco de la nacion Argentina en su
A7   cincuentenario. 1891-1941. [Buenos
              Aries, 1941].
              473p. illus. 31cm.

GREAT BRITAIN

VC30   Clapham, John Harold.
C5   The Bank of England, a history.
         Cambridge, University Press, 1966.
             2 vol. illus. 24cm.

VC30   Graham, William.
G7   The one pound note in the history of
         banking in Great Britain. Edinburgh,
         J. Thin, 1911.
             410p. illus. 23cm.

VC30   Mottram, R. H.
M6   The Westminster Bank, 1836-1936.
         London, 1936.
             28p. 19cm.

NETHERLANDS, BELGIUM, LIECHTENSTEIN, LUXEMBOURG

VC55   [History of R. Mees & Zoonen,
M4   bankers and insurance brokers,
             1720-1970.] Rotterdam, R. Mees
         & Zoonen, n.d.
             81p. illus. 22cm.

SOCIETIES, COMMISSIONS, ETC.

VD10
N3
Vol.1
National Monetary Commission.
Publications. Vol. 1
    Interviews on banking in England, France, Germany, Switzerland and Italy. Washington, GPO, 1912.
    539p.; separately paged sections. Charts. 23cm.

VD10
N3
V.2
National Monetary Commission.
Publications. Vol. 2
    financial laws of the U.S., 1778-1909. Washington, GPO, 1911.
    812p. 23cm.

VD10
N3
V.3
National Monetary Commission.
Publications. Vol. 3
    Digest of state banking laws; compiled by Samuel A. Welldon. Washington, GPO, 1911.
    746p. charts. 23cm.

VD10
N3
V.4
National Monetary Commission.
Publications. vol. 4.
    Banking in the United States before the Civil War. Washington, GPO, 1911.
    388p. 23cm.
    Contents.-The first and second bank of the U.S. by J.T. Holdsworth and P. R. Dewey.-State banking before the Civil War; by D. R. Dewey and R. F. Chaddock.

VD10
N3
V.5
National Monetary Commission.
Publications. vol. 5.
    The national banking system. Washington, GPO, 1911.
    484p. charts. 23cm.
    Contents.-The orgin of the national banking system, by A.M. Davis.-History of the natl. bank currency by A.D. Noyes.-History of crises under the Natl. banking system, by O.M.W. Sprague.

VD10   National Monetary Commission.
N3   Publications. vol. 6.
V.6   Clearing houses and credit
          instruments. Washington, GPO, 1910.
             229p. charts. 23cm.
             Contents.-Clearing house methods and
          practices, by J.G. Cannon.-The use
          of credit instruments in payments in
          the U.S., by D. Kinley.

VD10   National Monetary Commission.
N3   Publications. Vol. 7.
V.7   State banks, trust companies
          and independent treasury systems.
          Washington, GPO, 1910.
             366p. charts. 23cm.
             Contents.-State banks and trust
          companies since the passage of the
          natl. bank act, by G.E. Barnett.-
          The independent treasury system of
          the U.S., by D. Kinley.

VD10   National Monetary Commission.
N3   Publications. vol. 8.
V.8   The English banking system.
          Washington, GPO, 1911.
             297p. charts. 23cm.
             Contents.-The English banking
          system, by H. Withers, Sir R.H.I.
          Palgrave et.al.-History of the Bank
          of England, by E. Philippovich and
          H.S. Foxwell.

VD10   National Monetary Commission.
N3   Publications. Vol. 9
V.9   Banking in Canada. Washington,
          GPO, 1911.
             219p. charts. 23cm.
             Contents.-The history of banking in
          Canada by R.M. Breckenridge.-The
          Canadian banking system by J.F.
          Johnson.-Interviews on the banking
          and currency systems of Canada

VD10   National Monetary Commission.
N3   Publications. vol. 10.
V.10   The Reichsbank and renewal of its
          charter, 1876-1900. Washington,
          GPO, 1911.
             268p. 23cm.

VD10   National Monetary Commission.
N3   Publications. Vol. 11.
V.11   Articles on German banking and
          German banking laws. Washington,
          GPO, 1911.
              329p. 23cm.
              Contents.-Misc. articles on
          German banking.-German Imperial
          banking laws, by R. Koch.

VD10   National Monetary Commission.
N3   Publications. Vol. 12-13.
V.12-13   The German bank inquiry of 1908.
          Pts. 1 and 2. Washington, GPO,
          1910.
              1162p. 23cm.

VD10   National Monetary Commission.
N3   Publications. Vol. 14.
V.14   The great German banks; by
          J. Riesser. Washington, GPO, 1911.
              1042p. 23cm.

VD10   National Monetary Commission.
N3   Publications. Vol. 15.
V.15   Banking in France and the French
          bourse. Washington, GPO, 1911.
              276p. charts. 23cm.
              Contents: Evolution of credit
          and banks in France, by A. Liesse.-
          History and methods of the Paris
          Bourse, by E. Vidal.

VD10   National Monetary Commission.
N3   Publications. Vol. 16.
V.16   Banking in Belgium and Mexico.
          Washington, GPO, 1911.
              284p. charts. 23cm.
              Contents: The natl. bank of
          Belgium.-The banking system of
          Mexico, by Charles A. Conant.

VD10   National Monetary Commission.
N3   Publications. Vol. 17.
V.17   Banking in Sweden and Switzerland.
          Washington, GPO, 1911.
              269p. charts. 23cm.
              Contents.-The Swedish banking
          system, by A. W. Flux.-The Swiss
          banking law by Julius Landmann.

VD10   National Monetary Commission.
N3   Publications. Vol. 18.
V.18   Banking in Italy, Russia, Austro-
         Hungary, and Japan. Washington,
         GPO, 1911.
             214p. 23cm.
             Contents.-Italian banks of issue,
         by T. Canovai and C.F. Ferraris.-
         Banking in Russia, Austro-Hungary,
         Holland and Japan.

VD10   National Monetary Commission.
N3   Publications. Vol. 19.
V.19   Administrative features of national banking
         laws and European fiscal and postal savings
         systems. Washington, GPO, 1911.
             sections variously paged. charts. 23cm.

VD10   National Monetary Commission.
N3   Publications. Vol. 20.
V.20   Miscellaneous articles. Washington,
         GPO, 1911.
             205p. other sections variously
         paged. 23cm.

VD10   National Monetary Commission.
N3   Publications. Vol. 21.
V.21   Statistics for United States,
         Great Britain, Germany, and France.
         Washington, GPO, 1911.
             354p. charts. 29cm.
             Contents.-Statistics for the U.S.,
         by A. P. Andrew.-Special report
         from the Bank of the U.S., 1909.-
         Statistics for G.B. Germany & France,
         1867-1908 by R. H. I. Palgrave et. al.

VD10   National Monetary Commission.
N3   Publications. Vol. 22.
V.22   Seasonal variations in demands for
         currency and capital, by Edwin W.
         Kemmerer. Washington, GPO, 1911.
             517p. charts. 29cm.

VD10   National Monetary Commission.
N3   Publications. Vol. 23.
V.23   Financial diagrams and
         European bank summaries prepared
         by A. Piatt Andrew. Washington,
         GPO, 1912.
             22 charts, diagrams 39cm.

VD30   MacGregor, T. D.
M3   Money and banking through the ages.
          Philadelphia, MacGregor & Woodrow, 1939.
              23p. illus. 18cm.

VD30   Morris, James.
M6   The road to Huddersfield; a journey to
          five continents. New York, Pantheon,
          [1963].
              235p. illus., maps.

CHINA

VE30   Banyai, Richard A.
B3   Money and banking in China and
          Southeast Asia during the Japanese
          military occupation, 1937-1945. Taipei,
          Taiwan Enterprises Co., Ltd., 1974.
              150p. illus. 21cm.

<u>CHECKS</u>

BIBLIOGRAPHIES, DICTIONARIES, DIRECTORIES, ETC.

VM45   Check Collectors Round Table.
C5   Security printers. 1st ed.
            Cincinnati, Check Collectors
            Round Table, 1974, 1976.
               21p. 29cm.

SPECIAL - FORGERY

VM50   Hoffman, E. E.
H6   Billion dollar check racket.
            Tarzana, Ca., Renay Pub. Co., 1964.
               160p. illus. 23cm.

COLLECTING

VM60   Sowards, Neil, ed.
S6   The handbook of check collecting.
            Ft. Wayne, Ind., the author, 1975.
               97p. illus. 27cm.

BY COUNTRY, A-Z

VM90   Johanson, Erik.
R9J6   Type register of checks, money orders,
            Bons, talons and coupons in the Soviet
            Union, 1917-1924. Helsinki,
            Munkkiniemen Kopiolaitos, 1971.
               44p. illus. 21cm.

<u>ECONOMICS</u>

WORLD ECONOMICS

GENERAL WORKS

WA30   Brownell, Francis H.
B7   Brief on silver as money. n.p.,
            International monetary Fund, 1947.
                40p. 23cm.

WA30   Brownell, Francis H.
B7h   Hard money. N.Y., American
            Smelting and Refining Co., 1944.
                35p. tables. 23cm.

WA30   Croome, Honor.
C7   Introduction to money. London,
            Methuen & Co., Ltd., 1956.
                209p. 19cm. (Home Study Books,
            Series #25)

WA30   Fortune Magazine.
F6   An entire issue on money and
            inflation. Vol. XXXVII, #4.   Jersey
            City, N.J., Time Inc., 1948.
                215p. illus. 33cm.

WA30   Gayer, A. D., ed.
G3   The lessons of monetary experience;
            essays in honor of Irving Fisher.
            N.Y., Farrar & Rinehart Inc., 1937.
                450p. photo. 22cm.

WA30   Groseclose, Elgin.
G7d   The decay of money, a survey of western
            currencies, 1912-1962. Washington, D.C.,
            Institute for Monetary Research, 1962.
                32p. 23cm. (Institute for Monetary
            Research, Monograph no. 1)

WA30   Groseclose, Elgin.
G7m   Money and man; a survey of monetary
            experience. New York, F. Ungar, [1961].
                305p. 23cm.

WA30   Jevons, W. Stanley.
J4   Money and the mechanism of
        exchange. N.Y., D. Appleton,
        1875.
            349p. charts. 20cm. (International
        Scientific Series, v. 17)

WA30   Leavens, Dickson H.
L4   Silver money. Bloomington, Ind.,
        Principia, 1939.
            439p. 25cm.

WA30   Muhleman, Maurice L.
M8   Monetary systems of the world; a
        study of present currency systems and
        statistical information . . . by Maurice
        L. Muhleman. Revised ed. New York,
        Charles H. Nicoll, 1896.
            239p. 20cm.

WA30   Turner, W. E.
T8   Stable money; a conservative
        answer to business cycles. Ft.
        Worth, Tex., Marvin D. Evans, 1966.
            547p. illus. 24cm.

ANCIENT MONETARY SYSTEMS

WA50   Burns, A. R.
B8   Money and monetary policy in early
        times. New York, Knopf, 1927.
            517p. 16 pl.

WA50   Curtis, John B.
C8   Money and merchants in Ur III by
        Curtis and William W. Hallo. Off-print
        from Hebrew Union College Annual, vol. 30,
        1959.
            [39]p. illus. 24cm.

WA50   International Numismatic Convention, 1963.
I5   The patterns of monetary development
        in Phoenicia and Palestine in antiquity.
        Ed. by A. Kindler. Jerusalem, Schocken,
        [1967].
            325p. 22 pl. 24cm.

Lenormant, Francois.
    Essai sur l'organisation politique
et economique de la monnaie dans
l'antiquite. Reprint of the Paris
ed, 1863. Amsterdam, J.C. Gieben,
1970.
    192p. 23cm.

<u>UNITED STATES</u>

GENERAL WORKS

WB30   Bowers, Nathan A.
B6   Return to the gold standard.
Vert.   Reprinted from The Numismatist, August,
File   1955.
               unpaged. 23cm.

WB30   DeKnight, William F.
D4   History of the currency of the
          country and of the loans of the
          United States from the earliest period
          to June 30, 1900. 2nd. ed. Washington,
          GPO, 1900.
               277p. 29cm.

WB30   Dunbar, Charles F.
D8   Laws of the United States relating
          to currency, finance, and banking, from
          1789 to 1891, by Charles F. Dunbar.
          Boston, Ginn and Co., 1891.
               309p. 24cm.

WB30   Friedman, Milton.
F7   A monetary history of the United
          States, 1867-1960 by Friedman and Anna
          Jacobson. Schwartz. Princeton Univer-
          sity Press, 1963.
                860p. 23cm.

WB30   Gordon, Armistead C.
G6   Congressional currency; an outline of
          the Federal money system, by Armistead C.
          Gordon. New York, London, G. P. Putnam's
          Sons, 1895.
               ix, 234p. 20cm. (Questions of the
          day, 85)

WB30   Hepburn, A. Barton.
H4   History of coinage and currency in the
          United States and the perennial contest
          for sound money. New York, Macmillan, 1903, 1915.
               666p. 20cm.
               Bibliography

WB30   Laughlin, James Laurence.
L3   The history of bimetallism in the
        United States. New York, Appleton, 1886.
            257p. 22cm.

WB30   Nolan, R. M.
N6   The gold outflow--will it bankrupt the
Vert.   U.S.? Taken from Tracings, Summer, 1960,
File   Vol. 1, No. 3. East St. Louis, Illinois.
            6p. 18cm.

WB30   Nussbaum, Arthur.
N8   A history of the dollar. New York,
        Columbia University, [1957].
            308p.
            Bibliography

WB30   Sause, George G.
S2   Money, banking, and economic activity
        [by] George G. Sause. Boston, D.C. Heath & Co.,
        1966.
            507p. 24cm.

WB30   Sumner, William Graham.
S8   A history of American currency. New
        York, H. Holt, 1874, 1876.
            391p. 20cm.

WB30   U.S. Congress. House. Committee on Banking
U54   and Currency.
Vert.   A primer on money, [by the] Subcommittee on
File   Domestic Finance ... 88th Congress, 2d session.
        Washington, GPO, 1964
            144p. 23cm.

WB30   U.S. Treasury Secretary, Office of.
U58   Coins and currency of the United
Vert.   States by Office of the Secretary of the
File   Treasury. Washington, Treasury Dept., 1947.
            33p. 27cm.

WB30   Watson, David Kemper.
W3   History of American coinage. New
        York, Putnam's, 1899.
            xix, 278p. 19cm.

WB30   White, Horace.
W5   Money and banking illustrated by
        American history. Boston, Ginn &
        Company, 1896.
            x, 488p. illus. 19cm.
            Bibliography: p. [469]

WB40   Arrington, Leonard J.
A7   Great basin kingdom; an economic
          history of the Latter-Day Saints.
          Cambridge, Harvard University Press,
          1958.
              534p. illus., maps. 24cm.
              Bibliography

COLONIAL

WB50   Ernst, Joseph Albert.
E7   Money and politics in America, 1755-1775;
          a study in the Currency act of 1764 and the
          political economy of revolution. Chapel
          Hill, Published for the Institute of Early
          American History and Culture, by the
          University of North Carolina Press [1973]
              xix, 403p. illus. 24cm.
              Bibliography: p. 379-393.

WB50   Nettels, Curtis Putnam.
N4   The money supply of the American
          Colonies before 1720. New York, A. M.
          Kelley, 1964. Reprint of 1934 ed.
              318p. 22cm.
              Bibliography

NINETEENTH CENTURY

WB60   Barrett, Don C.
B3   The greenbacks and resumption of
          specie payments, 1862-1879, by Don C.
          Barrett. Cambridge, Mass., Harvard Univ.
          Press, 1931.
              259p. 24cm. (Harvard economic
          studies, v. 36)

WB60   Fowler, William Worthington.
F6   Twenty years of inside life in Wall
          Street, or revelations of the personal
          experience of a speculator . . . New York,
          Orange Judd Co., 1880.
              576p. 20cm.

WB60   Gresham, Otto.
G7   The Greenbacks or the money that won
            the Civil War and the World War.
            Chicago, Book Press, 1927.
                312p.   23cm.

WB60   Mitchell, Wesley Clair.
M5   A history of the greenbacks, with
            special reference to the economic con-
            sequences of their issue: 1862-65.
            University of Chicago Press, [1903].
                577p.   23cm.

WB60   Wells, David A.
W4   Robinson Crusoe's money or, the
            remarkable financial fortunes and mis-
            fortunes of a remote island community,
            with illustrations by Thomas Nast.   New
            York, Harper, 1896.
                118p.   illus.   20cm.

TWENTIETH CENTURY

WB70   Browne, Harry, 1933-
B7   You can profit from a monetary crisis.
            New York, Macmillan Publishing Co., 1974.
                397p.   illus.   24cm.

WB70   Goodman, George J. W.
G6   Supermoney.   New York, Random House, 1972.
                301p.   22cm.

WB70   Spahr, Walter E.
S6   Allied military currency; some queries
            and observations.   New York, Economists'
            National Committee on Monetary Policy,
            [1943].
                30p.   22cm.

WB70   Weber, Charles E.
W4   Perils of a debased coinage.
            n.p., American Numismatic Assn.,
            1965.   Reprinted from the
            Numismatist.
                unpaged.   illus.   23cm.

<u>EUROPE</u>

GENERAL WORKS

WC10   Hirst, Francis W.
H5   The paper moneys of Europe; their
          moral and economic significance. Boston,
          Houghton Mifflin Co., 1922.
              47p. 18cm.

WC10   Landis, Walter S.
L3   An engineer looks at inflation; its
          effects in Germany and France.
          N.P., The Duke Endowment, [1933.]
              56p. 21cm.

WC10   Wright, Philip G.
W7   Inflation and after; case studies of
          the effects of inflation in France,
          Germany and Austria...Condensed from
          a report prepared for the Duke
          Endowment. Charlotte, N.C., The
          Duke Endowment, n.d.
              66p. charts. 21cm.

GREAT BRITAIN

WC30   Feavearyear, Albert.
F4   The pound sterling, a history of
          English money. 2nd ed. Rev. by E. Victor
          Morgan. Oxford, Clarendon, 1963.
              446p. 22 pl.

WC30   Gould, J. D.
G6   The great debasement; currency and
          the economy in mid-tudor England.
          Oxford, Clarendon Press, 1970.
              198p. graphs. 23cm.

FRANCE

WC40   Harris, S. E.
H3   The assignats. Cambridge, Harvard
            University, 1930.
                293p. 22cm.
                Bibliography

WC40   White, Andrew Dickson.
W5   Fiat money inflation in France. New
            York, Appleton-Century, 1933. Reprinted,
            1959.
                68p. 21cm.

GERMANY

WC50   Banyai, Richard A.
B3   The legal and military aspects of
            German money, banking and finance;
            1938-1948. Phoenix, c1971.
                121p. illus. 28cm.
                Bibliography: pp. 118-121.

WC50   Elliott, E. B.
E4   Suggestions for the establishment
Vert.   of an international coinage on a
File   decimal and metric basis in
            Germany. n.p., 1869.
                14p. 23cm.

SWITZERLAND

WC52   Hofer, Paul F.
H6   Das munzwesen der Schweiz seit 1850.
            Heft 2. Bern, Gustav Grunau, 1937.
                62p. plates. 22cm.

ITALY

WC60   Gamberini di Scarfea, Cesare.
G3   Raccolta delle ... leggi ... relativi
          alla Carta monetata in Italia. Bologna,
          Forni, 1965.
              491p. 5 pl. 22cm.

<u>WESTERN HEMISPHERE</u>

WEST INDIES

WD50   Lacombe, Robert.
L3   Monetary history of Santo Domingo
        and the Republic of Haiti up to 1874.
        Paris, Larose, 1956.
            47p. 28cm.

SOUTH AMERICA

WD70   Lesseur, Carmelo Lauria.
L4   Recursos financieros y estrategia
        del desarrollo en Venezuela.
        Parlamar, Venezuela, Banco de
        Venezuela, 1975.
            77p. charts. 23cm.

WD70   Lesseur, Carmelo Lauria.
L4v   Venezuela 1975: la nueva
        dimension de sus recursos fin-
        ancieros y el fenomeno economico.
        Caracas, Banco de Venezuela, 1975.
            47p. 24cm.

<u>ASIA</u>

INDIA

WE30   Malhotra, D. K.
M3   History and problems of Indian
         currency, 1835-1959. New Delhi, Minerva
         Book Shop, 1960.
             287p. 22cm.
             Bibliography

CHINA

WE60   Leavens, Dickson H.
L4   Chinese money and banking. Phila-
         delphia, American Academy of Political
         and Social Science, 1930.
             8p. 24cm.

WE60   Miyashita, Tadao.
M5   The currency and financial system of
         mainland China. Tokyo, Institute of Asian
         Economic Affairs, [1966].
             278p. 8 pl. 24cm.

NEAR EAST

WE70   Ashtor, E.
A8   A social and economic history of
         the Near East in the Middle Ages [by]
         E. Ashtor. Berkeley, Ca., Univ. of
         California Press, 1976.
             384p. charts. graphs. 24cm.

PART IV
Periodicals

Periodicals and auction catalogues do not appear
in the index. These are both alphabetical listings.
Our inventories of periodicals and auction
catalogues depend upon the generosity of our
members, publishers, and auction houses. Collections may, therefore, be incomplete in some areas.
Please feel free to inquire concerning
specific dates and issues.

<u>PERIODICALS</u>

* Indicates incomplete holdings.

AMERICAN ASSN. OF MUSEUMS BULLETIN. WASHINGTON REPORT.
Washington, DC.
     Dec. 1972-Sept. 1973

AMERICAN JOURNAL OF NUMISMATICS. American Numismatic
and Archaeological Society, New York.
     v.1-53; May 1866-1924
     Title varies: 1866-1897, AMERICAN JOURNAL OF
     NUMISMATICS AND BULLETIN OF THE AMERICAN
     NUMISMATIC AND ARCHAEOLOGICAL SOCIETY.

AMERICAN NUMISMATIC AND ARCHAEOLOGICAL SOCIETY.
PROCEEDINGS. New York.
     30-48; 1888-1906

ANA CLUB BULLETIN. AMERICAN NUMISMATIC
ASSOCIATION. Colorado Springs, Colorado.
     v.11, no.3-; May 1962-
     Title varies: v.1-11, no.2, Oct 1951-
     Jan. 1962, AMERICAN NUMISMATIC ASSOCIATION.
     OFFICERS' BULLETIN.

AMERICAN NUMISMATIC ASSOCIATION. CONSTITUTION
AND BY-LAWS. Colorado Springs, Colorado.
     1891, 1939-
     Title varies: Published with Library List,
     Membership Directories, etc.

AMERICAN NUMISMATIC ASSOCIATION. LIBRARY
CATALOGUE. Colorado Springs, Colorado.
     1938-
     Title varies: Library List, etc.
     Published variously with Membership
     List, Constitution and By-Laws, etc.

AMERICAN NUMISMATIC ASSOCIATION. MEMBERSHIP
DIRECTORY. Colorado Springs, Colorado.
     1908, 1925-
     Title varies.

AMERICAN NUMISMATIC ASSOCIATION. OFFICERS'
BULLETIN. Colorado Springs, Colorado.
     See ANA CLUB BULLETIN.

AMERICAN NUMISMATIC ASSOCIATION. OFFICERS'
REPORT. Colorado Springs, Colorado.
     1942-*
     Title varies: Reports of Officers and
     Committees to the Annual Convention of
     the American Numismatic Association, etc.

AMERICAN NUMISMATIC ASSOCIATION. YEAR BOOK.
Colorado Springs, Colorado.
     v.1; 1910

AMERICAN NUMISMATIC SOCIETY. ANNUAL REPORT.
New York.
     1962-

AMERICAN NUMISMATIC SOCIETY. CERTIFICATE
OF INCORPORATION, CONSTITUTION AND BY-LAWS.
     1910, 1948, 1960, 1967, 1972

AMERICAN NUMISMATIC SOCIETY. MUSEUM NOTES.
New York.
     No.1-; 1945-

AMERICAN NUMISMATIC SOCIETY. PROCEEDINGS.
New York.
     See also AMERICAN NUMISMATIC SOCIETY.
     ANNUAL REPORT.
     1921-1923, 1926, 1934-1962
     Title varies: 1878-1907, AMERICAN NUMISMATIC
     AND ARCHAEOLOGICAL SOCIETY OF NEW YORK.

AMERICAN PHILATELIST. American Philatelic Society.
Phoenix, Arizona.
     v.86, no.9-; Sept. 1972-

AMERICAN TAX TOKEN SOCIETY NEWSLETTER. A.T.T.S.,
Azusa, Ca.
     1971-

AMERICAN TOPICAL ASSOCIATION.
     See TOPICAL TIME.

AMERICAN VECTURISTS ASSOCIATION.
     See FARE BOX.

ANALELE STIINTIFICE. Jassy. Universitatea. Rumania.
     v.12-20-; 1966-

THE ANTIQUITY. Mueller Publications. Hope, N.J.
     v.4, no.11-v.5, no.12; Nov. 72-Aug. 73

ANNALS OF THE NAPRSTEK MUSEUM. Prague.
     v.4, 5, 7; 1965, 1966, n.d.

ARETHUSE REVIEW. Jules Florange. Paris.
     no.1-29; 1923-1930

ART-N'-TIQUES TRENDS. Associated Business Coun-
sellors, Cleveland, Ohio.
     See also COLLECTIBLE TRENDS.
      Mar. 1973-Mar. 1975

ASIATIC SOCIETY OF BENGAL. JOURNAL AND PROCEEDINGS.
NUMISMATIC SUPPLEMENT. Calcutta.
     v.8, no.3-v.14, no.9.; Mar. 1912-April 1919

ANNUAL PROCEEDINGS. ASSAY COMMISSION. Washington, DC.
     1919, 1955-1963, 1966

AUSTRALIAN COIN REVIEW. P.J. Downie, Melbourne.
     July 1964-July 1970*

AUSTRALIAN COIN WORLD. Hawk Internat'l Pub. Co.,
Sydney.
     v.1, no.1-v.2, no.6.; Nov. 1966-Apr. 1968

AUSTRALIAN NUMISMATIC JOURNAL. Numismatic
Society of South Australia, Adelaide.
     See also: SOUTH AUSTRALIAN NUMISMATIC
     JOURNAL.
     v.9-23;   1958-1972

AUSTRALIAN NUMISMATIC SOCIETY REPORT. GPO, Sydney.
     v.25-; 1960-*

AUSTRALIAN NUMISMATIST. Numismatic Association
of Victoria, Melbourne.
     Aug. 1940, Feb. 1967-Dec 1970*

BANCO DE VENEZUALA. ECONOMIA I FINANZAS. BOLETIN
MENSUAL.
     Feb. 1972-

BANK NOTE REPORTER. Criswell's Publications, Citra,
Florida.
     1973-

BARILLA. Central Bank Money Museum. Manilla, Philippines.
     v.1-; July 1974-

BICENTENNIAL TIMES. American Revolution Bicentennial Administration, Washington, DC.
     April 1975-

BOLLETTINO NUMISMATTICO. Luigi Simonetti, Italy.
     1969-1971

BRITISH NUMISMATIC JOURNAL. British Numismatic
Society, London.
     1903-1957, 1970-1973

BUNYAN'S CHIPS. International Organization of
Wooden Money Collectors, Radnor, Ohio.
     v.7-; 1970-

C.O.I.N. COMPENDIUM OF INTERNATIONAL NUMISMATICS.
     #50, 51, 55-59, 61, 62, 66, 69; no date

CAB'S COIN COLLECTOR. Cab Atkins, Centralia, Mo.
     Nov. 1964-Mar. 1966*

CALCOIN NEWS. California State Numismatic Assn.
Berkeley.
     v.1-; 1947-

CANADA. ROYAL CANADIAN MINT. ANNUAL REPORT.
Department of Finance, Ottawa.
     1943, 1944, 1946-1960, 1962-1964

CANADIAN ANTIQUARIAN AND NUMISMATIC JOURNAL.
Numismatic and Antiquarian Society of Montreal.
     2nd series: v.2, no.2. (April, 1892)
     4th series: v.2-4. (1931-1933)

CANADIAN NUMISMATIC JOURNAL. Canadian Numismatic
Association, Ontario.
     v.1-; 1956-

CANADIAN PAPER MONEY JOURNAL. Canadian Paper Money Society, Toronto.
     1966-*

CENTINEL. Central States Numismatic Society.
     Title varies: Mar. 1955-Oct. 1959*, SENTINEL.
     Oct. 1959-Jan. 1972

CHANGE. BULLETIN TRIMESTRIAL D'INFORMATION. Paris.
     1963-1970*

CHECKLIST; CHECK COLLECTOR'S ROUND TABLE. Robert
Flaig, Cincinnati, Ohio.
     v.1-; 1970-

CHICAGO COIN CLUB BULLETIN.
     1936-1952, 1957, 1969

CIVIL WAR TOKEN SOCIETY JOURNAL.
     v.1-; 1967-

LE CLUB FRANCAIS DE LA MEDAILLE. Paris.
     1969, 1973-1975

COIN AND MEDAL BULLETIN. Edgar H. Adams and Wayte
Raymond, New York.
     April 1916-Mar. 1917

COIN AND MEDALLION NEWSLETTER. Crown Agents
Coin Bureau, Sutton, Surrey, England.
     no.32-; Mar. 1974-

COIN COLLECTOR'S JOURNAL. Scott Stamp and Coin
Co., New York.
     v.1-13; Dec. 1875-Dec. 1888
     New Series, v.1-21; Apr. 1934-Dec. 1954

COIN DEALER. Iola, Wisc.
     v.1 no.1-v.4, no.6; Sept. 1963-Aug. 1966

COIN DEALER NEWSLETTER. World Mint, Gardenia, Calif.
     1964-1970*

COIN GALLERIES.
     See NUMISMATIC REVIEW.

COIN HOBBY NEWS. Roy C. Lawrence, Anamosa, Iowa.
     June 1972-April 1974

COIN INVESTOR. Morland Lee, Ltd., London.
     no.1-13; 1969

THE COIN JOURNAL. Lancaster, Pa.
     v.1-3; 1880-1882*

COIN MARKET REPORT. N. Little Rock, Ark.
     2v.; June 1965-Jan. 1967

COIN MART. D. Benge, Burbank, Calif.
     1969-1973*

COIN MONTHLY. Numismatic Publishing Co., Brentwood Essex,
England.
     v.1-; Aug. 1966-*

COIN NEWS.
     See COIN PRESS.

COIN-ODDITY. Philadelphia, Pa.
     v.1-6,8,9; 1965-1967

COIN PRESS MAGAZINE. Chester L. Krause, Iola, Wisconsin.
     v.5-8; Dec. 1959-Dec. 1961
     Title varies: v.1, no.5-v.5, no.4, 1955-959, FLYING
     EAGLET; v.5, no.5-6, Sept.-Oct. 1959, COIN NEWS
     MAGAZINE; v.5, Nov. 1959-v.8, Dec. 1961, COIN PRESS
     MAGAZINE; v.9-, 1962-, COINS.

COIN, STAMP, ANTIQUE NEWS. Toronto.
     v.9-; 1971-*

COIN TOPICS. Wayte Raymond, New York.
     1936-37; 1936-40

COIN WHOLESALER. Kansas.
     v.1 no. 1-12; Sept. 18-Dec. 4, 1963

COIN WHOLESALER. Chattanooga, Tenn.
     1971-1974*

COIN WORLD. Sidney, Ohio.
    v.14-; 1973

COINAGE. Behn-Miller, Encino, Calif.
    v.1-; 1964-

COINS.
    See COIN PRESS MAGAZINE.

COINS. [British]
    See COINS AND MEDALS.

COINS AND MEDALS. Croyden, England.
    v.1-; 1964-
    Title varies: v.1-6, 11-; 1964-1969, 1974-
    COINS AND MEDALS. v.7-10, 1970-1973, COINS.

COINS AND MEDALS.
    See SEABY'S COIN AND MEDAL BULLETIN.

COINS DIGEST. Coins, medals and currency weekly, London.
    Aug. 1969-May 1970*

COINS, STAMPS AND COLLECTING.
    March 6, 1971-Jan. 22, 1972

COINS UNLIMITED. Houston, Texas.
    v.1, no.1-v.3, no.11; Aug. 1957-June 1960*

THE COAST COINER. Rockford, Washington.
    1954-1957*

COLLECTIBLE TRENDS MONTHLY NEWSLETTER. Cleveland, Ohio.
    v.4, no.4-; April 1875-
    See also ART N' TIQUES TRENDS for former issues.

COLONIAL NEWSLETTER. Huntsville, Alabama.
    March 1964-*

CURRENCY COLLECTOR; FOR COLLECTORS OF FOREIGN PAPER
MONEY. World Paper Currency Collectors.
    v.4-12, no.1; 1963-1971
    Index to v.1-4.
    Membership directory 1908, 1966

ELDER MONTHLY. Thomas Elder.
    March 1906-Jan. 1911*
    Title varies: March 1906-March 1908, ELDER MAGAZINE.
    Nov. 1909, NUMISMATIC PHILISTINE. Jan. 1910-
    Jan. 1911, ELDER MAGAZINE.

EMPIRE REVIEW. Empire Coin Co., Johnson City, New York.
    no. 14-19; Aug./Sept. 1961-Apr./May 1964.
    Title varies: no.1-11, 1958-60, EMPIRE TOPICS;
    1960-1961, BOWERS REVIEW; no. 14-19; Aug./Sept. 1961-
    Apr./May 1964, EMPIRE REVIEW.

EMPIRE TOPICS.
     See EMPIRE REVIEW.

ERRORSCOPE. Numismatic Error Collectors of America, Westminster, Calif.
     May 1966, July 1966, March 1967-

ERROR TRENDS. Oceanside, New York.
     v.1-; 1968-

ESSAY PROOF JOURNAL. Essay Proof Society.
     v.12-; 1955-

EX-SPAN-SION. Society of Philatelists and Numismatists,
Lima, Pa.
     v.3-; June/July 1970-

FAR EAST NUMISMATIC DIGEST. A.D. Craig, Berkeley, Calif.
     no. 1-5; Jan. 1957-Mar. 1961

FARE BOX. American Vecturist Association.
     v.9-; 1955-
     Membership roster AVA: 1964, 1967-68, 1970-72

FINANCE AND DEVELOPMENT. International Monetary Fund and
the World Bank Group, Washington, D.C.
     1969-1974*

THE FLYING EAGLET.
     See COIN PRESS MAGAZINE.

FOREIGN COIN BULLETIN.
     See WORLD COIN BULLETIN.

FOREIGN PAPER MONEY JOURNAL. Dwight Mussler, W. Virginia.
     v.1-2; July 1957-June 1959
     Title varies: v.3, July 1959-Nov. 1959, WORLD PAPER
     MONEY JOURNAL.

FORUM. Tulsa, Oklahoma.
     v.1, no.1-9,11; v.2, 1-4; July 1966-October 1967*

FRANCE. RAPPART AU MINISTRE DU FINANCE. ANNUAL REPORT.
     1957-1966

FRANKLIN MINT ANNUAL REPORTS.
     1968, 1972-74

THE GOBRECHT JOURNAL. Kamal M. Ahwash, Wallingford, Pa.
     December 1974-

GOLD BUG.
     See POLITICAL AMERICANA.

GREAT BRITAIN. ROYAL MINT. ANNUAL REPORTS.
     v.1-93, 98, 102, 103; 1870-1952, 1962, 1967, 1972-73

GUIDE DU COLLECTIONEUR.
     v.1-2, no. 2-23; October 1969-July 1971

HAMBURGER BEITRAGE ZUR NUMISMATIK. Hamburg.
     New series: v.1-5; 1951-1963*

HELVETISCHE MUNZEN ZEITUNG. Albert Meier, Lucerne.
     v.1-5; 1966-1970, Jan. 1971, Mar. 1971, Oct. 1972

HOBBIES. Lightner Publishing Co., Chicago.
     Feb. 1935-Dec. 1943, Feb. 1955-Dec. 1967*, 1968-

HUTT PNC NEWS. New Zealand.
     June 1974-

IL GAZZETTINO NUMISMATICO.
     1973-*

IMF SURVEY. International Monetary Fund, Washington.
     1972-

INTERCOIN. International Coin Society of San Diego.
     Feb. 1964; July 1964-Feb. 1967

INTERNATIONAL BANKNOTE SOCIETY. Essex, England.
     June 1962-
     Membership directories: 1965, 1968-1970

INTERNATIONAL COIN PRESS. International Coin Press, Inc.,
Butler, N.J.
     v.1, no.1-8; 1973-1974*

INTERNATIONAL FINANCIAL NEWS SURVEY. International Monetary Fund, Washington.
     v.23, no. 18-v.24, no. 25*; May 12, 1971-June 23
     1972*

IRISH NUMISMATICS. Stagecast Publications, Dublin.
     Jan. 1968-Dec. 1972*, Sept.-Oct. 1974

ITALIA NUMISMATICA. Oscar Renaldi, Mantova, Italy.
     Feb. 1960, April 1965-Dec. 1971

JASSY. UNIVERSITAE. ANALELE STIINTIFICE.
     See ANALELE STIINTIFICE.

JOURNAL OF INTERNATIONAL NUMISMATICS. Organization of
International Numismatics.
     1968-*
     Title varies: 1968-Oct. 1971, OIN-O-GRAM. Oct. 1971-
     JOURNAL OF INTERNATIONAL NUMISMATICS.

JOURNAL OF ISRAEL NUMISMATICS. UN Plaza, New York.
     Feb. 1966-April 1969

JOURNAL OF NUMISMATIC FINE ARTS.   Joel L. Malter, Encino,
California.
        January 1971-*

JOURNAL OF THE NUMISMATIC SOCIETY OF INDIA.   Bombay,
India.
        1940, 1943-46, 1952-July, 1953
        PROCEEDINGS;   1910-12, 1918, 1921, 1923, 1934, 1937

JOURNAL OF THE SOCIETY FOR INTERNATIONAL NUMISMATICS.
The Society for International Numismatics, Santa Monica,
California.
        Jan. 1968-Sept. 1969

KAYAK.   Coin Irregularity Association of Canada, Toronto.
        v.1, no.1-v.2, no.4; Jan. 1971-April 1972

KELLY'S COINS AND CHATTER.   James Kelly, Dayton, Ohio.
        July 1948-June 1961

MASON'S COIN COLLECTOR'S MAGAZINE.
        v.6, no.1-6; 1872
        Title varies: v.1-5, 1867-1871, MASON'S COIN AND
        STAMP COLLECTORS MAGAZINE. v.6, no. 1-6, 1872,
        MASON'S COIN COLLECTOR'S MAGAZINE.

MEDAL COLLECTOR.   Orders and Medals Society of America.
        v.3-4; 1952-1953*
        v.2-10; Apr. 1955-1969*
        Title varies: Jan/Mar. 1954-Mar. 1955
        MEDAL COLLECTOR BULLETIN.

MEDAL COLLECTOR BULLETIN.   Orders and Medals Society
of America.
        See MEDAL COLLECTOR.

MEDAL WORLD.   FBG Enterprises, Kermit, Texas.
        v.1-; Dec. 1974-

MEDALLIC MONTHLY.   Mandeville, La.
        v.1, no.1-7; Oct. 1967-Apr. 1968

MEHL'S NUMISMATIC MONTHLY; AN ILLUSTRATED NUMISMATIC
JOURNAL DEVOTED TO COINS, MEDALS, AND PAPER MONEY.
B. Max Mehl, Fort Worth, Texas.
        v.1-10; 1908-1919

MEMORIAS ACADEMIA MEXICANA DE ESTUDIOS.   Mexico City.
        v.1-v.2, no. 8; 1970-1973

MEXICO.   CASA DE MONEDA.   Annual Reports.
        1944-1946, 1948-1953, 1955-1956

MINTMARK.   Numismatic Society of Aukland Inc.
Aukland, New Zealand.
        no. 96-; 1967-*

MODERN COINS AND BANKNOTES. Spink & Son Ltd, London.
     v.1-v.3, no.3; Nov. 1970-June 1973*

MODERN MEDALS. FBG Enterprises, Kermit, Texas.
     1974-1975

MONEY TALKS. Superior Stamp and Coin Co., Los
Angeles.
     1970-*

MONEY TRENDS. INTERNATIONALE NUMISMATISCHE MON-
ATZEITSCHRIFT FUR DEUTSCHLAND, OSTERREICH, SCHWEIZ
UND LIECHTENSTEIN. Liechtenstein.
     Aug. 1972, Feb. 1973-*

MORAVSKE NUMISMATICKE SPRAVY. Czechoslavakia.
     1967-1973

MOUNTAIN STATES COIN COLLECTOR. Denver, Colorado.
     See WESTERN COIN COLLECTOR.

MUNZEN REVUE. Basel.
     v.3-; 1971-*

NATIONAL BANK OF ETHIOPIA. QUARTERLY BULLETIN.
     1972-1974

NATIONAL SCULPTURE REVIEW. National Sculpture
Society, New York.
     v.1:3- ;1952

NEW ZEALAND COIN COLLECTOR. Coin Publishing Co.,
Lower Hutt, N.Z.
     v.1, no.5-11; n.d.

NEW ZEALAND COIN NEWS. P.O. Box 12121, Wellington
North, N.Z.
     Oct. 1966-May 1968*

NEW ZEALAND NUMISMATIC JOURNAL. Proceedings of
the Numismatic Society. Wellington, N.Z.
     v.4-13; 1947-74
     INDEX; 1947-1966

99 NEWS. 99 Company, San Clemente, Calif.
     v.1-; July 1968-*

NORDISK NUMISMATISK ARSSKRIFT. SCANDANAVIAN NUM-
ISMATIC JOURNAL. The Royal Academy of Letters,
History and Antiquities in collaboration with the
Scandanavian Numismatic Union. Lund, Sweden.
     1960-*

NORTH AMERICAN JOURNAL OF NUMISMATICS. Argonaut,
Chicago.
     v.4-8; 1965-1969
     Title varies: Dec. 1964-Dec. 1966, THE VOICE
     OF THE TURTLE; Jan.-Jun. 1968, Jan.-Mar. 1969,
     THE TURTLE.

NUMISMA; AN OCCASIONAL NUMISMATIC PAMPHLET.
Privately printed, Pittsburg, Pa.
     1939-1948*

NUMISMA. Edward Frossard, Irvington, New York.
     v.1-9; 1877-1885

NUMISMA. Ibero-American Numismatic Society, Madrid.
     1953-1965*

NUMISMATIC AND ANTIQUARIAN SOCIETY OF PHILADELPHIA.
PROCEEDINGS.
     Annual: 1887-1924*

NUMISMATIC AND PHILATELIC JOURNAL OF JAPAN.
H.A. Ramsden, Yokahama.
     v.1, no.1-6, v.3, no.6; 1913-1914*

NUMISMATIC ASSOCIATION OF SOUTHERN CALIFORNIA
QUARTERLY. Santa Monica, Calif.
     v.1-; 1959-*

NUMISMATIC CHRONICLE. Royal Numismatic Society.
London.
     1881-

NUMISMATIC CIRCULAR. Spink, London.
     v.1-; Dec. 1892-

NUMISMATIC DIGEST.
     See WESTERN COIN COLLECTOR.

NUMISMATIC GAZETTE. Corbitt and Hunter Ltd, New-
castle-upon-Tyne, England.
     v.3-6; Aug. 1964-Mar. 1967

NUMISMATIC LITERARY GUILD NEWSLETTER. Numismatic
Literary Guild. Santa Ana, Calif.
     v.6-; 1973-*

NUMISMATIC LITERATURE. American Numismatic Society.
New York.
     no.1-; Oct. 1947-

NUMISMATIC MAGAZINE. C.H. Nunn, Bury St. Edmunds,
England.
     v.7; 1892

NUMISMATIC MESSENGER. Castenholz and Sons. Palisades,
Calif.
     v.1; 1971-1972*

NUMISMATIC NEWS WEEKLY. Krause Publications, Iola,
Wisconsin.
     v.1-; 1954-

NUMISMATIC REVIEW; A SCIENTIFIC DIGEST PERTAINING
TO COINS, MEDALS, AND PAPER MONEY. Stacks, New York.
     v.1-4; June 1943-Apr/Oct. 1947

NUMISMATIC REVIEW AND COIN GALLERIES FIXED PRICE
LIST. Coin Galleries. New York.
     v.1-13; 1960-1972*

NUMISMATIC SCRAPBOOK. Sidney Printing and Publishing Co., Sidney, Ohio.
     v.1-; 1935-
     TITLE INDEX; 1935-1964

NUMISMATIC SOCIETY OF INDIA. JOURNAL.
     See JOURNAL OF THE NUMISMATIC SOCIETY OF INDIA.

NUMISMATICA. P & P Santa Maria. Rome.
     1966

NUMISMATICA. REVISTA SOCIEDAD NUMISMATICA DEL
PERU. Lima.
     no. 14-; 1973-*

NUMISMATICKE LISTY. Narodni Muzeum a numismaticka
spolecnost Ceskoslovenska, Prague.
     v.17-; 1962-

NUMISMATICKY CASOPIS CESKOSLOVENSKY; REVUE
NUMISMATIQUE TCHECOSLOVAQUE. Prague.
     v.1-9; 1925-1933*

NUMISMATICS. Romano's Coin Shop, Springfield, Mass.
     Mar. 1931-Dec. 1932

THE NUMISMATIST. American Numismatic Association,
Colorado Springs, Colorado.
     v.1-; 1888-
     INDEX; v.1-51; 1888-1938
     INDEX: v.52-71; 1939-1958

NUMISMATOLOGY. T. Forster, London, Colchester.
     v.1-3; 1892-1894

OIN-O-GRAM.
     See JOURNAL OF INTERNATIONAL NUMISMATICS.

PACIFIC NORTHWEST NUMISMATIC ASSOCIATION NEWS.
Walla Walla, Washington.
     v.1-4; Apr. 1962-June 1964*

PAPER MONEY. Society of Paper Money Collectors, Anderson, S.C.
     v.1-; 1962-
     Index to v.1-10.

PARAMOUNT JOURNAL. Paramount International Coin Corp.,
Englewood, Ohio.
     v.1-; May 1973-

PENNY. Harry E. Parshall, Wheeling, W. Virginia.
     March 1963-May 1968*

PENNY-WISE; EARLY AMERICAN COPPERS. Brentwood, Long
Island, New York.
     v.2-; 1968*

A PERMUTA. Portuguese Numismatic Society, Portugal.
     1953-1961*

POLITICAL AMERICANA.
     March 1966-September 1970
     Title varies: March 1959-December 1965, GOLD BUG;
     March 1966-September 1970, POLITICAL AMERICANA.

PROOF COLLECTORS CORNER. World Proof Coins Association,
Pittsburgh, Pennsylvania.
     June 1967-December 1970, 1972-74

THE RAG PICKER. Paper Money Collectors of Michigan.
     v.10, no.1-; Jan.-Feb., 1975-

RARE COIN ADVISORY. First Coinvestors, Inc., Albertson,
New York.
     v.5-; 1971-*

RATION BOARD. Society of Ration Token Collectors, Plain-
field, New Jersey.
     1966-

REVIEW OF THE ECONOMIC SITUATION OF MEXICO. Banco Nacional
de Mexico, S.A., Mexico.
     v.48-; 1972-

REVISTA NUMISMATICA ARGENTINA. Asociacion Numismatica
Argentina, Buenos Aires.
     1960-1971*

REVUE BELGE DE NUMISMATIQUE. Societe Royale de Numismatique, Brussels.
     1895-1967*; 1969-

REVUE NUMISMATIQUE. Societe Francaise de Numismatique,
Paris.
     1906-1964*

SAN.   Society for Ancient Numismatics, Glendale,
California.
     v.1-; July 1969-

SCIENCE ON THE MARCH.   Buffalo Museum of Science, Buffalo.
     September 1974-February 1975

SEABY'S COIN AND MEDAL BULLETIN.
     1936-46*; 1947-
     Title varies: 1936-40, COINS AND MEDALS; 1940-
     1945, COIN AND MEDAL LIST; 1945-46*, 1947-,
     SEABY'S COIN AND MEDAL BULLETIN.

SENTINEL.
     See CENTINEL.

THE SHEKEL.   American Israel Numismatic Association, New
York.
     v.1- ; 1968-

SILVER INSTITUTE LETTER.   The Silver Institute, Washington.
     v.2, no.2-; 1971-

SIN FORMATION.   Society for International Numismatics,
Santa Monica, California.
     1964-1967*, 1972-*

SKANDINAVISK NUMISMATIK.   Numismatisk Monadstidskrift,
Stockholm.
     October 1972-

SOCIEDAD NUMISMATICA DE MEXICO.   BOLETIN.   Mexico City.
     October 1952-April 1967*; April 1967-

SOCIETY OF MEDALISTS, NEWS BULLETIN.   Weston, Connecticut.
     1971-

SOTHEBY PARKE BERNET NEWSLETTER.   New York.
     Jan.-April 1973, October-December 1973

SOUTH AFRICAN DIGEST.   Republic of South Africa, Pretoria.
     June 12, 1972-

SOUTH AUSTRALIAN NUMISMATIC JOURNAL.
     See AUSTRALIAN NUMISMATIC JOURNAL.

TAMS JOURNAL.   Token and Medal Society.
     v.1-; 1961-

TASMANIAN NUMISMATIC SOCIETY NEWSLETTER.   Hobart.
     October 1968-

TODAY'S COINS.   FBG Enterprises, Kermit, Texas.
     October 1, 1972-

TOPICAL TIME. American Topical Association, Milwaukee.
     1972-*

TRADE TOKEN TOPICS. Merchant Token Collectors Assoc.
     1971-72

U. K. COINS.
     1964-65*

U.S. DEPT. OF THE TREASURY. BUREAU OF THE MINT. ANNUAL
REPORTS.
     1868-1913*, 1924-

U.S. DEPT. OF THE TREASURY. BUREAU OF THE MINT NEWS.
     1973-

VOICE OF THE TURTLE.
     See NORTH AMERICAN JOURNAL OF NUMISMATICS.

WALL STREET COIN INVESTOR. Coin Investor, Vancouver,
Washington.
     1973-*

WESTERN COIN COLLECTOR. Denver, Colorado.
     April 1965-March 1968
     Title varies: Feb. 1965-April 1965, MOUNTAIN STATES
     COIN COLLECTOR; April 1965-March 1968, WESTERN COIN
     COLLECTOR; April 1968-, NUMISMATIC DIGEST.

WESTERN COIN JOURNAL. Western Coin Journal Pub. Co.,
Roseda, California.
     1959-1961*

WHITMAN COIN SUPPLY MERCHANDISER. Western Pub. Co.,
Racine, Wisconsin.
     October-November 1963, 1969-72*

WHITMAN NUMISMATIC JOURNAL. Whitman Publishing Co.,
Racine, Wisconsin.
     v.1-5; 1964-68

WHITMAN STAMP & COIN SUPPLY MERCHANDISER.
     See WHITMAN COIN SUPPLY MERCHANDISER.

WORLD COIN BULLETIN. Charles W. Amery, Peoria, Illinois.
     1960-March 1963
     Title varies: Oct.-Dec. 1959, FOREIGN COIN BULLETIN;
     1960-March 1963, WORLD COIN BULLETIN.

WORLD COIN NEWS. Krause Publications, Iola, Wisconsin.
     December 1973-

WORLD COINS. Sydney, Ohio.
     v.1-; 1964-

WORLD PAPER MONEY JOURNAL.
    See FOREIGN PAPER MONEY JOURNAL.

YOUNG NUMISMATIST. American Numismatic Association, Colorado Springs, Colorado.
    v.1-; 1971-

PART V

Auction Catalogues

<u>AUCTION</u> <u>CATALOGS</u>

Holdings may not be complete.
Prices realized are included with catalogs when available.
FPL indicates fixed price lists.

A-MARK (LOS ANGELES, CA)
     1972-1973
     Collection: Bitler (Mar. 1973)

ADAMS, CHARLES (LONDON) see MCSORLEY, CHARLES (NJ)

ADAMS, GEOFFREY CHARLTON (NY)
     1903-1906

AHLSTROM, B. (MYNT AND MEDALJER)
     FPL and auction catalogs are interfiled.
     1964-

AIELLO, JOHN (HEWITT, NJ)
     1972
     Collection: Morris

ALMANZAR'S (SAN ANTONIO, TX)
     FPL: 1964-
     Auction catalogs: 1970-1975
     Collections:
          King Farouk (Aug. 1972)
          Medina (1970, 1971)
          Schaaf (Septemember, 1974)

AMERICAN AUCTION ASSN. see BOWERS & RUDDY (HOLLYWOOD, CA)

AMERICAN NUMISMATIC ASSN. (COLORADO SPRINGS, CO)
     Convention programs: 1931-
     Convention auctions: 1935-

ANCIENT ARTS (BUFFALO, NY)
     FPL: 1965

ANCIENT COINS (BERKELEY, CA)
     1971-1975

ANTIQUITY IMPORTS (MINNEAPOLIS, MN)
     FPL: 1976-

ARS CLASSICA, S.A. (GENEVA, SWITZERLAND)
     1933-1934

ARS ET NUMMUS see NASCIA, GIUSEPPE (MILAN, ITALY)

ARTEMIS ANTIQUITIES (ST. PETERSBURG, FL)
     FPL: 1968?, 1970, no date

ASSOCIATED COIN AUCTION CO. (JERSEY CITY, NJ)
    1955-1957

BALL, ROBERT (BERLIN, GERMANY)
    1905, 1930-1934, 1937

BANGS, MERWIN & CO. (NY)
    1859-1897
    Collections:
        Bartow (1889)   Bogert (1859)
        Bushnell (1882)   Carter (1880)
        Chapman (1879)   Clark (1885)
        Cleveland (1872)   Haines-Hamlen (1887)
        Hibbard (1883)   Hitchcock (1881)
        Packer (1871)   Parker (1874)
        Palmer (1880)   Parmelee (1890)
        Smith (1880)   White (1876)
        Wiswell (1885)   Woodwide (1892)

BANK LEU (ZURICH, SWITZERLAND)
    FPL: 1972-
    Auction catalogs: 1962-
    Collections:
        Napolean Family (1974)
        Niggeler (1966, 1967)
        Stuker (1972)
        Vinzi (1973)

BANK LEU (ZURICH, SWITZERLAND) see also HESS, ADOLPH
    (FRANKFURT/MAIN, GERMANY)

BANK LEU (ZURICH, SWITZERLAND) see also KUNDIG, M. W.
    (GENEVA, SWITZERLAND)

BARANOWSKY, MICHELLE (MILAN, ITALY)
    1929-1932
    Collections:
        Martine (1931)
        Traverso (1931)

BARZAN, R. & RAG. M. RAVIOLA (TORINO, ITALY)
    1949-1952

BAUER, GEORGE J. (ROCHESTER, NY)
    1940-1951
    Collection: Gillette (1942)

BAYERISCHE VERINSBANK (MUNICH, GERMANY)
    1974, 1976

BEEBEE STAMP & COIN CO. (OMAHA, NE)
    FPL: 1943-1972
    Auction catalogs: 1954-1957
    Collection: Wade (1956)

BEN'S STAMP & COIN CO. (CHICAGO, IL)
    1944-1946, 1961

BERLINER MUNZ-CABINET (BERLIN, GERMANY)
    1972-1973

BERTRAND, ARTHUS (PARIS, FRANCE)
    FPL: 1925

BERUBE, HENRY J., CATALOGUER see NEW ENGLAND COIN CO.

BIRCH, THOMAS (PHILADELPHIA, PA)
    1869-1888
    Collections:
        Balmanno (1873)
        Bodey (1872)
        Dickeson (1870)
        Kirkpatrick (1887)
        Thorn (1869)

BLANC, DAVID, JR. (AUSTIN, TX)
    FPL: 1972-1975

BLASER-FREY, HELGA (FREIBURG, GERMANY)
    1962-1963, 1968

BLUESTONE, BARNEY (SYRACUSE, NY)
    FPL: 1937-1938, 1947
    Auction Catalogs: 1932-1946
    Collection: Grinnel (1944-1946)

BOLENDER, M. H. (SAN MARINO, CA)
    1928-1960
    Collections:
        Baird (1944)   Butterfield (1960)
        Clark (Nov. 1932)   Cox (1947)
        Erickson (1944)   Etting (1944)
        Feldmann (1951)   Fitzgerald (1942)
        Fox (1951)   Gray (1945)
        Harris (1948)   Hoffman (1951)
        Kennedy (1943)   Lau (1945)
        Long (1958)   McGill (1950-1951)
        Paget (1947)   Reis (1937)
        Savage (1950)   Schaef (1951)
        Schield (1943-1944)   Schuttte (1944)
        Smith (1935)   Smith (1945)
        Stuart (1960)   Thomas (1958)
        Vanarsdell (1944)   Williams (1950)
        Woods (1938)

BOURGEY, EMILE (PARIS, FRANCE)
        1944-
        Collections:
          Castaing (1976)
          Chevaillier (1973)
          France (1972)
          Maya, de Castro (1957)
          Schott (1972)

BOURGEY, ETIENNE (PARIS, FRANCE)
        1906-1932
        Collections:
        Cheabenot, Part 2 (1911)
        Salles (1929)

BOWERS AND RUDDY (CA)
    FPL: 1956
    FPL: "Bower's Reviews": 1960-1961
    FPL: "Special Coin Letter": 1975-
    FPL: "Rare Coin Reviews": 1971-
    Auction catalogs: 1972-
    Collections:
        Austin (1974)   Caldwell (1973)
        Champa (1972)   Dundee (1976)
        Hustal (1974)   Kensington (1975)
        Krugjohann (1976)   Larsen (1972)
        Marks (1972)   Montgomery (1976)
        Merriweather (1973)   Nagorka (1974)
        Num. Assn. of S. CA   Paxman (1974)
          (1974)   Ray (1973)
        Rothert (1973)   Terrell (1973)
        Winthrop (1975)

BRAUNSCHWEIGER MUNZVERKEHR (BRAUNSCHWEIG, GERMANY)
    1927-1928

BREEN, WALTER, CATALOGUER see
    AMERICAN NUMISMATIC ASSN. (1952-1971)
    HARMER-ROOKE (NOV. 1971)
    LESTER MERKIN (1963 FRACTIONAL CURRENCY LIST;
        Auctions 1964-1972)
    NEW NETHERLANDS (Auctions 39-56, 60)
    PINE TREE (Sept. 1973)
    STACK'S (1954 Dupont Sale I-II)

BULLOWA, C. E. (PHILADELPHIA, PA)
    FPL: no dates
    Auction catalogs: 1963-

BULLOWA, DAVID (PHILADELPHIA, PA)
    FPL: 1947-1959
    Auction catalogs: 1946-1958

BURGGRAFF, ROBERT (LOWDEN, WA)
    1963-1971

BUTTON, E. (FRANKFURT, GERMANY)
    1960-1972

CAHN, ADOLPH E. (FRANKFURT/MAIN, GERMANY)
    1926-1933
    Collections:
        Haeberlin (1932)
        Hahn (1928)
        Moritz (1930)
        Peltzer (1926)

CALDWELL, COL.
    1976-

CALICO, X. & F. (BARCELONA, SPAIN)
    1957-1974

CALIFORNIA STATE NUMISMATIC ASSN. (CA)
    1948-1969, 1971, 1975

CANADA COIN EXCHANGE (CANADA) see
    C.N.A. CONVENTION AUCTIONS
    CANADIAN PAPER MONEY SOCIETY (Feb. 1970)
    TORONTO COIN CLUB (Oct. 1964)
    EMPIRE STATE NUMISMATIC SOCIETY (May 1970)

C. N. A. CONVENTION AUCTIONS (CANADA COIN EXCHANGE)
    1954-1961, 1964-1972

CAYON, JUAN R. (MADRID, SPAIN)
    1967-1968, 1971

CELINA COIN CO. (LIMA, OH)
    FPL: 1948-1949, no dates
    Auction catalogs: 1945-1951

CHAPMAN, HENRY (PHILADELPHIA, PA)
    1907-1921
    Collections:
        Baldwin (April 1911)
        Bement, C. S. (Mar. 1916)   Butz (Dec. 1918)
        Davis (1916)   Earle (1912)
        Gable (1914)   Gray (1916)
        Heinrich (1917)   Hoare (1918)
        Jackman (1918)   Jenks (1921)
        Jerrems (1915)   Johnston (1918)
        Noegel (1915)   Nygren (1924)
        Ochme (1916)   Parsons (1914)
        Peabody (1916)   Siedlecki (1911)
        Sisson (1916)   Stickney (1907)
        White (1917)   Zabriskie (1909)

CHAPMAN, S. H. (PHILADELPHIA, PA)
     1907-1924
     Collections:
          Alvord (1924)   Beckwith (1923)
          Bindon (1907)   Brown (1911)
          Gregory (1916)   Hunter (1920)
          Jewett (1909)   Kingman (1920)
          Lambert (1910)   Simpson (1924)
          Wilson (1907)   Zimmerman (1907)
          Zug (1907, 1909)

CHAPMAN, S. H. & H. (PHILADELPHIA, PA)
1882-1906
     Collections:
          Alden (1896)   Barker (1904)
          Barton (June 1902)   Bourguin (Dec. 1897)
          Bushnell (1882)   Chapman (1879)
          Collier (1879)   Disbrow (1896, 1903)
          Elwell (1897)   Fletcher (1895)
          Haines (1888)   Hayes (1896)
          Humbert (1902)   Johnston (1897)
          Kassabaum (1895)   Kinney (1895)
          McCabe (1905)   Maris (1900)
          Mills (1904)   Morris (1905)
          Nexon (Dec. 1904)   Risse (June 1903)
          Schwartz (1898)   Seagrave (1898)
          Smith, H. (1906)   Smith, W. T. (1896)
          Snow (1888)   Steffan (1895)
          Stevaens (1902)   Warner (1891)
          Weeks (1902)   Wetmore (1906)
          Whitman (1893)   Winsor (1895)
          Wood (1896)

CHAPMAN, S. H. & H., CATALOGUERS (PHILADELPHIA, PA) see also
     BANGS, MERWIN & CO. (NY) (June 1882; Oct. 1879)

CHARLTON NUMISMATICS LTD. (TORONTO, ONTARIO)
     1972-1975
     Collection: Allan (Oct. 1972; Feb. 1973; Sept. 1973;
          Jan. 1974; June 1974)

CHRISTENSEN, HENRY (HOBOKEN, NJ)
     FPL: no dates, 1956-1957, 1965-1970
     Auction catalogs: 1956-
     Collections:
          Babbit (1963)   Bishop (1969)
          Brooke (1968)   Herding (1970)
          Krite (1968)   Lipno (1961)
          Nesmith (1970)   Parsons (1965-1966)
          Prober-Noronha (1963)   Roshom (1963)
          Rumhel (1959)   San Cristobal (1962)
          Sundstrum (1959)   Ubilla-Echenez (1964)
          Werner (1969)

CHRISTIE'S (LONDON, ENGLAND)
     1949-1950, 1962-
     Collections:
          Margadale-Wernher (1971)
          Monckton (1973)
          Northwick Park (Dec. 1965)
          O'Byrne (July 1962)
          Oman & Son (1972)
          Wentworth (1949)

CIANI, M. L. (PARIS, FRANCE)
     1924-1936
     Collection: Caron (1926)

CLARK'S ANCIENT COINS (DOUGLAS, WY)
     FPL: 1972-1974
     Auction catalogs: 1974-

CLEVELAND COIN AUCTIONS (CLEVELAND, OH)
     1962-1964

COBB, JOHN (LOS ALTOS HILLS, CA)
     1963-1966

COBB, JOHN, CATALOGUER (LOS ALTOS HILLS, CA) see also
     CA STATE NUMISMATIC ASSN. (Apr. 1964-Nov. 1967)

COHEN, JERRY, CATALOGUER see KREISBERG, ABNER (BEVERLY
     HILLS, CA)

COGAN, EDWARD, CATALOGUER see
     BANGS, MERWIN & CO. (NY) (Feb. 1871-May 1875)

COIN GALLERIES (NEW YORK, NY)
     FPL: 1955-1972
     Auction catalogs: 1954-
     Collections:
          Cole (1962)
          Collier (1956)
          Komm (1955)
          Ross (1954)
          Smullyan (1958)
          Swords-Miller (1958)

COINHUNTER see BULLOWA, C. E. (PHILADELPHIA, PA)

COIN IS KING (NY)
     1964-1965

COINQUEST (POMONA PARK, FL)
     1975

COIN SHOP, INC, (WASHINGTON, DC)
     1969
     Collection: Budde (1969)

THE COIN SHOP (ALAMEDA, CA)
    1938-1941, 1946

COINS & ANTIQUITIES, LTD. (LONDON, ENGLAND)
    FPL: 1970-

COINS AND CURRENCY see KABEALO, S. J. (PASADENA, CA)

COINS & CURRENCY, INC. (PHILADELPHIA, PA)
    FPL: 1955, 1957
    Auction catalogs: 1960-
    Collection: Wismer-Osmuer (1969)

COINS AND MEDALS OF THE WORLD see MARGOLIS (TEANECK, NJ)

COLLINS, JACK, CATALOGUER see
    A-MARK (LOS ANGELES, CA) (Mar, 1973)

COLONY COIN CO. (NEWTONVILLE, MA)
    1967-1973

CONN, ARTHUR - WHITENECK, HAROLD see
    AMERICAN NUMISMATIC ASSN. (Aug. 1960)

COPLEY COIN CO. (BOSTON, MA)
    FPL: 1953-1969

CRIPPA, CARLO (MILAN, ITALY)
    FPL: 1963-1965

CROWTHER, D. J., LTD. (LONDON, ENGLAND)
    FPL: 1966-1971

D & W see DOUGLAS, B. M. (WASHINGTON, DC)

DE FALCO, GIUSEPPE (NAPLES, ITALY)
    FPL: "Numismatica": 1949-1953, 1961-1964

DELAND, C. & L. (FT. WORTH, TX)
    FPL: 1969-

DE MEY, JEAN (BRUSSELS, BELGIUM)
    1974

DE NISE, GENE (SEATTLE, WA)
    1951
    Collection: Ecklund

DESVOUGES, MCANDRE (PARIS, FRANCE)
    1922-1923, 1932-1934

DEVINE, LAWRENCE see FOUNTAINHEAD OF FINE COINS (PORT
    JEFFERSON STATION, NY)

DILLINGHAM, PAUL M. (NASHVILLE, TN)
    FPL: no dates, 1976

DONLON, WILLIAM P. (UTICA, NY)
    1971-1974
    Collection: Donlon (1971)

DOOLEY, JOHN L. (TOPEKA, KS)
    1942-1948, 1954

DOROTHEUM (VIENNA, AUSTRIA)
    1955-1968
    Collection: Zeno (1955-1957)

DOUGLAS, B. M. (WASHINGTON, DC)
    FPL: no date, 1955
    Auction catalogs: 1957-1967

DOWNIE, P. J. (MELBOURNE, AUSTRALIA)
    1964-1968
    Collection: Kingston (1968)

DREIFUSS, J. (ZURICH, SWITZERLAND)
    FPL: 1953-1959

DUPRIEZ (BRUSSELS, BELGIUM)
    FPL: no dates
    Auction catalogs: 1925, 1928, 1934

EGGER, BRUDER (VIENNA, AUSTRIA)
    1912-1913
    Collection: Allerhochsten Kaiserhauses (1912)

EIDELSTEIN & HOLLAND (HAIFA, ISRAEL)
    1975

ELDER, THOMAS (NEW YORK, NY)
    1905-1939
    Collections:
        Adams (1935)   Barcky (1935)
        Bassett (1935)   Bement, C. S. (1923)
        Brevoort (1934)   Burgher (1934)
        Comstock-Gunter (1935)   Foster (1935)
        Gschwend (1908)   Lawrence (1929)
        Livingston (1936)   Miller (1920)
        Mongey (1910)   Parker (1935)
        Wilson-Pehrson (1918)   Stehlin (1917)

EMPIRE STATE NUMISMATIC ASSN.
    1951-1964

FEDERAL BRAND ENTERPRISES (CLEVELAND, OH)
    1961-1967
    Collection: FL United Numismatists (1963)

FEDERAL BRAND ENTERPRISES (CLEVELAND, OH) see also
    AMERICAN NUMISMATIC ASSN. (1964)

FEDERAL COIN EXCHANGE (CLEVELAND, OH)
    FPL: no date
    Auction catalogs: 1947-1961

FEDERAL COIN EXCHANGE (CLEVELAND, OH) see also
    AMERICAN NUMISMATIC ASSN. (1954, 1956-1957, 1959-1960)

FELLOWS, F. (BIRMINGHAM, AL)
    1966-1969

FEUARDENT FRERES (PARIS, FRANCE) see FLORANGE, J. (PARIS,
    FRANCE)

FINARTE (MILAN, ITALY)
    1968, 1972-1973, 1976

FISCHER, CHARLES H. (CLEVELAND, OH)
    1966-1969

FLORANGE, JULES (PARIS, FRANCE)
    1923-1928, 1935, 1937, 1953-1955
    Collections:
        Ciani (1928)
        D'Essling (1927)

FLORANGE (FAMILY) (PARIS, FRANCE)
    1932-1934

FLYNN, JOE, SR. COIN CO. (KANSAS CITY, KS)
    1973-

FORNI, ANRNALDO (BOLOGNA, ITALY)
    1967, 1971-1972

FOUNTAINHEAD OF FINE COINS (PORT JEFFERSON STATION, NY)
    1972-1974

FRANCESCHI, V. (BRUSSELS, BELGIUM)
    1967-1968

FRANKFURTER MUNZHANDLUNG see BUTTON, E. (FRANKFURT/MAIN,
    GERMANY)

FRENCH, A. (TROY, NY)
    1939-1943

FRENCH'S (JENSEN BEACH, FL)
    FPL: no date
    Auction catalogs: 1942-1974
    Collections:
        Colvin (1960)
        Curtis (1951, 1959)
        Lee (1966)
        Mckoy (1968)
        Penn-Ohio Fall Convention (1955)

FRENCH'S see also
    EMPIRE STATE NUMISMATIC ASSN. (May 1956)

FREY, H. P. R. (FREIBURG, GERMANY)
    1955

FROSSARD, ED (NEW YORK, NY)
    1893-1901

FROSSARD, ED, CATALOGUER (NY) see also
    BANGS, MERWIN & CO. (1882-1883)

GALERIE DES MONNAIES GMBH (DUSSELDORF, GERMANY)
    1969-1974

GALERIE DES MONNAIES SA (LAUSANNE, SWITZERLAND)
    1965

GANS, EDWARD see NUMISMATIC FINE ARTS (ENCINO, CA)

GIBBONS, STANLEY (LONDON, ENGLAND)
    FPL: no dates, 1946, 1975
    Auction catalogs: 1972-1973

GLENDINING & CO. (LONDON, ENGLAND)
    1927-
    Collections:
        Bauer (1963)   Bennett (1972)
        Bird (1974)   Brettell (1970)
        Burstal (1958)   Checkly (1965)
        Cotton (1955)   Doubleday (1972)
        Drewry (1971)   Duveen (1964)
        Elmore (1971)   Fishpool Hoard (1968)
        Ford (1975)   Forrer (1954)
        Foster (1953)   Glamis Castle (1974)
        Graham (1963)   Hall (1950)
        Harwood (1975)   Hird (1960)
        Jones (1971)   Lake (1964)
        Lawrence (Pts. 1-4: 1951)   Lawson (1954)
        Leistner (1970)   Lingford (1950-1951)
        Lockett (1955-1958)   Lockett (1974)
        Messinger (1951)   Morton (1951)
        Napier (1956)   Nightingale (1951)
        Parsons (1954)   Peltzer (1927)
        Rashleigh (1953)   Rawls (1970)
        Raymond (1964)   Ryan (1950, 1952)
        Smith (1951)   Symonds (1973)
        Taffs (1956)   Von Halle (1966)

GOLDSMITH & CO. (MONTREAL, CANADA)
    1971
    Collection: Meloche

GRABOW (BERLIN, GERMANY)
    1925-1926, 1934, 1939-1941, 1953-1957, 1967

GRAND CENTRAL see PARAMOUNT INTERNATIONAL (ENGLEWOOD, OH)

GRANT, HORACE M. (PROVIDENCE, RI)
    1938-1942, 1945-1946

GREEN, BEN G. (CHICAGO, IL)
    1902-1914

GREEN, C. E. (CHICAGO, IL)
    FPL: 1939-1940

GREEN, R. (CHICAGO, IL)
    FPL: 1949-1955
    Auction catalogs: 1949-1955

GRUNTHAL, HENRY (NEW YORK, NY)
    FPL: 1941-1952

GRUNTHAL, HENRY (NEW YORK, NY) see also NUMISMATIC FINE
    ARTS (ENCINO, CA)

HABELT, RUDOLF (BONN, W. GERMANY)
    1976

HAMBURGER, LEO (FRANKFURT/MAIN, GERMANY)
    1907-1928
    Collections:
        Ford (1912)
        Phillip (1928)
        Vogel (1925)

HARMER-ROOKE (NEW YORK, NY)
    1945, 1953, 1969-
    Collections:
        Dattari (1971)
        Parlin Gold Nugget Collection (1970)
        Pick (1970)
        Spellman (1970)

HARZFELD, S. K. (PHILADELPHIA, PA) see
    BANGS, MERWIN & CO. (Nov. 1880)

HASELTINE, J. W. (PHILADELPHIA, PA)
    1876

HASELTINE, J. W. (PHILADELPHIA, PA) see also
    BIRCH, THOMAS (JULY 1875, JUNE 1887)
    BANGS, MERWIN & CO. (OCT. 1882)

HATHAWAY & BOWERS GALLERIES, INC. (SANTA FE SPRINGS, CA)
    1969-1971

HELBING, OTTO (MUNICH, GERMANY)
    1913-1960
    Collections:
        Beyl (1928)   Goppl (1960)
        Hermann (1927)   Jager (1927)
        Julius (1932)   Seif (1928)
        Shapero (1971)   Zschiesche-Koder (1913)

HENKESL, STAN V. (PHILADELPHIA, PA)
    1886
    Collection: Maris

HESPERIA ART (PHILIDELPHIA, PA)
    1951-1953

HESPERIA ART (PHILADELPHIA, PA) see also
    EMPIRE NUMISMATIC ASSN. (May 1952)

HESS, ADOLPH (FRANKFURT/MAIN, GERMANY)
    1887-1974
    Collections:
        Desneux (1971)   Evzenberg (1936)
        Gibbs (1956-1957)   Holzmann (1910)
        Kubicki (1908)   Lobbecke (1926)
        Reimann (1891-1892)   Santiago (1961)
        Sedgwick-Berend (1887)   Trau (1935)

HESSLEIN (BOSTON, MA)
    FPL: no date, 1911-1915
    Auction catalogs: 1923-1930
    Collection: Cummings (1923)

HIRSCH, GERHARD (MUNICH, GERMANY)
    1955-1975
    Collection: Von Hohenzollern (1974)

HIRSCH, JACOB (GENEVA, SWITZERLAND)
    1906-1909
    Collections:
        Lobbecke (1906, 1908)
        Weber (1909)

HIRSCH, JACOB, CATALOGUER (GENEVA, SWITZERLAND) see also
    KUNDIG, M. W. (Mar. 1921)

HIRSH, M. C. (STOCKHOLM, SWEDEN)
    FPL: 1967-1971

HOFFMANN, M. H. (FLORENCE, ITALY)
    1885
    Collection: Bardini

HOLLINBECK COIN CO. (DES MOINES, IA)
    FPL: 1947, 1949, 1956
    Auction catalogs: 1940-1950

HOLLINBECK COIN CO. (DES MOINES, IA) see also
    HOLLINBECK-KAGIN

HOLLINBECK COIN CO. (DES MOINES, IA) see also
    KAGIN'S NUMISMATIC AUCTIONS.

HOLLINBECK-KAGIN (DES MOINES, IA)
    1951-1973

HOLLINBECK-KAGIN (DES MOINES, IA) see also
    KAGIN'S NUMISMATIC AUCTIONS.

HOLMBERGS, D. (STOCKHOLM, SWEDEN)
    FPL: 1938
    Auction catalogs: 1922-1935
    Collection: Bonniers (1906)

HOUSTON, W. P. (GERMANY)
    1975-

HUTTER, ALFRED (BALTIMORE, MD)
    FPL: 1953
    Auction catalogs: 1951-1952

INTERGOLD (CANADA) see CHARLTON NUMISMATICS (TORONTO)

INTERNATIONAL COIN CO. (CANADA)
    FPL: no date, 1958

INTERNATIONAL COIN CO. (CANADA) see also
    REGENCY COIN & STAMP CO. LTD (MANITOBA, CANADA)

IVY, STEVE RARE COIN CO. (DALLAS, TX)
    FPL: 1975-

JAMES, INC. (LOUISVILLE, KY)
    FPL: no date, 1955-1956
    Auction catalogs: 1956-1958

JEDSON INTERNATIONAL (SAN ANTONIO, TX)
    FPL: no date, 1969-1971

JOLIE COINS (ROSLYN HEIGHTS, NY)
    FPL: 1959-1967, 1973

KABEALO, S. J. (PASADENA, CA)
    1941, 1945, 1958-1973
    Collections:
        Gough (1951)
        Jory (1957)
        Scott (1963)
        Watson (1962)

KABEALO, S. J., CATALOGUER (PASADENA, CA) see also
    CA STATE NUMIS. ASSN. (Oct. 1948, Apr. 1949)
    NUMIS. ASSN. of S. CA (Feb. 1956, Feb. 1957)

KAGIN'S NUMISMATIC AUCTIONS, INC. (DES MOINES, IA)
    1974-1975

KAGIN'S NUMISMATIC AUCTIONS see also
    HOLLINBECK COIN CO.

KAGIN'S NUMISMATIC AUCTIONS see also
    HOLLINBECK-KAGIN

KAPLAN, SOL (CINCINNATI, OH)
    1943-1947

KASTNER, GITTA (MUNICH, GERMANY)
    1972-1975

KATEN, FRANK (WASHINGTON, DC)
    FPL: "Katen's Bargain List": 1947-1969
    Auction catalogs: 1946-
    Collection: Fuld (1971)

KEEBER, GEORGE W. (NEW YORK, NY)
    1924
    Collection: Dunlap

KELLY, JAMES (ENGLEWOOD, DAYTON, OH)
    FPL: no date, 1939-1947
    Auction catalogs: 1947-1965

KELLY, JAMES (ENGLEWOOD, DAYTON, OH) see also
    KELLY'S COINS & CHATTER (FPL in Periodicals Dept.)

KLENAU, GRAF (MUNICH, GERMANY)
    1969-1975

KLENOVA, KLENAU VON (GERMANY)
    FPL: no date
    Auction catalogs: 1965-1968

KNOBLOCH, FREDERICK S. (BRONX, NY)
    FPL: 1957-1964
    Auction catalogs: 1965-1969
    Collections:
        Bly (1965)   Cordoso (1963-1964)
        Gillespie (1965)   Stanton (1965)
        Umans (1963)   Walker (1965)
        Westervelt (1964)

KOLBE, G. FREDERICK (MISSION VIEJO, CA)
    1976-

KOLNER MUNZKABINETT (COLOGNE, GERMANY)
    1975

KOSOFF, ABE (CA)
    FPL: Kosoff's Coin Bulletin: 1954-1968
    FPL: Numis. Gallery Monthly: 1948-1953
    Auction catalogs: 1940-1973
    Collections:
        Burgett (1958)   Clarke (1956)
        Curtis (1950)   Donlon (1956)
        Epstein (1944)   Furthman (1965)
        Grimm (1961)   Higgy (1943)
        Hydeman (1961)   Kaplan (1943)
        Lahrman (1963)   Levy (1955)
        Marks (1971)   Melish (1956)
        Parks (1957)   Pearl (1944)
        Schwartz (1961)   Shufford (1968)
        Sloss (1959)   Sweyd (1963)
        Talmadge (1950)   Walrath (1948)

KOSOFF, ABE (CA) see also NUMISMATIC ENTERPRISES (CA) and
    NUMISMATIC GALLERY (CA)

KOSOFF, ABE, CATALOGUER
    see also
    CA STATE NUMIS. ASSN. (Oct. 1964, Oct. 1968, Nov. 1971)
    AMERICAN NUMIS. ASSN. (Aug. 1958, Aug. 1968)
    NUMIS. ASSN. of S. CA (Feb. 1966, Feb. 1968

KRAUS, FRNS. FERD. (BRAUNSCHWEIG, GERMANY) see
    BRAUNSCHWEIGER MUNZVERKEHR (GERMANY)

KREISBERG, ABNER (BEVERLY HILLS, CA)
    1955-
    Collections:
        Beck (Jan. 1975, Feb. 1976)
        Fraser (1957)
        Menjou (Jan. 1957)
        Williams (1963)

KREISBERG, ABNER (BERVERLY HILLS, CA) see also
    KOSOFF, ABE (NUMISMATIC GALLERY, CA)
    NUMIS. ASSN. OF S. CA (Feb.-Mar. 1958)

KRESS, KARL (MUNCHEN, GERMANY)
    1963-1975

KRICHELDORF, H. H. (STUTTGART, GERMANY)
    FPL: 1956-1973
    Auction catalogs: 1956-1975

KUNDIG (GENEVA, SWITZERLAND)
    1921-1938
    Collections:
        St. a S. (1936)
        Pozzi (1921)

KUNST UND MUNZEN, A. G. (LUGANO, ITALY)
    1969, 1973

L. & L. COINS (DENVER, CO)
    1976

LANGE, PAUL M. (ROCHESTER, NY)
    1928, 1930

LANZ, HERMANN (GRAZ, AUSTRIA)
    1958-1959, 1972-1975

LEAVITT (NH)
    1870-1893
    Collections:
        Clay (1871)   Groux (1874)
        Haines-Ferguson (1876)   Havana (1876)
        Idler (1870)   Macallister (1873)
        Phillips (1893)   Snow (1878)
        Stenz (1875)

LEISSERING, MANFRED MICHAEL (GERMANY) see
        BERLINER MUNZ-CABINET (BERLIN, GERMANY)

LELANDE (LOS ANGELES, CA)
    1928

LEONARD, JOSEPH (BOSTON, MA)
    1860-1861, 1870

LEPCZYK, JOSEPH (LANSING, MI)
    1974-

LOW, LYMAN H. (NEW ROCHELLE, NY)
    1882-1923
    Collections:
        Anderson (Apr. 1913)   Auerback (Sept. 1899)
        Balmanno (1903)   Brenneman (July 1917)
        Brown (Oct. 1904)   Castle (June 1906)
        Child (1908)   Courteau (1902)
        Cressingham (1887)   Ely (1886)
        Fisher (1896)   Furber (1913)
        Hallenbeck (1902)   Hills (1923)
        Horworth (1913)   Hoyt (1907)
        Johnson (1922)   Johnston (1902)
        Laurin (1906)   Lawrence (1902)
        Lindegard (1902)   Linderman (1887)
        Llewellyn (1902)   Low (1905)
        McCrea (1916)   Mills (1902)
        Morris (1901)   Patenaude (1900)
        Pearson (1902)   Perkins (1922)
        Peters, A. (1902)   Peters, G. (1923)
        Podhajski (1902)   Porcher (1886)
        Potts (1920-1921)   Raymond (1887)
        Steers-Breck (1920)   Tenney (1886)
        Thatcher (1906)   Ward (1906)
        West (1907)   Whittingham (1887)
        Wood (1887)   Zug (1907)

MCKINNEY, DAVIS (DALLAS, TX)
    1958-1967

MCSORLEY, CHARLES (CLOSTER, NJ)
    FPL: "Ancient Coins": no date

MALLOY, ALEX G. (NEW YORK, NY)
    FPL: "Germonica Caesar": 1968-
    FPL: "Medieval Coins": 1970-1975
    FPL: "Ancient Arts & Antiquities": 1972-1975
    Auction catalogs: 1972-

MALTER, JOEL (ENCINO, CA)
    FPL: 1965-1971
    Auction catalogs: 1969-1970, 1973

MARGOLIS, RICHARD (TEANECK, NJ)
    FPL: "Coins & Medals of the World": 1962-1975

MARGOLIS, RICHARD (TEANECK, NJ) see also
    EMPIRE STATE NUMIS. ASSN. (May 1960)

MAYFLOWER COIN AUCTIONS (BOSTON, MA)
    1956-1974
    Collections:
        ballou (1965)   Belcher (1964)
        Gaylord (1963)   Hodgdon (1969)
        Stearns (1973)   Ritter (1966)
        Thurlow (1967)

MEHL, MAX (FT. WORTH, TX)
    FPL: 1934, 1937-1940, 1942, 1948, 1950, 1953-1954, 1956
        1960
    Auction catalogs: 1908-1955
    Collections:
        Agurs (april 1937)   Alenius (Dec. 1917)
        Allenburger et al (Mar. 1948) Atwater (June 1946)
        Baldwin-Spencer (Mar. 1940)   Burton-High (1940)
        Burton, J. E. (April 1918)   Carlberg (Oct. 1917)
        Chatillou (1938-1939)   Collins (1955)
        Conover (1914)   Cowell (1911, 1923)
        Crichton (1919)   Dunham (1941)
        Elrod (1943)   Engstrom (1920)
        Faelten-Todd-Morse (1936)   King Farouk I (1948, 1951)
        French (no date)   Geiss (1947)
        Goette (1923)   Granberg (1919)
        Green-Smith (1949)   Griffith (1912)
        Grinnel (1943)   Hale (1939)
        Hartell (1927)   High-Burton, F. W. (1940)
        Hoffecker (1954)   Jansen (1921)
        Kern (1950)   Knapp (1945)
        Knoop (1931)   Lambert (1914)
        Lardner (1930)   McVitty (1938)
        Manst (1921)   May (1955)
        Morse (1936)   Neil (1947-1948)

MEHL, cont.

                Olsen (1944)   Philpott (1945)
                Porter (1942)   Rees (1928)
                Renz et al (Mar. 1948)   Roach (1944)
                Roe (1945)   Rosborough (1939)
                Rovensky (1954)   Ryan (1945)
                Sears (1918)   Shelton (1918)
                Slack (1925)   Smith, B. W. (1915)
                Smith, E.-Green (1949)   Smith, F. E. (1917)
                Smoots (1932)   Spencer-Baldwin (1940)
                Stevens (1923)   TenEyck (1922)
                Todd-Morse-Faelton (1936)   Truax (1917)
                Waltman (1945)   Walton (1930)
                Ware (1916)   Ware, W. (1902)
                Warner (1951)   Wasserman (1917)
                Wilharm (1921)   Wilson (1918)

MELNICK, HERBERT, CATALOGUER see
     PINE TREE AUCTIONS (Mar. 1976)

MERKIN, LESTER (NEWYORK, NY)
     FPL: 1961-1963, 1970
     Auction catalogs: 1964-1974
     Collection: Helfenstein (1964)

MERWIN-CLAYTON (NEW YORK, NY)
     1910-1911

MEUSS, HANS (HAMBURG, GERMANY)
     1925

MICHAEL, FRED & EDWARD (CHICAGO, IL)
     1912-1916

MIKE'S ERRORS (WANATAH, IN)
     1973-

MONNAIES & MEDAILLES (PARIS, FRANCE)
     FPL: 1921

MONNAIES & MEDAILLES (PARIS, FRANCE) see also
     MUNZEN UND MEDAILLEN (BASEL, SWITZERLAND)

MOREY, H. E. (BOSTON, MA)
     1891-1893, 1913

MORGENTHAU, J. C. (NEW YORK, NY)
     FPL: 1933
     Auction catalog: 1943
     Collection: Phillips

MORGENTHAU, J. C. (NEW YORK, NY) see also
     RAYMOND, WAYTE (NEW YORK, NY)

MUNZEN UND MEDAILLEN (BASEL, SWITZERLAND)
     FPL: 1948-1974
     Auction catalogs: 1946-1975

MYERS, ROBERT J. (LENOX HILL STATION, NY)
     FPL: "Ancient Coins": 1971-1975
     Collections:
          Rosen (1974)
          Weber (no date)

MYNT & MEDALJER (STOCKHOLM, SWEDEN) see AHLSTROM (STOCKHOLM,
     SWEDEN)

NASCIA, GIUSEPPE (MILAN, ITALY)
     FPL: "Ars et Nummus": 1968, 1972-

NETHAWAY COIN CO. (HOWE CAVE, NY)
     1962-1963

NETHAWAY COIN CO. (HOWE CAVE, NY) see also
     EMPIRE STATE NUMIS. ASSN. (May 1963)

NEW ENGLAND NUMISMATIC ASSN. (WORCHESTER, MA)
     1951-1956, 1958, 1963, 1966-1967, 1974-1975

NEW ENGLAND RARE COIN GALLERIES (FRAMINGTON, MA)
     1974-1975

NEW ENGLAND RARE COIN GALLERIES (FRAMINGTON, MA) see also
     NEW ENGLAND NUMISMATIC ASSN. (Nov. 1975)

NEW NETHERLANDS COIN CO. (NEW YORK, NY)
     FPL: 1937, 1939, 1943
     FPL: "Numisma": 1954-1960
     Auction catalogs: 1941-1975
     Collections:
          Cicero (1960)
          Landau (1958)

NEW YORK COIN AND STAMP (NEW YORK, NY)
     1903-1904

NEW YORK COIN AND STAMP (NEW YORK, NY) see also
     BANGS, MERWIN & CO. (Jan. 1889, Jan. 1890, June 1890,
          Apr. 1892, May 1892, Feb. 1893, Apr. 1896, May 1897)

NOBODY'S PERFECT (CLINTON, TN)
     FPL: 1976

NUMISMATIC ASSN. OF SOUTHERN CA (NASC)
     1956-
     Collections:
          Davies (1975)
          Niewoehner (1975)

NUMISMATIC ENTERPRISES (CA) see KOSOFF, ABE (CA)

NUMISMATIC FINE ARTS, INC. (ENCINO, CA)
    1975-

NUMISMATIC FINE ARTS (NEW YORK, NY)
    FPL: 1942-1963
    Auction catalogs: 1945-1960
    Collections:
        Herzfeld (1947)
        Orlowski (1947)
        Pond (1948)

NUMISMATIC FINE ARTS (NEW YORK, NY) see also
    AMERICAN NUMISMATIC ASSN. (Aug. 1952)

NUMISMATIC GALLERY (CA) see KOSOFF, ABE (CA)

NUMISMATICA (NAPLES, ITALY) see DE FALCO, GIUSEPPE (NAPLES,
    ITALY)

OGILVIE, JACK W. (HOLLYWOOD, CA)
    1940, 1945, 1954-1957, 1959

OVERTON, AL (PUEBLO, CO)
    FPL: 1949-1962
    Auction catalogs: 1943, 1945, 1947, 1949, 1952-1965
    Collections:
        Acree (1963)
        S. CO 6th Annual Convention (1964)

OVERTON, AL (PUEBLO, CO) see also
    AMERICAN NUMISMATIC ASSN. (Aug. 1963, Aug. 1965)

PACIFIC NORTHWEST NUMISMATIC ASSN. (OR-WA)
    1956-1965

PAGE, ALFRED (PARIS, FRANCE)
    FPL: no date, 1922, 1929
    Auction catalogs: 1930-1931, 1934

PARAMOUNT INTERNATIONAL (ENGLEWOOD, OH)
    FPL: "Rare Coin List": 1972-
    FPL: "Special Coin List" & misc.: 1966, 1968-1969,
        1972-1973, 1975-
    Auction catalogs: 1965-
    Collections:
        Burnheimer (1976)
        Grand Central Coin Convention (1966, 1973)
        Greater NY Coin Convention (1973)
        Long Beach Coin & Stamp Expo. (1974)

PARAMOUNT INTERNATIONAL (ENGLEWOOD, OH) see also
    AMERICAN NUMISMATIC ASSN. (1967, 1969, 1972, 1974)
    NEW ENGLAND NUMIS. ASSN. (Oct. 1966, Oct. 1967)
    NUMISMATIC ASSN. of S. CA (1967, 1969, 1971, 1973, 1975)
    TX NUMIS. ASSN. (Apr. 1967)

PARKE-BERNET (NEW YORK, NY)
    1946, 1950, 1967-1971
    Collections:
        Le Chameau (Dec. 1971)
        Schutz (1971)

PAYNE, PETER B. (SAN BERNARDINO, CA)
    1956-1958, 1960-1962

PENN-OHIO COIN CLUBS (OH)
    1954-1955, 1957-1959, 1962, 1968

PETEGHEM, C. VAN (PARIS, FRANCE)
    1880-1881, 1883, 1886

PETERS, JESS (DECATUR, IL)
    FPL: 1966, 1968, 1972
    Auction catalogs: 1965-
    Collections:
        Byrne (1975)
        C.O.I.N. (1973)
        FL United Numismatists (1974)
        Higgins (1975)
        Miami Beach Internat'l Midwinter Coin Convention
          (1972, 1974)

PETERS, JESS (DECATUR, IL) see also
    MICHIGAN STATE NUMIS. SOC. (Nov. 1974)
    TEXAS NUMIS. ASSN. (Apr. 1975, Apr. 1976)

PEUS, DR. BUSSO (FRANKFURT/MAIN, GERMANY)
    FPL: 1951, 1967-1973
    Auction catalogs: 1955, 1963, 1967-

PILARTZ, HEINRICH (COLOGNE, GERMANY)
    FPL: 1952-1954, 1964, 1966-1969
    Auction catalogs: 1964-1968

PINE TREE RARE COIN AUCTION SALES (ALBERTSON, NY)
    1973-
    Collection: Cohen (1976)

PLATT, MARCEL (PARIS, FRANCE)
    1957-1963, 1969, 1971

POINDESSAULT, BERNARD (PARIS, FRANCE)
    1967-1969, 1971, 1973

PROSKEY, DAVID see BANGS, MERWIN & CO. (Mar. 1887)

QUALITY SALES CORP. (CA) see KREISBERG, ABNER (BEVERLY
    HILLS, CA)

QUEEN CITY COIN SALES (CINCINNATI, OH)
    1950-1951

RANDALL, JAMES P. (CHICAGO, IL)
    FPL: no date, 1941, 1948, 1950, 1958
    Auction catalogs: 1942, 1950-1953

RARCOA-RARE COIN CO. OF AMERICA (CHICAGO, IL)
    FPL: 1962, 1967, 1975
    Auction catalogs: 1963, 1966-
    Collections:
        Boosel (1972)
        Central States Numis. Soc. Anniversary Convention (1969)
        Hausske (1969)
        Numismatic Assn. of S.CA (1972)
        Bell (1963)

RARCOA-RARE COIN CO. OF AMERICA (CHICAGO, IL) see also
    AMERICAN NUMIS. ASSN. (Aug. 1970)
    NUMISMATIC ASSN. OF S. CA (Feb. 1972)

RARE COIN REVIEW see BOWERS & RUDDY (CA)

RATTO, MARIO (MILANO, ITALY)
    1960-1972
    Collection: Curalto (Pt. 2-4: 1972)

RATTO, RODOLFO (SWITZERLAND)
    1911, 1928, 1930
    Collections:
        Hands (1928)
        Martini (1934)
        Morcom (1928)
        Wertheim (1928)

RAUCH, H. D. (VIENNA, AUSTRIA)
    1970-1975

RAYMOND, WAYTE (NEW YORK, NY)
    FPL: 1936, 1946
    Auction catalogs: 1925-1926, 1932-1947
    Collections:
        Morosini (1932)
        Newcomb (1945)
        Newcomer (1935, 1939, 1941)

REED, IRA S. (PHILADELPHIA, PA)
    1936-1946

REED, IRA S. (PHILADELPHIA, PA) see also
    AMERICAN NUMIS. ASSN. (Aug. 1941)

REGENCY COIN & STAMP CO., LTD. (MANITOBA, CANADA)
    FPL: 1958, 1960-1962, 1972-1975

RETTEW, JOEL (SANTA ANA, CA)
    1976

REICHMANN & CO. (HALLE, EAST GERMANY)
    1921, 1925

RIGGS, LU (CINCINNATI, OH)
    1948-1964, 1966, 1969

RINALDI, OSCAR (MANTOVA, ITALY)
    1949-1953, 1972

ROSE, FRANK (TORONTO, CANADA)
    1970, 1975-
    Collections:
        Flick (1975)
        McKay-Clements (1976)

ROSENBERG, H. S. (HANNOVER, GERMANY)
    1906, 1909, 1913, 1925, 1929
    Collections:
        Braunschweig-Luneberg (1925)
        Knigge (1929)
        Lehmann (1909)
        Mann (1906)
        Schwalbach (1913)

ROSENBERG, SALLY (FRANKFURT/MAIN, GERMANY)
    1906, 1926, 1932

RUCHER, GEORGE (NO PLACE GIVEN) see HESSLEIN

SAGE, A. B. (NEW YORK, NY)
    FPL: 1859

ST. LOUIS STAMP & COIN (ST. LOUIS, MO)
    FPL: no date 1-27, 1904
    Auction catalogs: 1902-1915

SALTON-SCHLESSINGER (NEW YORK, NY)
    1953-1962
    Collection: William (1955)

SALTON-SCHLESSINGER (NEW YORK, NY) see also
    EMPIRE STATE NUMIS. ASSN. (Oct. 1952)

SAMPSON, H. G. (NY) see BANGS, MERWIN & CO. (Jan. 1881,
    Oct. 1885)

SAN DIEGO COIN EXCHANGE (CA) see CA STATE NUMIS. ASSN.
    (Nov. 1969, Nov. 1971)

SANTAMARIA, P. & P. (ROME, ITALY)
    FPL: 1951-1953, 1960, 1964, 1967
    Auction catalogs: 1924, 1929, 1934, 1937, 1939, 1951,
        1959, 1961, 1963
    Collections:
        Gariazzo (1937)
        Nicola (1929)
        Signorelli (1951)
        Venturi-Ginori (1937)

SCHLESSINGER, FELIX (AMSTERDAM, HOLLAND)
    1929-1930, 1945-1935, 1939
    Collection: Chapelle (1939)

SCHULMAN COIN & MINT, INC. (NEW YORK, NY)
    FPL: 1972-
    Auction catalogs: 1971-
    Collections:
        Cann (1974)   King Farouk (1971)
        Freibrun (1971)   Gibbs (1971-1972)
        Gibbs-Kann (1971)   Harding (1972)
        Herdegen (1973)   Numis. & Antiquarian
        Orton (1973)   Soc. of Phila.
        Shapiro (1971)   (1973-1974)
        King Umberto II (1974)   Zack (1972)

SCHULMAN COIN & MINT, INC. (NEW YORK, NY) see also
    SCHULMAN, HANS (NEW YORK, NY)

SCHULMAN, HANS (NEW YORK, NY)
    FPL: no date, 1944, 1946, 1953-1956, 1960, 1964, 1967-1968
    Auction catalogs: 1914, 1940, 1950-1971
    Collections:
        Arlow (Nov. 1965)   Atomic (June 1961)
        Bowdoin College (Feb. 1972) Brand (1964)
        King Farouk (1950)   Gibbs (1951, 1960, 1962,
        Grogan (1914)   1966, 1970-1972)
        Horowitz (1961)   Ilton (1959)
        Johnson-Burdette (1951)   Kann (1953)
        Kays (1956)   Lara (1960)
        Lascano (1969)   Lee (Pt. 1-3: 1958)
        Lichtenfels (1964)   Loan-Gains (1968)
        Mabbott (1969-1970)   Mace (1968)
        Maguire (1959)   Medina (1968)
        Morgan (1951-1952)   Ovazza (1952)
        Rosenbach (Pt. 1-4:   Schulman (1951)
          1969-1970)   Tatnall (1962)
        Tracy (1951-1952)   Valdez (1968)
        Vanderwende (1942)   Vergara (1969)
        Vernon (1972)   Weill (1972)
        Woodward (1951-1952)

SCHULMAN, JACQUES (AMSTERDAM, HOLLAND)
    1905-1975
    Collections:
        Carvalho (1905)   Crone (1963)
        Dressmann (1956, 1967)   Eyndhoven (1924)
        Hermans (1925)   De Campos (1906)
        Dos Santos (1906)   Graham (1966)
        Kinberg (1910)   Koch (1932)
        Kortenbach (1963)   Lemos (1906)
        Langier (1913)   Leonardos (1927)
        Meili (1910)   Menso (1958)
        Rijswijck (1925)   King Umberto (1967)
        Vierordt (1923-1924)

SCHULMAN, JACQUES (AMSTERDAM, HOLLAND) see also
    KUNDIG, M. W. (Mar. 1921)

SCHULTZ, NORMAN (SALT LAKE CITY, UT)
    FPL: no date
    Auction catalogs: 1925, 1932, 1937, 1939, 1943, 1945,
        1946-1947, 1951

SCHWEIZERISCHER BANKVEREIN - SWISS BANK CORP. (SWITZERLAND)
    1975-

SCOTT STAMP & COIN CO. (NEW YORK, NY)
    FPL: 1894-1896, 1901-1902, 1933

SEABY, B. A., LTD. (LONDON, ENGLAND)
    1930, 1936, 1938

SEITZ, PAUL (GLEN ROCK, PA)
    1941, 1944-1945, 1947-1948, 1950-1952, 1954, 1962-1964,
    1966-1968

SISO, M. (LERIDA, SPAIN)
    1972-

SLADE, CHARLES (ORLANDO, FL)
    1963-1964

SLADE, CHARLES (ORLANDO, FL) see also
    MICHIGAN STATE NUMIS. SOC. (Apr. 1964)

SMITH, H. P. (NEW YORK, NY) see BANGS, MERWIN & CO.
    (Jan. 1880, Oct. 1881, Apr. 1883)

SMITH, HOWARD S. (CHICAGO, IL)
    1956, 1958, 1961-1974

SMITH, WILLIAM H., CATALOGUER see
    CA STATE NUMIS. ASSN. (Nov. 1959, Apr. 1960, Oct. 1960)

SOCIEDAD NUMISMATICA DE MEXICO (MEXICO CITY, MEXICO)
    1971-

SOTHEBY (TORONTO, CANADA)
    1968-1970

SOTHEBY & CO. (LONDON, ENGLAND)
    1817, 1924, 1880, 1889, 1903, 1912-1913, 1916, 1924,
        1930-1931, 1954, 1958, 1961-
    Collections:
        Assn. H.M.S. (Jan. 1970)   Bentley (Feb. 1970)
        Bridgewater House (1972)   Carlyton-Britton (1913)
        Chetwode (1973)   Cotton (1889)
        Dear (1972)   Denham (1972)
        Egypt-Palace Coll. (1954)   Garner (1973)
        Prince Georg (1973)   Hollis (1817)
        Houghton (1958)   Jungfleisch (1972)
        Metropolitan Art (1972)   Murdoch (1904)
        Reford (1968)   Pernt (1975)
        Scott-Taggart (1972)   Sharp (1966)
        Smith (1963)   Sparks (1880)
        Taellusson (1931)   Shetland Isles (1973)
        Wheeler (1930)   Williams (1969)

SOTHEBY & CO. (LONDON, ENGLAND) see also PARKE-BERNET
    GALLERIES (NEW YORK, NY)

SOTHEBY & CO. A. G. (ZURICH, SWITZERLAND) see SOTHEBY &
    CO. (LONDON, ENGLAND)

SOTHEBY PARKE-BERNET (NEW YORK, NY; LOS ANGELES, CA) see
    SOTHEBY & CO. (LONDON, ENGLAND)

SOUTH AFRICA COIN EXCHANGE (JOHANNESBURG, SOUTH AFRICA)
    1976-

SPINK & SON, LTD. (LONDON, ENGLAND)
    FPL: "Modern Coins": 1975-
    Auction catalogs: 1975-

SPINK & SON, LTD., CATALOGUER see
    GLENDINING & CO. (LONDON, ENGLAND)
    BOWERS & RUDDY (Feb. 1976)

STACK'S (NEW YORK, NY)
    FPL: 1939-1970
    Auction catalogs: 1936-
    Collections:
        Adams (1971)   Allan (1950)
        Alto (1970)   Aries (1960)
        Arnel (1967)   Arnold (1968)
        Baker (1964)   Baldenhofer (1955)
        Balderston (1948)   Bartlett (1966)
        Bauman (1966)   Bell (1944)
        Berlin (1952)   Berman (1964)
        Bolt (1966)   Bostic (1956)
        Brobston (1963)   Bryan (1973)
        California (1963)   Chapman (1951)
        Chase (1958)   Chien (1952)

Clarke (1975)
Cox (1962)
Dalton (1975)
Davis-Graves (Pt. 1-2: 1954)
Delta (1961)
Dines (1969)
Dupont (Pt. 1-2: 1954)
Emmons (1969)
Engel (1970)
Faelten-Reinhold (1938)
Flanagan (1944)
Ford (1951)
Forwalter (1970)
Frank (1956)
Gaston (Pt. 1-2: 1969-1970)
Globus (1972)
Goldsmith (1958)
Grasso (1950)
Guggenheimer (1953)
Harris (1950)
Hawn (1973)
Holmes (1960)
Hughs (1948)
Illinois (1969)
Johnson (1958)
Kerins (1936)
Klitgarrd (1948)
Knowles (1953)
Lee (1947)
Lohr (1956)
McKenzie (1938)
McKenzie, C. (1965)
McCullough (1967)
MA Hist. Soc.
  (1970-1973)
Metro. NY Numis. Con-
  vention (1956, 1971)
Myers (1972)
New Eng. Num. Assn.
  (1951-1956)
Patten (1973)
Perera (1942)
Pirtle (1953)
Proskey-McKenzie (1939)
Pryor (1971)
Raphael (1952)
Reuter (1959)
Robinson (1973)
Salman (1962)
Scanlon (1973)
Seeman (1970)
Slawson (1970)
Smith, L. (1973)
South (1951)

Copeland (1967)
Crosby (1958)
Davis, R. T. (1968)
Delp (1972)
Dietz (Pt. 1-2: 1946)
Dubblede (1950)
Egolf (1961)
Empire (1957)
Ewalt (1965)
Fairbanks (1960)
Ford (1951)
Forrest (1972)
Fowler (1969)
Garrabrant (1949)
Gies (1940)
Golding (1952)
Grand (1947)
Groves (1974)
Hall (1945)
Harvin (1959)
Heim (1972)
Horn (1950)
Hutchinson (1953)
Jay (1967)
Kaufman (1951)
Kingman (1965)
Knoblock (1970)
Laconte (1967)
Limpert (1955)
Lovi (1968)
McKenzie-Proskey (1939)
MacMurray (1958)
McPherson (1953)
Mathey (1973)
Mayfiled (1958)
Miles (1968-1969)
Miller (1966)
Neumoyer (1960)
Nicholson (1967)
Opezzo (1941)
Pelletreau (1959)
Pierce (1965)
Powers (1959)
Proskey (1939, 1943)
Ragee (1950)
Reed (1957)
Rise (1966)
Ross (1952-1953)
Sawicki (1954)
Schmandt (1957)
Slater (1947)
Smith, C. (1955)
Smith, T. (1957)
Spaulding (1960)

STACK'S, cont.

          Speir (1974)   Spence (1975)
          Stadium (1965)   Stack (1975)
          Steckler (1974)   Stewart (1972)
          Straus (1959)   Tanenbaum (1958)
          Thetford (1959)   Thomson (1967)
          Tice (1962)   Tollett (1971)
          Turrini (1972)   Van Roden (1968)
          Virginia (1973)   Walsh (1950)
          Walton (1963)   Ward (1964)
          Watson (1966)   Weihman (1951)
          Westchester (1973)   Wharton (1945)
          Williams (1947)   Wilson (1959)
          Wilson-Reuter (1959)   Windner (1958)
          Winter (1974)   Wolfson (Pt. 1-2:
          Zaremba (1970)   1962-1963)

STACK'S (NEW YORK, NY) see also
    AMERICAN NUMIS. ASSN. (Oct. 1939, Aug. 1940, Aug. 1971)
    NEW ENGLAND NUMIS. ASSN. (OCT. 1951, OCT. 1952, OCT.
        1953, OCT. 1954, OCT. 1955, OCT. 1956)

STEIGERWALT, CHARLES (LANCASTER, PA)
    FPL: 1809-1906, 1911
    Auction catalogs: 1893-1898
    Collections:
        Baker (1898)   Blair (1896)
        Childs (1894)   Crawford (1894)
        Lathrop (1896)   Luckenbach (1894)
        Mattern (1896)   Parter (1893)
        Ward (1897)   Wilson (1896)

STEINBERG, ROBERT L. (NEW YORK, NY)
    FPL: 1969, 1973-1974

STEINBERG, WILLIAM FOX (NEW YORK, NY) see STEINGERG, ROBERT L.
    (NEW YORK, NY)

STERNBERG, FRANK (ZURICH, SWITZERLAND)
    1973-1975

SUPERIOR GALLERIES - DIVISION OF SUPERIOR STAMP AND COIN
    (CA) see SUPERIOR STAMP AND COIN (LOS ANGELES, CA)

SUPERIOR STAMP AND COIN (LOS ANGELES, CA)
    FPL: 1970-1971, 1974
    Auction catalogs: 1970-
    Collections:
        Alexander (Pt. 1-2: 1970-1971) Durham (1973)
        A.N.A. (1975)   Praudeau (1970-1971)
        Bothamley (Pt. 1-3: 1970-1971) Ruby (1974)
        Dyan (Pt. 1-2: 1970-1971)

SWEENEY, FRED (KANSAS CITY, MO)
    1972-1973

SWISS BANK CORP. (SWITZERLAND) see SCHWEIZERISCHER BANK-
    VEREIN (ZURICH, SWITZERLAND)

SWISS CREDIT BANK (BERN, SWITZERLAND)
    1971-1974

SZEGO, ALFRED (NEW YORK, NY)
    1960-1961, 1963, 1965-1966

TATHAM STAMP AND COIN (SPRINGFIELD, MA)
    FPL: 1941, 1946, 1948-1949, 1951, 1955, 1969
    Auction catalogs: 1945-1947

TEXAS NUMISMATIC ASSN. (BROWNWOOD, TX)
    1960, 1967-1969, 1973-

THEIME, C. G. (LEIPZIG, AUSTRIA)
    FPL: 1872
    Auction catalog: 1871
    Collection: Hasse

THOMPSON, DON, CATALOGUER see CA STATE NUMIS. ASSN. (Apr.
    1961, Nov. 1961)

TOREX - TORONTO EXHIBITION (CANADA)
    1970-1971, 1975
    Collection: Flick (1975)

TRIPLE COIN CLUB OF NEW YORK (NY) see COIN IS KING (NY)

U.S. COIN CO. (NEW YORK, NY)
    FPL: 1914-1915
    Auction catalogs: 1913-1914, 1916-1918
    Collections:
        Crans (1918)
        Doughty (1914)
        Moore (1917)

VINCHON, J. & CIE. (PARIS, FRANCE)
    1953-
    Collections:
        Hindamain (1956)
        Vinchon (1962)

WALLIS & WALLIS (LEWES, SUSSEX, ENGLAND)
    1969-1971, 1974

WEBB, WALTER F. (ROCHESTER, NY)
    1936-1951

WINKEL, WOLFGANG (BIELEFELD, GERMANY)
    1971-1973

WITTLIN'S CATALOGUER (NO PLACE GIVEN) see CA STATE NUMIS.
    ASSN. (Apr. 1951, Nov. 1951, Apr. 1952)

WOODWARD, W. Elliot (NEW YORK, NY)
    1864, 1867, 1879-1890
    Collections:
        Abbey (1864)   Clogston (1881)
        Curtis (1880)   Day (1890)
        Dietrich (1882)   Dohrmann (1882)
        Doolittle (1881)   Emory (1864)
        Forbes (1890)   Hains (1880)
        Holstein (1884)   Howard (1884)
        Ilsley (1864)   Jenison (1881)
        Jenks (1880)   Lermann (1884)
        Levick (1864, 1885)   Maas (1882)
        Matthews (1885)   Mercer (1880)
        Mickley (1867)   Morgan (1882)
        Randall (1885)   Robinson (1879)
        Searing (1880)   Vickary (1883)
        Washburn (1882)   Woodward (1885)
        Woodward, W.E. (1879)

WOODWARD, W. ELLIOT, CATALOGUER see
    BANGS, MERWIN & CO. (1880, 1881, 1884-1885)

WORLD NUMISMATIQUES (OH) see KELLY, JAMES

WORLDWIDE COIN INVESTMENTS, LETC. (ATLANTA, GA)
    FPL: 1970-1973, 1975-

WRUCK, WALDEMAR (BERLIN, GERMANY)
    1941, 196801969, 1972-1973

YOUNG, LEO A. (OAKLAND, CA)
    1957-1962

YOUNG, LEO A., CATALOGUER see also
    AMERICAN NUMIS. ASSN. (Aug. 1959)
    CA STATE NUMIS. ASSN. (1953-1958)
    NUMIS. ASSN. OF S. CA (Feb. 1959)
    PACIFIC NORTHWEST NUMIS. ASSN. (May 1956, May 1957)
    PENN-OHIO COIN CLUBS CONVENTION (July 1958)

ZANDER, RANDOLPH (ALEXANDRIA, VA)
    FPL: 1954-1968

AUTHOR INDEX

Aamlid, Jan Olav..JC50.A2
Abbott, George H..AA80.A2
Abbott, Morris W..PA80.C6A2
Abbott, P. E..SE30.A2
Abdul Wali Khan, Mohammed..............KA60.A5b, KA60.A5q
Abeywardene, T. M. DeSilva............................BD20.A2
Abraham, Irwin R..SH40.A2
Academia Mexicana de Estudios Numismaticos.......FB40.A2
Academia Royale des Medailles....................RF80.L6F7
Academia Urguaya de Numismatica....................FE80.U2
Acharya, G. B...KA60.B6
Acworth, R. W. H..NB80.A3
Adams, Edgar H................FA10.G8c, GA90.A4, GB15.A3
        GB80,C3A3, PA70.A3, PA73.L6
Adams, Eva..GA85.A3
Adelson, Howard L..............BC85.A3, BE80.A3, GA10.A5
Adler, Jacob...GB80.H3A3
Adler, Jacob G. C......................................KA55.K8A3
Affleck, Charles J....................US60.A3, US80.V5A4
Agence Numismatique Interphilatelic...............JF30.A3
Ahlstrom, Bjarne......JC50.A4, JC50.B7, JC70.A4, JC85.A5
Ahmad, Shamsuddin...KA60.I5
Aichholz, V. Miller.......................................JK40.A5
Ainslie, George R...JB83.A4
Akerman, John Y......AA40.A4, AA50.A3, BA65.A4, BA70.A55
        BC40.A4, BC60.A4, BC67.A4, JB40.R8, BC97.A4
Akers, David W...........................GB10.A3, GB10.A3g
Albany Numismatic Society...........................GA40.A4
Albert, Alphaeus H.............QA20.A4, QA40.A5, SH30.A5
Albrecht, Gunther...JA80.A5
Album, Stephen...PA80.C3A4
Alef, Gustave..JM80.A5
Aleman, Miguel...FB50.A4
Alexander, David T......................................AA10.A44
Alexander and Co..AA50.A4
Allan, John.........BD10.B7, BD10.B7g, KA10.A4, KA60.I5
Allan, William...AA80.A5
Allen, Derek F................................JB20.B6, JB80.A4
Allen, Gina..AB30.A4
Allen, Harold D.......HA40.A5, PB30.A4, UI60.A4, US25.A3
Allen, J. J. Cullimore...................................JB63.A4
Allen, Lyman L...KB30.A5
Allen, W. Frank...FA23.A5
Allen and Ginter, Richmond, Va.....................SA20.A5
Allotte de la Fuye.......................................BD30.A4
Almanzar, Alcedo F...FA15.A4, FC75.A4, FD50.R4, FE55.A58
        FE70.A4, FE75.A4, FE80.A4, JB95.A3, LA20.A4
        RN50.E2A4, UK50.B6S4
Almeida, Basto and Piombino.........................JD60.A4
Almeida Ribeiro, Fernando...........................JD70.A4
Almirall, Juan...JD15.A4
Altz, Charles G..GA80.A5
American Bank Reporter..............................CC35.A54
American Bond and Currency Detector Co...........US30.A5

Atwood, Roland C.............PA40.A8a, PA40.A8c, PA40.A8n
Aulock, Hans von.......................BB20.S8d, BB20.S8de
Austria. State Printing Office....................RK20.A9
Avebury, John L...................................JB40.A8
Avila Martel, Alamiro de..........................RN70.A9
Azevedo, Vasco....................................LA40.A9

Barton, E. H...GA80.A5
Barzan, Rino...JI97.S2B3
Bascape, G. C...SF40.B3
Basmadjian, K. J.......................................KA20.A7B3
Basso, Aldo P...KB30.B3
Batalha Reis, Pedro............JD60.A4, JD70.B3, JD90.B3
Bates, George Eugene.................................BE40.B3
Batson, Alfred...SA30.B3
Batty, D. T..................................PE20.B3, PE20.B3i
Baum, J. W...................................PA30.B3, PA40.B3
Baumann, Charles A.....................................FE40.B3
Bausher, Jess..GA90.B39
Baxter, William J...GB10.B3
Bayerische Hypotheken und Wechsel Bank............UC20.B3
Beale, Gary...JD20.B4
Beard, Edward L..RG70.B4
Beaufoy, Henry...PE80.B8
Beauvais, Guillaume....................................BC40.C5
Beckenbauer, Egon..JG87.B4
Becker, J. Richard..HA85.B4
Becker, Thomas W...............AA40.B4, AA80.B4, AA90.B4
        CC70.B4, GB40.B4, JB94.B4, JC40.B4, JM70.B4
Becklake, J. T.............................LA30.B4, LA30.B44
Bedoukian, Paul Z.....................................KA20.A7B4m
Behn-Miller Publications.............................GB20.B44
Behrens, Kathryn L....................................US45.M2B4
Beierlein, J. B..JG90.B4
Beistle, Martin L...GB20.B4
Bekish, John I...JM40.B4
Belden, Bauman L..............GA80.B4, RM20.B4, RM85.I5B4
        SH30.B4, SH50.B4
Bell, Robert C......JB87.B4, PE60.B4, PE60.B4s, PE60.B4t
        PE70.B4
Bellevue (Ohio) First National Bank..............VA70.O3B4
Bellinger, Alfred R.........BA70.B4, BA80.T7B4, BB20.B44
        BB80.B4, BB90.B4, BC75.B42, BC75.B43, BC75.B46
        BC75.B48, BD34.B4, BE20.B4, BE70.B4, BE90.B4
Bellorius, Joannis Petri.............................BC80.B4
Bement, Clarence S.....................................BB20.B4
Benavides, Hector......................................UK10.C5G3
Bendixen, Kirsten.......................................JC20.B4
Benson, Frank S...BB40.B4
Beresford-Jones, R. D...............................JB83.B4
Beresiner, Yasha......................UA30.B4, UK10.C6B4
Berghaus, Peter...................JG98.D6B4, JG98.H4B4
Bergman, W..UP30.B4
Berlin Numismatic Society...........................JG10.B4
Berlincourt, Marjorie A...............................BA70.B4
Berliner Numismatische Zeitschrift................JG30.B4
Bernardi, Giulio...JI80.B4
Bernareggi, Ernesto....................................JI70.B4
Berriman, A. E...AA90.B42
Berry, Burton Y.....................BB20.S8b, BB80.B47
Berry, George................JB45.B4, NB60.B4, PE30.B4

Berson, Fred...GA55.B4
Berstett, Adrian....................................JG98.B3B4
Bertier de la Garde, A. L...........................JM92.B4
Bertram, Fred..........................KA40.B4, KA40.B4c
Berzins, Edgars.....................................UF40.B4
Betton, James L.....................................AA40.B42
Betts, Benjamin...............FB60.B4, RF80.L3B4, RN10.B4
Betts, Willys..........................GB50.B4, RM50.B4
Beule, Charles Ernest...............................BB40.B49
Bevan, David..UB30.B4
Beverley, James Andrew..............................NB40.B4
Biblical Museums Bulletin...........................BA65.B5
Bibliotheque Royale Albert............AA20.B5, JF90.B7B5
Bieber, Margarete.....................BA70.B5a, BA70.B5p
Bieciuk, Hank.......................................US80.T4B5
Bigot, Alexis.......................................JE82.B5
Bilinski, Robert....................................GA55.B5
Binder, Christian...................................JG96.B5
Birt, Hal....................PA80.A7B5a, PA80.A7B5t
Bisset, Ian...SE40.B5
Bizot, Pierre.......................................RD20.B5
Bjornstad, Ole C....................................JC50.B5
Blake, George H.....................................US20.B5
Blanchard, R. H.....................................QC30.B5
Blanchet, Adrien....................................JA79.B5
Blanchet, Jules A...................................JE80.B55
Bloesch, H..BA60.B5
Bloom, Murray T.....................................CC50.B55
Blunt, C. E...............................JB80.B58, JB80.G7s
Bobba, Cesare.......JI30.B6, JI40.B6, JI93.B6, JI97.S2B6
        UB50.B6
Bodenschatz, Herbert................................PG70.B6
Boehringer, Christofer..............................BB80.B64
Boggs, Winthrop S...................................US25.B6
Boissevain, Ursulla P...............................BB20.A5
Bolender, M. H......................................GB20.B6
Bolt, Conway A......................................AA58.B6B6
Bombay. Prince of Wales Museum of India..........KA60.B6
Bompois, H. Ferdinand...............................BB80.B6
Bonneville, Alphonse................................CC85.B6
Bonneville, Pierre..................................CC85.B65
Bononiensi, Philippo Argelato.......................BC85.B6S6
Boon, George C......................................BC60.B6
Boosel, Harry X.....................................GB70.B6
Borg, Erkki.............................JC90.B6, JC90.B6s
Boston. Museum of Fine Arts...BA20.B6, BB20.B6, RB50.B6
Boston Numismatic Society...........................GA10.B6
Boston. State Street Trust Co....................VA60.M3B6
Botsford, Robert K..................................AA60.B6
Boudard, P. Andre...................................JD40.B6
Boudeau, E.....................JE80,B6, JE82.B6, JE82.B6c
Boundy, Wyndham S...................................JB94.B6
Bowdoin College. Museum of Art.....................RA10.B6
Bowen, Harold L.....................................US80.M5B6

Bowen, Richard LeBaron...........................US45.R5B6
Bowers, Nathan..................................WB30.B6
Bowers, Q. David...............AA75.B6, GA50.B6, GA50.B6h
         GA55.B6, GA55.B6c, GB30.B6, NB80.B6, NB80.N6
Bowers and Ruddy Galleries......................AA78.B6
Bowker, Howard F.....................KB10.B6, KC20.C6e
Bowman, Fred................AA50.B5, HA40.B6c, HA40.B6d
         HA50.B6, PB40.B5, PB80.05B6
Bowring, Sir John...............................AA70.B6
Boy Scouts of American.........................AA60.B68
Boyce, Aline Abaecherli..............BC85.B6, BC93.B6
Boyne, William.............BC40.B6, PE55.W5, PE95.Y6B6
Bradbeer, William West..........................US60.B7
Bradfield, Elston...........AA60.A5, GA70.B7f, GA70.B7r
Bramsen, Ludwig Ernst...........................RF80.N3B7
Bramsen, William................................KD47.B7
Brandt, Tage....................................JC70.B7
Brasil, Banco do................................UK40.B7
Braun, Edmund Wilhelm...........................RG50.B7
Braun von Stumn, Gustaf.........................PG50.B7
Brazao, Arnaldo.................................JD70.B7
Breck, Samuel..................................US40.B7
Breckenridge, James Douglas.....................BE80.B7
Breen, Walter.....GA80.B7d, GA80.B7m, GA80.B7p, GA90.B7s
         GA90.B7u, GA90.G8, GA90.J8, GB10.B7d, GB10.B7e
         GB10.B7g, GB10.B7h, GB10.B7mg, GB10.B7mt
         GB10.B7q, GB10.B7t, GB10.B7vh, GB10.B7vq
         GB20.B7u, GB20.B7s, GB30.B7
Breglia, Laura.................................BC85.B65
Brekke, Bernhard F.............................JC50.B7
Brenner, Victor D..............................RA30.B7
Bressett, Kenneth E..........AA60.B68, AA60.B7, GA55.B65
         JB87.B7, PA80.A4G6
Breton, Pierre Napoleon...................HA35.B7, HA40.B7
Brett, Agnes Baldwin.........BB40.B7, BB60.B3, BB90.B65e
         BB90.B651, BB94.B7, BB97.B74, RB60.B3, RB60.B3i
         RB60.B3o, RB60.B3s
Brindley, H. H.................................QC50.B7
Brick, R. M....................................AB70.B7
Briggs, Geoffrey...............................SF40.G3
Bristow, Dick..................................QA60.B7
British Academy...BB20.S8f, BB20.S81, BB20.S8m, BB20.S8o
British Museum.......AA20.B7, AA90.B7, BA20.B7, BA20.B7s
         BB20.B7, BB20.B71, BB20.W7s, BB97.B7b, BC20.B7
         BC80.B7, BC85.B7, BD10.B7, BD10.B7a, BD10.B7g
         BE20.B7b, BE20.B7v, BE20.B7w, JB20.B7, JB67.B7
         JB80.B7, JB83.B7c, JB83.B7n, KA30.B7, KA50.B7
         KA60.B7m, KA60.B7s, PE20.B7, RE10.B7, RE20.B7
         RI10.B7i, RI10.B7m, RI10.B7s
Broeker, Peter W...............................AA80.B2
Bronson, Henry................................US45.C6B7
Brooke, George Cyril...................JB45.B7, JB83.B7n
Brooklyn Coin Club.............................CC35.B7
Brotman, Irwin F...............................PL40.B7

Browder, Tim J..KA90.M3B7
Browin, Frances..GA40.B7
Brown, Augustus.............................JB80.B4, JB80.B4r
Brown and Bigelow......................................AA40.B76
Brown, C. J...KA70.B7
Brown, Donald Frederick.................................BC70.B7
Brown, I. D...JB55.B7
Brown, Laurence A........................AA40.B7, AA60.B76
Brown, M. D..............................RA10.B7, RA80.B7
Brown, M. Ralph...UJ60.B7
Brown, Martin R..........................GA30.B7, GA50.B72
Browne, Harry..WB70.B7
Brownell, Francis H....................WA30.B7, WA30.B7h
Browning, A. W...GB20.B8
Bruck, Guido...BC67.B7
Brudin J. A..............................KC55.B7, RP50.B7
Brunatii, Joannis....................................JI97.P3B7
Brunetti, Lodovico.....................................AA70.B7
Brunk, Gregory........................AA50.B7, CC53.B7
Buchanan, Heinrich.....................................AA45.B8
Bucknill, John...JF95.B8
Budd, Robert C...PG70.B8
Bullowa, David M.......................................GB40.B8
Burgess, Frederick William.............................AA40.B8
Burke, Kenneth W.......................................PB40.C3s
Burkett, Russell.......................................AB30.B8
Burks, Paul Dore......................AA40.B87, AA60.B8
Burn, Jacob Henry......................................PE80.B8
Burn, Richard..BD10.B8
Burnett, Davis...FE55.B8
Burnie, Robert Harry...................................GB80.C3B8
Burns, A. R..WA50.B8
Burns, Edward..JB93.B8
Burns, Jack F..................FC65.B8, FD45.B8, PA40.B8
Burns, Thomas..NB40.B6
Burpee, Charles W......................................VA60.C6B8
Burzio, Humberto F............BC70.B8, FA15.B8d, FA20.B8
Bushnell, Charles Ira..................................PA70.B8
Bussell, Monica..JB67.S4b
Butak, Behzad..........KA20.T8B8, KA20,T8B8c, KA20.T8B8g
Buttrey, Theodore..BC80.B8, FA15.B82, FB67.B8c, FB67.B8g
     FB67.B82
Butts, Allison...AB40.B8
Byrne, Ray...........................FD50.B9, FD55.B9

Cabot, George D..PA40.C3
Cabre Aguilo, Juan.....................................JD43.C3
Cahn, Herbert A...............BA65.C3, BB80.C3, BB80.C3g
Cairola, Aldo..JI80.C35
Calbeto de Grau, Gabriel...............................JD35.C3
Caldecott, J. B..FD35.C3

Curtis, James. W...BC93.C8c, BC93.C8p, BC93.C8t, BD83.C8
        GA90.C8, GA90.C8u
Curtis, John B.......................................WA50.C8
Curto, J. J........PA70.C8i, PA70.C8m, PA70.C8p, PA75.C8
        PA75.C8s, UA50.C8, US35.C8c, US35.C8m
Cuttle, Cole S......................................PA70.C82
Czapski, Emeric Hutten..............................JJ20.C9
Czechoslovakia State Bank...........................JJ50.C8

Dalton, Charles.....................................SE40.D3
Dalton, George......................................QB40.D3
Dalton, Richard................PE60.W3, PE60.D3, PE70.D3
Daniel, Howard A...............................KB70.C3D3
Daniel, Russell.....................................US30.D3
Daniel Boone Bicentennial Commission.............GB40.D3
Dannenberg, Hermann.....................AA45.D3, JG80.D3
Dargent, Eduardo C..............................UK10.C6B4
Darrow, Rex...RM15.D3
Dartmouth College......................BC20.T4, BE20.S8
Dasi, Tomas...JD35.D3
Datlan, Giovanni....................................BB97.D3
Dattari, Giovanni...................................BB90.D3
Daughters of Utah Pioneers..........................VA40.D3
D'avant, Faustin Poey...............................JE82.D3
Davenport, J. S......JA83.D3, JA85.D3, JA87.D3, JA87.D32
        JG65.D3c, JG65.D3g, JG65.D3g2, JG65.D3o, JK50.D3
        LA10.D3d, LA10.D3s
Davis, Andrew McFarland................UN30.D3a, UN30.D3c
        US40.D3, US45.M3D3c, US45.M3D3t
Davis, Bruce..AA80.D3
Davis, Delores H....................................JJ50.D3
Davis, Holland A....................................GA40.D3
Davis, Norman........BB20.T7, BB40.D2, BB40.D22, GA50.D3
Davis, R. Edward.................................US80.I4D3
Davis, William John....................PE70.D32, PE95.W3D3
Deacon, James Hunt....................MA40.D4, MA50.D4
Dean, John..MA40.D45
DeBaene, Antoine....................................SH60.D4
De Jesus, P. I..............FB55.D4h, FB55.D4m, KB30.D4
        KB30.P5, KB40.D4, KB40.D4s
DeKay, Charles......................................RA30.D4
De Knight, William F................................WB30.D4
De la Bere, Ivan....................................SE40.D4
Delgado, Ricardo................................FB70.J3D4
Dellquist, Augustus Wilfrid.........................GA30.D4
Del Mar, Alexander..................................GB50.D4
Delmonte, A............................JF63.D4, JF65.D4
Del Monte, Jacques...AA40.F3, AA60.D4, AA60.F35, GA50.A6
Demole, Eugene......................RA60.C3D4, RD60.D4
Den Duyts, Francois.................................JF80.D85
Dennis, M. Wayne....................................PA40.H8s

Dennis, Virginia H....................................PA40.D4
Desmonde, William H..................................QB40.D4
De Sousa, Antonio B...............................KB70.H6D4
De Tabley, John B. L. W..............................BB40.D4
Deutch, Howard E.....................................GA55.D4
Deutsche Bundesbank, Frankfurt am Main..JG65.D4, UA30.D4
        UC55.D4d, UC55.D4p, UC60.D4
Deutschen Archaeologischen Institute.............BB20.S8d
Dewey, Frederick P...................................AB42.D4
Dewitt, John Doyle..........AA58.R6D4, QA20.D4, QA40.D4c
        QA40.D4e, QA40.D4m, QA40.D4p
DeWitte, Alphonse....................................JE20.D4
DiBella, Emil.....PA40.D5g, PA40.D5h, PA40.D5r, PA40.D5s
Dick, Robert...PE90.D5
Dickeson, Montroville................................GA40.D5
Dickinson, Willard Edward...........................GA40.D55
Dieffenbacher, Alfred................................CC50.D5
Dietzel, Heinz.......JA87.D5, JE87.D5, JF87.D5, JF87.D5m
        JG87.D5, JH87.D5, JJ20.D5, JJ50.D5, JJ70.D5
        JK87.D5
Diez, Guillermo E. Morales...........................FC65.D5
Dill, Earl..US30.D53
Dillistin, William H........US30.D55, US70.D5d, US70.D5n
        US80.G4D5, VA60.N4D5, VA60.N7D5
Dirkin, Milton.......................................GA50.D4
Dirks, Jacob...JF85.D5
Disraeli, Robert.....................................US25.D5
Dittrich, Karel...................................BA80.05H7
Divo, Jean-Paul...............JH65.D5, JH85.D5m, JH87.D51
        JH87.D51m, JL70.D5
Dodrill, Gordon......................................PA70.D6
Dodson, Oscar H......................................AA40.D6
Doering, David R.........................BC50.D6, BE30.D6
Dolley, Michael....................JB55.B7, JB80.G7s
        JB80.D6v, JB83.D6, JB90.D551
Domit, Moussa M...................................RM35.E2D6
Donaldson, Thomas Leverton...........................BA70.D6
Donati, Robert G.....................................FB50.D6
Donlop, William P.........................US70.D6, US90.D6
Donn, Albert I.......................................US35.D6
Dorfman, Ben......................................KC70.M3D6
Dorling, Henry Taprell......JA30.D6b, SA30.D6b, SA30.D6r
Dotti, Enrico..JI40.D6
Doughty, Francis Worcester...........................GB30.D6
Douglas, B. M............................US60.A3, US60.D6
Douglas, James.......................................UB30.D6
Douglas, Susan H.................................RM80.W3D6
Dow, Dottie..RM30.D6
Dowle, Anthony............................JB90.D6, JB96.G8
Dozy, Charles M......................................AA45.D6
Draper, Paul E.......................................US20.D7
Dressel, Heinrich....................................RB50.D7
Dreyfus, Gustave.....................................RA10.P6
Driscoll, R. E...................................VA70.S6D7

Drouin, Edmond...BD32.D7
Drowne, Henry Russell....................................US50.D7
Dryfhout, John H...GB10.D7
Dubois, Arthur E...SH60.D8
Du Bois, WIlliam Ewing...................................CC30.E3n
Duchalais, Adolphe.......................................RF40.D8
Dudik, Beda..JK20.D8
Dudley, Mayo...RA80.W3D8
Duffield, F. G...CC53.D8
Duggleby, Vincent..UB30.D8
Dunbar, Charles F..WB30.D8
Dunham, William F.........................GA50.D8, PA73.L6
Dunn, Hal V..PA80.N4D8
Dunn, John Wallace....................GA30.B7, GA50.B72
Duphorne, R..GB20.D9
Dupriez, Charles......................................AA45.D8
DuPuy, William Atherton..................................QB30.D8
Durand, Anthony......................................RA80.N8D8
Durst, Sanford J.....................CC63.D8, GB50.D8
Dusterberg, Richard B................................RM85.P7D8
Duve, Gebhard..JG98.B78D8
Duveen, Sir Geoffrey.................................JB63.D8
Duyts, Francois see Den Duyts, Francois
Dworschak, Fritz.........................JK80.M6, RK20.L6
Dye, John S....................AA30.D8, AA30.O8, AA50.D8
Dyer, G. P...JB87.D89

Eads, Ora W..............................AA80.E2, LA40.E2
Eastman, E. P..US30.W5
Ebner, J...RG50.E2
Eckfeldt, Jacob Reese...................CC30.E3m, CC30.E3n
Eckhel, Josepho..BA40.E25
Eddy, Samuel K...BC75.E3
Ede, James..CC83.E3
Edge, Brian..JB45.E4
Edmundson, Joseph..RE30.E3
Edwards, G. Roger..BB70.E3
Egenhoff, Elisabeth L...................................AB39.C2E4
Egg, Erich..JK80.E35
Egleston, Thomas..AA90.E3
Eglit, Nathan N...RM80.C6E4
Ehnbom, Ingvar..PI62.E3
Eidlitz, Robert J........RA80.A7E5, RE80.B6E4, RM80.J4E4
Einzig, Paul..QB40.E3
Eisenberg, Jerome M..........BC85.E4c, BC85.E4g, CC40.E5
Eklund, O. P..........FA27.E5, FB57.E4, JC30.E4, JC60.E5
        JC80.E5, JD37.E5, JD87.E4, JE67.E5, JE67.E4
        JG67.E4, JG67.E4c, JI67.E5, JI93.E5, JK67.E4
        JM67.E5, PC20.E4, PG70.E4, PG90.N8E4, PH40.E4
Elder, Thomas L...............AA40.E3c, AA60.E3, GB30.G5v
        QC30.E4, RM80.C5E4

Elizonda, Carlos A.......................................FA25.E5
Elliot, E. B...WC50.E4
Elliot, J. A...UI30.E4
Elliot, Walter...KA70.E4
Elliott, E. B..WC50.E4
Elmezian, Jorge..FE30.E4
Elwell, W. T...AB62.E3
Emergency Money Society..................................PG70.U6
Engel, Arthur....................CC30.E6, JA80.E5, JE82.E5
Engstrom, John Eric......................JB50.E6, RE80.C4E5
Erbstein, Albert...JA20.E7
Erbstein, Julius.........................JA20.E7, JA30.S3
Erickson, Erling A.....................................VA70.I8E7
Ernst, Barbara..........................JE85.E7, JE87.E7
Ernst, Joseph Albert.....................................WB50.E7
Erol, Mine...UM20.E7
Etienne, Francis......................................SI80.H3E8
Evans, Eva Knox.........................AA60.E8a, AA60.E8q
Evans, George G..GA80.E9
Evans, John..JB80.E9
Evelyn, John............................RA30.E9, RB20.E9
Exley, W...JB95.E9

Fabriczy, Cornelius von................................FI50.F3m
Fagerlie, Joan M...BE90.F3
Failor, Kenneth M..RM15.U5
Falcke, George...KA85.F3
Farquhar, Helen..JB85.F3
Fassbender, Dieter......................JA70.F3, JG87.F3
Fava, Anna Serena..BC80.F3
Feavearyear, Albert......................................WC30.F4
Federal Coin and Currency, Inc...........................CC63.F4
Federal Reserve Bank.....................................AA40.N4
Feely, Edward F.........................CC60.F4, CC67.F4
Feisel, Duane H.............NB20.F4, PA80.C3F4, PA80.N4D8
Felix, Ervin J...AA60.F4
Fellows, Charles...BD38.L9F4
Felt, Joseph B...US45.M3F4
Ferguson, Eugene S...................................... GA80.F4
Ferguson, Lewis K..PA80.I8F4
Ferguson, W. D...JB85.F4
Fernald, Kay...PA80.A4F4
Fernandez, R. I..UN30.F4
Ferraro Vaz, J.......JD70.F4, JD70.F4m, JD90.F4, KB25.V3
Ferreira, Virgilio.......................................LA40.F4
Feuardent, Gaston L......................................BC85.C6
Fiala, Eduard..AA20.F5
Fink, Clarence..........................AA40.F5m, AA40.F5p
Finland. Bank...........................JC90.F5, UB60.F5
Finlay, Walter L...AB62.F5
Finn, Patrick..JB96.G8

        JM92.F7c4, JM92.F7c5, JM92.F7i, JM92.F7o
        JM92.F7o2
Fromery and Fils, Berlin...........................RG80.F7F7
Frossard, Edouard............GB30.F7m, GB30.F7v, PF60.F7
Frost, Harwood....................................GA40.F7
Frye, Richard Nelson...................BD32.F7, BD38.T7F7
Fuchs, Gunter....................................BC80.F8
Fulco, William J...............................BA80.T4F8
Fuld, Melvin and George........NB80.F8, PA30.F8, PA40.F8
        PA60.F8, PA75.F8a, PA75.F8g, PA75.F8p, PA75.F8u
Fuller, Claud E..................................US60.F8
Fulop, Buck O...................................RK60.H8f
Funck, Walter.................JG67.F8, PG70.F8d, PG70.F8m
        PG70.F8n, PG70.F8no
Furber, E. A....................................FA15.F8
Furst, Mortiz...................................RM20.F8

Gabrici, Ettore.......................BB94.G32, BB94.G32t
Gadoury, Victor....................................JE40.G3
Gaebler, Hugo......................................BA40.F7
Gaillard, Victor...................................JF80.G3
Galbreath, Donald L................................SF40.G3
Galetovic, Jose M...............................UK10.C5G3
Gallatin, Albert..................................BB94.G3
Galletta, Gener...................................CC65.G3
Galster, Georg.................JB80.G3, JB80.G32, JC10.G3
        JC20.G2, JC20.G3c, JC20.G3m
Gama, Antonio Diez Soto y.........................RN20.G3
Gamberini di Scarfea, Cesare..........JI85.G3, JI97.V4G3
        PD30.G3, WC60.G3
Gans, Edward........................BB20.A53, RI50.G6
Ganz, David L.....................................GB40.G3
Ganzon de Legarda, Angelita.......................KB50.G3
Garcia, D. Valentin Gil y.........................RK65.G3
Garcia, Luis Pinto................................LA40.G3
Gardiakos, Soterios............JL40.G3, JL70.G3, JL90.G3
Gardner, C. T.....................................KD70.G3
Gardner, Percy.......BB20.B71, BB40.G3, BB55.G3, BB80.G3
        BB97.B7b, BD30.G3
Garner, Paul E...................................CC65.G37
Gartner, John.................MA20.G3, MA20.G3s, MA40.G3
Garza, J. Sanchez................................FB65.G3
Gaudenzi, Luciano................................JI30.G3
Gayer, A. D......................................WA30.G3
Gaytan, Carlos..............FB65.G32, JF30.G3p, UJ30.G3b
        UJ30.G3p, UJ30.G3P2
Gebert, Carl Friedrich..........................SD70.N8G4
Gebhart, Hans.....................................JG90.G4
Gedai, Istvan.....................................AA45.S4
Gelder, Hendrik........................JF40.G4, JF83.G4
Gelinas, Paul J...................................AA40.G4

Great Britain. Royal Mint..............JB20.G7, JB60.R6r
Greathouse, Thomas R...................................RM30.G7
Grebinger, James......................................US90.D6
Green, Benjamin Richard...............................BB60.G7
Green, Charles Elmore.................................GA40.G7
Green, Ronald A.......................................UI50.G7
Greenwell, William....................................BB90.G7
Gregore, Julius.......................................FC65.G7
Greiling Zigarettenfabrik, Dresden....................CC10.G7
Gresham, Otto...WB60.G7
Grieg, R. M...NB40.G7
Grierson, Philip..............AA40.G75, AA50.G7, BE20.B4
        JB80.G7, JI97.V4I9
Griffin, Clarence.....................................GB80.N6G7
Griffith, F. Llewellyn................................QC30.W3
Griffiths, William H..................................US25.G7
Grinnell, A. A..US20.G7
Grinsell, L. V.........................JB60.G7, JB80.G7s
Gritzner, Maximilian..................................SA50.G7
Groner, Egon..RK70.G7
Groom, Arthur...AA40.G76
Groseclose, Elgin......................WA30.G7d, WA30.G7m
Gross, Ruth Belov.....................................AA40.G73
Grossman, Lee...AA50.G76
Grosvenor, Gilbert....................................SH60.G7
Grosvenor Museum......................................JB80.P5
Grove, Frank W..RN20.G7
Grueber, Herbert Appold................BC80.B7, JB20.B7
Guadan, Antonio Manuel de.............JD40.G81, JD40.G8m
Guest, Montague John..................................PE20.B7
Guilloteau, Victor....................................JE40.G8
Guinovart, Jorge.......................JD33.G8, JD35.G8
Guioth, M...RD20.G8
Guiton, Harold H......................................GA50.G9
Gumowski, Marian.......................JJ20.G8, JJ20.G8h
        JJ30.G8, QC40.G8
Gupta, Parme Shavari Tal..............................KA70.G8
Gurdian, Raul...FC50.G8
Guren, Jay.............................RM85.M3G8, RM85.M3G8a
Guthrie, Hugh...FB65.G8
Guttag, Julius.........................FA10.G8c, PA75.H4
Guttag Bros...................CC35.G8, FA10.G9, GA30.G8r
        GA30.G8t, GB80.N4G8, PA73.G8

Habich, George.........................RG50.H3m, RG50.H3s
Hadziotis, Costas.....................................KA20.T8H3
Haeck, Aime...JF80.H3
Haevecker, Ulrich.....................................UC20.J3
Haffner, Sylvia.......................................KA40.H3
Haggenjos, Raymond....................................PA80.I5H3
Hahn, Wolfgang..BE40.M6

Halke, Heinrich.......................................JG40.H3
Hall, E. T...BA60.H3
Hall, Vernon...BE20.S8
Hallenbeck, Kenneth, Jr...................PA70.H3, PA75.H3
Halliday, G. R.......................................BA65.H3
Hamburg. Zirkel-correspondenz....................RA80.F7H3
Hamburger, Leo.......................................JI20.H3
Hamidi, Hakim.....................................KA20.A3H3
Hamilton, Peter F....................................FE40.H3
Hammer, S. H...PE60.D3
Hammer, Ted R...................AA40.H3, GB20.H3, GB35.H3
Hammett, A. B. J....................................AB30.H3
Hamson, Ray......................................KB70.H6H3
Hanauer, Albert M....................................PA40.K5
Handler, Susan.......................................BC70.H3
Hands, Alfred Watson.........BB40.H3, BB94.H3i, BB94.H3m
Hang Seng Bank Ltd., Hong Kong.....................KC20.H3
Hanks, William......................................FB67.H3
Hanley, Tom...MA40.H3
Hans, J.................................JK50.H3, JK50.H3e
Hanson, T..AA60.H25
Hargett, J. L....................................PA80.C6H3
Harduini, Joannis...................................BC40.H3
Hardy, Howard O.....................................GA90.H3
Hargreaves, R. P....................................MA70.H3
Harper, Terrence G...............................US80.V4H3
Harper's Magazine.......................GA80.M3, US40.H3
Harpes, Jean............................JF30.U4, JF95.H3
Harriman, Alan......................................GA55.C5
Harrington, Richard H...............................AB70.H3
Harris, N. Neil..................................RM85.A5H3
Harris, Robert P...............FA15.H3, FA23.H3, FA25.H3
        JA87.H3, JB96.H3, JM40.H3
Harris, S. E..WC40.H3
Harsche, Bert.......................................GA70.H3
Hart, A. M..US40.H32
Hartmann, John E....................................BB60.H3
Hartshorn, Derick S., III..........................KD10.H3
Harvard University. Fogg Art Museum...............BA20.H3
Haseltine, John....................BG20.H4c, GB20.H4e
        GB20.H4h, GB20.H4t, US60.H3
Haskin, Frederick J...............................AA40.H38
Hauser, Josef....................................RG90.M8H3
Hawkins, Edward.....................................JB65.H3
Haxby, J. A...HA30.H3
Haylings, George Wilfred...............GA55.C5, GA55.H3pb
        GA55.H3pm, GA55.H3po, GA55.H3py
Hays, W. W...GB30.F7v
Hazelton, Alan W....................................SG30.H3
Hazlitt, William Carew................AA60.H3, JA40.H35
Head, Barclay V..............BA20.B7s, BA40.C6, BA50.H4
        BB20.B7, BB20.B71, BB40.H4, BB40.H4s, BB40.R5
        BB97.H4, BD32.H4, JB40.J4e
Hearn, G..JB65.H42

Heath, G. A..................................AA60.H37, AA75.H3
Heath Publishing......................................US30.H4
Heath, Robert R.....................................RM90.M4H4
Heaton, A. G..GA80.H4
Hecht, E...JG90.H35
Hede, Holger..JC10.H4
Heiss, Aloiss..................JD40.H4, JD43.H41, JD43.H4r
Heisterkamp, David P..................................AA72.H4
Heller, Joseph..JG90.H4
Henckel, Paul...JG92.W9
Henderson, John Robertson...........................KA90.M8H4
Henderson, Kenn.......................................CC67.H4
Hendy, Michael F......................................BE40.H4
Henfrey, Henry William.....................JB40.H4, JB85.H4
Henkels, Stan V.......................................VA50.H4
Henry, J...................................JB65.H4, JB67.H4
Henseler, Antoine...................................RA50.B6H4
Henshall, John M......................................JB45.H4
Henze, Adolf...JA63.H45
Hepburn, A. Barton....................................WB30.H4
Herbert, Alan...GA90.H4
Herdman, Edward F.....................................PE70.H4
Herndon, James E......................................AA60.H4
Herrera, Adolfo.......................................JD35.H4
Herzfeld, Ernst Emil................................BD32.H45
Hessler, Gene...US40.H4
Hetrich, George.......................................PA75.H4
Heusinger, Friedrich..................................JG80.H4
Hewitt Bros...JA63.H4
Hewitt, Lee........GA40.W42, GA90.H48, GB30.H4, GB30.H4p
        GB30.H4u, PA80.N4H4, US90.D6
Hewlett, Lionel Mowbray...............................JB83.H4
Heyde, Gilbert C......................................AA50.H4
Heylen, Adrianus......................................JF40.H4
Hibler, Harold E......................................RM30.H5
Hickcox, John H.........................GB50.H5, US45.N5H5
Hickson, Howard.......................................GA80.H5
Hieronymussen, Poul Ohm...............................SB10.H5
Higgie, Lincoln W.......................FD60.G6, FD65.H5
Higgins, Francis Carlos.................JA67.H5, KC30.H5
Hildebrand, Bror Emil...................JB80.H4, JB80.H5
        RD50.H5m, RD50.H5s
Hill, George F........AA20.B7, AA70.B4, BA40.C6, BA45.H5
        BA50.H5, BB20.B71, BB20.H5, BB40.H4, BB40.W3
        BB50.H5, BB94.H5, BB97.B7a, BB97.B7c, BB97.H5
        BC40.H5, BD32.H5, BD38.A7H5, BD40.R42, CC55.H5
        JB80.H5, JE80.H5, RA10.H5, RA60.J4H5, RG20.H5
        RI10.B7m, RI35.P4H5, RI50.H5c, RI50.H5p
Hill, Leslie C......................................RE80.C6H5
Hill, Philip V..............BC60.H5b, BC67.H51, BC85.H5
Hirst, Francis W.....................................WC10.H5
Hobbs, Franklin......................................AB30.H6
Hobson, Burton...............AA40.H62, AA50.H62, AA50.R4
        AA60.A6m, AA60.H6, AA60.H6w, AA60.H6y

               AA60.H62w, AA60.R42c, AA60.R42h, AA70.H6
               AA96.H6, BA50.R4, CC63.H6, GA50.H55
               GA55.H55, GB40.H6, JC10.H6
Hoc, Marcel.................................JF83.G4, JF90.T6H6
Hoch, A. D...PB30.H6
Hocking, William John.....................JB20.G7, JB60.H6
Hodes, Alfred L....................................RA80.M3H6
Hodges, Daniel M...................................CC30.H6
Hodges, J. Tyler...................................US30.H6
Hodivala, Shahpurshan Hormasji.....................KA50.H6
Hofer, Paul F.............................JH85.H6, WC52.H6
Hoffman, E. E......................................VM50.H6
Hoffman, Lyle......................................US20.H6
Hohlfelder, Robert L...............................BE90.H6
Hoke, C. M...AB25.H6
Holloway, R. R...........................BA20.H6, BC97.H6
Holm, Johan C......JC10.H64, JC20.H6, KA90.T7H6, RD45.H6
Holmasato, Thure R....JM65.H6, JM93.H6, JM95.H6, JM97.H6
          UB60.H6
Holmberg, Berta..........................JC80.E5, JC80.H6
Holmberg, Daniel...................................JC70.H6
Holsen, Paul J.....................................FC60.Z4
Holst, Hans..JC50.B5
Holt, Susan Fraker.................................AA90.H4
Holzer, Hans W..........................BA20.H64, CC40.H6
Holzmair, Edward...............JK20.H6, JK87.H5, RA80.M4H6
Homans, Isaac Smith................................AA40.H6
Hoober, Richard T..............AA80.H6, US40.H6, US40.W4
          US45.M2H6, US45.N3H6, US45.N4H6, US45.V5H6
Hood, Clyde..GA50.H6
Hood, Jennings.....................................SH30.H6
Hook, Mary Jane....................................CC40.R8
Hooper, Joseph.....................................AA10.H6
Hoppe, Donald J....................................CC63.H65
Hopper, James......................................SH30.H66
Horn, Howard.......................................AB32.H6
Horn, Jeanne.......................................CC55.H6
Horn, Otto...JG67.H48
Hosch, Charles..........................CC60.H6, CC60.H6o
Hoskins, Charles R......................BA60.H6, CC65.H6
Houssayl, Noel.....................................BB60.H6
Howard, C. S.......................................UI30.H6
Howard-White, F. B.................................AB50.H6
Howell, Edgar M....................................SH50.C3
Howlett, C. J......................................JB95.H6
Howorth, Daniel F..................................JB96.H6
Hoyt, Samuel L.....................................AB25.H5
Hrbas, Milos.......................................BA80.05H7
Hubbard, Clyde.....................................FB67.B82
Hudson, Thomas..........................PA40.H8, PA40.H85
Hughes, B. H.......................................US60.D6
Huie, Byron S......................................KB30.H9
Hull, Donald B.....................................KA90.D4H8
Hulse, Granvyl G...................................KA45.H8

Hume, Edgar Erskine.....................RM80.W3H8, SH40.H8
Humphreys, Henry Noel..........AA40.H8, BA40.H8, BC70.H8
        JB40.H8, JB40.H8c, JB85.H8
Hungary. National Gallery............RK60.H8f, RK60.H8m
        RK60.H8me
Hunt, Inez...PA40.H88
Hunter, John...CC67.H9
Huntington, C. C.....................................VA70.O3H8
Hunzar, Lajos...JJ70.H8
Huntoon, Peter..................US20.O3, US90.G6, US90.W3
Hutchinson, William H................................AA40.H88
Hutten-Czapski, Comte Emeric see Czapski, Emeric
        Hutton-Comte
Hyman, Arthur.......................................PG90.N8H8

Icard, Severin...BB60.I3
Iliescu, O...BA20.I3
Illingworth Baquerizo, Gustavo...................RN50.E2I4
Imhoof-Blumer, Friedrich...............BB60.I5, BB97.I5
Imlay and Bicknell.....................................CC20.I4
Imperial Mint, Osaka...................KD40.J3g, KD40.J3h
India. Ministry of Finance.........................KA85.I5
Indian Museum. Calcutta............................KA60.I5
Ingholt, Harald.......................................AA40.A5
International Association of Professional Numismatists
        AA10.I5, CC50.I5
International Criminal Police Organization.......UA40.I5
International Currency Society.....................UN50.I5
International Nickel Company...AB50.I5, AB70.I5, CC67.I5
International Numismatic Commission..............AA40.I5
        AA40.S8
International Numismatic Company........KB10.I5, KD20.I5
        KD20.I5c
International Numismatic Convention...............WA50.I5
International Stamp and Coin Agency..............KB20.I5
Investimenti Trust Finanziario Numismatica.......JI30.I5
Irons, Charles F......................................SH20.I7
Irons, Kenneth J......................................MA40.D4
Israel Government Coins and Medals Corporation..KA40.I86
Israel Numismatic Society................BD40.I8, KA40.I8
Isthmian Numismatic Society.........................FC65.I8
Ittel, William.......................................UF70.S6
Ives, Herbert Eugene..................JA63.I8, JI97.V4I9

Jablonski, Tadensz...................................UF70.J3
Jacob, Kenneth A.........................AA60.J3, AA80.J3
Jacobs, Norman.......................................KD20.J3
Jaeckel, Peter.......................................JK40.J3

Kadman, Leo................BD50.K25, BD60.A3K3, BD60.A4K3
        BD60.C3K3, KA40.K3
Kagan, Arnold H.......................................KA40.K33
Kahler, Heinz...BC70.K3
Kalkowski, Taduesz....................................JJ20.K3
Kaminski, Czeslaw.....................................JJ20.K34
Kanael, Baruch..BD40.K3
Kann, Edward..........KC20.K3, KC40.K3, KC43.K3, KC45.K3
        KC60.K3, UN30.K3
Kaplan, Alec..LA30.K3
Kaplan, Sol...GB10.K3
Kappen, Charles V......................RM30.H5, US35.K3
Karys, Jonas.....................AA45.K3, JM95.K3, UF40.K3
Karyshkowski, P. O.........JM92.K3b, JM92.K3c, JM92.K3C2
        JM92.K3f, JM92.K3i, JM92.K3i2, JM92.K3m, JM92.K3o
        JM92.K3o2, JM92.K3o3, JM92.K3o4, JM92.K3v
Kassim Haji Ali, Mohammed...............KB25.S5, QB60.S5
Katsouros, Floros.....................................JL70.K3
Kaufman, Jerroll D....................................AB32.K3
Kavanaugh, Kevin F....................................KB20.K3
Kearney, W. L..RM85.M3K4
Keary, Charles F.....AA40.K4, JB40.H4, JB80.B7, RI10.B7i
Kelemen, G. Bela......................................JJ80.K4
Keller, Arnold........................PG70.K4, UA33.K4
        UA33.K4p, UC40.K4, UC40.K4d,UC40.K4n
        UC80.K4
Kelley, William D.....................................CC60.K4
Kellner, Hans-Jorg....................................JG90.K4
Kelly, P..AA90.K4
Kelman, Keith N.......................................GB20.K4
Kelpsh, A. E....................JE65.K4, JI83.K4, JM83.K4
Kemm, Theodore..US20.K4
Kemmerer, Edwin W.....................................VD10.N3
Kempf, Fred..KB70.T6K4
Kennepohl, Karl......................................JG98.H3K4
Kenner, Friedrich.....................................RK20.K4
Kenney, Richard D.....CC50.K4, GA70.K4, RM30.K4, RM60.K4
Kent, E. R. Jackson...................................JB85.K4
Kent, G. C..PE30.K4
Kent, J. P. C........................BC67.H51, JB20.B7
Kenyon, Robert Lloyd....................JB63.K4, JB65.H3
Kerr, R...PE90.K4
Kerrigan, Evans E......................SH30.K4, SH60.K4
Kessler, Alan...GB30.K4
Kestner-Museums.......................................BC85.K4
Kidd, J. A..RM30.G7
Kienast, Gunter W....................................RG35.G6K5
Kiezebrink, Th. H. R.................................JF90.O9K5
Kikusen, Nakahaski....................................KD20.K5
Kindler, Arie.......................BD60.T5K5, RG10.K5
King, Elizabeth W.....................................SH60.K5
King, Edward A..PA40.K5
King, Robert..GB40.K5
Kirby, Norman H.......................................JE65.K5

Kirschner, Bruno...RG10.K5
Kisch, Bruno.......................AA80.M4, AA90.K5, NB40.K5
Kisch, Guido........CC53.K5, RA40.K5, RA80.L3K5, RD60.K5
Kittlemann, E..JG65.K5
Klaasesz, Paul F...JJ60.K5
Klaes, F. X..GB20.K5
Klander, Charles...US15.K5
Klawans, Zander H.........................BB50.K5, BC85.K5
Kleinhaus, Philip L.....................................VA60.N4K5
Klenau, Armhard Graf....................................SD60.K54
Klenau, Tyra Giafin.....................................JG30.K5
Klietmann, K. G....................SD60.K55f, SD60.K55p
Knight, Hugh McCown.....................................GA50.K5
Knobloch, Fredrick S....................................BA20.M3
Knox, John Jay..US20.K6
Kobbe, Gustav...QA40.K6
Kocaer, Remzi..KA20.T8K6
Koch, Bernhard....................JK83.K6, JK90.S2K6
Koehler, Johann David...................................CC30.K6
Koenig, Marie E. P......................................JA79.K6
Kohl, Melvin J..LA50.K6
Kolbeinsson, Finnur.....................................JC40.K6
Kolman, Michael......................GA90.K6, GA90.K6f
Koper, Bert...HA57.P3
Korea.   Bank of..KD70.K6
Kortenbach, C. J..RF60.K6
Kortjohn, Martin F......................................CC67.K6
Kosoff, Abraham......GA40.K6, GA90.J8, GB15.K65, GB20.K6
        GB80.H3A3, JC70.K5, JM20.K6
Kotler, Joseph Mark.....................................PB40.K6
Kouymajian, Dickran K...................................KA10.K6
Kovel, Ralph M..RM15.K6
Kovel, Terry H..RM15.K6
Kozolubski, J...BB30.S4
Kozono, Hitoshi.....................KC20.C6e, KD20.K6
Kraay, Colin M....BB20.S8o, BB40.D22, BB40.K7a, BB40.K7g
        BB40.K7h, BB57.K7, BB90.K7, BC85.K7
Krakel, Dean Fenton.....................................GB40.K7
Kramer, Albert..GA90.K7
Krasnodebski, Jan J.....................................AA50.K7
Kratchkovski, V. A......................................JM40.K7
Kraus, Franz Ferdinand..................................JI97.K7
Krause, Chester L...............CC87.K7, GA50.C65, RM15.C8
        US50.C5
Krause, Delbert Ray.....................................RD60.K7
Krause, Hermann...AA50.K73
Kroha, Tyll...BA40.M45
Krueger, Leonard Bayliss................................VA70.W6K7
Krusy, Hans...JG80.K7
Kuhn, Hermann...JG70.K8
Kunz, George Frederick..................................RF35.R6K8
Kunz, Joseph...UF60.K8
Kurth, Howard H....HA57.K8, HA57.S8, PA40.K8, PA80.N42K8
Kustas, G. L..BC85.A3

Kuthmann, H..JG87.A7

LaBaume, Peter......................................JA79.L3
Lacombe, Robert.....................................WD50.L3
LaCouperie, Albert Terrien de see Terrien de la
        Couperie, Albert
Lagerquist, Lars O..................................JC70.L3
Lahiri, Amarendra Nath..............................BB97.L3
Lahore. Central Museum................KA60.L3r, KA60.L3w
Laing, Lloyd Robert.................................BA40.L3
Lake, Kenneth R.....................................UA50.L3
LaLoire, Edouard....................................RD20.L3
Lamb, J. A..PE90.K4
Lamb, Robert A.............................PF70.L3, PG70.L3
Lambros, Paul.......BB90.L3, JI95.L3, JL80.L3c, JL80.L3g
        JL80.L3u, JL90.L3
Landis, Walter S....................................WC10.L3
Lane-Poole, Stanley...........AA40.L3, KA50.L3, KA50.L3a
        KA50.L3m, KA50.L3u, KA50.P6, KA55.A4L3
        KA60.B7m, KA60.B7s
Lang, David Marshall...............................JM90.G4L3
Langdon, William Chauncy............................RN10.L3
Lange, Kurt...JG80.L3
Lanier, Henry Wysham...............................VA60.N7L3
Lannois, M..RF85.M4L3
Lapa, Frank A.................CC53.L3, JI93.L3, JM83.L3
        KA90.C4L3, NB40.L3
Lapp, A. Warren.....................................GB30.L3
LaTour, Henri de....................................JE80.L3
Lattimore, Steven...................................BB60.L3
Laughlin, James Laurence............................WB30.L3
LaVoix, Henri.......................................BD36.L3
Lawrence, Jimmie N..................................UA30.L3
Lawrence, Richard Hoe.............................RI35.C3L3
Leake, Stephen Martin..............................JB40.L4h
Leavens, Dickson H.....................WA30.L4, WE60.L4
Lebreton, M. Gaston.................................RF10.L4
Lee, Edward Melvin...................GB80.C3B8, GB80.C3L4
Lee, Kenneth W.....................GB80.C3L4, GB80.C3L42
Lee, Warren G.......................................QA60.L4
Leeds, Edward Thurlow...............................BC75.L4
Leeming, Joseph.....................................AA40.L4
Lees, W. A. D.......................................PB70.L4
Leggett, L. Candler...............................US80.M7L4
Leite de Vasconcellos, Jose.........................JD70.L4
Lelewel, Joachim....................................JA80.L4
Le Loux, S. A. M....................................JI93.L4
Le Marchant, R......................................UB30.L4
Le May, Reginald Stuart..........................KB70.T5L4
Lenormant, Francois............AA45.L4, BA40.L4, WA50.L4
Lenzi, Luciano......................JI97.L5C4, JI97.P5L4

Loubat, Joseph Florimond.............................RM60.L6
Low, Lyman H....................AA70.L6, FB60.L6, FB65.L6
        JI93.L6, PA73.L6, RM50.B4
Lowande, Joseph H...................................NB80.L5
Lowe, Geoffrey J....................................PE30.L6
Lund, Karl..UC40.L8
Luschin, Arnold...................................JK90.S7L8
Luscomb, Sally C....................................SA40.L8

Macalister, R. A. S.................................PE85.M3
McClure, R. A.......................................GA20.M3
McCormick-Goodhart, Leander......................RE80.V4M3
Macdonald, Georg................AA40.M3, BA40.M3, BB20.G5
        BB40.H4, BB60.H3, BB90.M3
McDowell, Kay.....................................PA80.A4F4
McDowell, Robert Harold.............................BD30.M3
McFarland, Cara Lee...............................VA80.06M3
McGarry, Sheridan L.................................US75.M3
McGregor, T. D......................................VD30.M3
McIlvaine, Arthur D.................................GB20.M3
Mack, Richard Paston.....................JB80.B58, JB80.M3
McKay, George L.....................................US40.M3
Mackay, James Alexander.............................AA30.M3
McKee, James L...................................US80.N3M3
McKenzie, Kenneth M..............................KA20.T8M3
McKinney, Willis J.................................GB40.M3
McLachlan, Robert W...........HA40.C3, HA40.M2, HA40.M3
        HA70.M2, HA70.M25, HA85.M3, JB85.M3, PB30.M3
        PB40.M3c, PB40.M3m, PB70.M3, RO60.M3, UI50.M3
McLaughlin, Lloyd A..............................RM85.M3M3
McLean, Janice.....................................SH60.W3
MacLennan, George A...............................PB40.M32
McNaught, James B..................................AA80.M3
McNeice, Roger V.................MA40.M3, UQ38.T3M3
MacNeil, Neil....................................RM85.P7M3
McNickle, A. J. Stanley................FA30.M3, FA30.M3e
Madai, David Samuel von.............................JA20.M3
Madden, Frederic....BC20.M3, BC45.S7, BD40.M3c, BD40.M3h
Madonia, Gail......................................CC40.M3
Madras. Government Museum.............BD10.M3, KA70.M3
Magain, Pierre...................................JF90.L5M3
Magnaguti, Alexander.................BA70.M3, BC80.M33
Mailliet, Prosper..................................CC53.M3
Maity, Sachindra Kumar.............................KA70.M35
Majer, Frederic....................................GA40.M2
Malhotra, D. K.....................................WE30.M3
Mallis, George A....................GB20.M35, GB20.V34
Malloy, Alex G...................................BD38.A5M3
Malter, Joel L.....................BD30.G3, BE50.M3
Mancini, Libero....................................UB50.M3
Mandel, Bill.......................................AA90.M3

Mandel, Edgar J..................KC47.M3, KD70.M3, PL50.M3
Mandel, Siegfried...BD40.W5h
Mangan, James Thomas......................................PA40.M35
Manhattan College, New York...............................BA20.M3
Mao, King O.....................................UN40.M3c, UN40.M3p
Marckhoff, Fred R...........................US80.I4M3c, US80.I4M3s
Marco, Jindrich...BA80.05H7
Marcon, Alfredo...UB50.M32
Margolis, Arnold.............GA90.M3c, GA90.M3n, GB20.M37
Maris, Edward...GB80.N4M3
Marple, Elliot..VA80.W3M4
Marshall, George..JB85.M37
Martin, Jean L..RD60.M3
Martin, Lee.....................................GA40.M3, RM30.M3
Martin, Peter Hugo..BA40.M37
Martin, Will..US20.H6
Martinez, Carlos..FB50.M3
Martinez del Rio, Pablo...................................FB65.M3
Marvin, William T. R......................................RM50.B4
Marx, Roger...RA10.M3
Mason, Don Walter..............................CC63.M3, GB10.M3
Massamore, George W.......................................US60.M3
Massey, J. Earl...GA40.M32
Masters, Robert V..........................AA40.M34, GA50.M3
Mateu y Llopis, Felipe........BD85.M3, JD43.M3, JD43.M3r
Mathews, George D...AA40.M35
Mathias, Peter..PE30.M3
Mathis, Rene..SB60.C9M3
Matravers, Brian..UN20.S6
Matsson, G. O...BA65.M3
Mattei, Luigi...RI50.M4M4
Mattingly, Harold.............BC20.B7, BC40.M35, BC75.M3
        BC80.M3, BC80.M3a, BC80.M3v, BC85.B7
        BC85.M3m, BC85.M3r
May, John Maunsell Frampton...............................BB94.M3
Mayer, Leo Ary..KA50.M3
Mayhew, Aubrey..RA60.K4M3
Mazard, Jean....................JE40.M32, JE95.M3, JE95.M3m
Mazerolle, Fernand..............................JE60.M3, RF35.B3M3
Mazio, Francesco..RI80.P6M3
Mazzulla, Fred and Jo.....................................PA40.M3
Medcalf, Gordon G........GB80.H3M4, SH70.H3M4, US80.H3M4
Medina, Jose Toribio...........FA15.M4, FA40.M4, RN10.M4
Medlar, Bob...US80.T4M4
Meek, W. F. W...PN40.M4
Mehl, B. Max.......AA50.S7, AA50.S7s, GA55.M4b, GA55.M4r
        GB20.H4h, GB40.M4
Mehl, Manfred...................................UC40.M4, UC40.M4p
Mendenhall, W. E..WB40.M4
Mercante, Luciano...RI50.M4M4
Merlub-Sobel, M...AB15.M4
Merrick, J. J...JA80.M4
Merrington, K. E..BC85.S8c
Mervis, Clyde D...AA95.M4

Molyneauz, Peter J................................GA55.M6
Montagu, Hyman.........................JB20.S6, JB67.M6
Morello,Theodore...............................RM10.M6
Moreno, Alvaro J...............................UJ40.M6
Morgan, Carl E................................GA90.M6
Morgan, E. Victor.............................WC30.F4
Morgan, J. McDowell...........................SH30.M6
Morgan, John Pierpont.........................BA20.R3
Morgentau, Bernard..........PA40.M6c, PA40.M6e, PA40.M6k
Morin, Francois...............................JF40.M6
Morin, Victor..............................RM85.I5M6
Morrieson, H. W..............................JB40.M6
Morris, James................................VD30.M6
Morris, Robert.............................JA80.M58
Morris, Thomas F.............................US25.M6
Morrison, Karl F.............................JA80.M6
Mort, Selwyn R...............................JK40.M6
Mosher, Stuart.................AA80.M6, GB40.M6, QB20.M6
Mosser, Sawyer McArthur................BA20.M6, BE50.M6
Mossop, Henry R..............................JB80.M6
Mottram, R. H................................VC30.M6
Moura Soares, Edgard.........................FE40.M6
Mowery, Thomas E.............................KC55.M6
Muhleman, Maurice L..........................WA30.M8
Muller, Johannes Heinrich....................JG80.M8
Muller, Ludwig.........................BB80.M8, BB94.M8
Muller - Wandau, August V....................UF30.M8
Mumey, Nolie.................GB80.C6M8, US80.C6M8
Munoz, Miguel.........................FB40.M8, FB65.M8
Munro, Neil Gordon...........................KD20.M8
Murari, Ottorino...........JI80.M8, JI97.P5M8, JI97.V5M8
Murphy, Claud.............................US80.G4C6
Murray, John...............................AA80.M8
Muscalus, John A.....UB30.M8, US20.M8, US20.M8p, US35.M8
        US50.M8, US50.M8p, US75.M8, US75.M8a
        US75.M8c, US75.M8d, US75.M8f, US75.M8il
        US75.M8inc, US75.M8inp, US75.M8inw, US75.M8l
        US75.M8p, US75.M8s, US75.M8s2, US75.M8u
        US77.B8M8, US77.C3M8, US77.C6M8, US77.D5M8
        US77.E3M8, US77.L3M8, US77.M4M8, US77.M6M8
        US77.P5M8, US77.P6M8, US77.R3M8, US77.R4M8
        US77.R6M8, US77.S5M8, US77.W5M8, US80.D5M8
        US80.N5M8, US80.V5M8, US85.L5M8, US85.M3M8
        US85.M4M8, US85.M5M8, US85.N5M8, US85.O3M8
        US85.P8M8, VA45.M8, VA50.M8
Musser, Dwight L................UA30.M8, UA50.M8, UN60.M8
Mussolini, Vittorio Emannele....................SF70.S207
Muszynski, Maurice....................UB40.M8, UP70.M8
Myers, Robert J...............................JE85.M8

Nahuys, Maurin................JF85.N3, RD20.N3h, RD20.N3m

Narain, A. K...............................BB97.N3, KA70.P7
Narbeth, Colin..................UA30.B4, UA50.N3, UB30.N3
Nasler, Paul...BB20.N3
Nathan, S...JD45.N3
Nathanson, Alan J....................................JB60.N3
National Bank of Detroit.............................AA20.N3
National Commemorative Society.......................RM15.N3
National Geographic Society..........................CC55.N3
National Monetary Commission.........................VD10.N3
National Portrait Gallery............................GB40.N3
National Sculpture Society.............RM10.N3a, RM10.N3c
Nau, Elisabeth.....................................JG98.S9N3
Navascues, Joaquin M.................................JD10.N3
Nazi Party...SD60.U5
Nebraska Numismatics....................RA20.N4, RA20.N4w
Nelson, Philip......................JB85.N4a, JB85.N4c
        JB85.N4g, JB90.N4, JB94.N4
Nemeskal, Lubomir....................................JJ60.N4
Nepal. Dept. of Archeology and Culture...........KB70.N4
Nesmith, Robert I....CC55.N4, FA30.N4, FB60.N4, JB85.N42
Neto, Fernando de Carvalho...........................FE40.N4
Netscher, E..JF95.N4
Nettels, Curtis Putnam...............................WB50.N4
Neuce, Ed..............................GA50.N4, US33.N4
Neumann, Josef.......................................CC67.N4
New York. Federal Reserve Bank.....................AA40.N4
New York. Numismatic Club..........................GA10.N4
New York. Public Library...........................AA50.N4
New York. State Library............................GA20.N4
New Zealand. Royal Numismatic Society...........PN40.N4
Newcomb, Howard R............GB30.C55b, GB30.N4, GB30.N4c
Newell, Edward T.....BA40.N4, BB40.N4, BB60.N4, BB70.N4f
        BB70.N4k, BB70.N4s, BB80.N4a, BB80.N4c, BB80.N4d
        BB80.N4e, BB80.N46, BB90.N4, BB90.N4s, BB90.N6
        BB97.N4s, BB97.N4t, BC75.N4f, BC75.N4t, BC95.N4
        BD30.N4, BD32.N4, BD34.N42, BD34.N44, BD34.N45
        BD34.N46, BD34.N47, BD34.N48, BD40.N4, BD83.N4
        BD83.N62, BE90.N4
Newlin, Harold P.....................................GB20.N4
Newman, E. G. V.....................................JB60.N49
Newman, Eric P......AA70.N4, GB20.N42, GB50.N4, GB50.N4c
        GB50.N4f, GB50.N4j, GB50.N4s, GB80.V4N4
        GB80.V5N4, US40.N4c, US40.N4e, US40.N4f, US40.N4n
Newman, W. A. C......................................JB60.N4
Nichols, Henry W.....................................BA60.N5
Niehaus, Fred R.....................VA80.C6N5d, VA80.C6N5s
Noe, Sydney P........AA70.N6, BB70.N6, BB90.N6, BB94.N6c
        BB94.N6m, BB94.N6t, BD32.N6, CC55.N6
        GB80.M4N6, GB80.M4N6n, GB80.M4N60, GB80.M4N6p
        GB80.M4N6s, PC20.E4, RM35.W4N6
Noehden, George Henry...............................BB94.N65
Noel, James A., Jr...................................JD45.N6
Nohejlova-Pratova, Emanuela.............JJ50.N6, RK40.N6
Nole, James E.......................US50.N6, US50.N6i

Petrie, W. M. F.............................QC30.P4, QC30.P4p
Petrov, V. I..JM40.P4
Pettit, William A...GB40.P4
Peyton, George..US30.P4
Pfeiffer, Philip A..US80.F5P4
Philadelphia. Numismatic Society...................PA70.P5
Philip, George..SE30.P4
Philippine Islands. (Government)......UM40.P5e, UM40.P5f
Philippine Numismatic and Antiquarian Society....KB30.P5
     KB30.P5g
Phillips, Arthur..AB70.B7
Phillips, C. H...KA11.P46
Phillips, Henry.....................US40.P5a, US40.P5p
Philpott, William A., Jr...................................US90.P5
Pick, Albert.................UA30.P5, UA33.P5c, UA33.P5s
     UA40.P5, UA50.P5, UC40.G4, UC40.K4
     UC55.P5, UC60.P5, UH20.P5
Pick, Monika..PG70.P5
Pilartz, Heinrich...JG98.C6P5
Pinerton, John...RA30.P5
Pink, Karl...JA79.P5
Piper, Richard...GB20.P5
Pirie, Anthony...UC60.P5
Pirie, Elizabeth J. E......................................JB80.P5
Piromya, Sompop..KB70.T5P5
Pitts, Edward H..FB55.P5
Plant, Richard J...KA50.P4
Plantijin, Christoffel.....................................JA80.P4
Platbarzdis, Aleksandrs..................JM97.P5, UB60.P5
Plenderleith, H. J...BA60.H6
Plumer, Warren Lloyd.......................................PC35.P5
Pohl, Arthur............................JJ70.P6, JJ80.P6
Polak, Arthur..RD20.P6
Polivka, Eduard..................JJ50.J3, JJ50.P6, JJ60.P6
Pollack, Foster B..PA70.P6
Pollack, Irving..GA55.P6
Pollard, Graham........................BB20.P64, RA10.H5
Pond, Shepard...................JE85.P6, JE85.P6p, RF30.P6
     RM90.M4P6, UB40.P6
Ponton d'Amecourt, Gustave.............JE82.P6d, JE82.P6r
Poole, Stanley Lane see Lane-Poole, Stanley
Poole, Reginald Stuart.......BB20.B71, BB97.B7b, KA30.B7
     KA55.A4L3, KA60.B7m, KA60.B7s, KC50.T4
Pope-Hennessy, John..RA10.P6
Porada, Edith..QC20.P6
Porcher, Hermann...FE40.P6
Porteous, John.........................AA40.P6c, AA40.P6h
Porter, A. S...GA50.Y42
Porto, E. J..JD90.P6
Posvar, Jaroslav.......................JJ60.P69, JK90.B6P6
Poulsom, Neville W..RE85.P6P6
Power, James R...SE30.P6
Pownall, Henry...SA60.P6
Pozzi, S...BB20.P6

Pradeau Aviles, Alberto F.....FB45.P72, FB50.P7, FB60.P7
        FB60.P7a, FB60.P7e, FB67.P7, PC20.L4
Prague. Numismaticke Spolecnost Ceskoslovenske..RK40.P7
Prakash, Vidya.....................................KA70.P7
Price, Martin......................................BB94.P7
Pridmore, F......................JB96.P7, JL90.P7, KB25.P7
Prime, William Cowper..............................AA40.P7
Prober, Kurt.................AA45.P7, FC55.P7, FD50.P7
        FE40.P7, FE40.P7c, FE40.P7p, RN60.P7
Probst, Romain.....................................JF40.P7
Probst, Gunter.............AA50.P7, JK40.P7, JK90.S2P7
        RK20.P7k, RK20.P7s
Prochazka, Roman Freiherr von...................SB60.A8P7
Promis, Deomenico...............................JI97.M6P7
Prow, M. Maurice..................................JE79.P7
Prowse, A. E......................................SD40.P7
Prucha, Francis Paul............................RM85.I5P7
Puerto Rico. Banco Credito........................FD60.P8
Purves, Alec A...................SA30.P8c, SA30.P8o
Purvey, Frank......................................AA60.P8
Pye, Charles....................PE60.P9, PE60.P9r

Quaker Currency Co.................................US15.Q8
Quarmby, Earnest..................................UB30.Q3
Quiggin, Alison Hingston.............AA40.Q8, QB40.Q5

Rabino, Hyacinth...................................KA30.R3
Rackus, Alexander M................................JA80.R3
Rada y Delgado, Juan...............................JD43.R3
Raeburn, G. Duncan....................KC30.R3, KC60.R3
Raisig, L. Miles...................................AA96.R2
Rama Rao, Mhd......................BD10.A5, KA60.A5s
Ramesan, Sri N.....................................KA60.A5v
Ramsay, Robert M...................................FA25.R3
Ramsden, Henry A......................KC47.R3, KC50.R3
        PL50.R3, PL60.R3, UN20.R3
Ranie, Hans.....................................AB66.S9R3
Raoul-Rochette, M..................................BB40.R3
Ratcliffe, E. E. JB50.R3
Ratto, Rodolfo................BB94.M6, BC67.S9c, BE20.R3
Rauta, Aurelio....................................JJ85.R3
Ravel, Oscar........................BB70.R3, BB90.R3a
Ravn, O. E..QC20.R3
Rawlings, Gertrude Burford..............AA40.R2, JB40.R3
Raymond, Doris........................AA40.R28, BB94.R3
Raymond, Rossiter.................................AB28.R3
Raymond, Wayte...............BA20.R3, BA30.R3a, BA30.R3g
        CC40.R3w, CC85.R3c, CC87.R3t, FA23.R3

        FA23.R3g, FA25.R35, FA25.R35s, FB30.R3, FC20.R3
        RD20.R3, FE20.R3, GA30.R3b, GA30.R3c, GA30.R3p
        GA30.R3r, GB20.R3, GA30.R3s, GA30.R3t, GA30.R3u
        GB10.R3u, GB15.R3, GB30.R3, GB30.R3s, HA35.R3
        JB65.R3, JB87,R3, JB96.R3, JB96.R3b, JD45.R3
        JD95.R3, JE65.R3, JE95.R3, JF40.R3, JF87.R3
        KA85.R3, LA20.R3, PA80.N42R3, RM80.W3R3
        US15.R3sc, US15.R3st, US70.R3
Rayner, Peter Alan.........................JB60.R3, JB65.S4b
Reagan, Lewis Martin..............................AA75.R4
Rebello, Fenelon..................................KA60.R4
Rebelo, Luis Manuel...............................UB55.R4
Reed, Fred Morton....AA60.R41, GA50.R4, GB40.R4, QB30.R4
Reed, Jeffrey.....................................SH60.W3
Regling, Kurt Ludwig...........BA40.R4, BA70.R4, BB20.R4
Reich, Joseph P...................................AA80.M4
Reifenberg, Adolf...........BD40.R4, BD50.R4i, BD50.R4p
Reimmann, Johann Friedrich Christian..............JA20.R4
Reinach, Theodore............BA40.R45, BB97.W3, BD40.R42
Reinfeld, Fred.....AA40.R4, AA40,R42, AA50.C4, AA60.H62p
        AA60.M34, AA60.R42c, AA60.R42h, BA50.R4
        GA40.R4, GA50.H55, GA50.M3, GA50.R45h, GA55.H55
        GB40.H6, US20.R4, US60.R4
Reinhardt, Hans...................................JH20.R4
Reitzenstein, Alexander Freiherr von...........SD70.B3S3
Remick, Jerome H......FD50.R4, FD55.B9, JB90.R4, JB96.G8
Remmelts, A. A....................................KC20.R4
Renauldin, Leop................................AA58.M4R4
Rengjeo, Ivan.....................................JL40.R4
Rentzmann, Wilhelm.......... AA50.R46, AA80.R4, AA80.R4w
Renz, Russell H...................................GB25.R4
Rethy, Ladislaus..................................JJ70.R4
Rhodes, N. G......................................KA10.07
Rhys-Davids, T. W.................................BD20.D3
Riccio, Gennaro...................................BC80.R5
Rice, Foster Wild.................................US25.R5
Rice, L. P..AB72.R5
Richardson, John M.............................GB80.V4R5
Richebe, R..RF30.R3
Richter, Gisela M.................................BB60.R5
Richter, R..UF60.P5
Rickard, T. A.....................................AB32.R5
Rickenbacker, William F...........................PA40.R5
Riddell, John Leonard.............................FA25.R5
Ridgeway, William.................................AA90.R5
Riesser, J..VD10.N3
Rinaldi, Alfio.................................RI80.P6R5
Rinaldi, Oscar....................................JI40.R5
Rink, Paul..VA40.R5
Risk, James Charles.....................SE30.R5, SE40.R5
Rittman, Herbert..................................CC35.R5
Ritzthaler, Robert E..............................QB60.R5
Rixen, Jens-Uwe.................................JG98.N6J3
Robb, Alistair T..................................MA70.R6

Robert, Charles...PF60.R6
Robert, Louis...BB40.R6
Roberts, Bruce..GB80.N6R6
Roberts, Jack...RO70.R6
Roberts, Travis L.....................................PA80.T4F6
Roberts, W. Rhys..BB40.R5
Robertson, Anne S.............BC85.R55, BC97.R6, JB80.R6
Robertson, John Drummond................................JB93.R6
Robertson, Ross M......................................VA30.R62
Robinson, Charles M.........................FC20.R6, FC55.R6
Robinson, David Moore......................BB56.R6, BB90.R6
Robinson, Edward S.G..........BB20.B7e, BB20.L6, BB20.R6
          BC80.M3
Robinson, Harry A.........................NB40.C6, PN40.R6
Robinson, John..KA10.R6
Robles de la Torre, Jose...............................FB60.R62
Rochesnard, Jean-Georges Forien de.................PF70.R6
Rochette, Edward C....................................RA60.K4R6
Rockholt, R. H..US80.M6R6
Rodgers, Charles James.................................KA60.L3r
Rodney, Richard S.....................................US45.D4R6
Rodriquez Lorenta, J. J.................................JD35.R6
Roest, Th. M...CC10.T4
Rogers, Edgar..................BB90.R63, BD34.R6, BD40.R6
Rogers, Edward Thomas...................................LA60.R6
Rohde, Theodore...BC85.R6
Rohlers, Johann...CC30.R6
Roll, Karl..RK20.R6
Rolla, Mario..JI40.D6
Rolland, Henri..BC80.R6
Rollin et Feuardent. Paris.............................JE83.R6
Romano, Don C...AA78.R6
Romanoff, Paul...BD40.R62
Rome. Museo Borgiano....................................BD83.R6
Romero de Terreros y Vincent, Manuel................FB40.R6
Romerstein, Herbert....................................US60.C7o
Roosa, Robert V.......................................VA30.R66
Roosbroech, Adelbert Van................................JG67.R6
Ros, Giuseppe...KC60.R6
Rosato, Angelo A......................................RM80.K4R6
Rosenberger, Mayer......................................BD45.R6
Rosichan, Richard H.....................................AA50.R6
Ross, Shelby C..SD60.R6
Ross, Thomas B..RM85.N4R6
Roth, Cecil...RA80.J4F7
Rothert, Matt...US50.R6
Rottinger, Bruno..PG70.R6
Roubier, Jean...AA80.B3
Royal Australian Mint...................................MA50.R6
Rua, Fernando Gimeno..................................JD50.C3R8
Ruby, Warren A..GB40.R8
Ruchlemer, Ruth...NB40.L3
Ruddy, James F........................GA50.R8, GB30.B6
Ruding, Rogers..JB40.R8

Rulau, Russell.............................CC40.R8, UA33.P5s
Rule, W. G..VA70.M6R8
Rupp, Robert O.....................................GB20.R8
Russell, Monica..................................PE30.S43
Russell, Solveig Paulson..........................AA40.R8
Russett, F. R.....................................US70.R8
Rutlader, James...................................UA60.R8
Rydberg, N. E.....................................UF30.O4
Ryder, Hillyer......................GB80.M4R9, GB80.V4R9
Rynearson, Paul F.................................BE30.R9
Rywell, Martin....................................AA60.S4

Saba Sumar, Wadi..................................FE75.S3
Sabatier, Justin.................................BE40.S2
Sabin, George....................................JE65.S6
Sadler, Jerry....................................CC55.S2
Saeman, C. C..................................... AA40.S2
Sahni, Birbal....................................BD10.S2
Said, Emmanuel...................................JN30.S2
Saint-Gaudens, Homer...........................RM35.S2S2
Salinas, Di Antonio.............................BB94.S2
Salles Oliviera, Alvarode......................FE40.S15
Sallet, Alfred......................JG20.F75, RG35.D8S3
Salmo, Helmer...................................JG79.S2
Salton, Mark...................................RA10.B6
Sambon, T......................................JI79.S2
Sams, Jack.....................................GA90.S2
San Jose. Uruguay. Banco.......................FE80.S2
Sanchez-Giron Blasco, Jose Maria.............KA55.M6S2
Sandham, Alfred................................HA40.S2
Sandwich, George Charles......................RA80.N3S3
Santamas, M. L.....................JC92.S2, KA20.T8S2
Santos, Ildefonso.............................KB50.S2
Santos Leitao and Co. (Rio de Janeiro)..........FE40.S2
Sarazin, Francois.............................KD43.S3
Satterlee, Alfred H...........................RM60.S3
Saulcy, Louis Felicien........ .BE40.S3, CC80.S2, JE82.S2
        JE82.S2c, JE82.S2d, JE90.M4S2, RF85.R4S2
Saurma-Geltsch, Hugo von......................JG98.S5S3
Sause, George G...............................WB30.S2
Saxton, Burton H..............................AA75.S2
Sbornik, I. Numismatickeho Symposia...........JJ60.S3
Scaife, J. Verner...................JB96.S3, PL40.S3
Scaligeri, Joseph.............................AA45.S3
Scates, Shelby................................VA40.S3
Schell, Frank R...............................PA80.I3S2
Schembri, H. Calleja..........................JA80.S28
Schenkman, David..............................PA70.S3
Schermerhoin, Charles W.......................AA60.S34
Scheuch, Karl..................JG67.S3, RG30.S3s, RG30.S3
Schilke, Oscar G..............................GB60.S3

Schimmel, Jerry F.....................................PA40.S3
Schive, C. I...JC50.S3
Schjoth, Fredrik.....................................KC20.S3
Schlumberger, Gustave Leon...............JA80.S3, JG80.S3
Schlumberger, Hans.....................JA63.S3, JA63.S3e
Schmall, Charles N...................................PA50.S3
Schmidt, Gunter Erik.............................SB60.A8S3
Schmitz, Hubert......................................UC40.S3
Schneider, Herbert...................................JB85.S3
Schneider, William A.................................CC65.S3
Scholes, I. R..AB62.E3
Scholten, C..JF95.S3
Scholtz, Josef.......................................BB20.S3
Schon, Gunter.........CC70.S3, CC85.S3, CC87.S3, JG87.S3
Schou, H. H..JC10.S3
Schreiber, Georg...................................SD70.B3S3
Schreiber, Otto Louis.............................RG80.L8S3
Schroeder, Albert..................KB70.A5S3a, KB70.A5S3g
Schrotter, Friedrich.................................JG92.S3
Schulman, Hans.......................................AA60.S3
Schulman, Jacques......................JF40.S3, RA80.P4S3
Schulten, Peter N....................................BC85.S3
Schulten, Wolfgang..................................JG85.S38
Schultess-Rechberg, K. G.............................JA20.S3
Schultz, Walter F....................................US50.S3
Schultz, William J.................................GB80.03S3
Schulze, Wolfgang...................................UC40.S38
Schumacher, Carolus..................................BB90.S3
Schwalbach, Carl.......................JG65.S3, JG67.S35
Schwan, Carlton F....................................UA60.T6w
Schwan, Fred...US90.G6
Schwartz, Frances M..................................JE85.M8
Schwartz, John L.....................................US90.G6
Schwartz, Max M......................................NB20.S3
Schwarz, Ted...AA40.S3
Schwarz, Winklhofer, I...............................AA80.S3
Schweikert, Helmut...................................LA70.S3
Schweizenscher, Bankverein...........................CC63.S3
Scott, J. W..AA30.S3c
Scott, Kenneth.......................GB50.S3, US45.C6S3
        US45.N5S3, US45.N6S3, US45.P4S3
Scott, Michael N.....................................JD45.S3
Scott Stamp and Coin Co...............AA30.S3p, AA30.S3s
        CC30.S3, CC67.S3, GA30.R3b, GA30.R3c, GA30.R3p
        GA30.R3s, US51.S3
Seaby, B. A.........BC30.S4c, JB30.S8, JB67.S4c, SE20.S4
Seaby, Herbert................BB30.S4, BC30.S4r, BC65.S4
        JB65.S4b, JB65.S4n, JB67.S4c, PE30.S4
Seaby, Peter.......................JB30.S82, JB45.S4
        JB67.S4b, JB90.S4, PE30.S43
Seager, Richard B....................................BB90.S4
Sear, David R................BB90.S42, BC30.S4r, BE30.S4
Sears, Deane...AA60.S4
Seaver, Charles H....................................AA40.G7

Seidenfaden, Eric....................................KB70.T5S4
Seidl, Johann Gabriel.................................BC67.S4
Seidler, Ned...AA40.S5
Sejbal, Jiri...JJ60.S4
Sellers, George Escol................................GA80.S4
Sellschopp, Arna.....................................FA20.S4
Sellschopp, Ernesto..................................FA20.S4
Sellwood, David......................................BD30.S4
Seltman, Charles....................BB40.S4b, BB40.S4g
        BB40.S4m, BB60.S4, BB70.S4, BB90.S43
Seltman, E. J..BD34.S35
Sem, Julius..UF70.S4
Senior, R. C...KA10.07
Seppa, Dale A..................FA15.S4, FE35.S4, FE55.A58
        FE60.S4, FE70.A4, FE75.A4, FE80.A4, RN50.E2A4
        UK40.S4, UK50.B6S4, UK50.S4, UK50.S4p, UK50.S4u
Serrure, Raymond.....CC30.E6, JA80.E5, JF80.S4, JF83.S4
Severin, H. M...............................JM63.S4, JM65.S4
Sey, Katalin B.......................................AA45.S4
Seymore, Dexter C....................................GB15.S4
Seyrig, Henri..BD36.S4
Shafer, Neil........................FB67.B8g, FB67.B82
        KB50.S5, UI60.S5, UM40.S5, UM40.S5p, US20.S5
        US90.S5
Shaw, E. M...LA30.S4
Shaw, William.......KB20.S4, KB25.S5, QB60.S5, UM45.M3S5
Shchukina, E...RJ80.P4S6
Sheheen, Austin M....................................US80.S6S5
Sheldon, John..GB20.S4
Sheldon, William H.......................GB30.S5e, GB30.S5p
Shelloff, D. B.......................................JM40.S5
Sheppard, Thomas.....................................AA90.S5
Sherwood, Earle D.............AA60.S5, BB50.S5, FA25.S45
Shiells, Robert......................................NB40.S4
Shih, Kalgan...KC60.S5
Shinkle, C. H..GA30.S5
Shipler, Guy...GA80.H5
Shliekler, Ed..FB67.S5
Shlosser, Franziska E................................BB20.W6
Shortt, W. T. P......................................BC97.S5
Siam Society Journal.................................KB70.T5S5
Sieg, Frovin...............................JC10.S5, UC60.S5
Siemsen, Carl..............................UB55.S5, UC40.K4
Sigler, Phares O...............AA50.S5, KC45.S5, QB30.S5
Silbermann, Reinhardt................................UC40.S5
Silver Institute.....................................CC65.S5
Simek, Eduard..JJ50.N6
Simon, James...JB90.S5
Simonetti, Luigi.........................JI80.S5, JI80.S5m
        JI80.S5mo, JI97.S2B3
Sinclair, James E....................................GB10.S5
Singh, Saran...KB20.S5
Singhal, C. R..............................KA60.B6, KA70.S5
Sircar, D. C...KA70.S55
Sivaramamurti, C.....................................KA80.S5

Skinner, Dion Hickson.........MA40.S5, MA40.S5r, MA70.S5
Skipton, Amy C....................................GB40.S4
Slabaugh, Arlie...............CC53.S5, CC53.S5p, GB40.S5
        PA80.I4S5, RM15.F7, RM85.C5S5, UC60.S6, UJ60.S5
        UN60.S5, US50.S5, US60.S5, US90.S55
Smart, Veronica...................................JB80.M6
Smedley, Glenn B..............AA60.A5, GA50.S6, US75.S6
Smith, Alice E....................................VA40.S6
Smith, Andrew M..............AA50.S6, GA80.S6c, GA80.S6v
Smith, Charles Roach..............................BC45.S7
Smith, David Eugene...............................NB60.S5
Smith, Ernest A...................................AB25.S6
Smith, Grant H.................................AB49.N3S6
Smith, Kenneth E.....................NB20.S6, NB20.S6c
Smith, Laurence Dwight............................US30.S6
Smith, Samuel, Jr.................................FA25.S6
Smith, Vincent A..................................KA60.I5
Smith, Ward D.....................................UN20.S6
Smithsonian Institution..................AA20.C5, AA40.S6
Smithsonian Institution. National Museum of History and
        Technology................................AA20.S6
Smyth, John.......................................SE40.S6
Smyth, William Henry..................BC80.S6, RB50.S6
Snelling, Thomas...............JB80.S6, JB90.S5, NB60.S6
Snider, D. M......................................PL70.S6
Snoek, Jhr. M. W..................................RD20.S6
Snow, Warren B....................................GB30.S6
Snowden, James Ross.........AA20.U5, GA80.S66, RM80.W3S6
Sobin, George.....................................JE65.S6
Sobrino, Jose Manuel..............................FB40.S6
Societa Italiana Acciai Speciali..................AB70.S6
Societe Francoise de Numismatique.................JE10.S6
Societe Royale de Numismatique..........JF10.S5, JF20.S6
Society of Ration Token Collectors................PA40.S6
Sollner, George...................................UB50.S6
Somod, Jorgen........................JC20.S6, PI66.S6
Sonakul, M. R. Ayumongol......................KB70.T5S6
Sondergaard, Tyge..............................JG65.D3o
Soohodolsky, Anatol...............................JM40.S6
Sorensen, Teije...................................JC50.S6
South African Gold Coin Exchange.......LA30.S6, LA30.S6s
South African Numismatic Society.................LA30.S65
South Carolina Legislature......................VA90.S6S6
South Kensington Museum. London..................JH20.P6
Sowards, Neil.....................................VM60.S6
Spadone, Frank G.....................GA90.S6m, GA90.S6v
Spadone, John G...................................KD10.S6
Spahr, Walter E...................................WB70.S6
Spajic, Dimitri...................................UF70.S6
Spanbauer, Larry..................................GA70.S6
Spanheim, Ezachiel................................BA40.S6
Spassky, I. G...............JM40.S65, RJ80.P4S6, SG50.S6
Spaziani Testa, Girolamo..........................JI50.S6
Spencer, William L................................FB67.S5

Sutherland, Allan..........................MA70.S8, PN40.S8
Sutherland, Carol H. V.........AA60.M5, AA80.S8, AB30.S9
        BA50.S8, BC40.S8, BC85.S8c, BC97.S9c
        BC97.S9r, JB45.S9, JB80.S8, RA30.S8
Svarstad, Carsten..................................RA80.A2S9
Svoronos, John.................AA70.S9, BB40.H4s, BB90.S9
Swails, Alfred J....................................UA60.S9
Sealwell, Irving V..................................GA90.S9
Sydenham, Edward.............BC67.S9a, BC80.S9c, BC85.S9
        BC85.S9c, BC95.S9
Sydney. Bank of New South Wales...................MA40.S9s
Sydney. Public Library of New S. Wales............AA50.S7
        AA50.S9, MA40.S9a
Symonds, Henry............................JB85.S9, JB85.S9s
Szego, Alfred.............................AA30.S3c, JK80.S9
Szego, Paul S......................................BB50.S9
Szwagrzyk, Josef Andrzej...........................JJ20.S9

Takaki, Masayoshi..................................UN50.T3
Talbot-Booth, E. C.................................SE30.T3
Tamplin, J. M. A...................................SE30.A2
Tannahill, Cecil Clifton..........................PB80.S3T3
Tantum, W. H.......................................SD40.T3
Targonsky, Paul....................................NB20.T3
Tatman, Charles T.......................GB50.T3, GB80.V5T3
Taullard, Alfredo..................................FE30.T3
Taurignac, Jean....................................SC40.T3
Taxay, Don...GA30.T3, GA70.T3, GA80.T3, GB40.T3, QB70.T3
Taylor, George P...................................KA83.T3
Taylor, H. C....................HA30.G8, JB87.T3
Teixeria de Aragao, Augusto C.....................JD70.T4
Temprano, Leo......................................FE55.T4
Terlecki, Wladyslaw................................JJ20.T4
Terrace, Edward Lee................................BC20.T4
Terrien de Lacouperie, Albert......................KC50.T4
Teyler Fondation, Harlem...........................CC10.T4
Theobald, Ormond E. C..............................JB85.T5
Thian, Raphael P...................................US60.T5
Thimonier, Argus.........................JE30.T5, JE87.T5
Thirion, Marcel.................BC75.T5, JF79.T5, JF87.T5
Thomas, E. R.......................................PN40.N4
Thomas, Edward.........................BD10.T5, BD10.T5e
Thomas, Eleanor....................................AA40.T5
Thomason, Edward...................................RE85.B5T5
Thompson, J..US30.T5
Thompson, J. D. A.............AA60.M5, CC20.T5, JB80.T5
Thompson, Margaret...........BB57.T45, BB70.E3, BB70.T5
Thompson, Thomas William...........................VA30.T5
Thompson, Walter........................GA80.T5, GA80.T52
Thorburn, William Stewart..........................JB40.T5
Thun, Norbert......................................JG87.T5

Thurman, Harrison E..............................AA80.T45
Till, William............................JB40.T55, RE30.T5
Timmons, William L.................................GB10.T5
Ting Fu-Pao..........................AA45.T5, KC50.T5
Tingstrom, Bertel...........JC70.T5, JC70.T5s, JC70.T59
Titus, Wright.....................................GA50.T5
Tobler, Edwin........................JC85.T5m, JH40.D5
Tochon d'Annecy, Joseph F.......................RB90.E3T6
Todd, Neil B......................................PE70.T6
Todd, Richard Cecil...............................US60.T6
Toderi, Guiseppi..................................JI87.C4
Tokai Bank, Ltd....................................KD50.T6
Token and Medal Society...........................PA30.T6
Tomasini, Wallace J...............................JA80.T6
Tomlinson, Geoffrey William.......................UQ30.T6
Tonkin, A. B......................................JC70.T6
Tonkin, W. A. R...................................JC75.T6
Tornberg, Carl Johan..............................KA50.T6
Torrey, Charles Cutler................BB80.T6, KA20.K5T6
Toy, Raymond S....................UA60.T6a, UA60.T6w
Toynbee, Jocelyn M. C.............................RB50.T6
Tracy, James E....................................KA90.P3T7
Tradewinds Evaluation System, Inc.................CC55.T7
Trapero, Maria Ruiz...............................JD40.T7
Trautman, Edwin S.................................RM15.F7
Trelde, F. von der....................UF60.T7, UF60.T7n
Trell, Bluma L.....................BA70.T7, BB60.T7
Tricou, J...PF90.L8T7
Trippe, Anton.....................................JG98.M41T7
Trowbridge, Richard J..................JB50.T7, JB65.T7
        JB70.T7, JB85.T7, JB87.T7, KA40.T7
Troxell, Hyla A...................................BB20.T7
Tsiang, C. C......................................KC20.T7
Tsukamoto, Toyojiro...............................KD20.T8
Tuckwood, Charles E...................BA65.T8, BA65.T82
Tufnell, R. H. C..................................KA70.T8
Turner, W. E......................................WA30.T8
Turner, W. W...................CC63.T8g, CC63.T8s, FA10.T8
        GA10.T8, GB10.T8, JB63.T8

Ugan, Richard....................................RM85.M3G8
Ulan, H. S..FB50.U3
L'Union des Trimbophiles de Luxembourg............JF30.U4
U.S. Army....................SH60.U5e, SH60.U5f, SH60.U5t
U.S. Bureau of the Mint..................AA20.J6, AA20.U5
        AA20.U5g, AB28.U5, CC10.U5, GA80.U5d
        GA80.U5do, GA80.U5f, GA80.U5i, GA80.U51
        GA80.U5m, GA85.U8c, GA85.U82i, GA85.U821
        GA85.U82p, RM15.U5
U.S. Comptroler of the Currency...................VA35.U5
U.S. Congress. House.................GA85.U41, GA85.U4L2

721

        GA85.U42c, GA85.U42s, GA85.U43c
        GA85.U44c, WB30.U54
U.S. Congress. Senate.................GA85.U72a, GA85.U72r
        GA85.U73c, SH30.U5, US10.U5
U.S. Federal Reserve System........................VA30.U5
U.S. Navy...SH60.U52
U.S. Secret Service...............................US30.U5
U.S. Supreme Court...............................GA85.U79g
        GA85.U8i, GA85.U8j, GA85.U8p
        GA85.U8t, GA85.U8w, US25.U5, WB30.U58
U.S. Treasury Dept......................GA85.U8b, GA85,U8g
Upton, Richard....................................PG70.U6
Utberg, Neil S.................FB20.U8, FB40.U8, FB40.U8r
        FB60.U8, FB65.U8, FB65.U8g, FB67.U8
        FB67.U8r, UJ30.G3p

Vacketta, Ore H...................................PA80.I4V3
Vaia, D...PA80.P6V3
Vaillant, Jean Foy see Foy-Vaillant, Jean
Valentine, Daniel W......................GB20.V3, US50.V3
Valentine, William H...........BD32.V3, KA50.V3, KA75.V3
Van Allen, Leroy C.....................GB20.V34, GB20.V35
Van Belkum, Louis......................US90.W3, VA50.V3
Vancouver Numismatic Society.........HA40.V3, PB80.B7V3r
        PB80.B7V3t
Vanderwende, George S.............................KB50.V3
Van Keymeulen, A........................JF40.V3, JF85.V3
        RA80.A5V8
Van Peteghem, C..................................RF90.A4V3
Van Roosbroeck, Adelbert see Roosbroeck, Adelbert Van
Varesi, Clelio....................................JI30.V3
Venn, Theodore J..................................GB70.V4
Verbanec, William R...............................CC63.V4
Vergora, Ruben W..................................BC70.V4
Vermeule, Cornelius C..........BA45.V4, BA60.V4, GB40.V4
        KD20.J3
Vero, Andrew J....................................US90.V4
Vertue, George....................................QC50.V4
Vettori, Francesco................................JI63.V4
Vicenti, Jose A.........................JD10.V5, JD10.V5b
        JD44.V5, JD44.V5c, UB53.V5
Vicker, Ray.......................................AB30.V5
Villaronga Garriga, Leandro............BC97.V5, JD40.V54
Villegaigne, J. G.................................CC35.V5
Vives y Escudero, Antonio.........................JD40.V5
Vlack, Robert A...................................GB50.V5
Vlasto, Michel P..................................BB94.V5
Voglhuber, Rudolf.................................JK65.V6
Vogt, George W....................................FB60.U8
Vollenweider, Marie-Louise........................BC80.V6
Von Allendorfer, Frederic.........................SE40.V6

Welch, Charles..RE90.L6W4
Welldon, Samuel A.......................................VD10.N3
Wells, David A..WB60.W4
Welter, Gerhard...AA95.W4
Wenzel, Alexander.......................................AA80.W4
Werlich, Robert.......SA30.W4, SG30.A5, SG30.W4, US15.W4
Wesch, H. J..CC65.W4
West, Allen Brown.......................................BB94.W4
West, Louis C..............................BC63.W4, BC93.W4
West, R. W..GA55.W3
Westdal, Stewart J......................................BC70.W4
Westerfield, Wiley......................................CC53.W4
Westervelt, Leonidas..................................RA60.L5W4
Westropp, M. S. Dudley..................................JB90.W4
Westrup, Alfred B.......................................VA45.W4
Wetton, J. L...PE55.W4
Weyl, Adolph...................CC10.F6, FA10.W4, JG92.W4
Wharton, Joseph...CC67.W5
White, Andrew Dickson...................................WC40.W5
White, Benjamin...............AA40.W5, AA60.W5, UB20.W5
White, Horace...WB30.W5
White, Peter J..AB30.W5
Whitehead, D. H. E......................................BB20.W6
Whitehead, Richard Bertram....BB97.W5, BD10.W4, KA60.L3w
        KA83.W5, KA83.W5m
Whiteley, Philip W....................................PA80.C6W5
Whiting, J. R. S.......................................RE30.W5
Whitting, Philip D......................................AA55.W5
        BE40.W46E5, BE40.W46G4
Widmer, Hans...RD60.W5
Wiebe, Carl..RA80.F7H3
Wielandt, Friedrich...................................JG98.B3W5
Wieschhoff, H. A.......................................QB20.W5
Wiggins, K. W,...KA10.07
Wilber, E. J...US30.W5
Wild, William J.......................................GB80.M4W5
Wilkinson, James.......................................SJ40.W5
Willem, John M...GB70.W5
Willey, Robert C...........................HA30.H3, HA35.C4
Williams, Caroline Ransom..............................QC30.W5
Williams, Dion...SH30.W5
Williams, Harry F......................................FA23.W5
Williams, Henry..RR35.C6C6
Williams, Roderick T...................................BB80.W5
Williamson, George Charles.............................PE55.W5
Wilson, George...US10.W5
Wilson, Neil C..VA80.C3W5
Wilson, R. A...GA30.W54
Windler, F. J., Jr.....................................BC85.W5
Winskowsky, Horst..........................AA60.W55, AA95.W5
Wirgin, Wolf........BA65.W5, BD40.W5h, BD50.W5p, RB60.W5
Wiseman, D. J..QC20.W5
Wismer, David C.............PA75.W5, US75.W5, US80.N4W5
        US80.N5W5, US80.04W5, US80.P4W5

Witte, A...RF35.D4W5
Wood, Howland.......FB65.W6c, FB65.W6m, FC60.W6, FD30.W6
         GB10.W6, GB40.W6, HA40.C3, KA20.T8W6
         KA90.C4W6, KC30.W6, LA50.W6, PB70.W6
Woodburn, Helen...PG70.E4
Woodford, Arthur M......................................VA70.M5W6
Woodin, William H.......................................GA90.A4
Woodside, William W.............NB40.C6, NB40.W6, PL30.W6
Woodward, A. M. Tracey..................KC55.W6, PL20.W6
Work, Eunice..BB94.W6
World Coins...KD20.W6
Wormser, Moritz................AA40.W6, AA55.W6, JG50.W6
         JG70.W6, JK90.T7W6
Wright, B. P..........................PA40.W7, PA70.W7
Wright, Glenn...GA55.W7
Wright, Henry N....................KA60.I5, KA90.D4W7
Wright, Laurence Victor W...........................JB96.W7
Wright, Philip G..WC10.W7
Wright, Richard...KC10.O7
Wroth, Warwick W.............BB20.B71, BB20.W7, BB20.W7s
         BB40.H4, BB97.B7g, BE20.B7b, BE20.B7v, BE20.B7w
Wurttembergische Bank. Stuttgart, Germany.......CC63.W8
Wurtzbach, Carl...GB80.M4W8
Wyllie, Robert E...........................SA30.W9, SH30.W9

Yahnin, V. L..JM60.Y3
Yale College. New Haven, Conn.....................AA20.Y3
Yamaga, Yos Ninori.....................................KD45.Y3
Yeoman, Richard S.............BA65.Y4, CC87.Y5c, CC87.Y4m
         GA50.W5, GA50.Y4, GA50.Y42, GA55.B65, GB80.C3Y4
Yernazarova, Tamara S...............................JM91.Y4
Young, Charles J..SH30.H6
Young, Derek...........................JB90.Y5, UB30.Y6
Young, Edward...RM15.Y6
Young, James...GA80.Y6
Yriarte y Oliva, Jose.........FA23.L6, JD33.L6, JD33.L6d
         JD33.L61, JD33.L6m, JD35.Y7

Zaloha, Jiri...JJ60.Z3
Zay, Ernest..JE95.Z3
Zegarowicz, Edward.....................................GA55.Z4
Zelaya, Manuel A.........................FC60.Z4, FC60.Z4a
Zerbe, Farran..QA40.Z4
Ziegesar, Anton Von....................................AA80.Z5
Zigrosser, Carl..RM35.D8Z5
Zimmerman, Walter J....................................AA60.Z5
Zimpfer, Michael.......................................GA90.S7
Zlatkovskaya, T. D.....................................BB94.Z5

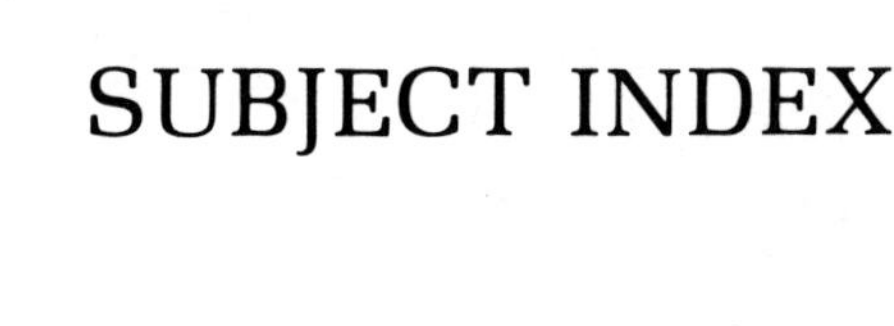

SUBJECT INDEX

OF NORTH AMERICA

AMERICAN NUMISMATIC ASSO-
  CIATION - MEDALS RM85

AMERICAN NUMISMATIC
  SOCIETY AA10

AMERICAN REVOLUTION -
  MEDALS RM85

AMERICAN VECTURISTS ASSO-
  CIATION PA40

AMISUS BD38

ANASTASIAN I, EMPEROR OF
  THE EAST BE80

ANCIENT AA, BB, BC, RA30
  see also GREECE, ANCIENT;
  ROME, ANCIENT; ISRAEL,
  ANCIENT; BYZANTINE;
  ASIA, ANCIENT; WEIGHTS
  AND MEASURES; HOARDS

ANDHRA DYNASTY BD10

ANDORRA JD20

ANDRITSAENA BB80

ANGLO-GALLIC JB67, JB83
  see also GREAT BRITAIN,
  MEDIEVAL; FRANCE

ANGLO-SAXON BC75, JB80
  see also GREAT BRITAIN,
  ANCIENT; ROMAN BRITAIN

ANGOLA LA40, UB55

ANHALT JG98

ANIMALS CC70, RA80

ANNAM KB10, KB70, KC20,
  KC50
  see also CHINA

ANNE, QUEEN OF GREAT
  BRITAIN JB85

ANTIOCH BC95

ANTONINIANI BC75

ANTWERP RF70

ARABIA KA50, KA55
  see also MOHAMMEDAN;
  ASIA
ARABIA, ANCIENT BB20, BD38,
  BE90

ARAMAIC LANGUAGE BB80

ARCADIA BB80

ARCHAEOLOGY BA40, BB55, KA55
  see also GREECE, ANCIENT;
  ROME, ANCIENT; ANCIENT;
  HOARDS

ARCHITECTURE BA70, BC70, RA80
  see also ICONOGRAPHY

ARGENTINA FE30

ARIZONA PA80

ARMENIA KA20
  see also ASIA; TURKEY

ART IN NUMISMATICS AA80, BB60,
  GB40, JG70, JG80, RM15,
  RM30, RM35, US77, US85

ASIA CC10, JA80, JB20, KA,
  LA10
  see also ORIENT
ASIA, ANCIENT BB97, BD
  see also ANCIENT; ASIA
  MINOR; GREEK ASIA;
  ORIENT; ROMAN ASIA MINOR
ASIA, ANCIENT - SEALS QC

ASIA MINOR BB20, BB40, BB97,
  BD
  see also ANCIENT; ASIA,
  ANCIENT; GREEK ASIA MINOR

ASSAM PL40

ATHENS BB90

ATTAMBELOS I BB97

AUGUSTUS, ROMAN EMPEROR
  27 B.C.-14 A.D. BC85

AURELIUS, LUCIUS DOMITIUS

BC85

AUSTRALIA CC10, JB96, MA, UQ30
  see also GREAT BRITAIN; NEW
  ZEALAND
AUSTRALIA - INVESTMENT CC40
AUSTRALIA - MEDALS RR
AUSTRALIA - PAPER UQ
AUSTRALIA - TOKENS NB40, PN

AUSTRIA JF, JG87, JJ, JK
AUSTRIA - BANKS AND BANKING
  UD10
AUSTRIA - MEDALS RK20
AUSTRIA, MEDIEVAL JK80
AUSTRIA - ORDERS & DECORATIONS
  SB60
AUSTRIA - PAPER UF60
AUSTRIA - SILVER JG65, JK65

BABELON, ERNEST RF35

BABYLONIA BD30
  see also ASIA, ANCIENT;
  GREECE, ANCIENT; PARTHIA;
  SELEUCIA

BACTRIA BB97

BADEN JG98

BAHMANI DYNASTY KA60

BALKAN STATES JL40
  see also BYZANTINE; GREECE

BALTIC STATES - ORDERS & DECO-
  RATIONS SB69
BALTIC STATES - PAPER UF40

BANKS AND BANKING VD10, VD30
  see also SPECIFIC COUNTRIES

BARBARIANS BC60-70

BARCELONA JD35

BAVARIA CC53, JG90
  see also GERMANY; SPECIFIC
  CITY
BAVARIA - ORDERS & DECORA-
  TIONS SD70

BECHTLER, CHRISTOPHER GB80

BECK, FULOP O. RK60

BECKER, CARL AA70, BC85

BELGIUM JF
  see also NETHERLANDS
BELGIUM - BANKS & BANKING
  VD10
BELGIUM - EMERGENCY MONEY
  JF87
BELGIUM - MEDALS JF40, RD20

BERG (GERMANY) JG98

BERLIN JG10, PG70

BERN (SWITZERLAND) JH90

BHARTPUR (INDIA) KA10

BIBLE AA80, BA65, BD40, RA60,
  RE85
  see also ISRAEL, ANCIENT;
  ANCIENT; CHRISTIANITY AND
  COINS; JUDAISM AND NUMIS-
  MATICS; ROME

BIBLIOGRAPHIES AA50, BA45,
  BE50, FA15, FD45,
  JJ50, KA50, KB10, KB30,
  NB40

BIBLIOTHEQUE, ALBERT (BRUS-
  SELS) BC75

BOHEMIA JG65, JK83, JK90

BOLEN, JAMES A. RM35

BOLIVIA FE35, UK50

BOONE, DANIEL GB40

BOULTON, MATTHEW RE80

BOVY, JEAN FRANCOISE ANTOINE
  RA50

BRABANT JF80
  see also NETHERLANDS

BRAZIL AA45, FE40, JD70
  see also PORTUGAL - COLO-
  NIES; SOUTH AMERICA
BRAZIL - MEDALS RN60
BRAZIL - PAPER UK40
BRAZIL - TOKENS NB80

BREMEN JG98

BRENNER, VICTOR D. RM35

BRITAIN see GREAT BRITAIN

BRITISH COLUMBIA - TOKENS PB80

BRITTANY JE82

BRUNSWICK JG65, JG98

BRUTUS BC85

BRYAN, WILLIAM J. QA40

BUKHARA BD38, KA20

BUNGTOWN PA50

BUTTONS SA
  see also SPECIFIC COUNTRY

BYZANTINE BA30, BE,
  JA80, JL40
  see also EUROPE, MEDIEVAL;
  MEDIEVAL

CAESAREA, ASIA MINOR BC95,
  BD60

CALIFORNIA AB39, GB80, PA80,
  VA80
  see also U.S. - GOLD

CALVIN, JEAN RA60

CANADA FA15, HA, JB96
  see also FRANCO-AMERICA;
  GREAT BRITAIN; NOVA SCOTIA;
  SPECIFIC PROVINCE
CANADA - BANKS & BANKING
  VB30, VD10
CANADA - BIBLIOGRAPHIES
  AA50
CANADA - COLLECTING GA, HA
CANADA - COUNTERFEITING UI40
CANADA - INVESTEMENT CC40
CANADA - MEDALS PB30, RM15,
  RO
CANADA - ORDERS & DECORATIONS
  SI20
CANADA - PAPER UH20, UI, US15,
  US20
CANADA - TOKENS AA40, PA40,

PA70, PB, PF60

CAPPADOCIA BB20

CARAUSIUS, MARCUS AURELIUS
  VALERIUS BC85, BC97

CARINTHIA RK20

CAROLINGIAN JA80
  see also EUROPE, MEDIEVAL

CARTHAGE BD80

CARYSTUS BB90

CATALAN JD50, JD43

CAVINO, GIOVANNI RI35

CELTIC JA79

CENTRAL AMERICA FA10, FC
  see also LATIN AMERICA;
  SPANISH AMERICA; SPECIFIC
  COUNTRY
CENTRAL AMERICA - COPPER
  FA27
CENTRAL AMERICA - PAPER
  UH20

CEYLON KA90
  see also INDIA
CEYLON, ANCIENT BD20
  see also INDIA,
  ANCIENT

CHANNEL ISLANDS JB95
  see also GREAT BRITAIN
CHANNEL ISLANDS - TOKENS
  PE70

CHAPMAN, JOHN G. RM35,
  US80

CHARACENE BD30

CHARITY TOKENS PH40

CHARLEMAGNE JE82

CHARLES V - EMPEROR OF GER-
  MANY JG65

CHARLES I - KING OF GREAT
  BRITAIN JB85

CHARLES XI - KING OF SWE-
   DEN JC80

CHECKS VM45
CHECKS - COLLECTING VM60
CHECKS - FORGERIES VM50

CHILE FA40, FE50
CHILE - MEDALS RN70

CHINA KB10, KD20, KD70
   see also JAPAN; KOREA;
   ORIENT
CHINA, ANCIENT KC50
CHINA - BANKS & BANKING
   VE30
CHINA - COUNTERFEITING
   UN30
CHINA - ECONOMICS VE30,
   WE60
CHINA - MEDALS RP50
CHINA - ORDERS SJ20
CHINA - PAPER UN
CHINA - TOKENS PL

CHIOS BB97, JL80

CHRISTIANITY & NUMSIMATICS
   AA80, BA65, RA

CHRISTMAS RM85

CHURCHILL, SIR WINSTON
   RE80

CIGOI, LUIGI AA70

CINCINNATI, SOCIETY OF THE
   RM80

CLARK, GRUBER & CO. GB80,
   VA80

CLAUDIUS, EMPEROR OF ROME
   BC97

CLAY, HENRY RM80

COAL MINES & MINING PA70

COINS - CATALOGUES AA30
   CC30
COINS - CLEANING & PRESER-
   VATION AA95, BA60
COINS - COLLECTING AA40-60,

    CC40, FE30, GA50, GB50,
    JB30, JB45
    see also U.S. - COLLECTING
COINS - COLLECTIONS AA20,
    CC10
COINS - DEALERS & DEALER-
    SHIPS AA75, GA55, JB45
COINS - GRADING AA96
COINS - INVESTMENT AA60
    CC40, CC55, CC63, GA55
COINS - PLATING AA90

COLE, W. E. RR35

COLOMBIA FE55
    see also SOUTH AMERICA
COLOMBIA - PAPER UK10

COLORADO GA80, GB80, PA80,
    VA80

COLUMBUS, CHRISTOPHER
    RM80

COMETS RA80

COMMEMORATIVE COINS AA80,
    CC70
    see also SPECIFIC COUNTRY;
    U.S., COMMEMORATIVE; ART IN
    NUMISMATICS; ICONOGRAPHY

COMMUNION TOKENS NB40,
    PB40, PE90

CONGO, BELGIAN JF40
    see also BELGIUM; AFRICA

CONNECTICUT GB80, US45, US75
    see also U.S., COLONIAL

CONSTANTINE THE GREAT
    BC85

COOCH BEHAR (INDIA) KA10

COOK, JAMES RR80

COPPER AB62
COPPER MINES AND MINING
    AB66

CORINTH BB70, BB90

CORITANI JB80

COSTA RICA FC50

COUNTERFEITING AA70, BC60,
  BC85, CC50, FA25, UA
    see also SPECIFIC COUNTRIES,
  PLACE OR PERIOD

COUNTERMARKED COINS CC53, FD,
  KA20, KB
    see also EMERGENCY MONEY

CRETE BB20, BB90, KA55, JL70
  see also GREECE

CROMWELL, OLIVER JB85

CRONDALL (ENGLAND) JB80

CRUSADERS CC80, JA80
    see also MEDIEVAL; EUROPE,
  MEDIEVAL; MALTA, KNIGHTS
  OF

CUBA FD45

CULION ISLANDS PL70

CURIUM BA80

CYPRUS BB20, BB90, JL70,
  JL90
    see also GREECE
CYPRUS - SOCIETIES JL92

CYRENAICA BB20

CYZICUS BB90

CZECH LANGUAGE JJ50

CZECHOSLOVAKIA JJ, UF70
CZECHOSLOVAKIA - BIBLIO-
  GRAPHIES AA50
CZECHOSLOVAKIA - MEDALS
  RK40
CZECHOSLOVAKIA - ORDERS &
  DECORATIONS SB60
CZECHOSLOVAKIA - PAPER UF70

DALMATIA JL40

DAMASTION BB94

DELAWARE US45

DELHI KA90

DEMANHUR BB80

DEMETRIUS POLIORCETES BB80

DENMARK JC
  see also SCANDINAVIA
DENMARK - COLONIES KA90
DENMARK - MEDALS RD45
DENMARK - ORDERS & DECORATIONS
  SB20
DENMARK - PAPER UC60

DEVREESE, GODEFROID
  RF35

DICTIONARIES AA50

DISTRICT OF COLUMBIA
  US80

DOLLAR SIGN FB50

DOMINICAN REPUBLIC FD50, WD50
  see also HAITI

DONEBAUER, MAX AA20

DORTMUND JG98

DUPRE, AUGUSTIN RM35

DURA-EUROPOS BC75, BD34

DURER, ALBRECHT RG35

DUTCH EAST INDIES JF95, KB20
  see also INDONESIA; NETHER-
  LANDS

EAKINS, THOMAS RM35

ECONOMICS WA30

ECUADOR FE60
ECUADOR - MEDALS RN50

EDWARD VII, KING OF GREAT
  BRITAIN JB96

EDWARD VIII, KING OF GREAT
  BRITAIN JB87

EGYPT KA50, KA55, LA60, QC30
  see also AFRICA
EQYPT, ANCIENT AA45, BB20,

BB80, BB93, BB97, BC93,
  BD83, QC30
EQYPT, ANCIENT - HOARDS
  BA80
EGYPT, ANCIENT - MEDALS
  RB90
EGYPT, ANCIENT - SCARABS
  QC30

EISENHOWER, DWIGHT D.
  GB40

ELONGATED COINS RM

EL SALVADOR see SALVADOR

EMERGENCY MONEY CC53, FA25,
  FA40, GB80, JB85, JF87,
  JG50, PF70, PG70, PG90,
  RF70, UB, UI, UM40, UQ38,
  US50

ENCASED POSTAGE STAMPS GA50,
  UA40, US50

ENGLAND see GREAT BRITAIN

ENGRAVING US25

ESTONIA JM97

ETHIOPIA LA50

EUBOIAN LEAGUE BB90

EUROPE AA45, CC, JA, JB20,
  JH20
    see also SPECIFIC COUNTRY;
    WORLD, MODERN
EUROPE, ANCIENT JA
EUROPE - BANKS & BANKING VD10
EUROPE - ECONOMICS WC10
EUROPE - MEDALS BA40, RA
EUROPE, MEDIEVAL BA40, BE20,
  JA, JD43, JG80
EUROPE - MILITARY CURRENCY
  UA60, UB20
EUROPE - ORDERS & DECORATIONS
  SB10, SE30
EUROPE - PAPER UA-UR
EUROPE - TOKENS NB, PD30

FAEROE ISLANDS JC10

FIJI MA

FINLAND JC, JG79
  see also SCANDINAVIA
FINLAND - ORDERS & DECORATIONS
  SB60
FINLAND - PAPER JC90, UB60

FIREMARKS CC55, SE50

FLANDERS JF80
  see also NETHERLANDS

FLORENCE RI10

FLORIDA US80

FOGG ART MUSEUM BA20

FRANCE CC40, JE, RF90
  see also ANGLO-GALLIC;
  CANADA; EUROPE; FRANCO-
  AMERICA; MEROVINGIAN
FRANCE, ANCIENT JE80
FRANCE - BANKS & BANKING VD10
FRANCE - ECONOMICS WC40
FRANCE - MEDALISTS RA50
FRANCE - MEDALS RE40, RF
FRANCE, MEDIEVAL JE82
FRANCE - ORDERS & DECORATIONS
  SC30, SC40
FRANCE - PAPER JE30, UB40
FRANCE - REVOLUTION RF85
FRANCE - SOCIETIES AA10
FRANCE - TOKENS PF, RF85

FRANCIS JOSEPH I JJ60

FRANCO-AMERICA FD30, HA
FRANCO-AMERICA - MEDALS RF,
  RO
FRANCO-AMERICA - TOKENS PF

FRANCONIA JG20

FRANKFURT JG98

FRANKLIN, BENJAMIN GA70,
  US40

FRASER, J. E. GB40

FREDERICK II RG80

FREEMASONS - MEDALS RA80
FREEMASONS - TOKENS PA40

FRITZ, JOHN RM80

FYFIELD (ENGLAND) BC75

GALATIA BB20

GALBA, EMPEROR OF ROME
  BC85

GAMBLING TOKENS PA, PL60
  see also NEVADA

GAND, UNIVERSITY OF JF80

GARHWAL (INDIA) KA10

GEORGE II, KING OF GREAT
  BRITAIN JB85

GEORGE VI, KING OF GREAT
  BRITAIN JB87

GEORGIA AB39, US80
GEORGIA - GOLD GB15
GEORGIA - PAPER US75, US85

GEORGIA (RUSSIA) JB90

GERMANY CC30, JA20, JA70,
  JG, UC40, WC50
    see also EUROPE; BAVARIA;
  PRUSSIA; SPECIFIC PROVINCE
GERMANY - BANKS & BANKING
  VD10
GERMANY - COLONIES JG67,
  JG92
GERMANY - COUNTERFEITING
  UC60
GERMANY - ECONOMICS WD50
GERMANY - MEDALS RG
GERMANY, MEDIEVAL JG80
GERMANY, MEDIEVAL - TOKENS
  PB50
GERMANY - ORDERS & DECORATIONS
  SD
GERMANY - PAPER PG70, UC20,
  UC40, UC55, UC60, WC50
GERMANY - PORCELAIN JG67
GERMANY - TOKENS PG70

GIANNINI, AMADEO PETER VA40

GOBRECHT, CHRISTIAN GA90

GOETHE, JOHANN WOLFGANG VON
  JG70

GOETZ, KARL RG35

GOLD AA50, AB30, AB32, CC50,
  CC55, CC63, GB10
    see also SPECIFIC COUNTRY

GOLD MINES & MINING AB30,
  AB32, AB39, AB49

GOTHS JA80

GOTLAND JC75

GREAT BRITAIN AA40, JB,
  WC30
    see also SCOTLAND; IRELAND;
    WALES; ISLE OF MAN; MAUNDY
    COINS
GREAT BRITAIN, ANCIENT BC97,
  JB80
    see also ANGLO-SAXON;
    ROMAN BRITAIN
GREAT BRITAIN - BANKS & BANKING
  VC30
GREAT BRITAIN - COLONIES
  CC40, GB50, JB85, JB96,
  JC80, KA85, KB25, KB70,
  LA20, MA20, MA40, MA50,
  RM85
GREAT BRITAIN - COLONIES -
  MEDALS RM85
GREAT BRITAIN - COMMONWEALTH
  JB65, JB96
    see also GREAT BRITAIN -
    COLONIES
GREAT BRITAIN - COPPER JB67
  PE20
GREAT BRITAIN - COUNTER-
  FEITING UC60
GREAT BRITAIN - ECONOMICS
  WC30
GREAT BRITAIN - INVESTMENT
  CC40
GREAT BRITAIN - MEDALS RA80
  RE, RR80
GREAT BRITAIN, MEDIEVAL AA70,
  BB20, JB, RA30
    see also ANGLO-GALLIC
GREAT BRITAIN - ORDERS &
  DECORATIONS SE
GREAT BRITAIN - PAPER JB45,
  UB30
GREAT BRITAIN - SEALS PE95,
  QC50
GREAT BRITAIN - TOKENS JB83,
  NB60, PE

GREECE BB60, JC, JL,
  see also BALKAN STATES;
  CRETE; CYPRUS; IONIAN
  ISLANDS
GREECE, ANCIENT AA30, AA45,
  BA, BA20, BB, BC65, BC75,
  BD34, BD60, BD83, JB40,
  KA20, KA60, QC30, RB10,
  WA
  see also ANCIENT; ROME,
  ANCIENT; ISRAEL, ANCIENT;
  PARTHIA; GREEK ITALY;
  HOARDS; ASIA, ANCIENT;
  BYZANTINE; SELEUCIA;
  ALEXANDER THE GREAT
GREECE, ANCIENT - ELECTRUM
  BB90
GREECE, ANCIENT - HOARDS
  BB70

GREEK ASIA BB20, BB97

GREEK ASIA MINOR BB20, BB97

GREEK EUROPE BC97

GREEK INDIA BB97

GREEK ITALY BB94

GREENLAND JC10, JC40

GRENNEL, ALBERT A. US10

GRIQUALAND LA30

GUATEMALA FC55
GUATEMALA - PAPER UK20
GUATEMALA - TOKENS PC37

GUILDS PF60, PH40

GUPTA DYNASTY (INDIA) BD10

GUSTAVUS I, KING OF SWEDEN
  JC80

HADRIAN, EMPEROR OF ROME
  BA70, RB60

HAITI FD50, WD50
  see also DOMINICAN REPUB-
  LIC; WEST INDIES
HAITI - ORDERS & DECORATIONS
  SI80

HAMBURG (GERMANY) JG98

HANNOVER (GERMANY) JG98

HAWAII GB80, US80
  see also UNITED STATES

HENRY VII, KING OF GREAT
  BRITAIN JB85

HENRY IX, KING OF GREAT
  BRITAIN JB85

HERACLEA LUCIANA BB94

HERALDRY AA80, JF40

HERFORD (GERMANY) JG98

HESSEN (GERMANY) JG98

HICKEY, WILLIAM AUGUSTUS
  PA70

HILDAGO, MIGUEL FB45

HINDUISM KA80
  see also INDIA

HISTIAEA BB90

HOARDS BA80, BB20, BB70,
  BB90, CC55, JA80, PG50,
  RB60
  see also ANCIENT -
  HOARDS; SPECIFIC PLACE OR
  PERIOD; GREECE, ANCIENT -
  HOARDS

HOHENZOLLERN JG96, PG70

HONDURAS FC60

HONG KONG KB70

HOOVER, HERBERT RM80

HUNGARY JJ, JK83
  see also AUSTRIA
HUNGARY - BANKS & BANKING
  VD10
HUNGARY - MEDALS RK60
HUNGARY - PAPER UF60

ICELAND JC10, JC40

ICONOGRAPHY AA80, BC70,
  FA30, JF40, KA10, RA80,
  RB70, RD60
  see also ART IN NUMISMA-
  TICS; SPECIFIC SUBJECTS;
  MEDICINE & PHYSICIANS;
  INSCRIPTIONS; SPECIFIC
  COUNTRIES; SHIPS & SEA-
  FARERS

IDAHO PA80

ILCHESTER JB83

ILLINOIS US80
ILLINOIS - TOKENS PA80

ILLYRO BB94

INDIA CC40, KA10, KA50-90
  see also KUTCH; MALDIVE
  ISLANDS
INDIA, ANCIENT BB97, BD10,
  BD15
  see also ANCIENT; ASIA,
    ANCIENT; GREECE,ANCIENT
INDIA, BRITISH KA85
INDIA - ECONOMICS WE30
INDIA, MEDIEVAL KA80
INDIA, PORTUGUESE KA60
  see also PORTUGAL
INDIA - TOKENS PL40

INDIANA PA80, VA70

INDIANS OF NORTH AMERICA
  PA70, QB70, RM85

INDOCHINA KB70

INDONESIA JF95, KB20, KB25
  see also MALAYSIA; DUTCH
  EAST INDIES
INDONESIA - TOKENS PL30

INSCRIPTIONS AA80, BB45, BB50
  see also ICONOGRAPHY

IONIAN ISLANDS JL

IONIAN LEAGUE BC85

IOWA PA80, VA70

IRAN KA30, KA50, KA60

LAFAYETTE, GILBERT MOTIER,
  MARQUIS DE RR80

LAGBE BE90

LAMPSAKOS BB90

LANDSEER, EDWIN US75

LATIN AMERICA CC10, FA
LATIN AMERICA - MEDALS RN

LATVIA JM93, JM97

LAW, JOHN RF80

LAW AND JURISPRUDENCE RA80

LEBANON KA45

LEGHORN JI97

LEPER COLONIES PL70

LESHER, JOSEPH PA80

LIBERCHIES (BELGIUM) BC75

LIECHTENSTEIN JF87, JG87,
  JH30, JH87

LIEGE JF80, JF90

LINCOLN, ABRAHAM GB40, US85

LIND, JENNY RA60

LITHUANIA JM95, JM97
  see also RUSSIA
LITHUANIA - PAPER JM97, UF40

LONDON - MEDALS RE90
LONDON - TOKENS PE80

LORRAINE JA80, JE82
  see also NETHERLANDS;
  EUROPE, MEDIEVAL

LOUIS XIV, KING OF FRANCE
  RF80

LOUISIANA US75

LOVE TOKENS NB80

LUNDY JB94

LUTHER, MARTIN JG70, RG80

LUXEMBOURG JF30,
  JF67, JF83, JF87, JG
  see also NETHERLANDS

LYCIA BB20, BB38

LYDIA BB20, BD32

LYSIMACHUS BB94

MACEDONIA BB20, BB94

MAESTRICHT JF90

MAGNA GRAECA BB94

MAINE US75

MALACCA KB25

MALAYSIA KB20-25, QB60
  see also INDONESIA

MALDIVE ISLANDS KA90

MALTA JN30

MALTA, KNIGHTS OF JA80

MANIPUR KA90

MARDI GRAS - MEDALS RM

MARIA THERESA, EMPRESS OF
  AUSTRIA RK20

MARRIAGE MEDALS RA80

MARYLAND US45

MASSACHUSETTS GB50, GB80
  RM90, US45, US75
  see also U.S. - COLONIAL

MAUNDY COINS JB50, JB65

MAURITANIA BD85

MAXIMILIAN I OF AUSTRIA JK80

MAXIMILIAN, EMPEROR OF
  MEXICO FB

MEARS, OTTO PA40

MECKLENBURG - SCHWERIN
  JG98

MEDALS AA20, AA30, AA80,
  BC60, CC10, RA-RM
  see also ORDERS &
  DECORATIONS
MEDALS, ANCIENT RB

MEDEBACH JG98

MEDICI FAMILY JI83, JI97

MEDICINE & PHYSICIANS AA80,
  RA80, RF85, RK40, SH40,
  US75

MEDIEVAL BA40, BE20, CC80,
  JG80
  see also EUROPE, MEDIEVAL;
  SPECIFIC COUNTRIES;
  BYZANTINE

MEGARA BB90

MEHL, B. MAX GA55

MELANESIA QB60

MELOS BB70

MENDE BB94

MERCANTE, LUCIANO RI50

MERCHANT TOKENS PA-PC, PE, PN

MEREAUX PH40

MEROVINGIAN JA80, JE82

MESOPOTAMIA BB20, BD38,
  BB97, WA50
  see also ASIA, ANCIENT;
  GREECE, ANCIENT

METALS AB15, AB25, AB72, CC60,
  see also SPECIFIC MET-
  ALS

METAPONTUM BB94

MEXICO FA10, FA30, FB
  see also SPANISH

    AMERICA; CENTRAL AMERICA;
    LATIN AMERICA
MEXICO - BANKS & BANKING VD10
MEXICO - MEDALS RN20
MEXICO - ORDERS & DECORA-
    TIONS SI40
MEXICO - PAPER UH20, UJ,
    US20
MEXICO - REVOLUTION FB65,
    FB70, UJ60
MEXICO - TOKENS PA70, PC20

MICHIGAN US35, US80,
    VA60

MIKHAILOVITCH, GEORG II,
    GRAND DUKE JM20

MILES, GEORGE C. GA10, KA10

MILITARY CURRENCY UB, US60,
    WB

MILITARY TOKENS PA70-75

MINNESOTA - PAPER US80

MINTS & MINTING AA90, CC40,
    GA80, JB60

MINTURINO (ITALY) BC75

MISSISSIPPI - PAPER US75

MOGUL EMPIRE KA60, KA83

MOHAMMEDAN BD60, JD43, JE67,
    KA, LA60
    see also INDIA; ARABIA;
    TURKEY; SPECIFIC COUNTRIES

MONACO JF97

MONTFERRAT (ITALY) JI97

MORELOS, JOSE FB45, FB60

MORMONS US75, WB40
MORMONS - BANKS & BANKING
    VA40

MOROCCO KA55

MORRIS, GOUVERNEUR GA70

MOZAMBIQUE LA40

MUNICH (GERMANY) RG90

MUSIC JA70

MYTHOLOGY BB60

NAMUR JF90

NAPOLEAN I JE83, JE85, JI85,
  JI97, JM70, RF70, RF80

NAPOLEAN, JOSEPH JD45

NAPOLEAN, LOUIS RD20

NAGUADA AND BALLAS QC30

NARBONNE JE80

NASSAU (GERMANY) JG98

NATIONAL MUSEUM OF IRELAND
  JB90

NEAR EAST CC35, KA10, SJ85

NEBRASKA US80

NEPAL KB70

NERO, CLAUDIUS CAESAR BC85

NETHERLANDS AA45, CC10, JA83,
  JF
  see also BRABANT; FLANDERS;
  BELGIUM; LUXEMBOURG; DUTCH
  EAST INDIES
NETHERLANDS - COLONIES JF95
NETHERLANDS - MEDALS RD20
NETHERLANDS, MEDIEVAL JF80
NETHERLANDS - TOKENS PH40

NEVADA PA80
NEVADA - BANKS & BANKING VA80
NEVADA - MINES & MINING AB49

NEW ENGLAND GB80

NEW ENGLAND NUMISMATIC
  ASSOCIATION RM85

NEW GUINEA MA20

NEW HAMPSHIRE US45, US75

NEW JERSEY GB80, QC60, US45,
  US80, VA60
  see also U.S. - COLONIAL

NEW YORK GA10, GA20, PA80,
  US45, US80, VA60
NEW YORK - BANKS & BANKING
  VA40, VA60

NEW ZEALAND MA
NEW ZEALAND - INVESTMENT
  CC40
NEW ZEALAND - MEDALS RR
NEW ZEALAND - TOKENS PN40,
  NB40

NEWTON, SIR ISAAC JB60

NICARAGUA FC80

NICKEL AB50, CC67
  see also SPECIFIC
  COUNTRY; U.S. - NICKEL

NIGERIA QB50

NORTH AMERICA - GOLD FA23
NORTH AMERICA - SILVER FA25

NORTH CAROLINA GB80,
  US45
  see also U.S. - COLONIAL
NORTH CAROLINA - PAPER
  US75

NORTHUMBRIA JB80

NORWAY JC10, JC50-60
  see also SCANDI-
  NAVIA

NOTGELD PG70, PG90, UA50,
  UC40

NOVA SCOTIA HA85, VB30

NUMISMATICS AA10, AA50,
  GA10, JG40, JK10
  see also
  COINS - COLLECTING

NUMISMATISTS AA10, AA58
  GA55, RA80

NUREMBURG PG90, SD70

OBSOLETE BANK NOTES UB30,
   US50, US75, US77, US85

OHIO GB80, US80, VA70

OKINAWA KB10

OKLAHOMA PA80

OLBIA BA80

OLYMPIC GAMES AA80

ONTARIO PB80

ORDERS & DECORATIONS JA30,
   SA

OREGON VA80

ORIENT KA10-11, KB
   see also ASIA; SPE-
   CIFIC COUNTRIES

OSORNO, JOSE FB60

OXFORD JB80

OXFORDSHIRE PE95

PACIFIC ISLANDS LA
   see also AUSTRALIA;
   PHILIPPINE ISLANDS

PAEONIA BB94

PANAMA FC65
   see also CENTRAL
   AMERICA
PANAMA - PAPER FC65, UK20

PANDYA (INDIA) KA90

PANTICAPAEUM BA80

PAPER MONEY UA50, US-US

PARAGUAY FE70
PARAGUAY - PAPER UK50

PARKING TOKENS NB20

PARTHIA BB20, BD30,
   BD32
   see also PERSIA; ASIA,
   ANCIENT; ANCIENT

PEACE RA80

PENNSYLVANIA US45
PENNSYLVANIA - PAPER US75

PERSIA BB20, BB97, BD32,
  KA
  see also IRAN; PARTHIA;
  ASIA, ANCIENT; ANCIENT
PERSIA - MEDALS RB90

PERU FE75

PETER THE GREAT JM83

PHILATELY AA50, AA99

PHILIPPI BB90

PHILIPPINE ISLANDS KB30-50
  see also SPAIN; UNITED
  STATES
PHILIPPINE ISLANDS - HOARDS
  FB55, KB30
PHILIPPINE ISLANDS - METALS
  RP20
PHILIPPINE ISLANDS - PAPER
  UM40
PHILIPPINE ISLANDS - SOCIETIES
  KB30
PHILIPPINE ISLANDS - TOKENS
  PL70

PHOENICIA BB20, WA50

PIEDMONT (ITALY) JI97

PILARTZ, HEINRICH JG98

PINCHES, JOHN RE15

PISA (ITALY) JI97

PISANELLO RI35

PISTRUCCI, BENEDETTO RI35

PLATINUM AA50, AB70
  see also GOLD

POLAND JJ20-30, JM67
POLAND - ORDERS & DECORA-
  TIONS SB60
POLAND - PAPER JJ20, UF70

POPES JA20, JF40, JI67,
  JI93
    see also VATICAN; ITALY
POPES - MEDALS RI80

PORCELAIN JG67, PL60, RG30

PORTUGAL JD
    see also SPAIN; INDIA,
    PORTUGUESE
PORTUGAL - COLONIES JD70,
  KB25, LA40, UB55
PORTUGAL, MEDIEVAL JD90
PORTUGAL, MODERN JD70
PORTUGAL - PAPER UB55
PORTUGAL - TOKENS PI30

POTOSI FA20

PRIMITIVE MONEY AA90, PA80,
  QB

PRINTING PE60

PRINZ, ERNST - COLLECTIONS
  BB20

PRIVATE GOLD GB15

PROOF COINS CC60
    see also WORLD - PROOF
    COINS; U.S. - PROOF
    COINS

PRUSSIA JG92, JG98

PSEUDONUMIA CC50, GA70, KC30,
  PE60, RI35

PTOLEMIES, KINGS OF EGYPT
  BB20, BD83

PUERTO RICO FD60, PA80
    see also UNITED STATES;
    WEST INDIES

PURKYNE, JAN E. RK40

QUEBEC PB80

RAJPUTANA (INDIA) KA90

RATION CURRENCY PA40

RAYY KA55

ROTY, LOUIS OSCAR RF35

RUMANIA JJ85
RUMANIA - MEDALS RK70
RUMANIA - PAPER UF50

RUSSIA JM
RUSSIA - BANKS & BANKING
  VD10
RUSSIA - CHECKS BM90
RUSSIA - COLONIES PA80
RUSSIA - JETONS SB30
RUSSIA - ORDERS & DECORA-
  TIONS JM, SG
RUSSIA - PAPER UF30

ST. JOHN OF JERUSALEM,
  HOSPITAL, ORDER OF
  JI95

ST. LOUIS, ORDER OF SC40

SALVADOR FC75

SALZBURG JK90

SAMOS BB90

SAN GENNARO, ORDER OF SF40

SAN MARINO JI30

SASKATCHEWAN PB80

SATAVAHANA DYNASTY BD10

SAVOY JI97
SAVOY - ORDERS AND DECORA-
  TIONS SF70

SAXONY JG94

SAXONY-LAURENBURG JG65, JG94

SCANDINAVIA BD90, JC
  see also SPECIFIC COUNTRY

SCARABS QC30, RB90

SCHLESWIG UC60

SCHOOL SCRIP US35

SCHWEIZER, J. OTTO RM35

SCOTLAND JB20-40, JB85, JB93
  see also GREAT BRITAIN
SCOTLAND, ANCIENT BC97
SCOTLAND - COPPER PE20
SCOTLAND - TOKENS JB30,
  NB40, PE90

SELEUCIA BD30, BD34, JK83
  see also PARTHIA; GREECE
  ANCIENT; BABYLONIA; SYRIA,
  ANCIENT

SELLERS, GEORGE ESCOL GA80

SELTZ, ALSACE BC75

SEVERNS, LUCIUS SEPTIMUS
  BC85

SHAKESPEARE, WILLIAM JB50

SHANGHAI PL20

SHIPS & SEAFARERS AA80, BB60,
  BC70, CC70, PB70, RA80,
  RE85, US77
  see also ICONOGRAPHY

SHIPWRECKS & TREASURE TROVES
  CC55
  see also HOARDS

SICILY BC85
SICILY, ANCIENT BB20, BB94
  see also ITALY; ROME,
  ANCIENT; GREEK ITALY

SICYON BB90

SIKKIM KA90

SILESIA JG98, JK83

SILVER AA50-60, AB40, AB42,
  CC65, FA25, QB70, WA30
  see also SPECIFIC COUNTRY,
  PLACE, PERIOD

SILVER MINES & MINING AB40,
  AB49, PA80

SIMON, THOMAS JB60, QC50

SIPHNOS BB70

SISTAN (PERSIA) KA30

SMITHSONIAN INSTITUTION
  AA20

SMYRNIA BC75

SOCIAL WAR CA. 355 B.C.
  BB80

SOUTH AFRICA LA30
  see also AFRICA, BRITISH
SOUTH AFRICA - PAPER UP30

SOUTH AMERICA CC35, FA, FE
  see also SPECIFIC COUN-
  TRIES; SPANISH AMERICA;
  LATIN AMERICA
SOUTH AMERICA - ORDERS & DEC-
  ORATIONS SI60
SOUTH AMERICA - PAPER MH20,
  UK10

SOUTH CAROLINA US80, VA90
SOUTH CAROLINA - BANKS &
  BANKING VA90

SOUTH DAKOTA VA70

SPAIN CC40, CC55, JD
  see also SPANISH AMERICA;
  ROMAN SPAIN; GREECE,
  ANCIENT
SPAIN, ANCIENT BC97, BC36,
  JC40, JE86
  see also ROMAN SPAIN
SPAIN - CATALOGS JD20, JD44
SPAIN - COLONIES KB30, KB50
SPAIN - GOLD JD33
SPAIN - MEDALS RH10, RH65
SPAIN - MEDIEVAL JD43, KA55
SPAIN - ORDERS & DECORATIONS
  SB20
SPAIN - SILVER JD35

SPANISH AMERICA CC55, FA
  FB55, FB60, FD35, JD,
  KB50, RN10
  see also SPAIN; LATIN AMERI-
  CA; MEXICO; CENTRAL AMERICA;
  SOUTH AMERICA; WEST INDIES

STAINLESS STEEL AB70

STATE BANK NOTES US75, US77,
  US85, VA90

STYRIA (AUSTRIA) JK90

SWEDEN AB66, JB80, JC10,
  JC60-80, KA50
  see also SCANDINAVIA
SWEDEN - BANKS & BANKING
  VD10
SWEDEN - COLONIES JC85
SWEDEN - MEDALS RD50
SWEDEN - PAPER JC70, JC75,
  UB60

SWITZERLAND JG, JH, WC52
SWITZERLAND - BANKS &
  BANKING VD10
SWITZERLAND - MEDALS JH90,
  RA50, RD60

SYRACUSE BB94, BD97

SYRIA BB20, BD36, KA55
SYRIA, ANCIENT BB20, BB97,
  BC75, BD34-36

TAIWAN KC60
  see also CHINA

TARANTO BB94

TARSOS BB97

TASMANIA MA40
TASMANIA - PAPER UQ38

TASSIE, JAMES & WILLIAM
  RE35

TELEPHONE TOKENS NB20

TENNESSE - PAPER US75

TERRITORIAL GOLD GB15

TEXAS CC55, US80
TEXAS - DEALERS & DEALER-
  SHIPS GA55
TEXAS - ECONOMICS WB80
TEXAS - GOLD GB10

THAILAND KB70
THAILAND - PAPER VM45
THAILAND - TOKENS PL60

THENOT, RENE RN70

THESSALY BB90

U.S. - POLITICANA PA70, QA
U.S. - PORTRAITS GB40
U.S. - PRESIDENTS RM60,
  RM85
U.S. - PRIVATE MINTS GA80,
  RM15
U.S. - PROOF COINS GA55,
  GA80, GB10
U.S. - SCRIP US35, US75,
  US80
U.S. - SILVER AB42, FA25,
  GA30, GA85, GB20, GB40,
  QC60, RM30
U.S. - STATE BANKS US75-80
  VA50
U.S. - TAX & REVENUE STAMPS
  PA40
U.S. - TERRITORIES KB50
U.S. - TOKENS NB80, PA, QA,
  US20
U.S. - TRADE DOLLAR CC85,
  GB70
UNITED STATES TREASURY US25
U.S. - TYPE COINS GA50

UR WA50

URTUKI TURKUMANS KA50

URUGUAY FD80
URUGUAY - PAPER UK50

UTAH US75
  see also MORMONS

UTRECHT JF90

VATICAN JF40, JI30, JI93
  see also POPES
VATICAN - PAPER UB50

VENTO (ITALY) JI97

VENEZUELA FE85

VENICE JI97, JL80
  see also ITALY

VERMONT GB80, US45, US75,
  US80
  see also U.S.- COLONIAL

VERNON, EDWARD (BRITISH AD-
  MIRAL) RE80

VICTORIA, QUEEN OF GREAT

BRITAIN JB87

VIENNA (AUSTRIA) JK10, JK20

VIJAYANAGAR DYNASTY KA60

VIKINGS JB80

VILLA, FRANCISCO RN20

VIRGIN ISLANDS FD65
    see also UNITED STATES

VIRGINIA GB80, US45, US60,
    US80
    see also U.S. - COLONIAL

VISIGOTHS JD43

WALES - MEDALS RE90

WAR PRISONERS CC53, US35

WARWICKSHIRE PE95

WASHINGTON, GEORGE RM80

WASHINGTON (STATE) VA40

WATKINS, FREDRICK M. BA20

WATT, JAMES RE80

WEIGHTS & MEASURES AA90,
    BC63, BD10, BD20, BE80,
    JM60, KA50, KA90, QC30

WEINMAN, ADOLPH GB10, RM35

WELLINGTON, ARTHUR WELLESLY
    PB70

WELLS FARGO VA40

WEST INDIES FA10, FA15, FD,
    JF95
    see also SPECIFIC COUN-
    TRIES; LATIN AMERICA;
    SOUTH AMERICA
WEST INDIES - PAPER UM20

WESTPHALIA JG98

WILLIAM III, KING OF GREAT
    BRITAIN JB85

WISCONSIN PA80
WISCONSIN - BANKS & BANKING
  VA70

WOOD, WILLIAM JB85

WOODEN MONEY PA40

WORLD, ANCIENT AA30-50
WORLD, ANCIENT - MEDALS
  AA40, RB20, RB70

WORLD BANK VD30

WORLD, MODERN AA30-50, AB70,
  CC, GA80, GA85, GB10, GB60
  see also SPECIFIC COUNTRIES
WORLD, MODERN - BANKS &
  BANKING VD10
WORLD, MODERN - COMMEMORA-
  TIVES RA40
WORLD, MODERN - COPPER CC67
WORLD, MODERN - INVESTMENT
  CC40, GA55, GB10, UA50
WORLD, MODERN - MEDALS AA40,
  CC85, RA10, RA40, RA80,
  RB20, RB70
WORLD, MODERN - ORDERS & DECO-
  RATIONS AA40, JA30
WORLD, MODERN - PAPER AA40,
  UA
WORLD, MODERN - TOKENS AA40,
  NB20, UA40

WORLD WAR I CC53, JE87, PF70,
  PG70, RA80, UB, UC
  see also GERMANY; EUROPE

WORLD WAR II UA60, UC, UI60,
  UM40, US35

WORLD'S FAIRS RM85

WURTTEMBERG JG96, PG70

WURZBURG JA98

WYON, WILLIAM RE35

YORKSHIRE PE95

YUGOSLAVIA JJ40,
YUGOSLAVIA - PAPER JJ40

ZAPATA, EMILIANO FB65, RN20